The OXFORD *Study* French DICTIONARY

Editorial Manager: Valerie Grundy
Editor: Jennifer Barnes

OXFORD
UNIVERSITY PRESS

OXFORD
UNIVERSITY PRESS

Great Clarendon Street, Oxford OX2 6DP

Oxford University Press is a department of the University of Oxford.
It furthers the University's objective of excellence in research, scholarship,
and education by publishing worldwide in

Oxford New York

Athens Auckland Bangkok Bogotá Buenos Aires Calcutta
Cape Town Chennai Dar es Salaam Delhi Florence Hong Kong Istanbul
Karachi Kuala Lumpur Madrid Melbourne Mexico City Mumbai
Nairobi Paris São Paulo Singapore Taipei Tokyo Toronto Warsaw

with associated companies in Berlin Ibadan

Oxford is a registered trade mark of Oxford University Press
in the UK and in certain other countries

British Library Cataloguing in Publication Data available

ISBN 0–19–910602–9

1 3 5 7 9 10 8 6 4 2

Typeset by Selwood Systems, Midsomer Norton
Printed in Spain

INTRODUCTION

Learning a new language is an exciting experience. However, it can also sometimes seem confusing and difficult. Feeling secure and at ease in using a bilingual dictionary is essential to the building of confidence in understanding and using a foreign language.

This dictionary has been specially written for students who are preparing for exams. We have paid particular attention to making the dictionary as user-friendly as possible. With the help of colour headwords, easy-to-follow signposts and examples, the right translation can quickly be found. French verbs on both sides of the dictionary are numbered to take the student straight to the appropriate pattern in the centre pages of the dictionary.

We have adopted a simplified version of traditional bilingual entry layout. This means that the dictionary is ideal for learning basic dictionary skills, which can subsequently be built upon as the student moves towards larger, more sophisticated dictionaries. We have done our best to make this dictionary a practical, easy-to-use tool for learning and understanding French.

Throughout the writing of this dictionary we have worked in close consultation with students, teachers, inspectors, and examining boards. We gratefully acknowledge the examining boards AQA (NEAB and SEG), OCR, and EDEXCEL (ULEAC), who have read and commented on the dictionary text.

HOW A BILINGUAL DICTIONARY WORKS

A bilingual dictionary is a dictionary that has two languages in it. When you look up a word in one of the languages, the dictionary gives the translation for that word in the other language. The two languages in this dictionary are English and French. This dictionary is divided into two halves separated by blue-edged pages in the middle. In the first half you look up French words to find out what they mean in English and in the second half you look up English words and find out how to say them in French.

The words you look up are in blue and in the first half of the dictionary you will find French words in alphabetical order from a to z and in the second half English words from a to z. In a dictionary, these are called **headwords** because each one of them comes at the **head** of an **entry**. In the entry you can find **translations** but also other sorts of information which you can use to make sure you get the correct translation. The different sorts of information are typed in different ways to help you see clearly which is which. Here is a guide to the different things you will find in an entry:

headword	a word you look up in the dictionary
translation	translations are the only things that are in 'ordinary' type in the dictionary. They are *always* typed like this, and something which is typed in a different way can *never* be a translation
noun	part of speech: tells you whether the word you are looking up is a noun, a verb, an adjective, or another part of speech. One headword can have more than one part of speech. For instance, **book** can be a noun *(she was reading a book)* or a verb *(I've booked the seats)*.
(signpost)	helpful information: to guide you to the right translation, to show you how to use the translation, or to give you extra information about either the headword or the translation.
example	a phrase or sentence using the word you have looked up. If these appear in the entry you are looking at, you should read through them carefully to see if they are close to what you want to understand or say.
M	gender: after a French noun to tell you that it is masculine
F	gender: after a French noun to tell you that it is feminine
●	indicates a phrasal verb such as *to carry on*
★	shows an idiomatic expression such as *over the moon*
[27]	verb number – tells you which verb pattern to look at in the centre of the dictionary

vi

You can think of a dictionary entry as being made out of different sorts of building bricks. In the entries below you can see how they fit together to help you to find what you need. The more you use your dictionary the more confident you will feel about finding your way around it.

verb number – shows you which pattern to look at in the verb tables *in the centre of the dictionary*

envoyer *verb* [40] to send; **envoyer quelque chose à quelqu'un** to send somebody something; **elle m'a envoyé une carte** she sent me a card; **elle m'a envoyé chercher les verres** she sent me to get the glasses.

essential usage for understanding French

examples of use

épais (F **épaisse**) *adjective* thick **une tranche épaisse** a thick slice.

part of speech

irregular forms in bold for easy look-up

épaisseur *noun* F thickness.

épargne *noun* F savings; **une banque d'épargne** a savings bank; **un compte d'épargne** a savings account.

gender

headwords in blue for easy reference

épatant *adjective* (*informal*) fantastic, great.

informal word or expression

A STEP-BY-STEP GUIDE TO FINDING THE TRANSLATION YOU NEED

Finding a word in the dictionary

You will be using this dictionary to do one of the following things:

1 look up a French word or phrase to find out what it means
2 look up an English word or phrase to find out how to say it in French.

1 Finding out what a French word means

First of all, look for it in the first half of the dictionary where you can find the French words and expressions with their English translations. You will see that the top of every page is marked like this.

No matter what you are using the dictionary to find out, you will always start by looking up a headword. Here are the French headwords **briller**, **brin**, **brindille**, **brioche**, **brique** and **briquet** with their entries.

> **briller** *verb* [1] to shine.
>
> **brin** *noun* M **1** sprig (*of herb or plant*);
> **un brin d'herbe** a blade of grass.
>
> **brindille** *noun* F twig.
>
> **brioche** *noun* F brioche, bun.
>
> **brique** *noun* F **1** brick; **2** carton (*of fruit-juice, milk, etc*).
>
> **briquet** *noun* M lighter.

Suppose you want to find out what the French word **matelas** means. You will look through the first half of your dictionary until you come to the bit which has all the French words beginning with **m**. You now need to find the page or pages containing French words beginning with **ma**, then **mat**, then **mate**. The dictionary helps you to do this by showing you the alphabetical range of words that you can find on the two pages you can see when you have the dictionary open.

For instance, if you look at pages 172–173, you will see **mariage** at the top of page 172 and **matin** at the top of page 173. This means that the first entry on page 172 is **mariage** and the last entry on page 173 is **matin**. The word you are looking for begins **mate-** so you will find it somewhere on these two pages.

If you look down the second column on page 173 you will find **matelas** between **match** and **matelassé**. Notice that hyphens, spaces between words, and accents on letters in French words make no difference to the alphabetical order.

> **mat** *adjective* matt.
>
> **mât** *noun* M mast; pole.
>
> **match** *noun* M match; **un match de foot** a football match; **faire match nul** to draw.
>
> **matelas** *noun* M mattress.
>
> **matelassé** *adjective* quilted.
>
> **matelot** *noun* M sailor.
>
> **matériaux** *plural noun* M materials; **les matériaux de construction** building materials.

When you look at the entry for **matelas** you will find the translation you are looking for: **matelas** means **mattress**.

> **matelas** *noun* M mattress.

You can also see that **matelas** is a *noun* and because all nouns are either masculine or feminine in French, you are given the gender M (F = feminine gender; M = masculine gender).

It often happens that a French word has more than one translation in English. If you look at the entry for **bouton** on page 36 you will see that it is divided into sections numbered **1** and **2**.

> **bouton** *noun* M **1** button; **2** spot, pimple.

The first translation is **button** and the second is **spot** or **pimple**. You will need to look at both translations and work out which one fits in best in the French sentence you are trying to understand. So:

il y a quatre boutons sur ma veste *means* there are four buttons on my jacket

BUT

j'ai un bouton sur le nez *means* I've got a spot on my nose

You add an **-s** to most French nouns to form the plural, as in **boutons** in the sentence above. There are exceptions to this and where the plural is not **-s** you will find the plural form after the headword.

For instance, if you are trying to find out what the French word **animaux** means you can see immediately that it is the plural of **animal**:

> **animal** (*plural* **animaux**) *noun* M animal.

Similarly, you usually add an **-e** to French adjectives to make them feminine to agree with a feminine noun. Where this is not the case, you will find the feminine form straight after the headword if it follows alphabetically, like **gazeuse** here:

> **gazeux** (F **gazeuse**) *adjective* fizzy;
> **eau gazeuse** fizzy mineral water.

As with nouns, you usually add an **-s** to the masculine or feminine form of an adjective to make it plural, but again there are exceptions to this. If you are trying to find out what **normaux** means, you will find that it is the masculine plural of **normal**:

> **normal** (M *plural* **normaux**)
> *adjective* **1** normal; **2** c'est
> **normal** it's natural; **3** ce n'est pas
> **normal** it's not right.

French like English has certain words that you would use when chatting with friends but not in more formal situations. French words like this are marked *informal* in the dictionary, like **bouquin** here:

bouquin *noun* M (*informal*) book.

Note that the usual word for **book** is **livre**.

2 Finding an English word and how to say it in French

You can see that it is quite easy once you know how the dictionary works to look up a French word and find out what it means. Students usually find it harder to use the dictionary to find out how to say something in French. This dictionary is written specially to help you do this and to make it easy to find the right way of saying things in French.

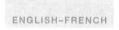
ENGLISH–FRENCH

Suppose you want to know how to say **garden** in French. Look up the word in the second part of the dictionary where the top of every page is marked like this.

If you follow the same method of going through the alphabetical order of the headwords as you did when you were looking up a French word, you will find **garden** on page 414.

gangster *noun* gangster M.

gap *noun* **1** (*hole*) trou M; **2** (*in time*) intervalle M; **a two-year gap** un intervalle de deux ans; **3 an age gap** une différence d'âge.

garage *noun* garage M.

garden *noun* jardin M.

gardener *noun* jardinier M; **he wants to be a gardener** il veut être jardinier.

gardening *noun* jardinage M.

garlic *noun* ail M.

Now you can see that the French word for **garden** is **jardin**. But if you want to make a sentence using a noun like **jardin** you need to know whether it is masculine or feminine. The **M** after **jardin** tells you that it is masculine so *in the garden* is **dans le jardin**.

It is not always as easy as this to know which French word you need. Sometimes there will be more than one French word for the English word you are looking up. When the dictionary entry gives you more than just one translation, it is very important to take the time to read through the whole entry. If you look up **plug** the entry looks like this:

> **plug** *noun* **1** (*electrical*) prise F;
> **2** (*in the bath or sink*) bonde F; **to**
> **pull out the plug** retirer la bonde.

You can see that **1** tells you that the French word for an electrical plug is **prise** and **2** tells you that the word for a bath plug or a sink plug is **bonde**.

Remember that information which is either in brackets or italics or both is there to help you, but it *will never be* the translation itself. Wherever there is more than one translation, depending on what meaning of the English word you are looking for, the dictionary will always help you to choose the right one.

Often it is not enough to find the translation of one word. In the case of more common words the dictionary also gives you a selection of common phrases you will often want to use. In the entry for **hair** below you can find out how to use the translation in different expressions:

> **hair** *noun* **1** cheveux M *plural*; **to have**
> **short hair** avoir les cheveux courts;
> **to brush your hair** se brosser les cheveux;
> **to wash your hair** se laver les cheveux;
> **to have your hair cut** se faire couper les
> cheveux; **she's had her hair cut** elle s'est
> fait couper les cheveux; **2 a hair** (*from the
> head*) un cheveu; (*from the body*) un poil.

How to use the verb table numbers

On the **FRENCH–ENGLISH** side of the dictionary all the headwords which are verbs look like this:

faire *verb* [10]

On the **ENGLISH–FRENCH** side of the dictionary all the verbs given as translations of English verbs look like this:

frighten *verb* effrayer [59]

If you look at the pages edged in blue in the centre of the dictionary, you will find tables showing you how to use the different types of French verbs. The verb **faire** above has the number 10. If you look at number 10 in the verb tables, you will see that because **faire** is a very common and very irregular verb it has a whole page to itself giving you all the tenses you will need.

The verb **effrayer** has number 59 after it. When you look up verb table number 59, you will see the verb **payer**. This means that the verb endings given for **payer** will also be the endings for **effrayer**. So **payer** is there to show you the pattern that other verbs like it, such as **effrayer**, will follow.

With practice you will soon be able to find your way easily around the dictionary and identify what you are looking for in an entry. Some entries may seem long and complicated at first glance. Reading carefully through the signposts and examples will lead you to the translation you need.

A a

a *verb* SEE **avoir**.

à *preposition* (*note that 'à + le'
becomes 'au' and 'à + les' becomes
'aux'*) **1** at; **à la maison** at home; **à
l'école** at school; **au bureau** at the
office; **à deux heures** at two
o'clock; **2** in; **à Londres** in London;
à la campagne in the country; **au
printemps** in the spring; **3** to; **aller
à Londres** to go to London; **donner
quelque chose à quelqu'un** to give
something to somebody; **4** by; **à la
main** by hand; **à vélo** by (or on a)
bicycle; **5** with; **une petite fille aux
yeux bleus** a little girl with blue
eyes; **6 à trois kilomètres d'ici**
three kilometres from here; **7 ce
bracelet est à Natalie** this bracelet
is Natalie's.

abandonner *verb* [1] **1** to give up;
elle a abandonné les maths she has
given up maths; **j'abandonne** I give
up; **2** to abandon; **un enfant
abandonné** an abandoned child.

abat-jour *noun* M lampshade.

abats *plural noun* M **les abats** offal
(*liver, kidneys, heart, etc*).

abattoir *noun* M slaughterhouse.

abattre *verb* [21] **1** to shoot down;
**deux policiers ont été abattus par
des gangsters hier** two policemen
were shot down by gangsters
yesterday; **2** to slaughter (*an
animal*); **3** to demolish (*a
building*).

abbaye *noun* F abbey; **l'abbaye de
Cluny** Cluny Abbey.

abbé *noun* M priest.

abcès *noun* M abscess.

abeille *noun* F bee; **une piqûre
d'abeille** a bee sting.

abîmer *verb* [1] **1** to damage; **la
pluie avait abîmé la porte** the rain
had damaged the door; **tu vas
t'abîmer les yeux** you'll ruin your
eyesight; **des fruits abîmés** fruit
which is going bad; **2 s'abîmer** to
get damaged; **les pommes vont
s'abîmer** the apples are going to go
bad; **la viande s'abîme vite** meat
goes off quickly.

aboiement *noun* M barking; **on
entendait des aboiements** we
could hear dogs barking.

abolir *verb* [2] to abolish.

abominable *adjective* abominable.

abondance *noun* F **une
abondance de** plenty of, lots of; **il y
a des fruits en abondance** there's
plenty of fruit.

abonné, abonnée *noun* M, F
1 season ticket holder;
2 subscriber (*to a magazine,
journal, etc*).
adjective **être abonné** to have a
subscription (*to a magazine, journal,
etc*); to have a season ticket (*for the
bus, train, theatre, etc*).

abonnement *noun* M
1 subscription; **2** season ticket.

abonner *verb* [1] **s'abonner à** to
subscribe to; **je me suis abonné
pour un an** I have a year's
subscription.

abord *noun* M **1 d'abord** first; **tout d'abord** first of all; **je vais d'abord faire du thé** I'll make some tea first; **2 d'abord** at first; **j'ai d'abord cru qu'il était français** I thought at first that he was French; **3 les abords** the surroundings.

abordable *adjective* **1 des prix abordables** affordable prices; **2 une personne abordable** an approachable person.

aborder *verb* [1] **1** to tackle (*a problem, a piece of work, a subject, etc*); **2** to approach.

aboutir *verb* [2] **1 aboutir à** to lead to; **la rue aboutit à une petite place** the street leads to a little square; **2 aboutir à** to end up in; **nous avons abouti à Paris** we ended up in Paris; **3** to succeed, to be successful (*of discussions or negotiations*).

aboyer *verb* [39] to bark.

abrégé *noun* M summary. *adjective* **la version abrégée** the abridged version.

abréger *verb* [15] to shorten.

abréviation *noun* F abbreviation.

abri *noun* M **1** shelter; **trouver un abri** to take shelter; **les sans-abri** the homeless; **2** shed; **3 à l'abri de** sheltered from; **à l'abri du vent** sheltered from the wind, out of the wind; **à l'abri de la lumière** in a dark place.

abricot *noun* M apricot; **de la confiture d'abricots** apricot jam; **une tarte aux abricots** an apricot tart.

abricotier *noun* M apricot tree.

abriter *verb* [1] **1** to shelter; **2 s'abriter** to take shelter.

abrupt *adjective* **1** steep; **une pente abrupte** a steep slope; **2** abrupt.

abrutir *verb* [2] **1** to deafen; **2** to stupefy.

absence *noun* F **1** absence; **pendant mon absence** while I was out, while I was away; **2 l'absence de** the lack of.

absent *adjective* **1 être absent** to be out, to be away; **je serai absent pendant une heure** I'll be out for an hour; **elle a été absente tout le mois de mai** she was away for the whole of May; **2** absent; **3** absent-minded.

absenter *verb* [1] **s'absenter** to go out, to go away; **je m'absente quelques minutes** I'm just popping out for a few minutes.

absolu *adjective* absolute.

absolument *adverb* absolutely.

absorbant *adjective* **1** absorbing; **un livre absorbant** an absorbing book; **2** absorbent (*material*).

absorber *verb* [1] **1** to absorb; **2** to take (*food or drink*).

abstenir *verb* [81] **s'abstenir de** to refrain from.

abstrait *adjective* abstract.

absurde *adjective* absurd.

absurdité *noun* F absurdity; **dire des absurdités** to talk nonsense.

abus *noun* M abuse; **l'abus d'alcool** alcohol abuse.

abuser *verb* [1] **1 abuser de** to misuse; **abuser de l'alcool** to drink too much (*regularly*); **2 abuser de** to take advantage of, to exploit; **elle abuse de ta gentillesse** she's taking advantage of your kindness.

abusif (F **abusive**) *adjective* **1** excessive; **2** unfair.

acajou *noun* M mahogany; **une table en acajou** a mahogany table.

accablant *adjective* overwhelming.

accabler *verb* [1] to overwhelm.

accéder *verb* [24] **1 accéder à** to reach, to get to ; **pour accéder à la salle de bains, il faut passer par la chambre** to get to the bathroom you have to go through the bedroom; **2 accéder au pouvoir** to come to power.

accélérateur *noun* M accelerator; **appuyer sur l'accélérateur** to accelerate.

accélération *noun* F acceleration.

accélérer *verb* [24] **1** to speed up (*the rhythm, process, etc*); **2** to accelerate (*in a car*).

accent *noun* M **1** accent; **un accent étranger** a foreign accent; **parler français sans accent** to speak French without an accent; **2** accent (*on a letter in written French*); **un accent aigu** an acute accent; **un accent grave** a grave accent; **un accent circonflexe** a circumflex; **3 mettre l'accent sur quelque chose** to stress something.

accentuer *verb* [1] to emphasize.

acceptation *noun* F acceptance.

accepter *verb* [1] **1** to accept; **accepter une invitation** to accept an invitation; **2 accepter de faire** to agree to do; **elle a accepté de m'aider** she agreed to help me.

accès *noun* M **1** access; **accès interdit** no entry; **2 un accès de colère** a fit of anger.

accessible *adjective* **1** accessible; **un livre accessible** a book which is easy to read; **2 des prix accessibles** affordable prices.

accessoire *noun* M accessory; **les accessoires** accessories (*gloves, handbags, etc*).
adjective incidental.

accident *noun* M **1** accident; **avoir un accident** to have an accident; **un accident de la route** a road accident; **2** hitch; **il y a eu un petit accident** there's been a slight hitch.

accidenté *adjective* **1** injured; **2** damaged; **3 'chaussée accidentée'** 'uneven road surface'.

acclamations *plural noun* F cheering.

accommodant *adjective* easy-going.

accompagnateur, accompagnatrice *noun* M, F **1** tourist guide; **2** courier (*for a group on a package holiday*); **3** accompanying adult (*with a child travelling alone*); **4** accompanist (*for example, a pianist accompanying a singer*).

accompagner *verb* [1] **1** to accompany; **je t'accompagne** I'll go with you, I'll come with you; **je t'accompagne jusqu'à chez toi** I'll see you home; **2 accompagné de** accompanied by; **elle est partie accompagnée de son frère** she left accompanied by her brother; **3** to accompany (*on the piano, for example*).

accomplir *verb* [2] to carry out (*a task, project, mission, etc*).

accord *noun* M **1** agreement; **2 d'accord** all right, OK; **je suis d'accord avec Rosie** I agree with Rosie; **Paul est d'accord pour venir avec nous** Paul's agreed to come with us; **3** chord (*in music*).

accordéon *noun* M accordeon; **jouer de l'accordéon** to play the accordeon.

accorder *verb* [1] **1** to grant (*a favour, permission, etc*); **2** to tune (*a musical instrument*); **3 s'accorder** to agree.

accotement *noun* M verge (*on the edge of the road*); hard shoulder (*on the motorway*); **'accotements non stabilisés'** 'soft verges' (*as road sign*).

accouchement *noun* M childbirth, delivery.

accoucher *verb* [1] to give birth.

accoutumé *adjective* **1** usual; **2 accoutumé à** used to, accustomed to;

accoutumer *verb* [1] **s'accoutumer à** to become accustomed to.

accro *noun* M (*informal*) addict. *adjective* (*informal*) **être accro de quelque chose** to be hooked on something.

accroc *noun* M **1** tear; **tu as un accroc à ta jupe** you've got a tear in your skirt; **2** hitch; **sans accroc(s)** without a hitch.

accrocher *verb* [1] **1** to hang; **accrocher un tableau au mur** to hang a picture on the wall; **accroché au mur** hanging on the wall; **2** to catch, to snag (*something on a nail or thorn, for example*).

accroupir *verb* [2] **s'accroupir** to crouch (down), to squat.

accueil *noun* M **1** welcome; **un accueil chaleureux** a warm welcome; **2** reception desk; **Madame Jones est priée de se présenter à l'accueil** would Ms Jones please go to the reception desk.

accueillant *adjective* **1** (*of a person*) hospitable, welcoming; **2** (*of a place*) inviting, friendly.

accueillir *verb* [35] **1** to welcome; **2** to receive, to greet.

accumuler *verb* [1] **1** to collect; **2 s'accumuler** to pile up.

accusation *noun* F accusation.

accusé de réception *noun* M **envoyer une lettre avec accusé de réception** to send a letter recorded delivery.

accuser *verb* [1] to accuse; **il m'a accusé d'avoir volé son stylo** he accused me of stealing his pen.

acharner *verb* [1] **s'acharner à faire** to persist in doing.

achat *noun* M purchase; **je te montre mes achats** I'll show you what I've bought.

acheter *verb* [16] **1** to buy; **je vais acheter du pain** I'm going to buy some bread; **2 acheter quelque chose à quelqu'un** to buy somebody something; **je t'achète un sandwich?** shall I buy you a sandwich?; **je lui ai acheté un cadeau** I bought him (or her) a present; **3 acheter quelque chose à quelqu'un** to buy something from somebody; **j'ai vendu ma voiture – c'est Lisa qui me l'a achetée** I've sold my car – Lisa bought it from me.

acheteur, acheteuse *noun* M, F buyer.

achever *verb* [50] **1** to finish (*a piece of work*); **2** to finish off (*meaning 'kill'*).

acide *noun* M acid. *adjective* sharp, sour.

acier *noun* M steel.

acné *noun* F acne.

acoustique *noun* F acoustics.

acquérir *verb* [17] to acquire.

âcre *adjective* pungent.

acrobate *noun* M & F acrobat.

acrobatie *noun* F acrobatics.

acte *noun* M act.

acte de naissance *noun* M birth certificate.

acteur, actrice *noun* M, F actor, actress.

actif (F **active**) *adjective* active; **la vie active** working life.

action *noun* F action, act; **une bonne action** a good deed.

activement *adverb* actively.

activer *verb* [1] **1** to speed up; **2 s'activer** to hurry up.

activité *noun* F activity.

activité professionnelle *noun* F occupation.

actualité *noun* F **1** current affairs; **2 les actualités** the news.

actuel (F **actuelle**) *adjective* present, current; **la situation actuelle** the present situation.

actuellement *adverb* at the moment; **elle est actuellement à Rome** she's in Rome at the moment.

adapté *adjective* **1** suitable; **adapté à** suitable for, suited to; **2** adapted.

adapter *verb* [1] **1** to adapt; **2 s'adapter à** to adapt to, to get used to.

additif *noun* M additive.

addition *noun* F **1** addition; **2** bill (*in a restaurant*); **l'addition, s'il vous plaît** can I have the bill please.

additionner *verb* [1] to add up.

adhésif (F **adhésive**) *adjective* adhesive; **ruban adhésif** sticky tape.

adieu (*plural* **adieux**) *noun* M goodbye, farewell (*the usual expression is "au revoir" since "adieu" is properly used to mean "goodbye for ever"*).

adjectif *noun* M adjective.

adjoint, adjointe *noun* M, F **1** assistant; **2** deputy.

admettre *verb* [11] **1** to admit; **j'admets qu'elle a raison** I admit that she's right; **2 admettre dans** to admit to (*a restaurant, a club, etc*).

administratif (F **administrative**) *adjective* administrative.

administration *noun* F administration.

admiratif (F **admirative**) *adjective* admiring; **des regards admiratifs** admiring glances.

admiration *noun* F admiration.

admirer *verb* [1] to admire.

adolescence *noun* F adolescence.

adolescent, adolescente *noun* M, F teenager, adolescent. *adjective* teenage, adolescent.

adopter *verb* [1] to adopt.

adoptif (F **adoptive**) *adjective* **un enfant adoptif** an adopted child.

adoption *noun* F adoption.

adorable *adjective* adorable.

adorer *verb* [1] to adore, to love.

adresse *noun* F **1** address; **quelle est ton adresse?** what's your address?; **se tromper d'adresse** to get (or go to) the wrong address; **2** skill; **elle l'a fait avec beaucoup d'adresse** she did it very skilfully; **3** speech, address.

adresser *verb* [1] **1 adresser une lettre à quelqu'un** to send somebody a letter; **2 adresser la parole à quelqu'un** to speak to somebody; **2 s'adresser à** to enquire at; **adressez-vous à la réception** enquire at reception; **4 s'adresser à** to be aimed at; **le**

film s'adresse aux adolescents the film is aimed at teenagers.

adroit *adjective* skilful.

adulte *noun* M & F, *adjective* adult.

adverbe *noun* M adverb.

adversaire *noun* M & F opponent.

adverse *adjective* opposing.

aérer *verb* [24] to air.

aérobic *noun* M aerobics.

aéro-club *noun* M flying club.

aérogare *noun* F (flight) terminal (*in an airport*).

aéroglisseur *noun* M hovercraft.

aéronautique *noun* F aeronautics.

aéroport *noun* M airport; **à l'aéroport** at (or to) the airport.

aérosol *noun* M aerosol.

affaire *noun* F **1** matter, business; **c'est une drôle d'affaire** it's a funny business; **c'est une autre affaire** that's another matter; **2** affair, political crisis.

affaires *plural noun* F **1 les affaires** business; **un homme d'affaires** a businessman; **une femme d'affaires** a businesswoman; **un voyage d'affaires** a business trip; **2** business; **occupe-toi de tes affaires!** mind your own business!; **3** belongings, things; **tu peux laisser tes affaires dans la chambre** you can leave your things in the bedroom.

affamé *adjective* starving.

affamer *verb* [1] to starve.

affecter *verb* [1] **1** to affect; **2 affecter de faire** to pretend to do.

affection *noun* F affection; **j'ai beaucoup d'affection pour lui** I'm very fond of him.

affectueusement *adverb* affectionately.

affectueux (F **affectueuse**) *adjective* affectionate.

affiche *noun* F **1** poster; **2** notice.

afficher *verb* [1] to put up (*a poster or a notice*).

affliger *verb* [52] **1** to distress, to grieve; **2 affliger de** to afflict with.

affluence *noun* F crowds; **aux heures d'affluence** at peak times.

affolant *adjective* (*informal*) frightening.

affoler *verb* [1] **1 affoler quelqu'un** to throw somebody into a panic; **2 s'affoler** to panic; **ne t'affole pas** don't panic.

affreux (F **affreuse**) *adjective* **1** awful, dreadful; **2** hideous.

afin *preposition* **1 afin de faire** in order to do; **2 afin que** in order that.

africain *adjective* African.

Africain, Africaine *noun* M, F African.

Afrique *noun* F Africa; **en Afrique** in (or to) Africa.

agaçant *adjective* annoying.

agacer *verb* [61] to annoy.

âge *noun* M age; **quel âge as-tu?** how old are you?; **à l'âge de cinq ans** at the age of five; **je ne sais pas son âge** I don't know how old he (or she) is; **il a l'âge de mon père** he's the same age as my father.

âgé *adjective* **1** old; **les personnes âgées** old people; **2 âgé de**; aged; **une femme âgée de trente ans** a woman aged thirty.

agence *noun* F **1** agency; **2** branch (*of a bank*).

agence de voyages *noun* F travel agent's.

agence immobilière *noun* F estate agent's.

agenda *noun* M diary.

agenouiller *verb* [1] **s'agenouiller** to kneel down.

agent *noun* M **1** official; **2** agent.

agent commercial *noun* M sales representative.

agent de police *noun* M police officer; **une femme agent de police** a woman police officer.

aggraver *verb* [1] **1** to make worse; **aggraver la situation** to make things worse; **2 s'aggraver** to get worse; **la situation s'aggrave** the situation is deteriorating, things are getting worse.

agir *verb* [2] **1** to act; **2** to behave; **3 il s'agit de** it is about; **il s'agit de ton frère** it's about your brother; **de quoi s'agit-il?** what's it about?

agitation *noun* F **1** hustle and bustle; **2** unrest; **3** restlessness.

agité *adjective* **1** restless, agitated; **2** rough (*sea*); **3** bustling (*street*);

4 mener une vie agitée to lead a hectic life.

agiter *verb* [1] to shake; **agiter la main** to wave your hand.

agneau (*plural* **agneaux**) *noun* M lamb; **un gigot d'agneau** a leg of lamb.

agrafe *noun* F **1** staple; **2** hook (*on a garment*).

agrafer *verb* [1] **1** to staple; **2** to fasten.

agrafeuse *noun* F stapler.

agrandir *verb* [2] to enlarge.

agrandissement *noun* M enlargement (*of a photo*).

agréable *adjective* pleasant, nice.

agréé *adjective* **1** registered; **2** authorized.

agréer *verb* [32] **1** to agree to; **2 veuillez agréer l'expression de mes sentiments distingués** Yours faithfully, Yours sincerely (*this is one of a number of fixed expressions used to end any formal or business letter*).

agresser *verb* [1] **1** to attack; **2** to mug.

agresseur *noun* M attacker.

agressif (F **agressive**) *adjective* aggressive.

agression *noun* F **1** attack; **2** mugging.

agressivité *noun* F aggressiveness.

agricole *adjective* agricultural.

agriculteur, agricultrice *noun* M, F farmer.

ahuri *adjective* amazed, stunned.

ai *verb* SEE **avoir**.

aide¹ *noun* M & F assistant.

aide² *noun* F **1** help; **avec l'aide de Claire** with Claire's help; **venir à l'aide de quelqu'un** to help somebody; **2** aid (*financial aid given to a person or a country*).

aider *verb* [1] **1** to help; **il m'a aidé à mettre la table** he helped me set the table; **est-ce que je peux t'aider?** would you like some help?; **2** to give aid to (*financial aid to a person, group, or country*).

aigle *noun* M & F eagle.

aiglefin *noun* M haddock.

aigre *adjective* **1** sour; **2** sharp.

aiguille *noun* F **1** needle; **une aiguille à coudre** a sewing needle; **une aiguille à tricoter** a knitting needle; **2** hand (*of a clock or watch*).

aiguilleur du ciel *noun* M air traffic controller.

aiguiser *verb* [1] to sharpen.

ail *noun* M garlic.

aile *noun* F wing; ★ **voler de ses propres ailes** to stand on your own two feet (*literally: to fly with your own wings*).

ailleurs *adverb* **1** elsewhere, somewhere else; **2 d'ailleurs** besides, moreover; **3 par ailleurs** also, in addition.

aimable *adjective* kind, nice; **vous êtes très aimable** that's very kind of you.

aimant *noun* M magnet.

aimer *verb* [1] **1** to like; **est-ce que tu aimes les fraises?** do you like strawberries?; **aimer faire quelque chose** to like doing something; **elle aime aller au cinéma** she likes going to the cinema; **elle aimerait aller au cinéma** she'd like to go to the cinema; **2 aimer mieux** to prefer; **j'aime mieux les fraises que les framboises** I prefer strawberries to raspberries, I like strawberries better than raspberries; **j'aimerais mieux aller au cinéma** I'd prefer to go to the cinema, I'd rather go to the cinema; **3** to love; **je t'aime** I love you; **4 s'aimer** to like each other, to love each other.

aîné, aînée *noun* M, F **l'aîné(e)** the eldest, the oldest (*child*). *adjective* elder, older (*of two*); eldest, oldest (*of more than two*); **leur fille aînée** their elder (or eldest) daughter.

ainsi *adverb* **1** thus; **2** in this way; **3 ainsi que** as well as, along with.

aïoli *noun* M garlic mayonnaise.

air *noun* M **1** air; **aller prendre l'air** to go out and get some fresh air; **2 un courant d'air** a draught; **3 avoir l'air (…)** to look (…); **avoir l'air bon** to look good; **avoir l'air fatigué** to look tired; **4 avoir l'air de** to look like; **il a l'air d'un policier** he looks like a policeman; **5 avoir l'air d'être** to look as if you are; **elle a l'air d'être perdue** she looks as if she's lost; **6 avoir l'air de faire** to look as if you are doing; **il a l'air de comprendre** he looks as if he

understands; **7 sourire d'un air heureux** to smile happily; **8** tune.

air bag™ *noun* M air bag (*in a car*).

aire de jeu *noun* F playground.

aire de pique-nique *noun* F picnic area.

aire de services *noun* F motorway service station.

aise *noun* F **être à l'aise** to be comfortable, to feel at ease; **être mal à l'aise** to feel uncomfortable.

aisselle *noun* F armpit.

ajout *noun* M addition.

ajouter *verb* [1] to add; **ajoutez un œuf** add an egg.

alarme *noun* F alarm; **sonner l'alarme** to sound the alarm.

album *noun* M album.

album de bandes dessinées *noun* M comic book.

album de photos *noun* M photograph album.

album de timbres *noun* M stamp album.

alcool *noun* M alcohol.

alcoolique *noun* M & F, *adjective* alcoholic.

alcoolisé *adjective* **une boisson alcoolisée** an alcoholic drink; **une boisson non alcoolisée** a non-alcoholic drink.

alcootest *noun* M Breathalyzer™.

alcôve *noun* F alcove.

alentours *plural noun* M **1** surroundings; **2 aux alentours**

de in the vicinity (or neighbourhood) of.

algèbre *noun* F algebra.

Algérie *noun* F Algeria.

algérien (F **algérienne**) *adjective* Algerian.

algues *plural noun* F seaweed.

aliment *noun* M food.

alimentaire *adjective* **des produits alimentaires** food products; **l'industrie alimentaire** the food industry.

alimentation *noun* F **1** groceries; **2** diet.

allée *noun* F path, drive.

alléger *verb* [15] **1** to lighten; **2** to reduce.

Allemagne *noun* F Germany.

allemand *noun* M, *adjective* German.

Allemand, Allemande *noun* M, F German (*person*).

aller¹ *verb* [7] **1** to go; **aller à Paris** to go to Paris; **je vais à Paris** I'm going to Paris, I go to Paris; **2** (*used with another verb in much the same way as 'going to' is used in English*) **je vais écrire à ma mère ce soir** I'm going to write to my mother this evening; **3 (comment) ça va?** how are you?; **ça va bien** I'm fine; **comment va ta mère?** how's your mother?; **elle va bien** she's fine; **4** to suit; **cette robe te va bien** that dress really suits you; **est-ce que jeudi te va?** does Thursday suit you?; **5 s'en aller** to leave; **je m'en vais!** I'm off!

aller² *noun* M **1 faire des allers et retours** to go to and fro; **2 un aller-simple** a single ticket; **un aller-retour** a return ticket; **Avignon aller simple, s'il vous plaît** a single to Avignon please.

allergie *noun* F allergy.

allergique *adjective* **être allergique à** to be allergic to.

alliance *noun* F **1** wedding ring; **2** alliance.

alligator *noun* M alligator.

allô hello (*only used on the telephone*).

allocation *noun* F benefit, allowance.

allocation chômage *noun* F unemployment benefit.

allocations familiales *plural noun* F family allowance.

allonger *verb* [52] **1** to lengthen; **2** to extend; **3 s'allonger** to lie down.

allumer *verb* [1] **1** to light; **allumer le feu** to light the fire; **2** to switch on; **allumer la lampe** to switch on the lamp; **3** to switch on the lights.

allumette *noun* F match; **une boîte d'allumettes** a box of matches.

allure *noun* F **1** speed; **à toute allure** at top speed; **2** appearance (*of a person*).

alors *adverb* **1** then, at that time; **elle travaillait alors à Paris** she was working in Paris then; **2** so; **alors, comment ça va?** so how are you?; **3 alors que** while; **alors qu'elle**

faisait ses devoirs while she was doing her homework.

alouette *noun* F skylark.

Alpes *noun* F **les Alpes** the Alps.

alphabet *noun* M alphabet.

alphabétique *adjective* alphabetical; **dans l'ordre alphabétique, par ordre alphabétique** in alphabetical order.

alpin *adjective* alpine.

alpinisme *noun* M mountaineering.

alternatif (F **alternative**) *adjective* alternative.

altitude *noun* F altitude.

alu *noun* M (*informal*) aluminium; **du papier alu** kitchen foil.

aluminium *noun* M aluminium.

amalgame *noun* M mixture.

amande *noun* F **1** almond; **2** kernel (*of a fruit stone*).

amant *noun* M lover.

amateur *noun* M enthusiast; **un amateur de musique** a music lover; *adjective* amateur; **un photographe amateur** an amateur photographer.

ambassade *noun* F embassy; **l'ambassade de France** the French Embassy.

ambassadeur *noun* M ambassador.

ambiance *noun* F atmosphere; **une bonne ambiance** a good atmosphere.

ambigu (F **ambiguë**) *adjective* ambiguous.

ambitieux (F **ambitieuse**) *adjective* ambitious.

ambition *noun* F ambition.

ambulance *noun* F ambulance.

ambulancier, ambulancière *noun* M, F ambulance driver.

âme *noun* F soul.

amélioration *noun* F improvement.

améliorer, s'améliorer *verb* [1] to improve.

aménagé *adjective* **1** equipped; **une cuisine aménagée** an equipped kitchen; **2** converted.

aménager *verb* [52] **1** to convert, to do up (*a building, a room, etc*); **2** to develop (*an area*); **3** to construct, to improve (*a road or road system*).

amende *noun* F fine; **une amende de 500 francs** a 500-franc fine.

amener *verb* [50] **1** to bring; **elle a amené son cousin** she brought her cousin (with her); **2** to take; **amener un enfant à l'école** to take a child to school.

amer (F **amère**) *adjective* bitter.

américain *adjective* American.

Américain, Américaine *noun* M, F American.

Amérique *noun* F America.

ami, amie *noun* M, F friend; **un ami à moi** a friend of mine; **un ami à Lisa** a friend of Lisa's. *adjective* friendly.

amiante *noun* M asbestos.

amical (M *plural* **amicaux**) *adjective* friendly.

amicale *noun* F association.

amicalement *adverb* **1** in a friendly way; **2** Best wishes (*at the end of a letter*).

amitié *noun* F **1** friendship; **faire quelque chose par amitié** to do something out of friendship; **2 amitiés** love (*at the end of a letter*).

amortisseur *noun* M shock absorber.

amour *noun* M love.

amoureux (F **amoureuse**) *adjective* in love; **être amoureux de** to be in love with.

amour-propre *noun* M self-esteem.

amovible *adjective* detachable.

amphi *noun* M (*informal*) lecture theatre (*in a university*).

amphithéâtre *noun* M **1** amphitheatre; **2** lecture theatre.

ample *adjective* **1** loose-fitting (*jacket, dress, etc*); **2** ample (*quantity*).

ampleur *noun* F size, scope.

ampli *noun* M (*informal*) amplifier.

amplificateur *noun* M amplifier.

ampoule *noun* F **1** light bulb; **2** blister.

amusant *adjective* **1** funny; **une histoire amusante** a funny story; **2** entertaining.

amuse-gueule *noun* M **des amuse-gueule** nibbles (*crisps, nuts, etc*).

amuser *verb* [1] **1** to amuse; **2** to entertain; **3 s'amuser** to play; **4 s'amuser** to enjoy oneself, to have a good time; **on s'est bien amusé** we really enjoyed ourselves, we had a really good time.

an *noun* M year; **elle a dix ans** she's ten (years old); **le nouvel an, le jour de l'an** New Year's Day; ★ **bon an, mal an** year in, year out (*literally: good year, bad year*).

analphabète *adjective* illiterate.

analyse *noun* F **1** analysis; **2 une analyse de sang** a blood test.

analyser *verb* [1] to analyse.

ananas *noun* M pineapple.

anatomie *noun* F anatomy.

ancêtre *noun* M & F ancestor.

anchois *noun* M anchovy.

ancien (F **ancienne**) *adjective* **1** (*coming before a noun*) former; **l'ancien président** the former president, the ex-president; **mon ancienne école** my old school; **un ancien élève** a former pupil; **2** (*coming after a noun*) old; **une maison ancienne** an old house; **une table ancienne** an antique table.

ancien combattant *noun* M war veteran.

âne *noun* M donkey.

anémone *noun* F anemone.

anesthésie *noun* F anaesthesia; **une anesthésie** an anaesthetic.

anesthésiste *noun* M & F anaesthetist.

ange *noun* M angel; ★ **être aux anges** to be over the moon, to be absolutely delighted (*literally: to be at the level of the angels*).

angine *noun* F throat infection; **avoir une angine** to have a throat infection.

anglais *noun* M English; **parler l'anglais** to speak English. *adjective* English.

Anglais, Anglaise *noun* M, F Englishman, Englishwoman; **les Anglais** the English; **il y a une Anglaise dans notre classe** there's an English girl in our class.

angle *noun* M **1** angle; **un angle droit** a right angle; **2** corner; **à l'angle de la rue** at the corner of the street; **le magasin qui fait l'angle** the shop on the corner.

Angleterre *noun* F England; **en Angleterre** in (or to) England; **aller en Angleterre** to go to England.

Anglo-Normande *adjective* **les îles Anglo-Normandes** the Channel Islands.

anglophone *noun* M & F English speaker. *adjective* English-speaking.

angoisse *noun* F anxiety.

angoissé *adjective* anxious.

anguille *noun* F eel.

animal (*plural* **animaux**) *noun* M animal.

animateur, animatrice *noun* M, F **1** group leader; **2** organizer; **3** presenter.

animation *noun* F **1** liveliness, life; **il y a beaucoup d'animation dans le quartier le soir** there's a lot going on in the area at night; **2** organization (*of a group, a programme, etc*).

animé *adjective* **1** lively (*person or discussion*); **2** busy (*place*).

animer *verb* [1] **1** to run (*a course*); **2** to lead (*a group*); **3** to present (*a programme or a show*); **4** to liven up (*an occasion*); **5** **s'animer** to liven up.

anis *noun* M aniseed.

anneau *noun* M ring.

année *noun* F year; **l'année prochaine** next year; **l'année dernière** last year; **les années 70** the seventies; **Bonne année** Happy New Year.

anniversaire *noun* M **1** birthday; **fêter son anniversaire** to celebrate one's birthday; **Bon anniversaire, Joyeux anniversaire** Happy Birthday; **2** anniversary.

annonce *noun* F **1** advertisement; **les petites annonces** the small ads (*in a newspaper*); **2** announcement; **3** sign.

annoncer *verb* [61] **1** to announce; **2** to forecast; **ils annoncent de la neige pour demain** snow is forecast for tomorrow.

annuaire *noun* M directory; **l'annuaire téléphonique** the telephone directory.

annuel (F **annuelle**) *adjective* annual, yearly.

annuler *verb* [1] to cancel; **le vol a été annulé** the flight has been cancelled.

anonyme *adjective* anonymous.

anorak *noun* M anorak.

anorexie *noun* F anorexia.

anormal (M *plural* **anormaux**) *adjective* abnormal.

anse *noun* F handle (*of a basket, cup, jug, or teapot*).

Antarctique *noun* M **l'Antarctique** the Antarctic.

antenne *noun* F **1** aerial (*for a radio or television*); **2** antenna (*of an insect, a radio mast, or a spacecraft*).

anthropologie *noun* F anthropology.

antibiotique *noun* M antibiotic; **prendre des antibiotiques** to be on antibiotics.

antichoc *adjective* shockproof; **un casque antichoc** a crash helmet.

anticiper *verb* [1] to foresee, to anticipate.

antidérapant *adjective* nonslip, nonskid.

antidote *noun* M antidote.

antigel *noun* M antifreeze.

antillais *adjective* West Indian.

Antilles *plural noun* F **les Antilles** the West Indies.

antilope *noun* F antelope.

antipathique *adjective* unpleasant.

antiquaire *noun* M & F antique dealer.

antiquité *noun* F antique.

antiseptique *noun* M, *adjective* antiseptic.

antitabac *adjective* antismoking.

antiterroriste *adjective* antiterrorist.

antivol *noun* M anti-theft device.

anxieux (F **anxieuse**) *adjective* anxious.

août *noun* M August; **en août, au mois d'août** in August.

apercevoir *verb* [66] **1** to catch sight of; **2 s'apercevoir de** to notice; **s'apercevoir que** to notice that.

aperçu *noun* M **1** insight; **2** glimpse.

apéritif *noun* M drink (*usually alcoholic, before a meal*).

aphte *noun* M mouth ulcer.

aplatir *verb* [2] **1** to flatten; **2** to smooth out.

apostrophe *noun* F apostrophe.

apparaître *verb* [57] **1** to appear; **2** to seem; **il apparaît que** it seems that.

appareil *noun* M **1** device, appliance, piece of equipment; **2** telephone; **c'est Paul à l'appareil** it's Paul speaking; **3 un appareil (dentaire)** a brace (*for teeth*).

appareil photo *noun* M camera.

apparemment *adverb* apparently.

apparence *noun* F appearance.

apparent *adjective* **1** visible, obvious; **2** apparent.

apparition *noun* F appearance.

appartement *noun* M flat; **'appartement à louer'** 'flat to let'.

appartenir *verb* [81] **appartenir à** to belong to; **est-ce que ce stylo t'appartient?** does this pen belong to you?, is this pen yours?; **à qui appartiennent ces chaussures?** who do these shoes belong to?

appel *noun* M **1** call, appeal; **un appel d'aide** a call for help; **2 un appel (téléphonique)** a telephone call; **3 faire appel à** to appeal to; **4 faire l'appel** to take the register (*at school*).

appeler *verb* [18] **1** to call; **ils l'ont appelé Roger** they called him Roger; **2 s'appeler** to be called; **il s'appelle Frank** he's called Frank, his name is Frank; **je m'appelle Anne** my name is Anne; **comment t'appelles-tu?, tu t'appelles comment?** what's your name?; **3** to phone; **4** to call; **appeler un taxi** to call a taxi.

appendicite *noun* F appendicitis.

appétissant *adjective* appetizing.

appétit *noun* M appetite; **'bon appétit'** 'enjoy your meal'.

applaudir *verb* [2] to applaud.

applaudissements *plural noun* M applause.

application *noun* F **1** care; **2** application.

appliquer *verb* [1] **1** to apply; **2 s'appliquer** to take care; **3 s'appliquer à** to apply to; **cela ne s'applique pas à vous** that doesn't apply to you.

apporter *verb* [1] to bring.

apprécier *verb* [1] to appreciate.

appréhender *verb* [1] **1** to arrest; **2** to dread.

apprenant, apprenante *noun* M, F learner.

apprendre *verb* [64] **1** to learn; **apprendre à lire** to learn to read; **2** to hear; **j'ai appris que tu vas partir** I hear you're leaving; **3** to teach; **apprendre quelque chose à quelqu'un** to teach somebody something; **elle leur apprend le français** she's teaching them French; **elle leur apprend à parler français** she's teaching them to speak French.

approche *noun* F approach.

approcher *verb* [1] **1** to move (something) closer; **approche ta chaise** move your chair closer; **approche ta chaise de la table** move your chair closer to the table; **2 approcher quelqu'un** to go up to somebody; **3 s'approcher de quelque chose** to go (or come) near to something.

approprié *adjective* appropriate.

approuver *verb* [1] **1** to approve of; **2** to approve (*a document, project, budget, etc*).

approximatif (F **approximative**) *adjective* approximate, rough.

approximativement *adverb* approximately, roughly.

appui *noun* M support.

appuyer *verb* [41] **1 appuyer sur quelque chose** to press something; **appuie sur le bouton** press the button; **2** to lean; **appuyer quelque chose contre le mur** to lean something against the wall.

après *adverb* afterwards, later; **une heure après** an hour later; **peu après** shortly afterwards; **longtemps après** a long time later. *preposition* **1** after **après dix heures** after ten o'clock; **après l'école** after school; **2 après avoir fait** after doing; **3 après que** after.

après-demain *adverb* the day after tomorrow.

après-midi *noun* M or F afternoon; **cet après-midi** this afternoon; **demain après-midi** tomorrow afternoon; **hier après-midi** yesterday afternoon; **tous les après-midi** every afternoon.

aquarelle *noun* F watercolours; **une aquarelle** a watercolour (painting).

aquarium *noun* M aquarium, fish tank.

arabe *noun* M Arabic. *adjective* **1** Arab; **2** Arabic.

Arabe *noun* M & F Arab.

araignée *noun* F spider; **une toile d'araignée** a spider's web.

arbitraire *adjective* arbitrary.

arbitre *noun* M referee, umpire.

arbre *noun* M tree.

arc *noun* M **1** bow (*as in 'bow and arrow'*); **2** arch.

arc-en-ciel *noun* M rainbow.

archéologie *noun* F archeology.

archéologue *noun* M & F archeologist.

archet *noun* M bow (*for a musical instrument such as a violin*).

archevêque *noun* M archbishop.

architecte *noun* M & F architect.

architecture *noun* F architecture.

Arctique *noun* M **l'Arctique** the Arctic.

ardoise *noun* F slate.

arène *noun* F **1** arena; **2** bullring.

arête *noun* F fishbone.

argent *noun* M **1** money; **dépenser de l'argent** to spend money; **2** silver; **une cuillère en argent** a silver spoon.

argent de poche *noun* M pocket money.

argot *noun* M slang.

aristocrate *noun* M & F aristocrat.

aristocratie *noun* F aristocracy.

arithmétique *noun* F arithmetic.

arme *noun* F weapon.

armé *adjective* **1** armed. **2 armé de** armed with, equipped with.

arme à feu *noun* F firearm.

armée *noun* F army.

armée de l'air *noun* F Air Force.

armée de terre *noun* F Army.

armoire *noun* F **1** cupboard; **2** wardrobe.

aromates *plural noun* M herbs and spices.

aromathérapie *noun* F aromatherapy.

aromatisé *adjective* flavoured.

arôme *noun* M **1** flavouring; **2** aroma.

arracher *verb* [1] **1 arracher quelque chose à quelqu'un** to snatch something from somebody; **2** to rip out, to rip off (*a page or pages*); **3** to pull up (*weeds or vegetables*).

arrangement *noun* M arrangement.

arranger *verb* [52] **1** to arrange; **arranger une réunion** to arrange a meeting; **2** to arrange (*flowers, books, etc*). **3** to sort out; **4** to fix; **5 s'arranger** to get better; **ça va s'arranger** it will sort itself out; **6 s'arranger avec quelqu'un** to sort it out with somebody; **tu t'arranges avec Paul** sort it out with Paul.

arrestation *noun* F arrest.

arrêt *noun* M **1** stop; **un arrêt de bus** a bus stop; **2 sans arrêt** non-stop.

arrêter *verb* [1] **1** to stop; **arrêter la voiture** to stop the car; **2** to switch off (*an engine, a machine, etc*); **3 arrêter de faire** to stop doing; **il a arrêté de fumer** he's stopped smoking; **elle n'arrête pas de travailler** she never stops working; **4 s'arrêter** to stop; **on va s'arrêter à**

la boulangerie we'll stop at the baker's.

arrhes *plural noun* F deposit; **verser des arrhes** to pay a deposit.

arrière *noun* M back; **à l'arrière** in the back (*of a car*); **regarder en arrière** to look back. *adjective* back (*door, pocket, etc*).

arrière-goût *noun* M aftertaste.

arrière-grand-mère *noun* F great-grandmother.

arrière-grand-père *noun* M great-grandfather.

arrière-grands-parents *plural noun* M great-grandparents.

arrière-petits-enfants *plural noun* M great-grandchildren.

arrivée *noun* F arrival.

arriver *verb* [1] **1** to arrive; **arriver à Londres** to arrive in London, to get to London; **je suis arrivé à cinq heures** I arrived at five o'clock, I got there (or here) at five o'clock; **j'arrive!** just coming!; **2** to happen; **un accident est arrivé** an accident has happened; **tu sais ce qui m'est arrivé?** do you know what happened to me?; **3 arriver à faire** to manage to do; **je n'arrive pas à tourner la clef** I can't manage to turn the key.

arrogant *adjective* arrogant.

arrondi *adjective* rounded.

arrondissement *noun* M arrondissement; **elle habite à Paris dans le neuvième arrondissement** she lives in Paris in the ninth arrondissement (*large French cities* *are divided into numbered administrative areas called 'arrondissements').*

arroser *verb* [1] to water; **arroser les plantes** to water the plants; **on va arroser l'anniversaire de mon frère** we're going to have a few drinks to celebrate my brother's birthday.

arrosoir *noun* M watering can.

art *noun* M art; **une galerie d'art** an art gallery; **l'art de faire** the art of doing.

art dramatique *noun* M drama.

artère *noun* F **1** artery; **2** arterial road; **3** main road.

arthrite *noun* F arthritis.

artichaut *noun* M artichoke.

article *noun* M **1** article (*in a newspaper, magazine, etc*). **2** item (*for sale*); **articles de sport** sports equipment; **articles de toilette** toiletries; **3** article (*in grammar*); **l'article défini** the definite article; **l'article indéfini** the indefinite article.

articulation *noun* F joint.

artificiel (F **artificielle**) *adjective* artificial.

artisan *noun* M craftsman.

artisanal (M *plural* **artisanaux**) *adjective* **1** traditional; **2** hand-crafted.

artisanat *noun* M arts and crafts.

artiste *noun* M & F **1** artist; **2** performer.

as[1] *verb* SEE **avoir**.

as[2] *noun* M ace.

ascenseur *noun* M lift; **prendre l'ascenseur** to take the lift.

asiatique *adjective* Asian.

Asie *noun* F Asia.

asile *noun* M **1** refuge; **2 le droit d'asile** political asylum.

aspect *noun* M **1** aspect; **2** appearance; **d'un aspect bizarre** strange-looking; **3** side; **l'aspect positif** the positive side.

asperger *verb* [52] to sprinkle.

asperges *plural noun* F asparagus.

asphyxier, s'asphyxier *verb* [1] to suffocate.

aspirateur *noun* M vacuum cleaner.

aspirine *noun* F aspirin.

assaisonnement *noun* M **1** seasoning; **2** dressing.

assaisonner *verb* [1] **1** to season; **2** to put the dressing on (*a salad*).

assassin, assassine *noun* M, F murderer.

assassinat *noun* M murder.

assassiner *verb* [1] to murder.

assemblée *noun* F meeting.

assembler *verb* [1] **1** to put together, to assemble (*a kit, a machine, etc*); **2** to gather together; **3 s'assembler** to gather (*of a group, crowd, demonstration, etc*); ★ **qui se ressemble s'assemble** birds of a feather flock together (*literally: those who are similar gather together*).

asseoir *verb* [20] **s'asseoir** to sit down; **s'asseoir sur une chaise** to sit down on a chair; **assieds-toi** take a seat; **asseyez-vous** do sit down; SEE ALSO **assis**.

assez *adverb* **1 assez de** enough; **assez de pain** enough bread; **2** enough; **elle ne mange pas assez** she doesn't eat enough; **3** enough; **est-ce que l'eau est assez chaude?** is the water hot enough?; **4** quite; **leur maison est assez grande** their house is quite big; **assez souvent** quite often; **assez joli** quite pretty; **5 j'en ai assez (de)** (*informal*) I'm fed up (with).

assiette *noun* F plate; **une assiette plate** a dinner plate; **une assiette creuse, une assiette à soupe** a soup plate; ★ **je ne suis pas dans mon assiette aujourd'hui** I'm not my usual self today.

assis *adjective* **être assis** to be sitting; **elle était assise dans un fauteuil** she was sitting in an armchair; **rester assis** to remain seated.

assistance *noun* F **1** audience; **dans l'assistance** in the audience; **2** assistance.

assistant, assistante *noun* M, F assistant.

assister *verb* [1] **1** to assist; **2** to aid (*a country, the poor, etc*); **3 assister à** to be present at, to be at; **j'ai assisté à leur mariage** I was at their wedding.

association *noun* F association.

associé, associée *noun* M, F associate, partner.

associer *verb* [1] **1 associer quelqu'un à quelque chose** to include somebody in something; **2 s'associer à un groupe** to join a group; **3 s'associer pour faire** to get together to do.

assommer *verb* [1] **1 assommer quelqu'un** to knock somebody senseless; **2 assommer quelqu'un** (*informal*) to bore somebody stiff; **3 être assommé par une nouvelle** to be stunned by a piece of news.

assorti *adjective* matching; **rideaux et coussins assortis** matching curtains and cushions; **une veste assortie à sa robe** a jacket to match her dress.

assortiment *noun* M assortment, selection.

assortir *verb* [2] **1** to match; **2 s'assortir à** to match.

assouplissant *noun* M fabric softener.

assourdir *verb* [2] **1** to deafen; **2** to muffle.

assourdissant *adjective* deafening.

assumer *verb* [1] **assumer la responsabilité de quelque chose** to take responsibility for something; **assumer une fonction** to hold a position.

assurance *noun* F **1** confidence; **avec assurance** confidently; **2** insurance.

assuré *adjective* **1** confident; **2** insured.

assurer *verb* [1] **1** to assure; **je vous assure que c'est vrai** I assure you it's true; **2** to insure; **assurer sa voiture** to insure one's car; **3** to provide (*a service*); **4** to carry out (*a task or a responsibility*); **5 s'assurer** to make sure.

astérisque *noun* M asterisk.

asthmatique *adjective* asthmatic.

asthme *noun* M asthma.

asticot *noun* M maggot.

astiquer *verb* [1] to polish.

astrologie *noun* F astrology.

astrologue *noun* M & F astrologer.

astronome *noun* M & F astronomer.

astronomie *noun* F astronomy.

astronomique *adjective* astronomical.

astuce *noun* F **1** cleverness; **2 une astuce** a trick (*for managing to do something*); **il doit y avoir une astuce** there must be a trick to it.

astucieux (F **astucieuse**) *adjective* clever.

atelier *noun* M **1** workshop; **2** studio (*of an artist, a sculptor, etc*); **3** work group.

athée *noun* M & F atheist.

Athènes *noun* Athens.

athlète *noun* M & F athlete.

athlétique *adjective* athletic.

athlétisme *noun* M athletics.

Atlantique *noun* M **l'Atlantique** the Atlantic.

atlas *noun* M atlas.

atmosphère *noun* F atmosphere.

atome *noun* M atom.

atomique *adjective* atomic.

atomiseur *noun* M spray, atomizer.

atout *noun* M **1** trump card; **c'est atout pique** spades are trumps; **2** asset, advantage.

atroce *adjective* dreadful, terrible.

atrocité *noun* F **1** atrocity; **2** monstrosity.

attachant *adjective* lovable.

attache *noun* F **1** tie, string, strap; **2 attaches familiales** family ties.

attacher *verb* [1] **1 attacher ses cheveux** to tie (or fix) your hair back; **2 s'attacher** to stick (*to the pan*).

attaque *noun* F attack.

attaquer *verb* [1] **1** to attack; **2** to tackle (*a job*).

attarder *verb* [1] **s'attarder** to linger.

atteindre *verb* [60] **1** to reach; **2** to achieve.

atteint *adjective* **être atteint d'une maladie** to be suffering from an illness.

attendant *in phrase* **en attendant** meanwhile, in the meantime.

attendre *verb* [3] **1** to wait; **tu peux attendre deux minutes?** can you wait for two minutes?; **2** to wait for; **j'attends le bus** I'm waiting for the bus; **je t'attends dehors** I'll wait for you outside; **3 s'attendre à** to expect.

attendrissant *adjective* touching.

attentat *noun* M **1 un attentat (à la bombe)** a bomb attack, a bombing; **2** assassination attempt.

attente *noun* F wait; **une attente de vingt minutes** a twenty-minute wait.

attentif (F **attentive**) *adjective* **1** attentive; **2** careful.

attention *noun* F **1** attention; **2 faire attention à** to be careful of; **3 attention!** watch out!

atterrir *verb* [2] to land.

atterrissage *noun* M landing.

attirant *adjective* attractive.

attirer *verb* [1] to attract; **attirer l'attention de quelqu'un sur quelque chose** to attract (or draw) somebody's attention to something.

attitude *noun* F attitude.

attraction *noun* F attraction.

attraper *verb* [1] **1** to catch; **2 attraper un rhume** to catch a cold; **3** to catch hold of.

attrayant *adjective* attractive.

attrister *verb* [1] to sadden.

au SEE **à**.

aube *noun* F dawn; **à l'aube** at dawn.

aubépine *noun* F hawthorn.

auberge *noun* F inn; ★ **on n'est pas sorti de l'auberge** our problems are not over yet (*literally: we're not out of the inn*).

auberge de jeunesse *noun* F youth hostel.

aubergine *noun* F aubergine.

aucun *adjective* no; **en aucun cas** under no circumstances; **sans aucun doute** without any doubt. *pronoun* none; **aucun des deux** neither of them; **aucun d'entre eux** none of them.

aucunement *adverb* in no way.

audace *noun* F daring.

audacieux (F **audacieuse**) *adjective* daring.

au-delà de *preposition* beyond.

au-dessous *adverb* **1** underneath; **2** below; **3 au-dessous de** underneath; **au-dessous de la table** underneath the table; **4 au-dessous de** below; **au-dessous de la limite** below the limit.

au-dessus *adverb* **1** above; **2 au-dessus de** above.

audience *noun* F audience.

audiovisuel (F **audiovisuelle**) *adjective* audiovisual.

auditeur, auditrice *noun* M, F listener.

audition *noun* F audition.

augmentation *noun* F increase; **l'augmentation des prix** the increase in prices; **une augmentation de salaire** a pay rise.

augmenter *verb* [1] **1** to raise, to increase; **augmenter les prix** to raise prices; **2** to rise, to go up; **le prix a augmenté** the price has gone up.

aujourd'hui *adverb* today; **nous sommes lundi aujourd'hui** today is Monday.

auparavant *adverb* before, beforehand.

auprès de *preposition* beside, next to.

auquel *pronoun* **le garçon auquel je parle** the boy I'm talking to.

aura, aurai, auras, aurez, aurons, auront *verb* SEE **avoir**.

au revoir *exclamation* goodbye.

aussi *adverb* **1** also, too; **moi aussi** me too; **j'ai aussi invité ton frère** I also invited your brother, I invited your brother as well;
2 aussi...que as...as; **mon panier est aussi lourd que le tien** my basket is as heavy as yours; **3 aussi bien que** as well as; **les enfants aussi bien que les adultes** children as well as adults.
conjunction so, therefore.

aussitôt *adverb* immediately.

Australie *noun* F Australia.

Australien, Australienne *noun* M, F Australian.

australien (F **australienne**) *adjective* Australian.

autant *adverb* **1** as much, so much; **je n'ai jamais mangé autant** I've never eaten so much; **2 autant que** as much as, as many as; **tu en as autant que moi** you have as much (or as many) as me; **3 autant de...que** as much...as, as many...as; **tu as autant de problèmes que moi** you have as many problems as I do.

autel *noun* M altar.

auteur *noun* M author.

authentique *adjective* genuine.

auto *noun* F car.

autobiographie *noun* F autobiography.

autobus *noun* M bus.

autocar *noun* M coach.

autocollant *noun* M sticker. *adjective* self-adhesive.

autodéfense *noun* F self-defence.

auto-école *noun* F driving school.

automate *noun* M robot.

automatique *adjective* automatic.

automatiquement *adverb* automatically.

automne *noun* M autumn; **en automne** in autumn.

automobile *noun* F car. *adjective* **l'industrie automobile** the car industry.

automobiliste *noun* M & F motorist.

autoradio *noun* M car radio.

autorisation *noun* F **1** permission; **2** permit.

autoriser *verb* [1] **1** to allow, to authorize; **2 autoriser quelqu'un à faire** to allow somebody to do.

autorité *noun* F authority.

autoroute *noun* F motorway; **l'autoroute de l'information** the information super-highway.

auto-stop *noun* M hitchhiking;
faire de l'auto-stop to hitchhike.

auto-stoppeur, auto-stoppeuse *noun* M, F
hitchhiker.

autour *adverb* 1 around; 2 **autour de** round, around; **autour de la table** round the table.

autre *adjective* 1 other; **l'autre couteau** the other knife; **l'autre jour** the other day; 2 **un/une autre** another; **tu peux me passer un autre verre?** can you pass me another glass?; 3 **quelqu'un d'autre** somebody else; **personne d'autre** nobody else.
pronoun 1 **un/une autre** another one; **donne-moi un autre** give me another one; 2 **les autres** the others; **où sont les autres?** where are the others?

autrefois *adverb* in the past, in the old days.

autrement *adverb* 1 differently; **autrement dit** in other words; 2 otherwise.

autre part *adverb* somewhere else.

Autriche *noun* F Austria.

Autrichien, Autrichienne *noun* M, F Austrian.

autrichien (F **autrichienne**) *adjective* Austrian.

autruche *noun* F ostrich.

aux SEE **à**.

auxiliaire *noun* M & F,
adjective auxiliary.

auxquelles *pronoun* **les filles auxquelles je parlais** the girls I was talking to.

auxquels *pronoun* **les garçons auxquels je parlais** the boys I was talking to.

avalanche *noun* F avalanche.

avaler *verb* [1] 1 to swallow; 2 to inhale.

avance *noun* F 1 advance, progress; 2 **je suis arrivé dix minutes en avance** I arrived ten minutes early; **avoir dix minutes d'avance** to be ten minutes early; 3 **être en avance** to be early; 4 **à l'avance** in advance.

avancer *verb* [61] 1 to move forward, to advance; 2 **avancer quelque chose** to move something forward; 3 **ma montre avance de cinq minutes** my watch is five minutes fast.

avant *adverb* 1 before; **longtemps avant** a long time before;
2 forward; **plus avant** further forward.
preposition 1 before; **avant Noël** before Christmas; **avant six heures** before six o'clock; **elle est arrivée avant moi** she arrived before me;
2 **avant de faire** before doing; **avant de partir, je vais téléphoner à ma mère** before leaving (or before I leave) I'll phone my mother;
3 **avant que** before.
noun M front.
adjective front; **la roue avant** the front wheel.

avantage *noun* M advantage.

avantageux (F **avantageuse**)
adjective **1 des prix avantageux**
attractive prices; **2 des conditions
avantageuses** favourable
conditions.

avant-bras *noun* M forearm.

avant-dernier, avant-dernière
noun M, F **l'avant-dernier** the last
but one.
adjective second last, last but one.

avant-hier *adverb* the day before
yesterday.

avare *noun* M & F miser.
adjective mean, miserly.

avec *preposition* with; **avec Marie**
with Marie; **avec un couteau** with a
knife; **avec ça?** anything else? (*in a
shop*).

avenir *noun* M future; **l'avenir** the
future; **à l'avenir** in the future.

aventure *noun* F adventure.

avenue *noun* F avenue.

averse *noun* F shower.

avertir *verb* [2] **1** to inform; **2** to
warn.

avertissement *noun* M warning.

aveuglant *adjective* blinding.

aveugle *adjective* blind.

aveuglément *adverb* blindly.

aveugler *verb* [1] to blind.

avez *verb* SEE **avoir**.

aviation *noun* F **1** aviation;
2 aircraft industry; **3** flying; **4** air
force.

avion *noun* M aeroplane, plane;
aller à Paris en avion to go to Paris
by plane, to fly to Paris; **par avion** by
airmail.

aviron *noun* M **1** rowing; **faire de
l'aviron** to row; **2** oar.

avis *noun* M **1** opinion; **à mon avis**
in my opinion; **2 changer d'avis** to
change one's mind; **3** notice.

avocat[1], **avocate** *noun* M, F
1 solicitor; **2** barrister.

avocat[2] *noun* M avocado (pear).

avoine *noun* F oats; **des flocons
d'avoine** porridge oats.

avoir *verb* [5] **1** to have (got); **elle a
trois frères** she has (or she's got)
three brothers; **tu as beaucoup de
livres** you have (or you've got) a lot
of books; **2** (*talking about age*)
avoir dix ans to be ten; **Claudie a
dix ans** Claudie's ten; **quel âge a-
t-il?** how old is he?; **3 avoir chaud**
to be hot; **j'ai chaud** I'm hot; **j'ai
froid** I'm cold; **4** (*used with another
verb, like 'have' in English, to form
past tenses*) **j'ai perdu mon stylo**
I have lost my pen; **j'ai vu ta mère
hier** I saw your mother yesterday;
5 j'en ai pour dix minutes it'll take
me ten minutes; **6 il y a** there is,
there are; **il y a un livre sur la table**
there's a book on the table; **il y a trois
livres sur la table** there are three
books on the table; **7 il y a** ago;
il y a trois ans three years ago;
8 qu'est-ce qu'il y a? what's the
matter?

avons *verb* SEE **avoir**.

avortement *noun* M abortion.

avouer *verb* [1] to confess, to admit.

avril *noun* M April; **en avril, au mois d'avril** in April.

azalée *noun* F azalea.

azote *noun* M nitrogen.

B b

babouin *noun* M baboon.

baby-foot *noun* M table football; **jouer au baby-foot** to play table football; **on va faire une partie de baby-foot** we're going to have a game of table football.

bac *noun* M 1 (*informal*) SHORT FOR **baccalauréat**; 2 tub.

bac à glace *noun* M ice tray.

baccalauréat *noun* M baccalaureate (*school-leaving certificate sat at the age of 17–18 and giving access to higher education*); **passer le baccalauréat** to sit the baccalaureate; **réussir au baccalauréat** to pass the baccalaureate.

bâche *noun* F tarpaulin.

badaud, badaude *noun* M, F passerby, onlooker.

baffe *noun* F (*informal*) slap.

baffle *noun* M speaker (*on a music system*).

bagage *noun* M **un bagage** a piece of luggage; **des bagages** luggage; **où sont tes bagages?** where is your luggage?; **j'ai fait mes bagages** I've packed.

bagarre *noun* F fight.

bagarrer *verb* [1] **se bagarrer** to fight.

bagnole *noun* F (*informal*) car.

bague *noun* F ring.

baguette *noun* F 1 baguette, French bread stick; 2 stick; 3 drumstick; 4 chopstick.

baguette magique *noun* F magic wand.

baie *noun* 1 bay (*on the sea*); 2 berry; 3 **une baie vitrée** a picture window.

baignade *noun* F swimming; **'baignade interdite'** 'no swimming'.

baigner *verb* [1] **se baigner** to go swimming.

baignoire *noun* F bath.

bail (*plural* **baux**) *noun* M lease; **un bail de trois ans** a three-year lease.

bâiller *verb* [1] to yawn.

bain *noun* M bath; **prendre un bain** to have a bath.

baiser *noun* M kiss; **bons baisers** love and kisses (*at the end of a letter*).

baisser *verb* [1] 1 to lower; **baisser le store** to lower (or pull down) the blind; **baisser le volume** to turn down the volume; **baisser la lumière** to turn down the lights; **baisser les prix** to cut prices; 2 **se baisser** to bend down.

bal *noun* M dance; **un bal populaire** a village dance (or disco).

balade *noun* F walk, drive; **faire une balade (à pied)** to go for a walk; **faire**

une balade (en voiture) to go for a drive; **faire une balade à la campagne** to go for a walk (or drive) in the country.

balader *verb* [1] **1 se balader** to go for a walk (or a drive); **se balader en Écosse** to tour around Scotland; **2 balader quelque chose** to carry something around.

baladeur *noun* M Walkman™, personal stereo.

balai *noun* M broom, (long-handled) brush; **passer le balai** to sweep the floor.

balance *noun* F scales; **une balance de cuisine** kitchen scales.

Balance *noun* F Libra (*sign of the Zodiac*).

balancer *verb* [61] **1** to sway; **2** to swing; **3** (*informal*) to throw, to chuck; **balance-moi les clés!** chuck me the keys!; **4** (*informal*) to chuck out; **je vais balancer tous ces vieux bouquins** I'm going to chuck out all these old books.

balançoire *noun* F **1** swing; **2** seesaw.

balayer *verb* [59] **1** to sweep; **balayer la cuisine** to sweep the kitchen floor; **2** to sweep up; **balayer les miettes** to sweep up the crumbs.

balayeur, balayeuse *noun* M, F roadsweeper.

balbutier *verb* [1] to mumble.

balcon *noun* M balcony.

baleine *noun* F whale.

baliser *verb* [1] **1** to signpost; **2** to mark out.

balle *noun* F **1** ball; **2** bullet.

ballerine *noun* F **1** ballerina; **2** ballerina shoe; **3** ballet shoe.

ballet *noun* M ballet.

ballon *noun* M **1** ball; **2** balloon; **3** (*informal*) Breathalyzer™; **souffler dans le ballon** to be breathalyzed.

balnéaire *adjective* seaside; **une station balnéaire** a seaside resort.

bambou *noun* M bamboo.

banal *adjective* ordinary; **peu banal** unusual.

banane *noun* F **1** banana; **2** bumbag.

banc *noun* M bench; **assis sur un banc** sitting on a bench.

bancaire *adjective* **1** banking; **2 une carte bancaire** a bank card.

bancal *adjective* **1** rickety; **2** wobbly.

bande *noun* F **1** group; **une bande de jeunes** a group of young people; **2** gang; **une bande de criminels** a criminal gang; **3** strip (*of fabric or paper*); **4** tape (*for recording*); **5** bandage.

bande-annonce *noun* F trailer (*for a film*).

bandeau (*plural* **bandeaux**) *noun* M **1** headband; **2** blindfold.

bande d'arrêt d'urgence *noun* F hard shoulder (*on motorway*).

bande de fréquence *noun* F wavelength (*on radio*).

bande dessinée *noun* F **1** comic strip; **2** comic book.

bande publique *noun* F Citizen's Band, CB radio.

bande rugueuse *noun* F rumble strip (*on motorway*).

bande sonore *noun* F **1** soundtrack (*of film*); **2** rumble strip (*on motorway*).

bandit *noun* M bandit.

banditisme *noun* M crime.

banlieue *noun* F **la banlieue** the suburbs; **une banlieue** a suburb; **une maison de banlieue** a house in the suburbs; **un train de banlieue** a commuter train.

banque *noun* F bank; **aller à la banque** to go to the bank.

banquette *noun* F **1** wall seat (*in a café or restaurant*); **2** seat (*in a car, bus, or train*).

banquier *noun* M banker.

baptême *noun* M christening.

baptiser *verb* [1] **1** to christen; **2** to name; **3** to nickname.

baquet *noun* M tub.

bar *noun* M bar.

baraque *noun* F (*informal*) house.

barbant *adjective* (*informal*) boring.

barbe *noun* F beard; ★ **c'est la barbe!** what a drag!; ★ **faire quelque chose à la barbe de quelqu'un** to do something behind somebody's back (*literally: to do something in somebody's beard*).

barbe à papa *noun* F candyfloss.

barbecue *noun* M barbecue.

barbelé *noun* M barbed wire.

barbouiller *verb* [1] **1** to smear; **tu es tout barbouillé de confiture** you've got jam all over your face; **2** to daub; **barbouillé de slogans** daubed with slogans.

barbu *noun* M **un barbu** a man with a beard.
adjective bearded.

barème *noun* M scale.

barmaid *noun* F barmaid.

barman *noun* M barman.

baromètre *noun* M barometer.

barque *noun* F rowing boat.

barquette *noun* F tub, container; **une barquette de fraises** a punnet of strawberries.

barrage *noun* M **1** dam; **2** roadblock.

barre *noun* F bar; **une barre de fer** an iron bar; **une barre de chocolat** a chocolate bar.

barreau (*plural* **barreaux**) *noun* M bar; **derrière les barreaux** behind bars (*in prison*).

barrer *verb* [1] **1** to block; **'route barrée'** 'road closed'; **2** to cross out; **barrer trois mots** to cross out three words; **3 se barrer** (*informal*) to clear off, to leave; **je me barre!** I'm off!; ★ **on est mal barré** (*informal*) we're in trouble.

barrette *noun* F hairslide.

barrière *noun* F **1** fence; **2** gate.

bar-tabac *noun* M café (*selling cigarettes, tobacco, and stamps as well as drinks and snacks*).

bas *noun* M **1** bottom, lower part; **en bas de la page** at the bottom of the page; **2** stocking.
adjective (F **basse**) low.
adverb **1** low; **plus bas** further down; **parler plus bas** to lower one's voice; **2 en bas** at the bottom; down below; downstairs; **les voisins d'en bas** the neighbours in the flat below.

bas-côté *noun* M verge (*on the roadside*).

basculant *adjective* **un camion à benne basculante** a dump truck.

bascule *noun* F **1** rocker; **un fauteuil à bascule** a rocking chair; **un cheval à bascule** a rocking horse; **2** seesaw.

basculer *verb* [1] to topple over.

base *noun* F **1** basis; **être à la base de quelque chose** to be at the root of something; **2** base; **à base de chocolat** chocolate-based; **3 de base** basic; **les ingrédients de base** the basic ingredients.

base-ball *noun* M baseball.

base de données *noun* F database.

baser *verb* [1] to base; **basé sur** based on.

basilic *noun* M basil; **une sauce au basilic** a basil sauce.

basket *noun* M **1** basketball; **2** sports shoe, trainer; ★ **lâche-moi les baskets!** (*informal*) get off my back!

basketteur, basketteuse *noun* M, F basketball player.

basque *noun* M, *adjective* Basque.

Basque *noun* M & F Basque (*person*).

basse *noun* F bass (*in music*). *adjective* SEE **bas**.

bassin *noun* M **1** pond; **2** pelvis.

bassine *noun* F bowl.

bassiste *noun* M & F bassist.

bataille *noun* F **1** battle; **la bataille de Trafalgar** the Battle of Trafalgar; **la bataille du pouvoir** the battle for power; **une bataille de boules de neige** a snowball fight; **2** a card game (*similar to beggar-my neighbour*); ★ **avoir les sourcils en bataille** to have bushy eyebrows; ★ **elle avait les cheveux en bataille** her hair was all over the place.

bateau (*plural* **bateaux**) *noun* M boat, ship; **faire du bateau** to go boating (or sailing).

bateau de plaisance *noun* M pleasure boat.

bateau-mouche *noun* M pleasure boat (*a large river boat for sightseeing trips*).

bateau pneumatique *noun* M rubber dinghy.

bâti *adjective* built; **bien bâti** well-built.

bâtiment *noun* M **1** building; **les bâtiments de l'école** the school buildings; **2 le bâtiment** the building trade; **travailler dans le**

bâtiment to work in the building trade; **3** ship.

bâtir *verb* [2] to build.

bâtisse *noun* F building.

bâton *noun* M stick.

bâton de ski *noun* M ski stick.

bâtonnet *noun* M stick.

bâtonnet de poisson *noun* M fish finger.

bâtonnet ouaté *noun* M cotton bud.

batte *noun* F bat (*cricket, baseball, etc*).

batterie *noun* F **1** battery; **2** drum kit, drums.

batterie de cuisine *noun* F pots and pans.

batteur *noun* M **1** drummer; **2** whisk.

battre *verb* [21] **1** to beat (*in a game*); **Nicole m'a battu au tennis** Nicole beat me at tennis; **2** to beat, to batter; **battre un chien** to beat a dog; **3** to beat (*a mixture*); **battre les œufs** to whisk the eggs; **battre la crème** to whip the cream; **4 se battre** to fight; **5 battre des mains** to clap your hands; **6 le cœur bat** the heart beats; **7 la porte bat** the door bangs.

bavard *adjective* talkative.

bavarder *verb* [1] to chat, to chatter.

baver *verb* [1] to dribble.

bazar *noun* M **1** general store; **2** (*informal*) mess.

B.D. *noun* F comic strip; SHORT FOR **bande dessinée**.

beau, bel (*before a vowel or silent 'h'*) (F **belle**) (M *plural* **beaux**) *adjective* **1** beautiful, lovely; **une belle maison** a beautiful house; **un bel homme** a handsome man; **fais de beaux rêves!** sweet dreams!; **2 il fait beau** it's a nice day; ★ **faire le beau** to sit up and beg (*of a dog*).

beaucoup *adverb* **1** a lot; **tu m'en as donné beaucoup** you've given me a lot; **tu ne m'en as pas donné beaucoup** you haven't given me much; **cinquante francs c'est beaucoup** fifty francs is a lot; **2** a lot; **il lit beaucoup** he reads a lot; **il ne lit pas beaucoup** he doesn't read much; **3** very much; **j'aime beaucoup ta robe** I like your dress very much, I really like your dress; **j'aime beaucoup aller au cinéma** I really like going to the cinema; **4 beaucoup de** a lot of; **beaucoup d'argent** a lot of money; **elle a beaucoup d'argent** she has a lot of money; **elle n'a pas beaucoup d'argent** she doesn't have much money; **il a beaucoup d'amis** he has a lot of friends; **il n'a pas beaucoup d'amis** he doesn't have many friends; **5 beaucoup plus** much more; **beaucoup moins** much less; **beaucoup trop** far too much; **beaucoup trop court** far too short.

beau-fils (*plural* **beaux-fils**) *noun* M **1** son-in-law; **2** stepson.

beau-frère (*plural* **beaux-frères**) *noun* M brother-in-law.

beau-père *noun* M **1** father-in-law; **2** stepfather.

beauté *noun* F beauty.

beaux-arts *plural noun* M fine arts; **école des beaux-arts** art school.

beaux-parents *plural noun* M parents-in-law, in-laws.

bébé *noun* M baby.

bec *noun* M beak.

bêche *noun* F spade.

bégayer *verb* [59] to stammer.

beige *adjective* beige.

beignet *noun* M **1** fritter; **2** doughnut.

bel *adjective* SEE **beau**.

belette *noun* F weasel.

belge *adjective* Belgian.

Belge *noun* M & F Belgian.

Belgique *noun* F Belgium.

bélier *noun* M ram.

Bélier *noun* M Aries (*sign of the Zodiac*).

belle *noun* F **1 ma belle** darling; **2 la Belle au bois dormant** Sleeping Beauty. *adjective* SEE **beau**.

belle-famille *noun* F in-laws.

belle-fille (*plural* **belles-filles**) *noun* F **1** daughter-in-law; **2** stepdaughter.

belle-mère *noun* F **1** mother-in-law; **2** stepmother.

belle-sœur (*plural* **belles-sœurs**) *noun* F sister-in-law.

bénédiction *noun* F blessing.

bénéfice *noun* M profit; **faire un bénéfice de dix mille francs** to make a profit of ten thousand francs.

bénéfique *adjective* beneficial.

bénévole *noun* M & F voluntary worker. *adjective* voluntary, unpaid.

bénir *verb* [2] to bless.

benne *noun* F skip (*for rubbish*).

béquille *noun* F crutch.

berceau (*plural* **berceaux**) *noun* M cradle.

bercer *verb* [61] to rock (*a baby*).

berceuse *noun* F **1** lullaby; **2** rocking chair.

béret *noun* M beret.

berge *noun* F bank (*of a river or canal*).

berger, bergère *noun* M, F shepherd, shepherdess.

berger allemand *noun* M Alsatian (dog).

besoin *noun* M need; **avoir besoin de quelque chose** to need something; **j'ai besoin d'un marteau** I need a hammer; **avoir besoin de faire** to need to do.

bestiole *noun* F (*informal*) creepy-crawly.

bétail *noun* M **1** livestock; **2** cattle.

bête *noun* F animal. *adjective* stupid.

bêtise *noun* F stupidity; **faire une bêtise** to do something stupid.

béton *noun* M concrete.

betterave (rouge) *noun* F beetroot.

beurre *noun* M butter; ★ **un œil au beurre noir** a black eye (*literally: an eye with black butter*).

beurrer *verb* [1] to butter.

bibelot *noun* M ornament.

biberon *noun* M (feeding) bottle.

bible *noun* F bible; **la Bible** the Bible.

bibliothécaire *noun* M & F librarian.

bibliothèque *noun* F 1 library; 2 bookcase.

bic™ *noun* M **un stylo bic™** a Biro™.

biche *noun* F doe.

bicyclette *noun* F bicycle; **faire de la bicyclette** to cycle.

bidet *noun* M bidet.

bidon *noun* M can.
adjective (*informal*) phoney.

bidonville *noun* M shanty town.

bidule *noun* M (*informal*) whatsit, thingamajig.

bien *noun* M 1 good; **le bien et le mal** good and evil; **ça te fera du bien** that'll do you good; 2 possession; **tous leurs biens** all their possessions.
adjective 1 good, nice; **des gens bien** nice people; **ce sera bien de le revoir** it will be nice to see him again; 2 well; **je ne me sens pas bien** I don't feel well; 3 happy, comfortable; **on est bien ici** it's nice here; **on est très bien dans ce fauteuil** this chair's really comfortable.
adverb 1 well; **elle chante bien** she sings well; **bien joué!** well done!; **tu vas bien?** are you well?; 2 well; **bien habillé** well dressed; **cette couleur te va bien** that colour suits you; 3 very, really; **bien triste** really sad; **bien chaud** really hot; 4 very much; **j'aime bien ta robe** I like your dress very much, I really like your dress; **j'aimerais bien savoir** I'd really like to know; **j'aimerais bien aller au cinéma** I'd really like to go to the cinema; **'veux-tu du thé?'** – **'oui, je veux bien'** 'would you like some tea?' – 'yes I'd love some'; **'tu aimes le poisson?'** – **'oui, je l'aime bien'** 'do you like fish?' – 'yes I do'; **je veux bien le faire** I'm quite happy to do it; 5 much; **bien mieux** much better; **bien plus chaud** much hotter; 6 **bien de** many, a number of; **bien des gens** many people; ★ **c'est bien fait pour elle!** serves her right!

bien entendu *adverb* of course.

bien-être *noun* M well-being.

bien que *conjunction* although.

bien sûr *adverb* of course.

bientôt *adverb* soon; **à bientôt** see you soon.

bienvenu, bienvenue¹ *noun* M, F **soyez le bienvenu (or la bienvenue)!** welcome!

bienvenue² *noun* F welcome; **bienvenue!** welcome!; **bienvenue en France!** welcome to France!; **souhaiter la bienvenue à quelqu'un** to welcome somebody.

bière *noun* F beer; **boire de la bière** to drink beer; **trois bières, s'il vous plaît** three beers, please.

bière blonde *noun* F lager.

bière brune *noun* F brown ale.

bifteck *noun* M steak.

bifurcation *noun* F fork (*in the road*).

bigoudi *noun* M hair curler.

bijou (*plural* **bijoux**) *noun* M jewel, piece of jewellery.

bijouterie *noun* F jeweller's (shop).

bijoutier, bijoutière *noun* M, F jeweller.

bilan *noun* M balance sheet;
★ **faire le bilan de quelque chose** to assess something.

bilingue *adjective* bilingual.

billard *noun* M **1** billiards; **jouer au billard** to play billiards; **2** billiard table.

billard américain *noun* M pool.

billard anglais *noun* M snooker.

billard électrique *noun* M pinball machine.

bille *noun* F **1** marble; **jouer aux billes** to play marbles; **2** billiard ball.

billet *noun* M **1** note, banknote; **un billet de cent francs** a hundred-franc note; **2** ticket; **un billet de train** a train ticket.

billion *noun* M billion.

biochimie *noun* F biochemistry.

biographie *noun* F biography.

biologie *noun* F biology.

biologique *adjective* **1** biological; **2** organically grown.

bip *noun* M beep; **'après le bip sonore'** 'after the tone' (*on an answering machine*).

biscotte *noun* F continental toast.

biscuit *noun* M biscuit.

bise *noun* F (*informal*) kiss; **faire la bise à quelqu'un** to kiss somebody on the cheek; **grosses bises** lots of love.

bissextile *adjective* **une année bissextile** a leap year.

bistro, bistrot *noun* M bistro, café.

bizarre *adjective* odd, strange.

blague *noun* F (*informal*) **1** joke; **sans blague!** no kidding!; **2** trick; **faire une blague à quelqu'un** to play a trick on somebody.

blaguer *verb* [1] (*informal*) to joke.

blaireau (*plural* **blaireaux**) *noun* M **1** badger; **2** shaving brush.

blâmer *verb* [1] **1** to criticize; **2** to blame.

blanc *noun* M **1** white; **peint en blanc** painted white; **2** white meat, breast; **3** white wine; **4** blank; **laisser un blanc** to leave a blank. *adjective* (F **blanche**) **1** white; **2** blank; **une feuille blanche** a blank sheet of paper.

blanche *adjective* SEE **blanc**.

Blanc, Blanche *noun* M, F white man, white woman.

blanchir *verb* [2] to whiten.

blé *noun* M wheat.

blessé, blessée *noun* M, F injured person, casualty. *adjective* injured.

blesser *verb* [1] **1** to hurt, to injure; **2 se blesser** to hurt oneself; **tu t'es blessé?** did you hurt yourself?

blessure *noun* F **1** injury; **2** wound.

bleu[1] *noun* M, *adjective* blue; **peint en bleu** painted blue; **bleu marine** navy blue.

bleu[2] *noun* M bruise.

bleuet *noun* M cornflower.

bloc *noun* M **1** block; **un bloc de ciment** a block of cement; **2 un bloc de papier à lettres** a writing pad.

bloc-notes *noun* M notepad.

blond *adjective* blonde, fair-haired.

bloqué *adjective* **1** blocked; **2** jammed; **3** stuck.

bloquer *verb* [1] **1** to block; **2** to jam.

blouse *noun* F overall.

blouson *noun* M jacket.

blue-jean *noun* M jeans; **j'ai acheté un blue-jean** I bought a pair of jeans.

bobine *noun* F reel.

bocal (*plural* **bocaux**) *noun* M jar.

bœuf *noun* M **1** bullock; **2** beef; **est-ce que tu aimes le bœuf?** do you like beef?

bof *exclamation* (*informal*) **'c'était bien hier soir?' – 'bof!'** 'did you have a good time last night?' – 'nothing special'.

bohémien, bohémienne *noun* M, F gipsy.

boire *verb* [22] to drink; **qu'est-ce que tu veux boire?** what would you like to drink?; **il n'y a rien à boire** there's nothing to drink.

bois *noun* M wood; **une table en bois** a wooden table; ★ **avoir la gueule de bois** (*informal*) to have a hangover (*literally: to have a mouth made of wood*).

boisson *noun* F drink; **une boisson fraîche** a cold drink.

boîte *noun* F **1** tin; **une boîte de sardines** a tin of sardines; **2** box; **une boîte d'allumettes** a box of matches; **3** (*informal*) **une boîte de nuit** a nightclub; **aller dans une boîte** to go to a club; **4** (*informal*) firm, company.

boîte aux lettres *noun* F post box.

boiter *verb* [1] to limp.

bol *noun* M **1** bowl; **un bol de riz** a bowl of rice; **2** (*informal*) luck; **un coup de bol** a stroke of luck; ★ **en avoir ras le bol** (*informal*) to be fed up (*literally: to have a bowlful*); **j'en ai ras le bol d'attendre** I'm fed up with waiting.

bombarder *verb* [1] **1** to bombard; **2** to bomb, to shell.

bombe *noun* F **1** bomb; **2** spray can (*containing hairspray, fly spray, etc*).

bon (F **bonne**) *adjective* **1** good; **un bon repas** a good meal; **bon en français** good at French; **2 un bon kilomètre** a good kilometre, at least a kilometre; **3** right; **le bon numéro** the right number; **la bonne adresse** the right address; **c'est bon** it's OK, it's fine.
noun **1** voucher; **2 cela a du bon** that has its good points; **pour de bon** for good.
adverb **sentir bon** to smell good (or nice); **il fait bon aujourd'hui** it's a nice day today; **il fait bon dans mon appartement** it's lovely and warm in my flat; SEE **bonne**².

bon anniversaire *greeting* happy birthday.

bon appétit *exclamation* enjoy your meal.

bonbon *noun* M sweet.

bonbonne *noun* F **1 une bonbonne à gaz** a gas cylinder; **2** demijohn.

bond *noun* M leap; **se lever d'un bond** to leap to your feet.

bondé *adjective* crowded, packed; **bondé d'étudiants** packed with students.

bonheur *noun* M **1** happiness; **2** pleasure; **avoir le bonheur de faire** to have the pleasure of doing.

bonhomme (*plural* **bonshommes**) *noun* M fellow, man.

bonhomme de neige *noun* M snowman.

bonjour *greeting* hello, good morning, good afternoon; ★ **être simple comme bonjour** to be really

easy, to be as easy as pie (*literally: to be as simple as hello*).

bon marché *adjective* cheap.

bonne *noun* F maid.
adjective SEE **bon**.

bonne année *greeting* happy New Year.

bonne chance *exclamation* good luck.

bonne heure *in phrase* **de bonne heure** early.

bonne nuit *greeting* goodnight.

bonnet *noun* M hat, bonnet.

bon retour *exclamation* safe journey back.

bon sens *noun* M common sense.

bonsoir *greeting* good evening.

bonté *noun* F kindness.

bon voyage *exclamation* have a good trip.

bord *noun* M **1** edge (*of a table, cliff, etc*); **2** rim (*of a glass, cup, vase, etc*); **3** side, edge (*of a road, path, etc*); **au bord de la route** on the edge of the road; **4** bank (*of a stream or lake*); **5 au bord de la mer** at the seaside.

bordeaux *adjective* maroon.

border *verb* [1] **1** to line; **bordé d'arbres** tree-lined; **2** to edge, to trim.

bordure *noun* F **1** border; **2** edge; **3 en bordure de** on the edge of.

borne *noun* F **1** kilometre marker (*the equivalent of a milestone*); **2** bollard.

Bosnie *noun* F Bosnia.

bosse *noun* F bump.

bosser *verb* [1] (*informal*) to work.

botanique *noun* F botany.
adjective **les jardins botaniques** the botanic gardens.

botte *noun* F **1** boot; **des bottes de cuir** leather boots; **des bottes de caoutchouc** wellington boots; **2 une botte de foin** a bale of hay.

bottine *noun* F ankle boot.

bouc *noun* M billy goat.

boucan *noun* M (*informal*) din, racket.

bouc émissaire *noun* M scapegoat.

bouche *noun* F mouth.

bouche-à-bouche *noun* M mouth-to-mouth resuscitation.

bouchée *noun* F mouthful.

boucher[1] *verb* [1] **1** to cork (*a bottle*); **2** to block up, to fill (*a hole, gap, or crack*); **3 se boucher** to get blocked up; **4 se boucher le nez** to hold one's nose.

boucher[2], **bouchère** *noun* M, F butcher.

boucherie *noun* F butcher's (shop).

bouchon *noun* M **1** cork; **2** screw-cap; **3** traffic jam.

boucle *noun* F **1** buckle; **2** curl.

bouclé *adjective* curly.

boucle d'oreille *noun* F earring.

Bouddha *noun* M Buddha.

bouddhisme *noun* M Buddhism.

bouder *verb* [1] **1** to sulk; **2 bouder quelque chose** to stay away from something.

boudin *noun* M black pudding.

boue *noun* F mud.

bouée *noun* F **1** rubber ring; **2** buoy.

bouée de sauvetage *noun* F lifebelt.

boueux (F **boueuse**) *adjective* muddy.

bouffe *noun* F (*informal*) food.

bouffée *noun* F **une bouffée d'air frais** a breath of fresh air.

bouffer *verb* [1] (*informal*) to eat.

bougeoir *noun* M candlestick.

bouger *verb* [52] to move.

bougie *noun* F **1** candle; **2** spark plug.

bouillabaisse *noun* F Mediterranean fish soup (*made with several varieties of fish and vegetables*).

bouillant *adjective* boiling; **faire cuire à l'eau bouillante** cook in boiling water.

bouillir *verb* [23] to boil; **faire bouillir le lait** to boil the milk; **le lait bout** the milk is boiling.

bouilloire *noun* F kettle.

bouillon *noun* M stock (*made with meat, fish, or vegetables*).

bouillon-cube *noun* M stock cube.

bouillotte *noun* F hot-water bottle.

boulanger, boulangère *noun* M, F baker.

boulangerie *noun* F bakery, baker's.

boule *noun* F bowl; **jouer aux boules** to play bowls.

bouleau *noun* M birch tree.

boule de neige *noun* F snowball.

boulette *noun* F pellet.

boulette de viande *noun* F meatball.

boulevard *noun* M boulevard.

boulevard périphérique *noun* M ring road.

bouleverser *verb* [1] **1** to overwhelm, to shatter; **être bouleversé** to be overwhelmed (or shattered) **2** to disrupt (*a schedule, plans, etc*); **3** to turn upside down.

boulot *noun* M (*informal*) **1** work; **j'ai trop de boulot** I've got too much work to do; **c'est un boulot immense** it's a huge amount of work; **2** job; **elle cherche du boulot** she's looking for a job.

boum *noun* F (*informal*) party.

bouquet *noun* M bunch, bouquet (*of flowers or herbs*).

bouquin *noun* M (*informal*) book.

bouquiner *verb* [1] (*informal*) to read.

bouquiniste *noun* M & F secondhand bookseller.

bourdon *noun* M bumblebee.

bourg *noun* M market town.

bourgeois, bourgeoise *noun* M, F middle-class person. *adjective* middle-class.

bourgeon *noun* M bud.

Bourgogne *noun* F Burgundy.

bourratif (F **bourrative**) *adjective* very filling.

bourré *adjective* **1** **bourré de** crammed with, stuffed with. **2** drunk.

bourrer *verb* [1] to cram.

bourse *noun* F grant.

Bourse *noun* F stock exchange.

bousculer *verb* [1] to push, to jostle.

boussole *noun* F compass.

bout *noun* M **1** end; **au bout de** at the end of; **2** tip (*of nose or finger*); **3** **un bout de papier** a scrap of paper; **un petit bout de fromage** a little bit of cheese; **4** **au bout de** after; **au bout d'une demi-heure** after half an hour.

bouteille *noun* F bottle.

boutique *noun* F shop.

bouton *noun* M **1** button; **2** spot, pimple.

bouton d'or *noun* M buttercup.

boxe *noun* F boxing.

boxeur *noun* M boxer.

bracelet *noun* M bracelet.

bracelet-montre *noun* M wristwatch.

braise *noun* F embers (*of a fire*).

brancard *noun* M stretcher.

branche *noun* F branch.

branché *adjective* (*informal*) trendy.

brancher *verb* [1] **1** to plug in (*an iron, a television, etc*); **2** to connect (*electricity, gas, water, telephone*).

bras *noun* M sleeve; **en bras de chemise** in one's shirtsleeves.

bras de fer *noun* M arm wrestling.

brasse *noun* F breaststroke.

brasserie *noun* F brasserie, café-restaurant.

brave *adjective* nice (*person*).

break *noun* M estate car.

brebis *noun* F ewe.

bref (F **brève**) *adjective* short, brief.

Brésil *noun* M Brazil.

Bretagne *noun* F Brittany.

bretelle *noun* F **1** strap; **2** slip road; **3** **des bretelles** braces.

brevet *noun* M certificate.

bribes *plural noun* F bits, fragments.

bricolage *noun* M DIY, do-it-yourself

bricoler *verb* [1] to do DIY.

bricoleur, bricoleuse *noun* M, F DIY enthusiast.

brièvement *adverb* briefly.

brillamment *adverb* brilliantly.

brillant *adjective* **1** shiny; **2** brilliant.

briller *verb* [1] to shine.

brin *noun* M sprig (*of herb or plant*); **un brin d'herbe** a blade of grass.

brindille *noun* F twig.

brioche *noun* F brioche, bun.

brique *noun* F **1** brick; **2** carton (*of fruit-juice, milk, etc*).

briquet *noun* M lighter.

brise *noun* F breeze.

briser *verb* [1] to break.

britannique *adjective* British.

Britannique *noun* M & F British person; **les Britanniques** the British.

brocante *noun* F **1** junk shop; **2** second-hand goods.

broche *noun* F **1** brooch; **2** spit (*for roasting*).

brochet *noun* M pike.

brochette *noun* F **1** skewer; **2** kebab; **une brochette de viande** a meat kebab.

brochure *noun* F **1** booklet; **2** brochure.

brocolis *plural noun* M broccoli.

broder *verb* [1] to embroider.

broderie *noun* F embroidery; **des broderies** embroidery.

bronchite *noun* F bronchitis; **avoir une bronchite** to have bronchitis.

bronzage *noun* M suntan.

bronzer *verb* [1] to tan.

brosse *noun* F brush.

brosse à cheveux *noun* F
hairbrush.

brosse à dents *noun* F
toothbrush.

brosser *verb* [1] **1** to brush; **2 se
brosser les dents** to brush your
teeth.

brouette *noun* F wheelbarrow.

brouillard *noun* M fog.

brouillon *noun* M rough draft.

bru *noun* F daughter-in-law.

brugnon *noun* M nectarine.

bruit *noun* M **1** noise; **entendre un
bruit** to hear a noise; **entendre le
bruit d'une voiture** to hear the
sound of a car; **2** rumour.

brûlant *adjective* **1** boiling hot;
2 burning hot.

brûlé *noun* M **un goût de brûlé** a
burnt taste; **ça sent le brûlé** there's
a smell of burning.

brûler *verb* [1] **1** to burn; **2 se
brûler** to burn yourself.

brûlure *noun* F burn.

brume *noun* F mist.

brun *adjective* **1** brown; **2** dark-
haired.

brushing *noun* M blow-dry; **se
faire faire un brushing** to have a
blow-dry.

brut *adjective* **1** raw (*material*);
2 crude (*oil*); **3** gross (*income*);
4 dry (*champagne*).

brutal (M *plural* **brutaux**) *adjective*
1 violent, brutal; **2** sudden.

brutalement *adverb* **1** suddenly;
2 violently.

Bruxelles *noun* Brussels.

bruyant *adjective* noisy, loud.

bruyère *noun* F heather.

bûche *noun* F log.

bu *verb* SEE **boire**.

budget *noun* M budget.

buffet *noun* M **1** sideboard;
2 buffet.

buisson *noun* M bush.

buissonnière *adjective* **faire
l'école buissonnière** to play truant.

Bulgarie *noun* F Bulgaria.

bulle *noun* F bubble.

bulletin *noun* M report, bulletin.

bulletin de salaire *noun* M
payslip.

bulletin scolaire *noun* M school
report.

bureau (*plural* **bureaux**) *noun* M
1 desk; **elle est à son bureau** she is
at her desk; **2** office; **au bureau** at
(or to) the office.

bureau de poste *noun* M post
office.

bureau de tabac *noun* M
tobacconist's.

bureau de tourisme *noun* M
tourist information office.

burin *noun* M chisel.

bus *noun* M bus.

buse *noun* F buzzard.

buste *noun* M bust.

but *noun* M **1** goal, aim, purpose; **2** goal (*in football, hockey*); **marquer un but** to score a goal; **3** target.

buté *adjective* stubborn.

buvable *adjective* drinkable.

buvard *noun* M blotter; **du papier buvard** blotting paper.

buvette *noun* F bar (*at a dance, village fair, etc*).

buvez, buvons *verb* SEE **boire**.

C c

ça *pronoun* **1** that, this; **donne-moi ça** give me that; **ça c'est un moineau** that's a sparrow; **2 comment ça va?, ça va?** how are you?; **ça va bien merci** I'm fine thanks; **3 c'est ça** that's right; **ça ne fait rien** it doesn't matter.

çà *adverb* **çà et là** here and there.

cabane *noun* F hut, shed.

cabas *noun* M shopping bag.

cabillaud *noun* M cod.

cabine *noun* F **1** cubicle; **cabine de douche** shower cubicle; **cabine d'essayage** fitting room (*in a clothes shop*); **2** cabin (*on a ship*).

cabinet *noun* M **1** office (*of a solicitor*); **2** surgery (*of a doctor or dentist*); **3 cabinet de médecins** medical practice.

cabine téléphonique *noun* F phone box.

cabinets *plural noun* M toilet.

câble *noun* M **1** cable; **2** rope.

câblé *adjective* **être câblé** to have cable television.

cabosser *verb* [1] to dent.

cacahuète *noun* F peanut; **des cacahuètes grillées** roasted peanuts.

cacao *noun* M cocoa.

cache *noun* F hiding place.

caché *adjective* hidden.

cache-cache *noun* M **jouer à cache-cache** to play hide and seek.

cachemire *noun* M **1** cashmere; **2 motif cachemire** paisley pattern.

cache-nez *noun* M (thick) scarf.

cache-pot *noun* M flowerpot holder.

cacher *verb* [1] **1** to hide; **cacher quelque chose** to hide something; **elle a caché son portefeuille dans un tiroir** she's hidden her wallet in a drawer; **2 se cacher** to hide; **il s'est caché derrrière la porte** he hid behind the door.

cachet *noun* M **1** tablet; **un cachet d'aspirine** an aspirin; **2** official stamp (*made with a rubber stamp*); **3 le cachet de la poste** the postmark.

cachette *noun* F **1** hiding place; **2 en cachette** secretly, on the sly.

cachot *noun* M dungeon.

cactus *noun* M cactus.

cadavre *noun* M corpse, body.

caddie *noun* M trolley (*in the supermarket*).

cadeau (*plural* **cadeaux**) *noun* M present; **faire un cadeau à quelqu'un** to give somebody a present; **du papier cadeau** wrapping-paper; **je vous fais un paquet-cadeau?** shall I gift-wrap it for you?

cadenas *noun* M padlock.

cadence *noun* F rhythm.

cadet, cadette *noun* M, F younger child, youngest child. *adjective* younger, youngest.

cadran *noun* M **1** face (*of a watch or clock*); **2** dial (*on an instrument such as the speedometer in a car*).

cadran solaire *noun* M sundial.

cadre *noun* M **1** frame (*of a picture, mirror, or window*); **2** surroundings, setting; **3** executive (*a person with a management job in a company*); **4** frame (*of a bicycle*).

cafard *noun* M **1** cockroach; **2** depression; **avoir le cafard** to be down in the dumps.

café *noun* M **1** coffee; **café instantané, café soluble** instant coffee; **café moulu** ground coffee; **café en grains** coffee beans; **café au lait** coffee with milk; **prendre un café** to have a coffee; **2** café.

café-crème *noun* M white coffee.

caféine *noun* F caffeine.

cafétéria *noun* F cafeteria.

cafetière *noun* F **1** coffee pot; **2** coffee maker.

cage *noun* F cage.

cageot *noun* M crate.

cagnotte *noun* F **1** kitty (*of money*); **2** jackpot.

cagoule *noun* F hood.

cahier *noun* M **1** exercise book; **2** notebook.

caille *noun* F quail.

cailler *verb* [1] to curdle.

caillou (*plural* **cailloux**) *noun* M pebble, stone.

caisse *noun* F **1** till, cash register; **2** cash desk; **3** checkout (*in a supermarket*); **4** box, crate.

caisse à outils *noun* F toolbox.

caisse d'épargne *noun* F savings bank.

caissier, caissière *noun* M, F **1** checkout assistant; **2** cashier.

cajou *noun* **une noix de cajou** a cashew nut.

cake *noun* M fruit cake.

calamar *noun* M squid.

calamité *noun* F disaster, calamity.

calcaire *noun* M **1** limestone; **2** furring (*the sediment which clogs up kettles, steam irons, etc*). *adjective* **eau calcaire** hard water; **l'eau ici est très calcaire** the water here is very hard.

calcium *noun* M calcium.

calcul *noun* M **1** calculation; **2** arithmetic.

calculatrice *noun* F pocket calculator.

calculer *verb* [1] to calculate, to work out.

calculette *noun* F pocket calculator.

caleçon *noun* M **1** boxer shorts; **2** leggings.

calembour *noun* M pun, play on words.

calendrier *noun* M **1** calendar; **2** schedule.

calepin *noun* M notebook.

caler *verb* [1] **1** to wedge; **2** to prop up; **3 ma voiture a calé** my car stalled.

calibre *noun* M **1** size, grade (*of eggs, fruit, or vegetables*); **2** calibre, bore (*of a gun*).

câlin *noun* M cuddle; **fais-moi un câlin** give me a cuddle (*usually said to a child*); **fais un câlin à ta grand-mère** give your gran a cuddle. *adjective* affectionate.

câliner *verb* [1] to cuddle.

calmant *noun* M sedative. *adjective* soothing.

calme *noun* M peace and quiet. *adjective* **1** calm; **2** quiet.

calmement *adverb* calmly.

calmer *verb* [1] **1 calmer quelqu'un** to calm somebody down; **2 se calmer** to calm down; **calme-toi** calm down; **3** to soothe; **l'aspirine a calmé la douleur** the aspirin soothed the pain.

calorie *noun* F calorie.

calque *noun* M **un calque** a tracing; **papier-calque** tracing paper.

calvados *noun* M calvados (*apple brandy made in Normandy*).

camarade *noun* M & F friend.

cambriolage *noun* M burglary.

cambrioler *verb* [1] **cambrioler une maison** to burgle a house; **ils ont été cambriolés** they were burgled.

cambrioleur, cambrioleuse *noun* M, F burglar.

caméra *noun* F cine-camera.

caméscope *noun* M camcorder.

camion *noun* M truck, lorry.

camion-citerne *noun* M tanker lorry.

camionnette *noun* F van.

camionneur *noun* M lorry driver, truck driver.

camp *noun* M camp.

campagnard, campagnarde *noun* M, F country person. *adjective* country; **la vie campagnarde** country life.

campagne *noun* F **1** country, countryside; **à la campagne** in the country, in the countryside; **aller se promener à la campagne** to go for a country walk; **2** campaign.

camper *verb* [1] to camp.

campeur, campeuse *noun* M, F camper.

camping *noun* M **1** camping; **faire du camping** to go camping; **2 un**

camping, un terrain de camping a campsite.

camping-car *noun* M camper van.

camping-gaz™ *noun* M camping stove.

Canada *noun* M Canada; **au Canada** in (or to) Canada.

canadien (F **canadienne**) *adjective* Canadian.

Canadien, Canadienne *noun* M, F Canadian.

canal (*plural* **canaux**) *noun* M canal.

canapé *noun* M sofa.

canapé-lit *noun* M sofa bed.

canard *noun* M duck.

canari *noun* M canary.

cancer *noun* M cancer; **avoir un cancer** to have cancer.

Cancer *noun* M Cancer (*sign of the Zodiac*).

candidat, candidate *noun* M, F **1** candidate; **2** applicant.

candidature *noun* F **poser sa candidature à un poste** to apply for a job.

cane *noun* F female duck.

caneton *noun* M duckling.

canette *noun* F **une canette de bière** a small bottle of beer.

canevas *noun* M canvas.

caniche *noun* M poodle.

canicule *noun* F scorching heat.

canif *noun* M penknife.

caniveau (*plural* **caniveaux**) *noun* M gutter.

canne *noun* F walking stick.

canne à pêche *noun* F fishing rod.

canne à sucre *noun* F sugar cane

cannelle *noun* F cinnamon.

canoë *noun* M **1** canoe; **2 faire du canoë** to go canoeing.

canon *noun* M **1** gun; **2** barrel (*of a gun*); **3** cannon.

canot *noun* M small boat, dinghy; **un canot pneumatique** a rubber (or inflatable) dinghy.

canot de sauvetage *noun* M lifeboat.

cantatrice *noun* F opera singer.

cantine *noun* F canteen; **manger à la cantine** to have school lunch.

caoutchouc *noun* M **1** rubber; **des bottes en caoutchouc** wellington boots; **2** rubber band.

cap *noun* M **1** cape, headland; **2** course (*of a ship*).

capable *adjective* capable; **être capable de faire** to be capable of doing.

capacité *noun* F **1** ability; **2** capacity.

cape *noun* F cape, cloak.

capitaine *noun* M captain.

capital (*plural* **capitaux**) *noun* M capital (*financial*). *adjective* **1 d'une importance capitale** of major importance; **2 une question capitale** a key question; **3 la peine capitale** capital punishment.

capitale *noun* F capital city; **la capitale française** the French capital.

capot *noun* M bonnet (*of a car*).

câpre *noun* F caper.

caprice *noun* M **1** whim; **2** tantrum; **faire un caprice** to throw a tantrum.

Capricorne *noun* M Capricorn (*sign of the Zodiac*).

capsule *noun* F **1** cap, top (*of a bottle*); **2** capsule.

capter *verb* [1] **1 capter une chaîne (de télévision)** to get a (television) channel; **2 capter l'attention de quelqu'un** to catch somebody's attention.

captif, captive *noun* M, F captive.

captivant *adjective* **1** fascinating; **2** gripping, riveting.

captivité *noun* F captivity; **en captivité** in captivity.

capturer *verb* [1] to capture.

capuche *noun* F hood.

capuchon *noun* M **1** hood; **2** top, cap (*of a pen*).

capucine *noun* F nasturtium.

car[1] *conjunction* because.

car[2] *noun* M coach, bus; **voyager en car** to travel by coach; **un voyage en car** a coach journey.

carabine *noun* F rifle.

caractère *noun* M **1** character, nature; **avoir mauvais caractère** to be bad-tempered; **2** character; **leur maison a beaucoup de caractère** their house has a lot of character; **3** character, letter; **en gros caractères** in large print.

caractéristique *noun* F, *adjective* characteristic.

carafe *noun* F carafe, jug (*for wine or water*).

caramel *noun* M **1** caramel; **2** toffee.

caravane *noun* F caravan.

carbone *noun* M **1** carbon; **2** carbon paper.

carbonisé *adjective* burnt to a cinder.

carburant *noun* M fuel.

carburateur *noun* M carburettor.

carcasse *noun* F carcass.

cardiaque *adjective* **une crise cardiaque** a heart attack.

cardinal (*plural* **cardinaux**) *noun* M **1** cardinal; **2** cardinal number.

carême *noun* M Lent.

caresser *verb* [1] to stroke, to caress.

cargaison *noun* F cargo.

caricature *noun* F caricature.

caricaturiste *noun* M & F caricaturist, cartoonist.

carie *noun* F **la carie dentaire** tooth decay; **avoir une carie** to have a hole in your tooth.

carillon *noun* M **1** church bells; **2** wind chimes.

caritatif (F **caritative**) *adjective* charitable; **une association caritative** a charity.

carnaval *noun* M carnival.

carnet *noun* M **1** notebook; **2** book (*of tickets or stamps*).

carnet de chèques *noun* M chequebook.

carotte *noun* F carrot.

carpe *noun* F carp.

carpette *noun* F rug.

carré *noun* M, *adjective* square; **un mètre carré** a square metre.

carreau (*plural* **carreaux**) *noun* M **1** floor tile; **2** wall tile; **3** windowpane; **4 du tissu à carreaux** checked fabric; **5 du papier à carreaux** squared paper; **6** diamonds (*suit of playing cards*); **le roi de carreau** the king of diamonds.

carrefour *noun* M crossroads, junction.

carrelage *noun* M **1** tiled floor; **2** tiling, tiles.

carrelet *noun* M plaice.

carrément *adverb* downright, completely; **c'est carrément malhonnête** it's downright dishonest.

carrière *noun* F **1** career; **2** quarry.

cartable *noun* M **1** satchel, schoolbag; **2** briefcase.

carte *noun* F **1** card; **2** playing card; **jouer aux cartes** to play cards;

un jeu de cartes a pack of cards; a card game; **3** map; **4** menu.

carte à jouer *noun* F playing card.

carte à mémoire *noun* F smart card.

carte d'abonnement *noun* F season ticket.

carte d'anniversaire *noun* F birthday card.

carte de crédit *noun* F credit card.

carte d'embarquement *noun* F boarding card.

carte de séjour *noun* F resident's permit.

carte de visite *noun* F business card.

carte de vœux *noun* F greetings card.

carte d'identité *noun* F identity card.

carte postale *noun* F postcard.

carte routière *noun* F road map.

carte téléphonique *noun* F phonecard

carton *noun* M **1** cardboard; **une chemise en carton** a cardboard folder; **carton ondulé** corrugated cardboard; **2** cardboard box.

cartouche *noun* F cartridge.

cas *noun* M **1** case; **au cas où tu oublierais** in case you forget; **en aucun cas** on no account; **en tout cas** in any case, at any rate. **2** case; **trois cas de rougeole** three cases of measles.

cascade *noun* F **1** waterfall;
2 stunt.

cascadeur, cascadeuse *noun*
M, F stuntman, stuntwoman.

case *noun* F **1** square (*on a board
game*); **2** box (*on a form*); **3** hut.

casher *adjective* kosher.

casier *noun* M **1** pigeonhole;
2 locker; **3** rack.

casino *noun* M casino.

casque *noun* M **1** crash helmet;
2 safety helmet, hard hat;
3 headphones, headset.

casquette *noun* F cap; **une
casquette de base-ball** a baseball
cap.

casse-croûte *noun* M snack.

casse-noisettes *noun* M
nutcrackers.

casser *verb* [1] **1** to break; **casser
un verre** to break a glass; **2** se
casser** to break; **le verre s'est
cassé** the glass broke; **3** se casser
la jambe** to break your leg; ★ **se
casser la tête** to go to a lot of trouble;
(*literally: to break your head*); **ne te
casse pas la tête!** don't go to a lot
of trouble!

casse-pieds *adjective* (*informal*)
elle est casse-pieds! she's a pain in
the neck!

casserole *noun* F saucepan.

casse-tête *noun* M **1** puzzle;
2 problem.

cassette *noun* F cassette, tape.

cassis *noun* M blackcurrant; **sirop
de cassis** blackcurrant cordial.

cassoulet *noun* M oven-baked
beans (*with meat and sausage*).

castor *noun* M beaver.

catalogue *noun* M catalogue.

catastrophe *noun* F disaster,
catastrophe.

catch *noun* M wrestling.

catcheur, catcheuse *noun* M, F
wrestler.

catégorie *noun* F category.

cathédrale *noun* F cathedral.

catholicisme *noun* M (Roman)
Catholicism.

catholique *noun* M & F,
adjective (Roman) Catholic.

cauchemar *noun* M nightmare;
faire un cauchemar to have a
nightmare.

cause *noun* F **1** cause; **la cause du
problème** the cause of the
problem; **2** à cause de** because
of; **3** la cause de quelque chose**
the reason for something; **fermé
pour cause de maladie** closed for
reasons of illness; **4** cause; **une
bonne cause** a good cause.

causer *verb* [1] **1** to cause; **2** to
talk, to chat; **causer de quelque
chose** to talk (or chat) about
something; **causer avec quelqu'un**
to talk (or chat) to somebody.

caution *noun* F **1** deposit (*when
renting a flat or house*); **2** bail.

cavalier, cavalière *noun* M, F
rider.

cave *noun* F cellar.

caverne *noun* F cave.

CE *noun* F SEE short for
Communauté Européenne EC.

ce¹, cet (*before a vowel or mute 'h'*),
cette *adjective* **1** this, that; **ce
stylo ne marche pas** this pen
doesn't work; **cette semaine** this
week; **ce couteau-ci** this knife;
2 that; **passe-moi cette assiette**
pass me that plate; **cette chaise-là**
that chair; **3 cette nuit** last night;
tonight.

ce², c' (*before an 'e'*) *pronoun* **1** this,
that, it; **qui est-ce?** who is it?; **c'est
moi** it's me; **qu'est-ce que c'est?**
what is it?; **c'est la première maison
à gauche** it's the first house on the
left; **2** he, she, they; **c'est un
médecin** he's a doctor; **ce sont les
enfants de Paul** they're Paul's
children; **3 ce qui** what; **mange ce
qui reste** eat what's left; **4 ce que**
what; **prends ce que tu veux** take
what you want; **5 c'est tout ce qui
reste** that's all that's left; **prends
tout ce que tu veux** take everything
you want.

ceci *pronoun* this; **ceci n'est pas à
moi** this is not mine.

céder *verb* [24] **1** to give in;
2 'cédez le passage' 'give way' (*at
a road junction*); **3 céder sa place**
to give up your seat; **4 céder à
quelque chose** to give in to
something.

cédille *noun* F cedilla.

cèdre *noun* M cedar.

ceinture *noun* F **1** belt;
2 waistband; **3** waist.

ceinture de sauvetage *noun* F
lifebelt.

ceinture de sécurité *noun* F
seatbelt.

cela *pronoun* this, that, it (*'cela' is
used in the same way as 'ça' but is more
formal*); **cela ne me concerne pas**
that does not concern me; **cela ne
fait rien** that doesn't matter.

célébration *noun* F celebration.

célèbre *adjective* famous.

célébrer *verb* [24] to celebrate.

céleri *noun* M celery.

célibataire *noun* M & F bachelor,
single woman.

celle *pronoun* SEE **celui**.

celle-ci *pronoun* SEE **celui-ci**.

celle-là *pronoun* SEE **celui-là**.

celles *pronoun* SEE **ceux**.

celles-ci *pronoun* SEE **ceux-ci**.

celles-là *pronoun* SEE **ceux-là**.

cellule *noun* F **1** (prison) cell;
2 cell (*in biology and medicine*);
3 unit.

celui, celle *pronoun* the one; **'quel
livre?'** – **'celui qui est sur la table'**
'which book?' – 'the one on the
table'; **'quelle casserole?'** – **'celle
qui est sur la cuisinière'** 'which
saucepan?' – 'the one on the
cooker'.

celui-ci, celle-ci this one.

celui-là, celle-là *pronoun* that
one.

cendre *noun* F ash; **les cendres**
the ashes.

cendrier *noun* M ashtray.

Cendrillon *noun* Cinderella.

censé *adjective* supposed; **être censé faire/être** to be supposed to do/be; **je suis censé être là à dix heures** I'm supposed to be there at ten o'clock.

cent *number* a hundred, one hundred; **trois cents personnes** three hundred people; **deux cent cinquante personnes** two hundred and fifty people (*note that there is no 's' on 'cent' when it is followed by another number*).

centaine *noun* F **une centaine de personnes** a hundred people, a hundred or so people; **plusieurs centaines de personnes** several hundred people; **des centaines de lettres** hundreds of letters.

centenaire *noun* M centenary.

centième *number* hundredth.

centime *noun* M centime (*the smallest unit of French money; there are 100 centimes to a franc*).

centimètre *noun* M **1** centimetre; **un centimètre carré** a square centimetre; **un centimètre cube** a cubic centimetre; **2** tape measure.

central *noun* M **un central téléphonique** a telephone exchange.
adjective (M *plural* **centraux**)
1 central; **2** main.

centrale *noun* F power station; **une centrale nucléaire** a nuclear power station.

centraliser *verb* [1] to centralize.

centre *noun* M centre; **au centre de** in the centre of.

centre commercial *noun* M shopping centre.

centre sportif *noun* M sports centre.

centre-ville *noun* M town centre, city centre.

cependant *adverb* however.

cercle *noun* M circle; **en cercle** in a circle.

cercueil *noun* M coffin.

céréale *noun* F cereal, grain.

cérémonie *noun* F ceremony.

cerf *noun* M stag.

cerf-volant *noun* M kite.

cerise *noun* F cherry.

cerisier *noun* M cherry tree.

certain *adjective* **1** certain, sure; **être certain de** to be certain (or sure) of; **2** certain; **un certain nombre de** a certain number of; **3** some; **certaines personnes** some people.
pronoun some; **certains de mes amis** some of my friends.

certainement *adverb* **1** most probably; **2** certainly; **3** of course.

certes *adverb* admittedly.

certificat *noun* M certificate.

certifier *verb* [1] to certify.

cerveau (*plural* **cerveaux**) *noun* M **1** brain; **2** mind.

ces *adjective* **1** these; **c'est Sara qui m'a acheté ces fleurs** it was Sara who bought me these flowers; **2** those; **ces livres que je t'ai**

prêtés those books I lent you; **ces arbres-là** those trees.

CES *noun* M (*Collège d'enseignement secondaire*) secondary school (*from 11 to 15, when students can go on to a 'lycée' for a further 3 years*).

cesse *noun* F **sans cesse** constantly.

cesser *verb* [1] to stop; **cesser de faire** to stop doing.

cessez-le-feu *noun* M ceasefire.

c'est-à-dire *phrase* that is, that's to say.

cet, cette *adjective* SEE **ce**.

ceux, celles the ones; **'quels livres?' – 'ceux qui sont sur la table'** 'which books?' – 'the ones on the table'; **'quelles chaussettes?' – 'celles que tu m'as prêtées hier'** 'which socks?' – 'the ones you lent me yesterday'; SEE **celui**.

ceux-ci, celles-ci these ones.

ceux-là, celles-là those ones.

chacal *noun* M jackal.

chacun, chacune *pronoun* **1** each; **ils ont chacun un billet** they each have a ticket; **2** everyone; **comme chacun sait** as everyone knows.

chagrin *noun* M grief.

chaîne *noun* F **1** chain; **2** channel (*on TV*).

chaîne hi-fi *noun* F hi-fi system.

chaîne laser *noun* F CD player.

chaîne stéréo *noun* F stereo system.

chair *noun* F **1** flesh; **2** meat; **la chair à saucisse** sausage meat; ★ **avoir la chair de poule** to have goose pimples (*literally: to have hen's flesh*).

chaise *noun* F chair.

châle *noun* M shawl.

chalet *noun* M chalet.

chaleur *noun* F heat, warmth.

chaleureux (F **chaleureuse**) *adjective* warm.

chambre *noun* F **1** bedroom; **dans ma chambre** in my bedroom; **2** (hotel) room; **une chambre pour une personne** a single room; **une chambre pour deux personnes** a double room; **3 la musique de chambre** chamber music.

chambre d'amis *noun* F spare bedroom.

chambre de commerce *noun* F chamber of commerce.

chambres d'hôte *plural noun* F bed and breakfast.

chameau (*plural* **chameaux**) *noun* M camel.

champ *noun* M field.

champagne *noun* M champagne.

champ de bataille *noun* M battlefield.

champ de courses *noun* M racetrack.

champignon *noun* M **1** mushroom; **des champignons de**

Paris button mushrooms;
2 fungus.

champion, championne *noun*
M, F champion.

championnat *noun* M
championship.

chance *noun* F **1** luck; **un coup de chance** a stroke of luck; **Bonne chance!** Good luck!; **j'ai eu la chance de pouvoir passer un an en France** I was lucky enough to be able to spend a year in France; **avoir de la chance** to be lucky; **tu as de la chance d'avoir une sœur pareille!** you're lucky to have a sister like that!; **2** chance.

chancelier *noun* M chancellor.

chandail *noun* M jumper.

chandelier *noun* M
1 candlestick; **2** candelabra.

change *noun* M exchange rate;
bureau de change bureau de change (*for changing money*).

changeant *adjective* changeable.

changement *noun* M change.

changer *verb* [52] **1** to change; **tu n'as pas changé** you haven't changed; **2 changer quelque chose** to change something; **changer les draps** to change the sheets; **changer une prise** to change a plug; **3 changer quelque chose** to exchange something (*in a shop*); **4 changer de** to change; **changer de train** to change trains; **changer d'avis** to change your mind; **j'ai changé d'avis** I've changed my mind; **5 se changer** to get changed, to change your clothes.

chanson *noun* F song.

chant *noun* M **1** singing; **2** song.

chantage *noun* M blackmail.

chanter *verb* [1] to sing.

chanteur, chanteuse *noun* M, F
singer.

chantier *noun* M **1** building site;
2 roadworks.

chantonner *verb* [1] to hum.

chaos *noun* M chaos.

chaotique *adjective* chaotic.

chapeau (*plural* **chapeaux**) *noun*
M **1** hat; **2 chapeau!** well done!

chapeau melon *noun* M bowler
hat.

chapelle *noun* F chapel.

chapelure *noun* F breadcrumbs.

chapiteau (*plural* **chapiteaux**)
noun M **1** marquee; **2** big top
(*circus tent*).

chapitre *noun* M chapter.

chaque *adjective* each, every.

char *noun* M **1** (military) tank;
2 carnival float.

charabia *noun* M (*informal*)
gobbledygook, rubbish.

charade *noun* F riddle.

charbon *noun* M coal.

charbon de bois *noun* M
charcoal.

charcuterie *noun* F **1** pork
butcher's (*selling salads and ready-
prepared dishes as well as pork,*

bacon, ham, sausages, etc); **2** pork products (*ham, salami, pâté, etc*).

charcutier, charcutière *noun* M, F pork butcher.

chardon *noun* M thistle.

charge *noun* F **1** load; **2** responsibility; **avoir la charge de** to be responsible for; **3 charges** costs, charges.

charger *verb* [52] **1** to load; **2** to charge (*a battery*).

chariot *noun* M trolley (*at the supermarket*).

charité *noun* F charity.

charmant *adjective* charming.

charme *noun* M **1** charm; **2** spell.

charmer *verb* [1] to charm.

charnière *noun* F hinge.

charpentier *noun* M carpenter.

charrette *noun* F cart.

charrue *noun* F plough.

charte *noun* F charter.

charter *adjective* **un vol charter** a charter flight.

chasse *noun* F hunting, shooting.

chasse d'eau *noun* F (toilet) flush; **tirer la chasse d'eau** to flush the toilet.

chasse-neige *noun* M snowplough.

chasser *verb* [1] to chase off.

chasseur *noun* M hunter.

chat *noun* M cat.

châtaigne *noun* F sweet chestnut.

châtaignier *noun* M sweet chestnut tree.

châtain *adjective* **les cheveux châtains** brown hair.

château (*plural* **châteaux**) *noun* M **1** castle; **2** large country house.

château d'eau *noun* M water tower.

chatouiller *verb* [1] to tickle.

chatte *noun* F (female) cat.

chaud *adjective* hot, warm; **du lait chaud** hot milk; **un pull chaud** a warm jumper; **j'ai chaud** I'm hot; **il fait chaud ici** it's hot here.

chaudière *noun* F boiler; **une chaudière à gaz** a gas boiler.

chauffage *noun* M heating.

chauffage central *noun* M central heating.

chauffe-eau *noun* M water heater.

chauffer *verb* [1] **1** to heat, to heat up; **2** to warm.

chauffeur *noun* M **1** driver; **un chauffeur de taxi** a taxi driver; **2** chauffeur.

chaumière *noun* F thatched cottage.

chaussée *noun* F roadway.

chaussette *noun* F sock.

chausson *noun* M **1** slipper; **2** ballet shoe.

chaussure *noun* F shoe.

chauve *adjective* bald.

chauve-souris *noun* F bat.

chavirer *verb* [1] to capsize.

chef *noun* M **1** leader; **2** head; **3** boss; **4** **chef de cuisine** chef.

chef-d'œuvre *noun* M masterpiece.

chemin *noun* M **1** country road; **2** track, path; **3** way; **perdre son chemin** to lose your way; **en chemin** on the way.

chemin de fer *noun* M railway.

cheminée *noun* F **1** chimney; **2** fireplace; **3** mantlepiece.

cheminot *noun* M railway worker.

chemise *noun* F shirt.

chemise de nuit *noun* F nightdress.

chemisier *noun* M blouse.

chêne *noun* M **1** oak tree; **2** oak; **une table en chêne** an oak table.

chenille *noun* F caterpillar.

chèque *noun* M cheque; **un carnet de chèques** a cheque book.

chèque de voyage *noun* M traveller's cheque.

chéquier *noun* M cheque book.

cher (F **chère**) *adjective* **1** dear; **Chère Anne** Dear Anne; **2** expensive, dear; **pas trop cher** reasonably priced.
adverb **coûter cher** to be expensive.

chercher *verb* [1] **1** to look for; **qu'est-ce que tu cherches?** what are you looking for?; **je cherche mes lunettes** I'm looking for my glasses; **je cherche un emploi** I'm looking for a job; **2** **chercher quelque chose** to look something up (*in a dictionary, for example*); **3** **aller chercher** to go and get (or fetch) (*somebody or something*); **je vais chercher des verres** I'll go and get some glasses; **4** to pick up; **je viendrai te chercher à l'école** I'll come and pick you up from school; **5** **chercher à faire** to try to do.

chercheur, chercheuse *noun* M, F scientist.

chéri, chérie *noun* M, F darling.

chérir *verb* [2] to cherish.

cheval (*plural* **chevaux**) *noun* M **1** horse; **à cheval** on horseback; **monter à cheval** to ride a horse; **2** **faire du cheval** to go horseriding.

cheval à bascule *noun* M rocking horse.

chevalet *noun* M easel.

chevet *noun* M **1** bedhead; **au chevet de quelqu'un** at somebody's bedside; **un livre de chevet** a bedside book; **une lampe de chevet** a bedside lamp; **2** bedside table.

cheveu (*plural* **cheveux**) *noun* M **1** **un cheveu** a hair; **2** **les cheveux** hair; **il a les cheveux blonds** he has blond hair; ★ **avoir un cheveu sur la langue** to have a lisp (*literally: to have a hair on one's tongue*); **couper les cheveux en quatre** to split hairs (*literally: to cut hairs in four*).

cheville *noun* F ankle.

chèvre[1] *noun* F goat, nanny-goat.

chèvre[2] *noun* M goat's cheese.

chèvrefeuille *noun* M honeysuckle.

chevreuil noun M **1** roe deer; **2** venison.

chez preposition **1 chez quelqu'un** at (or to) somebody's house; **je vais chez Paul ce soir** I'm going to Paul's this evening; **elle est chez les Brown** she's at the Browns'; **viens chez moi** come round to my place; **il est chez lui** he's at home; **je rentre chez moi maintenant** I'm going home now; **fais comme chez toi** make yourself at home; **2 chez le boucher** at (or to) the butcher's; **je l'ai rencontrée chez le coiffeur hier** I met her at the hairdresser's yesterday; **je vais chez le coiffeur demain** I'm going to the hairdresser's tomorrow.

chic adjective **1** chic, well-dressed; **2** nice; **c'était vachement chic de ta part** it was really nice of you; **3 Chic!** (informal) Cool!

chicorée noun F **1** endive; **2** chicory powder (for adding to coffee).

chien noun M dog; **'chien méchant'** 'beware of the dog'.

chien d'aveugle noun M guide dog.

chien de berger noun M sheepdog.

chien de garde noun M guard dog.

chienne noun F (female) dog, bitch.

chiffon noun M **1** rag; **2** duster.

chiffre noun M figure; **un numéro à cinq chiffres** a five-figure number.

chignon noun M bun, chignon.

chimie noun F chemistry.

chimique adjective chemical.

chimpanzé noun M chimpanzee.

Chine noun F China.

chinois noun M, adjective Chinese.

Chinois, Chinoise noun M, F Chinese man, Chinese woman; **les Chinois** the Chinese.

chiot noun M puppy.

chips noun F crisp; **un paquet de chips** a packet of crisps.

chirurgical (M plural **chirurgicaux**) adjective surgical; **une intervention chirurgicale** an operation.

chirurgie noun F surgery.

chirurgien noun M surgeon.

chirurgien-dentiste noun M dental surgeon.

choc noun M **1** shock; **ça m'a fait un choc** it gave me a shock; **2** crash.

chocolat noun M chocolate; **chocolat au lait** milk chocolate; **chocolat blanc** white chocolate; **chocolat en poudre** drinking chocolate; **un gâteau au chocolat** a chocolate cake; **un chocolat chaud** a hot chocolate.

chœur noun M **1** choir (professional); **2** chorus.

choisir verb [2] to choose.

choix noun M **1** choice; **un bon choix** a good choice; **2 un grand choix** a wide choice (or variety).

chômage *noun* M unemployment; **être au chômage** to be unemployed.

chômeur, chômeuse *noun* M, F unemployed person.

chope *noun* F beer mug.

choquer *verb* [1] to shock.

chorale *noun* F choir (*amateur*).

chose *noun* F thing; **les choses qui m'intéressent** the things that interest me; **j'ai plusieurs choses à te dire** I have several things to tell you; **je prends la même chose** I'll have the same.

chou (*plural* **choux**) *noun* M cabbage.

chouchou¹, chouchoute *noun* M, F teacher's pet.

chouchou² *noun* M scrunchy (*for holding back your hair*).

choucroute *noun* F sauerkraut (*pickled cabbage with different types of sausage, ham, and bacon*).

chou de Bruxelles *noun* M Brussels sprout.

chouette *noun* F owl. *adjective* (*informal*) great; **c'est chouette!** that's great!; **leur maison est très chouette** their house is really lovely.

chou-fleur (*plural* **choux-fleurs**) *noun* M cauliflower.

chrétien, chrétienne *noun* M, F, *adjective* Christian.

christianisme *noun* M Christianity.

chrome *noun* M chromium.

chronique *noun* F **1** column, page (*devoted to a particular journalist in a newspaper*); **2** (radio) programme. *adjective* chronic.

chronomètre *noun* M stopwatch.

chrysanthème *noun* M chrysanthemum.

chuchoter *verb* [1] to whisper.

chut *exclamation* shh!

chute *noun* F **1** fall; **faire une chute de 5 mètres** to fall 5 metres; **2 chutes de neige** snowfall; **chutes de pluie** rainfall; **3** fall, drop (*in price, value, temperature*).

chuter *verb* [1] to fall, to drop.

Chypre *noun* F Cyprus.

ci *adverb* **ce mois-ci** this month; **ces timbres-ci** these stamps; **ces jours-ci** these last few days.

cible *noun* F target.

ciboulette *noun* F **de la ciboulette** chives.

cicatrice *noun* F scar.

ci-contre *adverb* opposite.

ci-dessous *adverb* below.

ci-dessus *adverb* above.

cidre *noun* M cider.

ciel (*plural* **cieux**) *noun* M **1** sky; **au ciel** in the sky; **2** heaven.

cigale *noun* F cicada.

cigare *noun* M cigar.

cigarette *noun* F cigarette.

cigogne *noun* F stork.

ci-joint *adverb* **veuillez trouver ci-joint** please find enclosed (*in a letter*).

cil *noun* M eyelash.

ciment *noun* M cement.

cimetière *noun* M **1** cemetery; **2** graveyard.

cinéaste *noun* M & F film director.

ciné-club *noun* M film club.

cinéma *noun* M **1** cinema; **aller au cinéma** to go to the cinema; **2** (*informal*) play-acting; **arrête ton cinéma!** stop that nonsense!

cinéphile *noun* M & F keen cinema-goer.

cinglé *adjective* (*informal*) crazy.

cinq *number* five; **Lucie a cinq ans** Lucie's five; **à cinq heures** at five o'clock; **le cinq avril** the fifth of April.

cinquantaine *noun* F **une cinquantaine (de)** about fifty; **une cinquantaine de personnes** about fifty people; **avoir la cinquantaine** to be about fifty.

cinquante *number* fifty.

cinquantième *number* fiftieth.

cinquième *noun* F (*in a French school*) the equivalent of Year 8. *noun* M **au cinquième** on the fifth floor. *adjective* fifth.

cintre *noun* M clothes hanger.

cirage *noun* M shoe polish.

circonflexe *noun* M **un accent circonflexe** a circumflex.

circonstance *noun* F circumstance.

circuit *noun* M **1** circuit (*in an athletics stadium*); **2** tour; **3** (electrical) circuit.

circulaire *noun* F, *adjective* circular.

circulation *noun* F **1** traffic; **il y a beaucoup de circulation ce soir** there's a lot of traffic this evening; **2** circulation.

circuler *verb* [1] **1** to run (*of a bus or train*); **ce train ne circule pas le dimanche** that train doesn't run on Sundays; **2** to circulate.

cire *noun* F wax.

cirer *verb* [1] to polish.

cirque *noun* M circus; **au cirque** at (or to) the circus.

ciseaux *plural noun* M scissors; **une paire de ciseaux** a pair of scissors.

citadin, citadine *noun* M, F city dweller.

citation *noun* F quotation.

cité *noun* F **1** city, town; **2** housing estate; **3** **une cité universitaire** university halls of residence.

citer *verb* [1] to quote.

citerne *noun* F tank.

citoyen, citoyenne *noun* M, F citizen.

citron *noun* M lemon; **une tarte au citron** a lemon tart.

citronnade *noun* F still lemonade.

citronnier *noun* M lemon tree.

citron vert *noun* M lime.

citrouille *noun* F pumpkin.

civet *noun* M stew.

civil *noun* M 1 civilian; 2 **un policier en civil** a plain-clothes policeman.
adjective 1 civilian; 2 **un mariage civil** a civil wedding (*as opposed to a church wedding*).

civilisation *noun* F civilization.

civique *adjective* civic.

clair *adjective* 1 light; **bleu clair** light blue; 2 **la chambre est très claire** the bedroom is very light; 3 clear.
adverb clearly; **voir clair** to see clearly.

clair de lune *noun* M moonlight.

clairement *adverb* clearly.

clapier *noun* M rabbit hutch.

claque *noun* F slap.

claqué *adjective* (*informal*) exhausted, wiped out.

claquer *verb* [1] **claquer la porte** to slam the door.

clarifier *verb* [1] to clarify.

clarinette *noun* F clarinet; **jouer de la clarinette** to play the clarinet.

clarté *noun* F 1 light; 2 clarity.

classe *noun* F 1 class; **elle est dans ma classe à l'école** she's in my class (or year) at school; **en classe** in class; 2 classroom; 3 **première/deuxième classe** first/second class; 4 (social) class.

classement *noun* M 1 classification; 2 placing; 3 grading; 4 filing.

classer *verb* [1] 1 to classify; 2 to grade; 3 to file.

classeur *noun* M 1 ring binder, file; 2 filing cabinet.

classique *adjective* 1 classical; 2 classic; 3 usual; **c'est classique!** that's typical!

clavier *noun* M keyboard.

clé *noun* F 1 key; **fermer quelque chose à clé** to lock something; 2 spanner.

clef = CLÉ.

clémentine *noun* F clementine.

client, cliente *noun* M, F 1 customer; 2 client.

clientèle *noun* F customers.

cligner *verb* [1] **cligner des yeux** to blink.

clignotant *noun* M indicator (*on a motor vehicle*).

clignoter *verb* [1] to flash.

climat *noun* M climate.

climatisation *noun* F air-conditioning.

climatisé *adjective* air-conditioned.

clin d'œil *noun* M wink; **faire un clin d'œil à quelqu'un** to wink at somebody; ★ **en un clin d'œil** in a flash.

clinique *noun* F clinic, private hospital.

clip *noun* M **1** video clip; **2** clip brooch; **3** clip-on earring.

cliquer *verb* [1] **cliquer sur quelque chose** to click on something (*using a computer mouse*).

cliqueter *verb* [48] **1** to jingle; **2** to rattle.

clochard, clocharde *noun* M, F tramp, down-and-out.

cloche *noun* F bell.

clocher *noun* M **1** steeple; **2** bell tower.

cloison *noun* F **1** partition; **2** partition wall; **3** screen.

cloître *noun* M cloister.

clos *adjective* closed.

clôture *noun* F **1** fence; **2** close; **3** closing.

clou *noun* M **1** nail; **2** stud.

clou de girofle *noun* M clove.

clouer *verb* [1] **clouer quelque chose** to nail something down.

clown *noun* M clown.

club *noun* M club; **un club de foot** a football club.

cobaye *noun* M guinea pig.

Coca™ *noun* M Coke™.

cocaïne *noun* F cocaine.

coccinelle *noun* F ladybird.

cocher *verb* [1] to tick.

cochon *noun* M pig.
adjective (F **cochonne**) (*informal*) dirty (*joke, story*).

cochon d'Inde *noun* M guinea pig.

cocktail *noun* M **1** cocktail; **2** cocktail party.

coco *noun* M **une noix de coco** a coconut.

cocorico *noun* M cock-a-doodle-do.

cocotte *noun* F **1** casserole; **2** hen (*in baby talk*); **3** chocolate hen (*traditionally sold at Easter*).

cocotte-minute™ *noun* F pressure cooker.

code *noun* M **1** code; **le code de la route** the highway code; **2 codes** dipped headlights.

code postal *noun* M postcode.

cœur *noun* M **1** heart; **2** hearts (*suit of playing cards*); **le roi de cœur** the king of hearts; **3 par cœur** by heart; **apprendre quelque chose par cœur** to learn something by heart; ★ **avoir mal au cœur** to feel sick.

coffre *noun* M **1** chest; **2** safe; **3** boot (*of a car*).

coffre-fort *noun* M safe.

cogner *verb* [1] to bump, to bang; **se cogner la tête** to bang your head.

coiffer *verb* [1] **se coiffer** to brush (or comb) your hair.

coiffeur, coiffeuse¹ *noun* M, F hairdresser.

coiffeuse² *noun* F dressing table.

coiffure *noun* **1** hairdressing; **2** hairstyle; **tu as changé de coiffure** you've changed your hairstyle.

coin *noun* M **1** corner; **au coin** in the corner; **au coin de** in the corner of; **2 le café du coin** the local café; **les gens du coin** the local people; ★ **au coin du feu** by the fireside (*literally: in the corner of the fire*).

coincé *adjective* stuck, jammed.

coincer *verb* [61] to jam.

coïncidence *noun* F coincidence.

col *noun* M **1** collar; **2** neck; **3** (mountain) pass.

colère *noun* F anger; **être en colère** to be angry.

colin *noun* M hake.

colique *noun* F diarrhoea.

colis *noun* M parcel.

collant *noun* M **un collant** (a pair of) tights.
adjective sticky.

colle *noun* F **1** glue; **2** detention; **une heure de colle** an hour's detention.

collecte *noun* F collection (*of money*).

collection *noun* F collection.

collectionner *verb* [1] to collect.

collège *noun* M secondary school (*from 11 to 15, when students can either leave school altogether or go on to a 'lycée' for a further 3 years*).

collégien, collégienne *noun* M, F schoolboy, schoolgirl.

collègue *noun* M & F colleague.

coller *verb* [1] **1** to stick; **2** to stick down; **3** to glue; **4** to press.

collier *noun* M **1** necklace; **2** collar (*for a dog, cat, etc*).

colline *noun* F hill.

collision *noun* F collision.

colombe *noun* F dove.

colonie *noun* F colony.

colonie de vacances *noun* F holiday camp (*for children*).

colonne *noun* F column.

colonne vertébrale *noun* F spine.

colorant *noun* M colouring.

coloré *adjective* **1** coloured; **2** colourful.

colorer *verb* [1] to colour.

colorier *verb* [1] to colour in.

coloris *noun* M colour; **existe en plusieurs coloris** several colours available.

combat *noun* M **1** fighting; **2 un combat de boxe** a boxing match.

combattant *noun* M **un ancien combattant** a war veteran.

combattre *verb* [21] to fight.

combien *adverb* **1** how much; **tu en veux combien?** how much do you want?; **c'est combien?** how much is it?; **ça coûte combien?** how much does it cost?; **je vous dois combien?** how much do I owe you?, how much is that? **2** how many; **tu en veux combien?** how many do you want?; **3 combien de** how much; **combien d'argent?** how much money?; **4 combien de** how many; **combien de tasses?** how many cups?; ★ **nous sommes le combien**

aujourd'hui? what's the date today? (*literally: we are the how many today*)?

combinaison *noun* F
1 combination; 2 jumpsuit;
3 overalls; 4 slip, petticoat.

combiné *noun* M receiver (*of a telephone*).

comble *noun* M 1 **le comble de** the height of; **le comble du luxe** the height of luxury; 2 **ça c'est le comble!** that's the last straw!

comédie *noun* F comedy.

comédien, comédienne *noun* M, F actor, actress.

comestible *adjective* edible.

comique *noun* M comic, comedian.
adjective funny.

comité *noun* M committee.

commande *noun* F order; **sur commande** to order.

commander *verb* [1] 1 to order; **avez-vous commandé?** have you ordered?; 2 to be in charge.

comme *preposition* 1 like; **une montre comme la tienne** a watch like yours; 2 like; **comme ça** like this; 3 as a; **travailler comme serveur dans un café** to work as a waiter in a café; 4 **qu'est-ce que tu veux comme glace?** what kind of ice cream would you like?
conjunction 1 as; **comme tu veux** as you like; 2 as, since; **comme je suis malade** as (or since) I'm ill; 3 as; **comme je fermais la porte** as I was closing the door; 4 **comme si** as if.

adverb **comme il est gentil!** he's so nice!; **comme c'est bon!** it's so good!; **comme il fait chaud!** it's so hot!; ★ **blanc comme la neige** as white as snow; **fort comme un bœuf** as strong as an ox.

commencement *noun* M beginning, start.

commencer *verb* [61] 1 to begin, to start; **le film a commencé** the film has started; 2 **commencer à faire, commencer de faire** to start (or begin) to do; **elle a commencé à faire ses devoirs** she's started to do her homework; **je commence à comprendre** I'm beginning to understand; **il commence à pleuvoir** it's starting to rain.

comment *adverb* 1 how; **comment as-tu fait ce gâteau?** how did you make this cake?; **je ne sais pas comment le faire** I don't know how to do it; 2 **comment vas-tu?** how are you?; **comment ça va?** how are you?; **comment va ta mère?** how's your mother?; 3 **comment t'appelles-tu?** what's your name?; **il s'appelle comment, ton frère?** what's your brother's name?; 4 pardon?; 5 **comment est leur maison?, elle est comment, leur maison?** what's their house like?

commentaire *noun* M
1 comment; 2 commentary.

commenter *verb* [1] **commenter quelque chose** to comment on something.

commerçant, commerçante *noun* M, F shopkeeper.

commerce *noun* M **1** shop; **2** le
commerce business; **je fais des
études de commerce** I'm doing
business studies; **3 le commerce**
trade.

commercial (M *plural*
commerciaux) *adjective*
1 commercial; **2 un centre
commercial** a shopping centre.

commettre *verb* [11] **1 commettre
une erreur** to make a mistake;
2 commettre un crime to commit a
crime.

commissariat *noun* M police
station.

commission *noun* F
1 committee; **2** commission;
3 message; **4** errand; **5 faire les
commissions** to do the shopping.

commode *noun* F chest of drawers.
adjective **1** convenient, handy;
2 easy.

commun *adjective* **1** common;
2 shared; **3** joint; **4 en commun**
in common; **ils n'ont rien en
commun** they have nothing in
common; **5 en commun** jointly,
together; **6 les transports en
commun** public transport.

communauté *noun* F community.

communication *noun* F **1 une
communication téléphonique** a
telephone call; **2** communication.

communion *noun* F communion.

communiquer *verb* [1] **1** to
communicate; **2 communiquer
quelque chose** to pass something
on.

communisme *noun* M
communism.

communiste *noun* M & F,
adjective communist.

compact *adjective* **1** dense;
2 compact; **3 un disque compact**
a compact disc, a CD.

compagnie *noun* F **1** company,
firm; **2** company; **elle m'a tenu
compagnie** she kept me company.

compagnie aérienne *noun* F
airline.

compagnon *noun* M companion.

comparable *adjective* comparable.

comparaison *noun* F
comparison; **en comparaison de** in
comparison with.

comparatif (F **comparative**)
adjective comparative.

comparé *adjective* **comparé à**
compared to (or with).

comparer *verb* [1] to compare.

compartiment *noun* M
compartment.

compas *noun* M compass.

compatir *verb* [2] to sympathize.

compensation *noun* F
compensation.

compenser *verb* [1] **compenser
quelque chose** to compensate for
something.

compétence *noun* F **1** ability;
2 skill; **3** competence.

compétent *adjective* competent.

compétitif (F **compétitive**)
adjective competitive.

compétition *noun* F competition.

complémentaire *adjective* further, supplementary.

complet *noun* M suit. *adjective* (F **complète**) **1** complete; **2** total; **3** full (*speaking of a hotel or a train*); **4 le pain complet** wholemeal bread.

complètement *adverb* completely.

compléter *verb* [24] **1** to complete; **2** to fill in (*a form*).

complexe *noun* M, *adjective* complex.

complication *noun* F complication.

complice *noun* M & F accomplice.

compliment *noun* M compliment; **faire des compliments à quelqu'un** to compliment somebody.

compliqué *adjective* complicated.

compliquer *verb* [1] to complicate.

complot *noun* M plot.

comportement *noun* M behaviour.

comporter *verb* [1] **1** to include; **2** to consist of; **3 se comporter** to behave.

composé *adjective* **1 composé de** made up of; **2 une salade composée** a mixed salad.

composer *verb* [1] **1** to make up; **2** to put together; **3** to compose (*music*); **4 composer un numéro (de téléphone)** to dial a (telephone) number.

compositeur, compositrice *noun* M, F composer.

composition *noun* F composition.

composter *verb* [1] to punch (*a ticket*); **'n'oubliez pas de composter votre billet'** remember to punch your ticket (*in France it is an offence to get on a train without first punching your ticket in one of the machines provided for this at platform entrances*).

compote *noun* F stewed fruit; **la compote de pommes** apple puree.

compréhensible *adjective* understandable.

compréhensif (F **compréhensive**) *adjective* understanding.

comprendre *verb* [64] **1** to understand; **je comprends** I understand; **j'ai compris** I understood; **j'ai mal compris** I misunderstood; **2** to include; **3 se comprendre** to understand each other; **4 ça se comprend** that's understandable.

comprimé *noun* M tablet.

compris *adjective* **1** included; **service compris** service included; **non compris** not included; **2 y compris** including; **tout le monde y compris les enfants** everybody including the children.

compromis *noun* M compromise.

comptabilité *noun* F accounting, accountancy.

comptable *noun* M & F accountant.

compte *noun* M **1** account; **un compte bancaire** a bank account; **un compte d'épargne** a savings account; **j'ai cent livres sur mon compte** I have a hundred pounds in my account; **2 le compte est bon** the amount is correct; **3 se rendre compte de quelque chose** to realize something; **se rendre compte que** to realize that; **je me suis rendu compte que j'avais oublié mes clés** I realized I had forgotten my keys; **4 tenir compte de quelque chose** to take something into account; **5 en fin de compte** all things considered.

compter *verb* [1] **1** to count; **2 compter sur quelqu'un** to count on somebody.

compte rendu *noun* M report.

compteur *noun* M meter.

compteur de vitesse *noun* M speedometer.

comptine *noun* F nursery rhyme.

comptoir *noun* M **1** counter; **2** bar.

concentré *adjective* concentrated.

concentré de tomate *noun* M tomato puree.

concentrer *verb* [1] **se concentrer (sur)** to concentrate (on).

conception *noun* F design.

concernant *preposition* concerning.

concerner *verb* [1] to concern; **en ce qui me concerne** as far as I'm concerned.

concert *noun* M concert; **un concert de rock** a rock concert.

concessionnaire *noun* M & F dealer, agent.

concierge *noun* M & F caretaker.

conclure *verb* [25] to conclude.

conclusion *noun* F conclusion.

concombre *noun* M cucumber.

concours *noun* M competition.

concret (F **concrète**) *adjective* **1** concrete; **2** practical.

concurrence *noun* F competition; **il y a beaucoup de concurrence** there's a lot of competition.

concurrent, concurrente *noun* M, F competitor.

condamner *verb* [1] to sentence (*a criminal*).

condition *noun* F **1** condition; **en bonne condition** in good condition; **2 à condition de/que** provided that; **tu peux emprunter mon vélo à condition de me le rendre ce soir** you can borrow my bike provided you let me have it back this evening; **3 dans ces conditions** in that case.

conditionnel *noun* M conditional tense.

conditionner *verb* [1] to package.

conducteur, conductrice *noun* M, F driver.

conduire *verb* [26] **1** to drive; **apprendre à conduire** to learn to drive; **un permis de conduire** a driving licence; **je te conduis à la**

gare I'll drive you to the station;
2 to take; **je vous conduis à votre
chambre** I'll take you to your room;
3 se conduire to behave.

conduite *noun* F behaviour;
mauvaise conduite bad behaviour.

conférence *noun* F **1** lecture;
2 conference.

confesser *verb* [1] **se confesser** to
go to confession.

confiance *noun* F **1** trust; **avoir
confiance en quelqu'un, faire
confiance à quelqu'un** to trust
somebody; **je te fais confiance** I'll
leave it to you; **2** confidence.

confiant *adjective* confident.

confidence *noun* F secret.

confier *verb* [1] **1 confier quelque
chose à quelqu'un** to entrust
something to somebody; **2 se
confier à quelqu'un** to confide in
somebody.

confirmation *noun* F
confirmation.

confirmer *verb* [1] to confirm.

confiserie *noun* F sweet shop.

confisquer *verb* [1] to confiscate.

confit *adjective* **les fruits confits**
crystallized fruits.

confiture *noun* F jam; **la confiture
d'abricots** apricot jam.

conflit *noun* M conflict.

confondre *verb* [69] to confuse, to
mix up.

confort *noun* M comfort; **tout
confort** with all mod cons.

confortable *adjective* comfortable.

confrontation *noun* F
1 confrontation; **2** clash.

confus *adjective* **1** confused;
2 embarrassed.

confusion *noun* F **1** confusion;
2 embarrassment.

congé *noun* M holiday, leave (*from
work*); **Robert est en congé
aujourd'hui** Robert's on holiday
today; **je pars en congé le dix** I'm
on holiday from the tenth; **prendre
une semaine de congé** to take a
week's holiday; **Sylvie est en congé
de maladie** Sylvie is on sick leave.

congélateur *noun* M freezer.

congeler *verb* [45] to freeze.

congère *noun* F snowdrift.

congestion *noun* F congestion.

congrès *noun* M conference.

conifère *noun* M conifer.

conjoint, conjointe *noun* M, F
spouse (*husband or wife*).

conjonctivite *noun* F
conjunctivitis.

conjugaison *noun* F conjugation.

connaissance *noun* F
1 knowledge; **tes connaissances e
français** your knowledge of
French; **2** acquaintance;
3 consciousness; **perdre
connaissance** to lose
consciousness.

connaître *verb* [27] **1** to know; **es
ce que tu connais Gaby?** do you
know Gaby?; **je ne connais pas
Londres** I don't know London; **je l**

connais depuis trois ans I've known her for three years; **2 se connaître** to know each other; **on se connaît** we know each other; **3 s'y connaître en quelque chose** to know about something; **je ne m'y connais pas du tout en informatique** I know absolutely nothing about computers.

connecter *verb* [1] to connect.

connexion *noun* F connection.

connu *adjective* well-known; **elle est très connue en France** she's very well-known in France.

consacrer *verb* [1] to devote.

consciemment *adverb* consciously.

conscience *noun* F conscience; **avoir mauvaise conscience** to have a guilty conscience.

conscient *adjective* **1** aware; **être conscient de quelque chose** to be aware of something; **2** conscious.

conseil *noun* M **1** advice; **un conseil** a piece of advice; **des conseils** advice; **2** council.

conseiller¹, **conseillère** *noun* M, F adviser.

conseiller² *verb* [1] **1** to advise; **conseiller à quelqu'un de faire** to advise somebody to do; **je te conseille de voir un médecin** I advise you to see a doctor; **2** to recommend; **pouvez-vous me conseiller un dentiste?** Can you recommend me a dentist?

consentement *noun* M consent.

consentir *verb* [58] **consentir à quelque chose** to agree to something.

conséquence *noun* F **1** consequence; **2 en conséquence** consequently.

conséquent *adjective* **par conséquent** consequently.

conservateur, conservatrice *noun* M, F **1** conservative; **2** (museum) curator.

conservation *noun* F **1** conservation; **2 lait longue conservation** long-life milk.

conserve *noun* F **1 les conserves** canned food; **2 en conserve** canned; **des légumes en conserve** canned vegetables.

conserver *verb* [1] **1** to keep; **je t'ai conservé une place** I've kept you a seat; **'à conserver au frais'** 'keep in a cool place'; **2 se conserver** to keep; **ce fromage se conserve bien** this cheese keeps well.

considérable *adjective* considerable.

considérablement *adverb* considerably.

considération *noun* F consideration.

considérer *verb* [24] to consider.

consigne *noun* F **1** left luggage office; **2** deposit (*on a returnable bottle*); **3** instructions.

consistant *adjective* substantial; **un repas consistant** a substantial meal.

consister verb [1] **consister en** to consist of, to consist in.

consommateur, consommatrice noun M, F **1** consumer; **2** customer (in a café).

consommation noun F **1** consumption (of fuel, electricity, gas); **2** drink.

consommer verb [1] **1** to use (fuel); **2** to have a drink (in a café).

consonne noun F consonant.

conspiration noun F conspiracy.

conspirer verb [1] to conspire, to plot.

constamment adverb constantly.

constant adjective constant.

constater verb [1] to notice.

constipé adjective constipated.

construction noun F construction, building.

construire verb [26] to build; **construire une maison** to build a house; **faire construire une maison** to have a house built.

consul noun M consul.

consulat noun M consulate.

consultation noun F **1** consultation; **2** (doctor's) surgery hours.

consulter verb [1] **1** to consult; **2** to hold surgery.

contact noun M contact; **prendre contact avec quelqu'un** to contact somebody.

contacter verb [1] to contact.

contagieux (F **contagieuse**) adjective infectious.

contamination noun F contamination.

contaminer verb [1] to contaminate.

conte noun M tale, story; **un conte de fées** a fairy tale.

contempler verb [1] to look at, to contemplate.

contemporain, contemporaine noun M, F, adjective contemporary.

contenant noun M container.

conteneur noun M container.

contenir verb [77] to contain; **'ne contient pas de sucre'** 'does not contain sugar'.

content adjective pleased, glad, happy; **être content de quelque chose** to be pleased with something; **elle est très contente de son nouveau travail** she's very pleased with her new job; **je suis content de te voir** I'm pleased to see you.

contenter verb [1] **1** to satisfy; **2 se contenter de faire** to content oneself with doing.

contenu noun M contents.

contesté adjective controversial.

contester verb [1] to dispute, to challenge, to question.

contexte noun M context.

continent noun M continent.

continu adjective continuous.

continuation *noun* F
continuation.

continuer *verb* [1] to continue, to go
on (with); **continue!** go on!; **elle a
continué son histoire** she went on
with her story; **continuer à faire,
continuer de faire** to go on doing;
elle a continué à parler she went on
talking.

contour *noun* M outline, contour.

contourner *verb* [1] to go round.

contraceptif *noun* M
contraceptive.

contraception *noun* F
contraception.

contractuel, contractuelle
noun M, F traffic warden.

contradiction *noun* F
contradiction.

contradictoire *adjective*
contradictory.

contraindre *verb* [31] to force.

contraire *noun* M **1 le contraire**
the opposite; **c'est le contraire de
ce que je pensais** it's the opposite
of what I thought; **2 au contraire**
on the contrary.
adjective opposite.

contrairement *adverb*
contrairement à contrary to,
unlike; **contrairement à ce qu'il
nous a dit** contrary to what he told
us.

contrariant *adjective* annoying.

contrarier *verb* [1] **1** to upset;
2 to annoy.

contraste *noun* M contrast.

contraster *verb* [1] to contrast.

contrat *noun* M contract.

contravention *noun* F **1** parking
ticket; **2** speeding ticket.

contre *preposition* **1** against;
contre le mur against the wall;
2 être contre quelque chose to be
against something; **je suis plutôt
contre** on the whole, I'm against it;
3 jouer contre quelqu'un to play
against somebody; **4** versus;
5 échanger quelque chose contre
to exchange something for
(*something else*); **6 par contre** on
the other hand; ★ **le pour et le
contre** the pros and cons.

contrebande *noun* F
1 smuggling; **2** smuggled goods.

contrebasse *noun* F double bass.

contredire *verb* [47] to contradict.

contreplaqué *noun* M plywood.

contribuable *noun* M & F
taxpayer.

contribuer *verb* [1] **contribuer à** to
contribute to.

contribution *noun* F
contribution.

contrôle *noun* M **1** control;
2 class test (*at school*); **j'ai un
contrôle de français cet après-
midi** I've got a French test this
afternoon; **3 contrôle de police**
police check; **4 contrôle des
passeports** passport control;
contrôle des billets ticket
inspection.

contrôle continu *noun* M
continuous assessment.

contrôler *verb* [1] **1** to check; **2** to control.

contrôleur, contrôleuse *noun* M, F ticket inspector.

controversé *adjective* controversial.

convaincant *adjective* convincing.

convaincre *verb* [79] **1** to convince; **je ne suis pas convaincu** I'm not convinced; **2** to persuade; **je l'ai convaincu d'acheter un ordinateur** I persuaded him to buy a computer.

convenable *adjective* **1** suitable; **2** decent.

convenir *verb* [81] **1 convenir à** to suit, to be suitable for; **est-ce que dix heures te convient?** does ten o'clock suit you?; **2 convenir de faire** to agree to do.

convention *noun* F **1** agreement; **2** convention.

conversation *noun* F conversation.

convertir *verb* [2] to convert.

conviction *noun* F conviction.

convive *noun* M & F guest.

convivial (M *plural* **conviviaux**) *adjective* **1** friendly; **une atmosphère conviviale** a friendly atmosphere; **2** user-friendly.

convoi *noun* M **1** convoy; **2 'convoi exceptionnel'** 'dangerous load'.

convoquer *verb* [1] **1** to invite (*to a meeting*); **2** to summon.

coopératif (F **coopérative¹**) *adjective* cooperative.

coopération *noun* F cooperation.

coopérative² *noun* F cooperative.

coopérer *verb* [24] to cooperate.

coordonnées *plural noun* F address and telephone number.

coordonner *verb* [1] to coordinate.

copain *noun* M **1** friend, mate (*male*); **je sors avec les copains** I'm going out with my mates; **2** boyfriend; **elle est partie en vacances avec son copain** she's gone on holiday with her boyfriend.

copie *noun* F **1** copy; **2** paper (*on which an exam or class exercise has been written*); **j'ai un tas de copies à corriger ce soir** I've got a pile of marking to do this evening.

copier *verb* [1] to copy.

copieux (F **copieuse**) *adjective* hearty; **un petit déjeuner copieux** a hearty breakfast.

copine *noun* F **1** friend, mate (*female*); **je sors avec les copines** I'm going out with my mates; **2** girlfriend; **il est parti en vacances avec sa copine** he's gone on holiday with his girlfriend.

coq *noun* M cockerel.

coque *noun* F **1** hull (*of a boat*); **2** shell (*of a nut*); **3 un œuf à la coque** a soft-boiled egg.

coquelicot *noun* M poppy.

coqueluche *noun* F whooping-cough.

coquet (F **coquette**) *adjective* **1** flirtatious; **2** pretty.

coquetier *noun* M eggcup.

coquillage *noun* M **1** shellfish; **2** seashell.

coquille *noun* F **1** shell; **2** misprint.

coquille Saint-Jacques *noun* F scallop.

coquin *adjective* cheeky, naughty.

cor *noun* M horn (*musical instrument*).

corail (*plural* **coraux**) *noun* M coral.

Coran *noun* M **le Coran** the Koran.

corbeau *noun* M crow.

corbeille *noun* F basket; **une corbeille à papier** a wastepaper basket; **une corbeille à linge** a linen basket.

corbillard *noun* M hearse.

corde *noun* F **1** rope; **2** string (*of a racket, a bow, or an instrument such as a guitar or violin*); ★ **pleuvoir des cordes** to be raining cats and dogs (*literally: to be raining ropes*).

corde à linge *noun* F clothes line.

cordial (M *plural* **cordiaux**) *adjective* warm, cordial.

cordialement *adverb* **1** warmly; **2 cordialement à vous** Yours sincerely.

cordonnerie *noun* F shoe repairer's.

cordonnier *noun* M shoe repairer.

corne *noun* F horn.

cornemuse *noun* F bagpipes; **jouer de la cornemuse** to play the bagpipes.

cornet *noun* M **1 un cornet de glace** an ice cream cone; **2 un cornet de frites** a bag of chips (*in fact sold in a cardboard cornet*).

cornichon *noun* M gherkin.

Cornouailles *noun* F Cornwall.

corps *noun* M body.

correct *adjective* **1** correct; **2** reasonable, fine; **à un prix correct** at a reasonable price; **le repas était tout à fait correct** the meal was absolutely fine.

correctement *adverb* **1** correctly; **2** properly; **3** reasonably well.

correction *noun* F correction.

correspondance *noun* F **1** letters, correspondence; **2 acheter quelque chose par correspondance** to buy something by mail order; **3** connection (*a train or flight*); **j'ai raté ma correspondance** I missed my connection; **un vol en correspondance** a connecting flight.

correspondant, correspondante *noun* M, F pen friend.

correspondre *verb* [3] to correspond.

corrida *noun* F bullfight.

corriger *verb* [52] **1** to correct; **2** to mark; **elle est en train de corriger ses copies** she's doing her marking.

corsage *noun* M **1** blouse; **2** bodice.

corse *adjective* Corsican.

Corse *noun* F Corsica.

corsé *adjective* full-bodied, strong.

corvée *noun* F chore.

cosmétiques *plural noun* M cosmetics.

costaud *adjective* strong, sturdy.

costume *noun* M **1** suit; **2** costume.

côte *noun* F **1** coast; **2** hill; **3** rib; **4** chop; **une côte d'agneau** a lamb chop.

côté *noun* M **1** side; **de l'autre côté (de)** on the other side (of); **de l'autre côté de la rue** on the other side of the street; **2 d'un autre côté** on the other hand; **3 à côté** nearby; **mon frère habite à côté** my brother lives nearby; **4 à côté de** next to, beside; **elle était assise à côté de moi** she was sitting next to me.

Côte d'Azur *noun* F French Riviera.

côtelette *noun* F chop; **une côtelette de porc** a pork chop.

cotisation *noun* F **1** subscription; **2** contribution.

coton *noun* M **1** cotton; **un pull en coton** a cotton jumper; **2** sewing cotton; **3** cotton wool.

cou *noun* M neck.

couchage *noun* M **un sac de couchage** a sleeping bag.

couchant *adjective* **le soleil couchant** the setting sun; **au soleil couchant** at sunset.

couche *noun* F **1** layer; **2** coat (*of paint*); **3** nappy.

coucher *verb* [1] **1** to sleep; **tu peux coucher chez Sophie** you can sleep at Sophie's house; **2 se coucher** to go to bed; **elle se couche à dix heures** she goes to bed at ten o'clock; **3 coucher un enfant** to put a child to bed.

coucher de soleil *noun* M sunset; **un coucher de soleil magnifique** a magnificent sunset.

coucou *noun* M **1** cuckoo; **2** cowslip.

coude *noun* M elbow.

coudre *verb* [28] to sew; **coudre un bouton** to sew on a button.

couette *noun* F duvet, continental quilt.

couler *verb* [1] **1** to flow; **2 avoir le nez qui coule** to have a runny nose; **3 faire couler un bain** to run a bath; **4** to sink.

couleur *noun* F colour; **de quelle couleur est ta voiture?** what colour is your car?

couleuvre *noun* F grass snake.

coulisses *plural noun* F wings (*in a theatre*).

couloir *noun* M corridor.

coup *noun* M blow; **il a reçu un coup à l'estomac** he was hit in the stomach; ★ **boire un coup** (*informal*) to have a drink; ★ **donner un coup de balai** to sweep the floor; ★ **un coup de peinture** a lick of paint; ★ **sur le coup** at first;

★ **tenir le coup** to last out; ★ **tout d'un coup** all of a sudden.

coup de chance *noun* M stroke of luck.

coup de feu *noun* M (gun)shot.

coup de main *noun* M **donner un coup de main à quelqu'un** to give somebody a hand.

coup de pied *noun* M kick.

coup de poing *noun* M punch.

coup de soleil *noun* M **attraper un coup de soleil** to get sunburnt.

coup de téléphone *noun* M phone call.

coup de tonnerre *noun* M clap of thunder.

coup de vent *noun* M gust of wind.

coup d'œil *noun* M glance; **jeter un coup d'œil à quelque chose** to have a quick look at something.

coupable *noun* M & F culprit. *adjective* guilty.

coupe *noun* F **1** cup (*for sports*); **la Coupe du Monde** the World Cup; **2** haircut; **3** fruit dish.

couper *verb* [1] **1** to cut; **se faire couper les cheveux** to have your hair cut; **2 se couper** to cut yourself; **se couper le doigt** to cut your finger; **3** to cut off, to turn off (*gas, electricity*); **4 excuse-moi, je t'ai coupé la parole** sorry, I interrupted you.

couple *noun* M couple.

coupon *noun* M **1** remnant (*of fabric*); **2** coupon.

coupure *noun* F cut; **une coupure de courant** a power cut.

cour *noun* F **1** school playground; **2** inner courtyard (*in an apartment block or hotel*); **3** court (*of a king or queen*); **4** law court.

courage *noun* M **1** courage, bravery; **2** energy; **avoir le courage de faire** to have the energy to do; **3 bon courage!** good luck!

courageux (F **courageuse**) *adjective* brave.

couramment *adverb* fluently.

courant *noun* M **1 être au courant de quelque chose** to know about something; **est-ce que ta sœur est au courant?** does your sister know?; **je te tiens au courant** I'll let you know what happens; **2** current; **3** electricity; **couper le courant** to cut off (or turn off) the electricity; **une panne de courant** a power cut. *adjective* **1** common; **2** usual; **3** current.

courant d'air *noun* M draught.

courbe *noun* F curve.

courber *verb* [1] to bend.

coureur, coureuse *noun* M, F runner.

courge *noun* F (vegetable) marrow.

courgette *noun* F courgette.

courir *verb* [29] **1** to run; **traverser la rue en courant** to run across the street; **2 courir un risque** to run a risk.

couronne *noun* F crown.

courrier *noun* M mail, post.

courrier électronique *noun* M electronic mail, e-mail.

cours *noun* M **1** class, lesson; **le cours de français** the French lesson; **suivre des cours d'espagnol** to go to Spanish classes; **2** course (*of events*); **au cours de** in the course of.

course *noun* F **1** race; **2** running; **3 les courses** shopping; **faire des courses** to do some shopping; **je fais mes courses à midi** I do my shopping at lunchtime.

court *adjective* short.

court-circuit *noun* M short-circuit.

court de tennis *noun* M tennis court.

couru *verb* SEE **courir**.

cousin, cousine *noun* M, F cousin; **mon cousin germain** my first cousin.

coussin *noun* M cushion.

coût *noun* M cost; **le coût de la vie** the cost of living.

couteau (*plural* **couteaux**) *noun* M knife; **un couteau à pain** a bread knife.

coûter *verb* [1] to cost; **ça coûte combien?** how much is it?; **ça coûte dix francs** it's ten francs; **coûter cher** to be expensive; **est-ce que ça t'a coûté cher?** was it expensive?

coutume *noun* F custom.

couture *noun* F **1** sewing, dressmaking; **faire de la couture** to sew; **2** seam.

couturier *noun* M fashion designer.

couturière *noun* F dressmaker.

couvent *noun* M convent.

couvercle *noun* M **1** lid; **2** screwtop.

couvert *noun* M place setting; **les couverts** the cutlery; **mettre les couverts** to set the table. *adjective* **1** covered; **un marché couvert** a covered market; **2 couvert de** covered with; **3** overcast, cloudy.

couverture *noun* F **1** blanket; **2** cover (*of a book*).

couvre-lit *noun* M bedspread.

couvrir *verb* [30] to cover.

crabe *noun* M crab.

cracher *verb* [1] to spit.

crachin *noun* M drizzle.

craie *noun* F chalk.

craindre *verb* [31] to be afraid of.

crainte *noun* F fear.

crampe *noun* F cramp.

crâne *noun* M skull; **avoir mal au crâne** (*informal*) to have a headache.

crâner *verb* [1] (*informal*) to show off.

crapaud *noun* M toad.

craquement *noun* M creak.

craquer *verb* [1] **1** to split; **2** to creak; **3** (*informal*) to crack up; ★ **j'ai craqué** I couldn't resist it!

crasse *noun* F filth.

cravate *noun* F tie.

crawl *noun* M crawl (*in swimming*); **nager le crawl** to swim crawl.

crayon *noun* M pencil.

créatif (F **créative**) *adjective* creative.

création *noun* F creation.

crèche *noun* F **1** crèche, day nursery; **2** nativity scene (*as a Christmas decoration*).

crédit *noun* M **1** credit; **2** funding.

créer *verb* [32] to create.

crémaillère *noun* F chimney hook (*used in olden times to hang a pot for cooking over the fire*); ★ **pendre la crémaillère** to have a house-warming party (*literally: to hang the chimney hook*).

crème *noun* F, *adjective* cream.

crème Chantilly *noun* F whipped cream.

crémerie *noun* F cheese shop.

crémeux (F **crémeuse**) *adjective* creamy.

crêpe *noun* F pancake.

crépon *noun* M crepe paper.

crépuscule *noun* M twilight.

cresson *noun* M watercress.

creuser *verb* [1] **1** to dig; **2** to hollow out; ★ **se creuser la cervelle** (*informal*) to rack your brains.

creux *noun* M hollow. *adjective* (F **creuse**) **1** hollow; **2 une assiette creuse** a soup plate.

crevaison *noun* F puncture.

crevé *adjective* **1** burst; **2** (*informal*) knackered.

crever *verb* [50] **1** to burst; **un pneu crevé** a burst tyre, a puncture; **2** (*informal*) to die; **je crève de faim!** I'm starving!

crevette *noun* F prawn.

cri *noun* M cry, shout.

criard *adjective* garish.

cric *noun* M (car) jack.

cricket *noun* M cricket; **jouer au cricket** to play cricket.

crier *verb* [1] **1** to shout; **2** to scream.

crime *noun* M crime.

criminel, criminelle *noun* M, F, *adjective* criminal.

criquet *noun* M grasshopper.

crise *noun* F **1** crisis; **2** attack (*of an illness*).

crise cardiaque *noun* F heart attack.

cristal (*plural* **cristaux**) *noun* M crystal.

critère *noun* M criterion.

critique[1] *noun* M critic.

critique[2] *noun* F **1** criticism; **les critiques** criticism; **2** review (*of a film, book, etc*).

critique[3] *adjective* critical.

critiquer *verb* [1] to criticize.

Croatie *noun* F Croatia.

croche-pied noun M **faire un croche-pied à quelqu'un** (*informal*) to trip somebody up.

crochet noun M **1** hook; **2** detour; **3** crochet.

crocodile noun M crocodile.

croire verb [33] **1 croire que** to think that; **je crois qu'il est parti** I think he's left; **tu crois que c'est trop tard?** do you think it's too late?; **je ne crois pas** I don't think so; **2** to believe; **je n'arrive pas à le croire** I don't believe it; **3 croire à** to believe in; **4 je n'en croyais pas mes yeux!** I couldn't believe my eyes!

croiser verb [1] **1** to cross; **croiser les jambes** to cross your legs; **croiser les bras** to fold your arms; **2 croiser quelqu'un** to bump into somebody (*meet by chance*); **j'ai croisé Odile devant la banque** I bumped into Odile outside the bank.

croisière noun F cruise.

croissance noun F growth.

croissant noun M croissant.

croître verb [34] to grow.

croix noun F cross.

Croix-Rouge noun F Red Cross.

croquant adjective crunchy.

croque-monsieur noun M toasted ham sandwich with cheese sauce on top.

croque-mort noun (*informal*) M undertaker.

croquer verb [1] to munch.

croquis noun M sketch.

crottes plural noun F droppings; **des crottes de chien** dog dirt.

croustillant adjective crispy.

croûte noun F **1** crust; **2** rind (*of cheese*).

croûton noun M crouton.

croyance noun F belief.

cru[1] verb SEE **croire**.

cru[2] adjective raw, uncooked.

cruauté noun F cruelty.

cruche noun F (large) jug.

crudités plural noun F raw vegetables (*served with dips as a starter*).

cruel (F **cruelle**) adjective cruel.

crustacé noun M shellfish.

crypte noun F crypt.

cube noun M cube. adjective cubic; **un mètre cube** a cubic metre.

cueillir verb [35] to pick (*fruit or flowers*).

cuiller noun F **1** spoon; **2** spoonful.

cuillère noun F = **cuiller**.

cuillerée noun F spoonful.

cuir noun M leather; **des chaussures en cuir** leather shoes.

cuir chevelu noun M scalp.

cuire verb [36] to cook.

cuisine noun F **1** kitchen; **2** cooking; **faire la cuisine** to cook, to do the cooking.

cuisiner verb [1] to cook.

cuisinier, cuisinière[1] *noun* M, F cook.

cuisinière[2] *noun* F cooker; **une cuisinière à gaz** a gas cooker; **une cuisinière électrique** an electric cooker.

cuisse *noun* F thigh.

cuisse de poulet *noun* F chicken leg, chicken thigh.

cuit *adjective* cooked; **bien cuit** well done (*meat*).

cuivre *noun* M copper.

cuivre jaune *noun* M brass.

culot *noun* M (*informal*) cheek; **quel culot!** what a cheek!, what a nerve!; **elle a du culot!** she's got a nerve!

culotte *noun* F **une (petite) culotte** knickers.

culpabilité *noun* F guilt.

cultivateur, cultivatrice *noun* M, F farmer.

cultiver *verb* [1] **1** to grow; **2** to cultivate.

culture *noun* F **1** farming; **2** growing; **de culture biologique** organically produced; **3** crop; **4** culture.

culturel (F **culturelle**) *adjective* cultural.

culturisme *noun* M body-building.

cure *noun* F course of treatment.

curé *noun* M parish priest.

cure-dents *noun* M toothpick.

curer *verb* [1] **se curer les ongles** to clean your nails; **se curer les dents** to pick your teeth.

curieux (F **curieuse**) *adjective* **1** strange, odd; **2** curious, inquisitive.

curiosité *noun* F curiosity.

curseur *noun* M cursor (*on a computer screen*).

cuvette *noun* F bowl; **la cuvette des wc** the lavatory bowl.

cyclable *adjective* **une piste cyclable** a cycle track.

cycle *noun* M cycle.

cyclisme *noun* M cycling.

cycliste *noun* M & F cyclist.

cyclone *noun* M hurricane.

cygne *noun* M swan.

cylindre *noun* M **1** cylinder; **2** roller.

cynique *adjective* cynical.

cyprès *noun* M cypress (tree).

D d

d' *preposition* SEE **de**.

dactylo *noun* M & F typist.

daim *noun* M **1** suede; **des chaussures en daim** suede shoes; **2** fallow deer.

dalle *noun* F paving slab.

daltonien (F **daltonienne**) *adjective* colour-blind.

dame *noun* F **1** lady; **2** queen (*in cards or chess*).

dames *plural noun* F draughts;
jouer aux dames to play draughts.

dancing *noun* M dance hall.

Danemark *noun* M Denmark; **au
Danemark** to (or in) Denmark.

danger *noun* M danger.

dangereux (F **dangereuse**)
adjective dangerous.

danois *noun* M,
adjective Danish.

dans *preposition* **1** in; **elle est dans
la cuisine** she's in the kitchen;
2 into; **va dans la cuisine** go into
the kitchen; **3 dans trois mois** in
three months' time; **4 boire dans un
verre** to drink out of a glass.

danse *noun* F **1** dance; **2** dancing;
faire de la danse to go to dancing
classes.

danse classique *noun* F ballet.

danser *verb* [1] to dance.

danseur, danseuse *noun* M, F
dancer.

date *noun* F date.

date de naissance *noun* F date
of birth.

date limite *noun* F closing date.

date limite de vente *noun* F sell-
by date.

datte *noun* F date (*fruit*).

dauphin *noun* M dolphin.

davantage *adverb* **1** more;
2 longer.

de, d'(*before a vowel or a silent 'h'*)
(*note that 'de + le' becomes 'du'*)
preposition **1** of; **une boîte**

d'allumettes a box of matches; **le
pied de la table** the leg of the table,
the table leg; **2 le père de Marie**
Marie's father; **la maison de tes
parents** your parents' house;
3 from; **elle vient de Paris** she
comes from Paris; **elle rentre du
bureau à six heures** she comes
home from the office at six o'clock;
4 made from; **une table de bois** a
wooden table; **5** by; **le prix a
augmenté de vingt francs** the price
has gone up (by) twenty francs.
determiner **du café** (some) coffee;
veux-tu du café? would you like
(some) coffee?; **je n'ai pas de café** I
don't have any coffee; **nous avons
des pommes et des oranges** we
have apples and oranges; **veux-tu de
l'eau?** would you like some water?

dé *noun* M **1** dice; **2 un dé à
coudre** a thimble.

dealer *noun* M drug pusher.

déballer *verb* [1] to unpack.

débardeur *noun* M camisole top,
vest-style top.

débarquer *verb* [1] **1** to
disembark; **2** to land;
3 (*informal*) to turn up; **elle a
débarqué chez moi** she turned up
at my place.

débarras *noun* M junk room;
★ **bon débarras!** good riddance!

débarrasser *verb* [1] **1** to clear out
(*a room*); **débarrasser la table** to
clear the table; **2 se débarrasser de
quelque chose** to get rid of
something; **je me suis débarrassé
de tous ces vieux bouquins** I got
rid of all those old books.

débat noun M debate.

débattre verb [21] to discuss, to negotiate; **'prix à débattre'** 'price negotiable'.

débile adjective (informal) stupid, crazy; **tu es débile ou quoi?** are you stupid or something?; **c'est complètement débile!** that's completely crazy!

déblayer verb [59] to clear.

débordé adjective **être débordé** to be up to your eyes in work.

déborder verb [1] to overflow.

débouché noun M job prospect.

déboucher verb [1] **1** to uncork (a bottle); **2** to unblock (a drain or pipe); **3 déboucher sur** to lead into.

déboussoler verb [1] (informal) to confuse.

debout adverb **1** standing; **rester debout** to remain standing; **je suis resté debout toute la journée** I've been on my feet all day; **se mettre debout** to stand up; **tout le monde s'est mis debout** everybody stood up; **2** upright; **mettre quelque chose debout** to stand something upright; **3** up (out of bed); **je suis debout à six heures tous les jours** I'm up at six every day; ★ **ça ne tient pas debout** it doesn't make any sense (literally: it doesn't stand upright).

déboutonner verb [1] to unbutton.

débrancher verb [1] to unplug.

débris noun M **1** fragment; **2** piece of wreckage.

débrouiller verb [1] **se débrouiller** to manage; **je peux me débrouiller tout seul** I can manage by myself; **débrouille-toi!** get on with it!

début noun M beginning, start; **le début de** the beginning of; **au début** at the beginning, to start with; **on commencera début mars** we'll start at the beginning of March; **en début d'après-midi** in the early afternoon.

débutant, débutante noun M, F beginner.

débuter verb [1] to begin, to start.

décaféiné adjective decaffeinated.

décalage noun M **1** gap; **2** discrepancy.

décalage horaire noun M time difference (between time zones); **il y a une heure de décalage horaire entre la France et la Grande-Bretagne** there's an hour's time difference between France and Britain.

décaler verb [1] to move (forward or back).

décapiter verb [1] to behead.

décapotable adjective **une voiture décapotable** a convertible (car).

décéder verb [24] to die; **elle est décédée au mois de novembre** she died in November.

décembre noun M December; **en décembre, au mois de décembre** in December.

décemment adverb decently.

décennie noun F decade.

décent *adjective* decent.

déception *noun* F disappointment.

décès *noun* M death.

décevant *adjective* disappointing.

décevoir *verb* [66] to disappoint.

décharge *noun* F (public) rubbish tip.

décharger *verb* [52] to unload.

déchets *plural noun* M **1** waste; **les déchets nucléaires** nuclear waste; **2** rubbish.

déchiffrer *verb* [1] to decipher.

déchirant *adjective* heart-rending.

déchirer *verb* [1] **1** to tear; **j'ai déchiré mon pantalon** I've torn my trousers; **2** to tear up; **déchirer une enveloppe** to tear up an envelope; **3** to tear off; **déchirer une feuille** to tear off a sheet of paper; **4** to tear out; **déchirer une page** to tear out a page.

décidé *adjective* determined.

décidément *adverb* really.

décider *verb* [1] **1** to decide; **décider de faire** to decide to do; **j'ai décidé de vendre mon vélo** I've decided to sell my bike; **2 se décider** to make up your mind; **il faut qu'on se décide une fois pour toutes** we must make up our minds once and for all; **3 se décider à faire** to decide to do.

décimal (M *plural* **décimaux**) *adjective* decimal.

décimale *noun* F decimal.

décision *noun* F decision.

déclaration *noun* F **1** statement; **2** declaration.

déclarer *verb* [1] to declare.

déclencher *verb* [1] **1** to cause; **2** to set off; **déclencher l'alarme** to set off the alarm.

déclic *noun* M click.

décliner *verb* [1] to decline.

décollage *noun* M takeoff (*of a plane*).

décollé *adjective* ★ **avoir les oreilles décollées** to have sticking-out ears (*literally: to have ears which have come unstuck*).

décoller *verb* [1] **1** to take off (*of a plane*); **2 décoller quelque chose** to peel something off; **3 se décoller** to come unstuck, to peel off; **le papier peint est en train de se décoller** the wallpaper's peeling off.

décolleté *adjective* low-cut.

décolorer *verb* [1] **se décolorer** to fade; **se faire décolorer les cheveux** to have your hair lightened.

décombres *plural noun* M rubble.

décongeler *verb* [45] to defrost.

déconseillé *adjective* not recommended; '**déconseillé pour les enfants**' 'not recommended for children'.

déconseiller *verb* [1] **déconseiller à quelqu'un de faire** to advise somebody not to do; **nous lui avons déconseillé de voyager toute seule** we advised her not to travel alone.

décontracté *adjective* relaxed, laid-back; **mon patron est très décontracté** my boss is very laid-back.

décontracter *verb* [1] **se décontracter** to relax.

décor *noun* M **1** decor; **2** setting.

décorateur, décoratrice *noun* M, F interior designer.

décoratif (F **décorative**) *adjective* **1** ornamental; **2** decorative.

décoration *noun* F **1** decorating; **2** interior design.

décorer *verb* [1] to decorate.

découper *verb* [1] **1** to cut out; **découper un article dans un journal** to cut an article out of a newspaper; **2** to carve (*meat*); **c'est Marie-Laure qui va découper le poulet** Marie-Laure's going to carve the chicken.

décourageant *adjective* discouraging.

décourager *verb* [52] to discourage.

découvert *noun* M overdraft.

découverte *noun* F discovery.

découvrir *verb* [30] to discover.

décrire *verb* [38] to describe.

décrocher *verb* [1] **1** to lift the receiver (*of a telephone*); **'décrochez'** 'lift the receiver'; **il faut décrocher avant de composer le numéro** you have to lift the receiver before dialling; **2** to take down (*a picture, curtains, etc*).

déçu *adjective* disappointed; **nous sommes tous très déçus** we're all very disappointed.

dedans *adverb* inside; **1 elle a ouvert la boîte mais il n'y avait rien dedans** she opened the box but there was nothing in it; **2 là-dedans** in there.

dédommager *verb* [52] to compensate.

déduction *noun* F deduction.

déduire *verb* [26] **1** to deduce; **2** to deduct.

déesse *noun* F goddess.

défaire *verb* [10] **1** to undo; **2 se défaire** to come undone; **3 se défaire de** to get rid of.

défaite *noun* F defeat.

défaut *noun* M **1** flaw, defect; **2 à défaut de** for want of.

défavorisé *adjective* underprivileged; **les défavorisés** the underprivileged.

défectueux (F **défectueuse**) *adjective* faulty; **une prise défectueuse** a faulty plug.

défendre *verb* [3] **1** to forbid; **2** to defend.

défendu *adjective* forbidden.

défense *noun* **1 défense de fumer** no smoking; **2** defence; **3** protection; **la défense de l'environnement** the protection of the environment; **4** tusk (*of an elephant*).

défi *noun* M challenge.

déficit *noun* M deficit.

défigurer *verb* [1] to disfigure.

défilé *noun* M **1** parade;
2 procession; **3** march.

défiler *verb* [1] **1** to parade; **2** to march; **3** to come and go.

définir *verb* [2] to define.

définitif (F **définitive**) *adjective* final, definitive.

définition *noun* F definition.

définitivement *adverb* **1** for good; **2** definitely.

défoncer *verb* [61] to smash in (*a door*).

déformer *verb* [1] **1** to bend out of shape; **2** to distort. **3** to stretch (*a garment or shoes*).

défouler *verb* [1] **1 se défouler** to let off steam; **2** to unwind.

défunt *noun* M **le défunt** the deceased.

dégagé *adjective* **1** clear; **2** casual.

dégager *verb* [52] **1** to clear; **2** to free (*a trapped person*).

dégâts *plural noun* M damage.

dégel *noun* M thaw.

dégeler *verb* [45] to thaw.

dégénérer *verb* [24] **1** to degenerate; **2** to go from bad to worse.

dégivrer *verb* [1] **1** to defrost; **2** to de-ice.

dégonfler *verb* [1] to let down (*a tyre, an airbed, etc*).

dégouliner *verb* [1] to trickle.

dégourdi *adjective* smart, bright; **un gamin dégourdi** a bright kid.

dégoût *noun* M disgust.

dégoûtant *adjective* **1** filthy; **tes mains sont dégoûtantes** your hands are filthy; **2** disgusting.

dégoûté *adjective* disgusted.

dégoûter *verb* [1] **1** to disgust;
2 dégoûter quelqu'un de quelque chose to put somebody off something; **ça m'a dégoûté du poisson** that put me off fish.

dégrader *verb* [1] **1** to damage;
2 se dégrader to deteriorate.

dégraisser *verb* [1] to dryclean.

degré *noun* M degree.

dégringoler *verb* [1] (*informal*) to tumble down.

déguisé *adjective* **1** in fancy dress, in disguise; **2 une soirée déguisée** a fancy-dress party; **3** disguised.

déguiser *verb* [1] **1** to disguise;
2 se déguiser to dress up in fancy dress.

dégustation *noun* F tasting;
'dégustation de glaces' 'a fine selection of ice creams'.

déguster *verb* [1] **1** to savour, to enjoy; **2** to taste (*wine, cheese, etc*).

dehors *adverb* **1** outside; **je t'attends dehors** I'll wait for you outside; **j'ai passé toute la journée dehors** I've been outside all day;
2 en dehors de apart from; **en dehors de la salade, tout est prêt** everything's ready apart from the salad.

déjà adverb **1** already; **tu pars déjà?** are you leaving already?; **je t'ai déjà dit de ne pas faire ça!** I told you not to do that!; **2** before; **tu es déjà venu ici?** have you been here before?

déjeuner noun M lunch; **petit déjeuner** breakfast.
verb [1] **1** to have lunch; **nous déjeunons à une heure** we have lunch at one o'clock; **2** to have breakfast.

délabré adjective dilapidated.

délacer verb [61] to unlace.

délai noun M period of time, waiting period.

délavé adjective **1** faded; **2** washed-out.

délecter verb [1] **se délecter à faire** to delight in doing.

délégué, déléguée noun M, F **1** delegate; **2** representative.

délibéré adjective deliberate.

délibérer verb [24] to discuss.

délicat adjective **1** delicate; **2** tactful.

délice noun M delight; **c'est un vrai délice!** it's absolutely delicious!

délicieux (F **délicieuse**) adjective delicious.

délinquance noun F **1** crime; **2** delinquency.

délinquant, délinquante noun M, F offender.

délirant adjective (informal) crazy; **c'est complètement délirant!** it's completely crazy!

délire noun M **1** (informal) madness; **2** frenzy.

délirer verb [1] (informal) to be crazy; **il délire!** he's crazy!

délit noun M criminal offence.

délivrer verb [1] to free, to liberate.

déloyal (M plural **déloyaux**) adjective disloyal.

deltaplane noun M **1** hang-glider; **2 faire du deltaplane** to go hang-gliding.

déluge noun M **1** downpour; **2 le Déluge** the Flood (in the Bible).

demain adverb tomorrow; **à demain!** see you tomorrow!; **après-demain** the day after tomorrow.

demande noun F **1** request; **2** application; **faire une demande d'emploi** to apply for a job; **'demandes d'emplois'** 'situations wanted'; **3** demand.

demandé adjective **très demandé** very much in demand, very popular.

demander verb [1] **1 demander quelque chose** to ask for something; **2 demander quelque chose à quelqu'un** to ask somebody (for) something; **demande à ton père!** ask your father!; **il m'a demandé ton adresse** he asked me for your address; **3 demander à quelqu'un de faire** to ask somebody to do; **elle m'a demandé de téléphoner** she asked me to phone; **4 se demander** to wonder; **je me demande ce qu'elle est en train de faire** I wonder what she's doing.

demandeur d'emploi noun M job-seeker.

démangeaison *noun* F itch.

démanger *verb* [52] **ça me démange** it itches.

démanteler *verb* [45] to dismantle.

démaquillant *noun* M make-up remover.

démaquiller *verb* [1] **se démaquiller** to remove your make-up.

démarche *noun* F **1** walk; **2** step.

démarrer *verb* [1] **1** to start (*of engine or car*); **la voiture ne veut pas démarrer** the car won't start; **2** to drive off; **3** to start up, to start off; **le projet va démarrer en juin** the project will start up in June.

démarreur *noun* M starter (*in a car*).

démêler *verb* [1] to untangle.

déménagement *noun* M (house) move, removal.

déménager *verb* [52] **1** to move (house); **2 déménager quelque chose** to move something.

déménageur *noun* M removal man.

dément *adjective* crazy.

démentir *verb* [53] **1** to deny; **2** to refute.

démesuré *adjective* excessive.

demeurer *verb* [1] to reside, to live.

demi[1] *adjective* **1** half; **trois et demi** three and a half; **elle a trois ans et demi** she's three and a half; **une heure et demie** an hour and a half; **2 une demi-pomme** half an apple; **une demi-bouteille** half a bottle;

3 à deux heures et demie at half past two; **à trois heures et demie** at half past three.

demi[2] *noun* M half (*of beer*).

demi-cercle *noun* M semicircle.

demi-douzaine *noun* F half a dozen.

demie *noun* F half-hour; **à la demie** on the half-hour.

demi-écrémé *adjective* semi-skimmed.

demi-finale *noun* F semifinal.

demi-frère *noun* M half brother.

demi-heure *noun* F **une demi-heure** half an hour; **toutes les demi-heures** every half hour.

demi-journée *noun* F half a day.

demi-litre *noun* M half a litre.

demi-pension *noun* F half board.

demi-sel *adjective* slightly salted.

demi-sœur *noun* F half sister.

démission *noun* F resignation; **donner sa démission** to resign.

démissionner *verb* [1] to resign.

demi-tarif *adjective* half-price.

demi-tour *noun* M **faire demi-tour** to turn back.

démocrate *noun* M & F democrat. *adjective* democratic.

démocratie *noun* F democracy.

démocratique *adjective* democratic.

démodé *adjective* old-fashioned.

demoiselle *noun* F young lady.

demoiselle d'honneur *noun* F bridesmaid.

démolir *verb* [2] to demolish, to wreck.

démolition *noun* F demolition.

démon *noun* M demon.

démonstrateur, démonstratrice *noun* M, F demonstrator (*for products*).

démonstratif (F **démonstrative**) *adjective* demonstrative.

démonstration *noun* F
1 demonstration (*of a product, appliance, etc*); **2** display.

démonter *verb* [1] to dismantle, to take apart.

démontrer *verb* [1] to demonstrate, to prove.

démoraliser *verb* [1] to demoralize.

démouler *verb* [1] to turn out (*a cake, mousse, etc, from a tin or mould*).

dénoncer *verb* [61] to denounce.

dénouer *verb* [1] to undo.

denrée *noun* F foodstuff.

dense *adjective* dense.

densité *noun* F density.

dent *noun* F tooth; **avoir mal aux dents** to have toothache.

dentaire *adjective* dental.

dent de sagesse *noun* F wisdom tooth.

dentelle *noun* F lace.

dentier *noun* M denture, false teeth.

dentifrice *noun* M toothpaste.

dentiste *noun* M & F dentist.

déodorant *noun* M deodorant.

dépannage *noun* M repair;
'dépannages' 'emergency repairs';
le service de dépannage the breakdown service; **un véhicule de dépannage** a breakdown vehicle.

dépanner *verb* [1] **1** to fix, to repair; **2 dépanner quelqu'un** (*informal*) to help somebody out.

dépanneuse *noun* F breakdown truck.

départ *noun* M **1** departure; **je t'appellerai avant mon départ** I'll phone you before I leave; **elle m'a appelé avant son départ** she phoned me before she left; **2 au départ** at first, to start with.

département *noun* M department. (*As well as other sorts of department, this is a French numbered administrative area, rather like a county in Britain. The two numbers on the end of vehicle registrations in France show the number of the department where the car is registered.*)

dépassé *adjective* outdated, old-fashioned.

dépasser *verb* [1] **1** to overtake; **2** to exceed; **3 ça me dépasse!** it's beyond me!

dépêcher *verb* [50] **se dépêcher** to hurry up; **dépêche-toi!** hurry up!

dépendance *noun* F outbuilding.

dépendre *verb* [3] **1 dépendre de** to depend on; **ça dépend de l'heure**

it depends on the time; **ça dépend** it depends; **2** to be dependent on.

dépenser *verb* [1] to spend.

dépenses *plural noun* F
1 expenses; **2** spending.

dépensier (F **dépensière**) *adjective* extravagant.

dépilatoire *adjective* **une crème dépilatoire** a hair-removing cream.

dépistage *noun* M screening.

dépit *noun* M **en dépit de** in spite of.

déplacé *adjective* out of place.

déplacement *noun* M trip; **les frais de déplacement** travel expenses.

déplacer *verb* [61] **1** to move; **2 se déplacer** to travel.

déplaire *verb* [62] **déplaire à quelqu'un** to be displeasing to somebody; **cela me déplaît** I don't like that.

déplaisant *adjective* unpleasant.

dépliant *noun* M leaflet.

déplier *verb* [1] to unfold.

déporter *verb* [1] to deport.

déposer *verb* [1] **1** to put down; **2** to drop off; **il m'a déposé à la gare** he dropped me off at the station; **3 déposer un chèque** to pay in a cheque.

dépôt *noun* M **1** warehouse; **2** depot; **3** deposit.

dépôt d'ordures *noun* M rubbish tip.

dépoussiérer *verb* [24] to dust.

dépressif (F **dépressive**) *adjective* depressive.

dépression *noun* F depression.

déprimant *adjective* depressing.

déprimer *verb* [1] **1** to depress; **2** to get depressed; **elle déprime en ce moment** she's depressed at the moment.

depuis *preposition* **1** since; **depuis vendredi** since Friday; **je suis à Paris depuis mardi** I've been in Paris since Tuesday; **j'habite à Londres depuis avril** I've been living in London since April; **2** for; **elle habite à Londres depuis cinq ans** she's lived in London for five years; **je le connais depuis longtemps** I've known him for a long time; **3 tu es là depuis combien de temps?** how long have you been here?; **tu le sais depuis combien de temps?** how long have you known?; **depuis quand es-tu à Paris?** how long have you been in Paris?
adverb **1** since; **je ne l'ai pas revu depuis** I haven't seen him since; **2 depuis que** since; **depuis que ton frère est à Londres** since your brother's been in London.

député *noun* M deputy (*the French equivalent of a member of Parliament*).

déraciner *verb* [1] to uproot.

déranger *verb* [52] to disturb; **'ne pas déranger'** 'do not disturb'; **excusez-moi de vous déranger** sorry to bother you ; **est-ce que cela vous dérange si j'ouvre la fenêtre?** do you mind if I open the window?;

cela ne me dérange pas du tout I don't mind at all; **ça vous dérange de venir me chercher?** do you mind coming to pick me up?

déraper *verb* [1] **1** to skid; **2** to get out of control.

dérisoire *adjective* pathetic, trivial; **je l'ai acheté pour une somme dérisoire** I bought it for next to nothing.

dériveur *noun* M sailing dinghy.

dermatologue *noun* M & F dermatologist.

dernier (F **dernière**) *adjective* **1** last; **le dernier train part à minuit** the last train leaves at midnight; **jeudi dernier** last Thursday; **la semaine dernière** last week; **l'année dernière** last year; **2** latest; **leur dernier album** their latest album; **3 en dernier** last; **il est arrivé en dernier** he arrived last.

dernièrement *adverb* recently.

dérouler *verb* [1] **1** to unroll, to unwind; **2 se dérouler** to take place; **ça s'est très bien déroulé** it went very well.

déroutant *adjective* puzzling.

derrière *noun* M **1** back (*of an object or a house*); **2** bottom, backside.
preposition behind; **derrière la porte** behind the door.
adverb behind; **être derrière** to be in the back (*of the car*).

des *article* some, any; SEE **de, un**.

dès *preposition* **1** from; **dès l'âge de cinq ans** from the age of five; **2 dès que** as soon as.

désagréable *adjective* unpleasant.

désarroi *noun* M confusion.

désastre *noun* M disaster.

désavantage *noun* M disadvantage.

désavouer *verb* [1] **1** to deny; **2** to disown.

descendre *verb* [3] **1** to go down; **descendre les escaliers** to go down the stairs; **2** to come down; **je descends dans trois secondes!** I'll be down in a second!; **3** to get off (*a train or bus*); **je descends à Dijon** I'm getting off at Dijon; **4** to get down; **pouvez-vous descendre ma valise, s'il vous plaît?** could you get my case down for me, please?; **5** to take (or bring) downstairs; **je vais descendre mes bagages** I'm going to take my luggage downstairs; **est-ce que tu peux descendre une chaise de là-haut?** could you bring a chair down from upstairs?

descente *noun* F descent.

descriptif (F **descriptive**) *adjective* descriptive.

description *noun* F description.

déséquilibrer *verb* [1] **déséquilibrer quelqu'un** to throw somebody off balance.

désert *noun* M desert.
adjective deserted.

déserter *verb* [1] to desert.

désespéré *adjective* **1** desperate; **2** in despair; **3 une situation désespérée** a hopeless situation.

désespérer *verb* [24] to despair, to give up hope.

désespoir *noun* M despair.

déshabiller *verb* [1] **1 se déshabiller** to undress, to get undressed; **2 déshabiller quelqu'un** to undress somebody.

désherbant *noun* M weedkiller.

désherber *verb* [1] to weed.

déshérité *noun* M **les déshérités** the underprivileged.

déshériter *verb* [1] to disinherit.

déshydraté *adjective* dehydrated.

désigner *verb* [1] **1** to point out; **2** to denote.

désinfectant *noun* M disinfectant.

désinfecter *verb* [1] to disinfect.

désir *noun* M **1** wish; **2** desire.

désirer *verb* [1] to want; **que désirez-vous?** what would you like?

désobéir *verb* [2] **1** to be disobedient; **2 désobéir à quelqu'un** to disobey somebody.

désobéissant *adjective* disobedient.

désobligeant *adjective* unpleasant.

désodorisant *noun* M air freshener.

désolé *adjective* **être désolé** to be sorry; **je suis désolé** I'm sorry; **désolé de te déranger** sorry to disturb you.

désopilant *adjective* hilarious.

désordonné *adjective* untidy.

désordre *noun* M **1** untidiness, mess; **être en désordre** to be in a mess; **2** disorder.

désorganisé *adjective* disorganized.

désorienté *adjective* disorientated, confused.

désormais *adverb* **1** from now on; **2** from then on.

desquels, desquelles *pronoun* (= *de lesquels, de lesquelles*) which, whom.

dessécher *verb* [24] **1** to dry out; **2 se dessécher** to dry out.

dessert *noun* M dessert, pudding.

desservir *verb* [58] **le train dessert Vienne et Valence** the train calls at Vienne and Valence.

dessin *noun* M **1** drawing; **un cours de dessin** a drawing class; **2 un dessin** a drawing; **3** design.

dessin animé *noun* M (animated) cartoon.

dessin humoristique *noun* M cartoon.

dessiner *verb* [1] to draw.

dessous *noun* M **1** underside; **le dessous du pied** the sole of the foot; **2 les voisins du dessous** the neighbours below; **3 les dessous** underwear; **4 en dessous** underneath; **5 en dessous de** below.
adverb underneath.

dessus *noun* M **1** top; **le dessus du carton** the top of the box; **un pantalon gris et un dessus rose** grey trousers and a pink top; **2 les voisins du dessus** the neighbours above; **3 en dessus** above; **4 au-dessus de** above.

adverb on top; **quelqu'un a écrit dessus** somebody's written on it.

dessus-de-lit *noun* M bedspread.

destin *noun* M **1** fate; **2** destiny.

destinataire *noun* M & F addressee.

destination *noun* F destination; **le train à destination de Nice** the train for Nice; **les passagers à destination de Rome** passengers travelling to Rome.

destiner *verb* [1] **1 destiner quelque chose à** to design something for; **2 être destiné à** to be intended for; **3 être destiné à faire** to be intended to do.

détachable *adjective* detachable.

détachant *noun* M stain remover.

détacher *verb* [1] **1** to untie; **2** to undo; **3** to tear off; **4** to remove; **5** to remove the stains from; **6 se détacher** to come off, to come undone.

détail *noun* M **1** detail; **en détail** in detail; **2 regarder quelque chose dans le détail** to look closely at something; **3** retail.

détailler *verb* [1] to detail, to itemize; **une facture détaillée** an itemized bill.

détecter *verb* [1] to detect.

détective *noun* M detective.

éteindre *verb* [60] **1** to fade; **2** to run (*in the wash*).

étendre *verb* [3] **1** to be relaxing; **2** to relax; **3 se détendre** to relax.

détendu *adjective* relaxed.

détenir *verb* [81] **1** to detain; **2** to keep.

détente *noun* F relaxation.

détenu, détenue *noun* M, F prisoner, detainee.

détergent *noun* M detergent.

détériorer *verb* [1] **se détériorer** to deteriorate.

détermination *noun* F determination.

déterminer *verb* [1] to fix.

détestable *adjective* appalling, revolting.

détester *verb* [1] to hate.

détour *noun* M detour; ★ **ça vaut le détour** it's well worth seeing (*literally: it's worth the detour*).

détournement *noun* M **un détournement d'avion** a highjacking.

détourner *verb* [1] **1** to divert; **2 détourner un avion** to highjack a plane; **3 détourner les yeux** to look away.

détritus *plural noun* M rubbish, refuse.

détruire *verb* [26] to destroy.

dette *noun* F debt.

deuil *noun* M **1** bereavement; **2** mourning.

deux *number* **1** two; **deux enfants** two children; **elle a deux ans** she's two; **il est deux heures** it's two o'clock; **2 deux fois** twice; **3** second (*in dates*); **le deux juin** the second of June; **4** both; **les deux frères** both brothers; **tous les deux, toutes les deux** both; **ils sont malades tous les deux, tous les deux sont malades** they're both ill, both of them are ill.

deuxième *number* second; **pour la deuxième fois** for the second time; **au deuxième** on the second floor.

deuxièmement *adverb* secondly.

deux-points *noun* M colon.

dévaliser *verb* [1] to rob.

dévaluer *verb* [1] to devalue.

devant *noun* M front.
preposition **1** in front of; **elle était devant moi dans la queue** she was in front of me in the queue; **il l'a dit devant ses parents** he said it in front of his parents; **2** outside; **devant la boulangerie** outside the baker's.

développement *noun* M development; **les pays en voie de développement** developing countries.

développer *verb* [1] to develop.

devenir *verb* [81] to become; **devenir médecin** to become a doctor.

déviation *noun* F diversion

deviner *verb* [1] **1** to guess; **2** to foresee.

devinette *noun* F riddle.

devis *noun* M quote, estimate.

devises *plural noun* F (foreign) currency.

dévisser *verb* [1] to unscrew.

devoir *noun* M **1** exercise, test; **2 devoirs** homework; **faire ses devoirs** to do your homework; **3** duty.
verb [8] **1** to owe; **elle me doit vingt francs** she owes me twenty francs; **je vous dois combien?** how much do I owe you?; **2** to have to; **je dois partir à dix heures** I have to (or I must) leave at ten o'clock; **3 tu dois être fatigué** you must be tired; **elle doit avoir quarante ans** she must be forty; **il a dû oublier** he must have forgotten; **4 tu devrais partir** you ought to leave, you should leave; **tu aurais dû partir** you should have left; **5 elle doit arriver à cinq heures** she's supposed to arrive at five o'clock.

dévorer *verb* [1] to devour.

dévoué *adjective* devoted.

dévouement *noun* M devotion.

dévouer *verb* [1] **se dévouer à** to devote oneself to.

diabète *noun* M diabetes.

diabétique *noun* M & F, *adjective* diabetic.

diable *noun* M devil.

diabolo *noun* M fruit cordial and lemonade; **un diabolo menthe** a mint cordial and lemonade.

diagnostic *noun* M diagnosis.

diagnostiquer *verb* [1] to diagnos

diagonal (M *plural* **diagonaux**) *adjective* diagonal.

diagonale *noun* F diagonal; **en diagonale** diagonally.

diagramme *noun* M graph.

dialecte *noun* M dialect.

dialogue *noun* M dialogue.

dialyse *noun* F dialysis.

diamant *noun* M diamond.

diamètre *noun* M diameter.

diapo *noun* F (*informal*) slide;
SHORT FOR **diapositive**.

diapositive *noun* F slide.

diarrhée *noun* F diarrhoea.

dico *noun* M (*informal*) dictionary;
SHORT FOR **dictionnaire**.

dictateur *noun* M dictator.

dictature *noun* F dictatorship.

dictée *noun* F dictation.

dicter *verb* [1] to dictate.

dictionnaire *noun* M dictionary.

dicton *noun* M saying.

diesel *noun* M diesel.

diététique *noun* F **un magasin de diététique** a health-food shop.
adjective dietary.

lieu (*plural* **dieux**) *noun* M god.

Dieu *noun* M God; **mon Dieu!** good heavens!

différemment *adverb* differently.

différence *noun* F 1 difference;
quelle est la différence (entre)?
what's the difference (between)?;
2 **à la différence de** unlike.

différend *noun* M disagreement.

ifférent *adjective* 1 different;
différent de different from;
2 various, different; **différentes**
personnes various people,
different people.

difficile *adjective* 1 difficult, hard;
difficile à faire difficult to do; **leur maison est difficile à trouver** their house is difficult to find; **c'est difficile à imaginer** it's hard to imagine; 2 hard to please, fussy.

difficilement *adverb* with difficulty.

difficulté *noun* F difficulty; **avoir de la difficulté à faire** to have difficulty in doing; **j'ai eu de la difficulté à vous joindre** I had difficulty getting in touch with you.

difforme *adjective* deformed, misshapen.

difformité *noun* F deformity.

diffuser *verb* [1] 1 to broadcast;
2 to distribute; 3 to spread.

digérer *verb* [24] to digest.

digestif *noun* M (after-dinner) liqueur.

digestion *noun* F digestion.

digital (M *plural* **digitaux**) *adjective* digital.

digne *adjective* 1 worthy; **digne de** worthy of; **digne de foi** trustworthy; 2 dignified.

dignité *noun* F dignity.

digue *noun* F 1 sea wall; 2 dyke.

dilemme *noun* M dilemma.

diligent *adjective* diligent.

diluant *noun* M thinner.

diluer *verb* [1] 1 to dilute; 2 to thin (*paint*).

dimanche *noun* M **1** Sunday; **nous sommes dimanche aujourd'hui** it's Sunday today; **dimanche dernier** last Sunday; **dimanche prochain** next Sunday; **2** on Sunday; **je t'appellerai dimanche soir** I'll ring you on Sunday evening; **3** **le dimanche** on Sundays; **fermé le dimanche** closed on Sundays; **4** **tous les dimanches** every Sunday.

dimension *noun* F size.

diminuer *verb* [1] **1** to reduce; **2** to come (or go) down; **3** to decrease; **4** to die down.

dinde *noun* F turkey (*as meat*).

dindon *noun* M turkey (*when alive*).

dîner *noun* M dinner, supper; **inviter quelqu'un à dîner** to invite somebody to dinner.
verb [1] to have dinner; **viens dîner chez nous ce soir** come to dinner with us this evening.

dingue *adjective* (*informal*) crazy.

dinosaure *noun* M dinosaur.

diplomate *noun* M & F diplomat.
adjective diplomatic.

diplomatie *noun* F diplomacy.

diplomatique *adjective* diplomatic.

diplôme *noun* M **1** diploma, certificate; **2** (university) degree.

diplômé *adjective* qualified.

dire *verb* [9] **1** to say; **elle dit qu'elle est malade** she says she's ill; **2** to tell; **dire quelque chose à quelqu'un** to tell somebody something; **j'ai dit à Anne que tu l'appellerais** I told Anne you'd ring her; **dire à quelqu'un de faire** to tell somebody to do; **je leur ai dit de venir à cinq heures** I told them to come at five o'clock; **dire la vérité** to tell the truth; **dire l'heure** to tell the time; **dire des mensonges** to tell lies.

direct *adjective* **1** direct; **2** **en direct de** live from.

directement *adverb* **1** directly; **2** **aller directement à** to go straight to.

directeur, directrice *noun* M, F **1** director; **2** manager; **3** head (*of a school*).

direction *noun* F **1** direction; **en direction de** towards, in the direction of; **2** management; **3** steering (*of a vehicle*).

dirigeant, dirigeante *noun* M, F leader.

diriger *verb* [52] **1** to direct; **2** to manage; **3** to conduct (*an orchestra*); **4** **se diriger vers** to make for; **elle s'est dirigée vers la porte** she made for the door.

discerner *verb* [1] **1** to make out; **2** to detect.

discipline *noun* F **1** discipline; **2** subject (*of study*).

discipliner *verb* [1] **1** to discipline; **2** to control.

disco *noun* M **1** disco; **2** disco music.

discothèque *noun* F **1** disco, discotheque; **2** music library.

discours *noun* M speech.

discret (F **discrète**) *adjective*
1 discreet; 2 quiet; 3 subtle.

discrétion *noun* F discretion.

discrimination *noun* F
discrimination.

discussion *noun* F discussion.

discutable *adjective* questionable.

discuter *verb* [1] 1 to talk; **on peut
discuter tranquillement chez moi**
we can talk in peace at my house;
2 to argue; **ça se discute** it's
arguable; 3 **discuter de quelque
chose** to discuss something; **on va
en discuter demain** we'll discuss it
tomorrow.

disparaître *verb* [27] 1 to
disappear; 2 **faire disparaître
quelque chose** to get rid of
something; 3 to die.

disparition *noun* F
1 disappearance; 2 **une espèce en
voie de disparition** an endangered
species; 3 death.

disparu, disparue *noun* M, F
1 missing person; 2 **les disparus**
the dead.
adjective 1 missing; 2 lost;
3 dead.

dispenser *verb* [1] 1 to hand out;
2 to give; 3 **dispenser quelqu'un
de** to exempt somebody from.

disperser *verb* [1] 1 to break up (*a
crowd or demonstration*); 2 **se
disperser** to break up; **la foule s'est
dispersée** the crowd broke up.

disponibilité *noun* F availability.

disponible *adjective* available.

disposé *adjective* 1 arranged, laid
out; 2 **être disposé à faire** to be
willing to do.

disposer *verb* [1] 1 to arrange, to
lay out; 2 **disposer de quelque
chose** to have something (at your
disposal).

dispositif *noun* M 1 device;
2 system.

disposition *noun* F
1 arrangement, layout; 2 **à ta
disposition** at your disposal;
3 measure.

dispute *noun* F argument.

disputé *adjective* 1 contested;
2 controversial.

disputer *verb* [1] 1 **se disputer** to
argue; **ils se sont disputés** they had
an argument; 2 **se disputer
quelque chose** to fight over
something; 3 **se faire disputer**
(*informal*) to get told off; **je me suis
fait disputer par mon patron** I got
told off by my boss.

disqualifier *verb* [1] to disqualify.

disque *noun* M 1 record; **passer un
disque** to play a record (or CD);
2 disc; 3 (computer) disk.

disque compact *noun* M
compact disc, CD.

disque dur *noun* M hard disk (*of a
computer*).

disquette *noun* F (computer)
diskette.

disséquer *verb* [24] to dissect.

dissertation *noun* F essay.

dissident, dissidente noun M, F dissident.

dissimuler verb [1] to conceal.

dissocier verb [1] to separate.

dissolvant noun M **1** nail polish remover; **2** solvent.

dissoudre verb [67] **1 dissoudre quelque chose** to dissolve something; **2 se dissoudre** to dissolve.

dissuader verb [1] **1 dissuader quelqu'un de faire** to persuade somebody not to do, to put somebody off doing; **il m'a dissuadé d'y aller** he persuaded me not to go; **2** to deter; **pour dissuader les voleurs** in order to deter thieves.

distance noun F **1** distance; **une distance de cinq kilomètres** a distance of five kilometres; **c'est à quelle distance d'ici?** how far is it from here?; **à distance** from a distance; **l'enseignement à distance** distance learning; **2** gap.

distant adjective distant; **distant de** far away from; **un village distant de trois kilomètres** a village three kilometres away.

distiller verb [1] to distil.

distillerie noun F distillery.

distinct adjective distinct.

distinctif (F **distinctive**) adjective distinctive.

distinction noun F distinction.

distingué adjective distinguished.

distinguer verb [1] **1** to make out; **j'ai distingué un bateau à l'horizon** I made out a boat on the horizon; **2 distinguer entre** to distinguish between.

distraction noun F **1** entertainment; **on a besoin d'un peu de distraction** we need a bit of entertainment; **2** leisure; **3** leisure activity, form of entertainment; **4** absent-mindedness.

distraire verb [78] **1** to amuse, to entertain; **ça m'a distrait un peu** that cheered me up a bit; **2** to distract; **3 se distraire** to amuse yourself, to enjoy yourself.

distrait adjective absent-minded.

distribuer verb [1] **1** to hand out to distribute; **2 distribuer les cartes** to deal (in a card game); **3 distribuer le courrier** to deliver the mail.

distributeur noun M **1** distributor; **2 un distributeur automatique** a vending machine; **3 un distributeur de tickets** a ticket machine; **4 un distributeur de billets** a cash dispenser.

distribution noun F **1** distribution; **2** handing out; **3** delivery (of mail); **4** cast (of a play).

diverger verb [52] to diverge.

divers adjective various; **dans divers pays** in various countries.

divertir verb [2] **1** to amuse, to entertain; **2 se divertir** to amuse oneself.

divertissant adjective amusing, entertaining.

divin adjective divine.

diviser *verb* [1] to divide.

division *noun* F division.

divorce *noun* M divorce.

divorcer *verb* [61] to get divorced.

dix *number* ten; **elle a dix ans** she's ten; **il est dix heures** it's ten o'clock; **le dix juillet** the tenth of July.

dix-huit *number* eighteen; **il a dix-huit ans** he's eighteen; **à dix-huit heures** at six p.m.

dixième *noun* M **au dixième** on the tenth floor.
adjective tenth.

dix-neuf *number* nineteen; **elle a dix-neuf ans** she's nineteen; **à dix-neuf heures** at seven p.m.

dix-sept *number* seventeen; **elle a dix-sept ans** she's seventeen; **à dix-sept heures** at five p.m.

dizaine *noun* F **1** ten; **2 une dizaine de personnes** about ten people.

docteur *noun* M doctor.

document *noun* M document.

documentaire *noun* M, *adjective* documentary.

documentaliste *noun* M & F librarian.

documentation *noun* F **1** documentation; **2** material; **3** research.

documenter *verb* [1] **se documenter sur quelque chose** to gather information on something.

dodo *noun* M **faire dodo** (*baby talk*) to sleep; **on va faire dodo** time to tuck up in bed.

dogmatique *adjective* dogmatic.

doigt *noun* M finger; **se couper le doigt** to cut your finger; **avoir mal au doigt** to have a sore finger; ★ **être à deux doigts de** to be within an inch of (*literally: to be two fingers away from*).

doigt de pied *noun* M toe.

domaine *noun* M **1** estate; **2** field, domain.

dôme *noun* M dome.

domestique *noun* M & F servant. *adjective* domestic.

domicile *noun* M **1** place of residence; **2 à domicile** at home; **travailler à domicile** to work at home.

dominant *adjective* **1** dominant; **2** main.

dominer *verb* [1] **1** to dominate; **2** to control.

domino *noun* M domino; **jouer aux dominos** to play dominoes.

dommage *noun* M **1 c'est dommage** it's a pity; **c'est dommage qu'elle n'y soit pas allée** it's a pity she didn't go; **2 les dommages** damage.

dompter *verb* [1] to tame.

DOM-TOM SHORT FOR **départements et territoires d'outre-mer** (*French overseas departments and territories*).

don *noun* M **1** gift; **faire don de** to give; **2** gift, talent; **elle a un don pour les langues** she has a gift for languages; **avoir le don de faire** to have the gift of doing.

donc *conjunction* so, therefore.

donne *noun* F deal (*in card games*).

donné *adjective* given; **étant donné que** given that.

donnée *noun* F 1 fact; 2 **données** data.

donner *verb* [1] 1 to give; **donner quelque chose à quelqu'un** to give somebody something; **elle m'a donné dix francs** she gave me ten francs; **donne-moi ton adresse** give me your address; 2 to give away; **il a donné tous ses livres** he gave away all his books; 3 **ma fenêtre donne sur la rue** my window looks onto the street; 4 **se donner à quelque chose** to devote yourself to something.

dont *relative pronoun* whose, of which; **une personne dont j'ai oublié le nom** a person whose name I've forgotten; **la maison dont je parle** the house I'm talking about; **six verres dont l'un est cassé** six glasses, one of which is broken.

doré *adjective* 1 gold; 2 gilt; 3 golden.

dorénavant *adverb* from now on; **dorénavant je serai là tous les jours** from now on I'll be here every day.

dorer *verb* [1] 1 to gild; 2 **faire dorer** to brown (*meat or vegetables*).

dormir *verb* [37] to sleep; **tu as bien dormi?** did you sleep well?; **elle va dormir chez moi** she's going to spend the night at my house; **il dort** he's asleep.

dortoir *noun* M dormitory.

dos *noun* M back; **avoir mal au dos** to have backache; **faire quelque chose dans le dos de quelqu'un** to do something behind somebody's back; **elle me tournait le dos** she had her back to me; **il m'a tourné le dos** he turned his back on me.

dosage *noun* M 1 amount; 2 mixture.

dose *noun* F 1 dose; 2 measure.

dossier *noun* M 1 file; 2 application form; **remplir un dossier** to fill in an application form; 3 **dossier médical** medical records; 4 **le dossier d'une chaise** the back of a chair.

douane *noun* F **la douane** customs; **passer la douane** to go through customs.

douanier *noun* M customs officer.

double *noun* M 1 **le double (de)** twice as much, twice as many; 2 copy, duplicate; 3 double. *adjective* double.

doublé *adjective* 1 lined; 2 dubbed (*film*).

doublement *adverb* doubly.

doubler *verb* [1] 1 to double; 2 to overtake; **il m'a doublé dans un virage** he overtook me on a bend; 3 to line (*a garment*); 4 to dub (*a film*).

doublure *noun* F lining.

douce *adjective* SEE **doux**.

doucement *adverb* 1 gently; 2 slowly; 3 softly.

douceur *noun* F **1** softness;
2 gentleness; **3** mildness (*of weather*).

douche *noun* F shower; **prendre une douche** to take a shower.

doucher *verb* [1] **se doucher** to have a shower.

doué *adjective* gifted; **être doué pour quelque chose** to have a gift for something.

douillet (F **douillette**) *adjective* cosy.

douleur *noun* F **1** pain; **2** grief.

douloureux (F **douloureuse**) *adjective* painful.

doute *noun* M **1** doubt; **2 sans doute** probably.

douter *verb* [1] **1** to doubt; **douter de** to have doubts about; **2 se douter de** to suspect; **je m'en doutais** I thought as much.

douteux (F **douteuse**) *adjective* **1** doubtful; **2** dubious.

Douvres *noun* Dover.

doux (F **douce**) *adjective* **1** soft; **2** gentle; **3** mild; **4** sweet.

douzaine *noun* F **1** dozen; **2 une douzaine (de)** a dozen or so.

douze *number* twelve; **elle a douze ans** she's twelve; **le douze juillet** the twelfth of July.

douzième *noun* M **au douzième** on the twelfth floor.
adjective twelfth.

dragée *noun* F sugared almond.

draguer *verb* [1] (*informal*) **draguer quelqu'un** to chat somebody up; **il est toujours en train de draguer les nanas** he's always chatting up the girls; **se faire draguer** to get chatted up; **Carole s'est fait draguer par ton copain** Carole got chatted up by your mate.

dramatique *adjective* **1** tragic; **2** dramatic; **l'art dramatique** drama.

drame *noun* M **1** tragedy; **2** drama; **il en a fait tout un drame** he made a big scene about it.

drap *noun* M sheet.

drapeau *noun* M flag.

drap-housse *noun* M fitted sheet.

dresser *verb* [1] **1** to train (*an animal*); **2** to put up (*a tent*); **3** to draw up (*a list*); **4 se dresser** to stand up.

drogue *noun* F drug; **la drogue** drugs; **les drogues douces** soft drugs; **les drogues dures** hard drugs.

droguer *verb* [1] **1** to drug, to give drugs to; **2 se droguer** to take drugs.

droguerie *noun* F hardware shop.

droit *noun* M **1** right; **les droits de l'homme** human rights; **2 avoir le droit de faire** to be allowed to do; **je n'ai pas le droit de sortir ce soir** I'm not allowed to go out tonight; **3 avoir le droit de faire** to have the right to do; **tu n'as pas le droit de me critiquer** you have no right to criticize me; **4 le droit** law; **un étudiant en droit** a law student; **5** fee; **les droits d'inscription** enrolment fees.
adjective **1** straight; **une ligne droite** a straight line; **2** right; **ma**

main droite my right hand; **3 un angle droit** a right angle.
adverb straight; **continuez tout droit** go straight ahead.

droite *noun* F **1** right; **à droite** on the right; **tourner à droite** to turn right; **à ta droite** on your right; **2 la droite** the right (*in politics*).

droitier (F **droitière**) *adjective* right-handed.

drôle *adjective* **1** funny; **une histoire drôle** a funny story; **un film très drôle** a really funny film; **2** odd; **un drôle de film** an odd film.

drôlement *adverb* **1** (*informal*) really; **c'était drôlement bon !** it was really good!; **2** oddly, peculiarly.

du *article* some, any; SEE **de**.

dû, due, dus *verb* SEE **devoir**.

duc *noun* M duke.

duchesse *noun* F duchess.

duo *noun* M duet.

duplex *noun* M maisonette.

duquel *pronoun* (= **de lequel**).

dur *adjective* **1** hard; **2** tough (*meat*); **3** difficult, hard.
adverb **travailler dur** to work hard.

durant *preposition* **1** for; **des années durant** for years; **2** during.

durcir *verb* [2] **1** to harden; **2 se durcir** to harden.

durée *noun* F length.

durement *adverb* harshly.

durer *verb* [1] **1** to last; **2 durer pendant trois mois** to go on for three months.

dureté *noun* F **1** hardness; **2** toughness; **3** difficulty.

duvet *noun* M sleeping bag.

dynamique *adjective* dynamic, lively.

dyslexique *noun* M & F dyslexic.

E e

eau *noun* F water; **est-ce que tu veux de l'eau?** would you like some water?; **un verre d'eau** a glass of water; **eau gazeuse** sparkling mineral water; **eau plate** still mineral water; **'eau potable'** 'drinking water'; **'eau non potable'** 'not drinking water'; ★ **tomber à l'eau** to fall through (*literally: to fall into the water*); **nos projets sont tombés à l'eau** our plans have fallen through; ★ **mettre l'eau à la bouche de quelqu'un** to make somebody's mouth water; **ta sauce sent tellement bon que ça me met l'eau à la bouche** your sauce smells so good it's making my mouth water.

eau de Javel *noun* F bleach.

eau de toilette *noun* F toilet water.

eau minérale *noun* F mineral water.

ébaucher *verb* [1] **1** to sketch; **2** to outline.

ébéniste *noun* M & F cabinetmaker.

éblouir *verb* [2] to dazzle.

éblouissant *adjective* dazzling.

éboueur *noun* M refuse collector.

ébouillanter *verb* [1] to scald.

ébranler *verb* [1] to shake.

ébullition *noun* F boiling point; **porter à ébullition** to bring to the boil.

écaille *noun* F **1** scale (*of a fish or reptile*); **2** tortoiseshell.

écailler *verb* [1] **s'écailler** to flake; **la peinture s'écaille** the paint's flaking.

écart *noun* M **1** gap, distance; **2** difference; **3 à l'écart de** away from.

écarté *adjective* **1 un village écarté** a remote village; **2 les jambes écartées** with legs apart; **3 les bras écartés** with arms outstretched.

écarter *verb* [1] **1** to move apart; **écarter les rideaux** to open the curtains; **2** to move back.

échafaudage *noun* M scaffolding.

échalote *noun* F shallot.

échange *noun* M exchange; **en échange (de)** in exchange (for), in return for.

échanger *verb* [52] to exchange, to swap; **nous avons échangé nos adresses** we exchanged addresses.

échantillon *noun* M sample.

échapper *verb* [1] **1 échapper à** to escape, to escape from, to get away from; **le week-end nous échappons à la ville** at weekends we get away

from the town; **2 s'échapper** to escape.

écharde *noun* F splinter.

écharpe *noun* F scarf.

échasse *noun* F stilt.

échec *noun* M failure.

échecs *plural noun* M chess; **jouer aux échecs** to play chess.

échelle *noun* F **1** ladder; **2** scale.

échelon *noun* M **1** rung; **2** grade.

échiquier *noun* M chessboard.

écho *noun* M **1** echo; **2 des échos** rumours.

échographie *noun* F (medical) scan; **passer une échographie** to have a scan.

échouer *verb* [1] to fail; **échouer à un examen** to fail an exam.

éclabousser *verb* [1] to splash.

éclair *noun* M **1** flash of lightning; **2 un éclair au chocolat** a chocolate eclair.

éclairage *noun* M lighting.

éclaircie *noun* F sunny interval.

éclairer *verb* [1] to light (up).

éclat *noun* M **1** splinter, fragment; **2** brightness; **3** splendour; **4 un éclat de rire** a roar of laughter.

éclatant *adjective* brilliant; **des murs d'une blancheur éclatante** brilliant white walls.

éclater *verb* [1] **1** to burst; **un pneu a éclaté** a tyre has burst; **2** to shatter; **l'ampoule a éclaté** the bulb shattered; **3** to break out (*war or* *fighting*); **4 éclater de rire** to burst out laughing; **éclater en sanglots** to burst into tears.

écluse *noun* F lock (*on a canal or river*).

écœurant *adjective* sickly.

écœurer *verb* [1] to make (somebody) feel sick.

école *noun* F school; **aller à l'école** to go to school.

école maternelle *noun* F (state) nursery school (*age 2 – 6*).

école primaire *noun* F primary school (*age 6 – 11*).

écolier, écolière *noun* M, F schoolchild.

écologie *noun* F ecology.

écologique *adjective* **1** ecological; **2** environmentally friendly.

économe *noun* M potato peeler. *adjective* economical.

économie *noun* F **1** economy; **2** economics; **3 les économies** savings; **faire des économies** to save up.

économique *adjective* **1** economical; **2** economic.

économiser *verb* [1] to save.

économiste *noun* M & F economist.

écorce *noun* F **1** bark (*of a tree*); **2** peel (*of an orange or a lemon*).

écorcher *verb* [1] **s'écorcher le genou** to graze your knee.

écorchure *noun* F graze.

écossais *noun* M tartan (cloth). *adjective* **1** Scottish; **2** tartan; **une jupe écossaise** a tartan skirt.

Écossais, Écossaise *noun* M, F Scotsman, Scotswoman, Scot; **les Écossais** the Scots.

Écosse *noun* F Scotland; **elle habite en Écosse** she lives in Scotland.

écouter *verb* [1] to listen to; **j'écoute beaucoup la radio** I listen to the radio a lot; **écoute-moi** listen to me.

écouteur *noun* M **1** receiver (*on a telephone*); **2** headphones.

écran *noun* M **1** screen; **à l'écran** on the screen; **le petit écran** television; **2 la crème écran total** sun block.

écrasant *adjective* overwhelming.

écraser *verb* [1] **1** to crush; **écrasez les noix** crush the walnuts; **2** to squash; **tu vas écraser les pêches!** you'll squash the peaches!; **3 écraser une cigarette** to stub out a cigarette; **4 se faire écraser** to get run over; **Attention! Tu vas te faire écraser!** Watch out! You'll get run over!; **5 s'écraser** to crash; **leur voiture s'est écrasée contre un mur** their car crashed into a wall.

écrémé *adjective* **le lait écrémé** skimmed milk; **le lait demi-écrémé** semi-skimmed milk.

écrevisse *noun* F crayfish.

écrire *verb* [38] **1** to write; **elle m'a écrit une lettre** she wrote me a letter; **2 s'écrire** to write to each other; **ils s'écrivent tous les jours**

they write to each other every day;
3 s'écrire to be spelled; **comment
ça s'écrit?** how do you spell it?

écrit *noun* M **1** (piece of) writing;
2 written paper (*of an exam*); **il a
réussi à l'oral mais il a raté l'écrit**
he passed the oral but failed the
written paper; **3 à l'écrit** in writing.
adjective written.

écriture *noun* F handwriting.

écrivain *noun* M writer.

écrou *noun* M nut (*screwed onto a
bolt*).

écrouler *verb* [1] **s'écrouler** to
collapse.

écume *noun* F **1** foam, froth;
2 scum.

écureuil *noun* M squirrel.

écurie *noun* F stable.

eczéma *noun* M eczema.

EDF SHORT FOR **Électricité de France**
French electricity company.

Édimbourg *noun* Edinburgh.

éditer *verb* [1] to publish.

éditeur *noun* M publisher.

édition *noun* F **1** publishing; **elle
travaille dans l'édition** she works in
publishing; **2** edition; **une édition
de poche** a paperback edition.

édredon *noun* M eiderdown.

éducateur, éducatrice *noun* M,
F special needs teacher.

éducatif (F **éducative**) *adjective*
educational.

éducation *noun* F education; **elle a
reçu une bonne éducation** she had
a good education.

éducation physique *noun* F
physical education, PE.

éduquer *verb* [1] to educate.

effacer *verb* [61] to rub out.

effaceur *noun* M correction pen.

effarant *adjective* amazing.

effarer *verb* [1] to alarm.

effectivement *adverb* indeed
(*used to show agreement with what
someone has just said*); **il est
effectivement extrêmement gentil**
he is indeed extremely nice; **oui, elle
m'a effectivement téléphoné hier**
yes, that's right, she did phone me
yesterday; **'Tu as oublié tes clés'** –
'Ah oui, effectivement!' 'You've left
your keys behind' – 'Oh yes, so I
have!'; **'Il est maintenant trop tard
pour y aller'** – **'Oui,
effectivement'** 'It's too late to go
now' – 'Yes, so it is.'

effectuer *verb* [1] to make, to carry
out.

effet *noun* M **1** effect; **2 en effet**
indeed (*used to show agreement with
what someone has just said*); **elle
avait en effet raison** she was indeed
right; **'il fait très froid'** – **'Oui, en
effet'** 'It's very cold' – 'Yes, it is,
isn't it?'; **'Tu as laissé la porte
ouverte'** – **'Oui, en effet'** 'You've
left the door open' – ''Yes, so I have'.

efficace *adjective* **1** efficient; **elle
est très efficace** she's very
efficient; **2** effective; **c'est un**

remède très efficace it's a very effective remedy.

efficacité *noun* F **1** efficiency; **il est connu pour son efficacité** he's known for his efficiency; **2** effectiveness.

effondrer *verb* [1] **s'effondrer** to collapse.

efforcer *verb* [61] **s'efforcer de faire** to try hard to do; **elle s'efforce de rester calme** she tries hard to remain calm.

effort *noun* M effort; **faire un effort** to make an effort; **il n'a même pas fait l'effort de m'appeler** he didn't even make the effort to phone me.

effrayant *adjective* frightening.

effrayer *verb* [59] to frighten.

effroi *noun* M terror.

effronté *adjective* cheeky.

effroyable *adjective* dreadful.

égal, égale (M *plural* **égaux**) *noun* M, F equal.
adjective **1** equal; **une distance égale** an equal distance; **des quantités égales** equal quantities; **être égal à** to be equal to; **2** **ça m'est égal** I don't mind; **'Tu veux aller au cinéma ou rester à la maison?'** – **'Ça m'est égal'** 'Do you want to go to the cinema or stay at home?' – 'I don't mind'.

également *adverb* also; **elle est également prof d'allemand** she's also a German teacher.

égaler *verb* [1] to equal; **trois plus cinq égale huit** three plus five equals eight.

égalité *noun* F **1** equality; **2 les deux joueurs sont à égalité** the two players are level.

égard *noun* M **1 à l'égard de** towards; **à mon égard** towards me; **2 à cet égard** in this respect.

égaré *adjective* stray; **un chien égaré** a stray dog.

égarer *verb* [1] **1** to mislay; **j'ai égaré mes lunettes** I've mislaid my glasses; **2 s'égarer** to get lost; **nous nous sommes égarés dans les petites rues** we got lost in the back streets.

égayer *verb* [59] **1** to brighten up; **j'ai acheté quelques fleurs pour égayer la pièce** I've bought some flowers to brighten up the room; **2** to cheer up; **un peu de musique va nous égayer un peu** a bit of music will cheer us up a bit.

églantine *noun* F wild rose.

églefin *noun* M haddock.

église *noun* F church; **aller à l'église** to go to church.

égoïsme *noun* M selfishness.

égoïste *adjective* selfish.

égout *noun* M sewer.

égoutter *verb* [1] to drain (*vegetables or pasta*).

égratignure *noun* F scratch.

Égypte *noun* F Egypt.

eh bien *exclamation* well; **eh bien, ça me fait plaisir de te revoir** well, it's nice to see you again.

élancer *verb* [61] **s'élancer** to dash.

élargir *verb* [2] to widen.

élastique noun M **1** rubber band; **2** elastic.
adjective **1** elastic; **2** elasticated.

électeur, électrice noun M, F voter.

élection noun F election.

électricien, électricienne noun M, F electrician.

électricité noun F electricity.

électrique adjective **1** electric; **2** electrical.

électronique noun F electronics. adjective electronic.

élégant adjective elegant.

élément noun M **1** element; **2** part.

élémentaire adjective basic, elementary.

éléphant noun M elephant.

élevage noun M **1** farming (of livestock); **2** farm; **un élevage de porcs** a pig farm.

élève noun M & F student, pupil.

élevé adjective high; **une note élevée** a high mark.

élever verb [50] **1 élever un enfant** to bring up a child; **elle a été élevée en Écosse** she was brought up in Scotand; **2** to breed (animals); **3 élever la voix** to raise one's voice; **4 s'élever** to rise.

éleveur, éleveuse noun M, F breeder.

éliminer verb [1] **1** to eliminate; **2** to rule out; **nous ne pouvons pas éliminer cette possibilité** we cannot rule out that possibility.

élire verb [51] to elect.

elle pronoun **1** she; **où est Sylvie? – elle est dans la cuisine** where's Sylvie? – she's in the kitchen; **2** her; **Paul est avec elle** Paul's with her; **3** it (when referring to an object which is feminine in French); **où est ma tasse? – elle est sur la table** where's my cup? – it's on the table;

elle-même pronoun **1** herself; **elle me l'a dit elle-même** she told me herself; **2** itself (referring to an object which is feminine in French) **la pièce elle-même est jolie mais les meubles sont hideux** the room itself is pretty but the furniture is hideous.

elles pronoun they, them; **1** they (referring to female people or feminine objects); **elles sont arrivées** they've arrived; **2** them; **avec elles** with them.

éloigné adjective distant.

éloigner verb [1] **s'éloigner (de)** to move away (from).

Élysée noun M the Élysée Palace (the official residence of the French President).

émail noun M enamel.

emballage noun M wrapping.

emballer verb [1] **1** to wrap, to pack; **2** (informal) to get enthusiastic; **elle s'est vraiment emballée pour son nouveau boulot** she's got really enthusiastic about her new job; **ça ne m'emballe pas vraiment** I'm not that keen.

embarquement *noun* M
boarding; **une carte
d'embarquement** a boarding card.

embarquer *verb* [1] **1** (*informal*)
to go off with; **elle a embarqué
toutes mes chaises** she's gone off
with all my chairs; **2 s'embarquer**
to board.

embarrassé *adjective*
1 embarrassed; **2** cluttered.

embarrasser *verb* [1] **1** to
embarrass; **2** to clutter up.

embaucher *verb* [1] to take on (*an
employee*); **ils embauchent en ce
moment** they're taking people on at
the moment.

embêtant *adjective* annoying; **c'est
vraiment embêtant!** it's really
annoying!

embêter *verb* [1] **1** to annoy; **arrête
de m'embêter!** stop annoying me!;
2 s'embêter to be bored; **on ne
s'embête pas ici** there's plenty
going on here; **on ne s'embête pas!**
we're having a great time!

embouteillage *noun* M traffic
jam.

embrasser *verb* [1] to kiss; **je
t'embrasse** lots of love (*at the end
of a letter or said on the phone to a
friend*).

embrayage *noun* M clutch (*in a
vehicle*).

émeraude *noun* F emerald.

émerger *verb* [52] to emerge.

émeute *noun* F riot.

émission *noun* F programme (*on
television or radio*).

emménager *verb* [52] to move in (*to
a flat or house*); **nous avons
emménagé la semaine dernière** we
moved in last week.

emmener *verb* [50] to take; **c'est sa
sœur qui l'emmène à l'école** it's his
sister who takes him to school; **tu
veux que je t'emmène?** would you
like a lift?

émotif (F **émotive**) *adjective*
emotional.

émotion *noun* F emotion.

émouvant *adjective* moving.

emparer *verb* [1] **s'emparer de** to
seize.

empêcher *verb* [1] **1** to prevent, to
stop; **rien ne t'empêche d'essayer**
there's nothing to stop you trying;
**2 elle n'a pas pu s'empêcher de
rire** she couldn't help laughing.

empiler *verb* [1] to pile up.

empirer *verb* [1] to get worse.

emplacement *noun* M site.

emploi *noun* M **1** job; **2** use; **le
mode d'emploi** instructions for use.

emploi du temps *noun* M
timetable (*at school*).

employé, employée *noun* M, F
employee.

employer *verb* [39] **1** to employ;
2 to use.

employeur, employeuse *noun*
M, F employer.

empoisonné *adjective* poisoned.

empoisonner *verb* [1] to poison.

emporter *verb* [1] to take (away); **'plats à emporter'** 'takeaway meals'.

empreinte *noun* F footprint.

empreinte digitale *noun* F fingerprint.

emprisonner *verb* [1] to imprison.

emprunt *noun* M loan.

emprunter *verb* [1] to borrow.

EMT *noun* (= *éduation manuelle et technique*) technology (*at school*).

ému *adjective* moved.

en *preposition* **1** in; **elle habite en Écosse** she lives in Scotland; **en été** in summer; **en avril** in April; **un livre en anglais** a book in English; **habillé en noir** dressed in black; **j'étais en pyjama** I was in my pyjamas; **2** into; **aller en ville** to go into town; **traduire en anglais** to translate into English; **3** to; **aller en Italie** to go to Italy; **4** by; **en avion** by plane; **5** made of; **une table en bois** a table made of wood, a wooden table; **6 en vacances** on holiday; **7 en ami** as a friend; **8 en rentrant à la maison j'ai rencontré Tom** as I was coming home I met Tom; **je me suis brûlé en repassant ma chemise** I burned myself (while) ironing my shirt.
pronoun **1 j'en ai** I've got some; **je n'en veux pas** I don't want any; **tu en as combien?** how many (of them) do you have?, how much (of it) do you have?; **elle en a quatre** she's got four; **'qui a un stylo?'** – **'j'en ai un'** 'who's got a pen?' – 'I've got one' (*notice that in this sort of expression 'en' is often not translated*

at all); **2 elle m'en a parlé** she talked about it to me; **3 j'ai emprunté ton fer à repasser – est-ce que tu en as besoin?** I borrowed your iron – do you need it?

encadrer *verb* [1] to frame.

enceinte *adjective* pregnant.

encens *noun* M incense.

encercler *verb* [1] to surround, to circle.

enchanté *adjective* delighted.

enchère *noun* F bid; **une vente aux enchères** an auction sale.

encore *adverb* **1** still; **elle est encore au bureau** she's still at the office; **il reste encore de la viande** there's still some meat left; **2 pas encore** not yet; **il n'est pas encore rentré** he hasn't come home yet, he's not home yet; **3** again; **je l'ai encore oublié** I've forgotten it again; **4** more; **encore un peu** a little more; **encore une fois** one more time; **attendre encore une semaine** to wait for another week; **5** even; **encore mieux** even better.

encourageant *adjective* encouraging.

encouragement *noun* M encouragement.

encourager *verb* [52] to encourage; **elle m'a encouragé à suivre des cours de dessin** she encouraged me to go to drawing classes.

encre *noun* F ink.

encyclopédie *noun* F encyclopedia.

endive *noun* F chicory.

endommager *verb* [52] to damage.

endormi *adjective* asleep.

endormir *verb* [37] **1 endormir quelqu'un** to send somebody to sleep; **2 s'endormir** to fall asleep, to go to sleep.

endroit *noun* M **1** place; **un bon endroit pour** a good place for; **2** the right side (*of a garment*); **3 à l'endroit** the right way up.

énergie *noun* F energy.

énergique *adjective* energetic.

énervé *adjective* irritated, annoyed.

énerver *verb* [1] **1** to irritate, to annoy; **ça m'énerve!** this is getting on my nerves!; **2 s'énerver** to get annoyed.

enfance *noun* F childhood.

enfant *noun* M & F child; **un enfant unique** an only child.

enfantin *adjective* **1** easy; **2** childish.

enfer *noun* M hell.

enfermer *verb* [1] **1** to shut up; **2 s'enfermer** to shut yourself up; **elle s'est enfermée dans sa chambre** she shut herself up in her room.

enfiler *verb* [1] **1** to put on; **je vais juste enfiler mon pull** I'll just put my jumper on; **2 enfiler une aiguille** to thread a needle.

enfin *adverb* **1** at last; **je l'ai enfin fini** I've finished it at last; **2** finally; **elle a enfin réussi** she finally succeeded.

enflé *adjective* swollen.

enfoncer *verb* [61] **1** to push in; **2 s'enfoncer dans** to sink into.

engagement *noun* M commitment.

engager *verb* [52] **1** to take on (*an employee*); **2** to commit; **3 s'engager à faire** to promise to do; **je me suis engagé à organiser le repas** I promised to organize the meal.

engelure *noun* F chilblain.

engin *noun* M device.

engourdir *verb* [2] **s'engourdir** to go numb.

engrais *noun* M fertilizer.

engueuler *verb* [1] (*informal*) to tell off; **elle m'a engueulé** she gave me a telling off; **se faire engueuler** to get a telling off.

énième *adjective* umpteenth; **pour la énième fois** for the umpteenth time.

énigme *noun* F riddle.

enivrer *verb* [1] **1 enivrer quelqu'un** to make somebody drunk; **2 s'enivrer** to get drunk.

enjeu (*plural* **enjeux**) *noun* M **1** stake (*in a gambling game*); **2** what is at stake.

enlèvement *noun* M kidnapping.

enlever *verb* [50] **1** to take off (*garment*); **il a enlevé sa veste** he took off his jacket; **2** to remove; **enlever une tache** to remove a stain; **tu peux enlever les assiettes**

you can clear the plates; **3** to kidnap.

ennemi, ennemie *noun* M, F enemy.

ennui *noun* M **1** boredom; **2** problem; **avoir des ennuis** to have problems.

ennuyé *adjective* **1** bored; **2** embarrassed.

ennuyer *verb* [41] **1** to bore; **son discours m'a ennuyé** I found his speech boring; **2** to bother; **je t'ennuie?** am I bothering you?; **3 s'ennuyer** to be (or get) bored; **j'ai fini par m'ennuyer** I got bored in the end; **on s'ennuie ici** it's boring here.

ennuyeux (F **ennuyeuse**) *adjective* **1** boring; **2** annoying; **ça c'est vraiment ennuyeux** that's really annoying.

énorme *adjective* huge.

énormément *adverb* **1** tremendously; **2 énormément de** masses of; **j'ai énormément de choses à faire avant de partir** I've got masses of things to do before I leave.

enquête *noun* F **1** investigation; **2** inquiry; **3** survey.

enregistrement *noun* M **1** recording; **2** check-in (*at airport*).

enregistrer *verb* [1] **1** to record; **2** to register; **3** to check in (*at airport*).

enrhumer *verb* [1] **s'enrhumer** to catch a cold; **être enrhumé** to have a cold.

enrichir *verb* [2] **1** to make rich; **2** to enrich.

enrichissant *adjective* rewarding.

enrouler *verb* [1] to wind.

enseignant, enseignante *noun* M, F teacher.

enseigne *noun* F sign; **enseigne lumineuse** neon sign.

enseignement *noun* M **1** teaching; **2** education.

enseigner *verb* [1] to teach.

ensemble *noun* M **1** outfit; **j'ai acheté un joli ensemble pour le mariage** I've bought a lovely outfit for the wedding; **2 l'ensemble de** the whole of; **3 dans l'ensemble** on the whole.
adverb together; **on va y aller ensemble** we'll go together; **ils sont ensemble depuis trois ans** they've been together for three years.

ensoleillé *adjective* sunny.

ensommeillé *adjective* sleepy.

ensuite *adverb* then; **on va aller à la banque et ensuite chez Marianne** we'll go to the bank and then to Marianne's.

entamer *verb* [1] to start; **ce paquet n'a pas encore été entamé** this packet hasn't been started yet.

entasser *verb* [1] to pile up.

entendre *verb* [3] **1** to hear; **est-ce que tu l'entends?** can you hear it?; **se faire entendre** to make yourself heard; **2 j'ai entendu dire que...** I've heard that...; **3** to mean; **qu'est-ce que tu entends par là?**

what do you mean by that?;
4 s'entendre bien to get on well.

entendu *exclamation* **1** okay, fine;
2 bien entendu of course.

entente *noun* F **1** understanding;
2 agreement.

enterrement *noun* M funeral,
burial.

enterrer *verb* [1] to bury.

entêté *adjective* stubborn.

entêter *verb* [1] **s'entêter à faire** to
persist in doing.

enthousiasme *noun* M
enthusiasm.

enthousiasmer *verb* [1]
s'enthousiasmer to get
enthusiastic.

enthousiaste *adjective*
enthusiastic.

entier (F **entière**) *adjective* **1** whole;
une pomme entière a whole apple;
le monde entier the whole world;
2 je n'ai pas lu sa lettre en entier I
haven't read his letter right through;
3 le lait entier full-fat milk.

entièrement *adverb* completely,
entirely.

entorse *noun* F sprain; **se faire une
entorse à la cheville** to sprain your
ankle.

entouré *adjective* **entouré de**
surrounded by; **elle est entourée
d'amis** she's surrounded by friends.

entourer *verb* [1] to surround;
entourer de to surround with.

entracte *noun* M interval (*at the
theatre*).

entraînement *noun* M
1 training; **2** practice.

entraîner *verb* [1] **1** to lead to;
entraîner des problèmes to lead to
problems; **2** to take; **il m'a entraîné
chez sa copine** he took me off to his
girlfriend's; **3 entraîner une
équipe** to train a team; **4** to drag;
5 s'entraîner to train; **elle
s'entraîne tous les matins** she
trains every morning.

entre *preposition* **1** between; **entre
la porte et la fenêtre** between the
door and the window; **on va le
partager entre nous** we'll share it
between us; **2** among; **entre eux**
among themselves; **3 l'un d'entre
eux** one of them.

entrée *noun* F **1** entrance; **à
l'entrée de** at the entrance to;
billets à l'entrée tickets at the door;
2 hall(way); **3** admission;
4 starter, first course.

entremets *noun* M dessert.

entrepôt *noun* M warehouse.

entreprendre *verb* [64] **1** to
undertake; **2** to start.

entreprise *noun* F firm, business.

entrer *verb* [1] **1** to go in; **entrer
dans un magasin** to go into a shop;
entrer à l'hôpital to go into
hospital; **2** to come in; **entrer dans**
to come into; **Entrez!** Come in!

entre-temps *adverb* meanwhile.

entretenir *verb* [81] **1** to maintain
(*a building, a road, etc*); **2** to
support.

entretien *noun* M **1** interview; **elle
a été convoquée à un entretien** she

been invited for interview;
2 discussion; **j'ai eu un entretien avec mon patron** I had a discussion with my boss; **3** upkeep; **l'entretien de la maison** the upkeep of the house.

ntrevue *noun* F interview.

ntrouvert *adjective* ajar, half-open.

nvahir *verb* [2] to invade.

nveloppe *noun* F envelope; **une enveloppe matelassée** a padded envelope.

nvelopper *verb* [1] to wrap up.

nvers *noun* M **1** wrong side; **2** à l'envers upside down; inside out; back to front.
preposition towards, to.

nvie *noun* F **1** urge; **avoir envie de faire** to want to do, to feel like doing; **j'ai envie de te voir** I want to see you; **j'ai envie d'aller au cinéma** I feel like going to the cinema; **2** **avoir envie de quelque chose** to feel like something; **j'ai envie d'une glace** I feel like an ice cream; **3** **ces frites me font envie** I fancy some of those chips.

nvier *verb* [1] to envy.

nviron *adverb* about; **environ trente personnes** about thirty people.

nvironnement *noun* M environment.

nvirons *plural noun* M surroundings; **aux environs de** near.

envisager *verb* [52] **envisager de faire** to plan to do; **qu'est-ce que vous envisagez de faire?** what are you planning to do?

envoi *noun* M **1** dispatch; **faire un envoi de** to send; **2** consignment.

envoler *verb* [1] **s'envoler** to fly away.

envoyer *verb* [40] to send; **envoyer quelque chose à quelqu'un** to send somebody something; **elle m'a envoyé une carte** she sent me a card; **elle m'a envoyé chercher les verres** she sent me to get the glasses.

épais (F **épaisse**) *adjective* thick; **une tranche épaisse** a thick slice.

épaisseur *noun* F thickness.

épargne *noun* F savings; **une banque d'épargne** a savings bank; **un compte d'épargne** a savings account.

épatant *adjective* (*informal*) fantastic, great.

épaule *noun* F shoulder.

épaulette *noun* F **1** shoulder strap; **2** shoulder pad.

épave *noun* F wreck.

épée *noun* F sword.

épeler *verb* [18] to spell.

éphémère *adjective* fleeting.

épi *noun* M ear (*of corn*); **un épi de maïs** a corn cob.

épice *noun* F spice.

épicé *adjective* spicy, hot; **je n'aime pas les choses épicées** I don't like spicy food.

épicerie *noun* F grocer's (shop); **à l'épicerie** at the grocer's.

épicier, épicière *noun* M, F grocer.

épidémie *noun* F epidemic.

épilepsie *noun* F epilepsy.

épiler *verb* [1] **s'épiler les sourcils** to pluck your eyebrows; **une pince à épiler** eyebrow tweezers; **s'épiler les jambes** to shave your legs (*or use wax or cream to remove hair*).

épinards *plural noun* M spinach; **est-ce que tu aimes les épinards?** do you like spinach?

épine *noun* F thorn.

épingle *noun* F pin; **une épingle de sûreté** a safety pin.

épingler *verb* [1] to pin.

éplucher *verb* [1] to peel.

épluchures *plural noun* F peelings.

éponge *noun* F **1** sponge; **2** towelling.

éponger *verb* [52] **1** to mop up; **2** to sponge.

époque *noun* F time; **à cette époque-là** at that time.

épouse *noun* F wife.

épouser *verb* [1] to marry.

épouvantable *adjective* dreadful.

épouvantail *noun* M scarecrow.

épouvante *noun* F terror; **un film d'épouvante** a horror film.

époux *noun* M husband.

épreuve *noun* F **1** test; **2** exam; **l'épreuve de français** the French exam; **3** event (*sports*); **4** ordeal.

éprouver *verb* [1] to feel, to experience.

éprouvette *noun* F test tube.

EPS *noun* (= *éducation physique et sportive*) PE.

épuisant *adjective* exhausting; **c'est un travail épuisant** it's exhausting work.

épuisé *adjective* **1** exhausted, worn out; **je suis épuisé** I'm worn out; **2** out of stock; **3** out of print.

épuiser *verb* [1] to wear out; **cette discussion m'a épuisé** that discussion's worn me out.

équateur *noun* M equator.

équestre *adjective* **un centre équestre** a riding school.

équilibre *noun* M balance.

équilibré *adjective* balanced.

équipage *noun* M crew.

équipe *noun* F team.

équipé *adjective* **1** equipped; **2** **une cuisine équipée** a fitted kitchen.

équipement *noun* M equipment.

équipements *plural noun* M **les équipements sportifs** sports facilities.

équitation *noun* F riding.

équivalent *adjective* equivalent.

érable *noun* M maple tree; **le sirop d'érable** maple syrup.

rrer *verb* [1] to wander.

rreur *noun* F mistake; **par erreur** by mistake.

s *verb* SEE **être**[2].

scabeau *noun* M stepladder.

scalade *noun* F rock-climbing.

scalier *noun* M **1** stairs; **dans l'escalier** on the stairs; **2** staircase; **3 un escalier mécanique, un escalier roulant** an escalator.

scargot *noun* M snail.

scarpin *noun* M court shoe.

sclavage *noun* M slavery.

sclave *noun* M & F slave.

scorter *verb* [1] to escort.

scrime *noun* F fencing (*the sport*).

scroc *noun* M crook, swindler.

scroquer *verb* [1] to swindle.

space *noun* M space.

spacer *verb* [61] to space out.

spadon *noun* M swordfish.

spadrille *noun* F espadrille.

Espagne *noun* F Spain.

spagnol *noun* M, *adjective* Spanish.

Espagnol, Espagnole *noun* M, F Spaniard; **les Espagnols** the Spanish.

spèce *noun* F **1** sort; **une espèce de** a sort of; **on a mangé du poisson avec une espèce de sauce épicée** we had fish with a sort of spicy sauce; **2** species; **3 espèce d'idiot!** you idiot!; **4 en espèces** in cash.

espérer *verb* [24] to hope; **ils espèrent pouvoir venir** they're hoping to be able to come; **j'espère qu'elle n'a pas oublié** I hope she hasn't forgotten; **j'espère bien!** I certainly hope so.

espiègle *adjective* mischievous.

espion, espionne *noun* M, F spy.

espionnage *noun* M spying, espionage.

espionner *verb* [1] to spy on.

espoir *noun* M hope.

esprit *noun* M **1** mind; **ça ne m'est pas venu à l'esprit** it didn't cross my mind; **2** wit; **avoir de l'esprit** to be witty.

esquimau™ (*plural* **esquimaux**) *noun* M ice lolly.

esquisse *noun* F sketch.

esquisser *verb* [1] to sketch.

essai *noun* M **1** trial; **2** test; **3** attempt, try.

essaim *noun* M swarm.

essayer *verb* [59] **1** to try; **essayer de faire** to try to do; **j'ai essayé de t'appeler** I tried to phone you; **2** to try on; **essayer une robe** to try on a dress; **voulez-vous l'essayer?** would you like to try it on?; **3** to test;

essence *noun* F **1** petrol; **essence sans plomb** unleaded petrol; **2** essential oil.

essentiel (F **essentielle**) *adjective*
essential; **c'est l'essentiel** that's the
main thing.

essentiellement *adverb*
1 mainly; **2** essentially.

essorage *noun* M spin-dry.

essorer *verb* [1] to spin-dry.

essoufflé *adjective* out of breath.

essuie-glace *noun* M windscreen
wiper.

essuie-tout *noun* M (paper)
kitchen towel.

essuyer *verb* [41] to wipe; **essuyer
la vaisselle** to do the drying-up;
s'essuyer les mains to dry your
hands.

est[1] *verb* SEE **être**[2].

est[2] *noun* M east; **l'est de Paris** the
east of Paris; **dans l'est de la
France** in the east of France;
l'Europe de l'Est Eastern Europe.
adjective **1** east; **2** eastern.

est-ce que (*used for asking
questions*) **est-ce qu'il pleut?** is it
raining?; **est-ce que Julie est
partie?** has Julie left?; **où est-ce
qu'il habite?** where does he live?

esthéticienne *noun* F beautician.

estime *noun* F respect.

estimer *verb* [1] **1** to esteem; **2** to
value; **3 j'estime que...** I think
that...

estival (M *plural* **estivaux**) *adjective*
summer.

estivant, estivante *noun* M, F
summer visitor.

estomac *noun* M stomach; **avoir
mal à l'estomac** to have
stomachache.

Estonie *noun* F Estonia.

estrade *noun* F platform.

estragon *noun* M tarragon; **une
sauce à l'estragon** a tarragon sauce.

et *conjunction* and.

établir *verb* [2] **1** to establish;
2 établir une liste to draw up a list;
3 s'établir à son compte to set up
in business.

établissement *noun* M
1 institution; **établissement
scolaire** school; **2** organization.

étage *noun* M floor; **au premier
étage** on the first floor; **au dernier
étage** on the top floor; **à l'étage**
upstairs.

étagère *noun* F **1** shelf; **2** set of
shelves.

étain *noun* M **1** tin; **2** pewter.

étalage *noun* M window display.

étaler *verb* [1] **1** to spread; **2** to
spread out; **3** to roll out (*pastry*).

étanche *adjective* **1** watertight;
2 waterproof.

étang *noun* M pond.

étape *noun* F **1** stage; **2** stopping
place.

état *noun* M state, condition; **en
mauvais état** in a bad state; **en bon
état** in good condition; **en état de
marche** in working order; **être dans
tous ses états** to be in a state.

État *noun* M state, State.

États-Unis *plural noun* M **les États-Unis** the United States; **aux États-Unis** in (or to) the United States.

été¹ *verb* SEE **être²**.

été² *noun* M summer; **en été** in summer; **l'été dernier** last summer; **des vêtements d'été** summer clothes.

éteindre *verb* [60] **1** to turn off, to switch off; **éteindre la lumière** to turn out the lights; **2** to put out (*a fire or cigarette*); **3 s'éteindre** to go out.

étendre *verb* [3] **1** to spread out; **2** to stretch out (*your arms or legs*); **3 étendre le linge** to hang out the washing; **4 s'étendre** to stretch; **5 s'étendre** to spread.

éternel (F **éternelle**) *adjective* eternal.

éternité *noun* F eternity.

éternuer *verb* [1] to sneeze.

êtes *verb* SEE **être²**.

ethnie *noun* F ethnic group.

ethnique *adjective* ethnic.

étinceler *verb* [18] to sparkle, to twinkle.

étincelle *noun* F spark.

étiquette *noun* F **1** label; **2** etiquette.

étirer *verb* [1] to stretch.

étoffe *noun* F fabric.

étoile *noun* F star; **une étoile filante** a shooting star.

étonnant *adjective* **1** surprising; **2** astonishing.

étonnement *noun* M **1** surprise; **2** astonishment.

étonner *verb* [1] **1** to surprise; **ça m'a beaucoup étonné** that really surprised me; **ça ne m'étonne pas du tout** that doesn't surprise me at all; **2 s'étonner** to be surprised; **s'étonner de quelque chose** to be surprised at something.

étouffant *adjective* stifling.

étouffer *verb* [1] **1** to stifle; **2** to suffocate; **3 s'étouffer** to choke.

étourderie *noun* F **1** absent-mindedness; **2 une étourderie** a careless mistake.

étourdi, étourdie *noun* M, F scatterbrain.
adjective scatterbrained.

étourdir *verb* [2] to daze, to stun.

étourneau *noun* M starling.

étrange *adjective* strange.

étranger¹, étrangère *noun* M, F **1** foreigner; **2** stranger.
adjective foreign; **un pays étranger** a foreign country.

étranger² *noun* M **à l'étranger** abroad.

étrangler *verb* [1] **1** to strangle; **2** to choke.

être¹ *noun* M being; **un être humain** a human being.

être² *verb* [6] **1** to be; **nous sommes dans la cuisine** we're in the kitchen; **elle est malade** she's ill; **c'est moi** it's me; **2 elle est infirmière** she's a nurse; **3 être à quelqu'un** to belong to somebody, to be somebody's; **ce livre est à Paul** this book is Paul's; **ce livre est à moi** this book is mine; **4 il est 6 heures** it's 6 o'clock; **5 nous sommes le 7 mars** it's the 7th of March (today); **6** (*used with certain verbs to form past tenses: for a list of these, see the centre pages*) **je suis allé à Paris** I went to Paris; **nous sommes rentrés à 7 heures** we got home at 7 o'clock; **7** (*used to form the passive of verbs*) **ses robes sont faites par sa mère** her dresses are made by her mother.

étroit *adjective* **1** narrow; **2** close.

étroitement *adverb* closely.

étude *noun* F **1** study; **2 études** studies; **faire des études de médecine** to study medicine.

étudiant, étudiante *noun* M, F student.

étudier *verb* [1] to study.

étui *noun* M case.

eu *verb* SEE **avoir**.

Europe *noun* F Europe; **en Europe** in (or to) Europe.

européen (F **européenne**) *adjective* European.

euthanasie *noun* F euthanasia.

eux *pronoun* **1** them; **avec eux** with them; **des amis à eux** friends of theirs; **2** they.

eux-mêmes *pronoun* themselves.

évacuer *verb* [1] to evacuate.

évader *verb* [1] **s'évader** to escape.

évaluer *verb* [1] to assess.

évanouir *verb* [2] **s'évanouir** to faint.

évaporer *verb* [1] **s'évaporer** to evaporate.

évasion *noun* F escape.

éveillé *adjective* awake.

éveiller *verb* [1] **1** to arouse; **2** to awaken.

événement *noun* M event.

éventail *noun* M fan.

éventualité *noun* F possibility.

éventuel (F **éventuelle**) *adjective* possible.

éventuellement *adverb* **1** possibly; **2** if necessary.

évêque *noun* M bishop.

évidence *noun* F **être en évidence** to be clearly visible; **de toute évidence** clearly; **de toute évidence il a oublié de venir** he's clearly forgotten to come; **mettre quelque chose en évidence** to reveal something.

évidemment *adverb* of course.

évident *adjective* obvious.

évier *noun* M sink.

éviter *verb* [1] to avoid; **éviter de faire** to avoid doing; **ça t'évitera de sortir** that'll save you having to go out.

évolué *adjective* advanced.

évoluer *verb* [1] **1** to develop; **nous ne savons pas comment la situation va évoluer** we do not know how the situation will develop; **2** to progress; **l'informatique a beaucoup**

évolué ces dernières années computer science has progressed a great deal in recent years; **3** to change; **les choses ont évolué depuis** things have changed since.

volution *noun* F **1** development; **2** progress; **3** evolution.

xact *adjective* **1** correct; **c'est exact** that's absolutely right; **2** exact, precise.

xactement *adverb* exactly.

xagéré *adjective* **1** exaggerated; **2** excessive.

xagérer *verb* [24] **1** to exaggerate; **2** to go too far.

xamen *noun* M **1** exam; **passer un examen** to sit an exam; **réussir à un examen** to pass an exam; **un examen blanc** a mock exam; **2 un examen médical** a medical examination.

xaminateur, examinatrice *noun* M, F examiner.

xaminer *verb* [1] to examine.

xaspérant *adjective* exasperating.

xaspérer *verb* [24] to exasperate.

xcellence *noun* F excellence.

xcellent *adjective* excellent.

xcentrique *noun* M & F, *adjective* eccentric.

xcepté *preposition* except.

xception *noun* F exception; **à l'exception de** with the exception of.

xceptionnel (F **exceptionnelle**) *adjective* **1** exceptional; **2** special.

exceptionnellement *adverb* exceptionally.

excès *noun* M excess.

excès de vitesse *noun* M speeding.

excessif (F **excessive**) *adjective* excessive.

excessivement *adverb* excessively; **il est excessivement timide** he's incredibly shy.

excitant *noun* M stimulant. *adjective* exciting.

excitation *noun* F excitement.

excité *adjective* **1** frenzied; **2** over-excited; **3** thrilled.

exciter *verb* [1] **s'exciter** to get excited.

exclamation *noun* F exclamation.

exclamer *verb* [1] **s'exclamer** to exclaim.

exclu *adjective* **il n'est pas exclu que...** it's not impossible that...

exclusif (F **exclusive**) *adjective* exclusive.

excursion *noun* F excursion, trip.

excuse *noun* **1** apology; **présenter ses excuses** to apologize; **2** excuse.

excuser *verb* [1] **1** to forgive; **excusez-moi!** sorry!; **excusez-moi de vous déranger** sorry to disturb you; **2 s'excuser** to apologize; **je m'excuse** I'm sorry; **je m'excuse d'être en retard** sorry I'm late.

exécuter *verb* [1] **1** to execute; **2** to carry out.

exemplaire *noun* M copy; **six exemplaires du dictionnaire** six copies of the dictionary.

exemple *noun* M example; **par exemple** for example; **donner l'exemple** to set an example.

exercer *verb* [61] **1** to exercise (*a right*); **2** to practise (*an art or a profession*); **3** to exert (*authority*); **4** s'**exercer** to practise.

exercice *noun* M exercise.

exhiber *verb* [1] **1** to show off; **2** to display.

exhibitionniste *noun* M flasher.

exigeant *adjective* hard to please.

exiger *verb* [52] **1** to demand; **2** to require.

exil *noun* M exile.

exilé, exilée *noun* M, F exile.

existence *noun* F existence.

exister *verb* [1] to exist.

exotique *adjective* exotic.

expansion *noun* F **1** expansion; **2** growth.

expédier *verb* [1] to send (off); **expédier un paquet** to send off a package.

expéditeur, expéditrice *noun* M, F sender.

expédition *noun* F expedition.

expérience *noun* F **1** experience; **avoir de l'expérience** to be experienced; **2** experiment; **faire une expérience** to carry out an experiment.

expérimenté *adjective* experienced.

expert *noun* M expert.

explication *noun* F explanation.

explicite *adjective* explicit.

expliquer *verb* [1] to explain.

exploit *noun* M **1** achievement; **2** feat.

exploiter *verb* [1] **1** to exploit; **2** to use, to make use of.

explorer *verb* [1] to explore.

exploser *verb* [1] to explode, to blow up.

explosif (F **explosive**) *adjective* explosive.

explosion *noun* F **1** explosion; **2** boom.

export *noun* M export.

exportateur, exportatrice *noun* M, F exporter.

exporter *verb* [1] to export.

exposé *noun* M talk; **Gaby a fait un exposé sur le Japon** Gaby gave a talk about Japan.
adjective **1** exposed; **2** on display.

exposer *verb* [1] **1** to exhibit; **2** to expose; **3** to explain.

exposition *noun* F **1** exhibition; **une exposition d'art africain** an exhibition of African art; **2** exposure.

exprès *adjective* express.
adverb **1** deliberately; **tu l'as fait exprès** you did it deliberately, you did it on purpose; **il a fait exprès de le casser** he broke it on purpose;

c'est fait exprès it's meant to be like that; **2** specially; **je suis venu exprès pour te voir** I've come specially to see you.

express *noun* M **1** fast train; **2** espresso coffee.

expression *noun* F expression.

exprimer *verb* [1] **1** to express; **2 s'exprimer** to express yourself; **je m'exprime mal** I'm expressing myself badly.

expulser *verb* [1] **1** to evict; **2** to expel.

exquis *adjective* exquisite, delightful.

extase *noun* F ecstasy.

extensif (F **extensive**) *adjective* extensive.

extension *noun* F extension.

extérieur *noun* M **1** outside; **à l'extérieur** outside; **2** exterior. *adjective* **1** outside; **2** outer.

externat *noun* M day school.

externe *noun* M & F day pupil.

extincteur *noun* M fire extinguisher.

extra *adjective* (*informal*) great, fantastic; **ta sauce est vraiment extra!** your sauce is really fantastic!

extraction *noun* F **1** extraction; **2** mining.

extraire *verb* [78] **1** to extract; **2** to mine.

extrait *noun* M extract.

extraordinaire *adjective* extraordinary, amazing.

extravagant *adjective* **1** eccentric; **des vêtements extravagants** eccentric clothes; **2** extravagant.

extrême *noun* M, *adjective* extreme.

extrêmement *adverb* extremely.

Extrême-Orient *noun* M the Far East.

extrémité *noun* F **1** end; **2** tip; **3** edge; **4** extreme.

F f

F SHORT FOR **francs**; **30 F** 30 francs.

fabricant *noun* M manufacturer.

fabrication *noun* F manufacture.

fabriquer *verb* [1] to make; **fabriqué en France** made in France; **qu'est-ce que tu fabriques?** (*informal*) what are you up to?

fabuleux (F **fabuleuse**) *adjective* fabulous.

fac *noun* F (*informal*) university; **être en fac d'anglais** to be doing a degree in English.

face *noun* F **1** face; **face à face** face to face; **2 en face** opposite; **en face de l'école** opposite the school; **la maison d'en face** the house opposite; **le magasin en face de chez nous** the shop opposite our house; **3 faire face à quelque chose** to face up to something; **4 face à** facing; **face au mur** facing the wall; **5 pile ou face?** heads or tails?

fâché *adjective* **1** angry; **elle est fâchée contre moi** she's angry with me; **2 il est fâché avec son frère** he's fallen out with his brother.

fâcher *verb* [1] **1 se fâcher** to get angry; **se fâcher contre quelqu'un** to get angry with somebody; **elle s'est fâchée contre moi** she got angry with me; **2 se fâcher avec quelqu'un** to fall out with somebody.

facile *adjective* easy; **c'est facile** it's easy; **c'est facile à comprendre** it's easy to understand.

facilement *adverb* easily.

facilité *noun* F easiness.

faciliter *verb* [1] to make (something) easier; **ça devrait nous faciliter les choses** that should make things easier for us.

façon *noun* F **1** way; **il y a plusieurs façons de le faire** there are several ways of doing it; **d'une façon extraordinaire** in an extraordinary way; **de quelle façon?** in what way?; **2 de toute façon** anyway.

façonner *verb* [1] **1** to make; **2** to shape.

facteur[1] *noun* M factor.

facteur[2], **factrice** *noun* M, F postman, postwoman; **est-ce que le facteur est passé?** has the postman been?

facture *noun* F bill; **la facture d'électricité** the electricity bill.

facultatif (F **facultative**) *adjective* optional.

faculté *noun* F faculty.

fade *adjective* tasteless; **la sauce est un peu fade** the sauce is a bit tasteless.

faible *noun* M **avoir un faible pour** to have a soft spot for.
adjective **1** weak; **elle est encore très faible** she's still very weak; **2 elle est faible en chimie** she's not very good at chemistry; **3 un faible bruit** a faint noise.

faiblesse *noun* F weakness.

faiblir *verb* [2] **1** to weaken; **2 le vent a faibli** the wind's died down a bit.

faïence *noun* F earthenware; **des assiettes en faïence** earthenware plates.

faillir *verb* [42] **faillir faire** to nearly do; **j'ai failli tomber** I nearly fell; **j'ai failli rater le train** I nearly missed the train.

faillite *noun* F bankruptcy; **faire faillite** to go bankrupt.

faim *noun* F hunger; **avoir faim** to be hungry; **j'ai très faim** I'm really hungry; **je meurs de faim!** I'm starving!; **je n'ai plus faim** I've had enough to eat; **ces gâteaux me donnent faim** those cakes make me feel hungry.

fainéant *adjective* lazy.

faire *verb* [10] **1** to make; **faire un gâteau** to make a cake; **je vais me faire un café** I'm going to make myself a coffee; **faire du bruit** to make a noise; **2** to do; **qu'est-ce que tu fais?** what are you doing?; **il est en train de faire ses devoirs** he's doing his homework; **faire du français** to do French; **fais comme**

tu veux do as you like; **3 qu'as-tu fait du couteau?** what have you done with the knife?; **4 il fait froid** it's cold; **il fait chaud** it's hot; **5 quel temps fait-il?** what's the weather like?; **il fait beau** it's a nice day; **il fait beau en été ici** the weather's nice here in summer; **6 ça ne fait rien** it doesn't matter; **7 faire faire quelque chose** to have (or get) something done; **elle a fait réparer son vélo** she got her bike repaired; **il s'est fait couper les cheveux** he's had his hair cut; **8 faire chauffer de l'eau** to heat some water; **faire cuire quelque chose** to cook something; **9 ne t'en fais pas** don't worry.

faire-part noun M announcement (*of birth, marriage, or death*).

fais verb SEE **faire**.

faisan noun M pheasant.

faisons verb SEE **faire**.

fait[1] verb SEE **faire**.

fait[2] noun M **1** fact; **en fait** actually; **en fait je l'ai vu hier** in fact I saw him yesterday; **2 au fait** by the way; **au fait, est-ce que tu as fermé la porte?** by the way, did you shut the door?

fait d'actualité noun M news item.

faites verb SEE **faire**.

falaise noun F cliff.

fallait verb SEE **falloir**.

falloir impersonal verb [43] **1 il faut le faire** it has to be done, you must do it; **il ne faut pas faire ça** you mustn't do that; **il ne fallait pas faire ça** you shouldn't have done that; **il**

faudra partir à six heures we'll have to leave at six o'clock; **2 il me faut un stylo** I need a pen; **il leur faut une voiture** they need a car; **qu'est-ce qu'il te faut?** what do you need?; **3 il faut que tu le fasses** (*subjunctive*) you must do it; **il faut que tu prennes tes clés** you must take your keys; **4 comme il faut** properly; **tu ne l'as pas fait comme il faut** you haven't done it properly; **marche comme il faut!** walk properly.

famé adjective **un quartier mal famé** a rough area.

fameux (F **fameuse**) adjective first-rate; **le repas n'était pas fameux** the meal wasn't great.

familial (M plural **familiaux**) adjective family; **la vie familiale** family life; **les allocations familiales** child benefit.

familiariser verb [1] **se familiariser avec** to become familiar with.

familiarité noun F familiarity.

familier (F **familière**) adjective familiar; **un endroit familier** a familiar place.

famille noun F **1** family; **un déjeuner en famille** a family lunch; **une famille nombreuse** a big family; **2** relatives; **j'ai de la famille à Londres** I have relatives in London.

fanatique noun M & F fanatic.

fané adjective withered; **les fleurs sont fanées** the flowers are withered.

fanfare noun F brass band.

fantaisie *noun* F **1** imagination; **2 des bijoux de fantaisie** costume jewellery.

fantaisiste *adjective* **1** unreliable; **il est un peu fantaisiste** he's rather unreliable; **2 une idée fantaisiste** a wild idea.

fantastique *adjective* fantastic.

fantôme *noun* M ghost.

farce *noun* F **1** practical joke; **un magasin de farces et attrapes** a joke shop; **2** stuffing (*for a chicken, for example*).

farci *adjective* stuffed; **des tomates farcies** stuffed tomatoes.

farcir *verb* [2] to stuff (*a chicken, for example*).

fardeau (*plural* **fardeaux**) *noun* M burden.

farfelu *adjective* bizarre; **c'est un type farfelu** he's a bizarre bloke; **elle a toujours des idées farfelues** she always has crazy ideas.

farine *noun* F **1** flour; **2** baby cereal.

fascinant *adjective* fascinating; **son histoire était absolument fascinante** his story was absolutely fascinating.

fascination *noun* F fascination.

fasciner *verb* [1] to fascinate; **ça me fascine** I find that fascinating.

fascisme *noun* M fascism.

fastidieux (F **fastidieuse**) *adjective* tedious; **c'est un travail fastidieux** it's tedious work.

fatal *adjective* **1** inevitable; **c'était fatal** it was bound to happen; **2** fatal.

fatalité *noun* F fate.

fatidique *adjective* fateful.

fatigant *adjective* tiring.

fatigue *noun* F tiredness.

fatigué *adjective* tired; **je suis fatigué** I'm tired; **tu as l'air fatigué** you look tired.

fatiguer *verb* [1] **1** to tire (somebody) out; **la promenade m'a fatigué** the walk tired me out; **2 se fatiguer** to get tired.

faubourg *noun* M suburb.

fauché *adjective* (*informal*) broke; **je suis fauché cette semaine** I'm broke this week.

faucher *verb* [1] **1** to mow, to scythe; **2** (*informal*) to nick; **quelqu'un m'a fauché mon vélo** somebody's nicked my bike.

faucon *noun* M falcon.

faudra, faudrait *verb* SEE **falloir**.

faufiler *verb* [1] **se faufiler à travers la foule** to thread your way through the crowd.

faune *noun* F wildlife.

faussement *adverb* wrongly.

fausser *verb* [1] **1** to distort; **2** to bend.

faut *verb* SEE **falloir**.

faute *noun* F **1** mistake, error; **faire une faute** to make a mistake; **une faute d'orthographe** a spelling mistake; **2** fault; **c'est (de) ma**

faute it's my fault; **c'est la faute de Sophie** it's Sophie's fault; **3 faute de** for lack of; **faute de temps** for lack of time; **faute de mieux** for want of anything better; **4 sans faute** without fail.

fauteuil noun M armchair.

fauteuil roulant noun M wheelchair.

fautif (F **fautive**) adjective faulty.

fauve noun M wild animal. adjective tawny.

faux [1] (F **fausse**) adjective **1** wrong; **c'est faux** it's wrong; **2** untrue; **c'est totalement faux** it's totally untrue; **3** false; **une fausse barbe** a false beard; **4** imitation; **une table en faux marbre** an imitation marble table; **5 chanter faux** to sing out of tune.

faux [2] noun M fake, forgery; **cette pièce est un faux** this coin's a forgery.

faux [3] noun F scythe.

faux ami noun M false friend (a word in a foreign language which looks very like a word in your own language but does not mean the same thing at all).

faux-filet noun M sirloin.

faveur noun F favour; **en faveur de** in favour of.

favorable adjective favourable.

favorablement adverb favourably.

favori (F **favorite**) adjective favourite.

favoriser verb [1] to favour.

fax noun M **1** fax; **envoyer un fax** to send a fax; **2** fax machine.

fédéral (M plural **fédéraux**) adjective federal.

fédération noun F federation.

fée noun F fairy; ★ **avoir des doigts de fée** to have nimble fingers (literally: to have the fingers of a fairy).

féerique adjective magical.

feignant adjective (informal) lazy.

fêler verb [1] **se fêler** to crack.

félicitations plural noun F congratulations.

féliciter verb [1] to congratulate.

fêlure noun F crack.

femelle noun F, adjective female (animal).

féminin noun M **le féminin** the feminine (in French and other grammars); **au féminin** in the feminine.
adjective **1** female; **le sexe féminin** the female sex; **2** feminine; **elle est très féminine** she's very feminine; **3** women's; **les vêtements féminins** women's clothing; **la presse féminine** women's magazines; **les questions féminines** women's issues.

féministe noun M & F feminist.

femme noun F **1** woman; **c'est une femme très intéressante** she's a very interesting woman; **2** wife; **la femme de David** David's wife.

femme au foyer noun F housewife.

femme de ménage *noun* F cleaning lady.

fendre *verb* [3] **1** to split; **2** to crack.

fenêtre *noun* F window; **regarder par la fenêtre** to look out the window; ★ **jeter l'argent par les fenêtres** to throw your money away (*literally: to throw money out of the windows*).

fenouil *noun* M fennel.

fente *noun* F **1** slit; **2** slot; **3** crack.

fer *noun* M iron.

fer à cheval *noun* M horseshoe.

fer à repasser *noun* M iron (*for ironing things with*).

fer forgé *noun* M wrought iron.

férié *adjective* **un jour férié** a public holiday.

ferme[1] *noun* F **1** farm; **2** farmhouse.

ferme[2] *adjective* firm.

fermé *adjective* closed; **'fermé le dimanche'** closed on Sundays.

fermenter *verb* [1] to ferment.

fermer *verb* [1] **1** to close, to shut; **peux-tu fermer la porte, s'il te plaît** shut the door please; **il a fermé les yeux** he closed his eyes; **2** to turn off (*the lights, the tap, the water, etc*); **n'oublie pas de fermer les robinets** don't forget to turn off the taps; **3 se fermer** to close, to shut.

fermeture *noun* F **1** closing; **heures de fermeture** closing times; **2** fastening (*on a garment*).

fermeture éclair *noun* F zip.

fermier, fermière *noun* M, F **1** farmer; **2 la fermière** the farmer's wife.
adjective farm; **produits fermiers** farm produce; **un poulet fermier** a free-range chicken.

fermoir *noun* M clasp.

féroce *adjective* **1** fierce; **2** ferocious.

ferraille *noun* F scrap metal.

ferroviaire *adjective* rail; **le réseau ferroviaire** the rail network.

fertile *adjective* fertile.

fertilité *noun* F fertility.

fesse *noun* F buttock; **fesses** bottom.

festival *noun* M festival.

fête *noun* F **1** public holiday; **2** party; **faire la fête** to celebrate; **3 les fêtes de fin d'année** the festive season; **4** fête, fair; **5** saint' name day (*in France each day of the year is associated with the name of a saint and many people still celebrate the day of the saint they are named after*).

fête des Mères *noun* F Mother's Day (*in France on the last Sunday in May*).

fête des Pères *noun* F Father's Day.

fête foraine *noun* F funfair.

Fête Nationale *noun* F Bastille Day.

fêter *verb* [1] to celebrate.

feu *noun* M **1** fire; **faire du feu** to light a fire; **prendre feu** to catch fire; **2** light; **as-tu du feu?** have you got a light?; **3 les feux de signalisation;** the traffic lights; **un feu rouge** a red light; **4 faire cuire à feu doux** cook on a gentle heat; ★ **il n'y a pas le feu** there's no hurry (*literally: there isn't a fire*).

feu d'artifice *noun* M **1** firework; **2** firework display.

feuillage *noun* M leaves.

feuille *noun* F **1** leaf; **2 une feuille de papier** a sheet of paper.

feuilleté *noun* M savoury pasty. *adjective* **de la pâte feuilletée** puff pastry.

feuilleter *verb* [48] **feuilleter un livre** to leaf through a book.

feuilleton *noun* M serial, soap (*on television*).

feutre *noun* M **1** felt; **2 un feutre** a felt-tip pen.

fève *noun* F broad bean.

février *noun* M February; **en février, au mois de février** in February.

fiable *adjective* reliable.

fiançailles *plural noun* F engagement (*to be married*).

fiancé, fiancée *noun* M, F fiancé, fiancée. *adjective* **être fiancé à quelqu'un** to be engaged to somebody.

fiancer *verb* [61] **se fiancer** to get engaged.

fibre *noun* F fibre.

ficeler *verb* [18] to tie up.

ficelle *noun* F **1** string; **2** thin baguette (*of French bread*).

fiche *noun* F **1** form; **2** index card; **3** plug.

ficher *verb* (*informal*) [1] **1** to do; **qu'est-ce que tu fiches?** what do you think you're doing?; **2 je m'en fiche!** I don't care! **3 fiche-moi la paix!** leave me alone!

fichier *noun* M file.

fichu *adjective* (*informal*) done for; **ma voiture est fichue** my car's had it.

fiction *noun* F fiction.

fidèle *adjective* **1** faithful; **2** loyal.

fier[1] (F **fière**) *adjective* proud.

fier[2] *verb* [1] **se fier à** to trust.

fierté *noun* F pride.

fièvre *noun* F fever; **avoir de la fièvre** to have a temperature.

figer *verb* [52] **1 se figer** to congeal; **2** to freeze to the spot.

figue *noun* F fig.

figuier *noun* M fig tree.

figure *noun* F **1** face; **2** figure.

figurer *verb* [1] **1** to appear; **2 se figurer** to imagine.

fil *noun* M **1** thread; **du fil à coudre** sewing thread; **2** wire, flex (*of a telephone or electrical appliance*); **3 un coup de fil** (*informal*) a phone call; **passer un coup de fil** to make a phone call; **passe-moi un coup de fil** give me a ring.

fil de fer *noun* M wire; **fil de fer barbelé** barbed wire.

file *noun* F **1** **une file d'attente** a queue; **2** lane (*on a road*).

filer *verb* [1] **1** to speed along; **2** (*informal*) to give; **elle m'a filé deux CD** she gave me two CDs (*which she didn't want any more*).

filet *noun* M **1** net; **2** fillet; **un filet de poisson** a fish fillet.

fille *noun* F **1** girl; **une petite fille** a little girl; **une jeune fille** a young woman; **2** daughter.

fillette *noun* F little girl.

filleul, filleule *noun* M, F godson, goddaughter.

film *noun* M film.

film comique *noun* M comedy (*film*).

film d'épouvante *noun* M horror film.

filmer *verb* [1] to film.

film policier *noun* M thriller.

fils *noun* M son.

filtre *noun* M filter.

filtrer *verb* [1] to filter.

fin[1] *noun* F end; **à la fin** in the end; **à la fin du film** at the end of the film; **sans fin** endless.

fin[2] *adjective* **1** fine; **2** slender.

final (M *plural* **finaux**) *adjective* final.

finale *noun* F final, cup final.

finalement *adverb* **1** in the end, finally; **2** after all.

finance *noun* F finance.

financer *verb* [61] to finance.

fines herbes *plural noun* F mixed herbs.

finir *verb* [2] **1** to finish, to end; **le film finit à dix heures** the film finishes at ten o'clock; **2** **finir de faire** to finish doing; **j'ai fini de faire la vaisselle** I've finished doing the washing-up; **3** **finir quelque chose** to finish something; **as-tu fini tes devoirs?** have you finished your homework?; **j'ai fini le sucre** I've finished the sugar, I've used up all the sugar; **4** **finir par faire** to end up doing; **il a fini par accepter** he accepted in the end.

finlandais *noun* M, *adjective* Finnish.

Finlande *noun* F Finland.

firme *noun* F firm.

fisc *noun* M tax office.

fissure *noun* F crack.

fixe *adjective* **1** fixed; **2** **un emploi fixe** a steady job; **3** **aux heures fixes** at set times.

fixer *verb* [1] to fix.

flacon *noun* M (small) bottle.

flamant *noun* M flamingo.

flamand *noun* M, *adjective* Flemish.

Flamand, Flamande *noun* M, F Fleming (*Dutch-speaking Belgian*).

flamber *verb* [1] to blaze.

flamme *noun* F flame.

flan *noun* M custard tart.

flanc *noun* M side.

flâner *verb* [1] to stroll.

flaque *noun* F **une flaque d'eau** a puddle.

flash *noun* M **1** flash (*on a camera*); **2** newsflash.

flatter *verb* [1] to flatter.

flatteur (F **flatteuse**) *adjective* flattering.

flèche *noun* F **1** arrow; **2** spire.

fléchette *noun* F dart; **jouer aux fléchettes** to play darts.

fléchir *verb* [2] **1** to bend; **2** to weaken.

fleur *noun* F flower; **un tissu à fleurs** a flower-patterned fabric.

fleuri *adjective* **1** flowery; **du tissu fleuri** flowery material; **2 ton jardin est très fleuri** you've got lots of flowers in your garden.

fleurir *verb* [2] **1** to flower, to blossom; **2** to flourish.

fleuriste *noun* M & F florist.

fleuve *noun* M river.

flexible *adjective* flexible.

flic *noun* M (*informal*) policeman, cop.

flipper *noun* M pinball machine.

flirter *verb* [1] to flirt.

flocon *noun* M flake; **un flocon de neige** a snowflake.

flocons d'avoine *plural noun* M porridge oats.

floral (M *plural* **floraux**) *adjective* floral.

flotter *verb* [1] to float.

flou *adjective* **1** blurred; **une image floue** a blurred image; **2** vague; **ses projets sont un peu flous** her plans are a bit vague.

fluide *noun* M, *adjective* fluid.

fluo *adjective* (*informal*) fluorescent; **vert fluo** fluorescent green.

fluor *noun* M fluorine.

fluorescent *adjective* fluorescent.

flûte *noun* F flute; **jouer de la flûte** to play the flute.

flûte à bec *noun* F recorder.

focaliser *verb* [1] to focus.

foi *noun* F faith.

foie *noun* M liver; **une crise de foie** an upset stomach.

foin *noun* M hay.

foire *noun* F fair.

fois *noun* F **1** time; **une fois** once; **deux fois** twice; **trois fois** three times; **trois fois dix** three times ten; **plusieurs fois** several times; **la première fois** the first time; **trois fois plus grand** three times as big; **2 à la fois** at the same time; **trois à la fois** three at a time; **3 une fois que** once; **une fois que j'aurai pris une douche** once I've had a shower; **4 j'ai vu une fois...** I once saw...; **il était une fois...** once upon a time...

folie *noun* F madness; **c'est de la folie!** it's crazy!

folk *noun* M folk music.

folle *noun* F,
adjective SEE **fou**.

foncer *verb* [61] (*informal*) to rush;
tout le monde a foncé vers la porte
everybody rushed for the door.

fonction *noun* F **1** job; **une voiture
de fonction** a company car;
2 function.

fonctionnaire *noun* M & F civil
servant.

fonctionnel (F **fonctionnelle**)
adjective functional.

fonctionnement *noun* M
working; **comprendre le
fonctionnement de quelque chose**
to understand how something
works.

fonctionner *verb* [1] to work.

fond *noun* M **1** bottom; **au fond du
lac** at the bottom of the lake; **au
fond de la bouteille** in the bottom of
the bottle; **2** back; **au fond du tiroir**
at the back of the drawer; **au fond de
la salle** at the back of the room;
3 end; **au fond du couloir** at the end
of the corridor; **4** background;
5 au fond basically.

fondamental (M *plural*
fondamentaux) *adjective* basic,
fundamental.

fondateur, fondatrice *noun* M,
F founder.

fondation *noun* F foundation.

fond de teint *noun* M make-up,
foundation.

fonder *verb* [1] **1** to found; **2** to
base.

fondre *verb* [3] to melt.

fondu *adjective* melted.

font *verb* SEE **faire**.

fontaine *noun* F **1** fountain;
2 drinking fountain.

fonte *noun* F cast iron; **une poêle en
fonte** a cast iron frying pan.

foot *noun* (*informal*) **un match de
foot** a football match; **jouer au foot**
to play football.

football *noun* M football.

footballeur *noun* M footballer.

footing *noun* M jogging; **faire du
footing** to go jogging.

forain *noun* M fairground worker.
adjective **une fête foraine** a funfair.

force *noun* F **1** strength; **2** force;
de force by force; **3** force; **force de
vente** sales force; **4 à force de** by;
**à force de travailler toute la nuit,
elle a fini sa dissertation** she
finished her essay by working all
night.

forcément *adverb* **1** inevitably; **il
y a forcément une solution** there
has to be a solution; **2 pas
forcément** not necessarily.

forcer *verb* [61] **1** to force; **2 se
forcer** to force yourself.

forêt *noun* F forest.

forfait *noun* M fixed price.

forgeron *noun* M blacksmith.

formalité *noun* F formality.

format *noun* M format, size.

formation *noun* F training; **elle a
une formation d'infirmière** she's a
trained nurse.

formation continue noun F continuing education.

forme noun F **1** shape, form; **2 être en forme** to be on form; **tu as l'air en forme** you're looking well.

formel (F **formelle**) adjective **1** positive, categorical; **2** formal.

formellement adverb strictly; **formellement interdit** strictly forbidden.

former verb [1] **1** to form; **2** to train, to educate.

formidable adjective (informal) great, fantastic; **le film était formidable** the film was fantastic.

formulaire noun M form; **remplir un formulaire** to fill in a form.

fort adjective **1** strong; **il est très fort** he's very strong; **le café est très fort** the coffee's very strong; **2 être fort en quelque chose** to be good at something; **elle est très forte en maths** she's very good at maths; **3** stout.
adverb **1** extremely; **c'était fort bon** it was extremely good; **2** hard; **frapper fort** to knock (or hit) hard; **3** loudly; **chanter fort** to sing loudly; **parle plus fort** speak louder.

fortifiant noun M tonic.

fortifier verb [1] **1** to strengthen; **2** to fortify.

fortuit adjective accidental.

fortune noun F **1** fortune; **faire fortune** to make a fortune; **2 de fortune** makeshift; **un lit de fortune** a makeshift bed.

fossé noun M ditch.

fossette noun F dimple.

fou, folle noun M, F madman, madwoman; **un fou m'a doublé dans un virage** a madman overtook me on a bend.
adjective **1** mad; **devenir fou** to go mad; **2** crazy, amazing; **on a passé une soirée folle** we had an amazing evening; **il y avait un monde fou** there were masses of people; **3 être fou de** to be mad about;
★ **attraper un fou rire** to get the giggles.

foudre noun F lightning; **être frappé par la foudre** to be struck by lightning.

fouet noun M **1** whip; **2** whisk (for eggs, cream, etc).

fouetter verb [1] **1** to whip; **2** to whisk (eggs, cream, etc); ★ **avoir d'autres chats à fouetter** to have other fish to fry (literally: to have other cats to whip).

fougère noun F **1** fern; **2** bracken.

fouille noun F search.

fouiller verb [1] **1 fouiller quelqu'un** to search somebody; **2 fouiller dans quelque chose** to rummage through something.

fouillis noun M mess.

foulard noun M scarf.

foule noun F **1** crowd; **2 une foule de** masses of.

four noun M oven; **cuit au four** roasted, baked.

four à micro-ondes noun M microwave oven.

fourche *noun* F garden fork, pitchfork.

fourchette *noun* F fork.

fourgon *noun* M van.

fourmi *noun* F ant; ★ **avoir des fourmis dans les jambes** to have pins and needles in your legs (*literally: to have ants in your legs*).

fourmiller *verb* [1] **fourmiller de** to be swarming with.

fourneau (*plural* **fourneaux**) *noun* M stove.

fournir *verb* [2] to supply.

fournisseur *noun* M supplier.

fournitures *plural noun* F stationery; **les fournitures de bureau** office stationery.

fourré *adjective* **1** filled; **fourré au chocolat** with a chocolate filling; **2** fur-lined.

fourrure *noun* F **1** fur; **2** fur coat.

foyer *noun* M **1** home; **rester au foyer** to stay at home (*rather than going out to work*); **une femme au foyer** a housewife; **2** hearth; **3** household; **4** hostel.

fracas *noun* M crash.

fracasser *verb* [1] to smash.

fraction *noun* F fraction.

fracture *noun* F fracture.

fracturer *verb* [1] **1** to break open; **2** to fracture.

fragile *adjective* **1** fragile; **2** frail.

fragment *noun* M fragment.

fraîche *adjective* SEE **frais²**.

fraîcheur *noun* F **1** coolness; **2** freshness.

frais¹ *plural noun* M **1** expenses; **les frais de déplacement** travel expenses; **2** costs.

frais² (F **fraîche**) *adjective* **1** cool, cold; **il fait frais ce matin** it's a chilly morning; **2** cool; **'boissons fraîches'** 'cool drinks'; **servir frais** serve chilled; **conserver au frais** keep in a cool place; **3** fresh; **des légumes frais** fresh vegetables; **'peinture fraîche'** 'wet paint'.

fraise *noun* F strawberry; **une glace à la fraise** a strawberry ice-cream.

framboise *noun* F raspberry; **un yaourt à la framboise** a raspberry yoghurt.

franc¹ *noun* M franc (*the unit of currency in France, Belgium, and Switzerland; there are 100 centimes to the franc*).

franc² (F **franche**) *adjective* frank.

français *noun* M French; **j'apprends le français** I'm learning French; **Laura parle français** Laura speaks French.
adjective French; **un film français** a French film.

Français, Française *noun* M, F Frenchman, Frenchwoman; **les Français** the French.

France *noun* F France; **aller en France** to go to France; **habiter en France** to live in France.

franche *adjective* SEE **franc²**.

franchement *adverb* **1** frankly; **franchement, je ne le crois pas** frankly, I don't believe him; **2** really le film était franchement nul the film was really awful.

franchir *verb* [2] to cross.

franchise *noun* F **1** frankness, honesty; **2** franchise.

francophone *adjective* French-speaking.

frange *noun* F fringe.

frangin *noun* M (*informal*) brother.

frangine *noun* F (*informal*) sister.

frangipane *noun* F almond cream.

franglais *noun* M Franglais (*a mixture of French and English*).

frapper *verb* [1] **1** to hit; **2** frapper à la porte to knock on the door; **3** to strike; être frappé par to be struck by; ça m'a beaucoup frappé that made a big impression on me; **4** frappé par le chômage hit by unemployment.

fraude *noun* F **1** fraud; **2** cheating.

fredonner *verb* [1] to hum.

freezer *noun* M freezer compartment (*in a fridge*).

frein *noun* M brake; les freins the brakes; le frein à main the handbrake.

freiner *verb* [1] **1** to brake; **2** to slow down.

frêle *adjective* frail.

frelon *noun* M hornet.

frémir *verb* [2] **1** to shudder; **2** to tremble.

frêne *noun* M ash tree.

fréquemment *adverb* frequently.

fréquence *noun* F frequency.

fréquenté *adjective* **1** busy; un restaurant très fréquenté a very busy restaurant; **2** un quartier mal fréquenté a rough area.

fréquenter *verb* [1] **1** to go around with (*people*); **2** to go often to (*a place*).

frère *noun* M brother.

fric *noun* M (*informal*) money.

frictionner *verb* [1] to rub.

frigidaire™ *noun* M fridge.

frigo *noun* M (*informal*) fridge; au frigo in the fridge.

frileux (F **frileuse**) *adjective* être frileux to feel the cold; je ne suis pas frileuse I don't feel the cold.

frime *noun* F (*informal*) c'est de la frime! it's all show!

fringues *plural noun* F (*informal*) clothes.

fripé *adjective* crumpled.

frire *verb* [74] faire frire quelque chose to fry something.

frisé *adjective* **1** curly; **2** curly-haired.

frisée *noun* F curly endive, frisée (*a sort of lettuce*).

friser *verb* [1] to curl.

frisson *noun* M shiver.

frissonner *verb* [1] **1** to shiver; **2** to shudder.

frit *adjective* fried.

frite *noun* F chip, French fry; **steak frites** steak and chips.

friture *noun* F **friture de poissons** fried fish.

froid *noun* M **1** **le froid** the cold; **2** **avoir froid** to be cold; **j'ai froid** I'm cold; **3** **il fait froid aujourd'hui** it's cold today; **4** **prendre froid** to catch a chill.
adjective cold; **tes mains sont froides** your hands are cold.

froidement *adverb* coldly.

froideur *noun* F coldness.

froisser *verb* [1] **1** to crease; **2** **se froisser** to crease; **la soie se froisse facilement** silk crushes easily; **3** **se froisser** to take offence.

frôler *verb* [1] to brush against.

fromage *noun* M cheese.

fromagerie *noun* F cheese shop.

froment *noun* M wheat.

froncer *verb* [61] **froncer les sourcils** to frown.

front *noun* M **1** forehead; **2** **faire front à** to face up to.

frontière *noun* F border.

frotter *verb* [1] to rub; **se frotter les yeux** to rub your eyes.

fruit *noun* M **les fruits** fruit; **acheter des fruits** to buy some fruit; **un fruit** a piece of fruit; **veux-tu un fruit?** would you like any fruit?

fruité *adjective* fruity.

fruits de mer *plural noun* M seafood; **une omelette aux fruits de mer** a seafood omelette.

frustrant *adjective* frustrating.

frustrer *verb* [1] **1** to thwart; **2** to frustrate.

fugue *noun* F **1** **faire une fugue** to run away; **2** fugue.

fuir *verb* [44] **1** to run away, to flee; **2** **fuir quelque chose** to run away from something; **3** to leak; **la bouilloire fuit** the kettle's leaking.

fuite *noun* F **1** flight; **2** **prendre la fuite** to flee; **3** leak.

fulgurant *adjective* dazzling.

fumé *adjective* smoked; **du saumon fumé** smoked salmon.

fumée *noun* F smoke; ★ **il n'y a pas de fumée sans feu** there's no smoke without fire.

fumer *verb* [1] **1** to smoke; **2** **fumer une cigarette** to smoke a cigarette; **il fume la pipe** he smokes a pipe; ★ **fumer comme un pompier** to smoke like a chimney (*literally: to smoke like a fireman*).

fumeur, fumeuse *noun* M, F smoker; **zone non-fumeur** no-smoking area.

fumier *noun* M manure.

funambule *noun* M & F tightrope walker.

funèbre *adjective* **1** funeral; **pompes funèbres** undertaker's; **2** gloomy.

funérailles *plural noun* F funeral.

funiculaire *noun* M funicular.

fur *noun* M **1 au fur et à mesure** as you go along; **je corrige les erreurs au fur et à mesure** I correct the mistakes as I go along; **2 au fur et à mesure que** as.

furet *noun* M ferret.

fureur *noun* F **1** rage, fury; **2** frenzy; ★ **faire fureur** to be all the rage; **ces boucles d'oreilles font fureur en ce moment** these earrings are all the rage at the moment.

furibond *adjective* furious.

furieusement *adverb* furiously.

furieux (F **furieuse**) *adjective* furious; **elle est furieuse contre son copain** she's furious with her boyfriend.

furoncle *noun* M boil.

fusain *noun* M charcoal (*for drawing*).

fuseau *noun* M ski pants.

fusée *noun* F rocket.

fusible *noun* M fuse.

fusil *noun* M gun.

fusiller *verb* [1] to shoot.

fût *noun* M cask, barrel.

futé *adjective* **1** crafty; **2** bright, clever.

futur *noun* M, *adjective* future; **son futur mari** her husband-to-be.

G g

gâcher *verb* [1] **1** to waste; **gâcher la nourriture** to waste food; **2** to spoil; **ça m'a gâché la journée!** that's spoiled my day!

gâchis *noun* M waste.

gadget *noun* M gadget.

gaffe *noun* F (*informal*) blunder; **j'ai fait une gaffe** I've done something stupid; ★ **fais gaffe!** watch out!

gage *noun* M forfeit (*in a game*).

gagnant, gagnante *noun* M, F winner.
adjective winning.

gagner *verb* [1] **1** to win; **il a gagné** he's won; **gagner le match** to win the match; **2** to earn (*money*); **elle gagne bien sa vie** she makes a good living; **3 gagner du temps** to save time.

gai *adjective* cheerful.

gain *noun* M **1** earnings; **2 c'est un gain de temps** it saves time.

gaieté *noun* F cheerfulness.

galerie *noun* F gallery.

galerie marchande *noun* F shopping arcade.

galet *noun* M pebble.

galette *noun* F **1** biscuit; **2** round flat cake or loaf.

galette des Rois *noun* F Twelfth Night cake (*a cake eaten on Twelfth*

Night; it contains a 'fève', literally a bean, but usually a small ceramic figure; the person who gets this is the king or queen and is given a cardboard crown to wear).

Galles *noun* **le pays de Galles** Wales.

gallois *noun* M, *adjective* Welsh.

Gallois, Galloise *noun* M, F Welshman, Welshwoman; **les Gallois** the Welsh.

galoper *verb* [1] to galop.

gamba *noun* F king prawn.

gamin, gamine *noun* M, F (*informal*) kid; **elle a trois gamins** she has three kids.

gamme *noun* F **1** range; **la nouvelle gamme de produits de beauté** the new range of beauty products; **2** scale (*in music*).

gammé *adjective* **la croix gammée** the swastika.

gangster *noun* M gangster.

gant *noun* M glove.

gant de ménage *noun* M rubber glove.

gant de toilette *noun* M facecloth.

garage *noun* M garage.

garagiste *noun* M & F **1** garage owner; **2** motor mechanic.

garantie *noun* F guarantee.

garantir *verb* [2] to guarantee.

garçon *noun* M **1** boy; **2** young man; **un brave garçon** a nice

chap; **3** waiter; **4 un vieux garçon** a bachelor.

garçon de café *noun* M waiter (*in a café*).

garde *noun* M & F **1** guard; **2** nurse; **3 être de garde** to be on duty; **la pharmacie de garde** the duty chemist's; **mettre quelqu'un en garde** to warn somebody; ★ **prends garde!** watch out, be careful!

garder *verb* [1] **1** to keep; **est-ce que tu peux garder mon sac?** can you keep my bag for me?; **je t'ai gardé du gâteau** I've kept you some cake; **je t'ai gardé une place** I've kept you a seat; **2** to keep on; **elle a gardé son manteau** she kept her coat on; **3** to look after; **je garde mon petit-fils ce soir** I'm looking after my grandson this evening; **4 garder la maison** to guard the house.

garderie *noun* F day nursery.

garde-robe *noun* F wardrobe.

gardien, gardienne *noun* M, F **1** security guard; **2** caretaker; **3** attendant (*in a car park or museum*).

gardien de but *noun* M goalkeeper.

gardien de la paix *noun* M policeman.

gare *noun* F (railway) station.

garer *verb* [1] **1 garer une voiture** to park a car; **2 se garer** to park.

gare routière *noun* F coach station.

garni *adjective* **bien garni** full, well-stocked.

garnir *verb* [2] **1** to decorate; **2** to stock (*shelves, fridge*).

garniture *noun* F **1** side-dish; **2** trimming, decoration.

gars *noun* M (*informal*) guy.

Gascogne *noun* F Gascony.

gasoil *noun* M diesel (oil).

gaspiller *verb* [1] to waste.

gastronome *noun* M & F gourmet.

gastronomie *noun* F gastronomy.

gâteau *noun* M cake; **un gâteau au chocolat** a chocolate cake.

gâter *verb* [1] **1** to spoil; **2 se gâter** to go bad; **la viande se gâte** the meat is going bad; **le temps se gâte** the weather's breaking.

gauche *noun* F **1** left; **à gauche** on the left; **les Anglais conduisent à gauche** the English drive on the left; **tournez à gauche** turn left; **à ma gauche** on my left; **2 la gauche** the Left (*in politics*); **des idées de gauche** left-wing ideas. *adjective* left, left-hand; **sa main gauche** his left hand.

gaucher (F **gauchère**) *adjective* left-handed.

gaufre *noun* F waffle.

gaufrette *noun* F wafer.

gaz *noun* M gas; **le chauffage à gaz** gas central heating; **nous nous chauffons au gaz** we have gas heating.

gazeux (F **gazeuse**) *adjective* fizzy; **eau gazeuse** fizzy mineral water.

gazole *noun* M diesel (oil).

gazon *noun* M grass, lawn.

géant, géante *noun* M, F giant. *adjective* huge.

gel *noun* M **1** frost; **2 le gel des prix** the price freeze; **3** gel.

gelé *adjective* frozen.

gelée *noun* F **1** jelly; **œuf en gelée** egg in aspic; **2** frost.

geler *verb* [45] to freeze; **il gèle dehors** it's freezing outside.

gélule *noun* F capsule.

Gémeaux *plural noun* M Gemini (*sign of the Zodiac*).

gémir *verb* [2] to moan.

gênant *adjective* **1** annoying; **ce bruit est très gênant** that noise is very annoying; **2** awkward; **c'est une situation gênante** it's an awkward situation.

gencive *noun* F gum (*part of your mouth*).

gendarme *noun* M policeman.

gendarmerie *noun* F police station.

gendre *noun* M son-in-law.

gêne *noun* F **1** embarrassment; **2** inconvenience; **3** discomfort.

gêné *adjective* embarrassed.

gêner *verb* [1] **1** to bother; **est-ce que mon sac vous gêne?** is my bag in your way?; **2** to embarrass; **3** to block (*traffic*); **ta voiture gêne** your car's in the way.

général (*plural* **généraux**) *noun* M general.

adjective general; **en général** in general, generally; **de façon générale** generally.

généralement *adverb* generally.

génération *noun* F generation.

généreux (F **généreuse**) *adjective* generous.

générique *noun* M (film) credits.

générosité *noun* F generosity.

genêt *noun* M broom (*the bush*).

génétique *noun* F genetics.

Genève *noun* Geneva.

génial (M *plural* **géniaux**) *adjective*
1 brilliant; **une idée géniale** a brilliant idea; 2 (*informal*) great; **c'était génial!** it was great!

génie *noun* M 1 genius; 2 engineering.

genou (*plural* **genoux**) *noun* M knee; **avoir mal au genou** to have a sore knee; **être à genoux** to be kneeling; **se mettre à genoux** to kneel down; **sur mes genoux** on my lap.

genre *noun* M kind; **un genre de sauce épicée** a kind of spicy sauce; **un peu dans le genre de ton pull** a bit like your sweater.

gens *plural noun* M people; **beaucoup de gens** lots of people; **les gens disent que...** people say that...

gentil (F **gentille**) *adjective* 1 kind, nice; **elle est très gentille** she's really nice; 2 kind; **c'est très gentil de ta part** it's very kind of you; 3 good; **sois gentil et mange ta**

viande be a good boy and eat up your meat.

gentillesse *noun* F kindness.

gentiment *adverb* 1 nicely; **demande gentiment** ask nicely; 2 kindly.

géographie *noun* F geography.

géométrie *noun* F geometry.

gérant, gérante *noun* M, F manager, manageress.

gérer *verb* [24] to manage, to run.

germain *adjective* **un cousin germain** a first cousin.

gésier *noun* M gizzard.

geste *noun* M gesture.

gestion *noun* F management; **gestion de fichiers** file management (*on a computer*).

gibier *noun* M game (*for example, venison, pheasant*).

gifle *noun* F slap (*in the face*).

gifler *verb* [1] to slap (*in the face*).

gigantesque *adjective* huge, gigantic; **un repas gigantesque** a huge meal.

gigot *noun* M leg of lamb.

gilet *noun* M 1 cardigan; 2 waistcoat.

gilet de sauvetage *noun* M life-jacket.

gingembre *noun* M ginger.

girafe *noun* F giraffe.

gitan, gitane *noun* M, F gipsy.

gîte (rural) *noun* M holiday house.

glace *noun* F **1** ice cream; **une glace au chocolat** a chocolate ice cream; **2** ice; **3** mirror; **se regarder dans la glace** to look at yourself in the mirror; **4** window (*in a car*).

glacé *adjective* **1** icy cold; **j'ai les mains glacées** my hands are freezing; **2 un thé glacé** an iced tea.

glacier *noun* M glacier.

glacière *noun* F cool-box.

glaçon *noun* M ice cube.

glissant *adjective* slippery.

glisser *verb* [1] to slip, to slide; **attention, ça glisse!** be careful, it's slippery!

global *adjective* (M *plural* **globaux**) total.

gloire *noun* F fame, glory.

glorieux (F **glorieuse**) *adjective* glorious.

glossaire *noun* M glossary.

gobelet *noun* M cup, tumbler; **un gobelet en carton** a paper cup.

godasse *noun* F (*informal*) shoe.

gogo (*informal*) **à gogo** as much as you like; **pizza à gogo** as much pizza as you can eat.

golden *noun* F Golden Delicious (apple).

golf *noun* M **1** golf; **jouer au golf** to play golf; **2** golf course.

golfe *noun* M gulf.

gomme *noun* F rubber.

gommer *verb* [1] to rub out.

gonfler *verb* [1] **1** to pump up (*tyres*); **2** to blow up (*a balloon*).

gorge *noun* F **1** throat; **j'ai mal à la gorge** I've got a sore throat; **j'avais la gorge serrée** I had a lump in my throat; **il chantait à pleine gorge** he was singing at the top of his voice; **2** gorge.

gorgée *noun* F sip; **une gorgée de thé** a sip of tea.

gorille *noun* M gorilla.

gosse *noun* M & F kid.

goudron *noun* M tar.

gourde *noun* F water bottle.

gourmand *adjective* greedy.

gourmandise *noun* F **1** greed; **2 elle aime les gourmandises** she likes sweet things.

gousse *noun* F **une gousse d'ail** a clove of garlic.

goût *noun* M taste; **ça a un goût bizarre** it has a strange taste; **de bon goût** in good taste; ★ **chacun ses goûts** it takes all sorts to make a world.

goûter *noun* M **1** teatime snack; **2** children's party. *verb* [1] **1** to taste, to try; **est-ce que tu as goûté le gâteau?** have you tried the cake?; **2** to have a teatime snack.

goutte *noun* F drop; **une goutte de** a drop of; **goutte à goutte** drop by drop.

gouvernement *noun* M government.

gouverner *verb* [1] to govern, to rule.

grâce *noun* F **grâce à** thanks to; **la soirée a été un grand succès grâce à toi** the evening was a great success thanks to you.

gracieux (F **gracieuse**) *adjective* graceful.

grade *noun* M rank; **monter en grade** to be promoted.

gradins *plural noun* M terraces (*in a stadium*).

graduel (F **graduelle**) *adjective* gradual.

graffiti *plural noun* M graffiti.

grain *noun* M **1** grain; **un grain de sable** a grain of sand; **2** **du poivre en grains** peppercorns; **3** **du café en grains** coffee beans; **4** **un grain de beauté** a beauty spot; **5** **un grain de raisin** a grape.

graine *noun* F seed.

graisse *noun* F fat, grease.

grammaire *noun* F grammar.

gramme *noun* M gramme.

grand *adjective* **1** big; **une grande maison** a big house; **c'est ma grande sœur** she's my big sister; **2** tall; **un grand arbre** a tall tree; **ton frère est très grand** your brother's very tall; **elle est plus grande que moi** she's taller than me; **3** great; **un grand artiste** a great artist; **un grand ami** a great friend; **4** main; **les grandes lignes** main (railway) lines. *adverb* wide; **la porte était grande ouverte** the door was wide open.

grand-chose much; **pas grand-chose** not much; **il ne reste pas grand-chose** there's not much left.

Grande-Bretagne *noun* F Great Britain.

grande personne *noun* F grown-up.

grande surface *noun* F hypermarket.

grand magasin *noun* M department store.

grandes vacances *plural noun* F summer holidays.

grandeur *noun* F size; **grandeur nature** life-size.

grandir *verb* [2] to grow, to grow up.

grand-mère (*plural* **grands-mères**) *noun* F grandmother.

grand-père (*plural* **grands-pères**) *noun* M grandfather.

grands espaces *plural noun* M open spaces.

grands-parents *plural noun* M grandparents.

grange *noun* F barn.

grappe *noun* F **une grappe de raisin** a bunch of grapes.

gras (F **grasse**) *adjective* **1** fatty, greasy; **40% matière grasse** 40% fat (*on cheese or yoghurt label*); **2** **une peau grasse** oily skin; ★ **faire la grasse matinée** to have a lie-in.

gratitude *noun* F gratitude.

gratte-ciel *noun* M skyscraper.

gratter *verb* [1] **1** **gratter quelque chose** to scratch something; **2** **se**

gratter to scratch (yourself); **3** to itch; **ça gratte** it itches.

gratuit *adjective* free; **le concert est gratuit** the concert's free; **'entrée gratuite'** 'entrance free'.

grave *adjective* **1** serious; **un grave accident** a serious accident; **2 ce n'est pas grave** it doesn't matter; **3** serious; **une expression grave** a serious expression; **4** deep; **une voix grave** a deep voice.

gravement *adverb* seriously; **elle est gravement malade** she's seriously ill.

gravure *noun* F engraving, print.

gré *noun* M **contre son gré** against his will.

grec (F **grecque**) *adjective* Greek.

Grec, Grecque *noun* M, F Greek (person).

Grèce *noun* F Greece.

grêle *noun* F hail.

grelotter *verb* [1] to shiver.

grenade *noun* F **1** grenade; **2** pomegranate.

grenadine *noun* F grenadine (*pomegranate cordial*).

grenier *noun* M attic, loft; **au grenier** in the attic.

grenouille *noun* F frog; **les cuisses de grenouille** frogs' legs.

grève *noun* F strike; **une grève des trains** a train strike; **le métro est en grève** the underground's on strike; **faire grève** to go (or be) on strike.

gréviste *noun* M & F striker.

grièvement *adverb* seriously; **grièvement blessé** seriously injured.

griffe *noun* F claw.

griffonner *verb* [1] to scribble.

grillade *noun* F grilled meat, meat for grilling; **une grillade de porc** a pork steak.

grillage *noun* M wire netting.

grille *noun* F **1** metal gate; **2** railings; **3** wire fence.

grillé *adjective* **1** grilled; **2** toasted; **du pain grillé** toast.

grille-pain *noun* M toaster.

griller *verb* [1] **1** to grill; **2** to toast.

grillon *noun* M cricket (*the creature not the game*).

grimace *noun* F **faire des grimaces** to make faces.

grimper *verb* [1] to climb; **grimper dans un arbre** to climb a tree.

grincer *verb* [61] to creak, to squeak.

grincheux (F **grincheuse**) *adjective* grumpy.

grippe *noun* F flu; **avoir une grippe** to have flu; **une grippe intestinale** gastric flu.

gris *adjective* grey.

grogner *verb* [1] **1** to growl; **2** to grumble.

gronder *verb* [1] **1 gronder quelqu'un** to tell somebody off; **se faire gronder** to get a telling-off; **2** to rumble (*thunder, for example*).

gros (F **grosse**) *adjective* **1** big; **un gros morceau** a big piece; **un gros problème** a big problem; **2** fat; **un gros monsieur** a fat man; **3 un gros rhume** a bad cold; **4 un gros fumeur** a heavy smoker; **5 un gros mot** a swear word; **6 en gros** roughly.

groseille *noun* F redcurrant.

groseille à maquereau *noun* F gooseberry.

grosse *adjective* SEE **gros**.

grossesse *noun* F pregnancy.

grossier (F **grossière**) *adjective* **1** rude; **2** crude; **une idée grossière de** a rough idea of; **une erreur grossière** a bad mistake.

grossir *verb* [2] to put on weight; **il a beaucoup grossi** he's put on a lot of weight.

grosso modo *adverb* roughly.

grotesque *adjective* ridiculous.

grotte *noun* F cave.

groupe *noun* M group.

grouper *verb* [1] **1** to group; **2 se grouper** to gather, to form a group.

groupe sanguin *noun* M blood group.

grue *noun* F crane.

guépard *noun* M cheetah.

guêpe *noun* F wasp.

guère *adverb* ne...guère hardly; **je ne l'ai guère vu depuis Noël** I've hardly seen him since Christmas.

guérir *verb* [2] **1** to cure; **le médecin l'a guéri** the doctor cured him; **2** to

get better; **j'ai été malade mais je suis maintenant guéri** I've been ill but I'm better now.

guérison *noun* F recovery (*from a illness or injury*).

guerre *noun* F war; **le pays est actuellement en guerre** the country is at war at the moment; **la Seconde-Guerre mondiale** World War II.

guetter *verb* [1] to watch out for.

gueule *noun* F mouth (*of an animal; considered rude if used of a person*); **(ferme) ta gueule!** (*rude*) shut up!

gueule de bois *noun* F (*informa* **avoir la gueule de bois** to have a hangover.

gueuler *verb* [1] (*informal*) to yell.

gui *noun* M mistletoe.

guichet *noun* M **1** ticket office (*in station or museum*); **2** box office (*a a theatre or cinema*); **3** counter, window (*in a bank or post office*).

guichet automatique *noun* M cashpoint.

guide *noun* M guide.

guider *verb* [1] to guide.

guidon *noun* M handlebars.

guillemets *plural noun* M inverte commas; **entre guillemets** in inverted commas.

guirlande *noun* F **des guirlandes** tinsel; **des guirlandes en papier** paper chains.

guirlande électrique *noun* F fairy lights, Christmas-tree lights.

guitare *noun* F guitar; **jouer de la guitare** to play the guitar.

guitariste *noun* M & F guitarist.

gym *noun* F (*informal*) PE, gymnastics.

gymnase *noun* M gym; **je te verrai au gymnase** I'll see you in the gym.

gymnastique *noun* F gymnastics, exercises.

H h

habile *adjective* clever; **elle est habile de ses mains** she's clever with her hands; **de manière habile** cleverly.

habillé *adjective* **1** dressed; **je ne suis pas encore habillé** I'm not dressed yet; **2** smart (*for example, a dress or suit*).

habiller *verb* [1] **1 habiller quelqu'un** to dress somebody; **2 s'habiller** to get dressed; **habille-toi vite!** get dressed quick!; **3 s'habiller** to dress up; **s'habiller en clown** to dress up as a clown.

habitant, habitante *noun* M, F inhabitant.

habitation *noun* F house.

habiter *verb* [1] to live; **ils habitent à Paris** they live in Paris.

habitude *noun* F **1** habit; **c'est une mauvaise habitude** it's a bad habit; **2 d'habitude** usually; **d'habitude il arrive à midi** he usually arrives at twelve; **3 comme d'habitude** as

usual; **j'ai pris le bus comme d'habitude** I took the bus as usual; **4 avoir l'habitude de faire** to be used to doing; **j'ai l'habitude de travailler le soir** I'm used to working in the evening.

habitué, habituée *noun* M, F regular (*in a café, shop, etc*).

habituel (F **habituelle**) *adjective* usual.

habituer *verb* [1] **s'habituer à quelque chose** to get used to something; **je m'y suis habituée** I've got used to it.

hache *noun* F axe.

haché *adjective* chopped; **du bœuf haché** mince.

hacher *verb* [1] **1** to chop (*vegetables*); **2** to mince (*meat*).

hachis Parmentier *noun* M shepherd's pie.

haddock *noun* M smoked haddock.

haie *noun* F **1** hedge; **2 les haies** hurdles (*sport*).

haine *noun* F hatred.

haïr *verb* [46] to hate.

haleine *noun* F breath; **être hors d'haleine** to be out of breath.

hall *noun* M **1** (entrance) hall; **2** concourse (*in a station*).

halles *plural noun* F covered market.

halogène *adjective* halogen; **une lampe halogène** a halogen lamp.

halte *noun* F stop; **halte!** stop!; **faire une halte** to stop somewhere.

halte-garderie *noun* F playgroup.

haltérophilie *noun* F weightlifting.

hameau (*plural* **hameaux**) *noun* M group of houses.

hameçon *noun* M fish hook.

hamster *noun* M hamster.

hanche *noun* F hip.

handball *noun* M handball; **jouer au handball** to play handball.

handicap *noun* M handicap.

handicapé, handicapée *noun* M, F handicapped person. *adjective* handicapped, disabled.

hareng *noun* M herring.

haricot *noun* M bean; **haricot vert** French bean; **haricot blanc** haricot bean.

harmonica *noun* M mouth organ; **jouer de l'harmonica** to play the mouth organ.

harmonie *noun* F harmony.

harmoniser *verb* [1] to coordinate, to harmonize.

harnais *noun* M harness.

harpe *noun* F harp.

hasard *noun* M **1** chance; **par hasard** by chance; **je l'ai rencontré par hasard** I met him by chance; **2** **au hasard** at random; **elle a choisi un livre au hasard** she chose a book at random; **3** **à tout hasard** just in case; **prends un manteau à tout hasard** take a coat just in case; **4** **à tout hasard** on the off chance.

hasardeux (F **hasardeuse**) *adjective* risky.

hâte *noun* F **à la hâte** hurriedly; **elle est partie à la hâte** she left in a rush.

hausse *noun* F increase, rise; **une hausse des prix** a rise in prices; **les prix sont en hausse** prices are rising.

hausser *verb* [1] **1** to raise; **2** **hausser les épaules** to shrug your shoulders.

haut *noun* M **1** top **le haut de l'échelle** the top of the ladder; **regarder quelqu'un de haut en bas** to look somebody up and down; **2** **l'arbre fait 10 mètres de haut** the tree is 10 metres high; **3** **en haut** upstairs; **elle est en haut** she's upstairs; **4** **en haut de** at the top of; **en haut de l'escalier** at the top of the stairs. *adjective* **1** high; **la branche la plus haute** the highest branch; **2** **à haute voix** aloud; **lire à haute voix** to read aloud. *adverb* high; **plus haut dans l'arbre** higher up the tree; **'voir plus haut'** 'see above' (*in a book*); **haut les mains!** hands up!

hautbois *noun* M oboe.

hauteur *noun* F height; **la hauteur de la pièce** the height of the room; **dans le sens de la hauteur** upright; **l'avion prend de la hauteur** the plane's gaining height; **il n'est pas à la hauteur de son travail** he's not up to his job.

haut-parleur *noun* M loudspeaker.

aye *noun* **La Haye** The Hague.

ebdomadaire *noun* M weekly magazine.

éberger *verb* [52] to put up; **Jess va nous héberger** Jess'll put us up.

ein *exclamation* (*informal*) what?, eh?

élas unfortunately; **elle est déjà partie, hélas** she's already left, unfortunately; **hélas non** I'm afraid not.

élicoptère *noun* M helicopter.

émorragie *noun* F haemorrhage.

ennir *verb* [2] to neigh.

erbe *noun* F **1** **l'herbe** grass; **2** herb; **les fines herbes** mixed herbs; **les herbes de Provence** mixed herbs; **3** **une mauvaise herbe** a weed.

érisson *noun* M hedgehog.

éritage *noun* M inheritance.

ériter *verb* [1] to inherit.

ermétique *adjective* airtight.

éroïne *noun* F **1** heroine; **2** heroin.

éros *noun* M hero.

ésitation *noun* F hesitation.

ésiter *verb* [1] to hesitate; **à ta place, je n'hésiterais pas!** if I were you, I wouldn't hesitate!; **j'ai beaucoup hésité avant d'accepter** I thought about it for a long time before I agreed; **j'hésite entre le poulet et le poisson** I can't decide whether to have the chicken or the fish.

hêtre *noun* M **1** beech tree; **2** beech wood.

heure *noun* F **1** hour; **une heure plus tard** an hour later; **deux heures de train** two hours in the train; **une demi-heure** half an hour; **une heure et demie** an hour and a half; **Londres est à une heure d'avion de Paris** London is an hour from Paris by air; **toutes les quatre heures** every four hours; **payé à l'heure** paid by the hour; **cent kilomètres à l'heure** a hundred kilometres an hour; **2** time; **quelle heure est-il?** what time is it?; **il est sept heures** it's seven o'clock; **à huit heures du matin** at eight o'clock in the morning; **tu te lèves à quelle heure demain?** what time are you getting up tomorrow?; **à neuf heures** at nine o'clock; **à six heures et demie** at half past six; **3** **être à l'heure** to be on time; **4** **à l'heure du déjeuner** at lunchtime; ★ **de bonne heure** early; **je me lève de bonne heure demain** I'm getting up early tomorrow.

heures d'affluence *plural noun* F peak time, rush hour.

heureusement *adverb* fortunately.

heureux (F **heureuse**) *adjective* **1** happy; **elle est heureuse d'être ici** she's happy to be here; **2** lucky, fortunate.

heurter *verb* [1] to hit, to bump into; **la voiture a heurté un camion** the car collided with a lorry.

hexagone *noun* M **1** hexagon; **2** **l'Hexagone** France (*French journalists often refer to France as* *l'Hexagone as it has a six-sided shape on the map).*

hibou (*plural* **hiboux**) *noun* M owl.

hideux (F **hideuse**) *adjective* hideous.

hier *adverb* yesterday; **je l'ai vue hier** I saw her yesterday; **hier matin** yesterday morning; **avant-hier** the day before yesterday.

hi-fi *noun* F hi-fi; **une chaîne hi-fi** a stereo system.

hippique *adjective* equestrian; **un concours hippique** a horse show; **un club hippique** a riding school.

hippodrome *noun* M racecourse.

hippopotame *noun* M hippopotamus.

hirondelle *noun* F swallow.

histoire *noun* F **1** history; **l'histoire française** French history; **2** story; **l'histoire de ma vie** the story of my life; **3** matter **c'est une histoire d'argent** it's a matter of money; ★ **faire des histoires** to kick up a fuss.

historique *adjective* **1** historic; **un monument historique** a historic monument; **2** historical.

hit-parade *noun* M **le hit-parade** the charts (*pop music*).

hiver *noun* M winter; **en hiver** in winter.

HLM *noun* M or F (= *habitation à loyer modéré*) council flat; **nous habitons dans un HLM à Valence** we live in a council flat in Valence; **les HLM** council housing.

hocher *verb* [1] **hocher la tête** to shake your head, to nod.

hockey *noun* M hockey; **jouer au hockey** to play hockey; **le hockey sur glace** ice hockey.

hollandais *noun* M, *adjective* Dutch.

Hollandais, Hollandaise *noun* M, F Dutchman, Dutchwoman; **les Hollandais** the Dutch.

Hollande *noun* F Holland; **en Hollande** in (or to) Holland.

homard *noun* M lobster.

homéopathique *adjective* homeopathic.

hommage *noun* M tribute, homage.

homme *noun* M man.

homme d'affaires *noun* M businessman.

homme d'État *noun* M statesman.

homogénéisé *adjective* homogenized.

homosexuel, homosexuelle *noun*, M, F, *adjective* homosexual.

Hongrie *noun* F Hungary.

hongrois *noun* M, *adjective* Hungarian.

honnête *adjective* honest, respectable.

honnêtement *adverb* honestly, frankly; **honnêtement je ne sais pas ce que tu veux dire** I honestly don't know what you mean.

honnêteté *noun* F honesty; **en toute honnêteté** in all honesty.

honneur *noun* M honour.

honorer *verb* [1] to honour.

honte *noun* F shame; **avoir honte de quelque chose** to be ashamed of something; **j'ai vraiment honte** I'm really ashamed of myself; **tu n'as pas honte!** what a thing to say! (or do).

honteux (F **honteuse**) *adjective* disgraceful.

hôpital *noun* M hospital; **être à l'hôpital** to be in hospital.

hoquet *noun* M hiccup; **avoir le hoquet** to have hiccups.

horaire *noun* M timetable; schedule; **les horaires de train** the train timetable.

horizon *noun* M horizon; **à l'horizon** on the horizon.

horizontal (M *plural* **horizontaux**) *adjective* horizontal.

horloge *noun* F clock.

horodateur *noun* M parking ticket machine.

horoscope *noun* M horoscope.

horreur *noun* F 1 horror; **quelle horreur!** how awful!; 2 **avoir horreur de quelque chose** to hate something; **j'ai horreur d'être en retard** I hate being late; **j'ai horreur des escargots!** I can't stand snails!

horrible *adjective* horrible.

horrifier *verb* [1] to horrify.

hors *preposition* 1 **hors de** outside; **hors de France** outside France; 2 **les boutiques hors taxe** the duty-free shops; ★ **être hors de soi** to be beside yourself; **j'étais hors de moi** I was beside myself.

hors-d'œuvre *noun* M starter (*to a meal*).

hortensia *noun* M hydrangea.

hospitalier *adjective* **un centre hospitalier** a hospital.

hospitaliser *verb* [1] **elle a été hospitalisée** she's been taken into hospital.

hospitalité *noun* F hospitality.

hostilité *noun* F hostility.

hôte[1] *noun* M host.

hôte[2] *noun* M & F 1 guest; **hôte payant** paying guest; 2 host.

hôtel *noun* M hotel; **passer deux nuits à l'hôtel** to spend two nights in a hotel.

hôtel de ville *noun* M town hall.

hôtesse *noun* F 1 hostess; 2 receptionist.

hôtesse d'accueil *noun* F receptionist.

hôtesse de l'air *noun* F air hostess.

housse *noun* F cover (*for a chair or a machine*); **une housse de couette** a duvet cover.

houx *noun* M holly.

hublot *noun* M 1 window (*in a plane*); 2 porthole (*in a boat*).

huile *noun* F oil; **huile de tournesol** sunflower oil; **huile d'olive** olive oil; **huile solaire** suntan oil.

huit *number* **1** eight; **Paul a huit ans** Paul's eight; **le huit juillet** the eighth of July; **2 huit jours** a week; **il y a huit jours** a week ago.

huitième *noun* M; **au huitième** on the eighth floor.
adjective eighth.

huître *noun* F oyster.

humain *adjective* human.

humanitaire *adjective* humanitarian.

humeur *noun* F mood; **il est de bonne humeur** he's in a good mood; **elle est de mauvaise humeur** she's in a bad mood; **je ne suis pas d'humeur à faire ça** I'm not in the mood to do that.

humide *adjective* damp.

humidité *noun* F damp.

humoristique *adjective* humorous; **un dessin humoristique** a cartoon.

humour *noun* M humour; **avoir de l'humour** to have a sense of humour.

hurler *verb* [1] to yell, to howl.

hutte *noun* F hut.

hydratant *adjective* moisturizing.

hygiène *noun* F hygiene.

hygiénique *adjective* **1** hygienic; **2 une serviette hygiénique** a sanitary towel; **3 du papier hygiénique** toilet paper.

hymne *noun* M hymn; **l'hymne national** the national anthem.

hypermarché *noun* M hypermarket.

hypermétrope *adjective* long-sighted.

hypertension *noun* F high blood pressure.

hypnotiser *verb* [1] to hypnotize.

hypocondriaque *noun* M & F, *adjective* hypochondriac.

hypocrite *noun* M & F hypocrite.

hypothèse *noun* F hypothesis.

hystérie *noun* F hysteria.

I i

ici *adverb* **1** here; **il y a trop de monde ici** there are too many people here; **les gens d'ici** the local people; **2 jusqu'ici** this far; **les bus ne viennent pas jusqu'ici** the buses don't come this far; **3 jusqu'ici** so far; **jusqu'ici il a fait beau** so far the weather's been good.

idéal (*plural* **idéaux**) *noun* M, *adjective* ideal; **l'idéal serait de louer une voiture** the ideal thing would be to hire a car.

idée *noun* F idea; **quelle bonne idée!** what a good idea!; **je n'ai aucune idée** I've no idea; **se faire des idées** to imagine things.

identifier *verb* [1] to identify.

identique *adjective* identical.

identité *noun* F identity; **une carte d'identité** an identity card.

idiot, idiote *noun* M, F idiot; **ne fais pas l'idiot!** don't fool around!

adjective stupid; **c'est vraiment idiot!** it's really stupid!

gnorance *noun* F ignorance.

gnorant *adjective* ignorant.

gnorer *verb* [1] **1** not to know; **j'ignore leur adresse** I don't know their address; **j'ignore les détails** I don't know the details; **2** to ignore; **ils l'ont ignoré** they ignored him.

l *pronoun* **1** he, it; **il parle français** he speaks French; **2** it; **'où est mon sac?'** – **'il est sur la chaise'** 'where's my bag?' – 'it's on the table'; **il pleut** it's raining.

le *noun* F island.

légal (M *plural* **illégaux**) *adjective* illegal.

limité *adjective* unlimited.

lisible *adjective* illegible.

lumination *noun* F floodlighting; **les illuminations de Noël** the Christmas lights.

luminer *verb* [1] to floodlight.

lusion *noun* F illusion; **elle se fait des illusions** she's fooling herself.

lustration *noun* F illustration.

lustré *noun* M comic. *adjective* illustrated.

lustrer *verb* [1] to illustrate.

s *pronoun* they; **ils sont en vacances** they're on holiday.

y a SEE **avoir.**

mage *noun* F picture; **il y a de belles images dans ton livre** there are some lovely pictures in your book.

imaginaire *adjective* imaginary.

imagination *noun* F imagination.

imaginer *verb* [1] to imagine; **je n'arrive pas à l'imaginer** I can't imagine it; **elle va appeler, j'imagine** I suppose she'll phone.

imbattable *adjective* unbeatable.

imbécile *noun* M & F fool; **faire l'imbécile** to fool around. *adjective* idiotic.

imitation *noun* F imitation.

imiter *verb* [1] to imitate.

immangeable *adjective* inedible.

immatriculation *noun* F registration (*of a car*); **une plaque d'immatriculation** a numberplate.

immédiat *adjective* immediate; **dans l'immédiat** for the time being; **je n'ai pas de projets dans l'immédiat** I don't have any plans for the time being.

immédiatement *adverb* immediately.

immense *adjective* huge.

immeuble *noun* M **1** block of flats; **2** building; **un immeuble de six étages** a six-storey building; **3 un immeuble de bureaux** an office block.

immigration *noun* F immigration.

immigré, immigrée *noun* M, F immigrant.

immobile *adjective* motionless.

immobilier *noun* M property (*houses and land*); **une agence immobilière** an estate agent's.

immobiliser *verb* [1] to immobilise.

immodéré *adjective* excessive.

immoral (M *plural* **immoraux**) *adjective* immoral.

immuniser *verb* [1] to immunize.

impact *noun* M impact.

impair *adjective* odd; **un nombre impair** an odd number.

impardonnable unforgivable.

imparfait *noun* M imperfect (tense); **à l'imparfait** in the imperfect.
adjective imperfect.

impasse *noun* F dead end.

impatience *noun* F impatience.

impatient *adjective* impatient.

impeccable *adjective* **1** perfect; **un accent français impeccable** a perfect French accent; **2** spotless; **l'appartement est impeccable** the flat's spotless; **3** (*informal*) great; **'je viendrai te chercher chez toi à midi' – 'impeccable!'** 'I'll come and pick you up at your place at twelve' – 'great!'

impensable *adjective* unthinkable.

imper *noun* M (*informal*) SHORT FOR **imperméable** raincoat.

impératif *noun* M imperative; **à l'impératif** in the imperative.

imperfection *noun* F imperfection.

imperméable *noun* M raincoat.

impertinent *adjective* cheeky.

impitoyable *adjective* merciless.

impliquer *verb* [1] **1** to mean; **cela implique que nous n'aurons pas assez d'argent** this means that we won't have enough money; **2 être impliqué dans quelque chose** to be involved in something.

impoli *adjective* rude.

importance *noun* F importance; **ça n'a pas d'importance** it doesn't matter.

important *adjective* **1** important; **il est important de savoir que...** it's important to know that...; **2** considerable; **une réduction importante** a considerable reduction; **il y aura des retards importants** there will be considerable delays.

importations *plural noun* F imports.

importer *verb* [1] **1** to import (*goods*); **2** to matter; **'lequel veux-tu?' – 'n'importe!'** 'which one do you want?' – 'it doesn't matter!'; **n'importe où** anywhere; **viens n'importe quand** come any time; **n'importe qui sait faire ça** anyone can do that; **il dit n'importe quoi** he's talking nonsense; **elle le fait n'importe comment** she does it any old how.

imposant *adjective* imposing.

imposer *verb* [1] **1** to impose; **imposer à quelqu'un de faire quelque chose** to make somebody do something; **la maman de Katy lui a imposé de rester à la maison** Katy's mum made her stay at home; **2 s'imposer** to establish oneself.

impossibilité *noun* F impossibility.

impossible *adjective* impossible; *noun* **faire l'impossible** to do your utmost; **nous ferons l'impossible pour les contacter** we'll do our utmost to contact them.

impôt *noun* M tax.

imprécis *adjective* vague.

impression *noun* F impression; **sa première impression** his first impression; **elle a fait très bonne impression** she made a very good impression; **j'ai l'impression qu'il n'est pas heureux** I have a feeling he's not happy.

impressionnant *adjective* impressive.

impressionner *verb* [1] to impress.

imprévisible *adjective* unpredictable.

imprévu *adjective* unexpected.

imprimante *noun* F printer (*for a computer*).

imprimé *noun* M form (*to fill in*). *adjective* printed.

imprimer *verb* [1] to print.

improviser *verb* [1] to improvise.

improviste *noun* **à l'improviste** unexpectedly; **mon oncle est arrivé à l'improviste** my uncle arrived unexpectedly.

imprudent *adjective* **1** careless; **2** rash.

impuissant *adjective* helpless.

impulsif (F **impulsive**) *adjective* impulsive.

inabordable *adjective* **1** inaccessible; **2 des prix inabordables** prohibitive prices.

inacceptable *adjective* unacceptable.

inaccessible *adjective* inaccessible.

inachevé *adjective* unfinished.

inadapté *adjective* unsuitable.

inadmissible *adjective* intolerable.

inaperçu *adjective* **passer inaperçu** to go unnoticed; **son départ est passé inaperçu** her departure went unnoticed.

inattendu *adjective* unexpected; **une visite inattendue** an unexpected visit.

inattention *noun* F lack of attention; **une faute d'inattention** a careless mistake.

inaudible *adjective* inaudible.

inauguration *noun* F inauguration, opening.

inaugurer *verb* [1] **1** to open (*an exhibition, a new building*); **2** to unveil (*a monument*).

incapable *adjective* **1** incapable; **je suis incapable de bouger!** I'm incapable of moving!; **2** incompetent; **il est complètement incapable** he's completely incompetent.

incassable *adjective* unbreakable.

incendiaire *noun* M & F arsonist. *adjective* **une bombe incendiaire** an incendiary bomb.

incendie *noun* M fire; **l'incendie a détruit l'église** the fire destroyed the church.

incertain *adjective* **1** uncertain; **le résultat est toujours incertain** the result is still uncertain; **2** unsettled (*weather*).

incertitude *noun* F uncertainty.

incident *noun* M incident; **en cas d'incident** if anything should happen.

inciter *verb* [1] to encourage; **le père d'André l'a incité à apprendre la guitare** André's father encouraged him to learn to play the guitar.

inclure *verb* [25] **1** to include; **2** to enclose.

inclus *adjective* including; **il y aura trente invités, enfants inclus** there will be thirty guests, including children; **jusqu'à samedi inclus** up to and including Saturday.

incollable *adjective* **le riz incollable** easy-cook rice.

incolore *adjective* colourless.

incommode *adjective* **1** awkward; **2** uncomfortable.

incomparable *adjective* incomparable.

incompétent *adjective* incompetent.

incompréhensible *adjective* incomprehensible.

inconditionnel, inconditionnelle *noun* M, F devotee; **c'est un inconditionnel du jazz** he's a real jazz fan.
adjective unconditional.

inconfortable *adjective* uncomfortable.

inconnu, inconnue *noun* M, F stranger.
adjective unknown; **elle m'est inconnue** I don't know her.

inconsciemment *adverb* unconsciously.

inconscient *adjective* **1** unthinking; **2** unconscious (*in a faint*).

incontestable *adjective* unquestionable.

incontournable *adjective* unavoidable; **c'est un fait incontournable** it's an undeniable fact.

inconvénient *noun* M **1** drawback; **il y a plusieurs inconvénients** there are several drawbacks; **2 l'inconvénient, c'est que...** the difficulty is that...; **3 si vous n'y voyez pas d'inconvénient** if you have no objection.

incorporer *verb* [1] to blend in (*ingredients in cooking*); **incorporez l'huile une goutte à la fois** blend in the oil drop by drop.

incorrect *adjective* **1** incorrect; **2** rude.

incrédule *adjective* incredulous.

incroyable *adjective* incredible.

inculper *verb* [1] **inculper quelqu'un de** to charge somebody with (*a crime*); **elle a été inculpée de vol** she was charged with theft.

Inde *noun* F India; **en Inde** in (or to) India.

ndécis *adjective* **1** undecided; **elle est toujours indécise** she hasn't decided yet; **2** indecisive.

ndemne *adjective* unharmed.

ndemniser *verb* [1] to compensate; **demander à être indemnisé** to demand compensation.

ndéniable *adjective* undeniable.

ndépendamment *adverb* independently.

ndépendance *noun* F independence.

ndépendant *adjective* **1** independent; **2 cuisine indépendante** separate kitchen; **3 une maison indépendante** a detached house.

ndex *noun* M **1** index; **2** forefinger.

ndicateur *noun* M **1** timetable (*in a rail or coach station*); **l'indicateur des départs** the departures board; **2** street directory; **3** gauge (*for example, for oil levels*); **4 un panneau indicateur** a road sign.

ndicatif *noun* M **1** dialling code; **l'indicatif pour l'Espagne est 34** the dialing code for Spain is 34; **2** theme tune; **3** indicative (*of a verb*).

ndications *plural noun* F directions.

ndice *noun* M clue.

ndien (F **indienne**) *adjective* Indian.

ndifférent *adjective* indifferent.

ndigène *adjective* native; **les indigènes** the locals.

indigeste *adjective* indigestible.

indigestion *noun* F indigestion; **avoir une indigestion** to have indigestion.

indignation *noun* F indignation.

indigne *adjective* **1** unworthy; **2** disgraceful.

indigner *verb* [1] **s'indigner** to get indignant.

indiqué *adjective* recommended; **ce n'est pas très indiqué** it's not a very good idea.

indiquer *verb* [1] to point out, to show; **pouvez-vous m'indiquer la gare?** can you show me the way to the station?; **le nom est indiqué sur un grand panneau** the name is on a big sign; **cela indique que...** this shows that...

indirect *adjective* indirect.

indiscipliné *adjective* unruly.

indiscret (F **indiscrète**) *adjective* **1** indiscreet; **ne le lui dis pas, elle est très indiscrète** don't tell her, she can't keep a secret; **2 si ce n'est pas indiscret** if it's not being nosy.

indiscutable *adjective* unquestionable.

indispensable *adjective* essential; **les vêtements indispensables** essential clothing; **il est indispensable** it's essential.

indisposé *adjective* unwell.

individu *noun* M individual; **c'est un drôle d'individu** he's a funny bloke.

individuel (F **individuelle**) *adjective*
1 individual; 2 separate; **une
chambre individuelle** a single room;
une maison individuelle a detached
house.

indolore *adjective* painless.

indulgent *adjective* indulgent;
**notre prof de maths est trop
indulgent avec nous** our maths
teacher isn't strict enough with us.

industrialisé *adjective* **les pays
industrialisés** the industrialized
countries.

industrie *noun* F industry.

industriel (F **industrielle**) *adjective*
industrial; **une ville industrielle** an
industrial city.

inédit *adjective* unpublished.

inefficace *adjective* 1 inefficient;
**en tant que patron il est très
inefficace** as a boss he's very
inefficient; 2 ineffective; **un
remède inefficace** an ineffective
remedy.

inégal (M *plural* **inégaux**) *adjective*
1 uneven; 2 unequal.

inespéré *adjective* unhoped-for; **un
succès inespéré** an unhoped-for
success.

inévitable *adjective* 1 inevitable;
c'était inévitable it was bound to
happen; 2 unavoidable; **des
problèmes inévitables**
unavoidable problems.

inexact *adjective* 1 incorrect;
2 inaccurate.

inexpérimenté *adjective*
inexperienced.

infarctus *noun* M heart attack.

infect *adjective* foul; **le repas était
infect!** the meal was foul!

infecter *verb* [1] 1 to infect;
2 **s'infecter** to go septic.

infection *noun* F infection.

inférieur *adjective* 1 lower; **sur une
marche inférieure** on a lower step;
des prix inférieurs à la moyenne
lower than average prices;
2 smaller; **la taille inférieure** the
smaller size; 3 inferior, worse; **de
qualité inférieure** of a lower quality.

infernal (M *plural* **infernaux**)
adjective frightful, dreadful.

infini *adjective* infinite.

infinitif *noun* M infinitive (*in
grammar*); **à l'infinitif** in the
infinitive.

infirme *noun* **les infirmes** the
disabled; *adjective* disabled.

infirmerie *noun* F medical room.

infirmier, infirmière *noun* M, F
nurse.

inflammable *adjective* flammable.

inflation *noun* F inflation.

influence *noun* F influence; **il a
une bonne influence sur son frère**
he's a good influence on his brother.

influencer *verb* [61] to influence.

**informaticien,
informaticienne** *noun* M, F
computer scientist.

information *noun* F
1 information; **une information très
utile** a very useful piece of
information; 2 **les informations**

the news (*on TV or radio*); **les informations sont à vingt heures** the news is at eight o'clock.

informatique *noun* F computer science, IT.
adjective computer; **un système informatique** a computer system.

informatiser *verb* [1] to computerize.

informer *verb* [1] **1** to inform; **2 s'informer** to find out; **je peux m'informer si tu veux** I can find out if you like.

infrarouge *adjective* infra-red.

infusion *noun* F herbal tea.

ingénieur *noun* M engineer.

ingrat *adjective* **1** ungrateful; **2 un travail ingrat** unrewarding work.

ingrédient *noun* M ingredient.

inhabité *adjective* uninhabited.

inhabituel (F **inhabituelle**) *adjective* unusual.

inhumain *adjective* inhuman.

inimaginable *adjective* unimaginable, unthinkable.

ininterrompu *adjective* **1** uninterrupted; **2** continuous.

initial (M *plural* **initiaux**) *adjective* initial.

initiale *noun* F initial; **mes initiales sont là-dessus** my initials are on it.

initiation *noun* F introduction (*to a new place or skill*); **une journée d'initiation** an introductory day (*to a course, for example*); **une initiation**

à l'anglais an introduction to English.

initiative *noun* F initiative.

initier *verb* [1] **1 initier quelqu'un à** to introduce somebody to (*a skill*); **2** to initiate (*an idea or plan*); **3 s'initier à quelque chose** to learn about something; **elle s'initie à la photo** she's starting to learn photography.

injecter *verb* [1] to inject.

injection *noun* F injection.

injure *noun* F insult.

injurier *verb* [1] to insult; **il m'a injurié** he swore at me.

injuste *adjective* unfair.

innocent *adjective* innocent.

innombrable *adjective* countless.

innovation *noun* F innovation.

innover *verb* [1] to break new ground.

inoccupé *adjective* empty.

inondation *noun* F flood; **des inondations** flooding.

inonder *verb* [1] to flood.

inoubliable *adjective* unforgettable.

inouï *adjective* incredible.

inox *noun* M stainless steel; **une casserole en inox** a stainless steel pan.

inoxydable *adjective* **un évier en acier inoxydable** a stainless steel sink.

inquiet (F **inquiète**) *adjective* anxious, worried.

inquiétant *adjective* worrying.

inquiéter *verb* [24] **1** to worry; **je ne veux pas t'inquiéter** I don't want to worry you; **ça m'inquiète un peu** I find that a bit worrying; **ce qui m'inquiète, c'est qu'elle n'a pas téléphoné** what I find worrying is the fact that she hasn't phoned; **2 s'inquiéter** to worry, to be worried; **elle va s'inquiéter si nous sommes en retard** she'll worry if we're late; **ne t'inquiète pas!** don't worry!

inquiétude *noun* F anxiety.

insatisfait *adjective* dissatisfied.

inscription *noun* F **1** enrolment (*for a course or in a school*); **2** registration.

inscrire *verb* [38] **1** to enrol, to register (*someone for a course or school*); **elle m'a inscrit pour l'examen** she's entered me for the exam; **2 s'inscrire** to enrol; **s'inscrire au club de foot** to join the football club.

insecte *noun* M insect.

insertion *noun* F **1** insertion (*of an advertisement in a paper, for example*); **2** integration (*when somebody joins a new community*); **l'insertion des jeunes dans la société** the integration of young people into society.

insignifiant *adjective* insignificant.

insister *verb* [1] to insist; **il faut insister** keep on trying; **la clé est un peu tordue, il faut insister un peu**

the key's a bit bent, you have to push it really hard.

insolation *noun* F sunstroke; **attraper une insolation** to get sunstroke.

insolent *adjective* insolent.

insoutenable *adjective* unbearable.

inspecter *verb* [1] to inspect.

inspecteur, inspectrice *noun* M, F inspector.

inspection *noun* F **1** inspection; **2** inspectorate (*an official department*).

inspiration *noun* F inspiration.

inspirer *verb* [1] **1** to inspire; **ça ne m'inspire pas** that doesn't appeal to me; **2** to breathe in; **inspire fort!** breathe in deep!; **3 s'inspirer** to be inspired by; **il s'est inspiré de Picasso** he was inspired by Picasso.

instable *adjective* unstable; **il fait un temps instable** the weather's unsettled.

installation *noun* F **1** installation putting in; **2** move (*to a house or town*); **avant son installation à Paris** before he moved to Paris; **3 des installations sportives** sport facilities.

installer *verb* [1] **1** to install, to put in (*central heating or a dishwasher, for example*); to connect (*gas, electricity, a phone*); **2 s'installer** to settle, to settle in; **installez-vous** do sit down; **je me suis installée à mon bureau** I settled down at my desk.

instant *noun* M moment; **pour l'instant** for the moment; **à tout instant** all the time.

instantané *adjective* instant; **du café instantané** instant coffee.

instinct *noun* M instinct.

institut *noun* M institute; **un institut de beauté** a beautician's.

instituteur, institutrice *noun* M, F primary school teacher.

institution *noun* F **1** institution; **2** private school.

institutrice *noun* F SEE **instituteur**.

instructeur, instructrice *noun* M, F instructor.

instruction *noun* F **1** education; **instruction civique** civics; **2 instructions** instructions; **instructions de lavage** washing instructions.

instruire *verb* [26] **1** to teach, to train; **2 s'instruire** to learn.

instruit *adjective* educated.

instrument *noun* M **1** instrument; **un instrument de mesure** a measuring instrument; **les instruments de bord** the controls; **2 un instrument de musique** a musical instrument; **un instrument à cordes** a string instrument.

insu *noun* **à mon insu** without my knowing.

insuffisance *noun* F shortage.

insuffisant *adjective* **1** insufficient; **2** inadequate; **c'est insuffisant** it's not good enough.

insultant *adjective* insulting.

insulte *noun* F insult.

insulter *verb* [1] to insult.

insupportable *adjective* unbearable; **je la trouve insupportable** I can't stand her.

intact *adjective* intact.

intégral (M *plural* **intégraux**) *adjective* complete.

intégrale *noun* F complete works (*usually music*); **l'intégrale des Beatles** the complete Beatles collection.

intellectuel, intellectuelle *noun* M, F, *adjective* intellectual.

intelligence *noun* F intelligence.

intelligent *adjective* clever, intelligent.

intendance *noun* F administration (*in a school*).

intense *adjective* intense.

intensif (F **intensive**) *adjective* intensive.

intention *noun* F intention; **avoir l'intention de faire** to mean to do; **j'avais l'intention d'y aller mais je n'ai pas pu** I meant to go but I wasn't able to.

interdiction *noun* F ban; **'interdiction de fumer'** 'no smoking'.

interdire *verb* [47] to forbid; **je t'interdis de le faire** I forbid you to do it.

interdit *adjective* forbidden; **'entrée interdite'** 'no entry'; **il est interdit de fumer dans la salle** smoking is forbidden in the theatre.

intéressant *adjective*
1 interesting; **c'est un film très intéressant** it's a very interesting film; 2 **à un prix intéressant** at a good price.

intéressé *adjective* interested; **être intéressé par quelque chose** to be interested in something.

intéresser *verb* [1] 1 to interest; **ça ne m'intéresse pas** that doesn't interest me; 2 **s'intéresser à** to be interested in; **elle s'intéresse beaucoup à l'informatique** she's very interested in computing.

intérêt *noun* M 1 interest; **ce livre est sans intérêt** this book is really boring; 2 **tu as intérêt à faire** you'd better do; **tu as intérêt à le finir avant ce soir !** you'd better get it finished by this evening!

intérieur *noun* M inside, interior; **l'intérieur du placard** the inside of the cupboard; **où est-elle? – à l'intérieur** where is she? – inside (*in the house*).
adjective inside, internal; **le côté intérieur** the inside.

intermédiaire *noun* M & F go-between.
adjective intermediate; **avez-vous la taille intermédiaire?** do you have the size in-between?

internat *noun* M boarding school.

international (M *plural* **internationaux**) *adjective* international.

interne *noun* M & F boarder (*in a school*).
adjective internal.

Internet *noun* M Internet; **sur Internet** on the Internet.

interpeller *verb* [1] 1 to call out to; 2 **la police l'a interpellé** the police have taken him in for questioning.

interphone™ *noun* M entry phone.

interprète *noun* M & F 1 (*in the theatre*) actor; (*in music*) performer, soloist; 2 interpreter.

interpréter *verb* [24] 1 to perform, to play (*a role in the theatre or a piece of music*), to sing (*a song*); 2 to interpret (*a language or a remark*).

interrogatif *noun* M interrogative.

interrogation *noun* F 1 test (*at school*); 2 questioning.

interroger *verb* [52] 1 to question, to ask; **il m'a interrogé sur mon séjour en France** he asked me about my stay in France; 2 to test (*at school*).

interrompre *verb* [69] to interrupt; **interrompre quelqu'un** to interrupt somebody; **il a interrompu son travail** he broke off his work.

interrupteur *noun* M switch.

interruption *noun* F
1 interruption; 2 **sans interruption** without stopping.

intervalle *noun* M 1 interval; 2 **dans l'intervalle** in the meantime.

intervenir *verb* [81] to intervene.

intervention *noun* F intervention.

interview *noun* F interview (*on TV, radio, for a magazine*).

intestin *noun* M intestine.

intime *adjective* intimate; **un journal intime** a diary (*kept by somebody*).

intimider *verb* [1] to intimidate.

intimité *noun* F intimacy; **dans l'intimité** in private.

intolérable *adjective* intolerable.

intolérant *adjective* intolerant.

intoxication *noun* F poisoning.

intrigue *noun* F plot (*of a novel, play, etc*).

introduction *noun* F introduction.

introduire *verb* [26] **1** to introduce (*an idea, a measure, a new product*); **2 s'introduire** to get into; **un cambrioleur s'est introduit dans l'appartement** a burglar got into the flat.

intrus, intruse *noun* M, F intruder.

intuitif (F **intuitive**) *adjective* intuitive.

intuition *noun* F intuition.

inusable *adjective* hard-wearing.

inutile *adjective* pointless; **il est inutile de l'appeler** there's no point telephoning him; **inutile de dire que...** needless to say...

inutilement *adverb* pointlessly; **je l'ai cherché inutilement** I looked for it in vain.

inutilisable *adjective* unusable.

invalide *noun* M & F disabled person.

invasion *noun* F invasion.

inventer *verb* [1] to invent.

invention *noun* F invention.

inverse *noun* M **l'inverse** the opposite; **l'inverse est vrai** the opposite is true.
adjective opposite; **en sens inverse** in the opposite direction; **dans l'ordre inverse** in reverse order.

investigation *noun* F investigation.

investissement *noun* M investment.

invisible *adjective* invisible.

invitation *noun* F invitation.

invité, invitée *noun* M, F guest; **nous avons des invités ce soir** we have people coming round this evening.

inviter *verb* [1] to invite; **ils m'ont invité à dîner** they invited me to dinner.

involontaire *adjective* unintentional.

invraisemblable *adjective* **1** unlikely; **une explication invraisemblable** an unlikely explanation; **2** (*informal*) amazing.

ira, irai, iraient, irais, irait, iras *verb* SEE **aller**.

iris *noun* M iris.

irlandais *noun* M, *adjective* Irish.

Irlandais, Irlandaise *noun* M, F Irishman, Irishwoman; **les Irlandais** the Irish.

Irlande *noun* F Ireland; **la République d'Irlande** the Republic of Ireland.

Irlande du Nord *noun* F Northern Ireland.

ironie *noun* F irony.

ironique *adjective* ironic.

irons, iront *verb* SEE **aller**[1].

irradier *verb* [1] to irradiate.

irréel, irréelle *adjective* unreal.

irréfléchi *adjective* thoughtless.

irrégularité *noun* F irregularity.

irrégulier (F **irrégulière**) *adjective* irregular.

irrésistible *adjective* irresistible.

irresponsable *adjective* irresponsible.

irritable *adjective* irritable.

irritation *noun* F irritation.

irriter *verb* [1] **1** to irritate; **cela m'irrite** that makes me cross; **2 s'irriter** to get irritated.

islamique *adjective* Islamic.

isolation *noun* F insulation; **isolation acoustique** soundproofing.

isolé *adjective* **1** remote; **2** lonely.

isoler *verb* [1] **1** to insulate (*a room or building*); **2** to isolate (*a sick person or a prisoner*).

Israël *noun* M Israel.

israélien (F **israélienne**) *adjective* Israeli.

issue *noun* F exit; **issue de secours** emergency exit; **une rue sans issue** a dead end.

Italie *noun* F Italy; **en Italie** in (or to) Italy.

italien *noun* M, *adjective* Italian.

Italien, Italienne *noun* M, F Italian (*person*).

itinéraire *noun* M route.

itinérant *adjective* travelling.

ivoire *noun* M *adjective* ivory.

ivre *adjective* drunk.

ivresse *noun* F drunkenness.

ivrogne *noun* M & F drunkard.

J j

j' *pronoun* SEE **je**.

jacinthe *noun* F hyacinth.

jalousie *noun* F **1** jealousy; **2** slatted blind.

jaloux (F **jalouse**) *adjective* jealous.

jamais *adverb* **1** never; **elle ne fume jamais** she never smokes; **on ne sait jamais** you never know; **jamais plus!** never again!; **2** ever; **plus grand que jamais** bigger than ever; **si jamais il pleut** if by any chance it rains; **à jamais** forever.

jambe *noun* F leg; **se casser la jambe** to break your leg.

jambon *noun* M ham; **jambon blanc** cooked ham; **jambon de pays** cured raw ham.

janvier *noun* M January; **en janvier, au mois de janvier** in January.

Japon *noun* M Japan; **au Japon** in (or to) Japan.

japonais *noun* M, *adjective* Japanese.

Japonais, Japonaise *noun* M, F Japanese (*person*).

jardin *noun* M garden; **Patrick est au jardin** Patrick's in the garden; **une chaise de jardin** a garden chair.

jardinage *noun* M gardening.

jardinier, jardinière¹ *noun* M, F gardener.

jardinière² *noun* F (large) plant pot.

jardin public *noun* M park (*in a town*).

jaune *noun* M **1** yellow; **2 un jaune d'œuf** an egg-yolk. *adjective* yellow; **une robe jaune** a yellow dress.

jaunisse *noun* F jaundice.

Javel *noun* **eau de Javel** bleach.

jazz *noun* M jazz; **j'aime le jazz** I like jazz.

J.-C. *noun* M short for Jésus-Christ; **200 avant J.-C.** 200 BC; **400 après J.-C.** 400 AD.

e, j' (*before a vowel or silent 'h'*) *pronoun* I; **je sais où il habite** I know where he lives; **j'habite à Lyon** I live in Lyons.

jean *noun* M **1** (pair of) jeans; **j'ai acheté un jean** I've bought some jeans; **2** denim; **une jupe en jean** a denim skirt.

jet *noun* M **1** jet (*of water or steam*); **les jets d'eau de Versailles** the fountains at Versailles; **2** jet (plane).

jetée *noun* F jetty.

jeter *verb* [48] **1** to throw; **jette-moi le ballon** throw me the ball; **2** to throw away; **j'ai jeté ces vieilles chaussures** I've thrown away these old shoes; **3 jeter un coup d'œil** to have a look; **est-ce que tu peux jeter un coup d'œil aux pommes de terre?** can you have a look at the potatoes?

jeton *noun* M **1** counter (*for a board game*); **2** token (*for a machine*).

jeu (*plural* **jeux**) *noun* M game; **faire un jeu** to play a game; ★ **ce n'est pas du jeu!** (*informal*) that's not fair!

jeu-concours *noun* M competition.

jeu de cartes *noun* M **1** pack of cards; **2** game of cards.

jeu de mots *noun* M pun.

jeu de société *noun* M board game.

jeudi *noun* M **1** Thursday; **nous sommes jeudi aujourd'hui** it's Thursday today; **jeudi prochain** next Thursday; **jeudi dernier** last Thursday; **2** on Thursday; **je l'ai vu jeudi soir** I saw him on Thursday evening; **3 le jeudi** on Thursdays;

fermé le jeudi closed on Thursdays; **4 tous les jeudis** every Thursday.

jeune *noun* M & F young person; **une émission destinée aux jeunes** a programme aimed at young people. *adjective* young; **un jeune homme** a young man; **une jeune femme** a young woman; **une jeune fille** a girl.

jeunesse *noun* F **1** young people; **la jeunesse d'aujourd'hui** young people today; **2** youth; **dans ma jeunesse** in my youth.

jeu-vidéo *noun* M video game.

jogging *noun* M **1 faire du jogging** to go jogging; **2 un jogging** a track-suit.

joie *noun* F joy.

joindre *verb* [49] **1** to get hold of (*often by telephone*); **je n'ai pas pu la joindre** I wasn't able to get hold of her; **2** to enclose (*in a letter or parcel*); **3** to put together; **les pieds joints** feet together; ★ **joindre les deux bouts** to make ends meet (*financially*).

joli *adjective* pretty.

jonquille *noun* F daffodil.

joue *noun* F cheek.

jouer *verb* [1] **1** to play; **elle joue avec le chien** she's playing with the dog; **à toi de jouer!** your go!; **bien joué!** well done!; **2 jouer à** to play (*a sport*); **on va jouer au foot** we're going to play football; **3 jouer de** to play (*an instrument*); **Robert joue de la guitare** Robert plays the guitar; **4** to act; **il joue bien dans ce film** he's really good in this film.

jouet *noun* M toy.

joueur, joueuse *noun* M, F player.

jour *noun* M **1** day; **les jours de la semaine** the days of the week; **trois jours plus tard** three days later; **le jour où** the day when; **un de ces jours** one of these days; **2 de nos jours** nowadays; **3 mettre quelque chose à jour** to bring something up to date; **4** daylight, light; **il fait jour** it's daylight; **en plein jour** in broad daylight; **jour et nuit** night and day.

jour de l'an *noun* M New Year's Day.

jour férié *noun* M public holiday.

journal (*plural* **journaux**) *noun* M **1** newspaper, magazine; **le journal du soir** the evening paper; **du papier journal** newspaper (*for wrapping*); **2** news (*on TV or radio*); **le journal de vingt-deux heures** the ten o'clock news; **3 un journal intime** a diary.

journalisme *noun* M journalism.

journaliste *noun* M & F journalist.

journée *noun* F day; **toute la journée** all day, the whole day; **il est payé à la journée** he's paid by the day.

jour ouvrable *noun* M working day.

joyeux (F **joyeuse**) *adjective* happy; **Joyeux Anniversaire** Happy Birthday; **Joyeux Noël** Merry Christmas.

judicieux (F **judicieuse**) *adjective* sensible; **un choix judicieux** a wise choice.

judo *noun* M judo.

juge *noun* M judge.

juger *verb* [52] to judge.

juif, juive *noun* M, F Jew. *adjective* Jewish.

juillet *noun* M July; **en juillet, au mois de juillet** in July; **le quatorze juillet** Bastille Day (*July 14, a national holiday to celebrate the taking of the Bastille prison in Paris by the people at the beginning of the French Revolution in 1789*).

juin *noun* M June; **en juin, au mois de juin** in June.

juive *noun* F, *adjective* SEE **juif**.

jumeau (*plural* **jumeaux**), **jumelle** *noun* M, F twin.

jumeler *verb* [18] to twin (*towns*); **Oxford est jumelé avec Bonn** Oxford is twinned with Bonn.

jumelles *plural noun* F binoculars.

jument *noun* F mare.

jungle *noun* F jungle.

jupe *noun* F skirt.

jurer *verb* [1] to swear.

juridique *adjective* legal; **le système juridique** the legal system.

jury *noun* M **1** jury; **2** board of examiners.

jus *noun* M **1** juice; **un jus d'orange** an orange juice; **2** gravy.

jus de fruits *noun* M fruit juice.

jusqu'à *preposition* **1** as far as (*a place*); **ce train va jusqu'à Paris** this train goes as far as Paris; **nous avons marché jusqu'à la mer** we walked as far as the sea; **il m'a accompagné jusqu'à chez moi** he took me all the way home; **2** until; **elle reste jusqu'à mardi** she's staying until Tuesday; **jusqu'à quand reste-t-il?** how long is he staying for?; **jusqu'à présent, jusqu'à maintenant** up to now; **3** **jusqu'à ce que** until.

juste *adjective* **1** right, correct; **le mot juste** the right word; **ce que tu dis est juste** what you say is right; **2** fair; **ce n'est pas juste!** it's not fair!; **3** in tune; **elle chante juste** she sings in tune; **4** **c'est un peu juste** it's a bit tight; **une heure est un peu juste** an hour's a bit tight. *adverb* just; **juste à temps** just in time; **il vient tout juste d'arriver** he's only just arrived.

justement *adverb* **1** precisely; **2** just; **je parlais justement de toi** I was just talking about you; **3** correctly; **comme elle a dit très justement** as she so rightly said.

justesse *noun* F **1** correctness; **2** **de justesse** only just; **il a eu son avion, mais de justesse** he caught his plane, but only just.

justice *noun* F justice.

justifier *verb* [1] to justify.

juteux (F **juteuse**) *adjective* juicy.

juvénile *adjective* youthful.

K k

kaki *noun* M persimmon.
adjective khaki.

kangourou *noun* M kangaroo.

karaté *noun* M karate.

karting *noun* M go-karting.

kascher *adjective* kosher.

kermesse *noun* F (school) fête.

kidnapper *verb* [1] to kidnap.

kidnappeur, kidnappeuse
noun M, F kidnapper.

kilo *noun* M kilo; **deux kilos de
pommes** two kilos of apples; **j'ai pris
trois kilos** I've put on three kilos.

kilogramme *noun* M kilogramme.

kilomètre *noun* M kilometre; **à dix
kilomètres d'ici** ten kilometres
from here; **Paris est à combien de
kilomètres de Dijon?** how many
kilometres is it from Paris to Dijon?

kinésithérapeute *noun* M & F
physiotherapist.

kinésithérapie *noun* F
physiotherapy.

kiosque *noun* M kiosk.

kiwi *noun* M kiwi (*the bird and the
fruit*).

klaxon™ *noun* M horn (*on a car*).

klaxonner *verb* [1] to sound the
horn (*in a car*).

km SHORT FOR **kilomètre**; **km/h** kph
(*kilometres per hour*).

K.O. *adjective* **1 mettre quelqu'un
K.O.** to knock somebody out (*in
boxing*); **2 je suis complètement
K.O.** (*informal*) I'm completely
knackered.

kraft *noun* M **le papier kraft** brown
paper.

K-way™ *noun* M cagoule.

L l

la, l' (*before a vowel or silent 'h'*)
definite article,
pronoun SEE **le**.

là *adverb* **1** there; **est-ce que Paul
est là?** is Paul there?; **c'est là
qu'habite mon frère** that's where my
brother lives; **2** here; **viens là** come
here; **Danielle n'est pas là en ce
moment** Danielle's not here at the
moment; **3** then; **c'est là que j'ai
pensé à toi** that's when I thought of
you.

-là *adverb* **cette maison-là** that
house; **ces gens-là** those people; **à
ce moment-là** at that moment.

là-bas *adverb* **1** there; **qu'est-ce
que vous avez fait là-bas?** what did
you do there?; **2** over there; **notre
maison est là-bas** our house is over
there.

labo *noun* M (*informal*) lab.

laboratoire *noun* M laboratory.

laboratoire de langues *noun* M
language laboratory.

labourer *verb* [1] to plough.

labyrinthe *noun* M maze, labyrinth.

lac *noun* M lake; **le lac d'Annecy** Lake Annecy.

lacer *verb* [61] **lacer ses chaussures** to tie your shoelaces.

lacet *noun* M lace (*for shoes*); **des chaussures à lacets** lace-up shoes.

lâche *adjective* **1** cowardly; **2** loose (*a belt or rope, for example*).

lâcher *verb* [1] **1** to drop (*an object*); to let go of (*a rope or branch*); **lâche-moi!** let go of me!; **ne lâche pas la corde!** don't let go of the rope!; **2** to drop; **elle a lâché son sac** she dropped her bag; **3** to give way; **la corde a lâché** the rope gave way.

lâcheté *noun* F cowardice.

lacrymogène *adjective* **le gaz lacrymogène** teargas.

là-dedans *adverb* in there; **il y a un oiseau là-dedans** there's a bird in there; **il n'y a rien là-dedans** there's nothing inside.

là-dessous *adverb* under there; **les verres sont là-dessous** the glasses are under there.

là-dessus *adverb* **1** on there; **tu peux mettre les assiettes là-dessus** you can put the plates on there; **2** about it; **ils sont d'accord là-dessus** they agree about it; **a-t-il dit quelque chose là-dessus?** did he say anything about it?; **3** with that; **là-dessus il est sorti** with that, he went out.

là-haut *adverb* **1** up here, up there; **il est là-haut dans l'arbre** he's up there in the tree; **2** upstairs; **maman est là-haut** Mum's upstairs.

laid *adjective* ugly.

laideur *noun* F ugliness.

laine *noun* F wool; **un pull en laine** a woollen jumper.

laine vierge *noun* F pure new wool.

laïque *adjective* **une école laïque** a state school.

laisse *noun* F lead (*for a dog*).

laisser *verb* [1] **1** to leave; **j'ai laissé mes clés chez toi** I've left my keys at your house; **bon, je vous laisse** right, I must be off now; **2 laisser quelqu'un faire** to let somebody do; **laisse-le parler!** let him speak!; **laissez-la faire, elle reviendra** leave her alone, she'll come back; **3 il se laisse insulter** he puts up with being insulted; **elle s'est laissée aller** she's let herself go.

laisser-aller *noun* M carelessness.

lait *noun* M milk; **un thé au lait** a cup of tea with milk; **un café au lait** a white coffee.

lait demi-écrémé *noun* M semi-skimmed milk.

lait écrémé *noun* M skimmed milk.

laitier (F **laitière**) *adjective* **les produits laitiers** milk products (*such as yoghurt*).

laitue *noun* F lettuce.

lame *noun* F blade.

lamelle *noun* F thin strip.

lamentable *adjective* awful.

lampadaire *noun* M **1** standard lamp; **2** street lamp.

lampe *noun* F lamp, light; **allumer la lampe** to turn on the lamp.

lampe de poche *noun* F torch.

lampe électrique *noun* F torch.

lancement *noun* M launch.

lancer *verb* [61] **1** to throw; **il m'a lancé le ballon** he threw the ball to me; **2** to launch; **ils vont lancer leur nouveau produit en juin** they're going to launch their new product in June; **3 se lancer dans quelque chose** to embark on something.

landau *noun* M pram.

lande *noun* F moor.

langage *noun* M language, type of language; **le langage administratif** official jargon.

langouste *noun* F crayfish.

langue *noun* F **1** tongue; **tirer la langue** to stick your tongue out; **2** language; **une langue étrangère** a foreign language; **ma langue maternelle** my mother tongue; ★ **je l'ai sur le bout de la langue** it's on the tip of my tongue.

lanière *noun* F strap.

lapin *noun* M rabbit; ★ **il m'a posé un lapin** (*informal*) he stood me up.

laque *noun* F **1** hairspray; **2** lacquer, gloss paint.

laquelle *pronoun* SEE **lequel**.

lard *noun* M streaky bacon.

lardons *plural noun* M diced bacon; **salade aux lardons fumés** green salad with diced smoky bacon.

large *noun* M open sea; **au large** offshore.
adjective wide; **un large sourire** a broad smile; **deux mètres de large** two metres wide.

largement *adverb* **c'est largement suffisant** that's more than enough; **j'ai largement le temps** I've got plenty of time.

largeur *noun* F width.

larme *noun* F tear; **en larmes** in tears; **rire aux larmes** to laugh till you cry.

laryngite *noun* F laryngitis.

lasagnes *plural noun* F lasagna; **manger des lasagnes** to eat lasagna.

laser *noun* M laser; **une platine laser** a compact disc player.

lasser *verb* [1] **se lasser** to get tired.

lassitude *noun* F weariness.

latin *noun* M, *adjective* Latin.

laurier *noun* M laurel; **un laurier commun** a bay tree; **une feuille de laurier** a bay leaf.

laurier-rose *noun* M oleander.

lavable *adjective* washable; **lavable en machine** machine-washable.

lavabo *noun* M washbasin.

lavage *noun* M **1** washing; **2** wash (*on a washing-machine programme*); **3** car wash.

lavande *noun* F lavender.

lave-linge *noun* M washing machine.

laver *verb* [1] **1** to wash; **2 se laver** to wash; **se laver les mains** to wash your hands; **se laver les dents** to brush your teeth.

laverie *noun* F launderette.

lave-vaisselle *noun* M dishwasher.

le, la, l', les *definite article* **1** the; **le chat** the cat; **la maison** the house; **les enfants** the children; **'quelle chemise?'** – **'la verte'** 'which shirt?' – 'the green one'; **2** (*'les' is often not translated*) **je n'aime pas les chiens** I don't like dogs; **3 elle se lave les cheveux** she's washing her hair; **4 le père de mon ami** my friend's father; **5** a, an; **5 francs le kilo** five francs a kilo.
pronoun him, her, it, them; **je la vois tous les soirs** I see her every evening; **je le vois tous les soirs** I see him every evening; **où est-ce que tu les as mis?** where did you put them?; **il l'a acheté chez Meyer** he bought it at Meyer's.

lécher *verb* [1] to lick.

lèche-vitrines *noun* M **faire du lèche-vitrines** to go window-shopping.

leçon *noun* F lesson; **une leçon de géographie** a geography lesson.

lecteur, lectrice *noun* M, F **1** reader (*of a book*); **2** foreign language assistant (*in a university*).

lecteur de cassettes *noun* M cassette player.

lecteur de disquettes *noun* M disk drive.

lecteur laser *noun* M CD player.

lecture *noun* F reading; **j'aime la lecture** I like reading; **le soir il fait de la lecture** he reads in the evenings.

légal *adjective* (M *plural* **légaux**) legal.

légende *noun* F **1** caption (*to a picture*); **2** key (*to a map*); **3** legend.

léger (F **légère**) *adjective* **1** light; **une veste légère** a light jacket; **un repas léger** a light meal; **2** slight; **un léger retard** a slight delay; **3** weak; **un café léger** a weak coffee; ★ **faire quelque chose à la légère** to do something without thinking.

légèrement *adverb* **1** lightly; **légèrement parfumé** lightly perfumed; **2** slightly; **il est légèrement blessé** he's slightly hurt; **elle est légèrement plus grande que moi** she's slightly taller than me.

légèreté *noun* F lightness.

législatif (F **législative**) *adjective* legislative; **les élections législatives** the general election.

légume *noun* M vegetable; **des légumes verts** green vegetables.

lendemain *noun* M **le lendemain** the next day; **Marc est arrivé le lendemain** Marc arrived the next day; **le lendemain matin** the next morning; **le lendemain de**

l'accident the day after the accident.

lent *adjective* slow.

lentement *adverb* slowly.

lenteur *noun* F slowness; **avec lenteur** slowly.

lentille *noun* F 1 lentil; **soupe aux lentilles** lentil soup; 2 lens; **lentilles de contact** contact lenses; **elle met ses lentilles** she's putting in her contact lenses.

léopard *noun* M leopard.

lequel, laquelle, lesquels, lesquelles *pronoun* 1 which one?, which?; **'passe-moi les verres' – 'lesquels?'** 'pass me the glasses' – 'which ones?'; 2 which, who; **la voiture dans laquelle ils roulaient** the car they were driving in, the car in which they were driving; **le monsieur avec lequel je discutais** the man to whom I was talking (*often not translated*) the man I was talking to.

les *definite article, pronoun* SEE **le**.

lessive *noun* F 1 washing; **faire la lessive** to do the washing; 2 washing powder, washing liquid.

lettre *noun* F 1 letter; **écrire une lettre** to write a letter; 2 letter (*of the alphabet*); **une lettre minuscule** a small letter; **une lettre majuscule** a capital letter; ★ **il prend tout ce qu'on lui dit à la lettre** he takes everything you say literally.

lettres *plural noun* F arts (*at university*).

leur *pronoun* them (*meaning 'to them'*); **je leur donne de l'argent** I give them money.
adjective (*plural* **leurs**) their; **leur voiture** their car; **leurs enfants** their children.
pronoun **le leur, la leur, les leurs** theirs; **ça, c'est notre maison, et ça, c'est la leur** that's our house and that's theirs; **nous avons appelé nos parents et ils ont appelé les leurs** we phoned our parents and they phoned theirs.

levant *adjective* **le soleil levant** the rising sun.

lever [1] *verb* [50] 1 to lift, to raise; **levons nos verres!** let's raise our glasses!; **levez la main!** put your hand up!; **il a levé les yeux** he looked up; 2 **se lever** to get up (*out of bed or from a chair*); **je me lève à sept heures** I get up at seven o'clock; **nous nous sommes levés tôt** we got up early; **quand le soleil se lève** when the sun rises.

lever [2] *noun* M **au lever du soleil** at sunrise.

lève-tard *noun* M late riser.

lève-tôt *noun* M early riser.

levier *noun* M lever.

lèvre *noun* F lip.

lévrier *noun* M greyhound.

levure *noun* F yeast.

lexique *noun* M word list.

lézard *noun* M lizard.

liaison *noun* F 1 link, connection; **une liaison routière** a road link; **une liaison radio** radio contact; **une**

liaison satellite a satellite link;
2 (love) affair.

liasse noun F wad, bundle (of papers or banknotes).

libellule noun F dragonfly.

libération noun F release, liberation; **la libération des femmes** women's liberation; **la Libération (de 1944)** the Liberation (of 1944) (the end of the German occupation of France).

libérer verb [24] **1** to free, to release (a prisoner or hostage); **2** to vacate (a hotel room or flat).

liberté noun F freedom.

libraire noun M & F bookseller.

librairie noun F bookshop.

librairie-papeterie noun F bookseller's and stationer's.

libre adjective free; **1 vous êtes libre de partir** you are free to go; **2** free (of a seat or telephone); **est-ce que cette place est libre?** is this seat free?

librement adverb freely.

libre-service noun M self service, self-service shop or restaurant; **un libre-service bancaire** a cashpoint.

licence noun F degree (at university); **elle a une licence de chimie** she has a chemistry degree.

licencier verb [1] **licencier quelqu'un** to make somebody redundant.

lien noun M link; **mes liens avec la famille** my links with my family; **un lien d'amitié** a bond of friendship.

lierre noun M ivy.

lieu (plural **lieux**) noun M **1** place; **un lieu public** a public place; **date et lieu de naissance** date and place of birth; **lieu de travail** place of work; **2 en premier lieu** in the first place; **3 avoir lieu** to take place; **le mariage aura lieu en juin** the marriage will take place in June; **4 au lieu de** instead of; **au lieu de prendre le bus, il est parti à pied** instead of taking the bus, he went off on foot; **5 les lieux** the premises; **peut-on visiter les lieux?** can one visit the premises?; **la police est arrivée sur les lieux** the police are now at the scene.

lièvre noun M hare.

lifting noun M face-lift.

ligne noun F **1** line; **une ligne droite** a straight line; **une ligne blanche** a white line (on the road); **à la ligne!** new paragraph! (in a dictation); **2** line (of a bus or train); **la ligne Paris-Dijon** the Paris-Dijon line; **une ligne de chemin de fer** a railway line; **les grandes lignes** the main lines (sign at a railway station); **3** cable; **ligne électrique** electric cable; **4** (telephone) line; **la ligne est mauvaise** it's a bad line; **restez en ligne, monsieur** hold the line, sir; **5** figure; **pour garder la ligne** to keep your figure, to stay slim.

lilas noun M lilac.

limace noun F slug.

lime noun F file; **une lime à ongles** a nail file.

limite *noun* F **1** limit; **une limite d'âge** an age limit; **2 la date limite** the closing date; **3 sans limites** endless; **une patience sans limites** endless patience; **4 à la limite** if it comes to it, at a pinch; **à la limite, je peux te prêter l'argent** if it comes to it, I can lend you the money; **5 dans la limite de** within the limits of; **dans la limite des places disponibles** subject to available seating space; **dans la limite du possible** as far as possible; **6** boundary; **les limites du village** the village boundaries; **7** maximum, last; **vitesse limite** maximum speed; **âge limite** maximum age; **date limite de vente** sell-by date.

limiter *verb* [1] **1** to limit; **2 se limiter** to limit oneself; **je me limite à deux cafés par jour** I limit myself to two coffees a day.

limonade *noun* F lemonade.

lin *noun* M linen; **une jupe en lin** a linen skirt.

linge *noun* M **1** linen (*sheets, towels, etc*); **linge de maison** household linen; **du linge sale** dirty linen; **2** washing; **as-tu du linge pour la machine?** have you any washing for the machine?; **une corde à linge** a washing line; ★ **elle était blanche comme un linge** she was white as a sheet.

lingerie *noun* F lingerie.

lion *noun* M lion.

Lion *noun* M Leo (*sign of the Zodiac*).

liqueur *noun* F liqueur.

liquidation *noun* F clearance sale, closing-down sale; **'liquidation totale!'** 'everything must go!'

liquide *noun* M **1** liquid; **2** cash; **payer quelque chose en liquide** to pay cash for something. *adjective* liquid.

lire *verb* [51] to read; **lire un roman** to read a novel; **elle sait lire maintenant** she can read now; **elle m'a lu une histoire** she read me a story; **un auteur qui est très lu** a popular author; **lire à haute voix** to read aloud; ★ **lire entre les lignes** to read between the lines.

lis *verb* SEE **lire**.

lisible *adjective* legible.

lisse *adjective* smooth.

liste *noun* F list; **faire une liste** to make a list; **faire la liste de** to make a list of.

liste d'attente *noun* F waiting list.

lit¹ *verb* SEE **lire**.

lit² *noun* M bed; **aller au lit** to go to bed; **faire son lit** to make one's bed; **un lit à une place** a single bed; **un lit à deux places** a double bed; **une chambre à deux lits** a twin-bedded room; **au lit!** bedtime!

literie *noun* F bedding.

litière *noun* F litter (*for an animal's bed*); **la litière pour chat** cat litter.

litre *noun* M litre; **un litre d'eau** a litre of water.

littéralement *adverb* literally.

littérature *noun* F literature; **la littérature française** French literature.

livraison *noun* F delivery; **'livraisons à toute heure'** 'we deliver any time'; **'livraisons à domicile'** 'we deliver'.

livre[1] *noun* M book; **un livre pour enfants** a children's book; **un livre de poche** a paperback.

livre[2] *noun* F **1** pound (*in money*); **une livre sterling** a pound sterling; **2** pound (*in France = 500 grammes*); **une livre de tomates** a pound of tomatoes.

livrer *verb* [1] to deliver, to hand over.

livret *noun* M booklet.

livret de famille M *noun* family record book (*with details of births, marriages, and deaths*).

livret scolaire *noun* M school report book.

local (*plural* **locaux**) *noun* M place (*usually a building*); **locaux commerciaux** business premises; **dans les locaux du lycée** on school premises.
adjective local; **un journal local** a local paper; **dix heures heure locale** ten a.m. local time.

locataire *noun* M & F tenant.

location *noun* F **1** renting; **un appartement de location** a rented flat; **'locations'** 'to rent'; **2** hire, rental; **location de voitures** car hire; **location de vidéos** video rental; **3** reservation, booking (*of theatre seats*).

locomotive *noun* F engine, locomotive.

loge *noun* F **1** lodge (*for the caretaker in a block of flats*); **2** (*in a theatre*) dressing-room (*for an actor*); box (*for a spectator*).

logement *noun* M
1 accommodation; **il a trouvé un logement tout près** he's found somewhere to live just nearby;
2 housing; **la crise du logement** the housing crisis.

loger *verb* [52] **1** to put up; **peux-tu me loger ce soir?** can you put me up tonight?; **2** to stay; **pour l'instant elle loge chez mes parents** for the moment she's staying with my parents.

logiciel *noun* M **1** software; **2** program (*for a computer*); **un logiciel de jeux** a games program.

logique *noun* F logic.
adjective logical.

loi *noun* F law.

loin *adverb* **1** (*in distance*) a long way, far off; **c'est loin** it's a long way; **c'est trop loin** it's too far; **c'est loin d'ici** it's a long way from here; **le cinéma est plus loin** the cinema is further on; **2** (*in time*) far off; **les vacances sont loin** the holidays are a long way off; **il n'est pas loin de midi** it's almost twelve; **3** **de loin** from a long way off; **on voit leur maison de loin** you can see their house from a long way off; **4** **de loin** by far; **c'est de loin le plus cher** it's by far the most expensive; **5** **au loin** in the distance.

lointain *adjective* distant.

loisirs *plural noun* M **1** spare time; **je dessine pendant mes loisirs** I draw in my spare time; **2** spare-time activities.

Londonien, Londonienne *noun* M, F Londoner.

Londres *noun* London; **à Londres** in (or to) London; **les rues de Londres** the London streets.

long *noun* M **1** **une corde de cinq mètres de long** a rope five metres long; **2** **le long de** all along; **le long de la route** all along the road; **3** **tout le long du film** all the way through the film.
adjective (F **longue**) long; **une longue vie** a long life; **un long silence** a long silence; **un long voyage** a long journey; **la rue la plus longue de Paris** the longest street in Paris; **une chemise à manches longues** a long-sleeved shirt; **la pièce est longue de quatre mètres, la pièce fait quatre mètres de long** the room is four metres long;
★ **marcher de long en large** to walk up and down; ★ **à la longue** in the long run.

longtemps *adverb* (for) a long time; **elle est restée longtemps** she stayed for a long time; **longtemps après** a long time after; **elle est là depuis longtemps** she's been here for a long time; **j'y suis allé, mais il y a longtemps** I've been there, but a long time ago; **ça fait longtemps qu'on ne s'est pas vu!** it's ages since we've seen each other!; **je n'en ai pas pour longtemps** I won't be long.

longuement *adverb* for a long time.

longueur *noun* F **1** length; **de quelle longueur est le couloir?** how long is the corridor?; **2** **avoir des longueurs** to drag; **le film est intéressant mais il a des longueurs** it's an interesting film but it drags in places.

longueur d'onde *noun* F wavelength.

lorsque, lorsqu' (*before a vowel or silent 'h'*) *conjunction* when; **lorsque j'étais petite** when I was a little girl.

lot *noun* M **1** batch; **un lot de trois boîtes** a pack of three cans; **2** prize (*in a lottery*); **elle a gagné le gros lot** she won the jackpot.

loterie *noun* F **1** lottery; **2** raffle.

lotion *noun* F lotion.

lotissement *noun* M housing estate.

loto *noun* M lottery.

lotte *noun* F monkfish.

louche[1] *noun* F ladle.

louche[2] *adjective* fishy; **il y a un type louche à la porte** there's a fishy-looking guy at the door.

louer *verb* [1] **1** to let (*a house or flat*); **pendant mon absence j'ai loué mon appartement** while I was away I let my flat; **'à louer'** 'to let'; **2** to rent; **nous avons loué un appartement à Lille** we've rented a flat in Lille; **3** to hire; **nous avons loué une voiture** we hired a car; **4** to praise.

loup *noun* M wolf; ★ **j'ai une faim de loup** I'm absolutely starving

(*literally: I'm as hungry as a wolf*);
★ **quand on parle du loup (on en voit la queue)** speak of the devil (*literally: when you speak of the wolf (you see its tail)*).

loupe *noun* F magnifying glass.

louper (*informal*) *verb* [1] **1** to miss (*a train*); **on a loupé le train de dix heures** we missed the ten o'clock train; **2** to fail; **elle a loupé son permis** she failed her driving test.

loup-garou *noun* M werewolf.

lourd *adjective* **1** heavy; **ta valise est très lourde** your case is very heavy; **le repas était un peu lourd** the meal was a bit heavy; **2 une lourde erreur** a serious mistake.

loutre *noun* F otter.

loyal (M *plural* **loyaux**) *adjective* faithful.

loyauté *noun* F loyalty.

loyer *noun* M rent; **payer le loyer** to pay the rent.

lu *verb* SEE **lire**.

lucarne *noun* F skylight.

luge *noun* F sledge.

lugubre *adjective* gloomy.

lui *pronoun* **1** him; **c'est lui** it's him; **Hélène travaille avec lui** Hélène works with him; **est-ce qu'il a aimé le bouquin que je lui ai prêté?** did he like the book I lent him?; **2** to him; **Pierre est en colère – qu'est-ce que tu lui as dit?** Pierre's angry – what did you say to him?; **3** to her; **Nadine est en colère – qu'est-ce que tu lui as dit?** Nadine's angry – what did you say to her?;

4 (*for emphasis*) **lui, il n'est jamais content!** he's never pleased!

lui-même *pronoun* **1** himself; **il l'a fait lui-même** he did it himself; **2** (*on telephone*) **'Monsieur Dubois?' – 'lui-même'** 'Monsieur Dubois?' – 'speaking'.

lumière *noun* F light.

lumineux (F **lumineuse**) *adjective* luminous; **un panneau lumineux** an electronic display board; **une enseigne lumineuse** a neon sign.

lunch *noun* M buffet (*lunch or supper*).

lundi *noun* M **1** Monday; **nous sommes lundi aujourd'hui** it's Monday today; **lundi prochain** next Monday; **lundi dernier** last Monday; **2** on Monday; **je l'ai vu lundi soir** I saw him on Monday evening; **3 le lundi** on Mondays; **fermé le lundi** closed on Mondays; **4 tous les lundis** every Monday.

lune *noun* F moon; ★ **il est dans la lune** he's got his head in the clouds; ★ **il m'a promis la lune** he promised me the earth.

lune de miel *noun* F honeymoon.

lunettes *plural noun* F glasses; **une paire de lunettes** a pair of glasses; **mets tes lunettes!** put on your glasses!; **je porte des lunettes pour lire** I wear glasses to read.

lunettes de natation *plural noun* F swimming goggles.

lunettes de soleil *plural noun* F sun-glasses.

lutte *noun* F fight, struggle; **la lutte contre la drogue** the fight against drugs.

lutter *verb* [1] to fight, to struggle; **ils luttaient pour la liberté et contre l'oppression** they were fighting for freedom and against oppression.

luxe *noun* M luxury; **une voiture de luxe** a luxury car.

luxueux (F **luxueuse**) *adjective* luxurious.

lycée *noun* M secondary school (*for ages 15–18*).

lycéen, lycéenne *noun* M, F secondary school student.

M m

M. SHORT FOR **Monsieur; M. Dupont** Mr Dupont.

ma *adjective* my; SEE **mon.**

macaronis *plural noun* M macaroni; **manger des macaronis** to have macaroni.

mâche *noun* F lamb's lettuce.

mâcher *verb* [1] to chew.

machin *noun* M (*informal*) whatsit, thingumajig; **tu n'as pas un machin pour ouvrir les enveloppes?** don't you have a whatsit for opening envelopes with?

machine *noun* F **1** machine; **2 taper à la machine** to type.

machine à coudre *noun* F sewing machine.

machine à écrire *noun* F typewriter.

machine à laver *noun* F washing machine.

machine à sous *noun* F fruit machine.

mâchoire *noun* F jaw.

mâchonner *verb* [1] to chew.

maçon *noun* M **1** builder; **2** bricklayer.

Madame (*plural* **Mesdames**) *noun* F **1 Madame Jones** Ms Jones, Mrs Jones; **2 Madame,...** Dear Madam,...; **3 bonsoir madame** good evening (*when greeting a person you do not know well in French, it is polite to add 'Madame', 'Monsieur', or 'Mademoiselle' to the greeting*).

Mademoiselle (*plural* **Mesdemoiselles**) *noun* F **1** Miss, Ms; **2 bonsoir mademoiselle** good evening; SEE ALSO **Madame.**

magasin *noun* M shop; **un grand magasin** a department store; **un magasin de vêtements** a clothes shop; **un magasin de sport** a sport shop; **faire les magasins** to go round the shops.

magazine *noun* M magazine.

maghrébin *adjective* North African.

Maghrébin, Maghrébine *noun* M, F North African.

magicien, magicienne *noun* M F magician.

magie *noun* F magic.

magique *adjective* **1** magic; **2** magical.

magistral (M *plural* **magistraux**) *adjective* **un cours magistral** a lecture (*at university*).

magnétique *adjective* magnetic.

magnétiser *verb* [1] **1** to magnetize; **2** to hypnotize.

magnétophone *noun* M tape recorder.

magnétoscope *noun* M video recorder.

magnifique *adjective* splendid.

magouille *noun* F (*informal*) fiddling.

magret de canard *noun* M duck breast.

mai *noun* M May; **en mai, au mois de mai** in May; **le premier mai** May Day.

maigre *adjective* thin, skinny; ★ **maigre comme un clou** as thin as a rake (*literally: as thin as a nail*).

maigrir *verb* [2] to lose weight; **il a beaucoup maigri** he's lost a lot of weight.

maille *noun* F stitch (*in knitting*).

maillot *noun* M **1** shirt, jersey (*in sports such as football*); **2 maillot (de corps)** vest.

maillot de bain *noun* M **1** swimsuit; **2** swimming trunks.

main *noun* F hand; **avoir quelque chose à la main** to have something in your hand; **serrer la main à quelqu'un** to shake hands with somebody; **se serrer la main** to shake hands; **nous nous sommes serré la main** we shook hands; **se donner la main** to hold hands; **haut les mains!** hands up!; **donner un coup de main à quelqu'un** to give somebody a hand; **tu veux un coup de main?** do you want a hand?; **fait à la main** handmade.

main-d'œuvre *noun* F labour.

maintenant *adverb* **1** now; **il est maintenant trop tard pour sortir** it's too late to go out now; **2** nowadays; **maintenant presque tout le monde a le téléphone** nowadays nearly everybody has a phone.

maintenir *verb* [81] **1** to maintain; **2** to support.

maire *noun* M mayor.

mairie *noun* F **1** town hall; **2** town council.

mais *conjunction* **1** but; **j'ai essayé de t'appeler mais tu n'étais pas là** I tried to phone you but you weren't there; **2 mais oui** yes of course; **mais non** of course not.

maïs *noun* M **1** maize; **2** sweetcorn; **3 des épis de maïs** corn on the cob.

maison *noun* F **1** house; **leur maison est petite mais très confortable** their house is small but very comfortable; **2** home; **rester à la maison** to stay at home; **rentrer à la maison** to go home.

maître, maîtresse *noun* M, F **1** master, mistress; **2** teacher.

maître-nageur *noun* M swimming instructor.

maîtresse *noun* SEE **maître**.

maîtrise noun F **1** mastery;
2 command; **la maîtrise de soi** self-control; **3** master's degree.

maîtriser verb [1] **1** to control;
2 to master.

majestueux (F **majestueuse**)
adjective majestic.

majeur adjective **1** major; **2 être
majeur** to be over 18.

majorité noun F majority.

majuscule noun F capital (letter);
en majuscules in block capitals; **un
R majuscule** a capital R.

mal (plural **maux**) noun M **1** pain,
ache; **faire mal** to hurt; **se faire mal**
to hurt yourself; **avoir mal à la
gorge** to have a sore throat; **j'ai mal
au dos** my back hurts; **ça fait mal** it
hurts; **2 faire mal à quelqu'un** to
hurt somebody; **aïe! tu me fais mal!**
ouch! you're hurting me!; **3 avoir du
mal à faire** to have difficulty in
doing; **j'ai du mal à comprendre ce
qu'il dit** I have difficulty in
understanding what he says; **se
donner du mal à faire** to go to a lot
of trouble to do; **elle s'est donné
beaucoup de mal pour contacter
tout le monde** she went to a lot of
trouble to contact everybody;
4 evil.
adjective **1 pas mal** not bad;
2 être mal to be uncomfortable.
adverb **1** badly; **écrire mal** to write
badly; **2 je t'entends mal** I can't
hear you very well; **3 j'ai mal
compris** I misunderstood; **4 être
mal à l'aise** to feel uncomfortable.

malade noun M & F patient.
adjective ill, sick; **tomber malade** t
fall ill.

maladie noun F **1** illness;
2 disease.

maladresse noun F
1 clumsiness; **2** blunder.

maladroit adjective clumsy.

malaise noun M **1 avoir un
malaise** to feel faint, to pass out;
2 créer un malaise to make peopl
feel uncomfortable; **ça a créé un
malaise** it made everybody feel
uncomfortable.

malaxer verb [1] **1** to knead; **2** to
cream.

malchance noun F bad luck.

mal de mer noun M **avoir le mal
de mer** to be seasick.

mal du pays noun M **avoir le ma
du pays** to be homesick.

mâle noun M,
adjective male.

malédiction noun F curse.

malencontreux (F
malencontreuse) adjective
unfortunate.

malentendu noun M
misunderstanding.

malfaiteur noun M criminal.

mal famé adjective **un quartier m
famé** a rough area.

malgré preposition **1** in spite of;
malgré le froid in spite of the cold
2 malgré tout all the same; **mais
malgré tout nous avons décidé d'**

aller but we decided to go all the same.

alheur *noun* M misfortune; **porter malheur** to bring bad luck.

alheureusement *adverb* unfortunately; **Vincent était déjà parti, malheureusement** unfortunately, Vincent had already eft.

alheureux, malheureuse *noun* M, F poor thing; **la malheureuse!** poor woman! *adjective* **1** unhappy; **avoir l'air malheureux** to look unhappy; **rendre quelqu'un malheureux** to make somebody unhappy; **2** unfortunate; **un choix malheureux** an unfortunate choice.

alhonnête *adjective* dishonest.

alice *noun* F mischief.

alicieux (F **malicieuse**) *adjective* mischievous.

alin (F **maligne**) *adjective* **1** clever; **ce n'était pas très malin ça** that wasn't very clever; **elle se croit maligne** she thinks she's clever; **2** malignant (*tumour*).

alle *noun* F trunk.

alodorant *adjective* smelly.

alpoli *adjective* rude.

alpropre *adjective* dirty.

alsain *adjective* unhealthy.

altraiter *verb* [1] to ill-treat; **les enfants maltraités** battered children.

alveillance *noun* F malice.

alveillant *adjective* malicious.

maman *noun* F mum, mummy.

mamie *noun* F granny, gran, nan.

mammifère *noun* M mammal.

manager *verb* [52] to manage.

manageur *noun* M manager.

manche[1] *noun* M handle (*of a tool*).

manche[2] *noun* F **1** sleeve; **une chemise à manches courtes** a short-sleeved shirt; **sans manches** sleeveless; **2** leg (*of a match*).

Manche *noun* F **la Manche** the Channel; **le tunnel sous la Manche** the Channel Tunnel.

mandarine *noun* F mandarin orange.

mandat *noun* M money order.

manège *noun* M **1** merry-go-round; **2** riding school.

manette *noun* F lever.

mangeable *adjective* edible.

manger *noun* M food. *verb* [52] to eat; **qu'est-ce qu'on va manger?** what shall we have to eat?; **manger au restaurant** to go out for a meal; **j'ai déjà mangé** I've already eaten; **j'ai assez mangé** I'm full, I've had enough; **donner à manger à** to feed; ★ **manger ses mots** to mumble (*literally: to eat your words*).

mangue *noun* F mango.

maniaque *noun* M & F fusspot. *adjective* extremely fussy.

manie *noun* F **1** odd habit; **2** mania.

manier *verb* [1] to handle.

manière *noun* F **1** way; **une manière plus facile** an easier way; **on ne peut pas le faire d'une manière plus facile?** isn't there an easier way of doing it?; **de cette manière** like this, like that; **d'une autre manière** in another way; **d'une manière ou d'une autre** one way or another; **d'une certaine manière** in a way; **2 de toute manière** in any case; **3 de manière à faire** so as to do; **de manière à éviter de dépenser de l'argent** so as to avoid spending money; **4 manières** manners; **ne fais pas de manières!** don't make a fuss!

manifestant, manifestante *noun* M, F demonstrator.

manifestation *noun* F demonstration; **une manifestation contre le racisme** a demonstration against racism.

manifester *verb* [1] **1** to demonstrate, to take part in a demonstration; **2 manifester quelque chose** to express something.

manipuler *verb* [1] **1** to handle; **2** to manipulate.

manivelle *noun* F handle.

mannequin *noun* M **1** fashion model; **2** dummy (*either in a shop window or as used by a dressmaker*).

manoir *noun* M manor house.

manque *noun* M **manque de** lack of, shortage of; **leur manque d'imagination** their lack of imagination; **être en manque**

d'affection to be in need of affection.

manqué *adjective* **1** failed; **un acteur manqué** a failed actor; **2** missed; **une occasion manquée** missed opportunity.

manquer *verb* [1] **1 manquer quelque chose** to miss something; **a manqué son train** he missed his train; **2 manquer un examen** to fail an exam; **3 manquer à quelqu'un** to be missed by somebody; **tu me manques** I miss you; **Londres leur manque** they miss London; **4 il manque quelque chose** something's missing; **il manque trois fourchettes** there are three forks missing, we're three forks short; **5 manquer de** to lack; **nous ne manquons pas de verres** there's no shortage of glasses; **6 manquer de faire** to fail to do; **il a manqué de fermer la porte à clé** he failed to lock the door.

mansarde *noun* F attic room.

manteau (*plural* **manteaux**) *noun* M coat.

manuel *noun* M **1** manual; **2** textbook; **un manuel scolaire** a school book. *adjective* (F **manuelle**) manual.

manufacture *noun* F **1** factory; **2** manufacture.

manuscrit *noun* M manuscript. *adjective* handwritten; **un petit mot manuscrit** a handwritten note.

maquereau (*plural* **maquereaux**) *noun* M mackerel.

maquette *noun* F scale model.

maquillage *noun* M make-up.

maquiller *verb* [1] **se maquiller** to put on your make-up.

marais *noun* M marsh.

marathon *noun* M marathon.

marbre *noun* M marble; **une cheminée en marbre** a marble fireplace.

marc de café *noun* M coffee grounds.

marchand, marchande *noun* M, F **1** shopkeeper; **la marchande de fromage** the woman in the cheese shop; **2** stallholder (*on a market*).

marchand de journaux *noun* M newsagent.

marchander *verb* [1] to haggle (over).

marchandise *noun* F goods.

marche *noun* F **1** walking; **faire de la marche** to go walking; **2** march; **3** step; **les marches d'escalier** the stairs; **attention à la marche** mind the step; **4** **mettre en marche** to start up (*a machine*); **être en état de marche** to be in working order.

marche arrière *noun* F reverse; **faire marche arrière** to reverse.

marché *noun* M **1** market; **aller au marché** to go to market; **le marché aux fleurs** the flower market; **un marché aux puces** a flea market; **le marché de l'emploi** the job market; **2** deal.

marchepied *noun* M step (*on a train*).

marcher *verb* [1] **1** to walk; **on va marcher jusqu'à la gare** we'll walk as far as the station; **2** **marcher dans quelque chose** to tread in something; **marcher sur quelque chose** to tread on something; **3** to march; **4** to work; **ça a marché** it worked; **la machine à laver ne marche pas** the washing machine doesn't work; **les trains ne marchent pas aujourd'hui** the trains are not running today; **5** **et ton boulot, ça marche?** (*informal*) and is your job going all right?; ★ **faire marcher quelqu'un** to pull somebody's leg.

marcheur, marcheuse *noun* M, F walker.

mardi *noun* M **1** Tuesday; **nous sommes mardi aujourd'hui** it's Tuesday today; **mardi prochain** next Tuesday; **mardi dernier** last Tuesday; **2** on Tuesday; **je t'appellerai mardi soir** I'll ring you on Tuesday evening; **3** **le mardi** on Tuesdays; **c'est fermé le mardi** it's closed on Tuesdays; **4** **tous les mardis** every Tuesday.

Mardi gras *noun* M Shrove Tuesday.

mare *noun* F pond.

marée *noun* F tide; **la marée monte** the tide's coming in; **la marée descend** the tide's going out.

margarine *noun* F margarine.

marge *noun* F **1** margin; **2** **en marge de** on the fringe of.

marguerite *noun* F **1** marguerite; **2** oxeye daisy.

mari *noun* M husband; **le mari de Claire** Claire's husband.

mariage *noun* M **1** marriage;
2 wedding; **être invité à un
mariage** to be invited to a wedding.

Marianne *noun* F Marianne (*a
woman figure representing the
French Republic in statues and
paintings*).

marié, mariée *noun* M, F
bridegroom, bride; **les jeunes
mariés** the newlyweds.
adjective married.

marier *verb* [1] **1 se marier** to get
married; **ils se sont mariés à
Londres** they got married in
London; **elle s'est mariée avec
Frank** she married Frank; **2 le
prêtre qui les a mariés** the priest
who married them.

marin *noun* M sailor.
adjective sea.

marine *adjective* **bleu marine** navy
blue.

mariner *verb* [1] to marinate.

marionnette *noun* F puppet.

marjolaine *noun* F marjoram.

marketing *noun* M marketing.

marmelade *noun* F **marmelade
d'oranges amères** orange
marmalade.

marmite *noun* F cooking pot.

marmonner *verb* [1] to mutter, to
mumble.

Maroc *noun* M Morocco.

marocain *adjective* Moroccan.

maroquinerie *noun* F **1** leather
shop; **2** leather goods.

marquant *adjective* outstanding.

marque *noun* F **1** brand; **une
marque de nourriture pour chats** a
brand of cat food; **2** make; **c'est une
marque de jean bien connue** it's a
well-known make of jeans; **3** mark
4 point.

marque déposée *noun* F
registered trademark.

marquer *verb* [1] **1** to mark; **2** to
write down; **j'ai marqué ton nom**
I've written down your name;
3 marquer un but to score a goal.

marqueur *noun* M marker pen.

marraine *noun* F godmother.

marrant *adjective* (*informal*) funny

marre *adverb* (*informal*) **j'en ai
marre** I'm fed up; **j'en ai marrre
d'écrire** I'm fed up with writing.

marrer *verb* [1] **1 se marrer** to have
a great time; **2 se marrer** to have a
good laugh.

marron *noun* M **1** (sweet)
chestnut; **2** (horse) chestnut.
adjective brown; **des chaussures
marron** brown shoes; **marron clair**
light brown; **marron foncé** dark
brown.

marronnier *noun* M chestnut tree

mars *noun* M March; **en mars, au
mois de mars** in March.

Marseillaise *noun* F **la
Marseillaise** the Marseillaise (*the
French national anthem*).

Marseille *noun* Marseilles.

marteau *noun* M **1** hammer;
2 doorknocker.

arteau piqueur *noun* M pneumatic drill.

arteler *verb* [45] to hammer.

artinet *noun* M swift.

artin-pêcheur *noun* M kingfisher.

artyrisé *adjective* **un enfant martyrisé** a battered child.

ascotte *noun* F mascot.

asculin *noun* M masculine (*in French and other grammars*); **au masculin** in the masculine. *adjective* **1** male; **le sexe masculin** the male sex; **2** men's; **les vêtements masculins** men's clothing; **3** masculine.

asque *noun* M mask.

asquer *verb* [1] to hide.

assacre *noun* M massacre.

assacrer *verb* [1] to massacre.

assage *noun* M massage; **faire un massage à quelqu'un** to give somebody a massage.

asse *noun* F **1** mass; **2 une masse de** (*informal*) masses of; **j'ai une masse de boulot à faire avant lundi** I've got masses of work to do for Monday.

asser *verb* [1] **1** to massage; **2 se masser** to assemble.

assif (F **massive**) *adjective* **1** solid; **une table en pin massif** a solid pine table; **2** massive.

ass media *plural noun* M **les mass media** the mass media.

astic *noun* M **1** putty; **2** filler.

mastiquer *verb* [1] **1** to chew; **2** to putty (*a window*); **3** to fill (*a crack*).

mat *adjective* matt.

mât *noun* M **1** mast; **2** pole.

match *noun* M match; **un match de foot** a football match; **faire match nul** to draw.

matelas *noun* M mattress.

matelassé *adjective* quilted.

matelot *noun* M sailor.

matériaux *plural noun* M materials; **les matériaux de construction** building materials.

matériel *noun* M equipment; **matériel de sport** sports equipment.

maternel (F **maternelle**) *adjective* **1** motherly; **2** maternal; **ma tante maternelle** my aunt on my mother's side of the family.

maternelle *noun* F (state) nursery school (*for ages 2–6*); **aller en maternelle** to go to nursery school.

maternité *noun* F **1** motherhood; **2** pregnancy; **être en congé de maternité** to be on maternity leave; **3** maternity unit.

mathématiques *plural noun* F mathematics.

maths *plural noun* F maths.

matière *noun* F subject; **la matière que j'aime le mieux c'est l'histoire** the subject I like best is history.

matières grasses *plural noun* F fat.

matin *noun* M morning; **à quelle heure est-ce que tu te lèves le**

matin? what time do you get up in the morning?; **à six heures du matin** at six o'clock in the morning; **du matin au soir** from morning till night; **de bon matin** early in the morning.

matinal (M *plural* **matinaux**) *adjective* **1** morning; **2** **être matinal** to be an early riser.

matinée *noun* F **1** morning; **au cours de la matinée** during the morning; **2** matinée.

matou *noun* M tomcat.

matraque *noun* F truncheon, club.

matrimonial *adjective* **une agence matrimoniale** a marriage bureau.

maturité *noun* F maturity.

maudire *verb* to curse.

maussade *adjective* **1** sullen; **2** dull, dreary (*weather*).

mauvais *adjective* **1** bad; **une mauvaise expérience** a bad experience; **ça sent mauvais ici** there's a nasty smell here; **ça a mauvais goût** it tastes horrible; **c'est du mauvais goût** it's bad taste; **2** wrong; **le mauvais numéro** the wrong number; **la mauvaise adresse** the wrong address; **3** **il fait mauvais** the weather's bad; **4** **elle a mauvaise mine** she doesn't look well.

mauvaise herbe *noun* F weed.

maux *plural noun* M **des maux de tête** headaches.

maximum *noun* M, *adjective* maximum; **au maximum** as much as possible; **au maximum** at the most; **faire le maximum** to do your utmost.

mayonnaise *noun* F mayonnaise.

mazout *noun* M fuel oil.

me, m' (*before a vowel or silent 'h'*) *pronoun* me; **1** **elle me déteste** she hates me; **il m'a vu** he saw me; **2** to me; **elle ne me parle jamais** she never speaks to me; **elle m'a donné son adresse** she gave me her address; **il me l'a donné** he gave it to me; **3** myself; **je me fais une salade** I'm making myself a salad; **me suis blessé** I hurt myself; **je me lève à sept heures** I get up at seven o'clock; **je me brosse les dents** I brush my teeth (*literally: I brush to myself the teeth*).

mec *noun* M (*informal*) guy.

mécanicien, mécanicienne *noun* M, F **1** mechanic; **2** train driver.

mécanique *noun* F **1** mechanics; **2** mechanism. *adjective* **1** mechanical; **2** clockwork.

mécanisme *noun* M mechanism.

méchamment *adverb* spitefully, nastily.

méchanceté *noun* F **1** nastiness; **2** spite.

méchant *adjective* **1** nasty; **elle a été vraiment méchante avec moi** she was really nasty to me; **2** spiteful; **3** vicious; **'chien méchant'** 'beware of the dog'.

mèche *noun* F **1** lock (*of hair*); **2** wick.

éconnaissable *adjective* unrecognizable.

écontent *adjective* dissatisfied.

écontentement *noun* M **1** annoyance; **2** displeasure.

édaille *noun* F medal.

édecin *noun* M doctor; **aller chez e médecin** to go to the doctor's.

édecine *noun* F medicine; **faire des études de médecine** to go to medical school.

édias *plural noun* M **les médias** the media.

édiathèque *noun* F multimedia library.

édical (M *plural* **médicaux**) *adjective* medical.

édicament *noun* M drug.

édiéval (M *plural* **médiévaux**) *adjective* medieval.

édiocre *adjective* second-rate, poor; **un travail médiocre** a second-rate piece of work.

éditation *noun* F meditation.

éditer *verb* [1] **1** to meditate; **2 méditer quelque chose** to mull something over.

éditerranée *noun* F **la Méditerranée** the Mediterranean.

éditerranéen (F **méditerranéenne**) *adjective* Mediterranean; **la cuisine mediterranéenne** Mediterranean cooking.

éduse *noun* F jellyfish.

méfait *noun* M **1** crime; **2 les méfaits de la pollution** the detrimental effects of pollution.

méfiance *noun* F suspicion.

méfiant *adjective* suspicious.

méfier *verb* [1] **se méfier de quelqu'un** not to trust somebody; **méfie-toi!** watch out!

mégère *noun* F shrew.

mégot *noun* M cigarette end.

meilleur *noun* M best; **c'est le meilleur** it's the best one; **le meilleur des deux** the better of the two. *adjective* better; **le climat est bien meilleur au sud** the climate's much better in the south; **meilleur que** better than; **ton écriture est meilleure que la mienne** your writing's better than mine; **c'est meilleur que l'autre** it's better than the other one.

mélange *noun* M mixture.

mélanger *verb* [52] **1** to mix; **2** to mix up; **j'ai mélangé les dates** I got the dates mixed up.

mélasse *noun* F black treacle.

mêlée *noun* F scrum.

mêler *verb* [1] **1 se mêler à** to mingle with; **2 se mêler de** to meddle in; ★ **mêle-toi de ce qui te regarde!** mind your own business!

mélodie *noun* F melody, tune.

mélomane *noun* M & F music lover.

melon *noun* M **1** melon; **2 un chapeau melon** a bowler hat.

membre *noun* M **1** member;
2 limb.

même *adjective* **1** same; **j'ai le
même anniversaire que toi** I have
the same birthday as you; **ils avaient
des chapeaux de la même couleur**
they had the same colour hats; **2 en
même temps** at the same time;
3 tout de même all the same.
adverb even; **il n'a même pas
demandé** he didn't even ask.

mémé *noun* (*informal*) F
1 granny; **2 une vieille mémé** an
old lady.

mémoire *noun* F memory.

mémoriser *verb* [1] to memorize.

menace *noun* F threat.

menacer *verb* [61] to threaten.

ménage *noun* M **1** housework;
faire le ménage to do the cleaning;
une femme de ménage a cleaning
lady; **2** household.

ménager¹ *verb* [52] **ménager
quelqu'un** to handle somebody
tactfully.

ménager² (F **ménagère**) *adjective*
household; **les appareils ménagers**
household appliances; **les travaux
ménagers** housework.

mendiant, mendiante *noun* M,
F beggar.

mendier *verb* [1] to beg.

mener *verb* [50] **1** to lead; **mener à**
to lead to; **le chemin qui mène à la
ferme** the track which leads to the
farm; **2 mener une société** to run
a company; **3 mener une
campagne** to conduct a campaign.

méningite *noun* F meningitis.

menottes *plural noun* F handcuff

mensonge *noun* M lie; **dire des
mensonges** to tell lies.

mensualité *noun* F monthly
payment.

mensuel (F **mensuelle**) *adjective*
monthly.

mental (M *plural* **mentaux**)
adjective mental.

mentalité *noun* F mentality.

menteur, menteuse *noun* M, F
liar.
adjective untruthful.

menthe *noun* F mint; **le sirop de
menthe** mint cordial.

mention *noun* F **1** mention;
2 grade (*in an exam or a degree*); **e**
a eu son bac avec mention bien s
got a grade B pass in her
baccalaureate.

mentionner *verb* [1] to mention.

mentir *verb* [53] to lie, to tell lies.

menton *noun* M chin.

menu¹ *noun* M menu; **qu'est-ce
qu'il y a au menu?** what's on the
menu?; **le menu du jour** today's
menu.

menu² *adjective* very small.

menuiserie *noun* F woodwork.

menuisier *noun* M joiner.

mépris *noun* M contempt.

mépriser *verb* [1] to despise.

mer *noun* F sea; **aller à la mer** to go to the seaside; **au bord de la mer** at the seaside.

mercerie *noun* F haberdashery.

merci[1] *exclamation* thank you, thanks; **merci beaucoup, merci bien** thank you very much; **merci de m'avoir rappelé** thank you for calling me back.

merci[2] *noun* F mercy.

mercredi *noun* M **1** Wednesday; **nous sommes mercredi aujourd'hui** it's Wednesday today; **mercredi prochain** next Wednesday; **mercredi dernier** last Wednesday; **je t'appellerai mercredi soir** I'll ring you on Wednesday evening; **3 le mercredi** on Wednesdays; **c'est fermé le mercredi** it's closed on Wednesdays; **tous les mercredis** every Wednesday.

mercure *noun* M mercury.

mer du Nord *noun* F North Sea.

mère *noun* F mother; **la mère de Sophie** Sophie's mother.

merguez *noun* F spicy lamb sausage.

méridional (M *plural* **méridionaux**) *adjective* southern.

meringue *noun* F meringue.

mérite *noun* F merit.

mériter *verb* [1] to deserve.

merle *noun* M blackbird.

merveille *noun* F **1** wonder; **ton gâteau est une vraie merveille** your cake's absolutely wonderful; **2 à merveille** wonderfully.

merveilleux (F **merveilleuse**) *adjective* marvellous.

mes *adjective* SEE **mon**.

Mesdames *noun* SEE **Madame**.

Mesdemoiselles *noun* SEE **Mademoiselle**.

mesquin *adjective* petty, mean.

message *noun* M message.

messager, messagère *noun* M, F messenger.

messe *noun* F mass; **aller à la messe** to go to mass.

Messieurs *noun* SEE **Monsieur**.

mesure *noun* F **1** measurement; **prendre les mesures de la pièce** to take the measurements of the room; **2 sur mesure** tailor-made; **3** measure; **prendre des mesures pour faire** to take measures to do; **le conseil municipal va prendre des mesures pour contrôler la pollution** the town council is going to take measures to control pollution; **4 être en mesure de faire** to be in a position to do; **nous ne sommes pas en mesure de vous aider** we are not in a position to help you.

mesurer *verb* [1] to measure.

met *verb* SEE **mettre**.

métal (*plural* **métaux**) *noun* M metal.

métallique *adjective* metallic.

métallisé *adjective* metallic; **bleu métallisé** metallic blue.

météo *noun* F weather forecast.

méthode *noun* F **1** method; **une méthode de faire** a method of doing; **2** manual, tutor.

métier *noun* M **1** job; **2** un métier à tisser a weaving loom.

mètre *noun* M **1** metre; **2** metre rule.

métrique *adjective* metric.

métro *noun* M underground; **une station de métro** an underground station.

mets *verb* SEE **mettre**.

metteur en scène *noun* M **1** director (*of a film*); **2** producer (*of a play*).

mettre *verb* [11] **1** to put; **où as-tu mis le sel?** where have you put the salt?; **2** to put on; **je vais mettre mon manteau** I'm going to put my coat on; **3** to wear; **mets ta jupe rose** wear your pink skirt; **4** to turn on (*radio, television, heating*); **mettre le réveil** to set the alarm clock; **5** mettre quelqu'un en colère to make somebody angry; **6** j'ai mis trois heures pour le faire it took me three hours to do it; **7** se mettre quelque part to stand (or sit) somewhere; **8** se mettre debout to stand up; **9** se mettre à faire to start to do; **elle s'est mise à chanter** she started to sing.

meuble *noun* M **1** des meubles furniture; **2** un meuble a piece of furniture.

meublé *adjective* furnished.

meule *noun* F **1** millstone; **2** une meule de foin a haystack.

meurtre *noun* M murder.

meurtrier, meurtrière *noun* M, F murderer.
adjective **1** deadly; **2** fatal.

Mexico *noun* Mexico City.

Mexique *noun* M Mexico; **aller au Mexique** to go to Mexico.

mi- *prefix* **1** half-; **mi-clos** half-shut; **2** mid-; **à la mi-février** in mid-February.

mi-bas *noun* M knee sock.

mi-chemin *noun* **à mi-chemin** halfway.

micro *noun* M microphone.

microbe *noun* M germ.

micro-ondes *noun* M microwave; **faire cuire quelque chose au micro-ondes** to cook something in the microwave.

micro-ordinateur *noun* M microcomputer.

microscope *noun* M microscope.

midi *noun* M **1** midday, noon; **il es midi vingt** it's twenty past twelve; **je viendrai vers midi** I'll come around twelve; **2** lunchtime; **je fais mes courses à midi** I do my shopping i my lunch hour.

Midi *noun* M **le Midi** the South of France.

miel *noun* M honey.

mien, mienne, miens, mienne *pronoun* **le mien, la mienne, les miens, les miennes** mine; **'à qui sont ces chaussures?'** – **'ce son les miennes'** 'whose shoes are these?' – 'they're mine'; **Puis-je**

t'emprunter ton vélo? Le mien est chez moi Can I borrow your bike? Mine's at home.

miette *noun* F crumb.

mieux *adjective,* *adverb* **1** better; **tu la connais mieux que moi** you know her better than I do; **je me sens mieux** I feel better; **mon père va mieux maintenant** my father's better now; **c'est mieux comme ça** it's better like that; **2 il vaut mieux que tu restes chez toi** it would be better if you stayed at home. **3** best; **c'est le rouge que j'aime le mieux** I like the red one best.
noun M **le mieux est de revenir** the best thing is to come back; **au mieux** at best, at least; **pour le mieux** for the best.

mignon (F **mignonne**) *adjective* sweet.

migraine *noun* F headache, migraine.

mijoter *verb* [1] to simmer.

milieu *noun* M **1** middle; **au milieu de** in the middle of; **2** background; **il vient d'un milieu pauvre** he comes from a poor background; **3** environment.

militaire *noun* M serviceman. *adjective* military; **le service militaire** military service.

mille *number* a thousand; **mille personnes** a thousand people; **deux mille personnes** two thousand people.

millefeuille *noun* M vanilla slice.

mille-pattes *noun* M centipede.

milliard *noun* M thousand million.

milliardaire *noun* M & F multimillionaire.

millier *noun* M thousand; **des milliers de francs** thousands of francs.

milligramme *noun* M milligramme.

millimètre *noun* M millimetre.

million *noun* M million; **deux millions de francs** two million francs.

millionnaire *noun* M & F millionaire.

mime *noun* M & F mime artist.

mimer *verb* [1] **1** to mime; **2** to mimic.

minable *adjective* (*informal*) **1** pathetic; **ses plaisanteries sont minables** her jokes are pathetic; **2** crummy; **un film minable** a crummy film.

mince *adjective* **1** thin; **une mince tranche de viande** a thin slice of meat; **2** slim; **3 mince alors!** (*informal*) oh bother!

minceur *noun* F **1** thinness; **2** slimness.

mine *noun* F **1 avoir bonne mine** to look well; **tu as mauvaise mine** you don't look well; **2** expression; **3** mine; **une mine de charbon** a coalmine; **4** pencil lead.

minéral (*plural* **minéraux**) *noun* M mineral.
adjective mineral; **eau minérale** mineral water.

minet, minette *noun* M, F
pussycat.

mineur[1] *noun* M miner.

mineur[2], **mineure** *noun* M, F
person under 18.
adjective **1** minor; **2** under 18.

minijupe *noun* F mini-skirt.

minimal (M *plural* **minimaux**)
adjective minimal.

minimiser *verb* [1] **1** to minimize;
2 to play down.

minimum *noun* M,
adjective minimum; **au minimum** at
the very least.

ministère *noun* M ministry.

ministre *noun* M minister.

Minitel™ *noun* M (*Minitel is
France Telecom's online data service;
subscribers have a small computer
linked to the telephone and can use it
to access a large number of services
including the telephone directories*).

minorité *noun* F minority.

minou *noun* M pussycat.

minuit *noun* M midnight; **à minuit**
at midnight.

minuscule *noun* F small letter (*as
opposed to a capital letter*).
adjective tiny.

minute *noun* F minute; **dans dix
minutes** in ten minutes; **dix
minutes plus tard** ten minutes later;
d'une minute à l'autre any minute
now.

minuterie *noun* F time-switch.

mirabelle *noun* F small yellow
plum.

miracle *noun* M miracle; **par
miracle** miraculously.
adjective wonder.

miraculeux (F **miraculeuse**)
adjective miraculous.

miroir *noun* M mirror; **au miroir i**
the mirror.

mis *verb* SEE **mettre**.

miser *verb* [1] to bet.

misérable *adjective* poor.

misère *noun* F destitution, extrem
poverty.

missionnaire *noun* M & F
missionary.

mistral *noun* M mistral (*a strong
cold north wind which blows down
the Rhône valley to the
Mediterranean*).

mite *noun* F clothes moth.

mi-temps[1] *noun* M part-time job
travailler à mi-temps to work part
time.

mi-temps[2] *noun* F half-time (*in a
match*).

miteux (F **miteuse**) *adjective* seedy
shabby.

mitraillette *noun* F submachine
gun.

mixer *verb* [1] to mix.

mixte *adjective* **1** mixed;
2 coeducational.

Mlle SHORT FOR **Mademoiselle**.

Mme SHORT FOR **Madame**.

mobile *noun* M **1** motive;
2 mobile.
adjective **1** mobile; **2** **feuilles**

mobiles loose sheets (*as opposed to a pad of paper*).

mobilier *noun* M furniture.

mobylette *noun* F moped.

mocassin *noun* M 1 loafer; 2 moccasin.

moche *adjective* (*informal*) 1 awful; 2 ugly.

mode¹ *noun* F fashion; **être à la mode** to be fashionable.

mode² *noun* M way, mode.

mode d'emploi *noun* M instructions for use.

mode de vie *noun* M way of life.

modèle *noun* M 1 model; 2 style; **ce modèle existe en plusieurs coloris** this style is available in several colours.

modéré *adjective* moderate.

moderne *adjective* modern.

moderniser *verb* [1] to modernize.

modernité *noun* F modernity.

modeste *adjective* 1 modest; 2 humble.

modestie *noun* F modesty.

modifier *verb* [1] to change.

modiste *noun* F milliner.

module *noun* M 1 module; 2 kitchen unit.

moelle *noun* F marrow (*of bone*).

moelleux (F **moelleuse**) *adjective* 1 soft; 2 mellow.

mœurs *plural noun* F 1 customs; 2 morals.

moi *pronoun* 1 me; **c'est pour moi** it's for me; **pas moi** not me; 2 **moi, je pense que...** I think that...; 3 **à moi** mine; **ce n'est pas à moi** it's not mine; **un ami à moi** a friend of mine.

moi-même *pronoun* myself; **je l'ai fait moi-même** I did it myself.

moindre *adjective* slightest; **le moindre problème** the slightest problem; **je n'ai pas la moindre idée** I haven't the slightest idea.

moine *noun* M monk.

moineau (*plural* **moineaux**) *noun* M sparrow.

moins *preposition* 1 minus; **sept moins deux égale cinq** seven minus two equals five; 2 **il est dix heures moins cinq** it's five to ten. *adverb* 1 less; **tu en as moins que moi** you've got less than me; **de moins en moins** less and less; **il est moins grand que son frère** he's not as tall as his brother; **c'est moins loin** it's not as far; **j'aime moins le bleu** I don't like the blue one as much; 2 **le moins** the least; **le moins difficile** the least difficult; **le moins gros** the smallest; 3 **moins de** less, fewer; **moins de beurre** less butter; **moins de voitures** fewer cars; 4 **au moins** at least; 5 **du moins** at least; 6 **à moins que** (+ *subjunctive*) unless; **à moins qu'elle soit malade** unless she's ill.

mois *noun* M month; **au mois de mai** in May; **le mois dernier** last month; **le mois prochain** next month.

moisi *noun* M mould. *adjective* mouldy.

moisir *verb* [2] to go mouldy.

moisson *noun* F harvest.

moite *adjective* **1** damp; **2** muggy.

moitié *noun* F **1** half; **la moitié d'une pomme** half an apple; **donne-moi la moitié** give me half; **la moitié du temps** half the time; **2 à moitié** half; **à moitié vide** half empty.

moitié-moitié *adverb* half-and-half; **partager moitié-moitié** to go halves.

molaire *noun* F molar, back tooth.

molle *adjective* SEE **mou**.

mollet *noun* M calf (*of the leg*). *adjective* **un œuf mollet** a soft-boiled egg.

molleton *noun* M flannel, flannelette.

môme *noun* M & F (*informal*) kid.

moment *noun* M moment; **un moment, s'il vous plaît** just a moment please; **en ce moment** at the moment; **par moments** at times; **pour le moment** for the moment; **au moment où** at the time when; **à ce moment-là** just at that moment, just then; **j'ai attendu un bon moment** I waited for a good while.

mon, ma, mes *adjective* my; **mon fils** my son; **ma fille** my daughter; **mes enfants** my children.

monarchie *noun* F monarchy.

monastère *noun* M monastery.

monde *noun* M **1** world; **2** people; **il y a beaucoup de monde** there are a lot of people; **peu de monde** not many people; **tout le monde** everybody.

mondial (M *plural* **mondiaux**) *adjective* **1** world; **la Seconde Guerre mondiale** the Second World War; **2** worldwide.

monétique *noun* F electronic banking.

moniteur[1] *noun* M monitor.

moniteur[2], **monitrice** *noun* M, F **1** instructor (*sports or driving*); **un moniteur de ski** a ski instructor; **2** camp leader.

monnaie *noun* F **1** currency; **2 une pièce de monnaie** a coin; **3** change; **je n'ai pas de monnaie** I don't have any change.

monopoliser *verb* [1] to monopolize.

monotone *adjective* monotonous.

Monsieur (*plural* **Messieurs**) *noun* M **1 Monsieur Lejay** Mr Lejay; **bonsoir monsieur** good evening (*when greeting somebody you do not know well in French it is polite to add 'Monsieur', 'Madame',* ‹ *'Mademoiselle' to the greeting*); **2** man; **un grand monsieur** a tall man; **les deux messieurs assis à la table** the two men sitting at the table.

monstre *noun* M monster. *adjective* huge; **un travail monstre** a huge amount of work.

monstrueux (F **monstrueuse**) *adjective* monstrous.

mont *noun* M mountain; **le mont Blanc** Mont Blanc.

montagne *noun* F **1** mountain; **la montagne** the mountains; **2 une montagne de** a mountain of.

montagneux (F **montagneuse**) *adjective* mountainous.

montant *noun* M sum. *adjective* rising.

monter *verb* [1] **1** to go up, to come up; **monter l'escalier** to go (or come) up the stairs; **monter la colline** to go up the hill; **monter se coucher** to go up to bed; **2 monter dans** to get on (*a bus, train, etc*); **3 monter quelque chose** to bring (or take) something up; **je vais monter tes valises** I'll take your cases up; **4** to assemble (*a kit*); **5** to rise; **les prix ont monté** prices have risen; **6** to increase; **7 monter à cheval** to ride a horse.

montgolfière *noun* F hot-air balloon.

montre *noun* F watch.

montrer *verb* [1] **1** to show; **montrer quelque chose à quelqu'un** to show somebody something; **montre-moi ton cadeau** show me your present; **2** to point out; **montrer quelque chose du doigt** to point to something.

monture *noun* F frames (*of glasses*).

monument *noun* M **1** monument; **un monument aux morts** a war memorial; **2** historic building.

moquer *verb* [1] **1 se moquer de** to make fun of; **tout le monde s'est moqué de moi** everybody made fun of me; **2 se moquer de** not to care about; **je m'en moque** I couldn't care less.

moquette *noun* F fitted carpet.

moqueur (F **moqueuse**) *adjective* mocking.

moral (*plural* **moraux**) *noun* M morale; **je n'ai pas le moral** I'm feeling really down. *adjective* **1** moral; **2** mental.

morale *noun* F **1** moral; **2** morality.

morceau (*plural* **morceaux**) *noun* M piece, bit; **un morceau de pain** a piece of bread; **un morceau de sucre** a sugar lump.

mordre *verb* [3] to bite.

mordu *adjective* **être mordu de quelque chose** (*informal*) to be mad about something.

morne *adjective* **1** gloomy; **2** dismal, dreary.

morsure *noun* F bite.

mort[1] *noun* F death; **trois mois avant sa mort** three months before he died.

mort[2], **morte** *noun* M, F dead man, dead woman. *adjective* dead.

mort-aux-rats *noun* F rat poison.

mortel (F **mortelle**) *adjective* **1** deadly; **2** fatal.

morue *noun* F **1** cod; **2** salt cod.

mosaïque *noun* F mosaic.

Moscou *noun* Moscow.

mosquée *noun* F mosque.

mot *noun* M **1** word; **mot à mot** word for word; **2 un petit mot** a note.

motard, motarde *noun* M, F (*informal*) motorcyclist.

mot de passe *noun* M password.

moteur *noun* M engine.

motif *noun* M **1** motive; **2** pattern.

motiver *verb* [1] to motivate.

moto *noun* F motorbike.

motocycliste *noun* M & F motorcyclist.

mots croisés *plural noun* M crossword.

mou, mol (*before a vowel*) (F **molle**) *adjective* **1** soft; **2** flabby.

mouche *noun* F fly.

moucher *verb* [1] **se moucher** to blow your nose.

moucheron *noun* M midge.

mouchoir *noun* M **1** handkerchief; **2** tissue.

moue *noun* F pout; **faire la moue** to pout.

mouette *noun* F seagull.

mouiller *verb* [1] **1** to wet; **2 se mouiller** to get wet.

moulant *adjective* tight-fitting.

moule[1] *noun* M mould.

moule[2] *noun* F mussel.

mouler *verb* [1] to mould.

moulin *noun* M mill.

moulin à vent *noun* M windmill.

moulu *adjective* ground; **le café moulu** ground coffee.

moulure *noun* F moulding.

mourir *verb* [54] to die; **elle est morte en février** she died in February; **je meurs de faim!** I'm starving!; **je meurs d'envie d'y aller** I'm dying to go there.

mousquetaire *noun* M musketeer.

moussant *adjective* foaming.

mousse *noun* F **1** foam; **mousse à raser** shaving foam; **2** lather; **3** froth; **4 mousse au chocolat** chocolate mousse; **5** moss.

mousser *verb* [1] to foam.

mousseux (F **mousseuse**) *adjective* **du vin mousseux** sparkling wine.

moustache *noun* F moustache.

moustique *noun* M mosquito.

moutarde *noun* F mustard.

mouton *noun* M **1** sheep; **2** mutton.

mouvement *noun* M **1** movement; **2** activity, bustle.

mouvementé *adjective* hectic, eventful; **j'ai eu une semaine mouvementée** I've had a hectic week.

moyen *noun* M **1** means; **un moyen de transport** a means of transport; **un moyen de faire** a means of doing; **je n'ai aucun moyen de le contacter** I have no means of contacting him; **2 les moyens** the

means, the wherewithal; **je n'ai pas les moyens de m'acheter un ordinateur** I can't afford to buy a computer; **3** way.
adjective (F **moyenne**) **1** medium; **2** medium-sized; **3** average.

moyenne *noun* F **1** average; **en moyenne** on average; **2 avoir la moyenne** to pass (*an exam*).

Moyen-Orient *noun* M Middle East.

muet (F **muette**) *adjective* **1** speechless, dumb; **2** silent.

muguet *noun* M lily of the valley.

mulet *noun* M mule.

multifonction *adjective* multipurpose.

multiple *adjective* **1** multiple; **2** various.

multiplication *noun* F **1** multiplication; **2 multiplication de** increase in the number of.

multiplier *verb* [1] **1** to multiply; **2** to increase.

municipal (M *plural* **municipaux**) *adjective* **1** local, town; **2** municipal.

municipalité *noun* F **1** town (or local) council; **2** municipality.

mur *noun* M wall.

mûr *adjective* **1** ripe; **2** mature.

mûre *noun* F blackberry.

mûrir *verb* [2] **1** to ripen; **2** to mature; **3** to develop.

murmure *noun* M murmur.

murmurer *verb* [1] to murmur.

musc *noun* M musk.

muscade *noun* F nutmeg; **une noix de muscade** a nutmeg.

muscle *noun* M muscle.

musclé *adjective* muscular.

musculation *noun* F bodybuilding.

museau (*plural* **museaux**) *noun* M muzzle, snout.

musée *noun* M museum.

musical (M *plural* **musicaux**) *adjective* musical.

musicien, musicienne *noun* M, F musician.

musique *noun* F music; **mettre de la musique** to put on some music.

musulman, musulmane *noun* M, F,
adjective Muslim.

mutuel (F **mutuelle**) *adjective* mutual.

myope *adjective* short-sighted;
★ **être myope comme une taupe** to be as blind as a bat (*literally: to be as short-sighted as a mole*).

myopie *noun* F short-sightedness.

myosotis *noun* M forget-me-not.

myrtille *noun* F bilberry.

mystère *noun* M mystery.

mystérieux (F **mystérieuse**) *adjective* mysterious.

mystifier *verb* [1] to fool.

mystique *adjective* mystical.

mythe *noun* M myth.

mythologie *noun* F mythology.

N n

n' *adverb* SEE **ne**.

nacre *noun* F mother-of-pearl.

nage *noun* F swimming.

nager *verb* [52] to swim.

nageur, nageuse *noun* M, F swimmer.

naïf (F **naïve**) *adjective* naïve.

nain, naine *noun* M, F, *adjective* dwarf.

naissance *noun* F birth; **date de naissance** date of birth.

naître *verb* [55] to be born; **elle est née en 1975** she was born in 1975.

nana *noun* F (*informal*) girl.

naphtaline *noun* F mothballs.

nappe *noun* F tablecloth.

narcisse *noun* M narcissus.

narine *noun* F nostril.

natal *adjective* native; **mon pays natal** my native country.

natalité *noun* F **le taux de natalité** the birthrate.

natation *noun* F swimming; **faire de la natation** to go swimming.

natif (F **native**) *adjective* native.

nation *noun* F nation.

national (M *plural* **nationaux**) *adjective* national.

nationaliser *verb* [1] to nationalize.

nationalité *noun* F nationality.

natte *noun* F **1** plait; **2** mat.

nature *noun* F nature. *adjective* **yaourt nature** plain yoghurt; **un thé nature** a cup of tea without milk or sugar.

naturel *noun* M **1** nature; **2 au naturel** plain. *adjective* (F **naturelle**) natural.

naturellement *adverb* of course.

nausée *noun* F nausea; **avoir la nausée** to feel sick.

nautique *adjective* water; **faire du ski nautique** to go water-skiing.

navet *noun* M turnip.

navette *noun* F shuttle; **j'ai pris la navette de l'aéroport** I took the shuttle from the airport; **faire la navette** to travel back and forth.

naviguer *verb* [1] to sail.

navire *noun* M ship.

navré *adjective* sorry; **je suis vraiment navré** I'm terribly sorry.

ne, n' (*before a vowel or silent 'h'*) *adverb* **1 ne + pas** not; **je n'aime pas le lait** I don't like milk; **2 ne + jamais** never; **je ne vais jamais à Londres** I never go to London; **3 ne + que** only; **je n'ai que dix francs**

only have ten francs; **4 ne + plus** no longer; **elle n'habite plus à Londres** she no longer lives in London; **5 ne + rien** nothing; **il ne mange rien** he eats nothing; **rien ne t'empêche d'y aller** there's nothing to stop you going; **6 ne + personne** nobody; **il n'y a personne** there's nobody; **personne n'a compris** nobody understood.

né, née verb SEE **naître**.

néanmoins adverb nevertheless.

nécessaire noun M **faire le nécessaire** to do the necessary. adjective necessary; **il est nécessaire de faire** it is necessary to do; **est-ce qu'il est nécessaire de réserver?** is it necessary to book?

nécessairement adverb necessarily.

nécessité noun F necessity.

nécessiter verb [1] to require.

néerlandais noun M, adjective Dutch.

nef noun F nave (of a church).

négatif noun M, adjective (F **négative**) negative.

négligé adjective scruffy.

négligent adjective careless.

négliger verb [52] **1** to neglect; **2 il a négligé de le faire** he didn't bother to do it.

négociant noun M merchant.

négocier verb [1] to negotiate.

neige noun F snow; **un bonhomme de neige** a snowman.

neiger verb [52] to snow; **il neige** it's snowing.

nénuphar noun M waterlily.

néon noun M neon.

néo-zélandais adjective New Zealand.

Néo-Zélandais, Néo-Zélandaise noun M, F New Zealander.

nerf noun M nerve.

nerveux (F **nerveuse**) adjective nervous.

n'est-ce pas? adverb **il fait froid ce soir, n'est-ce pas?** it's cold this evening, isn't it?; **il habite à Paris, n'est-ce pas?** he lives in Paris, doesn't he?; **tu as déjà mangé, n'est-ce pas?** you've already eaten, haven't you?

net (F **nette**) adjective **1** clear; **c'est très net** it's quite clear; **2** distinct; **une nette différence** a distinct difference; **une nette amélioration** a distinct improvement. adverb **1 s'arrêter net** to stop dead; **2 refuser net** to refuse flatly.

nettement adverb far; **nettement meilleur** much better.

nettoyage noun M cleaning; **le nettoyage à sec** dry cleaning.

nettoyer verb [39] to clean.

neuf[1] number nine; **il est neuf heures du matin** it's nine o'clock in the morning; **Julie a neuf ans** Julie's nine; **le neuf juillet** the ninth of July.

neuf[2] (F **neuve**) adjective new; **une voiture toute neuve** a brand new car.

neutre *adjective* neutral.

neuvième *noun* M, **au neuvième** on the ninth floor; *adjective* ninth.

neveu (*plural* **neveux**) *noun* M nephew.

nez *noun* M nose.

ni *conjunction* **ni…ni** neither…nor; **ni lui ni son frère** neither he nor his brother; **il n'y a ni pain ni lait** there's neither bread nor milk; **ni Frank ni Paul ne le sait** neither Frank nor Paul knows; **ni moi non plus** me neither.

niche *noun* F **1** kennel; **2** niche.

nid *noun* M nest.

nièce *noun* F niece.

nier *verb* [1] to deny.

n'importe *adverb* **1** either, it doesn't matter; **'tu veux une aile ou une cuisse?' – 'n'importe'** 'do you want a wing or a leg?' – 'either, it doesn't matter'; **2 n'importe qui** anybody; **n'importe qui peut le faire** anybody can do it; **3 n'importe quoi** anything; **je ferai n'importe quoi pour t'aider** I'll do absolutely anything to help you; **elle a fait n'importe quoi** she's made a real mess of it; **tu dis n'importe quoi** you're talking complete rubbish; **4 n'importe quand** any time; **tu peux m'appeler n'importe quand** you can ring me any time; **5 n'importe comment** any old how; **tu peux jeter tous ces papiers dans un tiroir n'importe comment** you can throw all these papers into a drawer any old how; **6 n'importe où** anywhere; **pose tes valises**

n'importe où put your cases down anywhere you like; **je ne peux pas habiter n'importe où** I can't live just anywhere.

niveau (*plural* **niveaux**) *noun* M level; **au même niveau** at the same level.

niveau de vie *noun* M standard of living.

noble *adjective* noble.

noces *plural noun* F wedding.

nocif (F **nocive**) *adjective* harmful.

nocturne *noun* F late-night opening. *adjective* nocturnal.

Noël *noun* M Christmas; **Joyeux Noël** Merry Christmas; **un cadeau de Noël** a Christmas present; **le sapin de Noël** the Christmas tree.

nœud *noun* M knot; **faire un nœud** to tie a knot.

noir *noun* M **1** black; **2 le noir** the dark. *adjective* **1** black; **2** dark; **il fait noir** it's dark.

Noir, Noire *noun* M, F black man, black woman; **les Noirs** black people.

noirceur *noun* F blackness.

noircir *verb* [2] to blacken.

noisette *noun* F hazelnut.

noix *noun* F **1** walnut; **2 une noix de beurre** a knob of butter.

noix de cajou *noun* F cashew nut

noix de coco *noun* F coconut.

nom *noun* M **1** name; **nom de famille** surname; **nom de jeune fille** maiden name; **2** noun.

nombre *noun* M number; **bon nombre de** a good many.

nombreux (F **nombreuse**) *adjective* many; **de nombreuses personnes** many people; **ils étaient nombreux** there were a lot of them; **ils étaient peu nombreux** there weren't many of them; **une famille nombreuse** a big family.

nombril *noun* M navel.

nommer *verb* [1] **1** to appoint; **2** to name.

non *adverb* **1** no; **elle a dit non** she said no; **2 non seulement** not only; **non loin de** not far from; **moi non plus** me neither.

non- *combining form* **un non-fumeur** a nonsmoker.

nord *noun* M north; **le nord de l'Espagne** northern Spain; **le vent du nord** the north wind. *adjective* north, northern; **le côté nord** the north side.

nord-est *noun* M north-east.

nord-ouest *noun* M north-west.

normal (M *plural* **normaux**) *adjective* **1** normal; **2 c'est normal** it's natural; **3 ce n'est pas normal** it's not right.

normalement *adverb* **1** normally; **2** according to plan; **normalement, elle doit être à Rome actuellement** if things have gone according to plan, she should be in Rome at the moment.

normand *adjective* Norman; **la côte normande** the Normandy coast.

Normandie *noun* F Normandy.

norme *noun* F **1** norm; **2** standard; **selon les normes européennes** according to European standards.

Norvège *noun* F Norway.

norvégien (F **norvégienne**) *adjective* Norwegian.

nos *adjective* SEE **notre**.

notaire *noun* M notary public.

notamment *adverb* in particular.

note *noun* F **1** bill; **la note, s'il vous plaît** can I have the bill please; **2** mark; **j'ai eu une bonne note en allemand** I got a good mark in German; **3 prendre des notes** to take notes.

noter *verb* [1] **1** to write down; **2** to notice.

notice *noun* F instructions.

notion *noun* F **1** idea; **2 des notions** basic knowledge; **j'ai des notions d'espagnol** I have a basic knowledge of Spanish.

notre (*plural* **nos**) *adjective* our; **notre fille** our daughter; **nos enfants** our children.

nôtre *pronoun* **le nôtre, la nôtre, les nôtres** ours.

nouer *verb* [1] to tie, to knot.

nougat *noun* M nougat.

nouilles *plural noun* F noodles, pasta.

nounours *noun* M (*baby talk*) teddy bear.

nourrice *noun* F childminder.

nourrir *verb* [2] to feed.

nourrissant *adjective* nourishing.

nourrisson *noun* M infant.

nourriture *noun* F food.

nous *pronoun* **1** we; **nous apprenons le français** we are learning French; **2** us; **viens avec nous** come with us; **elle nous aide** she helps us; **elle nous a aidés** she helped us; **3** to us; **elle ne nous a pas parlé** she didn't speak to us; **elle nous a donné son adresse** she gave us her address; **4** ourselves **nous nous ferons une salade** we'll make ourselves a salad; **5** (*reflexive*) **nous nous levons à sept heures** we get up at seven o'clock.

nous-mêmes *pronoun* ourselves.

nouveau, nouvel (*before a vowel or silent 'h'*) (F **nouvelle**) (M *plural* **nouveaux**) *adjective* **1** new; **viens voir mon nouvel appartement** come and see my new flat; **2 à nouveau, de nouveau** again.

nouveauté *noun* F **1** novelty; **2** new release.

Nouvel An *noun* M New Year.

nouvelle *adjective* SEE **nouveau**. *noun* F **1 une nouvelle** news; **j'ai une bonne nouvelle!** I've got good news!; **2** short story; **nous étudions une nouvelle de Camus** we're doing a Camus short story; **3 des nouvelles** news; **nous n'avons pas de nouvelles pour l'instant** we have no news for the moment; **as-tu des nouvelles de lui?** have you heard from him?

Nouvelle-Zélande *noun* F New Zealand.

novembre *noun* M November; **en novembre, au mois de novembre** in November.

noyau (*plural* **noyaux**) *noun* M **1** stone (*in fruit*); **2** nucleus.

noyer[1] *verb* [39] **1** to drown; **2 se noyer** to drown, to drown oneself.

noyer[2] *noun* M **1** walnut tree; **2** walnut; **une table en noyer** a walnut table.

nu *adjective* **1** naked; **2** bare.

nuage *noun* M cloud.

nuageux (F **nuageuse**) *adjective* cloudy.

nuance *noun* F **1** shade (*of a colour*); **2** nuance.

nucléaire *adjective* nuclear; **l'énergie nucléaire** nuclear power.

nuisible *adjective* harmful.

nuit *noun* F **1** night; **cette nuit** last night, tonight; **dans la nuit** in the night; **toute la nuit** all night; **travailler la nuit** to work at night; **2 il fait nuit** it's dark; **avant la nuit** before dark; **la nuit tombe à sept heures** it gets dark at seven o'clock.

nul (F **nulle**) *adjective* **1** (*informal*) hopeless, awful; **le film était nul** the film was awful; **je suis nul en histoire** I'm hopeless at history; **2 un match nul** a draw.

nulle part *adverb* nowhere; **je ne trouve nulle part mon dictionnaire** I can't find my dictionary anywhere.

numéro *noun* M number; **ils habitent au numéro vingt-cinq** they live at number twenty-five.

numéro de téléphone *noun* M telephone number.

nu-pieds *noun* M open sandal.

nutritif (F **nutritive**) *adjective* nourishing, nutritious; **valeur nutritive** nutritional value.

nylon *noun* M nylon.

O o

obéir *verb* [2] **obéir à** to obey.

obéissance *noun* F obedience.

obéissant *adjective* obedient.

objectif *noun* M objective. *adjective* (F **objective**) objective.

objection *noun* F objection.

objet *noun* M object.

objets trouvés *plural noun* M lost property; **aller aux objets trouvés** to go to the lost property office.

obligatoire *adjective* compulsory.

obligé *adjective* **être obligé de faire** to have to do; **je suis obligé de partir** I have to go.

obliger *verb* [52] **obliger quelqu'un à faire** to force somebody to do.

obscène *adjective* obscene.

obscur *adjective* **1** dark; **2** obscure.

obscurité *noun* F **1** darkness; **dans l'obscurité** in the dark; **2** obscurity.

obséder *verb* [24] to obsess; **être obsédé par quelque chose** to be obsessed by something.

obsèques *plural noun* F funeral.

observateur, observatrice *noun* M, F observer. *adjective* observant.

observation *noun* F **1** comment; **2** remark.

observatoire *noun* M observatory.

observer *verb* [1] **1** to watch; **elle nous observait de loin** she was watching us from a distance; **2** to observe (*rules*).

obstacle *noun* M obstacle.

obstination *noun* F obstinacy.

obstiné *adjective* stubborn.

obtenir *verb* [77] to get.

occasion *noun* F **1** opportunity; **avoir l'occasion de faire** to have the opportunity to do; **2 acheter quelque chose d'occasion** to buy something second hand; **une voiture d'occasion** a second-hand car; **3** bargain; **une bonne occasion** a good bargain; **4** occasion; **à l'occasion de** on the occasion of; **5 à l'occasion** some time.

occasionner *verb* [1] to cause.

Occident *noun* M **l'Occident** the West.

occidental (M *plural* **occidentaux**) *adjective* western.

occupation *noun* F occupation.

occupé *adjective* **1** busy; **je suis occupé en ce moment** I'm busy at the moment; **2** engaged (*of a telephone line or toilet*); **3** **cette place est occupée** this seat is taken.

occuper *verb* [1] **1** to occupy; **2** **s'occuper** to keep yourself busy; **3** **s'occuper de** to deal with, to see to; **je vais m'occuper du dîner** I'll go and see to dinner; **je m'en occupe** I'll see to it; **4** **s'occuper de quelqu'un** to attend to somebody; **est-ce qu'on s'occupe de vous?** are you being attended to?

occurrence *noun* F **1** case; **plusieurs occurrences de typhoïde** several cases of typhoid; **2** occurrence.

océan *noun* M ocean.

octet *noun* M byte (*in computing*).

octobre *noun* M October; **en octobre, au mois d'octobre** in October.

odeur *noun* F smell; **des odeurs de cuisine** cooking smells.

odorat *noun* M sense of smell.

œil (*plural* **yeux**) *noun* M eye; ★ **cela saute aux yeux** it's obvious (*literally: it jumps into your eyes*).

œillet *noun* M carnation.

œuf *noun* M egg; **un œuf à la coque** a boiled egg; **un œuf dur** a hard-boiled egg; **un œuf mollet** a soft-boiled egg; **un œuf sur le plat** a fried egg; **des œufs brouillés** scrambled eggs.

œuvre *noun* F work (*of art or literature*); **une œuvre d'art** a work of art.

offenser *verb* [1] to offend.

office *noun* M **1** office; **2** **office religieux** religious service.

officiel *noun* M official. *adjective* (F **officielle**) official.

officier *noun* M officer.

offre *noun* F **1** offer; **2** **'offres d'emploi** 'situations vacant'.

offrir *verb* [56] **1** **offrir quelque chose à quelqu'un** to give something to somebody; **elle m'a offert une montre pour mon anniversaire** she gave me a watch for my birthday; **2** **s'offrir quelque chose** to treat yourself to something; **je vais m'offrir un nouveau dictionnaire** I'm going to treat myself to a new dictionary; **3** to offer.

oie *noun* F goose.

oignon *noun* M onion.

oiseau (*plural* **oiseaux**) *noun* M bird.

olive *noun* F olive; **l'huile d'olive** olive oil.

olivier *noun* M olive tree.

ombragé *adjective* shaded (*from the sun*).

ombre *noun* F **1** shade; **à l'ombre** in the shade; **2** shadow.

ombre à paupières *noun* F eyeshadow.

ombrelle *noun* F sun umbrella.

omelette *noun* F omelette; **une omelette aux champignons** a mushroom omelette.

omoplate *noun* F shoulder blade.

on *pronoun* **1** we; **on va au cinéma** we're going to the cinema; **on a oublié de fermer la porte** we forgot to shut the door; **2** you; **de la terrasse on voit la mer** from the terrace you can see the sea; **on ne devrait pas mentir** you shouldn't tell lies; **3** on leur a dit que... they were told that...; **on a volé leur voiture** their car's been stolen.

oncle *noun* M uncle.

onde *noun* F wave (*on radio*).

ondée *noun* F shower (*of rain*).

onéreux (F **onéreuse**) *adjective* costly.

ongle *noun* M nail; **se faire les ongles** to do your nails; **je me suis coupé les ongles** I've cut my nails.

ONU *noun* F SHORT FOR **Organisation des Nations unies** UN, United Nations.

onze *number* eleven; **onze personnes** eleven people; **Marie-Ange a onze ans** Marie-Ange is eleven; **le onze juillet** the eleventh of July.

onzième *noun* M **au onzième** on the eleventh floor. *adjective* eleventh.

opéra *noun* M **1** opera; **2** opera house.

opérateur, opératrice *noun* M, F operator.

opération *noun* F **1** operation; **2** calculation.

opérer *verb* [24] to operate; **opérer quelqu'un** to operate on somebody; **se faire opérer** to have an operation.

opinion *noun* F opinion.

opposant, opposante *noun* M, F opponent.

opposé *noun* **l'opposé** the opposite. *adjective* **1** opposite; **2** être **opposé à quelque chose** to be opposed to something.

opposer *verb* [1] **1** le match de samedi prochain oppose les Anglais et les Français the English are playing the French in next Saturday's match; **2** s'opposer à quelque chose to oppose something.

opposition *noun* F opposition.

opter *verb* [1] to opt.

opticien, opticienne *noun* M, F optician.

optimisme *noun* M optimism.

optimiste *noun* M & F optimist. *adjective* optimistic.

option *noun* F option.

optionnel (F **optionnelle**) *adjective* optional.

or[1] *noun* M **1** gold; **une montre en or** a gold watch; **2** une occasion en or a golden opportunity.

or[2] *conjunction* now.

orage *noun* M storm.

orageux (F **orageuse**) *adjective*
1 stormy; **2** thundery.

oral (*plural* **oraux**) *noun* M oral
(exam); **l'oral de français** the
French oral.
adjective oral; **une épreuve orale**
an oral exam.

orange *noun* F,
adjective orange.

oranger *noun* M orange tree.

orbite *noun* F orbit.

orchestral (M *plural* **orchestraux**)
adjective orchestral.

orchestre *noun* M **1** orchestra;
2 band.

orchidée *noun* F orchid.

ordinaire *noun* M **1** 2-star petrol;
2 sortir de l'ordinaire to be out of
the ordinary; **ça sort un peu de
l'ordinaire** it's a bit out of the
ordinary; **3 à l'ordinaire,
d'ordinaire** usually.
adjective ordinary; **une journée
ordinaire** an ordinary day.

ordinateur *noun* M computer.

ordonnance *noun* F prescription.

ordonné *adjective* tidy.

ordonner *verb* [1] to order.

ordre *noun* M **1** order; **donner des
ordres** to give orders; **2** order; **par
ordre alphabétique** in alphabetical
order; **mettre de l'ordre** to tidy up;
mettre en ordre to tidy.

ordures *plural noun* F rubbish.

oreille *noun* F ear.

oreiller *noun* M pillow.

oreillons *plural noun* M mumps.

organe *noun* M organ (*of the body*).

organique *adjective* organic.

organisateur, organisatrice
noun M, F organizer.

organisation *noun* F
organization.

organiser *verb* [1] **1** to organize;
2 s'organiser to get organized.

organisme *noun* M
1 organization; **2** body;
3 organism.

organiste *noun* M & F organist.

orge *noun* F barley; **le sucre d'orge**
barley sugar.

orgeat *noun* M **le sirop d'orgeat**
barley water.

orgue *noun* F organ; **jouer de
l'orgue** to play the organ.

orgueil *noun* M pride.

orgueilleux (F **orgueilleuse**)
adjective proud.

Orient *noun* M **l'Orient** the East.

oriental (M *plural* **orientaux**)
adjective **1** eastern; **2** oriental.

orientation *noun* F
1 orientation; **2 l'orientation
professionnelle** careers advice;
3 avoir le sens de l'orientation to
have a good sense of direction.

orienter *verb* [1] **1** to position;
2 to direct; **3 s'orienter** to find
one's bearings; **4 s'orienter vers** to
move towards; **Bernard s'oriente
vers les langues** Bernard's going in
for languages.

originaire *adjective* **être originaire de** to be a native of; **Giselle est originaire de Dijon** Giselle comes from Dijon.

original (*plural* **originaux**) *noun* M original.
adjective **1** original; **le film est en version originale** the film isn't dubbed; **2** eccentric; **c'est une vieille dame assez originale** she's rather an eccentric old lady.

originalité *noun* F **1** originality; **2** eccentricity.

origine *noun* F **1** origin; **2** elle est d'origine écossaise she's Scottish; **3 à l'origine** originally; **à l'origine la maison appartenait à mon oncle** the house originally belonged to my uncle.

orme *noun* M elm tree.

orné *adjective* **orné de** decorated with.

ornemental (M *plural* **ornementaux**) *adjective* ornamental.

orphelin, orpheline *noun* M, F orphan.

orphelinat *noun* M orphanage.

orteil *noun* M toe; **gros orteil** big toe.

orthographe *noun* F spelling.

ortie *noun* F nettle.

os *noun* M bone.

osé *adjective* daring; **c'était un peu osé de dire ça** it was a bit daring to say that.

oseille *noun* F sorrel.

oser *verb* [1] to dare.

osier *noun* M wicker; **un panier en osier** a wicker basket.

otage *noun* M hostage; **être pris en otage** to be taken hostage.

OTAN *noun* F SHORT FOR **Organisation du traité de l'Atlantique Nord** NATO.

ôter *verb* [1] **1** to take off; **je vais ôter ma veste** I'll take off my jacket; **2** to take away; **3** to remove.

otite *noun* F earache; **avoir une otite** to have earache.

ou *conjunction* **1** or; **est-ce que vous voulez le fromage ou le dessert?** would you like cheese or dessert?; **2 ou…ou** either…or; **c'est ou dans ma chambre ou dans le salon** it's either in my bedroom or in the sitting-room; **3 ou bien** or else; **on peut se retrouver au cinéma ou bien chez moi, si tu veux** we can meet at the cinema or else at my place, if you like.

où *adverb* where; **où es-tu?** where are you?; **ton frère habite où?** where does your brother live?; **tu l'as trouvé où ton sac?** where did you find your bag?; **je sais où elle habite** I know where she lives.
pronoun **1** where; **le village où elle habite** the village where she lives; **la ville d'où il vient** the town he comes from; **2** when, that; **le jour où je suis arrivé** the day I arrived.

ouate *noun* F cotton wool.

oubli *noun* M **1** forgetfulness; **2 l'oubli de quelque chose** forgetting something; **3** oversight;

c'était un oubli I (or you etc.) forgot about it.

oublier *verb* [1] **1** to forget; **j'ai oublié leur adresse** I've forgotten their address; **2** to leave; **j'ai oublié mes clefs chez Jérôme** I've left my keys at Jérôme's.

ouest *noun* M west; **à l'ouest de Paris** west of Paris; **dans l'ouest de la France** in the west of France; **l'Ouest** the West; **l'Europe de l'Ouest** Western Europe.
adjective **1** west; **le côté ouest** the west coast; **2** western.

ouf *exclamation* phew!

oui *adverb* yes; **elle a dit oui** she said yes; **dire oui de la tête** to nod.

ouragan *noun* M hurricane.

ourlet *noun* M hem.

ours *noun* M bear.

oursin *noun* M sea urchin.

outil *noun* M tool.

outre *preposition* in addition to.

outré *adjective* outraged.

outremer *noun* M, *adjective* ultramarine.

outre-mer *adverb* overseas.

ouvert *adjective* **1** open; **laisse la porte ouverte** leave the door open; **'ouvert le dimanche'** 'open on Sundays'; **2 laisser le robinet ouvert** to leave the tap on.

ouvertement *adverb* openly.

ouverture *noun* F **1** opening; **les heures d'ouverture** opening hours; **2** openness; **ouverture d'esprit** open-mindedness.

ouvre-boîte *noun* M tin-opener.

ouvre-bouteille *noun* M bottle-opener.

ouvrier, ouvrière *noun* M, F worker.
adjective **la classe ouvrière** the working class.

ouvrir *verb* [30] **1** to open; **ouvrir la fenêtre** to open the window; **2 ouvrir le robinet** to turn on the tap; **3 elle n'a pas ouvert la bouche** she didn't say a word; **4 s'ouvrir** to open; **ça s'ouvre comment?** how do you open it?

ovale *adjective* oval.

ovni *noun* M SHORT FOR **objet volant non identifié** UFO.

oxygène *noun* M oxygen.

ozone *noun* F ozone.

P p

Pacifique *noun* M **l'océan Pacifique** the Pacific Ocean.

pagaille (*informal*) *noun* F mess; **quelle pagaille!** what a mess!

page *noun* F page; **à la première/dernière page** on the first/last page; **les Pages Jaunes** the Yellow Pages.

paie (or **paye**) *noun* F pay; **un bulletin de paie, une fiche de paie** a payslip.

paiement *noun* M payment.

paillasson *noun* M doormat.

paille *noun* F straw.

pain *noun* M **1** bread; **une tranche de pain** a slice of bread; **2 un pain** a loaf of bread; **trois pains** three loaves of bread; **un petit pain** a roll; ★ **ils se vendent comme des petits pains** they're selling like hot cakes (*literally: like rolls*).

pain au chocolat *noun* M chocolate pastry.

pain complet *noun* M wholemeal bread.

pain de mie *noun* M sandwich loaf.

pain d'épices *noun* M gingerbread.

pain de seigle *noun* M rye bread.

pain grillé *noun* M toast.

pair *adjective* **1** even (*number*); **2 au pair** au pair; **une jeune fille au pair** an au pair; **travailler au pair** to work as an au pair.

paire *noun* F pair; **une paire de chaussures** a pair of shoes.

paix *noun* F peace.

palais *noun* M **1** palace; **2** palate.

palais de justice *noun* M law courts.

pâle *adjective* pale; **bleu pâle** pale blue.

Palestine *noun* F Palestine.

palier *noun* M landing (*on a staircase*).

pâlir *verb* [2] **1** to turn pale; **2** to fade.

palme *noun* F flipper (*for swimming*).

palmier *noun* M palm tree.

palpitant *adjective* thrilling.

pamplemousse *noun* M grapefruit.

panaché *noun* M shandy. *adjective* **une salade panachée** a mixed salad.

pancarte *noun* F notice, sign.

pané *adjective* coated in breadcrumbs.

panier *noun* M basket.

panier à salade *noun* M salad shaker.

panique *noun* F panic.

paniquer *verb* [1] to panic.

panne *noun* F breakdown (*of a car or machine*); **la voiture est en panne** the car's broken down; **la photocopieuse est en panne** the photocopier's not working; **tomber en panne** to break down; **nous sommes en panne d'essence** we've run out of petrol; **une panne de courant** a power cut.

panneau (*plural* **panneaux**) *noun* M sign, notice board.

panneau indicateur *noun* M signpost.

panneau publicitaire *noun* M advertisement hoarding.

panorama *noun* M **1** panorama; **2** viewpoint.

pansement *noun* M **1** sticking plaster; **2** dressing.

panser *verb* [1] to put a dressing on (*a wound*).

pantalon *noun* M trousers; **mon pantalon gris** my grey trousers; **un pantalon neuf** a new pair of trousers; **deux pantalons** two pairs of trousers.

panthère *noun* F panther.

pantoufle *noun* F slipper.

paon *noun* M peacock.

papa *noun* M Dad, Daddy, father.

pape *noun* M pope.

paperasse *noun* F (*informal*) paperwork, bumph.

papeterie *noun* F stationer's.

papi *noun* M (*informal*) granddad.

papier *noun* M paper; **du papier blanc** white paper; **vos papiers, s'il vous plaît monsieur** your (identity) papers please, sir.

papier à lettres *noun* M writing paper.

papier aluminium *noun* M kitchen foil.

papier cadeau *noun* M gift wrap.

papier-calque *noun* M tracing paper.

papier hygiénique *noun* M toilet paper.

papier peint *noun* M wallpaper.

papiers d'identité *plural noun* M identity papers.

papillon *noun* M butterfly.

paquebot *noun* M liner.

pâquerette *noun* F daisy.

Pâques *noun* M Easter; **à Pâques** at Easter; **un œuf de Pâques** an Easter egg; **les vacances de Pâque** the Easter holidays; **le lundi de Pâques** Easter Monday.

paquet *noun* M **1** packet; **un paquet de sucre** a packet of sugar **2** parcel; **il y a un paquet pour vou** there's a parcel for you; **3** bundle (*clothes or papers*).

paquet-cadeau *noun* M gift-wrapped parcel; **est-ce que je vou fais un paquet-cadeau?** shall I gif wrap it for you?

par *preposition* **1** by; **par moi** by m **par la poste** by post; **payer par chèque** to pay by cheque; **par accident** by accident; **par hasard** by chance; **deux par deux** two by two; **jeter quelque chose par la fenêtre** to throw something out of the window; **aller par Paris** to go v (or by) Paris; **par ennui** out of boredom; **2** in; **par endroits** in places; **par cette chaleur** in this heat; **3** per; **50 francs par personne** 50 francs per person; **deux repas par jour** two meals a day; **deux fois par semaine** twice week.

parachute *noun* M parachute.

parachutiste *noun* M & F parachutist.

paradis *noun* M heaven.

paragraphe *noun* M paragraph.

paraître *verb* [57] **1** to seem; **ça n paraît étrange** that seems strange to me; **il paraît qu'il est mort** it seems he's dead; **2 paraît-il** apparently; **elle est à Nice, paraît-** she's in Nice, apparently; **3** to appear; **paraître en public** to appe in public; **4** (*of a book*) to come out, to be published; **le roman va paraître en juin** the novel will come out in June.

arallèle *adjective* parallel.

aralysé *adjective* paralysed.

arapente *noun* M **1** paraglider; **2** paragliding.

arapluie *noun* M umbrella.

arasite *noun* M **1** parasite; **2 des parasites** interference (*on TV or radio*).

arasol *noun* M parasol.

arc *noun* M **1** park; **aller au parc** to go to the park; **2** grounds (*of a large house*).

arc d'attractions *noun* M amusement park.

arce que *conjunction* because; **parce qu'elle est malade** because she's ill; **c'est parce que je t'aime** it's because I love you.

ar-ci *adverb* **par-ci par-là** here and there.

arcmètre *noun* M parking meter.

arc naturel *noun* M nature park.

arcourir *verb* [29] to go all over, to travel all over; **j'ai parcouru l'Europe** I travelled all over Europe.

arcours *noun* M **1** route (*for a bus or a traveller*); **2** course (*for a race*).

ar-derrière *adverb* from the back, behind; **elle est passée par-derrière** she went round the back.

ar-dessous *adverb* underneath.

pardessus *noun* M overcoat.

par-dessus *adverb* **1** on top; **2** over it; **il a sauté par-dessus** he jumped over it.
preposition over; **elle a sauté par-dessus le ruisseau** she jumped over the stream; **j'aime ça par-dessus tout!** I like that best of all!

par-devant *adverb* by the front.

pardon *noun* M **1** pardon, forgiveness; **je te demande pardon** I'm sorry; **2** excuse me, sorry.

pardonner *verb* [1] to forgive.

pare-balles *adjective* bullet-proof; **un gilet pare-balles** a bullet-proof vest.

pare-brise *noun* M windscreen.

pare-chocs *noun* M bumper (*on a car*).

pareil (F **pareille**) *adjective* **1** the same; **les deux voitures sont presque pareilles** the two cars are almost the same; **c'est toujours pareil** it's always the same; **mais ce n'est pas du tout pareil!** but it's not the same at all!; **2** such; **je n'ai jamais dit une chose pareille** I never said any such thing; **tu ne peux pas sortir par un temps pareil** you can't go out in weather like this.

parent *noun* M **1** parent; **mes parents** my parents; **2** relation; **parents et amis** friends and relations.

parenthèse *noun* F bracket; **entre parenthèses** in brackets.

paresse *noun* F laziness.

paresseux (F **paresseuse**)
adjective lazy.

parfait *adjverb* perfect.

parfaitement *adverb* **1** perfectly;
tu le sais parfaitement! you know
perfectly well!; **parfaitement faux**
totally wrong; **2 parfaitement!**
absolutely!

parfois *adverb* sometimes.

parfum *noun* M **1** perfume;
2 flavour; **tu veux quel parfum de
yaourt?** what flavour yoghurt would
you like?

parfumé *adjective* **1** perfumed,
fragrant; **parfumé à la lavande**
lavender-scented; **2** flavoured; **une
glace parfumée au chocolat** a
chocolate ice-cream.

parfumerie *noun* F perfume shop.

pari *noun* M bet; **faire un pari** to
make a bet.

parier *verb* [1] to bet.

Paris *noun* Paris; **à Paris** in (or to)
Paris.

parisien (F **parisienne**) *adjective*
1 Parisian; **2** Paris; **un restaurant
parisien** a Paris restaurant.

parking *noun* M car park; **dans le
parking** in the car park.

Parlement *noun* M Parliament.

parler *verb* [1] **1** to speak; **parler (le)
français** to speak French; **parler en
italien** to speak in Italian; **parler
fort/doucement** to speak
loudly/softly; **parler à quelqu'un** to
speak to someone; **2** to talk; **il parle
très vite** he talks very fast; **parler
cinéma** to talk (about) films;

3 parler de to talk about, to
mention; **tout le monde en parle**
everyone's talking about it; **non, il
n'en a pas parlé** no, he didn't
mention it; **n'en parlons plus!** let's
say no more about it!; **se parler**
to talk to each other; ★ **tu parles!**
(*informal*) you must be joking!

parmi *preposition* among; **parmi le
invités** among the guests.

parole *noun* F **1 les paroles** the
lyrics; **les paroles de la chanson**
the lyrics of the song; **2 elle m'a
donné sa parole** she gave me her
word; **3** speech; **perdre la parole**
lose the power of speech.

parquet *noun* M **1** wooden floor;
2 parquet.

parrain *noun* M godfather.

parrainer *verb* [1] to sponsor.

parsemer *verb* [50] to sprinkle.

part *noun* F **1** portion, helping; **un
part de pizza** a portion of pizza;
2 share; **il a payé sa part** he paid h
share; **elle a fait sa part du travail**
she did her share of the work; **3** sid
de toutes parts from all sides;
4 pour ma part, je pense que... f
my part, I think that...; **5 à part**
separate, separately; **une chambre
part** a separate bedroom; **j'ai mis
l'argent à part** I put the money
aside; **à part ça, qu'est-ce qu'il t'a
dit?** apart from that, what did he
say?; **6 de la part de quelqu'un** o
behalf of somebody, for somebody;
c'est de la part de qui? who's

...alling?; **dis-lui bonjour de ma part**
...ay hello to him from me.

...**rtager** verb [52] **1** to share
(*possessions or food*); **2** to divide; **je**
partage mon temps entre mon
travail et les enfants I divide my
time between my job and the
children.

...**rtenaire** noun M & F partner.

...**rterre** noun M **1** flower bed;
2 stalls (*in a theatre*).

...**rti** noun M **1** party, group; **le parti**
communiste the communist
party; **2** side.

...**rticipation** noun F
participation.

...**rticipe** noun M participle;
participe passé past participle.

...**rticiper** verb [1] **participer à**
quelque chose to take part in
something.

...**rticulier** noun M private
individual.
adjective (F **particulière**) **1** special;
en de particulier nothing special;
2 private; **une voiture particulière** a
private car; **3** en particulier in
particular; **rien en particulier**
nothing in particular; **4** en
particulier in private.

...**rticulièrement** adverb
particularly.

...**rtie** noun F **1** part; **une partie de**
ma vie part of my life; **la première**
partie the first part; **2** en partie
partly; **3** faire partie de quelque
chose to be part of something; **ce**
bâtiment fait partie du musée this
building is part of the museum; **elle**

fait partie de la famille she's one of
the family; **4** game; **faire une partie**
de tennis to have a game of tennis;
gagner la partie to win the game.

partir verb [58] **1** to leave, to go;
partir à pied to go on foot; **tu pars**
déjà? are you leaving already?; **elle**
est partie en Italie she's gone to Italy;
il est parti à Londres he's gone to
London; **elle est partie au travail**
she's left for work; **partir en**
vacances to go away on holiday;
elle est partie pour huit jours she's
gone away for a week; **ils sont partis**
en courant they ran off; **2** à partir
de from; **à partir de lundi** from
Monday (onwards).

partition noun F score (*in music*).

partout adverb **1** everywhere; **j'ai**
cherché partout I've looked
everywhere; **2** trois buts partout
three goals all.

parvenir verb [81] **1** parvenir à to
reach; **2** parvenir à faire to
manage to do; **il est parvenu à ouvrir**
la porte he managed to open the
door.

pas¹ adverb **1** (*used with 'ne' to put*
verbs into the negative) **je ne suis**
pas I am not; **je n'ai pas de stylo**
I don't have a pen; **je ne pense pas**
I don't think so; **ils n'ont pas le**
téléphone they haven't got a
phone; **2** not; **c'est lui qui paie, pas**
moi he's paying, not me; **pas du**
tout not at all; **pas vraiment** not
really; **une radio pas chère** a cheap
radio; **pas de chance!** bad luck!;
pas possible! I don't believe it!

pas² noun M **1** step; **faire un**
grand/petit pas to take a big/small

step; **j'habite à deux pas d'ici** I live very near here; **2** pace; **ralentir le pas** to slow down; **'roulez au pas!'** 'dead slow' (*road sign*).

passage *noun* M **1** traffic; **une rue où il y a beaucoup de passage** a street where there's a lot of traffic; **passage interdit** no through traffic; **2** visit; **je peux te prendre au passage** I can pick you up on my way.

passage à niveau *noun* M level crossing.

passage pour piétons *noun* M pedestrian crossing.

passager, passagère *noun* M, F passenger.
adjective passing, temporary.

passage souterrain *noun* M subway (*under a road*).

passant, passante *noun* M, F passer-by.

passé *noun* M **1** past; **c'est dans le passé** it's in the past now; **2** past tense; **le passé composé** the present perfect.
adjective **1** **l'année passée** last year; **2** past; **il est dix heures passées** it's past ten o'clock.

passeport *noun* M passport.

passer *verb* [1] **1** to pass; **le temps passe vite** time passes quickly; **2** to spend (*time*); **j'ai passé deux jours à Paris** I spent two days in Paris; **3** **en passant** in passing; **4** **passer quelque chose à quelqu'un** to pass somebody something; **passe-moi le sel** pass me the salt; **5** to cross; **passer le pont** to cross the bridge; **6** to drop

in; **Pierre est passé ce matin** Pier dropped in this morning; **est-ce qu le facteur est passé?** has the postman been?; **je passerai te prendre à huit heures** I'll pick you up at eight; **7** to get through; **laissez passer l'ambulance!** let th ambulance through!; **8** to go; **passer à la caisse** to go to the checkout; **passons au salon** let's g through to the sitting room; **le film est passé à la télé lundi** the film was on telly on Monday; **9** to give; **m'a passé son vélo** he gave me hi bike; **je te passe Michel** I'll put yo on to Michel (*on the telephone*); **10** to put (on) (*a garment*); **11** **passer l'aspirateur** to vacuum; **12** to take, to sit (*a test or an exam*; **13** **passer par** to go through; **nou sommes passés par Paris** we wer through (or via) Paris; **14** **se passer** to happen; **qu'est-ce qui s passe?** what's happening?; **ça s'e passé en Chine** it happened in China; **15** **se passer de** to do without; **se passer d'un manteau** do without a coat.

passerelle *noun* F **1** footbridge; **2** gangway.

passe-temps *noun* M hobby.

passif *noun* M passive (*in grammar*).
adjective (F **passive**) passive.

passion *noun* F passion.

passionnant *adjective* exciting.

passionné, passionnée *noun* F enthusiast; **c'est un passionné tennis** he's a tennis enthusiast.
adjective keen; **c'est une**

musicienne passionnée she's a keen musician.

passionner *verb* [1] **l'histoire me passionne** history fascinates me.

passoire *noun* F strainer.

patate (*informal*) *noun* F potato.

pâte *noun* F **1** pastry; **pâte feuilletée** puff pastry; **2** dough; **3** batter; **pâte à crêpes** pancake batter; **4** paste; **5** **les pâtes** pasta; **on va manger des pâtes ce soir** we're having pasta tonight.

pâte à modeler *noun* F Plasticine™.

patience *noun* F patience.

patient, patiente *noun* M, F, *adjective* patient.

patienter *verb* [1] to wait; **patientez, s'il vous plaît** would you hold the line please?

patin *noun* M skate.

patinage *noun* M skating; **patinage artistique** figure skating.

patin à glace *noun* M ice skate.

patin à roulettes *noun* M roller skate.

patiner *verb* [1] to skate.

patinoire *noun* F ice rink.

pâtisserie *noun* F **1** cake shop; **2** cake.

patois *noun* M dialect.

patrie *noun* F homeland, country.

patron[1] *noun* M pattern (*for dressmaking*).

patron[2], **patronne** *noun* M, F boss.

patronner *verb* [1] to sponsor.

patte *noun* F **1** paw; **2** leg (*of an animal*); ★ **à quatre pattes** on all fours.

paume *noun* F palm (*of the hand*).

paumer *verb* [1] (*informal*) **1** to lose; **2** **se paumer** to get lost.

paupière *noun* F eyelid; **le fard à paupières** eyeshadow.

pause *noun* F **1** break; **faire une pause** to take a break; **la pause café** the coffee break; **2** pause.

pauvre *noun* M & F poor man, poor woman; **les pauvres** the poor; **le pauvre!** poor thing! *adjective* poor.

pauvreté *noun* F poverty.

pavé *noun* M cobblestone.

pavillon *noun* M **1** detached house; **un pavillon de banlieue** a house in the suburbs; **2** wing (*in a hospital*).

payant *adjective* **1** (*of a show or event*) not free; **c'est payant?** do you have to pay to get in?; **un parking payant** a pay-and-display car park; **2** **un hôte payant** a paying guest.

paye *noun* F wages.

payer *verb* [59] **1** to pay (*a bill or a person*); **c'est moi qui paie** I'm paying; **être mal payé** to be badly paid; **être payé à l'heure** to be paid by the hour; **2** to pay for; **il a payé le repas** he paid for the meal; **3** (*informal*) **je te paie à boire** I'll buy you a drink; **4** **je me suis payé**

une semaine à Paris I treated myself to a week in Paris.

pays *noun* M **1** country; **la France est un beau pays** France is a beautiful country; **2** region; **des fruits du pays** locally grown fruit.

paysage *noun* M landscape.

paysan, paysanne *noun* M, F farmer.

Pays-Bas *plural noun* M **les Pays-Bas** the Netherlands.

pays de Galles *noun* M Wales; **au pays de Galles** in (or to) Wales.

PC *noun* M PC, personal computer.

péage *noun* M **1** toll; **autoroute à péage** toll motorway (*motorists have to pay to travel on motorways in France*); **2** tollbooth.

peau (*plural* **peaux**) *noun* F **1** skin; **avoir la peau sèche** to have dry skin; **2** peel (*of fruit*); **peau d'orange** orange peel.

pêche *noun* F **1** peach; **2** fishing; **aller à la pêche** to go fishing.

péché *noun* M sin.

pêcher[1] *verb* [1] **1** to fish for (*trout, salmon, etc*); **2** to catch; **Denise a pêché trois truites** Denise caught three trout.

pêcher[2] *noun* M peach tree.

pêcheur *noun* M fisherman.

pédagogique *adjective* educational; **méthode pédagogique** teaching method.

pédale *noun* F pedal; ★ **perdre les pédales** (*informal*) to lose your grip.

pédaler *verb* [1] to pedal.

pédalo™ *noun* M pedalo, pedal boat.

pédestre *adjective* **faire une randonnée pédestre** to go walking (*on a long-distance public footpath*).

peigne *noun* M comb.

peigner *verb* [1] **1** to comb; **2 se peigner** to comb your hair.

peindre *verb* [60] to paint.

peine *noun* F **1** effort, trouble; **se donner de la peine** to go to a lot of trouble; **il n'a même pas pris la peine d'appeler** he didn't even take the trouble to ring; **2 ce n'est pas peine** it's not worth it; **3** difficulty **elle a eu beaucoup de peine à trouver un logement** she had a lot of difficulty finding somewhere to live; **4 faire de la peine à quelqu'un** to upset somebody; **5** penalty (*in law*); **sous peine d'amende** offenders will be fined; **6 à peine** hardly, scarcely; **je le connais à peine** I hardly know him; **il était à peine cinq heures** it was barely five o'clock.

peine de mort *noun* F death penalty.

peintre *noun* M painter.

peinture *noun* F **1** paint; **'peinture fraîche'** 'wet paint'; **2** painting; **faire de la peinture** to paint; **3 une peinture** a painting.

pelle *noun* F **1** spade; **2** shovel.

pelle à poussière *noun* F dustpan.

pelle mécanique *noun* F mechanical digger.

ellicule *noun* F **1** film (*for a camera*); **une pellicule couleur** a colour film; **2 les pellicules** dandruff.

elouse *noun* F lawn; **'pelouse interdite'** 'keep off the grass'.

eluche *noun* F soft toy.

encher *verb* [1] **1** to tilt; **2** to lean; **3 se pencher** to bend down; **4 se pencher par la fenêtre** to lean out of the window.

endant *preposition* **1** for; **je t'ai attendu pendant deux heures** I waited for you for two hours; **2** during; **pendant l'hiver** during the winter; **3 pendant que** while; **pendant que les enfants sont à l'école** while the children are at school.

endentif *noun* M pendant.

enderie *noun* F wardrobe, hanging cupboard.

endre *verb* [3] **1** to hang; **2 pendre quelque chose** to hang something up; **3** to hang down.

endule *noun* F clock.

énétrer *verb* [24] **1 pénétrer dans** to enter; **un voleur a pénétré dans le bureau** a thief got into the office; **2** to penetrate.

énible *adjective* **1** difficult, hard; **2 il est pénible** he's a pain.

éniche *noun* F barge.

énis *noun* M penis.

ensée *noun* F **1** thought; **2** pansy.

penser *verb* [1] **1** to think; **je pense que tu as raison** I think you're right; **oui, je pense** yes, I think so; **je ne pense pas** I don't think so; **2** to intend; **il pense arriver mardi** he's intending to arrive on Tuesday; **3 penser de** to think of; **qu'est-ce que tu penses de mon idée?** what do you think of my idea?; **4 penser à** to think about; **à quoi penses-tu?** what are you thinking about?; **5 cette chanson me fait penser à ta mère** this song reminds me of your mother; **6** to remember; **pendant que j'y pense** while I remember; **fais-moi penser à acheter des citrons** remind me to buy lemons.

pension *noun* F **1** boarding school; **2** boarding house; **3** pension; **4 pension complète** full board; **demi-pension** dinner, bed and breakfast.

pensionnaire *noun* M & F boarder.

pente *noun* F slope; **en pente** sloping.

Pentecôte *noun* F Whitsun; **à la Pentecôte** at Whitsun.

pépin *noun* M **1** (grape) pip; **2** (*informal*) slight problem.

perçant *adjective* **1** piercing; **2** sharp.

perce-neige *noun* M or F snowdrop.

percer *verb* [61] to pierce; **avoir les oreilles percées** to have pierced ears; **se faire percer les oreilles** to have your ears pierced; **percer un trou** to make a hole.

perceuse *noun* F drill.

perdant, perdante *noun* M, F
loser.

perdre *verb* [3] **1** to lose; **notre
équipe a perdu** our team lost;
2 perdre quelque chose to lose
something; **j'ai perdu mes clefs** I've
lost my keys; **j'ai perdu mon chemin**
I've lost my way; **3 être perdu** to be
lost; **4 se perdre** to get lost; **je me
suis perdu dans les petites rues** I
got lost in the back streets; **5 perdre
du temps** to waste time.

perdu *adjective* **1** lost; **un enfant
perdu** a lost child; **2** stray; **un chien
perdu** a stray dog; **3 c'est du temps
perdu** it's a waste of time.

père *noun* M father; **le père Noël**
Father Christmas.

perfectionner *verb* [1] to perfect.

performant *adjective* **1** efficient;
2 high-performance.

périmé *adjective* out-of-date.

période *noun* F period.

périphérique *noun* M ring road.

perle *noun* F **1** pearl; **2** bead.

permanence *noun* F **1** service;
'**permanence de 8h à 19h**' 'open
from 8 a.m. to 7 p.m.'; **2 en
permanence** permanently, all the
time.

permanent *adjective*
1 permanent; continuous.

permettre *verb* [11] **permettre à
quelqu'un de faire** to allow
someone to do; **elle leur a permis de
partir** she allowed them to leave;
permettez-moi de vous aider let me
help you.

permis *noun* M permit, licence.

permis de conduire *noun* M
driving licence; **passer son permis**
to sit your driving test.

permission *noun* F
1 permission; **2** leave (*from the
army*).

perroquet *noun* M parrot.

perruche *noun* F budgie.

perruque *noun* F wig.

persécution *noun* F persecution.

persévérer *verb* [24] to persevere.

persil *noun* M parsley.

persister *verb* [1] to persist.

personnage *noun* M **1** character
(*in a book, film, or play*); **2** figure,
person; **un personnage célèbre** a
famous person.

personnalité *noun* F personality.

personne[1] *pronoun* **1** nobody;
personne ne sait nobody knows;
2 anybody; **je ne vois personne** I
can't see anybody; **je n'ai parlé à
personne** I didn't speak to anybody.

personne[2] *noun* F person; **vingt
personnes** twenty people; **les
personnes âgées** the elderly; **en
personne** in person.

personnel *noun* M **1** staff; **2 le
service du personnel** the personnel
department.
adjective (F **personnelle**) personal.

personnellement *adverb*
personally.

perspective *noun* F
1 perspective; **2** view; **3** prospect.

persuader *verb* [1] **1** to persuade; **persuader quelqu'un de faire** to persuade somebody to do; **2 être persuadé** to be sure.

perte *noun* F **1** loss; **2** waste; **une perte de temps** a waste of time.

perturber *verb* [1] to disrupt.

pèse-personne *noun* M bathroom scales.

peser *verb* [50] **1 peser quelque chose** to weigh something; **2** to weigh; **je pèse 60 kilos** I weigh 60 kilos.

pessimiste *noun* M & F pessimist. *adjective* pessimistic.

pétale *noun* M petal.

pétanque *noun* F bowls (*the French version, played outdoors with metal bowls; also called 'boules'*).

pétard *noun* M firecracker, banger.

pétillant *adjective* sparkling (*wine or mineral water*).

petit *adjective* **1** little, small; **une petite fille** a little girl; **une toute petite maison** a tiny house; **2** short; **une petite distance** a short distance.
noun (F **petite**) little boy, little girl; **les petits** the children; ★ **petit à petit** little by little.

petit ami *noun* M boyfriend.

petit déjeuner *noun* M breakfast.

petite amie *noun* F girlfriend.

petite annonce *noun* F small ad.

petite-fille *noun* F granddaughter.

petit-fils *noun* M grandson.

petit mot *noun* M note.

petit pois *noun* M garden pea.

petits-enfants *plural noun* M grandchildren.

pétrole *noun* M **1** oil, petroleum; **2** paraffin.

peu *adverb* **1** not much; **il dort peu** he doesn't sleep much; **elle gagne très peu** she earns very little; **2** not very; **peu intéressant** not very interesting; **3 peu de** not much, not many; **il reste peu de temps** there's not much time left; **peu de voitures** not many cars; **4 un peu de** a little, a bit; **il reste un peu de café** there's a bit of coffee left; **5 parle un peu plus fort** speak a little louder; **juste un petit peu** just a little; **6 à peu près** about; **il y avait à peu près vingt personnes** there were about twenty people.

peuple *noun* M people, nation.

peuplier *noun* M poplar.

peur *noun* F fear; **avoir peur de** to be afraid of; **Nadine a peur des souris** Nadine's afraid of mice; **n'ayez pas peur!** don't be afraid!; **faire peur à quelqu'un** to frighten somebody; **tu m'as fait peur!** you gave me a fright!

peut *verb* SEE **pouvoir**[1].

peut-être *adverb* perhaps.

peuvent, peux *verb* SEE **pouvoir**[1].

phare *noun* M **1** headlight; **allumer les phares** to turn the headlights on; **2** lighthouse.

pharmacie *noun* F chemist's.

pharmacien, pharmacienne *noun* M, F chemist, pharmacist.

phénomène *noun* M phenomenon.

philo (*informal*) *noun* F SHORT FOR **philosophie**.

philosophie *noun* F philosophy.

phoque *noun* M seal.

photo *noun* F **1** photo, photograph; **une photo d'identité** a passport photo; **2** photography.

photocopie *noun* F photocopy.

photocopier *verb* [1] to photocopy.

photocopieuse *noun* F photocopier.

photographe *noun* M & F photographer; **Sean est photographe** Sean's a photographer.

photographie *noun* F **1** photography; **2** photograph.

photographier *verb* [1] to photograph.

photomaton™ *noun* M photo booth.

phrase *noun* F sentence.

physique[1] *noun* F physics.

physique[2] *adjective* physical.

pianiste *noun* M & F pianist.

piano *noun* M piano; **jouer du piano** to play the piano.

piano à queue *noun* M grand piano.

pichet *noun* M jug.

pièce *noun* F **1** room; **notre maison a quatre pièces** our house has four rooms; **2** coin; **une pièce de cinq francs** a five-franc coin; **3** play; **une pièce de Molière** a play by Molière; **4** bit, piece; **les pièces d'un puzzle** the pieces of a jigsaw; **5** item; **dix francs (la) pièce** ten francs each.

pièce détachée *noun* F spare part.

pièce de théâtre *noun* F play.

pièce d'identité *noun* F identification (*such as a passport or identity card*).

pied *noun* M **1** foot; **être pieds nus** to be barefoot; **aller à pied** to go on foot; **un coup de pied** a kick; **donner un coup de pied à quelqu'un** to kick someone; **2** bottom, foot; **au pied du lit** at the foot of the bed; **3** le **pied de la table** the table leg.

piège *noun* M trap.

piéger *verb* [15] to trap; **voiture piégée** a car bomb.

pierre *noun* F stone.

piéton, piétonne *noun* M, F pedestrian; **un passage pour piétons** a pedestrian crossing.

piétonnier (F **piétonnière**) *adjective* pedestrian; **une rue piétonnière** a pedestrian street.

pieuvre *noun* F octopus.

pile[1] *noun* F **1** battery; **2** pile; **une pile de vêtements** a pile of clothes; **3** tails (*when tossing a coin*); **pile ou face?** heads or tails?

pile[2] (*informal*) *adverb* **1** exactly; **à dix heures pile** at ten o'clock on the dot; **2 s'arrêter pile** to stop dead.

pilote *noun* M **1** pilot; **2 un pilote de course** a racing driver.

piloter *verb* [1] to fly (*a plane*).

pilule *noun* F pill.

piment *noun* M chilli.

pin *noun* M pine tree; **une pomme de pin** a pine cone.

pince *noun* F **1 une pince** a pair of pliers; **2** dart (*in a garment*); **3** pincer (*of a crab*).

pince à épiler *noun* F tweezers.

pince à linge *noun* F clothes peg.

pinceau (*plural* **pinceaux**) *noun* M paintbrush.

pincée *noun* F pinch (*of salt, for example*).

pincer *verb* [61] to pinch.

pingouin *noun* M penguin.

ping-pong *noun* M ping-pong.

pintade *noun* F guinea fowl.

pion *noun* M **1** counter (*in a board game*); **2** pawn (*in chess*); **3** piece (*in draughts*).

pipe *noun* F pipe; **fumer la pipe** to smoke a pipe.

pipi (*informal*) *noun* M wee; **faire pipi** to have a wee.

piquant *adjective* **1** prickly; **2** spicy.

pique *noun* M spades (*in a pack of cards*); **le trois de pique** the three of spades.

pique-nique *noun* M picnic.

pique-niquer *verb* [1] to have a picnic.

piquer *verb* [1] **1** to sting; **j'ai été piqué par une guêpe** I've been stung by a wasp; **2** to bite; **piqué par des moustiques** bitten by mosquitoes; **3 se piquer** to prick yourself; **je me suis piqué le doigt** I've pricked my finger; **4** (*informal*) to pinch; **quelqu'un a piqué mon stylo** somebody's pinched my pen; ★ **piquer une crise (de nerfs)** (*informal*) to throw a fit.

piquet *noun* M **1** post; **2** peg.

piqûre *noun* F **1** injection; **faire une piqûre à quelqu'un** to give somebody an injection; **2** bite, sting (*of an insect*).

pirate *noun* M pirate.

pirate informatique *noun* M computer hacker.

pire *adjective* **1** worse; **pire que** worse than; **c'est pire que ça!** it's worse than that!; **c'est encore pire** it's even worse; **2** worst; **le pire** the worst; **au pire** if the worst comes to the worst.

pis *in phrase* **tant pis** too bad; **tant pis pour lui!** that's his bad luck!

piscine *noun* F swimming-pool.

pissenlit *noun* M dandelion.

pistache *noun* F pistachio.

piste *noun* F **1** trail (*left by an animal or fugitive*); **la police est sur sa piste** the police are on his trail; **2** track (*for racing or sport*); **faire un tour de piste** to do a lap; **3** piste, trail (*in skiing*); **4** runway (*at an airport*).

piste cyclable *noun* F cycle lane.

pistolet *noun* M pistol.

pitié *noun* F pity; **avoir pitié de quelqu'un** to feel sorry for someone.

pittoresque *adjective* picturesque.

placard *noun* M cupboard.

place *noun* F **1** space, room; **il y a assez de place pour deux** there's enough room for two; **2** seat (*in a theatre, cinema, train, or bus*); **trois places pour ce soir** two seats for this evening's performance; **3** place; **remettez tous les livres à leur place!** put all the books back in their places!; **si j'étais à ta place** if I were you; **4** place; **en troisième place** in third place; **5** square; **la place Rouge** the Red Square; **la place du village** the village square; **6** à la place de instead of; **il y est allé à ma place** he went instead of me; **7** être sur place to be on the spot.

placer *verb* [61] **1** to place; **2** to seat (*a person*); **elle m'a placé à côté de Louis** she put me next to Louis.

plafond *noun* M ceiling.

plage *noun* F beach; **on va à la plage** we're going to the beach.

plaie *noun* F wound.

plaindre *verb* [31] **1** to feel sorry for; **je te plains** I feel sorry for you; **2** se plaindre to complain; **je ne me plains pas** I'm not complaining.

plaine *noun* F plain.

plainte *noun* F complaint; **porter plainte** to complain.

plaire *verb* [62] **1** s'il te plaît, s'il vous plaît please; **deux billets, s'il vous plaît** two tickets, please; **2** le tissu me plaît I like the material; la **chambre vous plaît?** do you like your room?; **le film a beaucoup plu à mon père** my father liked the film very much.

plaisanter *verb* [1] to joke.

plaisanterie *noun* F joke.

plaisir *noun* M pleasure; **le plaisir de lire** the pleasure of reading; **'vous venez avec nous?' – 'oui, avec plaisir'** 'will you come too?' – 'yes, with pleasure'; **faire plaisir à quelqu'un** to please someone; **j'y suis allé pour faire plaisir à ma mère** I went to please my mother.

plan *noun* M **1** map (*of a town or underground system*); **le plan du métro** the underground map; **2** plan; **le plan du bâtiment** the plan of the building; **3** au premier plan in the foreground, in the forefront.

planche *noun* F plank.

planche à repasser *noun* F ironing board.

planche à roulettes *noun* F skateboard.

planche à voile *noun* F windsurfing board; **faire de la planche à voile** to go windsurfing.

plancher *noun* M floor.

plan d'eau *noun* M artificial lake (*often for swimming and other water sports*).

laner *verb* [1] **1** to glide; **2** (*informal*) to have your head in the clouds.

lanète *noun* F planet.

lante *noun* F plant; **une plante verte** a houseplant.

lanter *verb* [1] **1** to plant (*a tree, shrub, or plant*); **2** to hammer in (*a nail*); **3 se planter** (*informal*) to make a blunder.

laque *noun* F **1** patch (*of damp or ice*); **2** plate, sheet (*of metal or glass*).

laqué *adjective* **plaqué or** gold-plated; **plaqué argent** silver-plated.

laque d'immatriculation *noun* F number plate (*on a car*).

lastique *noun* M plastic; **un sac en plastique** a plastic bag.

lat *noun* M **1** dish; **un plat chaud/froid** a hot/cold dish; **le plat du jour** the dish of the day; **2** course (*of a meal*); **le plat principal** the main course; ★ **faire tout un plat de quelque chose** (*informal*) to make a big deal of something.
adjective **1** flat; **à plat ventre** flat on your stomach; **2 l'eau plate** still water.

latane *noun* M plane tree.

lateau (*plural* **plateaux**) *noun* M **1** tray; **2** plateau.

late-bande *noun* F flower bed.

lâtre *noun* M plaster; **il a une jambe dans le plâtre** he has a leg in plaster.

lein *adjective* **1** full; **le panier est plein** the basket's full; **elle est pleine d'idées** she's full of ideas; **2 en pleine nuit** in the middle of the night; **en plein été** at the height of summer; **en plein centre-ville** right in the middle of town; **en pleine mer** on the open sea.
noun M **faire le plein** to fill up (*a car with petrol*); **le plein, s'il vous plaît** a full tank, please.
adverb **plein de** (*informal*) loads of; **elle a plein d'amis** she's got loads of friends.

pleurer *verb* [1] to cry.

pleut *verb* SEE **pleuvoir**.

pleuvoir *verb* [63] to rain; **il pleut** it's raining; **il va pleuvoir** it's going to rain; **il a plu cette nuit** it rained last night.

pli *noun* M **1** fold; **2** pleat; **3** crease (*in trousers*).

plier *verb* [1] **1** to fold; **2** to bend (*your arm or leg, or a stem*); ★ **être plié en deux/en quatre** (*informal*) to be doubled up (*with laughter or pain*).

plomb *noun* M **1** lead; **de l'essence sans plomb** unleaded petrol; **2** fuse; **faire sauter les plombs** to blow the fuses.

plombage *noun* M filling (*in a tooth*).

plombier *noun* M plumber.

plongée *noun* F diving; **faire de la plongée** to go diving.

plongeoir *noun* M diving board.

plonger *verb* [52] **1** to dive; **2** to plunge.

plongeur, plongeuse *noun* M, F **1** diver; **2** washer-up.

plu *verb* SEE **plaire; pleuvoir**.

pluie *noun* F rain; **un jour de pluie** a rainy day; **sous la pluie** in the rain.

plume *noun* F 1 feather; 2 ink pen.

plupart *noun* F **la plupart de** most; **la plupart des gens** most people; **la plupart du temps** most of the time.

pluriel *noun* M plural; **au pluriel** in the plural.

plus *adverb* 1 **plus de** more; **voulez-vous un peu plus de fromage?** would you like a little more cheese?; 2 **plus de** more than; **il y avait plus de cent personnes** there were more than a hundred people; 3 **plus que** more than; **il mange plus que moi** he eats more than I do; **le film est plus intéressant que le livre** the film's more interesting than the book; **leur maison est plus grande que la nôtre** their house is bigger than ours; 4 **le plus rapide** the fastest; **le plus joli** the prettiest; 5 **plus...plus** the more...the more; **plus je gagne, plus je dépense** the more I earn the more I spend; 6 **en plus** more; **il nous faut trois côtelettes en plus** we need three more chops; 7 **de plus** more; **trois chaises de plus** three more chairs; **une fois de plus** one more time; 8 **de plus en plus** more and more; **elle fume de plus en plus** she smokes more and more; **je deviens de plus en plus fatigué** I'm getting more and more tired; **il fait de plus en plus chaud** it's getting hotter and hotter; 9 **plus ou moins** more or less; **la cuisine est plus ou moins propre** the kitchen's more or less

clean; 10 **le plus** the most; **c'est lu qui gagne le plus** he earns the mos **au plus** at the most; 11 **ne ... plus** no longer; **elle n'habite plus ici** she no longer lives here; 12 **je ne veux plus y aller** I don't want to go there any more; 13 **il n'y a plus de lait** there's no milk left; 14 plus; **deux plus trois égalent cinq** two plus three is five.

plusieurs *adjective* several; **plusieurs personnes** several people; **plusieurs fois** several time

plutôt *adverb* 1 rather; **prends le jaune plutôt que le vert** take the yellow one rather than the green one; 2 instead; **demande plutôt à Anne** ask Anne instead; 3 pretty; l **repas était plutôt bon** the meal wa pretty good; **plutôt bien** pretty good; 4 rather; **elle est plutôt maigre** she's rather thin.

pluvieux (F **pluvieuse**) *adjective* rainy.

pneu *noun* M tyre.

poche *noun* F pocket; **un livre de poche** a paperback; **l'argent de poche** pocket money; ★ **c'est dans la poche** (*informal*) it's in the bag; ★ **je connais Paris comme m poche** (*informal*) I know Paris like the back of my hand.

poêle¹ *noun* M stove (*for heating*); **un poêle à bois** a wood-burning stove.

poêle² *noun* F frying pan.

poème *noun* M poem.

poésie *noun* F poetry.

poète *noun* M poet.

poids *noun* M weight; **prendre du poids** to put on weight; **perdre du poids** to lose weight.

poids lourd *noun* M lorry.

poignée *noun* F **1** handful; **une poignée de cailloux** a handful of pebbles; **2** handle; **3** **une poignée de main** a handshake.

poignet *noun* M wrist.

poil *noun* M hair; **un poil** a hair; **le chat perd ses poils** the cat's moulting; ★ **être de bon/mauvais poil** to be in a good/bad mood.

poilu *adjective* hairy.

poing *noun* M fist; **un coup de poing** a punch.

point *noun* M **1** point; **et mon dernier point** and my last point; **un point de détail** a minor point; **un point faible** a weak point; **2** **un point de rencontre** a meeting-place; **3** **être sur le point de faire** to be just about to do; **j'étais sur le point de t'appeler** I was on the point of phoning you; **4** dot; **un petit point sur la carte** a tiny dot on the map; **5** full stop; **6** point (*when scoring*); **six points contre sept** six points to seven; **marquer/perdre des points** to win/lose points; **7** mark (*in a test*); **8** **à point** just in time; **tu es arrivé à point** you arrived just in time; **un steak cuit à point** a medium-rare steak.

point chaud *noun* M trouble spot.

point de départ *noun* M starting point.

point de vue *noun* M point of view; **d'un point de vue politique** from a political point of view.

point d'exclamation *noun* M exclamation mark.

point d'interrogation *noun* M question mark.

pointe *noun* F **1** point; **la pointe d'un couteau** the point of a knife; **sur la pointe des pieds** on tip-toe; **être en pointe** to be pointed; **2** **les heures de pointe** the rush hour, peak time; **3** **une pointe de** a touch of; **une pointe d'ail** a touch of garlic. ★ **être à la pointe du progrès** to be in the forefront of progress.

pointillé *noun* M dotted line.

point mort *noun* M neutral (*gear*); **tu es au point mort** you're in neutral.

pointu *adjective* pointed.

pointure *noun* F size (*of shoes*); **quelle est votre pointure?** what size do you take?

point-virgule *noun* M semi-colon.

poire *noun* F pear.

poireau (*plural* **poireaux**) *noun* M leek.

poirier *noun* M pear tree; **faire le poirier** to stand on your head.

pois *noun* M **1** pea; **des petits pois** (garden) peas; **2** **à pois** spotted; **un tissu à pois** a spotted fabric.

pois chiche *noun* M chick pea.

pois de senteur *noun* M sweet pea.

poison *noun* M poison.

poisson *noun* M fish; **j'aime le poisson** I like fish.

poisson d'avril *noun* M April fool; **il m'a fait un poisson d'avril** he played an April fool trick on me.

poissonnerie *noun* F fishmonger's.

poisson rouge *noun* M goldfish.

poissonnier, poissonnière *noun* M, F fishmonger.

Poissons *plural noun* M Pisces (*sign of the Zodiac*).

poitrine *noun* F **1** chest; **2** bust; **quel est votre tour de poitrine?** what is your bust size?

poivre *noun* M pepper; **poivre noir en grains** whole black peppercorns.

poivrier *noun* M pepper pot.

poivron *noun* M pepper (*red, green, or yellow*).

polar (*informal*) *noun* M detective story.

pôle *noun* M pole; **le pôle Nord/Sud** the North/South Pole.

poli *adjective* polite; **être poli avec quelqu'un** to be polite to somebody.

police *noun* F **1** police; **appeler la police** to call the police; **2** (insurance) policy.

policier *noun* M police officer; **une femme policier** a woman police officer.
adjective **un roman policier** a detective story.

poliment *adverb* politely.

politesse *noun* F politeness; **par politesse** out of politeness.

politicien, politicienne *noun* M, F politician.

politique *noun* F **1** politics; **2** policy; **la politique sociale/étrangère** social/foreign policy.
adjective **1** political; **2** **un homme politique** a politician.

polluer *verb* [1] to pollute.

pollution *noun* F pollution.

polo *noun* M polo shirt.

Pologne *noun* F Poland; **en Pologne** in (or to) Poland.

polonais *noun*, *adjective* Polish.

pommade *noun* F ointment.

pomme *noun* F **1** apple; **une tarte aux pommes** an apple tart; **2** potato; **pommes frites** chips; ★ **tomber dans les pommes** (*informal*) to faint (*literally: to fall into the apples*).

pomme de terre *noun* F potato.

pommier *noun* M apple tree.

pompe *noun* F pump.

pompe à essence *noun* F petrol pump.

pompes funèbres *plural noun* F undertaker's.

pompier *noun* M fire fighter; **appeler les pompiers** to call the fire brigade.

pompiste *noun* M & F petrol pump attendant.

poncer verb [61] to sand (*wood*).

ponctuation noun F punctuation.

poney noun M pony.

pont noun M **1** bridge; **2** deck (*of a ship*); ★ **faire le pont** to take a long weekend (*usually when the Thursday before or the Tuesday after is a public holiday*).

populaire adjective **1** working-class (*family, housing, or area*); **2** popular (*art or writing*); **3** folk; **la culture populaire** folk culture; **4** popular.

population noun F population.

porc noun M **1** pig; **un élevage de porcs** a pig farm; **2** pork; **manger un rôti de porc** to have roast pork.

porcelaine noun F china, porcelain.

port noun M **1** port; **2** harbour.

portable adjective portable; **un ordinateur portable** a laptop computer.

portail noun M gate.

portatif (F **portative**) adjective portable.

porte noun F **1** door; **la porte d'entrée** the front door; **2** gate (*in an airport*); **la porte numéro douze** gate number twelve; **3** **l'entreprise a fermé ses portes** the business has closed down; **mettre quelqu'un à la porte** to sack somebody.

porte-bagages noun M luggage rack.

porte-clés noun M key-ring.

portée noun F **à portée de main** within reach.

porte-fenêtre noun F French window.

portefeuille noun M wallet; **une jupe en portefeuille** a wrapover skirt.

porte-jarretelles noun M suspender belt.

portemanteau (*plural* **portemanteaux**) noun M coat rack.

portemine noun M propelling pencil.

porte-monnaie noun M purse.

porte-parole noun M spokesperson.

porter verb [1] **1** to carry; **porter une valise** to carry a suitcase; **2** to take; **porter un paquet à la poste** to take a parcel to the post office; **3** to wear; **elle portait une robe bleue** she was wearing a blue dress; **4** **se porter bien** to be well; **se porter mal** to be in a bad way; ★ **porter bonheur/malheur** to bring good/bad luck.

portière noun F door (*of a car*).

portion noun F portion, helping.

porto noun M port (*wine*).

portrait noun M portrait.

portugais noun M, adjective Portuguese.

Portugal noun M Portugal; **au Portugal** in (or to) Portugal.

poser verb [1] **1** to put down; **il a posé sa tasse sur la table** he put his cup down on the table; **pose ta valise** put your case down; **2 cela nous pose un problème** that's a problem for us; **3 poser une question** to ask a question.

positif (F **positive**) *adjective* positive.

position *noun* F position.

posséder *verb* [24] to own.

possibilité *noun* F **1** possibility; **c'est une possibilité** it's a possibility; **2** opportunity; **la possibilité de voyager** the opportunity to travel.

possible *adjective* possible; **aussi grand que possible** as big as possible; **le moins possible** as little as possible; **dès que possible** as soon as possible; **ce n'est pas possible!** I don't believe it!; ★ **faire tout son possible** to do your best.

poste[1] *noun* M **1** job, post; **un poste de secrétaire** a job as a secretary; **2 un poste de radio/télévision** a radio/television set; **3** extension (*on a telephone system*); **le poste 578, s'il vous plaît** extension 578, please.

poste[2] *noun* F post office; **il travaille pour la poste** he works for the post office; **mettre quelque chose à la poste** to post something.

poste de police *noun* M police station.

pot *noun* M **1** jar; **un pot de confiture** a jar of jam; **2** carton; **un pot de crème** a carton of cream; **3 un pot de peinture** a tin of paint; ★ **prendre un pot** to have a drink.

potable *adjective* **eau (non) potable** (not) drinking water.

potage *noun* M soup; **potage aux légumes** vegetable soup.

potager *noun* M vegetable garden.

pot-au-feu *noun* M boiled beef with vegetables.

pot d'échappement *noun* M exhaust, silencer (*for a car*).

poteau (*plural* **poteaux**) *noun* M post.

potelé *adjective* chubby.

poterie *noun* F **1** pottery; **2** piece of pottery.

pou (*plural* **poux**) *noun* M louse; ★ **chercher des poux** (*informal*) to nitpick.

poubelle *noun* F dustbin; **mettre quelque chose à la poubelle** to throw something in the dustbin.

pouce *noun* M **1** thumb; **2** inch; ★ **se tourner les pouces** (*informal*) to twiddle your thumbs.

poudre *noun* F powder.

pouffer *verb* [1] **pouffer de rire** to burst out laughing.

poulain *noun* M foal.

poule *noun* F hen; ★ **quand les poules auront des dents** (*informal*) when pigs can fly (*literally: when hens have teeth*).

poulet *noun* M chicken; **une cuisse de poulet** a chicken leg; **du poulet rôti** roast chicken.

poulet fermier *noun* M free-range chicken.

pouls *noun* M pulse.

poumon *noun* M lung; **crier à pleins poumons** to shout at the top of your voice.

poupée *noun* F doll.

pour *preposition* **1** for; **un cadeau pour Marie-Laure** a present for Marie-Laure; **un billet pour Calais** a ticket for Calais; **le train pour Londres** the train for London; **ce sera prêt pour samedi?** will it be ready for Saturday?; **être pour** to be in favour; **je n'y suis pour rien** I had nothing to do with it; **je n'en ai pas pour longtemps** it won't take long; **2 pour faire cela** in order to do that; **je suis allé au marché pour acheter des légumes** I went to the market to buy some vegetables; **je suis là pour t'aider** I'm here to help you; **c'était juste pour rire!** it was only meant as a joke!; **pour ainsi dire** so to speak; ★ **le pour et le contre** the pros and cons.

pour cent per cent; **dix pour cent** ten per cent.

pourboire *noun* M tip.

pourcentage *noun* M percentage.

pourquoi *adverb* why; **pourquoi ont-ils refusé?** why did they refuse?; **je veux savoir pourquoi** I want to know why; **pourquoi pas?** why not?

pourri *adjective* rotten.

pourrir *verb* [2] to go bad.

poursuivre *verb* [75] **1** to chase; **2** to continue.

pourtant *adverb* **1** though; **et pourtant c'est vrai** it's true

though; **2** yet; **et pourtant ça aurait pu être bien** and yet it could have been good.

pourvu que *conjunction* (*followed by subjunctive*) **1** providing, as long as; **pourvu que tu reviennes samedi** providing you come back on Saturday; **2** let's hope that; **pourvu que ça dure!** let's hope it lasts!

pousser *verb* [1] **1** to push; **elle a poussé la porte** she pushed the door shut (or open) ; **2 pousser un cri** to let out a cry, to cry out; **3** to grow (*of a child, hair, or a plant*); **mes tomates poussent bien** my tomatoes are growing well; **4 se pousser** to move over; **pousse-toi!** move over!

poussette *noun* F pushchair.

poussière *noun* F dust; ★ **dix francs et des poussières** ten francs something, just over 10 francs.

poutre *noun* F beam.

pouvez *verb* SEE **pouvoir**[1].

pouvoir[1] *verb* [12] can; **je peux être là à dix heures** I can be there at ten; **peux-tu m'aider?** can you help me?; **je ne peux pas l'ouvrir** I can't open it; **ils ne pouvaient pas téléphoner avant** they couldn't phone before; **je n'ai pas pu réserver** I wasn't able to book; **elle aurait pu nous le dire** she could have told us; **puis-je parler à Cécile, s'il vous plaît** may I speak to Cécile, please; **tu peux toujours essayer** there's no harm in trying.

pouvoir[2] *noun* M power; **après dix ans au pouvoir** after ten years in power.

pouvons *verb* SEE **pouvoir**[1].

prairie *noun* F meadow.

pratique *noun* F practice; **mettre quelque chose en pratique** to put something into practice; **il manque de pratique** he lacks practical experience.
adjective practical, convenient; **cet ouvre-boîte n'est pas très pratique** this can opener isn't very practical; **le nouvel appartement est très pratique pour les magasins** the new flat's very handy for the shops.

pratiquement *adverb* practically; **c'est pratiquement fini** it's practically finished.

pratiquer *verb* [1] **1** to play, to do (*a sport or hobby*); **je pratique le yoga** I do yoga; **2** to practise; **pendant mon séjour à Lille j'aurai la possibilité de pratiquer mon français** during my stay in Lille I'll be able to practise my French.

pré *noun* M meadow.

précaution *noun* F precaution; **par précaution** as a precaution; **prendre ses précautions** to take precautions.

précédent *adjective* previous; **l'année précédente** the previous year, the year before.

précieux (F **précieuse**) *adjective* precious, valuable; **une pierre précieuse** a precious stone; **des renseignements précieux** extremely useful information.

précipice *noun* M precipice.

précipitation *noun* F haste.

précipiter *verb* [1] **se précipiter** to rush; **ils se sont précipités vers la porte** they rushed for the door.

précis *adjective* precise.

préciser *verb* [1] **1** to specify (*details or one's intentions*); **2** to explain; **pouvez-vous préciser comment?** could you explain exactly how?

précision *noun* F **1** precision; **2** detail; **voici quelques précisions sur le voyage** here are some details about the journey.

précuit *adjective* precooked.

préfecture *noun* F prefecture (*France is divided into 96 'départements', which are roughly equivalent to British counties. The administration of each of these is done at the local level from the prefecture.*)

préférable *adjective* preferable.

préféré *adjective* favourite; **mon plat préféré** my favourite dish.

préférence *noun* F **1** preference; **2 de préférence** preferably; **de préférence avant le dix mai** preferably before the tenth of May.

préférer *verb* [24] to prefer; **elle préfère le poisson à la viande** she prefers fish to meat.

préfet *noun* M prefect (*official with overall responsibility for running a French department*); SEE ALSO **préfecture**.

préjugé *noun* M prejudice.

prélavage *noun* M prewash.

prématuré *adjective* premature.

premier (F **première**) *adjective*
1 first; **la première fois** the first
time; **c'est la première fois que je le
fais** it's the first time I've done it;
Michel, tu passes le premier
Michel, you go first; **le premier juin**
the first of June; **2** top; **de première
qualité** top quality; **3** **au premier
étage** on the first floor; **4** **en
premier** first; **arriver en premier** to
arrive first.

première *noun* F **1** première (*of a
film or play*); **2** **une première
mondiale** a world first (*an
important event or achievement*);
3 **voyager en première** to travel
first-class; **4** (*in a French school*)
the equivalent of Year 12.

premièrement *adverb* firstly.

Premier ministre *noun* M prime
minister.

prendre *verb* [64] **1** to take; **prends
celui-ci!** take this one!; **prendre un
taxi** to take a taxi; **2** **prendre
quelque chose à quelqu'un** to take
something from somebody; **qui m'a
pris mon vélo?** who's taken my
bike?; **3** to have (*something to eat or
drink*); **je prends une bière** I'll have
a beer; **qu'est-ce que tu prends?**
what would you like?; **4** to bring;
**est-ce que tu as pris ton
parapluie?** did you bring your
umbrella?; **5** **passer prendre
quelqu'un** to pick somebody up; **je
passerai te prendre à dix heures** I'll
pick you up at ten; ★ **c'est à
prendre ou à laisser** take it or leave
it.

prénom *noun* M first name.

préparatifs *plural noun* M
preparations; **les préparatifs du
voyage** the preparations for the
journey.

préparation *noun* F preparation,
training.

préparer *verb* [1] **1** to prepare; **je
vais préparer les légumes** I'll go and
prepare the vegetables; **Françoise
est en train de préparer le dîner**
Françoise is busy making dinner; **as-
tu préparé tes affaires pour le
matin?** have you got your things
ready for the morning?; **on a préparé
une petite surprise pour elle** we've
got a little surprise ready for her; **des
plats préparés** ready-to-eat meals;
2 **se préparer** to get ready; **je vais
me préparer pour partir** I'll go and
get ready to leave.

préposition *noun* F preposition.

près *adverb* **1** nearby; **il y a un
village tout près** there's a village
nearby; **2** **près de** near; **près de la
gare** near the station; **près de toi**
near you; **près de chez nous** near
our house, near where we live;
3 **près de** nearly, almost; **près de
mille francs** nearly a thousand
francs; **4** **de près** closely; **regarder
quelque chose de près** to look
closely at something; **5** **à peu près**
more or less; **à peu près deux
heures** two hours, more or less; **j'ai
à peu près fini** I've more or less
finished.

présence *noun* F presence.

présent *noun* M **1** present (tense);
au présent in the present; **2** **à
présent** now; **à présent je n'ai pas
le temps** I haven't got time just now.

adjective present (*at an event*);
toute la famille était présente the
whole family was there.

présentateur, présentatrice
noun M, F **1** presenter (*of a
broadcast or programme*);
2 newsreader.

présentation *noun* F
1 presentation; **2** introduction (*to
someone you haven't met before*).

présenter *verb* [1] **1** to introduce;
je vous présente mon père may I
introduce my father?; **Alain, je te
présente Raphaël** Alain, this is
Raphaël; **2** to present (*a ticket, pass,
or document*); **il faut présenter votre
passeport** you must show your
passport; **3** **présenter ses
excuses** to apologize; **4** **se
présenter** to go, to come; **en
arrivant, présentez-vous à la
réception** when you get there (or
here), go (or come) to reception;
5 **se présenter à quelqu'un** to
introduce yourself to somebody.

préservatif *noun* M condom.

préserver *verb* [1] to protect, to
preserve.

président *noun* M **1** president;
2 chairman.

présidente *noun* F **1** president;
2 chairwoman.

présidentielles *plural noun* F **les
présidentielles** the presidential
elections.

presque *adverb* **1** nearly; **j'ai
presque fini** I've nearly finished;
2 **presque rien** hardly anything; **il
ne reste presque rien** there's hardly
anything left; **3** **presque pas de**

hardly any; **il ne reste presque pas
de lait** there's hardly any milk left.

presqu'île *noun* F peninsula.

pressant *adjective* urgent.

presse *noun* F **la presse** the press,
the newspapers; **que dit la presse?**
what do the papers say?

pressé *adjective* **1** **être pressé** to
be in a hurry; **2** urgent; **ce n'est pas
pressé** it's not urgent; **3** **un citron
pressé** a fresh lemon juice (*served
with water and sugar*).

presser *verb* [1] **1** to urge (*someone
to do something*); **2** to squeeze;
presser une orange to squeeze an
orange; **3** **ça ne presse pas** there's
no hurry; **presser le pas** to hurry
(on); **4** **se presser** to hurry.

pressing *noun* M dry cleaner's.

pression *noun* F **1** pressure; **sous
pression** pressurized; **2** press
stud; **3** (*informal*) draught beer; **un
demi pression** a half of draught
beer.

**prestidigitateur,
prestidigitatrice** *noun* M, F
conjurer.

présumer *verb* [1] to assume, to
presume.

prêt *noun* M loan.
adjective ready; **le dîner est prêt!**
dinner's ready!; **être prêt à partir** to
be ready to leave.

prêt-à-porter *noun* M ready-to-
wear (clothes).

prétendre *verb* [3] to claim; **elle
prétend que ce n'est pas sa faute**
she claims it's not her fault.

prêter *verb* [1] **1** to lend; **prêter quelque chose à quelqu'un** to lend somebody something; **je te prêterai mon vélo** I'll lend you my bike; **2 prêter attention** to pay attention; **3 prêter l'oreille** to listen.

prétexte *noun* M excuse.

prêtre *noun* M priest.

preuve *noun* F **1** proof; **la preuve, c'est que...** the proof is that...; **2 faire preuve de** to show; **ils ont fait preuve de beaucoup d'intelligence** they showed considerable intelligence.

prévenir *verb* [81] **1** to tell (*in advance*); **prévenez-moi de ta visite** tell me when you're coming; **ils arrivent toujours sans nous prévenir** they always arrive without letting us know; **2** to call (*the police or a doctor*); **3** to warn; **je te préviens** I warn you.

prévention *noun* F prevention.

prévision *noun* F forecast, forecasting; **les prévisions météorologiques** the weather forecast.

prévoir *verb* [65] **1** to predict (*an event or change*); **2** to plan (*a journey or an arrangement*); **3 tout a été prévu** everything's been taken care of; **4 le départ est prévu pour huit heures** departure is scheduled for eight o' clock; **5** to allow (*time or money*); **prévoyez 50 francs pour le taxi** allow 50 francs for the taxi.

prier *verb* [1] **1 prier quelqu'un de faire** to ask someone to do; **il m'a prié d'excuser son retard** he asked me to forgive him for being late; **les clients sont priés de ne pas fumer** customers are kindly requested not to smoke; **2 je vous en prie** you're welcome, it's nothing; **'merci beaucoup' – 'je vous en prie'** 'thank you very much' – 'you're welcome'; **3** to pray.

prière *noun* F **1** prayer; **2** request; **'prière de fermer la porte'** 'please close the door'.

primaire *adjective* primary; **l'école primaire** primary school.

prime *noun* F **1** bonus; **2** free gift.

primevère *noun* F primrose.

prince *noun* M prince; **le prince Charles** Prince Charles.

princesse *noun* F princess.

principal (M *plural* **principaux**) *adjective* principal, chief.

principe *noun* M **1** principle; **2 en principe** as a rule; **en principe je rentre à six heures** as a rule I get back at six; **3 en principe** in theory; **en principe tout le monde a été informé** in theory, everybody's been informed.

printanier (F **printanière**) *adjective* spring-like (*weather*).

printemps *noun* M spring; **au printemps** in (the) spring.

priorité *noun* F **1** priority; **2** right of way; **'vous n'avez pas la priorité'** 'you do not have right of way' (*sign at a roundabout*).

pris *verb* SEE **prendre**. *adjective* **1** busy; **je suis très pris ce matin** I'm very busy this morning;

2 taken; **toutes les places sont prises** all the seats are taken;
3 overcome (*with an emotion or a feeling*); **être pris de panique** to be panic-stricken.

prise *noun* F **1** socket, plug (*for an electric appliance*); **2** capture; **la prise de la Bastille** the storming of the Bastille.

prise de courant *noun* F power point.

prise de sang *noun* F blood test.

prise multiple *noun* F adaptor plug.

prison *noun* F prison.

prisonnier, prisonnière *noun* M, F prisoner.

privé *noun* M **1** private sector (*of business or the school system*); **2 en privé** in private; off the record. *adjective* **1** private; **'propriété privée'** 'private property';
2 without; **nous sommes privé d'électricité** we are without electricity; **privé de sens** senseless.

priver *verb* [1] **1 priver quelqu'un de quelque chose** to deprive someone of something; **2 se priver de quelque chose** to do without something.

privilège *noun* M privilege.

privilégié *adjective* privileged, special, fortunate.

privilégier *verb* [1] **1** to favour;
2 to give priority to.

prix *noun* M **1** price; **quel est le prix des places?** what price are the seats?; **le prix a augmenté** the price

has gone up; **2 à tout prix** at all costs; **3** prize; **le premier prix** first prize.

probable *adjective* likely; **c'est peu probable** it's unlikely.

probablement *adverb* probably.

problème *noun* M problem; **sans problème!** no problem!

procédé *noun* M process.

procès *noun* M **1** trial; **2** lawsuit.

prochain *adjective* next; **la prochaine fois** the next time; **le mois prochain** next month; **jeudi prochain** next Thursday; **à la prochaine!** see you soon!

prochainement *adverb* soon.

proche *adjective* **1** near; **la ville la plus proche est Valence** the nearest town is Valence; **2** close; **c'est une amie très proche de Julie** she' a very close friend of Julie's;
3 proche de near; **ils ont acheté une maison proche de Nice** they've bought a house near Nice.

Proche-Orient *noun* M **le Proche-Orient** the Middle East.

proches *plural noun* M close family and friends.

procurer *verb* [1] **se procurer quelque chose** to get something.

producteur, productrice *noun* M, F producer.

production *noun* F production.

produire *verb* [26] **1** to produce;
2 se produire to happen; **ça s'est produit au mois de mai** that happened in May.

produit *noun* M product; **les produits de beauté** beauty products; **les produits d'entretien** household products; **les produits laitiers** dairy produce.

prof *noun* M (*informal*) SHORT FOR **professeur** teacher; **notre prof de français** our French teacher.

professeur *noun* M **1** teacher; **ma sœur est professeur de physique** my sister's a physics teacher; **2** university lecturer; **3** university professor.

profession *noun* F profession, occupation.

professionnel (F **professionnelle**) *adjective* professional.

profil *noun* M profile.

profit *noun* M **1** profit; **les profits de la société** the company's profits; **2 au profit de** in aid of; **au profit des sans-abri** in aid of the homeless.

profiter *verb* [1] **1 profiter de** to take advantage of (*an opportunity*); **j'ai profité des soldes pour m'acheter un manteau** I took advantage of the sales to buy myself a coat; **2** to make the most of; **profite bien de tes vacances !** make the most of your holiday!; **3 profiter à** to benefit.

profond *adjective* deep; **un trou profond de 3 mètres** a hole three metres deep; **la France profonde** provincial France.

profondément *adverb* deeply, profoundly.

profondeur *noun* F depth; **la piscine a une profondeur de 3 mètres** the swimming pool is 3 metres deep; **étudier quelque chose en profondeur** to study something in depth.

programme *noun* M **1** programme; **ce n'est pas au programme** it's not on the programme; **2** program (*for a computer*); **3** syllabus; **le programme de maths** the maths syllabus.

programmer *verb* [1] **1** to schedule; **2** to program (*on a computer*).

progrès *noun* M progress; **les progrès de l'informatique** advances in computer science; **faire des progrès** to make progress.

progresser *verb* [1] **1** to progress; **2** to make progress.

projecteur *noun* M **1** floodlight; **2** spotlight; **3** projector.

projet *noun* M **1** plan; **mes projets pour l'été** my plans for the summer; **2** project; **3** rough draft.

projeter *verb* [48] **1** to throw, to hurl; **le choc l'a projeté de sa voiture** the impact hurled him out of his car; **2** to show (*a film*); **3** to cast (*a shadow*); **4 projeter de faire** to plan to do.

prolongation *noun* F continuation.

prolongé *adjective* lengthy; **une discussion prolongée** a lengthy discussion.

prolonger *verb* [52] **1** to extend; **elle a prolongé son congé de maladie** she's extended her sick leave; **2 se prolonger** to go on; **les discussions se sont prolongées jusqu'à 23 h** discussions went on till 11 p.m.

promenade *noun* F **1** walk; **faire une promenade** to go for a walk; **une promenade en voiture** a drive; **une promenade à vélo** a bike ride; **2** promenade (*by the sea*).

promener *verb* [50] **1 promener un enfant** to take a child for a walk; **promener le chien** to walk the dog; **2 promener quelque chose** to carry something around; **3 se promener** to go for a walk; **se promener en voiture** to go for a drive; **se promener à vélo** to go for a bike ride.

promesse *noun* F promise; **il m'a fait une promesse** he made me a promise; **tenir sa promesse** to keep your promise.

prometteur (F **prometteuse**) *adjective* promising.

promettre *verb* [11] to promise; **promettre de faire** to promise to do; **il a promis de téléphoner ce soir** he promised to ring this evening; **j'ai promis à ma mère de lui écrire une fois par semaine** I promised my mother I would write to her once a week.

promotion *noun* F **1** special offer; **les fraises sont en promotion cette semaine** strawberries are on special offer this week; **2** promotion (*to a higher job*); **avoir une promotion** to be promoted.

pronom *noun* M pronoun.

prononcer *verb* [61] **1** to pronounce (*a word*); **2** to mention (*a name*); to say (*a word or phrase*); **3** to make (*a speech*); **4 se prononcer pour/contre quelque chose** to declare oneself for/against something.

prononciation *noun* F pronunciation.

propagande *noun* F propaganda.

proportion *noun* F proportion; **en proportion de** in proportion to.

propos *noun* M **1 à propos** by the way; **à propos, as-tu appelé maman?** by the way, did you ring Mum?; **2 à propos de** about; **il n'a rien dit à propos de son père** he said nothing about his father; **3 des propos** remarks.

proposer *verb* [1] **1 proposer quelque chose à quelqu'un** to suggest something to somebody; **je leur ai proposé une petite promenade** I suggested we went for a little walk; **2 proposer quelque chose à quelqu'un** to offer somebody something; **on lui a proposé un poste de technicien** she (or he) has been offered a job as a technician.

proposition *noun* F offer.

propre *adjective* **1** (*when it comes after the noun*) clean; **une chemise propre** a clean shirt; **2** (*when it comes before the noun*) own; **ma propre voiture** my own car; **leurs propres enfants** their own children.

proprement *adverb* **1** properly; **mange proprement!** eat properly!; **2 à proprement parler** strictly speaking.

propreté *noun* F cleanliness.

propriétaire *noun* M & F **1** owner (*usually of a building or a business*); **2** landlord, landlady.

propriété *noun* F **1** property; **propriété privée** private property; **2** ownership.

prospectus *noun* M leaflet.

prospère *adjective* prosperous.

protecteur, protectrice *noun* M, F protector. *adjective* protective; **une crème protectrice** protective cream.

protection *noun* F protection; **des lunettes de protection** protective goggles.

protéger *verb* [15] to protect; **pour protéger l'environnement** to protect the environment; **se protéger du soleil** to protect yourself from the sun.

protestant, protestante *noun* M, F, *adjective* Protestant.

protestation *noun* F protest.

protester *verb* [1] to protest; **protester contre quelque chose** to protest against something.

prouver *verb* [1] to prove.

provenance *noun* F origin; **du fromage en provenance de France** cheese from France; **un passager en provenance de Madrid** a passenger arriving from Madrid.

proverbe *noun* M proverb.

province *noun* F province; **en province** in the provinces; **une ville de province** a provincial town.

provision *noun* F **1** supply; **nous avons fait provision de bois** we've laid in a supply of wood; **2 des provisions** food; **maman est partie prendre des provisions** Mum's gone off shopping for food.

provisoire *adjective* temporary.

provocateur, provocatrice *noun* M, F agitator. *adjective* provocative.

provoquer *verb* [1] **1** to cause; **provoquer un accident** to cause an accident; **provoquer une discussion** to spark off a discussion; **2 provoquer quelqu'un** to provoke somebody.

proximité *noun* F nearness; **à proximité de** near.

prudemment *adjective* carefully.

prudence *noun* F caution; **conduisez avec prudence!** drive carefully!

prudent *adjective* **1** careful; **soyez prudents par mauvais temps!** be careful in bad weather!; **2** wise; **il est plus prudent de réserver** it's wiser to book.

prune *noun* F plum.

pruneau (*plural* **pruneaux**) *noun* M prune.

prunier *noun* M plum tree.

psychanalyste *noun* M & F psychoanalyst.

psychiatre *noun* M & F
psychiatrist.

psychologie *noun* F psychology.

psychologique *adjective*
psychological.

psychologue *noun* M & F
psychologist.

pu *verb* SEE **pouvoir**[1].

pub *noun* F (*informal*) SHORT FOR
publicité advert.

public *noun* M **1** public; **en public**
in public; **ouvert au public** open to
the public; **'interdit au public'** 'no
admission'; **2** audience,
spectators; **pour un public jeune** for
a young audience; **3** fans (*of a
performer*).
adjective (F **publique**) public; **dans
un lieu public** in a public place; **une
école publique** a state school.

publicitaire *adjective*
1 advertising; **une campagne
publicitaire** an advertising
campaign; **2** promotional
(*material*).

publicité *noun* F **1** advertising;
elle travaille dans la publicité she
works in advertising; **2** advert; ad
(*in a magazine, a newspaper, on
television, or at the cinema*).

publier *verb* [1] to publish.

puce *noun* F **1 une puce
électronique** a microchip; **une
carte à puce** a smart card; **2** flea;
un marché aux puces a
fleamarket.

puer *verb* [1] to stink.

puis *adverb* then; **nous allons à
Cannes, puis à Nice** we're going to
Cannes, then Nice.

puisque, puisqu' (*before a vowel or
silent 'h'*) *conjunction* since;
puisqu'il pleut je prendrai le bus
since it's raining I'll take the bus.

puissance *noun* F power; **un
moteur d'une forte puissance** a
high-power engine; **une puissance
étrangère** a foreign power.

puissant *adjective* powerful,
strong.

puits *noun* M well.

pull, pull-over *noun* M jumper.

pulvérisateur *noun* M spray.

punaise *noun* F **1** drawing-pin;
2 bug.

punir *verb* [2] to punish.

punition *noun* F punishment.

pur *adjective* **1** pure; **un
shampooing très doux, très pur** an
ultra-mild, ultra-pure shampoo; **un
croissant pur beurre** an all-butter
croissant; **2** sheer, total; **c'est de la
folie pure** it's sheer madness.

purée *noun* F mashed potatoes.

puzzle *noun* M jigsaw puzzle.

PV *noun* M SHORT FOR **procès verbal**
parking ticket.

pyjama *noun* M (pair of) pyjamas;
où est mon pyjama? where are my
pyjamas?; **un pyjama propre** a clean
pair of pyjamas.

pyramide *noun* F pyramid.

Pyrénées *plural noun* F Pyrenees.

Q q

quai *noun* M **1** platform; **le train à destination de Paris va arriver au quai numéro trois** the train for Paris is about to arrive at platform number three; **2** quay.

qualifié *adjective* **1** qualified; **2** skilled.

qualifier *verb* [1] to qualify.

qualité *noun* F quality; **des fruits de première qualité** top quality fruit.

quand *conjunction,*
adverb when; **quand est-ce que ton frère arrive?** when is your brother arriving?; **quand tu auras dix-sept ans, tu pourras apprendre à conduire** when you're seventeen you'll be able to learn to drive.

quand même *adverb* all the same; **il pleut mais je vais sortir quand même** it's raining but I'm going to go out all the same; **quand même!** honestly!

quant à *preposition* as for; **quant à moi, je reste** as for me, I'm staying here.

quantité *noun* F amount.

quarantaine *noun* F **1** about forty; **une quarantaine de personnes** about forty people; **j'approche la quarantaine** I'll soon be forty; **2** quarantine.

quarante *number* forty.

quart *noun* M **1** (*in time expressions*) quarter; **un quart d'heure** a quarter of an hour; **dix heures et quart** quarter past ten; **2** quarter; **le quart du gâteau** a quarter of the cake; **un quart d'eau minérale** a quarter-litre bottle of mineral water; **trois quarts** three quarters; **les trois quarts du temps** most of the time.

quartier *noun* M area (*of a town*); **un quartier résidentiel** a residential area; **les gens du quartier** the local people.

quartz *noun* M quartz.

quasi *adverb* almost; **quasi parfait** almost perfect.

quasiment *adverb* **1** practically; **c'est quasiment neuf** it's practically new; **2 quasiment jamais** hardly ever; **il n'est quasiment jamais chez lui** he's hardly ever at home.

quatorze *number* fourteen; **Céline a quatorze ans** Céline's fourteen; **le quatorze juin** the fourteenth of June.

quatre *number* four; **Louis a quatre ans** Louis is four; **le quatre mars** the fourth of March.

quatre-vingts *number* eighty; **quatre-vingts personnes** eighty people; **quatre-vingt-trois** eighty-three (*note that the 's' is dropped when another number is added*); **quatre-vingt-seize** ninety-six.

quatre-vingt-dix *number* ninety; **quatre-vingt-dix-neuf** ninety-nine.

quatrième *noun* F (*in a French school*) the equivalent of Year 9.

noun M **au quatrième** on the fourth floor.
adjective fourth.

que *conjunction, pronoun, adverb*
1 that (*often left out in English*); **elle dit que c'est vrai** she says (that) it's true; **je sais qu'il y habite** I know he lives there; **je veux que tu sois heureux** I want you to be happy; **2** whether; **qu'ils arrivent demain ou mardi, n'importe** whether they come tomorrow or on Tuesday, it doesn't matter; **3** **que tout le monde se lève!** everybody stand up!; **4** **plus...que** more...than; **elle est plus grande que Marie** she's taller than Marie; **5** **aussi...que** as...as; **elle est aussi grande que moi** she's as tall as me; **6** **ne...que** only; **je n'ai que dix francs** I've only got ten francs; **7** that, which, whom (*often left out in English*); **le livre que je lis** the book (that) I'm reading; **la chemise qu'il a achetée** the shirt (which) he's bought; **8** what; **que veut-il?** what does he want?; **je ne sais pas ce qu'il veut** I don't know what he wants; **9** **qu'est-ce que...?** what...?; **qu'est-ce que tu as trouvé?** what have you found?; **qu'est-ce que c'est?** what's that? **qu'est-ce qu'il y a?** what's the matter?; **qu'est-ce qu'elle a?** what's the matter with her?; **10** how (*in an exclamation*); **que tu as grandi!** how you've grown!

quel, quelle *adjective* **1** (*in a question*) what; which; **quel livre?** which book?; **quelle voiture?** which car?; **quelle heure est-il?** what time is it?; **quel âge as-tu?** how old are you?; **dans quels pays?** in which countries?; **pour quelles raisons?** for what reasons?; **2** (*in an exclamation*) what; **quel beau temps!** what lovely weather!; **quelle coïncidence!** what a coincidence!; **quelle horreur!** how dreadful!

quelconque *adjective* any; **si tu as un problème quelconque** if you have any sort of a problem; **si pour une raison quelconque** if for any reason.

quelle *adjective* SEE **quel**.

quelque chose *pronoun*
1 something; **il faut manger quelque chose, Claire** you must eat something, Claire; **il y a quelque chose de bizarre** there's something strange; **voulez-vous boire quelque chose?** would you like something to drink?; **2** anything; **est-ce que tu as vu quelque chose?** did you see anything?

quelquefois *adverb* sometimes.

quelque part *adverb*
1 somewhere; **quelque part dans le jardin** somewhere in the garden; **2** anywhere; **est-ce que tu as vu mes lunettes quelque part?** have you seen my glasses anywhere?

quelques *adjective* **1** some; **je vais te donner quelques cerises** I'll give you some cherries; **2** a few; **il reste quelques fraises** there are a few strawberries left; **elle est partie pour quelques jours** she's gone away for a few days.

quelques-uns, quelques-unes *plural pronoun* some; **quelques-**

uns des enfants some of the children.

quelqu'un *pronoun* **1** somebody; **quelqu'un a appelé pour toi** somebody rang for you; **quelqu'un d'autre** somebody else; **2** anybody; **il y a quelqu'un?** is there anybody there?

quels, quelles *adjective* SEE **quel**.

querelle *noun* F quarrel.

qu'est-ce que SEE **que**.

qu'est-ce qui SEE **qui**.

question *noun* F **1** question; **poser une question à quelqu'un** to ask somebody a question; **elle n'a pas répondu à mes questions** she didn't answer my questions; **2** matter, question; **c'est une question de goût** it's a matter of taste; **c'est hors de question** it's out of the question; **pas question!** no way!

questionnaire *noun* M questionnaire.

questionner *verb* [1] to question.

queue *noun* F **1** tail; **la queue du chat** the cat's tail; **2** queue; **faire la queue** to queue; **3** la queue du train** the rear of the train; **4** stalk (*of a flower or a fruit*).

queue de cheval *noun* F ponytail.

qui *pronoun* **1** who; **qui a fermé la porte?** who closed the door?; **qui voulez-vous voir?** who do you want to see?; **la personne qui vous a écrit n'est pas là aujourd'hui** the person who wrote to you is not here today; **2** that; **prends la casserole qui est** sur l'évier take the pan that's on the sink; **3** à qui?** whose?; **à qui est ce pull?** whose is this jumper?; **4** à qui parles-tu?** who are you talking to?; **5** qu'est-ce qui…?** what…?; **qu'est-ce qui t'amène?** what brings you here?

quincaillerie *noun* F hardware shop.

quinzaine *noun* F **1** about fifteen; **une quinzaine d'enfants** about fifteen children; **2** une quinzaine de jours** a fortnight; **dans une quinzaine** two weeks from now.

quinze *number* **1** fifteen; **Marise a quinze ans** Marise is fifteen; **le quinze juillet** the fifteenth of July; **2** quinze jours** two weeks; **tous les quinze jours** every two weeks.

quitter *verb* [1] **1** to leave; **je quitte le bureau à cinq heures** I leave the office at five; **j'ai quitté l'école à seize ans** I left school at sixteen; **2** se quitter** to part; **3** ne quittez pas** hold the line please (*on the telephone*).

quoi *pronoun* **1** what; **quoi encore?** what now?; **tu es sourd ou quoi?** are you deaf or what?; **à quoi penses-tu?** what are you thinking about?; **pour quoi faire?** what for?; **à quoi bon continuer?** what's the point in going on?; **il n'y a pas de quoi se fâcher** there's no reason to get angry; **il n'y a pas de quoi** don't mention it; **2** which; **après quoi, il est parti** after which, he left.

quoique *conjunction* although, though; **quoique petit, il est fort** although he's small he's strong.

quotidien (F **quotidienne**) *adjective* daily; **la vie quotidienne** daily life. *noun* M daily newspaper.

R r

rabais *noun* M discount; **au rabais** at a discount.

raccompagner *verb* [1] **raccompagner quelqu'un** to see somebody home.

raccourci *noun* M short cut.

raccrocher *verb* [1] to hang up (*telephone*).

race *noun* F **1** race; **la race humaine** the human race; **2** breed; **un chien de race** a pedigree dog.

racheter *verb* [16] **1** to buy more; **il faut racheter du pain** we'll have to buy more bread; **2 il m'a racheté ma voiture** he bought my car off me.

racine *noun* F root.

raciste *noun* M & F, *adjective* racist; **des propos racistes** racist remarks.

racler *verb* [1] to scrape.

raconter *verb* [1] to tell (*a story*); **raconte-nous ce qui s'est passé** tell us what happened.

radar *noun* M radar.

radiateur *noun* M radiator.

radio *noun* F **1** radio; **je l'ai entendu à la radio** I heard it on the radio; **2** X-ray; **passer une radio** to have an X-ray.

radiocassette *noun* M or F radio cassette player.

radio-réveil *noun* M clock radio.

radis *noun* M radish.

rafale *noun* F gust (*of wind or rain*) flurry (*of snow*).

raffoler *verb* [1] **raffoler de** to be mad about; **je ne raffole pas des huîtres** I'm not mad about oysters.

rafraîchir *verb* [2] **1 le temps se rafraîchit** the weather's getting cooler; **2** to cool (somebody) down

rage *noun* F **1** rabies; **2 une rage de dents** raging toothache.

ragoût *noun* M stew.

raide *adjective* **1** stiff (*body, arm, leg*); **2** straight (*hair*); **3 une pente raide** a steep slope.

raie *noun* F **1** parting (*in your hair*); **2** skate (*the fish*).

rail *noun* M rail (*for trains*); ★ **remettre quelque chose sur les rails** to put something back on the right track.

raisin *noun* M grapes; **j'ai acheté du raisin noir** I bought some black grapes; **une grappe de raisin** a bunch of grapes; **un grain de raisin** a grape; **le jus de raisin** grape juice

raisin de Corinthe *noun* M currant.

raisin sec *noun* M raisin.

raison *noun* F **1** reason; **pour cette raison** for this reason; **pour raisons de santé** for health reasons; **2 avoir raison** to be right; **oui, tu as raison** yes, you're right.

raisonnable *adjective* sensible.

raisonnement *noun* M reasoning.

rajouter *verb* [1] to add; **on peut rajouter de l'eau si on veut** you can add water if you want.

ralentir *verb* [2] to slow down.

ralentissement *noun* M slowing down.

ralentisseur *noun* M speed bump.

râler (*informal*) *verb* [1] to moan; **arrête de râler!** stop moaning!

rallonge *noun* F **1** extension cord; **2** extra leaf (*for a table*).

ramasser *verb* [1] **1** to pick up; **est-ce que tu peux ramasser tous ces papiers, s'il te plaît** can you pick up all these papers please; **2** to pick (*fruit*); **ils ont déjà ramassé les framboises** they've already picked the raspberries; **3** to collect; **on va ramasser des châtaignes dans les bois** we're going to go and collect chestnuts in the woods; **4** collect in (*books, homework*); **Anne, veux-tu ramasser tous les cahiers?** Anne, would you collect in all the exercise books?

rame *noun* F **1** oar; **2 une rame de métro** an underground train.

rameau (*plural* **rameaux**) *noun* M branch; **le dimanche des Rameaux** Palm Sunday.

ramener *verb* [50] **1 ramener quelqu'un (en voiture)** to give somebody a lift home; **tu veux que je te ramène?** do you want a lift home?; **elle m'a ramené en voiture** she gave me a lift back; **2** to take back; **je dois ramener les livres à la bibliothèque** I must take these books back to the library.

ramer *verb* [1] to row.

rampe *noun* F banister.

rançon *noun* F ransom.

rancune *noun* F resentment, grudge.

randonnée *noun* F **faire une randonnée pédestre** to go walking (*on public footpaths*); **on a fait une randonnée de vingt kilomètres** we did a twenty-kilometre walk; **faire une randonnée à cheval** to go pony-trekking; **une randonnée à vélo** a long-distance bike ride.

randonneur, randonneuse *noun* M, F walker, rambler.

rang *noun* M row; **au cinquième rang** in the fifth row.

rangée *noun* F row; **une rangée de maisons** a row of houses.

ranger *verb* [52] **1** to put away; **ranger la vaisselle** to put away the dishes; **2** to tidy; **je vais ranger ma chambre** I'm going to tidy my room; **3** to arrange; **il range ses livres par ordre alphabétique** he arranges his books alphabetically.

râper *verb* [1] to grate; **le fromage râpé** grated cheese.

rapide *noun* M express train. *adjective* quick; **prends le métro,**

c'est plus rapide take the underground, it's quicker.

rapidement *adverb* quickly, rapidly.

rappel *noun* M **1** reminder (*for a bill*); **'dernier rappel'** 'final demand'; **2** booster (*vaccination*).

rappeler *verb* [18] **1** to remind; **rappelle-moi de passer par la banque** remind me to go to the bank; **le paysage me rappelle la France** the countryside reminds me of France; **2** to ring back (*on the telephone*); **il va te rappeler dans une heure** he'll ring you back in a hour; **3 se rappeler** to remember; **je ne me rappelle plus** I can't remember; **je me rappelle qu'elle avait les cheveux longs** I remember she had long hair.

rapport *noun* M **1** report; **un rapport officiel** an official report; **2** connection; **je ne vois pas le rapport** I don't see the connection; **3 être en rapport avec quelqu'un** to be in touch with someone; **4 par rapport à** compared with; **il a fait très beau par rapport à l'année dernière** the weather's been very good compared with last year.

rapporter *verb* [1] **1** to bring back; **est-ce que tu peux le rapporter demain?** can you bring it back tomorrow?; **2** to bring in; **son travail ne rapporte pas beaucoup** her job doesn't bring in much money.

rapprocher *verb* [1] **1** to move (something) closer; **peux-tu rapprocher la lampe de ma chaise?** can you move the lamp closer to my chair?; **2** to bring

together (*different people*); **des efforts pour rapprocher les deux pays** efforts to bring the two countries together; **3 se rapprocher** to come (or go) closer; **elle s'est rapprochée de la table** she moved closer to the table.

raquette *noun* F **1** racket (*for tennis*); **2** bat (*for ping-pong*).

rare *adjective* rare; **une fleur rare** a rare flower; **il est rare qu'elle arrive à l'heure** she very rarely arrives on time.

rarement *adverb* rarely.

ras *adjective* **1** short (*hair or fur*); **il a les cheveux coupés ras** his hair cut short; **2 en rase campagne** in open country; **3 au ras de l'eau/du sol** at water/ground level; ★ **j'en ras le bol!** (*informal*) I'm fed up!

raser *verb* [1] **1** to shave, to shave off; **il a rasé sa barbe** he's shaved his beard; **la mousse à raser** shaving foam; **2 se raser** to shave; **se raser les jambes** to shave your legs.

ras-le-cou *noun* M crew-neck sweater.

rasoir *noun* M razor.

rassemblement *noun* M meeting, rally.

rassembler *verb* [1] to gather (together); **j'ai rassemblé les enfants près de l'entrée** I gathered all the children together by the main entrance; **tout le village s'est rassemblé pour l'écouter** the whole village gathered to listen to him.

ssis *adjective* **du pain rassis** stale bread.

ssurer *verb* [1] **1** to reassure; **ah, cela me rassure!** oh, that sets my mind at rest!; **2 rassure-toi** don't worry.

t *noun* M rat.

teau (*plural* **râteaux**) *noun* M rake.

ter *verb* [1] **1** to fail; **Sophie a raté son permis** Sophie failed her driving test; **2** to miss; **j'ai raté mon train** I've missed my train.

tionner *verb* [1] to ration.

ttacher *verb* [1] **1** to (re)fasten; **attache ta ceinture** (re)fasten your seat-belt; **2** to attach; **plus rien ne me rattache ici** I no longer have any ties here.

ttraper *verb* [1] **1** to catch up with (*a person*); **ne t'inquiète pas, s nous rattraperont** don't worry, they'll catch up with us; **2** to make up for (*lost time*); **3 se rattraper** to make up for it; **j'ai très peu joué cet été mais je vais me rattraper** I've played very little this summer but I'll make up for it.

ture *noun* F crossing-out.

vi *adjective* delighted; **je suis ravi e vous voir** I'm delighted to see ou.

visseur, ravisseuse *noun* M, kidnapper.

vé *adjective* striped (*fabric*).

ver *verb* [59] **1** to cross out (*a mistake*); **j'ai rayé ton nom de la liste** I crossed your name off the list; **2** to scratch (*a surface*).

rayon *noun* M **1** shelf; **un rayon pour mes livres** a shelf for my books; **2** department (*in a department store*), section (*in a supermarket*); **au rayon fraîcheur** in the chilled foods section; **3** ray; **un rayon de soleil** a ray of sunshine; **les rayons X** X-rays; **4** radius.

rayure *noun* F **1** stripe; **2** scratch.

RC *noun* M SHORT FOR **rez-de-chaussée** ground floor.

réacteur *noun* M **1 un réacteur nucléaire** a nuclear reactor; **2** jet engine.

réaction *noun* F reaction.

réagir *verb* [2] to react; **elle n'a pas réagi** she didn't react.

réalisateur, réalisatrice *noun* M, F director (*of a film or TV programme*).

réalisation *noun* F **1** carrying out (*of a plan or project*); **2** production (*of a film or a radio/TV programme*).

réaliser *verb* [1] **1** to carry out (*a project*); **2** to fulfil; **réaliser un rêve** to fulfil a dream; **3** to make (*a film*); **4** to realize.

réaliste *adjective* realistic.

réalité *noun* F reality; **en réalité** in reality.

réanimation *noun* F resuscitation; **(service de) réanimation** intensive care (unit).

rebondir *verb* [2] to bounce.

rebord noun M **1 le rebord de la fenêtre** the window ledge; **2** edge; **le rebord de la baignoire** the edge of the bath.

récemment adverb recently.

récent adjective recent.

réception noun F **1** reception desk; **demandez la clé à la réception** ask for the key at the reception desk; **2** reception (party).

réceptionniste noun M & F receptionist.

recette noun F recipe; **la recette du gâteau** the recipe for the cake.

recevoir verb [66] **1** to receive, to get; **j'ai reçu ta lettre** I got your letter; **2** to welcome (a visitor or guest); **3** to see (a patient or client); **le dentiste reçoit entre 9h et 17h** the dentist sees patients between 9 a.m. and 5 p.m.; **4 être reçu à un examen** to pass an exam; **elle a été reçue première à l'examen** she came top in the exam.

rechange noun M **de rechange** spare; **une pièce de rechange** a spare part.

recharge noun F refill.

réchaud noun M stove.

réchauffer verb [1] **1** to warm up (food); **peux-tu mettre la soupe à réchauffer?** can you put the soup on to warm?; **2** to warm (hands or feet); **3 se réchauffer** to get warm; **va te réchauffer près du feu** go and get warm by the fire.

recherche noun F **1** research; **2 être à la recherche de quelque**

chose to be looking for something; **je suis à la recherche d'un logement** I'm looking for somewhere to live.

rechercher verb [1] to look for; **la police le recherche** the police are looking for him; **elle recherche un travail plus flexible** she's looking for a more flexible job.

récipient noun M container.

réciproque adjective mutual.

récit noun M story; **il nous a fait le récit de son voyage** he told us all about his journey.

réciter verb [1] to recite.

réclame noun F **1** advertisement; **une réclame pour le nouveau modèle** an advertisement for the new model; **2 en réclame** on (special) offer; **le jambon est en réclame cette semaine** the ham is on special offer this week.

réclamer verb [1] to demand; **ils réclament trois jours de plus de vacances** they're demanding three more days' holiday.

récolte noun F **1** harvest; **2** crop.

récolter verb [1] **1** to harvest; **récolter le blé** to harvest the wheat; **2** to collect (money); **3** (information) to get; **récolter une amende** to get a fine.

recommandé adjective registered; **une lettre recommandée** a registered letter; **je voudrais l'envoyer en recommandé** I'd like to send it by registered post.

recommander verb [1] **1** to advise; **je te recommande de ne ri**

ire I advise you to say nothing;
to recommend.

commencer *verb* [61] **1** to start
gain; **j'ai recommencé ma lettre** I
tarted my letter again; **il a
ecommencé à neiger** it's started
nowing again; **2** to do it again; **si tu
e fais pas attention, elle va
ecommencer** if you don't watch
ut, she'll do it again; **ça
ecommence!** here we go again!

compense *noun* F reward.

compenser *verb* [1] to reward.

concilier *verb* [1] **se réconcilier
vec quelqu'un** to make it up with
omebody.

confortant *adjective*
omforting.

connaissable *adjective*
ecognizable.

connaissance *noun* F
gratitude; **en reconnaissance de
** appreciation of; **2** recognition.

connaissant *adjective* grateful.

connaître *verb* [27] **1** to
ecognize; **je ne l'ai pas reconnue** I
idn't recognize her; **je l'ai reconnu
sa voix** I recognized him by his
oice; **2** to admit; **il faut reconnaître
ue c'est difficile** it must be
dmitted that it's difficult; **elle
econnaît qu'elle a menti** she
dmits she lied.

construire *verb* [26] to rebuild.

opier *verb* [1] to copy out.

ord *noun* M record; **un record
ondial** a world record; **battre un
ecord** to break a record.

recouvrir *verb* [30] to cover.

récréation *noun* F break; **la cour
de récréation** the playground.

rectangle *noun* M rectangle.

rectangulaire *adjective*
rectangular.

rectifier *verb* [1] to correct.

reçu *noun* M receipt.
verb SEE **recevoir**.

recueil *noun* M collection (*of
poems or essays*).

reculer *verb* [1] **1** to move back; **elle
a reculé de quelques pas** she moved
back a few steps; **2** to reverse (*in a
car*); **3 reculer la date d'une
réunion** to postpone a meeting.

reculons *in phrase* **à reculons**
backwards.

récupérer *verb* [24] **1** to get back;
**je vais chez Brigitte pour récupérer
le bouquin que je lui ai prêté** I'm
going round to Brigitte's to get back
the book I lent her; **2** to recover
(*from an illness*).

recycler *verb* [1] to recycle.

rédaction *noun* F essay.

redemander *verb* [1] **1** to ask
again; **tu devrais redemander** you
should ask again; **2** to ask for more;
**il faut qu'on redemande des
cahiers** we'll have to ask for more
exercise books.

redescendre *verb* [3] **1** to go (or
come) back down; **elle est
redescendue à la cave** she went
back down to the cellar; **je monte à
Glasgow demain et je redescends
lundi** I'm going up to Glasgow

tomorrow and I'm coming back down on Monday; **2** to bring or take back down; **est-ce que tu peux redescendre ma valise?** can you bring my suitcase back down?

rédiger *verb* [52] to write (*an article*); to write up (*notes*).

redonner *verb* [1] to give again; **je leur ai redonné mon adresse** I gave them my address again; **est-ce que je te redonne un peu de salade?** can I give you a bit more salad?

redoubler *verb* [1] to repeat a year (*at school*).

réduction *noun* F **1** reduction; **une réduction du nombre d'étudiants** a reduction in the number of students; **2** (price) reduction; **une réduction de 20%** a 20% reduction.

réduire *verb* [68] to cut (*prices*); **réduire les impôts** to cut taxes; **des vêtements à prix réduits** cut-price clothing.

rééducation *noun* F physiotherapy.

réel (F **réelle**) *adjective* real.

réellement *adverb* really.

refaire *verb* [10] **1** to redo; **je dois refaire mon devoir de maths** I have to redo my maths homework; **c'est tout à refaire** it has to be completely redone; **il ne faut pas refaire la même erreur** we mustn't make the same mistake again; **2** to make more; **elle est en train de refaire du café** she's making some more coffee.

référence *noun* F reference; **faire référence à quelque chose** to refer to something;

réfléchi *adjective* **1** reflexive (*verb*); **2** considered (*decision*).

réfléchir *verb* [2] to think; **il faut bien réfléchir avant d'accepter** you should think carefully before accepting; **j'ai réfléchi au problème** I've thought about the problem.

reflet *noun* M **1** reflection; **2 des cheveux aux reflets blonds** hair with blond highlights.

refléter *verb* [24] to reflect.

réflexe *noun* M, *adjective* reflex.

réflexion *noun* F **1** thought; **2** comment; **il m'a fait des réflexions désagréables** he made some nasty comments to me.

refrain *noun* M chorus.

réfrigérateur *noun* M refrigerator.

refroidir *verb* [2] to cool down.

refroidissement *noun* M drop in temperature.

refuge *noun* M **1** mountain hut (*for climbers*); **2** animal sanctuary; **3** traffic island; **4** refuge.

réfugié, réfugiée *noun* M, F refugee.

réfugier *verb* [1] **se réfugier** to take shelter, to take refuge.

refus *noun* M refusal; ★ **ce n'est pas de refus** I wouldn't say no;

veux-tu boire quelque chose?' – ce n'est pas de refus' 'would you like a drink?' – 'I wouldn't say no'.

refuser verb [1] **1** to refuse; **refuser de faire** to refuse to do; **elle a refusé de répondre** she refused to answer; **2** to turn down; **ils ont refusé sa candidature** they turned him down for the job.

regagner verb [1] **nous avons regagné nos places** we went back to our seats.

régal noun M feast; **ça a été un véritable régal** it was a real feast.

régaler verb [1] **on s'est vraiment régalé!** the food was absolutely wonderful!

regard noun M look.

regarder verb [1] **1** to look at; **je vais regarder la carte** I'll look at the map; **2** to watch; **regarder la télé** to watch telly; **veux-tu regarder le film?** do you want to watch the film?; **3** to look; **regarder par la fenêtre** to look out of the window; **regarde!** look!; **4** to concern; **cela ne nous regarde pas** that doesn't concern us; **cela ne le regarde pas** that's none of his business.

régime noun M **1** diet; **un régime sans sel** a salt-free diet; **je fais un régime** I'm on a diet; **2 un régime de bananes** a bunch of bananas; **3** régime.

région noun F region; **les vins de la région** the local wines.

régional (M plural **régionaux**) adjective regional.

registre noun M register.

réglable adjective adjustable.

règle noun F **1** ruler; **2** rule; **selon les règles** according to the rules; **les règles de sécurité** the safety regulations; **en règle générale** as a general rule; **3 en règle** in order (valid); **4 les règles** period (menstruation); **j'ai mes règles** I've got my period.

règlement noun M regulations.

régler verb [24] **1** to pay (a debt or a bill); **vous réglez comment, monsieur?** how would you like to pay, sir?; **2** to sort out (details or a problem); **3** to adjust; **on peut régler la hauteur** you can adjust the height.

réglisse noun F liquorice.

règne noun M reign.

régner verb [24] to reign.

regret noun M regret; **avec/sans regret** with/without regret; **mille regrets** I'm terribly sorry.

regretter verb [1] **1** to be sorry; **je regrette** I'm sorry; **nous regrettons beaucoup de partir** we're very sorry to be leaving; **2** to regret; **elles regrettent avoir quitté Paris** they regret having left Paris; **je ne regrette rien** I have no regrets; **3** to miss; **je regrette la vie à Paris** I miss the Parisian way of life.

regrouper verb [1] **1** to group together; **les débutants sont regroupés ensemble** beginners are grouped together; **2 se regrouper** to regroup; **les enfants se sont regroupés autour d'elle** the children gathered around her.

régularité noun F regularity.

régulier (F **régulière**) adjective
1 regular; **à intervalles réguliers** at
regular intervals; **2 vols réguliers à
New York** scheduled flights to New
York.

régulièrement adverb regularly.

rein noun M 1 kidney; **2 les reins**
the back; **j'ai mal aux reins** I've got
back-ache.

reine noun F queen; **la reine
Elisabeth** Queen Elizabeth.

reine-claude noun F greengage.

rejeter verb [48] to reject.

rejoindre verb [49] 1 to meet up
with; **je vous rejoins au bar** I'll meet
you in the bar; **2** to join (*other
people, a group, or a movement*);
3 se rejoindre to meet up; **alors on
se rejoint à onze heures?** so shall
we meet up at eleven?

relâcher verb [1] 1 to loosen (*a grip
or hold*); **2** to set free (*a prisoner,
hostage, or animal*); **3** to relax (*your
attention or discipline*).

relais noun M 1 restaurant, hotel;
2 prendre le relais (de quelqu'un)
to take over (from someone); **il a pris
le relais au volant** he took over the
driving; **3** relay race.

relatif (F **relative**) adjective relative.

relation noun F 1 connection; **en
relation avec** in connection with;
2 acquaintance; **une relation de
mon frère** an acquaintance of my
brother's; **3** relationship; **il a de
bonnes relations avec son patron**
he has a good relationship with his

boss; **4 les relations publiques**
public relations.

relativement adverb relatively;
relativement à in relation to.

relax (*informal*) adjective casual,
laid back.

relaxer verb [1] to relax.

relent noun M lingering smell.

relevé noun M 1 **faire le relevé d**
quelque chose to make a list of
something; **2 un relevé de compt**
a bank statement.

relever verb [50] 1 to raise;
2 relever la tête to look up; **3** to
notice (*details, mistakes, or
interesting facts*); **4 relever le
compteur** to read the meter; **5 se**
relever to pick yourself up (*after a
fall*).

religieux, religieuse noun M, F
monk, nun.
adjective religious.

religion noun F religion.

relire verb [51] to re-read, to read
over.

remarquable adjective
remarkable, striking.

remarque noun F remark,
comment.

remarquer verb [1] 1 to notice; **je**
n'ai rien remarqué I didn't notice
anything; **j'ai remarqué qu'elle es**
arrivée en retard I noticed she
arrived late; **2 se faire remarquer**
to draw attention to yourself; **il
n'aime pas se faire remarquer** he
doesn't like drawing attention to
himself; **3 faire remarquer quelq**

chose à quelqu'un to point something out to somebody; **elle lui a fait remarquer que c'était déjà trop tard** she pointed out to him that it was already too late.

rembobiner verb [1] to rewind (a tape or video).

remboursement noun M repayment, refund.

rembourser verb [1] **1** to pay back; **je te rembourserai demain** I'll pay you back tomorrow; **2** to refund the price of; **ils m'ont remboursé les billets** they refunded me the price of the tickets; **3** to reimburse; **nous vous rembourserons le voyage** we'll pay your travelling expenses.

remède noun M remedy.

remerciement noun M thanks; **tous mes remerciements** many thanks; **une lettre de remerciement** a thank-you letter.

remercier verb [1] **1** to thank; **je l'ai remerciée pour les fleurs** I thanked her for the flowers; **remercier quelqu'un d'avoir fait quelque chose** to thank somebody for doing something; **il nous a remerciés de l'avoir aidé** he thanked us for helping him.

remettre verb [11] **1** to put back; **remets la bouteille au frigo** put the bottle back in the fridge; **il a remis la photo sur la table** he put the photo back on the table; **as-tu remis tous les livres à leur place?** have you put all the books in their place?; **2** to put back on; **je vais remettre ma veste** I'm going to put my jacket back on; **3** to hand over; **pouvez-**

vous me remettre les clés demain? can you hand over the keys to me tomorrow?; **4** to put off; **ils ont remis la réunion à jeudi** they've put the meeting off until Thursday; **5 se remettre** to start again; **elle s'est remise au piano** she's started playing the piano again; **il s'est remis à pleuvoir** it's started raining again; **6 se remettre de** to recover; **ils ne se sont toujours pas remis du choc** they still haven't recovered from the shock.

remise noun F **1** handing out; **la remise des prix** the prizegiving; **2** discount; **nous faisons une remise de 20% sur tous les CD** we're giving a 20% discount on all CDs; **3** garden shed.

remonte-pente M noun ski lift.

remonter verb [1] **1** to go (or come) back up; **Nathalie est remontée dans sa chambre** Nathalie's gone back up to her room; **je descends à Londres ce soir et je remonte lundi** I'm going down to London tonight and coming back up on Monday; **2** to take (or bring) back up; **veux-tu remonter les chaises?** would you take the chairs back upstairs?; **3** to put back up; **il m'a remonté ma valise au filet** he put my case up in the luggage rack for me; **4 remonter la pente** to go back up the hill; **5** to get or climb back in; **ils sont remontés dans le car** they got back into the coach; **6 remonter quelqu'un**, **remonter le moral à quelqu'un** to cheer someone up.

remords noun M remorse.

remorque *noun* F **1** trailer (*for a car*); **2** tow-rope.

remplaçant, remplaçante *noun* M, F **1** replacement (*for another person*); **2** supply teacher.

remplacer *verb* [61] **1** to stand in for (*a person*); **2** to replace; **il faut remplacer les piles** you need to replace the batteries.

remplir *verb* [2] **1** to fill; **il a rempli son verre de vin** he filled his glass with wine; **la salle était remplie de jeunes** the hall was full of young people; **2 remplir un formulaire** to fill in a form; **3** to carry out (*a duty or a role*).

remue-ménage *noun* M commotion.

remuer *verb* [1] **1** to move (*your head or hand, for example*); **le vent remuait les branches** the wind was shaking the branches; **2** to stir; **peux-tu remuer la sauce, s'il te plaît?** can you stir the sauce, please?

rémunérer *verb* [24] to pay (*a person*); to pay for (*work*).

renard *noun* M fox.

rencontre *noun* F **1** meeting; **elle est venue à ma rencontre** she came to meet me; **2** (*in sport*) match; **la rencontre entre la France et l'Allemagne** the match between France and Germany.

rencontrer *verb* [1] **1** to meet (*a person*); **je l'ai rencontrée en 1993** I met her in 1993; **2** to play (*an opponent or a team*); **3 se rencontrer** to meet; **nous nous sommes rencontrés à Londres** we met in London.

rendez-vous *noun* M **1** appointment; **prendre rendez-vous** to make an appointment; **j'ai rendez-vous chez le dentiste** I've got a dentist's appointment; **le médecin voit les malades sur rendez-vous** the doctor sees patients by appointment; **2** date; **Marc a rendez-vous avec sa copine à trois heures** Marc's got a date with his girlfriend at three; **3 donner rendez-vous à quelqu'un** to arrange to meet somebody; **il m'a donné rendez-vous au café** he arranged to meet me at the café.

rendormir *verb* [37] **se rendormir** to go back to sleep; **elle s'est rendormie** she went back to sleep.

rendre *verb* [3] **1** to give back; **je te rendrai les clés demain** I'll give you back the keys tomorrow; **2 rendre quelqu'un heureux** to make somebody happy; **3** to hand in (*homework*); **4 se rendre** to give oneself up; **les voleurs se sont rendus à la police** the thieves gave themselves up to the police; **5 se rendre compte de quelque chose** to realize something; **je me suis rendu compte du fait que j'avais oublié mes clés** I realized I had forgotten my keys.

renifler *verb* [1] to sniff.

renne *noun* M reindeer.

renommé *adjective* famous.

renoncer *verb* [61] **1** to give up; **c'est trop difficile, je renonce!** it's too difficult, I give up!; **2 renoncer à quelque chose** to give something up.

renouveler *verb* [18] to renew (*a passport or a subscription, for example*).

renover *verb* [1] **1** to renovate (*a house*); **2** to restore (*furniture*).

renseignement *noun* M **1** un renseignement a piece of information; un renseignement utile a useful piece of information; **2** les renseignements information; je cherche des renseignements I'm looking for information; adressez-vous aux renseignements ask at the information desk; **3** renseignements directory enquiries.

renseigner *verb* [1] **1** renseigner quelqu'un to give someone information; la brochure vous enseigne sur les horaires the brochure gives you timetable information; il était très bien renseigné sur le projet he was very well-informed about the project; **2** se renseigner to find out; je vais me renseigner au bureau de tourisme I'm going to find out at the tourist office.

rentable *adjective* profitable.

rentrée *noun* F la rentrée (des classes) the start of the new school year.

rentrer *verb* [1] **1** to get home; Maman rentre à dix-huit heures Mum will be home at six; je vais rentrer chez moi I'm going home; **2** to get back; ils rentrent de Paris jeudi they'll be back from Paris on Thursday; **3** to come (or go) in; entrez! do come in!; elles sont rentrées dans un magasin they've gone into a shop; **4** rentrer dans quelque chose to go in something; tout ça ne rentrera jamais dans ton sac! all that will never go in your bag!; **5** rentrer dans quelque chose to crash into something; la voiture est rentrée dans un mur the car crashed into a wall; **6** rentrer quelque chose to bring something in (*from outside*); rentre les chaises, il pleut! bring the chairs in, it's raining!

renverser *verb* [1] **1** to knock over; il a renversé sa chaise he knocked his chair over; **2** être renversé par une voiture to be knocked down by a car; **3** to spill; j'ai renversé mon thé I've spilled my tea.

renvoyer *verb* [40] **1** to send back; as-tu renvoyé le formulaire? have you sent back the form?; on m'a renvoyé à l'hôpital they sent me back to hospital; **2** to throw back (*a ball*); **3** to dismiss; la secrétaire a été renvoyée the secretary has been dismissed.

réouverture *noun* F reopening.

répandu *adjective* widespread.

réparation *noun* F repair.

réparer *verb* [1] to repair.

repartir *verb* [58] **1** to go off again; ils ont déposé les enfants et ils sont repartis they dropped the children and went off again; **2** to go again; je suis reparti chez moi I went home again; **3** repartir à zéro to start from scratch.

repas *noun* M meal; **le repas de midi** lunch; **le repas du soir** the evening meal.

repassage *noun* M ironing.

repasser *verb* [1] **1** to drop in again; **il a dit qu'il repasserait demain** he said he'd drop in again tomorrow; **2** to iron; **Frank est en train de repasser sa chemise** Frank's busy ironing his shirt; **une planche à repasser** an ironing board; **3** to resit (*an exam or test*).

repeindre *verb* [60] to repaint.

repère *noun* M **un point de repère** a landmark; a reference point.

repérer *verb* [24] **1** (*informal*) to spot; **j'ai repéré trois erreurs dans son article** I spotted three mistakes in his article; **2** to locate (*a place*).

répertoire *noun* M notebook (*with a thumb index*); **un répertoire d'adresses** an address book.

répéter *verb* [24] **1** to repeat; **elle l'a répété trois fois** she repeated it three times; **faire des essais répétés** to make repeated attempts; **2** to rehearse (*a play*); **3** to practise (*a piece of music*); **4 se répéter** to repeat oneself; **5 se répéter** to happen again; **espérons que cela ne se répétera pas** let's hope it doesn't happen again.

répétition *noun* F **1** rehearsal; **la répétition générale** the dress rehearsal; **2** repetition.

replier *verb* [1] **1** to fold up; **elle a replié la carte** she folded up the map (*a sheet*); **2 elle a replié ses jambes** she tucked her legs up (under her).

répondeur *noun* M answering machine; **j'ai laissé un message s**▮ **le répondeur** I left a message on th▮ answering machine.

répondre *verb* [3] **1** to answer; **il n'a pas répondu** he didn't answer; **je ne lui ai pas répondu** I didn't answer him; **2 répondre à une question** to answer a question; **3 répondre à une lettre** to reply to a letter.

réponse *noun* F answer; **la bonne réponse** the right answer.

reportage *noun* M **1** report; **un reportage sur la drogue** a report o▮ drugs; **2** (news) story.

reporter[1] *verb* [1] to postpone; **on a reporté le match à jeudi** the match has been postponed until Thursday.

reporter[2] *noun* M reporter.

repos *noun* M rest; **dix jours de repos** ten days' rest.

reposant *adjective* restful.

reposer *verb* [1] **1 reposer quelq**▮ **chose** to put something back dow▮ **elle a reposé le livre sur la table s**▮ put the book back down on the table; **2 se reposer** to have a rest; **j'ai besoin de me reposer** I need a rest; **repose-toi bien!** have a good rest!

repousser *verb* [1] **1** to grow aga▮ **tes cheveux ont vite repoussé** you▮ hair's grown quickly; **2** to push back; **3** to postpone; **le match a é**▮ **repoussé** the match has been postponed.

reprendre verb [64] **1** to have some more (food or drink); **reprends du poulet** have some more chicken; **2** to take back; **est-ce que je peux reprendre les verres que je t'avais prêtés?** can I take back the glasses I lent you?; **3** to start again; **l'école reprend en septembre** school starts again in September; **4 reprendre le travail** to go back to work; **j'ai repris le travail lundi** I went back to work on Monday; **5 reprendre la route** to set off again.

représentant, représentante noun M, F sales rep.

représentation noun F performance (of a play); **prochaine représentation à 20h** next performance 8 p.m.

représenter verb [1] **1** to depict; **2** to represent.

réprimander verb [1] to tell off, to reprimand.

réprimer verb [1] to suppress.

reprise noun F **1** resumption (of work or discussions); **2** rerun (of a play or film); repeat (of a broadcast); **3 à plusieurs reprises** on several occasions.

reproche noun M criticism; **il m'a fait des reproches** he criticized me.

reprocher verb [1] **1** to criticize; **il a reproché à son fils de ne pas travailler** he criticized his son for not working; **2 se reprocher** to blame oneself.

reproduction noun F reproduction.

reproduire verb [26] **1** to reproduce; **2 se reproduire** to happen again.

républicain adjective republican.

république noun F republic; **la République française** the French Republic.

répugnant adjective revolting.

réputation noun F reputation; **il a la réputation d'être très sévère** he has a reputation for being very strict.

requin noun M shark.

RER noun M SHORT FOR **réseau express régional** (the fast suburban network on the Paris underground).

rescousse noun F **aller à la rescousse de quelqu'un** to go to someone's rescue.

réseau (plural **réseaux**) noun M network.

réservation noun F reservation.

réserve noun F **1** stock; **des réserves de charbon** stocks of coal; **j'ai deux bouteilles en réserve** I have put aside two bottles; **2** reserve (for birds or animals); **une réserve ornithologique** a bird sanctuary.

réservé adjective reserved.

réserver verb [1] **1** to reserve, to book; **j'ai réservé deux places pour ce soir** I've booked two seats for this evening; **2** to keep; **Philippe t'a réservé du poulet** Philippe's kept some chicken for you.

réservoir noun M **1** tank; **réservoir à essence** petrol tank; **2** reservoir.

résidence *noun* F **1** home, residence; **une résidence secondaire** a holiday home; **2** block of flats.

résident, résidente *noun* M, F resident.

résidentiel (F **résidentielle**) *adjective* residential.

résistant, résistante *noun* M, F Resistance fighter (*in France during World War II*). *adjective* tough.

résister *verb* [1] **résister à** to resist.

résolu *adjective* **1** determined; **elle est résolue à démissionner** she is determined to resign; **2** resolved; **le problème est résolu** the problem is resolved.

résoudre *verb* [67] **1** to solve (*a problem*); **2 se résoudre à faire** to make up one's mind to do; **elle s'est résolue à partir** she made up her mind to leave.

respect *noun* M respect.

respecter *verb* [1] to respect.

respectueux (F **respectueuse**) *adjective* respectful.

respiration *noun* F breathing.

respirer *verb* [1] to breathe.

responsabilité *noun* F **1** responsibility; **2 avoir la responsabilité de quelque chose** to be responsible for something; **il a la responsabilité des livraisons** he's responsible for deliveries.

responsable *noun* M & F **1** person in charge; **le responsable du projet** the person in charge of the project;

2 person responsible; **les responsables de la catastrophe** those responsible for the disaster. *adjective* responsible; **il est responsable de l'accident** he's responsible for the accident.

ressemblance *noun* F similarity

ressembler *verb* [1] **1 ressemble à** to look like; **elle ressemble beaucoup à sa mère** she looks ver like her mother; **cela ressemble à du bois mais c'est du plastique** it looks like wood but it's plastic; **2 s ressembler** to be alike; **les deux sœurs ne se ressemblent pas du tout** the two sisters are not at all alike.

ressentiment *noun* M resentment.

resserrer *verb* [1] **1** to tighten (*a knot or screw, for example*); **2 se resserrer** to move closer together; **resserrez-vous un peu!** squeeze u a bit!

resservir *verb* [58] **1** to give another helping; **je vous ressers u peu?** shall I give you a little more? **2 se resservir** to help yourself to more; **ressers-toi de la salade** he' yourself to some more salad; **je me suis déjà resservi, merci** I've already helped myself to more, thank you.

ressort *noun* M spring (*in a bed o a chair*).

ressortir *verb* [58] to go out again **est revenu pour les clés et il est ressorti** he came back for the keys and went out again.

essource *noun* F **1** resource; **des ressources énergétiques** energy resources; **2 il est sans ressources** he has no means of support.

estaurant *noun* M restaurant; **on mange au restaurant ce soir** we're going out for a meal tonight.

estauration *noun* F **1** catering; **la restauration rapide** the fast-food industry; **2** restoration.

estaurer *verb* [1] to restore.

este *noun* M **1 le reste** the rest; **le reste du temps** the rest of the time; **et tout le reste, tu le sais déjà** and you know all the rest already; **2 les restes** the leftovers; **j'ai fait un curry avec les restes du poulet** I made a curry with the leftover chicken.

ester *verb* [1] **1** to stay; **reste là, je reviens tout de suite !** stay there, I'll be right back!; **Camille est restée à la maison** Camille stayed at home; **je ne peux pas rester longtemps** I can't stay long; **hier je suis resté sans manger** I didn't have anything to eat yesterday; **2 rester debout** to remain standing; **je préfère rester debout** I prefer to stand; **3 rester assis** to remain seated; **je suis resté assis toute la journée** I've been sitting down all day; **4** to be left; **il reste du fromage** there's some cheese left; **il nous reste combien d'argent?** how much money have we got left?; **il ne reste pas beaucoup à faire** there's not much left to do.

striction *noun* F restriction.

résultat *noun* M result; **les résultats des examens** the exam results.

résulter *verb* [1] **résulter de** to result from.

résumé *noun* M summary, résumé.

résumer *verb* [1] to summarize, to sum up.

rétablir *verb* [2] **1** to restore; **2 se rétablir** to recover (*after an illness*).

retaper *verb* [1] to do up (*a house*).

retard *noun* M **1** delay; **ils annoncent un retard d'une heure sur notre vol** they say there's an hour's delay on our flight; **sans retard** without delay; **2 avoir du retard** to be late; **excusez mon retard** I'm sorry I'm late; **ils sont arrivés avec trois heures de retard** they arrived three hours late; **3 être en retard** to be late; **nous sommes en retard** we're late.

retarder *verb* [1] **1** to hold up, to delay; **la grève nous a retardés** the strike held us up; **l'avion était retardé** the plane was delayed; **2** to put off, to postpone; **il a retardé son départ** he put off his departure.

retenir *verb* [77] **1** to hold up; **j'ai été retenu au bureau** I was held up at the office; **je ne vous retiendrai pas longtemps** I won't keep you long; **2 retenir son souffle** to hold your breath; **elle ne pouvait pas retenir ses larmes** she couldn't hold back her tears; **3** to book; **j'ai retenu des places** I've booked seats; **4** to remember; **je ne retiens jamais leur**

adresse I can never remember their address.

réticence *noun* F 1 reluctance; 2 reticence.

retirer *verb* [1] 1 to take off; **je vais d'abord retirer ma veste** I'll take my jacket off first; 2 to take away; **ils ont retiré son permis** they took away his licence; 3 **retirer de l'argent** to take out some money (*from your bank account*).

retouche *noun* F alteration (*to a garment*).

retour *noun* M 1 return; **un billet aller-retour** a return ticket; **dès mon retour** as soon as I get back; 2 **être de retour** to be back; **elle sera de retour vers onze heures** she'll be back about eleven.

retourner *verb* [1] 1 to go back; **elle est retournée à l'école** she went back to school; **je n'y suis jamais retourné** I've never been back there again; 2 to turn over; **est-ce que je retourne les steaks?** shall I turn the steaks over?; 3 to overturn.

retraite *noun* F retirement; **prendre sa retraite** to retire; **une maison de retraite** an old people's home.

retraité, retraitée *noun* M, F pensioner.

rétrécir *verb* [2] to shrink.

retrouver *verb* [1] 1 to find; **as-tu retrouvé tes clés?** did you find your keys?; 2 to meet; **je te retrouve à la sortie** I'll meet you at the exit; 3 **se retrouver** to meet; **on se retrouve devant le cinéma?** shall we meet ouside the cinema?; **on se retrouvera**

à Noël we'll see each other again at Christmas; 4 **se retrouver** to end up; **on s'est retrouvé chez Amanda** we ended up at Amanda's place; 5 **se retrouver** to find one's way around; **je n'arrive jamais à me retrouver à Londres** I can never find my way around London.

rétroviseur, rétro *noun* M rearview mirror.

réunion *noun* F meeting.

réunir *verb* [2] **se réunir** to meet; **on s'est réuni pour discuter du problème** we met to discuss the problem.

réussi *adjective* successful.

réussir *verb* [2] 1 to succeed; **j'espère qu'elle va réussir** I hope she'll succeed; 2 **réussir un examen** to pass an exam; 3 to be successful; **ça a très bien réussi** tha was very successful; 4 **réussir à faire** to manage to do; **je n'ai pas réussi à les persuader** I didn't manage to persuade them.

réussite *noun* F success.

revanche *noun* F 1 return match 2 **prendre sa revanche** to get your own back; 3 **en revanche** on the other hand.

rêve *noun* M dream; **faire un rêve** to have a dream; **votre maison de rêve** your dream house.

réveil *noun* M alarm clock.

réveille-matin *noun* M alarm clock.

réveiller *verb* [1] 1 **réveiller quelqu'un** to wake somebody up; **elle m'a réveillé à sept heures** sh woke me at seven; **2 se réveiller** to wake up; **d'habitude je me réveille à sept heures** I usually wake up at seven.

éveillon *noun* M **le réveillon du Nouvel An** the New Year's Eve celebrations.

éveillonner *verb* [1] **1** to celebrate Christmas Eve; **2** to see the New Year in.

éveler *verb* [24] to reveal.

evenant, revenante *noun* M, F ghost.

evendre *verb* [3] to sell, to resell.

evenir *verb* [81] **1** to come back; **elles sont revenues très tard** they came back very late; **tu reviendras nous voir?** will you come back and see us?; **2** to come to; **ça revient à cent francs** that comes to a hundred francs; **ça revient au même** it comes to the same thing; **3 je n'en reviens pas!** I can't get over it!

evenu *noun* M income.

ever *verb* [1] to dream.

everbère *noun* M street lamp.

evers *noun* M **1** lapel (*on a jacket*), turn-up (*of trousers*), cuff (*on a sleeve*); **2** backhand (*in tennis*); **3** setback; **4 le revers de la médaille** the other side of the coin.

viser *verb* [1] **1** to revise; **2** to service (*a car or machine*).

vision *noun* F **1** revision; **2** service (*for a car*).

revoici *preposition* (*informal*) **me revoici!** here I am again!

revoir[1] *verb* [13] **1** to see again; **et nous ne l'avons jamais revue** and we never saw her again; **2** to revise; **je dois revoir ma chimie** I have to revise my chemistry.

revoir[2] *noun* M **au revoir** goodbye.

révolte *noun* F revolt, rebellion.

révolter *verb* [1] to appal.

révolution *noun* F revolution.

révolutionner *verb* [1] to revolutionize.

revolver *noun* M revolver, handgun.

revue *noun* F magazine; **une revue d'art** an art magazine; **une revue scientifique** a scientific journal.

rez-de-chaussée *noun* M ground floor (*literally: level with the road*); **la réception est au rez-de-chaussée** reception is on the ground floor.

RF SHORT FOR **République française** French Republic.

Rhin *noun* M **le Rhin** the Rhine.

rhinocéros *noun* M rhinoceros.

rhubarbe *noun* F rhubarb.

rhum *noun* M rum.

rhume *noun* M cold; **attraper un rhume** to catch a cold; **un rhume de cerveau** a head cold.

rhume des foins *noun* M hay fever.

ri *verb* SEE **rire**.

ricaner *verb* [1] to snigger, to giggle.

riche *adjective* well-off; **1 nous ne sommes pas très riches** we're not terribly well-off; **2** rich; **riche en vitamines** rich in vitamins.

richesse *noun* F **1** wealth; **2 les richesses naturelles** natural resources.

ride *noun* F wrinkle (*on skin*), ripple (*on water*).

rideau (*plural* **rideaux**) *noun* M curtain.

ridicule *adjective* ridiculous; **mais c'est totalement ridicule!** but that's completely ridiculous!

rien¹ *pronoun* **1** nothing; **'qu'est-ce qu'elle a dit?' – 'rien'** 'what did she say?' – 'nothing'; **il n'a rien** he has nothing; **je n'ai rien vu** I didn't see anything; **ce n'est rien** it's nothing; **il ne reste plus rien** there's nothing left; **rien du tout** nothing at all; **'merci' – 'de rien'** 'thank you' – 'it's nothing'; **rien d'autre** nothing else; **rien de bon** nothing good; **2 rien que** just; **rien que les livres pèsent 20 kilos** the books by themselves weigh 20 kilos; **'que reste-t-il à faire?' – 'rien que la vaisselle'** 'what's left to do?' – 'just the washing-up'; ★ **rien à faire!** it's no good!

rien² *noun* M little thing; **elle se met à hurler pour un rien** the slightest thing starts her shouting.

rigide *adjective* rigid, stiff.

rigoler (*informal*) *verb* [1] **1** to laugh; **elle en a beaucoup rigolé** she had a good laugh about it; **2** to have a good time; **nous avons bien rigolé** we had a great time; **3** to be joking; **je rigolais!** I was only joking!

rigolo *adjective* (F **rigolote**) (*informal*) funny.

rillettes *plural noun* F **les rillettes de porc** potted pork.

rime *noun* F rhyme.

rincer *verb* [61] to rinse; **se rincer le cheveux** to rinse one's hair.

rire *noun* M laughter; **un rire** a laugh.
verb [68] **1** to laugh; **il nous fait rire** he makes us laugh; **2** to have fun; **on va rire ce soir** we'll have some fun this evening; **c'était pour rire** it was meant as a joke.

ris *noun* M **les ris de veau** calf's sweetbreads.

risque *noun* M risk; **risque d'incendie** fire risk; **c'est sans risque** it's safe.

risqué *adjective* risky.

risquer *verb* [1] **1** to risk; **vas-y, tu ne risques rien** go on, it's quite safe; **2 il risque de pleuvoir** it might well rain; **tu risques de te brûler** you might burn yourself,

rivage *noun* M shore.

rive *noun* F **1** bank (*of a river*); **la Rive gauche** the Left Bank (*when talking about the Seine in Paris and other rivers which flow through cities, the left bank is the left side of the river when you are facing downstream*); **2** shore (*by the sea*)

rivière *noun* F river.

riz *noun* M rice; **riz cantonais** fried rice; **gâteau de riz** rice pudding.

RN *noun* F SHORT FOR **route
nationale** A road.

obe *noun* F dress; **une robe d'été**
a summer dress; **une robe de
mariée** a wedding dress.

obe de chambre *noun* F
dressing gown.

obinet *noun* M tap; **l'eau du
robinet** tap water.

bot *noun* M robot; **robot
ménager** food processor.

buste *adjective* robust, sturdy.

che *noun* F rock.

cher *noun* M rock.

ck *noun* M rock (music).

der *verb* [1] to prowl.

gnons *plural noun* M kidneys
(*for cooking*).

i *noun* M king; **le roi Charles** King
Charles; **les Rois mages** the Three
Wise Men; **la fête des Rois** Twelfth
Night.

le *noun* M role.

main *adjective* Roman.

man *noun* M novel; **un roman
olicier** a detective story.

mancier, romancière *noun* M,
novelist.

mantique *adjective* romantic.

marin *noun* M rosemary.

mpre *verb* [69] to split up; **Claire
David ont rompu** Claire and
avid have split up; **Anne a rompu
vec son copain** Anne's broken up
ith her boyfriend; **rompre ses**

fiançailles to break off your
engagement.

ronce *noun* F bramble.

rond *noun* M circle; **tourner en
rond** to go round in circles.
adjective round.

rondelle *noun* F **1** slice; **une
rondelle de tomate** a slice of
tomato; **2** washer (*for a tap or
screw*).

rond-point *noun* M roundabout.

ronfler *verb* [1] to snore.

ronger *verb* [52] **1** to gnaw; **2 se
ronger les ongles** to bite one's nails.

ronronner *verb* [1] to purr.

rosbif *noun* M roast beef.

rose *noun* F rose.
adjective pink; **rose pâle** pale pink.

rosé *noun* M rosé (wine); **un verre
de rosé** a glass of rosé.

rosée *noun* F dew.

rosier *noun* M rosebush.

rossignol *noun* M nightingale.

rôti *noun* M roast; **du rôti de bœuf**
roast beef; **un rôti de bœuf** a joint of
beef.

rôtir *verb* [2] to roast.

roucouler *verb* [1] to coo.

roue *noun* F wheel; **la roue de
secours** the spare wheel; ★ **faire
la roue** to turn a cartwheel.

rouge *noun* M **1** (the colour) red; **le
rouge ne me va pas** red doesn't suit
me; **2** red traffic light; **il est passé
au rouge** he jumped the lights; **le feu
est passé au rouge** the light

changed to red; **3** red wine. **un verre de rouge** a glass of red wine; *adjective* red; **tes chaussettes rouges** your red socks.

rouge à lèvres *noun* M lipstick.

rouge-gorge *noun* M robin.

rougeur *noun* F redness.

rougir *verb* [2] **1** to blush; **2** to turn red.

rouille *noun* F rust.

rouillé *adjective* rusty.

rouiller, se rouiller *verb* [1] to go rusty.

roulant *adjective* **un fauteuil roulant** a wheelchair.

rouleau (*plural* **rouleaux**) *noun* M roll; **un rouleau d'essuie-tout** a roll of kitchen towel.

rouleau à pâtisserie *noun* M rolling pin.

rouler *verb* [1] **1** to go; **nous roulons très vite** we're going very fast; **2** to drive; **il faut rouler à droite en France** in France you must drive on the right; **nous avons roulé toute la nuit** we drove all night; **3** to roll; **4** to roll up; **il faut rouler le tapis** we must roll up the carpet; **5** (*informal*) to cheat; **on m'a roulé!** I've been done!

Roumanie *noun* F Romania.

rousse *adjective* SEE **roux**.

route *noun* F **1** road; **une grande route** a main road; **un accident de la route** a road accident; **Rouen est à trois heures de route d'ici** Rouen is three hours' drive from here;

2 route; **il a changé de route à cause de la neige** he changed his route because of the snow; **3** **en route** on the way; **être en route** to be on the way; **nous sommes en route pour Nice** we're on our way t Nice; **4** **se mettre en route** to set off.

route départementale *noun* F secondary road, B road.

route nationale *noun* F A road.

routier, routière *noun* M, F lorr driver.
adjective road; **le transport routie** road transport; **la gare routière** th bus station.

routine *noun* F routine.

roux (F **rousse**) *adjective* red-haire ginger.

royal (*plural* **royaux**) *adjective* royal.

royaume *noun* M kingdom.

Royaume-Uni *noun* M United Kingdom.

ruban *noun* M ribbon.

rubéole *noun* F German measles

ruche *noun* F beehive.

rudement *adverb* (*informal*) rea **il est rudement bon ton gâteau** your cake's really good.

rue *noun* F street; **une rue piéton** a pedestrian street; ★ **mettre quelqu'un à la rue** to put someon out on the street.

rugby *noun* M rugby; **jouer au rugby** to play rugby.

ugbyman (*plural* rugbymen) *noun* M rugby player.

uine *noun* F ruin; une maison en ruine(s) a ruined house.

uiner *verb* [1] to ruin.

uisseau (*plural* ruisseaux) *noun* M stream.

umeur *noun* F 1 rumour; 2 murmur.

umsteck *noun* M rump steak.

upture *noun* F break-up.

ural (M *plural* ruraux) *adjective* country; la vie rurale country life.

use *noun* F 1 trick; les ruses du métier the tricks of the trade; 2 cunning.

usé *adjective* cunning, crafty.

usse *noun* M, *adjective* Russian.

usse *noun* M & F Russian person).

ussie *noun* F Russia.

thme *noun* M rhythm; marquer le ythme to beat time.

S s

pronoun SEE se.

adjective SEE son.

ble *noun* M sand.

blé *noun* M shortbread biscuit. *djective* la pâte sablée shortcrust astry.

sac *noun* M 1 bag; un sac de sucre a bag of sugar; un sac de sport a sports bag; 2 sack; un sac de charbon a sack of coal; ★ vider son sac (*informal*) to get something off one's chest (*literally: to empty one's bag*).

sac à dos *noun* M rucksack.

sac à main *noun* M handbag.

sac de couchage *noun* M sleeping bag.

sachet *noun* M sachet; un sachet de thé a teabag.

sacoche *noun* F 1 bag; la sacoche du facteur the postman's bag; 2 pannier (*for a bike*).

sacré *adjective* 1 (*informal*) c'est un sacré problème it's a hell of a problem; elle a eu une sacrée chance she's been damn lucky; 2 sacred.

sacrifier *verb* [1] to sacrifice.

sage *adjective* 1 good, well-behaved; Tom, sois sage be a good boy, Tom; 2 wise, sensible; il serait sage de se renseigner sur le prix it would be wise to enquire about the price.

sagesse *noun* F wisdom; une dent de sagesse a wisdom tooth.

Sagittaire *noun* M Sagittarius (*sign of the Zodiac*).

saignant *adjective* rare (*beef*).

saigner *verb* [1] to bleed.

sain *adjective* healthy; ★ sain et sauf safe and sound.

saint, sainte *noun* M, F saint.
adjective holy; **le Saint-Esprit** the
Holy Spirit; **le vendredi saint** Good
Friday; **la Sainte Vierge** the Virgin
Mary.

Saint-Jacques *noun* **une coquille
Saint-Jacques** a scallop.

Saint-Jean *noun* F Midsummer's
Day (*June 24th*).

Saint-Sylvestre *noun* F New
Year's Eve.

sais *verb* SEE **savoir**[1].

saisir *verb* [2] **1** to grab; **il m'a saisi
par le bras** he grabbed my arm;
2 saisir l'occasion to seize the
opportunity; **3** to understand; **je
n'ai pas tout à fait saisi...** I didn't
entirely understand...; **4** to catch,
(*to hear*); **je n'ai pas saisi votre
nom** I didn't catch your name.

saison *noun* F season; **il fait froid
pour la saison** it's cold for the time
of year.

sait *verb* SEE **savoir**[1].

salade *noun* F **1** lettuce; **une
salade** a lettuce ; **2** salad; **une
salade de fruits** a fruit salad.

saladier *noun* M salad bowl.

salaire *noun* M salary; wages.

salarié, salariée *noun* M, F
salaried employee.

sale *adjective* **1** (*after the noun*)
dirty; **les mains sales** dirty hands;
2 (*before the noun*) (*informal*)
horrible; **quel sale temps!** what
horrible weather!; **il a une sale tête**
he looks awful.

salé *adjective* **1** salty; **la sauce est
un peu trop salée** the sauce is a bit
salty; **2** savoury; **des petits gâteau
salés** savoury biscuits; **3 du
beurre salé** salt butter.

saler *verb* [1] to salt.

saleté *noun* F dirt.

salir *verb* [2] to dirty, to get
(something) dirty; **tu vas salir ta
robe** you'll get your dress dirty.

salle *noun* F **1** room (*'salle' by itse
is no longer used to mean a room in
a house*); **2** dining-room (*in a
restaurant*); **3** hall; **4** auditorium
(*in a theatre or cinema*).

salle à manger *noun* F **1** dining
room; **2** dining-room suite.

salle d'attente *noun* F waiting
room.

salle de bains *noun* F bathroom

salle de classe *noun* F
classroom.

salle d'eau *noun* F shower room

salle d'embarquement *noun*
departure lounge.

salle de jeux *noun* F games roo

salle de séjour *noun* F living
room.

salle des fêtes *noun* F
community centre.

salon *noun* M **1** sitting room;
2 living-room suite; **3** trade fair;
4 salon; **salon de coiffure** hair
salon.

salon de thé *noun* M tea-room

salopette *noun* F **1** dungarees;
2 overalls.

aluer *verb* [1] **1** to say hello to; **je l'ai salué, mais il ne m'a pas entendu** I said hello to him but he didn't hear; **elle l'a salué de la main** she waved at him; **2** to say goodbye to.

alut *greeting* M Hi!

amedi *noun* M **1** Saturday; **samedi prochain** next Saturday; **samedi dernier** last Saturday; **2** on Saturday; **samedi soir** on Saturday evening; **3 le samedi** on Saturdays; **fermé le samedi** closed on Saturdays; **4 tous les samedis** every Saturday.

AMU *noun* M SHORT FOR **Service d'assistance médicale d'urgence** ambulance service.

andale *noun* F sandal.

andwich *noun* M sandwich; **un sandwich au jambon** a ham sandwich.

ang *noun* M blood; **être en sang** to be covered in blood.

ang-froid *noun* M calm.

anglier *noun* M wild boar.

anglot *noun* M sob; **éclater en sanglots** to burst into tears.

anisette™ *noun* F automatic public lavatory.

anitaire *adjective* **les conditions sanitaires** sanitary conditions; **les règlements sanitaires** health regulations.
noun M **les sanitaires** the toilet block (*in a campsite*).

ans *preposition* without; **une maison sans téléphone** a house without a telephone; **un café sans sucre** a coffee with no sugar; **sans hésiter** without hesitating.

sans-abri *noun* M & F homeless person; **les sans-abri** the homeless.

sans-emploi *noun* M & F unemployed person; **les sans-emploi** the unemployed.

santé *noun* F **1** health; **être en bonne santé** to be in good health; **2 à votre santé!** cheers!

sapeur-pompier *noun* M fireman; **appeler les sapeurs-pompiers** to call the fire brigade.

sapin *noun* M fir tree; **un sapin de Noël** a Christmas tree.

sardine *noun* F sardine.

satellite *noun* M satellite.

satin *noun* M satin.

satisfaction *noun* F satisfaction.

satisfaire *verb* [10] to satisfy.

satisfaisant *adjective* satisfactory.

satisfait *adjective* satisfied; **êtes-vous satisfaits de votre séjour?** are you satisfied with your stay?

sauce *noun* F **1** sauce; **2** gravy.

saucisse *noun* F sausage.

saucisson *noun* M salami.

sauf¹ *preposition* **1** except; **tous les jours sauf le lundi** every day except Monday; **sauf quand il pleut** except when it rains; **2 sauf si** unless; **c'est tout, sauf s'il y a des questions?** that's all, unless there are any questions?; **3 sauf que** except that; **tout va bien, sauf que ta sœur n'est pas encore arrivée**

everything's fine, except that your sister hasn't arrived yet.

sauf[2] *adjective* SEE **sain**.

saule *noun* M willow; **un saule pleureur** a weeping willow.

saumon *noun* M salmon.

saupoudrer *verb* [1] to sprinkle.

saut *noun* M jump.

saut à la perche *noun* M pole vault.

saut à l'élastique *noun* M bungee jumping.

saut en hauteur *noun* M high jump.

saut en longueur *noun* M long jump.

sauter *verb* [1] **1** to jump, to jump over; **elle a sauté la barrière** she jumped over the gate; **elle a sauté dans un taxi** she jumped into a taxi; **2** **sauter à la corde** to skip (*with a rope*); **3** to skip; **nous avons sauté trois pages** we've skipped three pages; **4** to blow up; **les terroristes ont fait sauter l'avion** the terrorists blew up the plane; **faire sauter les plombs** to blow the fuses; ★ **ça saute aux yeux!** it's blindingly obvious!

sauterelle *noun* F grasshopper.

sauvage *adjective* wild, savage.

sauvegarder *verb* [1] **1** to safeguard; **2** to save, to back up (*on a computer*).

sauver *verb* [1] **1** to save; **vous m'avez sauvé la vie** you saved my life; **2** **se sauver** to run away; **ils se**

sont sauvés they ran away; **3** **je me sauve!** (*informal*) I'm off!

sauvetage *noun* M rescue, life-saving.

savent, savez *verb* SEE **savoir**[1].

savoir[1] *verb* [70] **1** to know; **je sais qu'il habite à Londres** I know he lives in London; **je ne savais pas qu'elle était médecin** I didn't know she was a doctor; **tu sais très bien que…** you know very well that …; **je n'en sais rien** I know nothing about it; **comment l'avez-vous su?** how did you find out about it?; **allez savoir!** who knows!; **2** **savoir faire** to know how to do; **je ne sais pas le faire** I don't know how to do it; **savoir lire et écrire** to be able to read and write; **tu sais jouer du piano?** can you play the piano?

savoir[2] *noun* M knowledge.

savoir-faire *noun* M know-how.

savon *noun* M soap.

savonnette *noun* F cake of soap.

savons *verb* SEE **savoir**[1].

savoureux (F **savoureuse**) *adjective* tasty.

scandale *noun* M scandal; **le discours du ministre a fait scandale** the minister's speech caused a scandal.

scandinave *adjective* Scandinavian.

Scandinavie *noun* F Scandinavia.

scanner *noun* M scanner.

scarabée *noun* M beetle.

scénariste *noun* M & F scriptwriter.

scène *noun* F **1** stage (*in a theatre*); **être sur scène** to be on stage; **mettre en scène** to stage (*a play*); to direct (*a film*); **2** scene; **sur la scène politique** on the political scene; **des scènes de panique** scenes of panic; **faire (toute) une scène** to throw a fit.

sceptique *adjective* sceptical.

schéma *noun* M diagram.

scie *noun* F saw.

science *noun* F science.

sciences naturelles *plural noun* F biology.

scientifique *noun* M & F scientist. *adjective* scientific.

scier *verb* [1] to saw.

scolaire *adjective* school; **les vacances scolaires** the school holidays; **le livret scolaire** the school report.

scolarité *noun* F schooling, education.

Scorpion *noun* M Scorpio (*sign of the Zodiac*).

Scotch™ *noun* M Sellotape™.

scout, scoute *noun* M, F boy scout, girl guide.

scrutin *noun* M **1** ballot; **2** polls; **le jour du scrutin** polling day.

sculpteur *noun* M sculptor.

sculpture *noun* F sculpture.

SDF *noun* M & F SHORT FOR **sans domicile fixe** of no fixed abode; **les SDF** the homeless.

se, s' (*before a vowel or silent 'h'*) *reflexive pronoun* **1** himself; **il se regarde** he's looking at himself; **2** herself; **elle se regarde** she's looking at herself; **3** itself; **le chien s'est fait mal** the dog has hurt itself; **4** themselves; **ils se sont fait mal** they've hurt themselves; **5** each other; **ils se regardaient** they were looking at each other; **6** yourself, oneself; **se faire mal** to hurt yourself (or oneself); **7** (*sometimes not translated*) **Claudie se lave les cheveux** Claudie's washing her hair; **Jules se brosse les dents** Jules is brushing his teeth.

séance *noun* F **1** session; **2** showing (*of a film*); **la séance de vingt heures** the eight o'clock showing.

seau (*plural* **seaux**) *noun* M bucket.

sec (F **sèche**) *adjective* **1** dry; **mes cheveux ne sont pas secs** my hair's not dry; **un vin blanc sec** a dry white wine; **2** dried; **des abricots secs** dried apricots.

sèche-cheveux *noun* M hair dryer.

sèche-linge *noun* M tumble dryer.

sèche-mains *noun* M hand dryer.

sécher *verb* [1] to dry; **des fleurs séchées** dried flowers.

sécheresse *noun* F drought.

second *noun* M **au second** on the second floor; **il est arrivé en second** he arrived second.
adjective second; **la seconde fois** the second time.

secondaire *adjective* secondary; **une école secondaire** a secondary school; **des effets secondaires** side effects.

seconde *noun* F **1** second; **je reviens dans une seconde** I'll be back in a moment; **2** second class; **voyager en seconde** to travel second class; **un billet de seconde** a second class ticket; **3** (*in a French school*) the equivalent of Year 11.

secouer *verb* [1] to shake; **secouer la tête** to shake your head.

secourir *verb* [29] to rescue.

secourisme *noun* M first aid.

secouriste *noun* M & F first aider.

secours *noun* M **1** help; **au secours!** help!; **elle a crié au secours** she shouted for help; **2 les premiers secours** first aid; **3 une sortie de secours** an emergency exit; **4 la roue de secours** the spare wheel.

secret *noun* M secret; **garder un secret** to keep a secret; **en secret** in secret.
adjective (F **secrète**) secret.

secrétaire[1] *noun* M & F secretary.

secrétaire[2] *noun* M writing desk.

secrétariat *noun* M secretary's office.

secteur *noun* M sector; **dans le secteur privé** in the private sector; **dans le secteur public** in the public sector.

sécu (*informal*) *noun* F SHORT FOR **Sécurité sociale** Social Security.

sécurité *noun* F **1** safety; **pour votre sécurité** for your own safety; **les règles de sécurité** safety regulations; **la sécurité routière** road safety; **une ceinture de sécurité** a seatbelt; **2 être en sécurité** to be safe; **3** security; **un système de sécurité** a security system; **la sécurité de l'emploi** job security.

Sécurité sociale *noun* F Social Security.

séduisant *adjective* attractive, appealing.

seigle *noun* M rye; **le pain de seigle** rye bread.

seigneur *noun* M lord; **le Seigneur** the Lord.

sein *noun* M **1** breast; **avoir un cancer du sein** to have breast cancer; **2** within; **au sein du gouvernement** within the government.

seize *number* sixteen; **Corinne a seize ans** Corinne's sixteen; **le seize juillet** the sixteenth of July.

seizième *number* sixteenth.

séjour *noun* M **1** stay; **pendant votre séjour en France** during your stay in France; **2 la salle de séjour** the living room.

sel *noun* M salt; **une pincée de sel** a pinch of salt.

sélection *noun* F selection.

sélectionner *verb* [1] to select.

self *noun* M (*informal*) self-service restaurant.

self-service (*informal*) M *noun* self-service restaurant.

selle *noun* F saddle.

selon *preposition* according to; **selon la météo, il va pleuvoir** according to the forecast, it's going to rain.

semaine *noun* F week; **cette semaine** this week; **la semaine prochaine/dernière** next/last week; **elle est payée à la semaine** she's paid by the week.

semblable *adjective* similar.

semblant *noun* M **faire semblant de faire** to pretend to do; **elle fait semblant de ne pas entendre** she's pretending not to hear.

sembler *verb* [1] to seem; **la maison semble vide** the house seems empty; **il semble bon d'attendre leur retour** it seems a good idea to wait till they get back.

semelle *noun* F sole (*of a shoe*).

semer *verb* [1] **1** to sow (*seeds*); **2 semer la panique** to spread panic.

semestre *noun* M semester.

semi-remorque *noun* M articulated truck.

semoule *noun* F semolina; **le sucre semoule** caster sugar.

sens *noun* M **1** direction; **dans les deux sens** in both directions; **dans le sens Calais-Paris** in the Calais-Paris direction; **dans tous les sens** in all directions; **sens dessus dessous** upside down; **mets-le dans le bon sens!** put it the right way up!; **2** meaning; **le sens d'un mot** the meaning of a word; **cela n'a pas de sens** it doesn't make sense, it's absurd.

sensation *noun* F **1** feeling; **2** sensation; **le film a fait sensation à Cannes** the film was a sensation at Cannes.

sensationnel (F **sensationnelle**) *adjective* sensational, fantastic.

sens commun *noun* M common sense.

sens de l'humour *noun* M sense of humour; **avoir le sens de l'humour** to have a sense of humour.

sensé *adjective* sensible.

sensibiliser *verb* [1] **sensibiliser les gens à un problème** to increase people's awareness of a problem.

sensible *adjective* **1** sensitive; **c'est une fille très sensible** she's a very sensitive girl; **je suis sensible au froid** I feel the cold; **2** noticeable; **une différence sensible** a noticeable difference.

sensiblement *adverb* noticeably.

sens interdit *noun* M no entry sign; one-way street.

sens unique *noun* M one-way street.

sentier *noun* M path.

sentier de randonnée *noun* M long-distance footpath (*a marked route for ramblers*).

sentiment noun M feeling;
sentiments affectueux best wishes;
**veuillez croire à mes sentiments les
meilleurs** yours sincerely, yours
faithfully (*one of a number of fixed
formulae for ending a formal letter*).

sentimental (M *plural*
sentimentaux) *adjective*
sentimental.

sentir *verb* [58] **1** to smell; **ça sent
bon!** that smells good!; **2** to smell
of; **ça sent les roses** it smells of
roses; **tu sens la cigarette** you smell
of cigarettes; **3** to feel; **je ne sens
rien** I can't feel anything; **on sent
que l'hiver s'approche** you can feel
it will soon be winter; **je sens qu'elle
est sincère** I feel she's sincere; **4 se
sentir** to feel; **je ne me sens pas
bien** I don't feel well; ★ **je ne peux
pas le sentir!** I can't stand him!

séparé *adjective* **1** separated; **mes
parents sont séparés** my parents
are separated; **2** separate; **dans une
chambre séparée** in a separate
bedroom.

séparément *adverb* separately.

séparer *verb* [1] **1** to separate;
séparez les œufs separate the eggs;
séparer les filles des garçons to
separate the girls from the boys;
2 se séparer to separate, to split up;
mes parents se sont séparés my
parents have separated.

sept *number* seven; **Yasmin a sept
ans** Yasmin's seven; **il est sept
heures** it's seven o'clock; **le sept
mars** the seventh of March.

septante *number* seventy (*used in
Belgium and Switzerland, instead of*
soixante-dix); **septante-sept**
seventy-seven.

septembre *noun* M September; **en
septembre, au mois de
septembre** in September.

septième *noun* M **au septième** on
the seventh floor;
adjective seventh.

sera, serai, seras, serez *verb*
SEE **être**[1].

série *noun* F series.

sérieusement *adverb* seriously.

sérieux *noun* **prendre quelque
chose au sérieux** to take something
seriously.
adjective (F **sérieuse**) **1** serious;
vraiment? tu es sérieux? really? are
you serious? **2** reponsible; **Camilla
est une jeune fille sérieuse** Camilla
is a reponsible young woman;
3 reliable; **il n'est pas sérieux** he's
unreliable; **4 un travail sérieux** a
careful piece of work; ★ **garder son
sérieux** to keep a straight face.

serin *noun* M canary.

seringue *noun* F syringe.

séronégatif *adjective* (F
séronégative) HIV-negative.

serons, seront *verb* SEE **être**[1].

séropositif (F **séropositive**)
adjective HIV-positive.

serpent *noun* M snake.

serpillière *noun* F floorcloth.

serre *noun* F greenhouse; **l'effet de
serre** the greenhouse effect.

serré *adjective* **1** tight; **ma jupe est
trop serrée** my skirt's too tight; **un**

budget serré a tight budget;
2 close (*match or competition*).

serrer *verb* [1] **1** to grip; **elle serrait
le volant** she gripped the steering
wheel; **il m'a serrée dans ses bras**
he hugged me; **2 serrer la main à
quelqu'un** to shake somebody's
hand; **nous nous sommes serré la
main** we shook hands; **3 serrer
quelqu'un dans ses bras** to hug
somebody; **4 serrer les poings** to
clench your fists; **5** to tighten (*a
screw or belt*); **6** to be too tight; **mes
chaussures me serrent** my shoes
are too tight; **7** to push closer
together; **serrez les tables** move
the tables closer together; **8 se
serrer** to squeeze up; **serrez-vous
un peu!** squeeze up a bit!

serrure *noun* F lock.

serveur, serveuse *noun* M, F
waiter, waitress.

service *noun* M **1** favour; **peux-tu
me rendre un petit service?** could
you do me a small favour?; **2** service
(*bus, train*); **service de dimanche**
Sunday service; **3 être en service**
to be working; **il n'y a qu'un
ascenseur en service** there's only
one lift working; **être hors service**
to be out of order; **l'ascenseur est
hors service** the lift is out of order;
4 duty, service; **la pharmacie de
service** the duty chemist; **je suis de
service ce soir** I am on duty this
evening; **le service militaire**
national service; **5** service (*charge*);
le service est compris service is
included; **6** department (*in a town
hall or hospital, for example*); **le
service des urgences** the casualty
department.

service après-vente *noun* M
after-sales service.

serviette *noun* F **1** towel; **une
serviette de bain** a bath towel;
2 napkin; **3** briefcase.

serviette hygiénique *noun* F
sanitary towel.

servir *verb* [71] **1** to serve (*in a shop,
for example*); **merci, on me sert**
thank you, I'm being served; **2** to
serve (*with food or drink*); **est-ce
que je peux vous servir du poulet?**
can I give you some chicken?; **'servir
frais'** 'serve chilled'; **3 se servir** to
help yourself; **sers-toi de riz** help
yourself to rice; **4 se servir de** to
use; **est-ce que tu sais te servir
d'une machine à coudre?** do you
know how to use a sewing
machine?; **5** to serve (*in tennis or in
the army*); **à toi de servir!** your
service!; **6 servir à** to be used for; **à
quoi ça sert?** what's it for?; **ça ne
sert à rien!** it's no use!; **ça ne sert à
rien de pleurer** there's no point in
crying; **7 se servir** to be served
(*food or drink*); **ce vin se sert frais**
this wine should be served chilled.

ses *adjective* SEE **son**.

set de table *noun* M place mat.

seul *adjective* **1** only; **la seule
personne** the only person; **c'est le
seul Anglais que je connaisse** he's
the only English person I know;
j'étais le seul à aimer le film I was
the only one who liked the film;
2 alone; **il ne faut pas y aller seul**
you mustn't go there alone; **j'étais
tout seul à la maison** I was all alone
in the house; **3 se sentir seul** to
feel lonely; **4 tout seul** all by

yourself; **il l'a fait tout seul** he did it all by himself; **Sophie sait s'habiller toute seule maintenant** Sophie can get dressed all by herself now.

seulement *adverb* **1** only; **trois fois seulement** only three times; **2 non seulement…mais** not only…but; **non seulement elle n'est pas venue, mais elle n'a même pas appelé** not only did she not come, but she didn't even phone; **3 si seulement je l'avais su** if only I'd known.

sévère *adjective* strict.

sexe *noun* M **1** sex; **2** genitals.

sexuel (F **sexuelle**) *adjective* **1** sexual; **2 l'éducation sexuelle** sex education.

shampooing *noun* M shampoo.

short *noun* M (pair of) shorts; **où est mon short?** where are my shorts?; **trois shorts** three pairs of shorts.

si, s' (*before il or ils*) *conjunction* if; **si tu veux** if you like; **s'il pleut** if it rains.
adverb **1** so; **je suis si fatigué!** I'm so tired!; **tu chantes si bien!** you sing so well!; **2** yes (*when you are contradicting somebody*); **'tu ne viens pas avec nous?' – 'si!'** 'you're not coming with us?' – 'yes I am!'; **'il ne reste pas manger' – 'mais si!'** 'he's not staying for a meal' – 'of course he is!'; **elle ne les aime pas du tout, moi si** she doesn't like them at all, but I do.

Sicile *noun* F Sicily.

sida *noun* M SHORT FOR **syndrome immuno-déficitaire acquis** AIDS; **avoir le sida** to have AIDS.

siècle *noun* M century; **au vingtième siècle** in the twentieth century.

siège *noun* M **1** seat; **le siège d'avant** the front seat; **2** head office (*of a company*).

sien, sienne, siens, siennes *pronoun* **le sien, la sienne, les siens, les siennes 1** his; **j'ai prêté mon vélo à Paul, le sien est chez lui** I've lent Paul my bike, his is at home; **'est-ce que ces chaussures sont à Bernard?' – 'oui, ce sont les siennes'** 'are these shoes Bernard's?' – 'yes, they're his'; **2** hers; **j'ai prêté mon vélo à Annie, le sien est chez elle** I've lent Annie my bike, hers is at home; **'est-ce que ces chaussures sont à Nathalie?' – 'oui, ce sont les siennes';** 'are these shoes Nathalie's?' – 'yes, they're hers'.

sieste *noun* F nap; **faire la sieste** to have a nap.

siffler *verb* [1] to whistle.

sifflet *noun* M whistle.

signal (*plural* **signaux**) *noun* M signal.

signaler *verb* [1] **1** to point out; **je vous signale que je serai absent ce jour-là** I'd like to point out that I shall be away that day; **2** to report; **3** to indicate (*roadworks or danger, for example*).

signalisation *noun* F signalling; signals.

signalisation routière *noun* F road signs and markings.

signature *noun* F signature; **je vous demande une petite signature** just sign here, would you?

signe *noun* M signe; **c'est bon/mauvais signe** it's a good/bad sign; **faire signe à quelqu'un** to wave to someone; **il m'a fait signe de m'approcher** he beckoned me over to him; **d'un signe de main elle a montré la sortie** she pointed to the exit.

signer *verb* [1] **1** to sign; **2 se signer** to cross oneself.

signification *noun* F meaning.

signifier *verb* [1] to mean.

silence *noun* M silence; **en silence** in silence.

silencieux (F **silencieuse**) *adjective* silent.

silhouette *noun* F **1** silhouette, outline; **2** figure.

similarité *noun* F similarity.

simple *noun* M **le simple messieurs/dames** the men's/women's singles (*in tennis*). *adjective* simple; **un repas simple** a simple meal; **un simple coup de téléphone** just a telephone call.

simplement *adverb* simply.

simplicité *noun* F simplicity.

simplifier *verb* [1] to simplify.

simuler *verb* [1] to simulate.

simultané *adjective* simultaneous.

sincère *adjective* sincere.

sincérité *noun* F sincerity.

singe *noun* M monkey.

singulier *noun* M singular; **au singulier** in the singular.

sinistre *noun* M accident, disaster (*for example, a fire or flood*). *adjective* **1** sinister; **2** gloomy.

sinistré, sinistrée *noun* M, F disaster victim. *adjective* stricken; **de l'aide pour les familles sinistrées** help for the families stricken by the disaster.

sinon *conjunction* otherwise; **il faut partir, sinon on sera en retard** we must leave, otherwise we'll be late.

sirène *noun* F **1** siren; **une sirène d'alarme** a fire alarm; **2** mermaid.

sirop *noun* M **1** syrup; **sirop pectoral** cough mixture; **2 sirop de menthe** mint cordial.

site *noun* M site, area; **site touristique** place of interest (*to visit*); **site classé** conservation area.

sitôt *adverb* as soon as; **sitôt rentrée, elle s'est couchée** as soon as she got home, she went to bed; **sitôt après** immediately afterwards; ★ **sitôt dit, sitôt fait** no sooner said than done.

situation *noun* F **1** situation; **2** job; **il a perdu sa situation** he's lost his job.

situer *verb* [1] **1 être situé** to be situated; **l'hôtel est situé au bord de la mer** the hotel is situated on the edge of the sea; **bien situé** well situated; **2 se situer** to be situated; **la maison se situe dans un quartier résidentiel** the house is in a residential area; **3 se situer** to be set; **le roman se situe à Moscou** the novel is set in Moscow.

six *number* six; **Rosie a six ans** Rosie's six; **il est six heures** it's six o'clock; **le six juillet** the sixth of July.

sixième *noun* F (*in a French school*) the equivalent of Year 7.
noun M **au sixième** on the sixth floor.
adjective sixth.

ski *noun* M **1** ski; **où sont mes skis?** where are my skis? **2** skiing; **il adore le ski** he loves skiing; **on va faire du ski ce week-end** we're going skiing this weekend.

ski de fond *noun* M cross-country skiing.

ski de piste *noun* M downhill skiing.

skier *verb* [1] to ski; **il skie plutôt bien** he skis pretty well; **skier hors piste** to ski off-piste.

skieur, skieuse *noun* M, F skier.

ski nautique *noun* M water-skiing.

slip *noun* M **1** underpants; **2** knickers.

Slovaquie *noun* F Slovakia.

Slovénie *noun* F Slovenia.

SMIC *noun* M guaranteed minimum wage; **elle touche le SMIC** she's on the legel minimum wage.

smoking *noun* M dinner jacket.

SNCF *noun* F SHORT FOR **Société nationale des chemins de fer français** (*French railways*).

snob *noun* M & F snob.
adjective snobbish (*of a person*); posh (*of a restaurant*).

sobre *adjective* sober.

sociable *adjective* friendly, sociable.

social (M *plural* **sociaux**) *adjective* social.

socialiste *noun* M & F, *adjective* socialist.

société *noun* F **1** society; **dans notre société** in our society; **2** company; **il travaille pour une grande société** he works for a big company.

sociologie *noun* F sociology.

socquette *noun* F ankle sock.

sœur *noun* F sister; **ma grande sœur** my big sister, my older sister.

soi *pronoun* **1** one, oneself; **des ami autour de soi** friends around one; **2** **avoir confiance en soi** to have confidence in oneself; **3** itself; **pas très intéressant en soi** not very interesting in itself; **cela va de soi** that goes without saying.

soi-disant *adjective* **1** so-called; **c'est le soi-disant champion** he's the so-called champion; **2** supposedly; **elle est soi-disant malade** she's supposedly ill.

soie *noun* F silk; **un foulard en soie** a silk scarf; **le papier de soie** tissue paper.

soif *noun* M thirst; **avoir soif** to be thirsty.

soigner *verb* [1] to look after.

soigneusement *adverb* carefully.

soi-même *pronoun* yourself, oneself; **il faut le faire soi-même** you have to do it yourself.

soin *noun* M **1** care; **2 prendre soin de quelque chose** to take care of something. **3 les soins** treatment; **4 les premiers soins** first aid.

soir *noun* M evening, night; **ce soir** tonight; **hier soir** last night; **demain soir** tomorrow night; **je sors tous les samedis soirs** I go out every Saturday night; **par un beau soir d'été** one fine summer's evening; **à six heures du soir** at six in the evening; **à ce soir!** see you tonight!

soirée *noun* F **1** evening; **pendant la soirée** during the evening; **2** party; **elle donne une petite soirée** she's having a little party; **3 en tenue de soirée** in evening dress.

sois *verb* SEE **être**[1]; **sois gentil** be good.

soit *conjunction* **soit…soit** either…or; **soit demain, soit jeudi** either tomorrow or Thursday.

soixantaine *noun* F **1** about sixty; **une soixantaine de personnes** about sixty people; **2 avoir la soixantaine** to be in your sixties.

soixante *number* sixty.

soixante-dix *number* seventy; **soixante-dix-huit** seventy-eight.

soja *noun* M soya bean; **la sauce de soja** soy sauce.

sol *noun* M **1** floor; **2** soil.

solaire *adjective* **1** solar; **2 la crème solaire** sun cream.

soldat *noun* M soldier.

solde *noun* M **1 les soldes** the sales; **faire les soldes** to go round the sales; **2 être en solde** to be reduced; **les pulls sont en solde** the jumpers are reduced; **3** balance in a bank account.

soldé *adjective* reduced.

sole *noun* F sole (*fish*).

soleil *noun* M sun; **au soleil** in the sun; **il fait soleil** it's sunny; **en plein soleil** in full sun; **attraper un coup de soleil** to get sunburnt.

solfège *noun* M musical theory.

solide *adjective* **1** strong; **2** solid.

soliste *noun* M & F soloist.

solitaire *adjective* **1** lonely, isolated; **2 un navigateur solitaire** a solo yachtsman.

solution *noun* F solution.

sombre *adjective* dark, gloomy.

somme[1] *noun* F sum; **une somme d'argent** a sum of money.

somme[2] *noun* M nap; **faire un somme** to have a nap.

sommeil *noun* M sleep; **avoir sommeil** to feel sleepy; **je n'ai plus sommeil** I'm not sleepy any more.

sommes *verb* SEE **être**[1].

sommet *noun* M summit.

somnambule *noun* M & F sleepwalker; **être somnambule** to walk in your sleep.

son¹, sa, ses *adjective* **1** his; **son fils** his son; **sa fille** his daughter; **ses enfants** his children; **2** her; **son fils** her son; **sa fille** her daughter; **ses enfants** her children; **3** its; **le chat a perdu son collier** the cat's lost its collar.

son² *noun* M **1** sound; **le son d'un piano** the sound of a piano; **2** volume (*on a radio or hi-fi*); **baisser le son** to turn the volume down; **3** bran.

sondage *noun* M survey; **un sondage d'opinion** an opinion poll.

sonner *verb* [1] to ring; **le téléphone sonne** the phone's ringing; **on sonne à la porte** somebody's ringing the doorbell.

sonnerie *noun* F bell; **la sonnerie d'alarme** the alarm bell; **la sonnerie du téléphone** the ring of the telephone.

sonnette *noun* F bell, doorbell.

sono *noun* F (*informal*) sound system.

sophistiqué *adjective* sophisticated.

sorbet *noun* M sorbet; **un sorbet au cassis** a blackcurrant sorbet.

sorcière *noun* F witch.

sort *noun* M fate; ★ **tirer au sort** to draw lots.

sorte *noun* F sort; **c'est une sorte de poudre** it's a sort of powder; **toutes sortes d'activités** all sorts of activities.

sortie *noun* F **1** exit; **il nous attend à la sortie** he's waiting for us at the exit; **sortie de secours** emergency exit; **2** outing; **3** launching (*of a new product*); release (*of a film*); publication of a book.

sortir *verb* [72] **1** to go out; **tout le monde est sorti dans la rue** everybody went out into the street; **ils sont sortis déjeuner** they've gone out for lunch; **elle est sortie en courant** she ran out; **2** to come out; **c'est l'heure où les gens sortent du cinéma** it's the time when people are coming out of the cinema; **son nouveau film sortira en mai** her new film is coming out in May; **3** to go out (*for pleasure*); **mes parents sortent peu** my parents don't go out much; **4** **sortir avec** to be going out with; **il sort avec ma sœur** he's going out with my sister; **5** to take out; **elle a sorti une bouteille du frigo** she took a bottle out of the fridge; **j'ai oublié de sortir le chien** I forgot to take the dog out; **6** **s'en sortir** to manage; **je m'en sortirai d'une manière ou d'une autre** I'll manage one way or another.

sottise *noun* F **1** silliness; **2** **dire des sottises** to talk nonsense; **ne fais pas de sottises** don't do anything silly.

sou *noun* M **j'ai dépensé tous mes sous** I've spent all my money; **je n'ai pas un sou** I'm broke; **une machine à sous** a fruit machine; ★ **être près de ses sous** to be tight-fisted.

souci *noun* M **1** worry, **se faire du souci** to worry; **mon fils me donne bien des soucis** my son's a great worry to me; **j'ai d'autres soucis à présent** I've got other problems just now; **2** marigold.

soucieux (F **soucieuse**) *adjective* worried.

soucoupe *noun* F saucer.

soudain *adjective* sudden. *adverb* suddenly.

souffle *noun* M breath; **être à bout de souffle** to be out of breath; **couper le souffle à quelqu'un** to take someone's breath away.

soufflé *noun* M soufflé; **un soufflé au fromage** a cheese soufflé.

souffler *verb* [1] **1** to blow; **le vent soufflait fort** there was a strong wind; **2** to blow out (*a candle*); **3** to whisper; **elle me soufflait quelque chose à l'oreille** she was whispering something in my ear; ★ **souffler dans le ballon** (*informal*) to be breathalysed.

souffrir *verb* [73] **1** to suffer; **a-t-elle beaucoup souffert?** did she suffer much?; **il souffre souvent du dos** he often has back pain; **2 je ne peux pas le souffrir!** (*informal*) I can't stand him!

souhait *noun* M wish; ★ **à tes souhaits!** bless you! (*when somebody sneezes*).

souhaiter *verb* [1] to wish; **je te souhaite bonne chance** I wish you luck; **il nous a souhaité la bienvenue** he welcomed us; **il souhaite se marier** he'd like to get married.

soûl *adjective* drunk.

soulagé *adjective* relieved.

soulagement *noun* M relief.

soulager *verb* [52] to relieve.

soulever *verb* [50] **1** to lift; **je n'arrive pas à soulever ta valise** I can't lift your case; **2** to raise (*problems, objections, or difficulties*); **personne n'a soulevé la question** nobody raised the question.

soulier *noun* M shoe.

souligner *verb* [1] **1** to underline; **2** to emphasize.

soupçon *noun* M **1** suspicion; **2** spot, drop (*of food or drink*); **juste un soupçon de lait** just a drop of milk.

soupçonner *verb* [1] to suspect.

soupe *noun* F soup; **la soupe aux oignons** onion soup.

souper *verb* [1] to have supper.

soupir *noun* M sigh.

soupirer *verb* [1] to sigh.

souple *adjective* **1** supple (*person*); **2** flexible (*system*); **3** soft (*hair or clean washing*).

source *noun* F spring; **l'eau de source** spring water.

sourcil *noun* M eyebrow.

sourd *adjective* **1** deaf; **2** dull, muffled (*noise*); ★ **faire la sourde oreille** to turn a deaf ear.

souriant *adjective* cheerful.

sourire *noun* M smile; **il faut garder le sourire** you must keep smiling. *verb* [68] to smile; **sourire à quelqu'un** to smile at somebody.

souris *noun* F mouse (*also for a computer*).

sous *preposition* under, underneath; **sous la chaise** under the chair; **sortir sous la pluie** to go out in the rain; **sous terre** underground; ★ **sous peu** before long.

sous-entendu *noun* M innuendo. *adjective* implied.

sous-estimer *verb* [1] to underestimate.

sous-marin *noun* M submarine. *adjective* under-water; deep-sea.

sous-sol *noun* M basement; **au sous-sol** in the basement.

sous-tasse *noun* F saucer.

sous-titre *noun* M subtitle.

soustraction *noun* F subtraction.

sous-vêtements *plural noun* M underwear.

soutenir *verb* [77] **1** to support; **elle m'a soutenu à la réunion** she supported me at the meeting; **2 soutenir que** to maintain that; **3 soutenir une conversation** to keep up a conversation; **4** to withstand (*a shock or attack*).

souterrain *adejctive* underground.

soutien *noun* M support.

soutien-gorge *noun* M bra.

soutif *noun* M (*informal*) bra.

souvenir *noun* M **1** memory; **mes souvenirs de Londres** my memories of London; **garder un bon souvenir de quelque chose** to have happy memories of something; **je n'ai aucun souvenir de l'avoir rencontrée** I have no memory of meeting her; **2** souvenir.

verb [81] **se souvenir de** to remember; **je me souviens d'elle** I remember her; **je me souviens de l'avoir rencontrée** I remember meeting her; **t'en souviens-tu?** do you remember that?

souvent *adverb* often; **je ne la vois pas très souvent** I don't see her ver~ often; **le plus souvent** more often than not

spacieux (F **spacieuse**) *adjective* spacious.

spaghettis *plural noun* M spaghetti; **manger des spaghettis** to have spaghetti.

sparadrap *noun* M sticking plaster.

speaker, speakerine *noun* M, F announcer.

spécial (M *plural* **spéciaux**) *adjective* **1** special; **rien de spécial** nothing special; **les effets spéciaux** special effects; **2** odd; **il est vraiment très spécial** he's really very odd.

spécialement *adverb* specially.

spécialiser *verb* [1] **se spécialiser** to specialize; **elle se spécialise dan~ la génétique** she's specializing in genetics.

spécialiste *noun* M & F specialist

spécialité *noun* F speciality.

spécifier *verb* [1] to specify.

spectacle *noun* M show.

spectaculaire *adjective* spectacular.

spectateur, spectatrice *noun* M, F **1** member of the audience; **2** spectator.

spéléologie *noun* F potholing.

spirituel, spirituelle *adjective* **1** witty; **2** spiritual.

splendeur *noun* F splendour.

splendide *adjective* magnificent.

sponsoriser *verb* [1] to sponsor.

spontané *adjective* spontaneous.

sport *noun* M sport; sports; **aimez-vous le sport?** do you like sport?; **il fait beaucoup de sport** he does a lot of sport; **mon maillot de sport** my sports shirt; **les sports d'hiver** winter sports.

sportif, sportive *noun* M, F sportsman, sportswoman. *adjective* **1** sports; **un club sportif** a sports club; **une rencontre sportive** a sports meeting; **2** sporty, athletic.

spot *noun* M **1** spotlight; **2** **un spot publicitaire** a commercial.

square *noun* M public garden.

squelette *noun* M skeleton.

stable *adjective* **1** stable; **2** **un emploi stable** a steady job.

stade *noun* M stadium.

stage *noun* M **1** course; **un stage intensif d'anglais** an intensive English course; **2** **un stage professionnel** work experience; **j'aimerais faire un stage professionnel dans une société britannique** I'd like to do work experience in an British company.

stand *noun* M **1** stand (*in a market or an exhibition*); **2** stall (*in a fairground*).

standard *noun* M switchboard; **il faut passer par le standard** you have to go through the switchboard.

standardiste *noun* M & F switchboard operator.

standing *noun* M **un appartement de standing** a luxury flat.

star *noun* F star (*in a film or show*).

starter *noun* M choke (*in a car*).

station *noun* F **1** **une station de métro** an underground station; **2** **une station de taxis** a taxi rank; **3** resort; **une station de ski** a ski resort; **4** **une station de radio** a radio station.

station de travail *noun* F (computer) work station.

stationnement *noun* M parking; **'stationnement interdit'** 'no parking'.

stationner *verb* [1] to park.

station-service *noun* F service station.

statistique *noun* F statistic(s).

statue *noun* F statue.

steak *noun* M steak; **un steak frites** steak and chips; **un steak haché** a burger steak.

sténodactylo *noun* M & F shorthand typist.

stéréo *noun* F, *adjective* stereo.

stérile *adjective* sterile.

stériliser *verb* [1] to sterilize.

stimulant *adjective* stimulating.

stock *noun* M stock; **en stock** in stock.

stop *noun* M **1** stop sign; **2 faire du stop** to hitch-hike.

stopper *verb* [1] to stop.

store *noun* M **1** blind; **2** awning.

strapontin *noun* M fold-down seat.

stratégie *noun* F strategy.

stratégique *adjective* strategic.

stress *noun* M stress.

stressant *adjective* stressful.

stressé *adjective* stressed; **elle avait l'air stressé** she looked stressed; **je suis très stressé en ce moment** I'm stressed out at the moment.

strict *adjective* **1** strict; **2** severe.

studieux (F **studieuse**) *adjective* studious.

studio *noun* M **1** studio flat; **2** studio.

stupéfait *adjective* astounded.

stupéfiants *plural noun* M narcotics.

stupeur *noun* F astonishment.

stupide *adjective* stupid.

stupidité *noun* F stupidity.

style *noun* M style; **c'est bien son style!** that's just like him!

styliste *noun* M & F designer.

stylo *noun* M fountain pen.

stylo-bille *noun* M ball-point pen.

stylo-feutre *noun* M felt pen.

stylo-plume *noun* M fountain pen.

su *verb* SEE **savoir**[1].

subir *verb* [2] **1** to be subjected to; (*change, violence, or pressure*); to suffer (*defeat or damage*); **2 subir une opération** to have an operation.

subitement *adverb* suddenly.

subjonctif *noun* M subjunctive; **au subjonctif** in the subjunctive.

subordonné, subordonnée *noun* M F subordinate.

substituer *verb* [1] to replace, to substitute.

subtil *adjective* subtle.

subvention *noun* F subsidy.

succès *noun* M success; **c'est un grand succès!** it's a big success!

succursale *noun* F branch (*of a company*).

sucer *verb* [61] to suck.

sucette *noun* F lollipop.

sucre *noun* M **1** sugar; **du jus d'orange sans sucre** unsweetened orange juice; **2 un sucre** a lump of sugar.

sucré *adjective* sweet; **c'est trop sucré pour moi** it's too sweet for me.

sucre cristallisé *noun* M granulated sugar.

sucre d'orge *noun* M barley sugar.

sucre en morceaux *noun* M sugar lumps.

sucre en poudre *noun* M caster sugar.

sucre glace *noun* M icing sugar.

sucrerie *noun* F **des sucreries** sweet things.

sucre roux *noun* M brown sugar.

sucrier *noun* M sugar bowl.

sud *noun* M south; **au sud de l'Écosse** in the south of Scotland; **au sud de Calais** south of Calais; **un vent du sud** a south wind. *adjective* 1 south; **la côte sud** the south coast; 2 southern; **la partie sud** the southern part.

sud-africain *adjective* South African.

sud-américain *adjective* South American.

sud-est *noun* M, *adjective* south-east.

sud-ouest *noun* M, *adjective* south-west.

Suède *noun* F Sweden.

suédois *noun* M, *adjective* Swedish.

Suédois, Suédoise *noun* M, F Swede.

suer *verb* [1] to sweat.

sueur *noun* F sweat; **je suis en sueur** I'm sweating.

suffire *verb* [74] 1 to be enough; **un kilo suffit** one kilo's enough; **ça suffit!** that's enough!; 2 **il suffit de faire** all you have to do is; **il suffit de nous téléphoner** all you have to do is give us a call.

suffisamment *adverb* enough; **ce n'est pas suffisamment cuit** it's not cooked enough; **il n'y a pas suffisamment de verres** there aren't enough glasses.

suffisant *adjective* 1 sufficient; **c'est bien suffisant!** that's quite enough!; 2 smug; **je la trouve un peu suffisante** I find her a bit smug.

suffoquer *verb* [1] to suffocate; to choke.

suggérer *verb* [24] to suggest.

suggestion *noun* F suggestion.

suicider *verb* [1] **se suicider** to commit suicide.

suis *verb* SEE **être**[1]; SEE **suivre**.

suisse *adjective* Swiss.

Suisse *noun* F Switzerland; **en Suisse** in (or to) Switzerland; **la Suisse romande** French-speaking Switzerland; **la Suisse allemande** German-speaking Switzerland.

suite *noun* F 1 rest; **je te raconterai la suite plus tard** I'll tell you the rest later; **et on connaît la suite** and we all know what happened next; 2 continuation; **'suite page 67'** 'continued on page 67'; **regardez la suite jeudi** watch the next instalment on Thursday; 3 suite (*in a hotel*); 4 in succession; **trois fois de suite** three times in succession; 5 **tout de suite** straightaway; **j'arrive tout de suite!** I'll be right there!; 6 **par la suite** later; **on s'est rendu compte par la suite que c'était une erreur** we realized later that it was a mistake.

suivant, suivante *noun* M, F next one; **pas ce lundi mais le suivant** not this Monday but the next. *adjective* following; **le jour suivant** the following day.

suivre *verb* [75] **1** to follow; **suivez-moi** follow me; **2 suivre l'actualité** to keep up with the news; **3 'à suivre'** 'to be continued'; **4 faire suivre son courrier** to have your mail forwarded; **5 suivre un cours** to do a course; **6 suivre un régime** to be on a diet.

sujet *noun* M **1** subject; **au sujet de** about; **c'est au sujet de votre fils** it's about your son; **c'est à quel sujet?** what's it about?; **un sujet de conversation** a topic of conversation; **2 un sujet d'examen** an exam question. *adjective* (F **sujette**) **être sujet à** to suffer from; **elle est sujette à des crises d'asthme** she suffers from asthma attacks.

super *noun* M four-star petrol. *adjective* (*informal*) fantastic; **mais c'est super!** but that's fantastic!

superficie *noun* F area.

superficiel (F **superficielle**) *adjective* superficial.

supérieur, supérieure *noun* M, F superior. *adjective* **1** upper; **l'étage supérieur** the upper floor; **la lèvre supérieure** the upper lip; **2** greater; **la taille supérieure** the bigger size; **à une vitesse supérieure** at a faster speed; **à une température supérieure** at a higher temperature; **un prix supérieur** a higher price;

3 better, superior (*work, quality*); **c'est de loin supérieur à l'autre!** it's much better than the other one!; **4 supérieur à** greater than; **un nombre supérieur à trois** a number higher than three.

superlatif *noun* M superlative.

supermarché *noun* M supermarket.

superposer *verb* [1] **1** to stack up; **des lits superposés** bunk beds; **2** to superimpose (*an image*).

superstitieux (F **superstitieuse**) *adjective* superstitious.

superstition *noun* F superstition.

supplément *noun* M extra charge; **le vin est en supplément** wine is extra.

supplémentaire *adjective* **1** additional; **2 faire des heures supplémentaires** to do overtime.

supplier *verb* [1] to beg.

support *noun* M **1** support; **2** back-up (material); **un support audiovisuel** audiovisual aids.

supportable *adjective* bearable.

supporter *verb* [1] **1** to stand; **il ne supporte pas qu'on le critique** he can't stand being criticized; **je ne peux plus la supporter!** I can't stand any more of her!; **2** to support (*a weight*).

supposer *verb* [1] to suppose.

supprimer *verb* [1] **1** to get rid of; **2 supprimer des emplois** to cut jobs; **supprimer un train** to cancel a train.

sur *preposition* **1** on; **c'est sur ton lit** it's on your bed; **un débat sur le racisme** a discussion on racism; **le cinéma est sur la droite** the cinema's on the right; **2** over; **un pont sur la Loire** a bridge over the Loire; **3** by (*in measurements*); **c'est deux mètres sur trois** it's two metres by three; **4** out of; **trois femmes sur cinq** three women out of five; **5** out of; **j'ai eu douze sur vingt en géographie** I got twelve out of twenty in geography.

sûr *adjective* **1** sure; **tu es sûr?** are you sure?; **oui, bien sûr!** yes, of course!; **sûr et certain** certain; **j'en étais sûr!** I knew it!; **2 il est très sûr de lui** he's very self-confident; **3** safe; **en lieu sûr** in a safe place; **le plus sûr est de tout fermer à clé** the safest thing is to lock everything.

surcharger *verb* [52] to overload.

surdité *noun* F deafness.

sûrement *adverb* **1** certainly; **sûrement pas!** certainly not!; **2 il doit sûrement arriver à tout instant** he's bound to arrive at any moment; **elle est sûrement partie** she's bound to have left.

sûreté *noun* F safety, security.

surf *noun* M surfing.

surface *noun* F **1** surface; **2** area; **3 une grande surface** a supermarket.

surgelé *noun* M **les surgelés** frozen food.
adjective frozen; **les légumes surgelés** frozen vegetables.

sur-le-champ *adverb* right away.

surlendemain *noun* M **elle est arrivée le surlendemain** she arrived two days later.

surmonter *verb* [1] to overcome.

surnaturel (F **surnaturelle**) *adjective* supernatural.

surnom *noun* M nickname.

surnommer *verb* [1] to nickname.

surpeuplé *adjective* overpopulated.

surprenant *addjective* surprising.

surprendre *verb* [64] **1** to surprise; **ça m'a beaucoup surpris** I found that really surprising; **2 surprendre quelqu'un en train de faire quelque chose** to catch somebody doing something; **je l'ai surprise en train de lire mon courrier** I caught her reading my mail.

surpris (F **surprise**) *adjective* surprised; **je suis surpris de te voir** I'm surprised to see you.

surprise *noun* F surprise; **quelle surprise!** what a surprise!; **faire une surprise à quelqu'un** to give somebody a surprise.

surréaliste *noun* M & F surrealist. *adjective* surreal.

surtout *adverb* **1** especially; **il y a beaucoup de touristes, surtout en été** there are lots of tourists, especially in the summer; **2** above all; **il faut surtout rester calme** above all, we must stay calm.

surveillant, surveillante *noun* M, F supervisor (*in a school, responsible for maintaining school discipline outside the classroom*).

surveiller *verb* [1] **1** to watch, to keep an eye on; **est-ce que tu peux surveiller mon sac deux secondes?** can you keep an eye on my bag for a couple of minutes?; **2 surveiller une maison** to keep a house under surveillance; **3** to supervise; **surveiller le travail des élèves** to supervise the students' work (*work or progress*); **4 surveiller un examen** to invigilate an exam; **5 je surveille ma ligne** I'm watching my figure.

survêtement *noun* M tracksuit.

survie *noun* F survival.

survivant, survivante *noun* M, F survivor.

survivre *verb* [82] to survive; **survivre à un accident** to survive an accident.

survoler *verb* [1] to fly over.

suspect, suspecte *noun* M, F suspect.
adjective suspicious.

suspense *noun* M suspense (*as in a thriller*).

suture *noun* F **un point de suture** a stitch (*in a wound*).

svelte *adjective* slender.

SVP SHORT FOR **s'il vous plaît;** please.

syllabe *noun* F syllable.

symbole *noun* M symbol.

symbolique *adjective* symbolic; **un geste symbolique** a token gesture.

sympa *adjective* (*informal*) nice; **je le trouve très sympa, ton copain** he's really nice, your boyfriend.

sympathie *noun* F **j'ai beaucoup de sympathie pour elle** I like her a lot.

sympathique *adjective* nice; **c'est un type sympathique** he's a nice guy.

sympathiser *verb* [1] **sympathiser avec quelqu'un** to get on well with someone.

symptôme *noun* M symptom.

syndicat *noun* M trade union.

syndicat d'initiative *noun* M tourist information office.

synthétique *adjective* synthetic.

système *noun* M system; **un système d'éclairage** a lighting system.

T t

ta *adjective* SEE **ton**.

tabac *noun* M **1** tobacco; **2 un bureau de tabac** a tobacconist's.

table *noun* F table; **à table!** dinner's ready!; **se mettre à table** to sit down to eat; **mettre la table** to lay the table.

tableau *noun* M **1** painting; **un tableau de Renoir** a painting by Renoir; **2 le tableau noir** the blackboard; **3 le tableau d'affichage** the notice board.

tableau de bord *noun* M dashboard.

able de chevet, table de nuit *noun* F bedside table.

able des matières *noun* F (list of) contents (*in a book*).

ablette *noun* F **une tablette de chocolat** a bar of chocolate.

ablier *noun* M apron.

abouret *noun* M stool.

ache *noun* F stain.

âche *noun* F task.

ache de rousseur *noun* F freckle.

acher *verb* [1] to stain.

act *noun* M tact; **il l'a fait avec beaucoup de tact** he did it very tactfully.

actique *noun* F tactics. *adjective* tactical.

aie *noun* F **une taie d'oreiller** a pillowcase.

aille *noun* F **1** size; **qu'est-ce que vous avez à ma taille?** what have you got in my size?; **quelle taille faites-vous?** what size are you?; **'taille unique'** 'one size'; **la taille au-dessus/au-dessous** the next size up/down; **2** height; **un homme de grande taille** a tall man; **3** waist; **avoir la taille fine** to have a slim waist.

aille-crayon *noun* M pencil sharpener.

ailleur *noun* M **1** suit (*for a woman*); **2** tailor; ★ **s'asseoir en tailleur** to sit cross-legged (*literally: like a tailor*).

taire *verb* [76] **se taire** to stop talking; **taisez-vous!** be quiet!

talent *noun* M talent; **c'est un jeune musicien de talent** he's a talented young musician.

talon *noun* M **1** heel (*of your foot or a shoe*); **2** stub (*of a ticket or cheque book*).

talon aiguille *noun* M stiletto heel.

tambour *noun* M drum.

Tamise *noun* F **la Tamise** the Thames.

tampon *noun* M **1** pad (*for sponging*); **un tampon à récurer** a scouring pad; **2** **un tampon (hygiénique)** a tampon.

tamponneuse *adjective* **les autos tamponneuses** the dodgems.

tandis que *conjunction* while.

tant *adverb* **1** so much; **j'ai tant mangé que...** I've eaten so much that...; **ce qu'elle avait tant espéré** what she had so much hoped for; **je ne les aime pas tant que ça** I don't like them as much as that; **2** **tant de** so much; so many; **tant d'argent** so much money; **tant d'amis** so many friends; **tant de monde** so many people; **3** **tant pis** never mind; **4** **tant mieux** so much the better; **5** **tant que** while; **tant que tu y es, passe-moi un stylo** while you're there, pass me a pen; **6** **tant que** as long as; **tant que Jacques ne sera pas rentré, je ne peux pas sortir** I can't go out until Jacques gets back.

tante *noun* F aunt.

tantôt *adverb* sometimes; **tantôt chez elle, tantôt chez moi** sometimes at her place and sometimes at mine.

taper *verb* [1] **1 taper quelqu'un** to hit somebody; **ça tape aujourd'hui** the sun's really beating down today; **2 taper à la machine** to type; **taper une lettre** to type a letter; **3 taper des mains** to clap your hands; **taper du pied** to tap your foot; **4 taper à la porte** to knock on the door; **5** (*informal*) **se taper dessus** to knock each other about.

tapis *noun* M carpet.

tapis de bain *noun* M bathmat.

tapis roulant *noun* M **1** walkway; **2** carousel (*for airport luggage*); conveyor belt.

tapisser *verb* [1] **1** to wallpaper; **2** to upholster.

tapisserie *noun* F **1** tapestry; **2** wallpaper.

taquiner *verb* [1] to tease.

tard *adverb* late; **couche-toi, il est tard** go to bed, it's late; **plus tard** later; **trop tard** too late; **pas plus tard que mardi** no later than Tuesday; **ce sera pour plus tard** there'll be other times.

tarder *verb* [1] to be a long time; **ta mère ne va pas tarder** your mother won't be long.

tardif (F **tardive**) *adjective* late.

tarif *noun* M **1** rate; **tarif de nuit** night rate (*for the phone*); **2** fare; **plein tarif** full fare; **tarif réduit** reduced fare; **3** price list.

tarte *noun* F tart; **une tarte aux abricots** an apricot tart.

tartine *noun* F slice of bread and butter (*and/or jam*).

tartiner *verb* [1] to spread (*on bread*).

tas *noun* M **1** pile; **un tas de bois** a pile of wood; **2** (*informal*) **un tas de** stacks of; **j'ai un tas de choses à faire ce soir** I've got stacks of things to do tonight.

tasse *noun* F cup; **une tasse de thé** a cup of tea.

tatie *noun* F (*informal*) auntie.

taupe *noun* F mole (*animal*).

taureau (*plural* **taureaux**) *noun* M bull.

Taureau *noun* M Taurus (*sign of the Zodiac*).

taux *noun* M rate; **le taux mensuel** the monthly rate; **le taux de change** the exchange rate.

taxe *noun* F tax; **la boutique hors taxes** the duty-free shop.

taxi *noun* M taxi; **appeler un taxi** to call a taxi.

tchèque *adjective* Czech; **la République tchèque** the Czech Republic.

te, t' (*before a vowel or silent 'h'*) *pronoun* you; **1 Gaby te cherche** Gaby's looking for you; **il t'a vu** he saw you; **elle m'a donné son adresse** she gave me her address; **il te l'a donné** he gave it to you; **2** to you; **3** yourself; **tu peux te faire une salade** you can make yourself a salad; **tu t'es blessé?** have you hurt yourself? **tu te lèves quand?** what time do you get up?

echnicien, technicienne *noun* M, F technician.

echnique *noun* F technique. *adjective* technical.

echnologie *noun* F technology.

eckel *noun* M dachshund.

ee-shirt *noun* M T-shirt.

eint *noun* M complexion; **avoir le teint clair** to have a fair complexion.

einturier, teinturière *noun* M, F dry-cleaner's.

el, telle *adjective* **1** such; **avec un tel intérêt** with such interest; **une telle aventure** such an adventure; **de tels mensonges** such lies; **2 tel que** such as; **les grandes villes telles que Paris et Lyon** large towns such as Paris and Lyons; **3 rien de tel que** nothing like; **il n'y a rien de tel qu'un bon repas** there's nothing like a good meal; **4 servir le saumon tel quel** serve the salmon just as it is; **je l'ai acheté tel quel** I bought it just as it was.

élé *noun* F (*informal*) telly; **je l'ai vu à la télé** I saw it on telly.

élécarte™ *noun* F phonecard.

élécommande *noun* F remote control.

élécopie *noun* F fax.

élécopieur *noun* M fax machine, fax.

éléphérique *noun* M cable car.

éléphone *noun* M telephone; **un numéro de téléphone** a phone number; **Bruno est au téléphone.** Bruno's on the phone.

téléphone portable *noun* M mobile phone.

téléphoner *verb* [1] to phone; **je vais téléphoner à Robert** I'll phone Robert.

téléphonique *adjective* **une cabine téléphonique** a phone box; **un appel téléphonique** a phone call.

télésiège *noun* M chairlift.

téléski *noun* M ski-tow.

téléspectateur, téléspectatrice *noun* M, F viewer (*of TV*).

téléviser *verb* [1] to televize.

téléviseur *noun* M television (set); **un téléviseur couleur** a colour television.

télévision *noun* F television; **à la télévision** on television.

telle *adjective* SEE **tel**.

tellement *adverb* **1** so; **c'est tellement compliqué!** it's so complicated!; **2** so much; **c'est tellement mieux payé** it's so much better paid; **'tu aimes lire?' – 'pas tellement'** 'do you like reading?' – 'not much'; **3 tellement de** so much, so many; **j'ai tellement de travail!** I've got so much work!; **il y a tellement de choses à voir!** there are so many things to see!; **il y avait tellement de monde** there were so many people there.

tels, telles *adjective* SEE **tel**.

témoignage noun M **1** story, account; **selon les témoignages de l'accident** according to accounts of the accident; **2** evidence (*in court*); **3 un témoignage d'amitié** a token of friendship.

témoigner verb [1] to give evidence.

témoin noun M witness.

température noun F temperature.

tempête noun F storm.

temple noun M **1** temple; **2** (Protestant) church.

temporaire adjective temporary.

temps noun M **1** weather; **quel temps fait-il?** what's the weather like? **par temps de pluie** in rainy weather; **2** time; **je n'ai pas le temps** I haven't got time; **il est temps de partir** it's time to go; **arriver à temps** to arrive in (or on) time; **de temps en temps** from time to time; **en même temps** at the same time; **ça a pris beaucoup de temps** it took a long time; **il nous reste combien de temps?** how much time do we have left?; **c'est du temps perdu** it's a waste of time; **il était temps!** about time too!; **ces derniers temps** recently; **un travail à plein temps** a full-time job; **un travail à temps partiel** a part-time job; **3** tense (*of a verb*).

tendance noun F **1** tendency; **avoir tendance à faire** to tend to do; **2** trend.

tendre¹ verb [3] **1** to stretch (*something elastic*); **2** to hold out; **elle m'a tendu un crayon** she held out a pencil to me; **tendre la main à quelqu'un** to hold out one's hand to someone; **3 tendre le bras** to reach out.

tendre² adjective tender.

tendresse noun F tenderness.

tendu adjective tense.

tenir verb [77] **1** to hold; **peux-tu tenir la corde?** can you hold the rope? **elle tenait l'enfant par la main** she was holding the child by the hand; **2** to run (*a shop, a business*); **3** to keep; **elle tenait les yeux baissés** she kept her eyes down; **'tenir hors de la portée des enfants'** 'keep out of reach of children'; **4** to take up; **cela tient la place de deux personnes** it takes u the space of two people; **5 tenir à** to be attached to; **elle tient beaucoup à ses petits-enfants** she's very attached to her grandchildren; **6 tenir à faire quelque chose** to be determined t do something; **je tiens à le finir aujourd'hui** I'm determined to finish it today; **7 tiens!** oh!; **tiens, il est déjà midi!** oh, it's twelve already!; **tiens! est-ce que je t'ai raconté...?** listen! have I told you...?; **tiens, tiens, c'est toi!** well well, it's you!; **tiens, prends le mien** here, take mine; **8 tenir de quelqu'un** to take after someone; **elle tient de sa mère** she takes after her mother; **9 se tenir** to hold; **ils se tenaient par la main** they were holding each other by the hand; **10 se tenir** to stand; **elle se tenait devant l'entrée** she was standing b the entrance; **tiens-toi tranquille!** be quiet!; **tiens-toi droit!** stand up straight!; **11 se tenir pour** to think yourself; **il se tient pour un génie** he thinks he's a genius.

tennis *noun* M **1** tennis; **jouer au tennis** to play tennis; **un terrain de tennis, un tennis** a tennis court; **tennis de table** table tennis; **2** tennis shoe.

tension *noun* F **1** tension; **2** blood pressure.

tentant *adjective* tempting.

tentation *noun* F temptation.

tentative *noun* F attempt.

tente *noun* F tent.

tenter *verb* [1] **1** to attempt; **il a tenté de s'échapper** he tried to escape; **tenter sa chance, tenter le coup** (*informal*) to give it a try; **2** to tempt.

tenu *adjective* **1** **bien/mal tenu** well/badly cared for; **2** **être tenu de faire** to be required to do.

tenue *noun* F clothes; **être en tenue de sport** to be in sports kit; **en tenue de soirée** in evening dress.

terme *noun* M **1** word, term; **un terme technique** a technical term; **les termes du contrat** the terms of the contract; **2** end; **à court terme** short-term; **à long terme** long-term.

terminale *noun* F (*in a French school*) the equivalent of Year 13.

terminer *verb* [1] **1** to finish; **2** to end; **la réunion s'est terminée à dix-huit heures** the meeting ended at six p.m.; **ça va mal se terminer!** it'll end in tears!

terminus *noun* M terminus.

terrain *noun* M **1** ground, land; **il a acheté du terrain** he's bought some land; **2** pitch, ground (*for sports*); **un terrain de football** a football pitch; **un terrain de golf** a golf course; **3** piece of ground; **un terrain à bâtir** a building plot.

terrain de camping *noun* M campsite.

terrain de jeu(x) *noun* M playground.

terrain de sport(s) *noun* M sports ground.

terrain vague *noun* M waste ground.

terrasse *noun* F terrace.

terre *noun* F **1** ground; **s'asseoir par terre** to sit on the floor; **tomber par terre** to fall down; **2** **la Terre** the Earth; **3** soil; **4** land (*not sea*); **aller à terre** to go ashore.

terre cuite *noun* F terracotta.

terrible *adjective* **1** terrible; **des événements terribles** terrible events; **2** (*informal*) terrific; **'c'était bien, le film?' – 'pas terrible'** 'was the film any good?' – 'not great'.

terrifiant *adjective* terrifying.

terrine *noun* F pâté.

territoire *noun* M **1** territory; **2** country; **'il fera beau sur l'ensemble du territoire'** 'it will be fine over the whole country'.

terrorisme *noun* M terrorism.

terroriste *noun* M & F terrorist.

tes *adjective* your; SEE **ton**.

test *noun* M test.

testament *noun* M will.

tester *verb* [1] to test.

tétanos *noun* M tetanus.

têtard *noun* M tadpole.

tête *noun* F **1** head; **se laver la tête** to wash your hair; **j'ai la tête qui tourne** my head's spinning; **2** face; **je n'aime pas sa tête** I don't like his face; **3** top; **tu es en tête de la liste** you're first on the list; **4** mind; **j'ai quelque chose en tête** I have something in mind; **où avais-tu la tête?** what were you thinking of?; **5** front (*of a train*); **les deux wagons de tête sont à destination de Bourges** the two front coaches are for Bourges; ★ **faire la tête** to sulk; ★ **un dîner en tête à tête** a private dinner for two; ★ **j'en ai par-dessus la tête!** I'm fed up to the back teeth!

têtu *adjective* stubborn.

texte *noun* M text.

TGV *noun* M SHORT FOR **train à grande vitesse** high-speed train.

thalassothérapie *noun* F seawater treatment (*at a health spa*).

thé *noun* M tea; **un thé au lait** tea with milk.

théâtre *noun* M **1** theatre; **des costumes de théâtre** stage costumes; **un coup de théâtre** a dramatic turn of events; **2** plays; **le théâtre de Molière** Molière's plays; **3 faire du théâtre** to belong to a drama group.

théière *noun* F teapot.

thème *noun* M **1** subject; **2** prose (*a text to translate into the foreign language*).

théorie *noun* F theory.

thérapie *noun* F **1** (medical) treatment; **2** therapy.

thermal (M *plural* **thermaux**) *adjective* thermal; **une station thermale** a spa.

thermomètre *noun* M thermometer.

thon *noun* M tuna.

thym *noun* M thyme.

tibia *noun* M **1** shin; **2** shinbone.

tic *noun* M nervous twitch.

ticket *noun* M **1** ticket; **un ticket de métro** an underground ticket; **2** **un ticket de caisse** a till receipt.

tiède *adjective* **1** warm; **2** lukewarm.

tien, tienne, tiens, tiennes *pronoun* **le tien, la tienne, les tiens, les tiennes** yours; **est-ce que ce stylo est le tien?** is this pen yours?; **ma voiture et la tienne** my car and yours; **mes lettres et les tiennes** my letters and yours.

tiens *verb* SEE **tenir**. *pronoun* SEE **tien**.

tiers *noun* M third; **les deux tiers de la population** two-thirds of the population. *adjective* (F **tierce**) third.

tiers-monde *noun* M Third World.

tige *noun* F stem.

tigre *noun* M tiger.

lleul *noun* M **1** lime tree; **2** lime flower tea.

mbre *noun* M stamp.

mide *adjective* shy.

midité *noun* F shyness.

quer *verb* [1] **sans tiquer** without batting an eyelid.

r *noun* M **1** shooting; **2** shot (*in football*).

rage *noun* M **le tirage au sort** the draw (*in a lottery, for example*); **par tirage au sort** by drawing lots.

r à l'arc *noun* M archery.

re-bouchon *noun* M corkscrew.

relire *noun* F money box.

rer *verb* [1] **1** to pull; **il m'a tiré par le bras** he pulled my arm; **elle m'a tiré les cheveux** she pulled my hair; **2** to draw; **tirer les rideaux** to draw the curtains; **il a tiré la lettre de sa poche** he drew the letter from his pocket; **tirer un trait** to draw a line; **tirer des conclusions** to draw conclusions; **tirer au sort** to draw lots; **3** to fire; **ils ont tiré sur les policiers** they fired on the police; **tirer plusieurs coups de feu** to fire several shots.

ret *noun* M dash.

roir *noun* M drawer.

sane *noun* F herbal tea.

ssu *noun* M material, fabric.

tre *noun* M **1** title; **2** headline; **les titres de l'actualité** the news headlines; **3** **à juste titre** quite rightly; **à titre d'exemple** as an example.

titre de transport *noun* M travel ticket.

tituber *verb* [1] to stagger.

toast *noun* M **1** piece of toast; **servir avec des toasts** serve with toast; **2** toast (*to someone's health*).

toboggan *noun* M slide.

toi *pronoun* you; **c'est toi!** it's you!; **avec toi** with you; **plus grand que toi** bigger than you; **c'est à toi de jouer** it's your turn; **assieds-toi** sit down; **est-ce que ces chaussettes sont à toi?** are these socks yours?

toile *noun* F **1** cloth; **toile de lin** linen; **une toile cirée** an oilcloth; **2** painting, canvas; **une toile de Picasso** a painting by Picasso.

toile d'araignée *noun* F spider's web, cobweb.

toilette *noun* F **1** **faire sa toilette** to have a wash; **2** outfit; **je me suis acheté une toilette pour le mariage de ma sœur** I've bought an outfit for my sister's wedding.

toilettes *plural noun* F toilet; **aller aux toilettes** to go to the toilet.

toi-même *pronoun* yourself; **l'as-tu fait toi-même?** did you do it yourself?

toit *noun* M roof.

tolérant *adjective* tolerant.

tolérer *verb* [24] to tolerate.

tomate *noun* F tomato; **une salade de tomates** a tomato salad.

tombe *noun* F grave.

tombeau (*plural* **tombeaux**) *noun* M tomb.

tomber *verb* [1] **1** to fall; **attention, tu vas tomber!** careful, you'll fall!; **la chaise est tombée** the chair fell over; **Noël tombe un lundi** Christmas falls on a Monday; **2 laisser tomber** to drop; **j'ai laissé tomber mon porte-monnaie** I've dropped my purse; **3 laisser tomber** to give up (*an activity*); **elle a laissé tomber l'espagnol** she's given up Spanish; **4 tomber malade** to fall ill; **tomber amoureux** to fall in love; **5 tomber sur** to bump into; **je suis tombé sur Georges devant la poste** I bumped into Georges outside the post office; **6 ça tombe bien** that's lucky; ★ **je tombe de sommeil** I can't keep my eyes open (*literally: I'm dropping with sleep*).

ton[1], **ta, tes** *adjective* your; **ton chat** your cat; **ta sœur** your sister; **tes pieds** your feet.

ton[2] *noun* M **1** tone of voice; **2** colour.

tondeuse *noun* F lawnmower.

tondre *verb* [3] to mow.

tonique *adjective* bracing.

tonne *noun* F tonne, metric ton (*1,000 kg*); ★ **j'ai des tonnes de choses à faire** (*informal*) I've loads of things to do.

tonneau (*plural* **tonneaux**) *noun* M barrel.

tonnerre *noun* M thunder.

tonton *noun* M (*informal*) uncle.

tonus *noun* M energy (*for a person*); tone (*for your muscles*).

toque *noun* F chef's hat.

torchon *noun* M cloth; tea towel.

tordre *verb* [3] to twist; **se tordre la cheville** to twist your ankle.

tordu *adjective* **1** bent; **2** crooked; **3** weird; **une histoire tordue** a weird story.

torrent *noun* M waterfall; mountain stream.

torse *noun* M chest, upper body; **il s'est mis torse nu** he stripped to the waist.

tort *noun* M **1 avoir tort** to be wrong; **je crois que tu as tort** I think you're wrong; **il a tort de dire ça** he's wrong to say that; **2 à tort** wrongly; **à tort ou à raison** rightly or wrongly.

torticolis *noun* M stiff neck; **avoir le torticolis** to have a stiff neck.

tortiller *verb* [1] **se tortiller** to wriggle.

tortue *noun* F tortoise, turtle.

torture *noun* F torture.

torturer *verb* [1] to torture.

tôt *adverb* **1** early; **on va partir tôt** we're leaving early; **tôt le matin** early in the morning; **2** soon; **le plus tôt possible** as soon as possible; **tôt ou tard** sooner or later.

total (*plural* **totaux**) *noun* M total **au total** in total.
adjective total.

totalement *adverb* totally.

totalité *noun* F **la totalité des élèves** all the pupils; **la totalité du groupe** the whole group.

touchant *adjective* touching.

touche *noun* F **1** key (*on a piano or keyboard*); **2** button (*on a machine*); **appuyez sur la touche** press the button marked; **3 (ligne de) touche** touchline.

toucher *verb* [1] **1** to touch; **ne touche pas à ma peinture** don't touch my painting; **2** to touch; **cette histoire m'a beaucoup touché** that story really touched me; **3** to affect, to concern; **ce problème nous touche tous** this problem affects us all; **4** to get (*money or wages*); **il touche 2 000 francs par semaine** he's getting 2,000 francs a week.

touffu *adjective* bushy, thick.

toujours *adverb* **1** always; **il est toujours en retard** he's always late; **comme toujours** as always; **2** still; **nous habitons toujours au même endroit** we're still living in the same place; **ton paquet n'est toujours pas arrivé** your parcel still hasn't come; **3 pour toujours** for ever.

tour[1] *noun* M **1 faire le tour de** to go round; **faire le tour des magasins** to go round all the shops; **faire le tour du monde** to go round the world; **2 faire un tour** to go for a walk; **on va faire un petit tour** we'll go for a little walk; **3 faire un tour à vélo** to go for a bike ride; **4 faire un tour en voiture** to go for a drive; **5** turn; **c'est ton tour de jouer** it's your turn to play; **à qui le tour?** whose turn is it?

tour[2] *noun* F **1** tower; **la tour Eiffel** the Eiffel Tower; **2** tower block; **3** castle, rook (*in chess*).

tourbillon *noun* M whirlwind, whirlpool.

tourisme *noun* M tourism.

touriste *noun* M & F tourist.

touristique *adjective* **un guide touristique** a tourist guide(book); **une ville touristique** a town which attracts tourists.

tourmenter *verb* [1] to tease.

tourne-disque *noun* M record player.

tournée *noun* F **1** round (*of a postman or baker, for example*); **2** round (*of drinks*); **c'est ma tournée** it's my round; **3** tour (*of a performer*); **être en tournée** to be on tour.

tourner *verb* [1] **1** to turn; **tournez à gauche à l'église** turn left at the church; **2** to toss (*a salad*); **3 mal tourner** to go wrong; **4 se tourner** to turn; **elle s'est tournée vers moi** she turned to face me; **5 tourner le dos à quelqu'un** to have your back to somebody.

tournesol *noun* M sunflower.

tournevis *noun* M screwdriver.

tournoi *noun* M tournament.

tous *adjective, pronoun* SEE **tout**.

Toussaint *noun* F All Saints' Day (*November 1st*).

tousser *verb* [1] to cough.

tout, toute, tous, toutes *adjective* **1** all; **tout le pain** all the bread; **toute la classe** all the class, the whole class; **tous les garçons** all the boys; **toutes les filles** all the girls; **ils sont tous là** they're all

there; **tout le monde** everybody;
toute la journée all day; **tous les
deux** both; **je les achète tous les
trois** I'll buy all three of them;
pendant toute une année for a
whole year; **2** any; **à tout âge** at
any age; **à tout instant** at any
moment; **'service à toute heure'**
'service at any time'; **tous
les jours** every day; **prenez un
comprimé toutes les quatre
heures** take one pill every four
hours.
pronoun **1** everything; **ils ont tout
pris** they took everything; **tout va
bien** everything's fine; **2** all; **54 en
tout** 54 in all; **et tout ça** and all that;
tout ce que je sais, c'est que... all
I know is that...; **tous ensemble** all
together; **elles étaient toutes là**
they were all there; **3** pas du tout
not at all.
adverb **c'est tout prêt** it's all ready;
il est tout seul he's all alone; **tout
doucement** very slowly; **tout
droit** straight ahead.

tout à coup *adverb* suddenly.

tout à fait *adverb* completely,
absolutely; **ce n'est pas tout à fait
sec** it's not absolutely dry.

tout à l'heure *adverb* **1** just now;
je l'ai vu tout à l'heure I saw him
just now; **2** in a little while; **à tout à
l'heure!** see you later!

tout de même *adverb* all the same;
c'est tout de même bizarre all the
same, it is odd.

tout de suite *adverb* at once; **fais-
le tout de suite!** do it at once!

tout d'un coup *adverb* suddenly.

toutefois *adverb* however.

toutes *adjective,*
pronoun SEE **tout**.

toux *noun* F cough.

toxicomane *noun* M & F drug
addict.

trac *noun* M (*informal*) **avoir le
trac** to feel nervous.

trace *noun* F **1** tracks; **des traces
de skis** ski-tracks; **des traces de
pas** footprints; **2** mark; **des traces
de doigts** finger marks.

tracer *verb* [61] to draw.

tracteur *noun* M tractor.

tradition *noun* F tradition.

traditionnel (F **traditionnelle**)
adjective traditional.

traducteur, traductrice *noun* M
F translator.

traduction *noun* F translation.

traduire *verb* [26] to translate;
traduire en français to translate
into French.

trafic *noun* M **1** **le trafic de
drogue** drug dealing; **2** traffic.

trafiquant, trafiquante *noun* M
F dealer (*in drugs or arms*).

tragédie *noun* F tragedy.

tragique *adjective* tragic.

trahir *verb* [2] to betray.

trahison *noun* F betrayal.

train *noun* M **1** train; **monter dans
le train** to get on the train;
descendre du train to get off the
train; **le train de dix heures** the te

o'clock train; **2 être en train de faire** to be (busy) doing; **Henri est en train de faire la vaisselle** Henri's doing the washing-up.

traîner *verb* [1] **1** to wander round; **2** to lie around; **il laisse ses affaires traîner partout** he leaves his things lying around everywhere; **3** to dawdle; **ne traînez pas, le train arrive** don't be long, the train's coming; **4** to drag on; **j'ai des projets qui traînent** I've got some projects that are dragging on; **5** to drag; **elle traînait sa valise derrière elle** she was dragging her suitcase behind her; **6 traîner les pieds** to drag your feet.

traire *verb* [78] to milk.

trait *noun* M **1** line; **2 les traits** features (*of a face*); **avoir des traits fins** to have delicate features; **3 d'un seul trait** at one go; **il l'a bu d'un seul trait** he drank it all at one go.

trait d'union *noun* M hyphen.

traitement *noun* M **1** treatment; **2** processing; **le traitement de texte** word processing; **3** salary.

traiter *verb* [1] **1** to treat; **il la traite très mal** he treats her very badly; **le médecin qui me traite** the doctor who's treating me; **2** to deal with (*a question or problem*); **3 traiter de** to call; **il m'a traité de menteur** he called me a liar.

traiteur *noun* M caterer.

trajet *noun* M **1** journey; **c'est un trajet de deux heures** it's a two-hour journey; **2** route.

tramway *noun* M tram, tramway.

tranchant *adjective* sharp.

tranche *noun* F **1** slice; **deux tranches de jambon** two slices of ham; **2** phase, period (*of time*).

trancher *verb* [1] **1** to slice; **2** to decide.

tranquille *adjective* **1** quiet; **une rue tranquille** a quiet street; **tiens-toi tranquille!** be quiet! **2 laisse-moi tranquille!** leave me alone! **3 maman n'est pas tranquille si je n'appelle pas** Mum worries if I don't ring.

tranquillité *noun* F peace.

transat *noun* M (*informal*) deck chair.

transférer *verb* [24] to transfer.

transfert *noun* M transfer.

transformer *verb* [1] **1** to change; **ils ont transformé leur jardin** they've completely changed their garden; **nous avons transformé cette chambre en bureau** we've turned this bedroom into a study; **2 se transformer en** to change into; **le têtard se transforme en grenouille** the tadpole changes into a frog.

transfusion *noun* F **une transfusion sanguine** a blood transfusion.

transistor *noun* M transistor.

transmettre *verb* [11] **1 transmettre quelque chose à quelqu'un** to pass something on to somebody; **2** to transmit.

transpiration *noun* F perspiration, sweat.

transpirer *verb* [1] to sweat.

transport *noun* M **1** transport; **les frais de transport** transport costs; **2 les transports en commun** public transport.

transporter *verb* [1] **1** to transport; **2** to carry.

trappe *noun* F trap door.

travail (*plural* **travaux**) *noun* M **1** work; **j'ai beaucoup de travail à faire** I've got a lot of work to do; **2** job; **je cherche un travail** I'm looking for a job.

travailler *verb* [1] to work.

travailleur, travailleuse *noun* M, F worker.
adjective hard-working.

travailliste *adjective* Labour; **le parti travailliste** the Labour party (*in Britain*).

travaux *plural noun* M **1** work; **des travaux de construction** building work; **ils font faire des travaux chez eux** they're having some work done on the house; **2** roadworks; **3 les travaux ménagers** housework; **4 les travaux dirigés** classwork; **les travaux manuels** handicrafts.

travers *noun* M **1 à travers** through; **j'ai regardé à travers les rideaux** I looked through the curtains; **voyager à travers le monde** to travel all over the world; **2 de travers** crooked, wrong; **c'est boutonné de travers** it's buttoned up wrong.

traversée *noun* F crossing; **une traversée de l'Atlantique** an Atlantic crossing.

traverser *verb* [1] **1** to cross; **regarde avant de traverser la rue** look before you cross the road; **2** to go through; **traverser la France pour aller en Italie** to go through France on the way to Italy; **la pluie a traversé ma veste** the rain's gone right through my jacket; **ils ont traversé une crise** they went through a crisis.

traversin *noun* M bolster.

trébucher *verb* [1] to stumble.

trèfle *noun* M **1** clover; **2** clubs (*in cards*); **la dame de trèfle** the queen of clubs.

treize *number* thirteen; **Aurélie a treize ans** Aurélie's thirteen; **à treize heures** at one p.m.; **le treize juillet** the thirteenth of July.

treizième *number* thirteenth.

tremblement de terre *noun* M earthquake.

trembler *verb* [1] to shake, to tremble.

trempé *adjective* soaked.

tremper *verb* [1] to soak.

tremplin *noun* M springboard.

trentaine *noun* F **1** about thirty; **une trentaine de personnes** about thirty people; **2 elle a la trentaine** she's in her thirties.

trente *number* thirty; **elle a trente ans** she's thirty; **le trente juillet** the thirtieth of July.

très *adverb* very; **très heureux** very happy; **j'ai très faim** I'm very hungry; **très bien fait** very well done.

trésor noun M treasure.

tresse noun F plait.

tréteau (*plural* **tréteaux**) noun M trestle.

tribu noun F tribe.

tribunal (*plural* **tribunaux**) noun M court; **paraître devant le tribunal** to appear in court (*on a charge*).

tricher verb [1] to cheat.

tricolore adjective three-coloured; **le drapeau tricolore** the French flag (*which is three-coloured, blue, white, and red, in vertical stripes*).

tricoter verb [1] to knit.

trier verb [1] to sort (out); **hier soir nous avons trié toutes les photos** last night we sorted out all the photographs.

trimestre noun M term.

triomphe noun M triumph.

triompher verb [1] to triumph.

tripes plural noun F tripe.

triple noun M **le triple** three times as much.

tripler verb [1] to treble.

triplés plural noun M triplets.

triste adjective sad.

tristesse noun F sadness.

trognon noun M **un trognon de pomme** an apple core.

trois number three; **Tom a trois ans** Tom's three; **à trois heures** at three o'clock; **le trois mars** the third of March; ★ **être haut comme trois pommes** to be knee-high to a grasshopper (*literally: as tall as three apples*).

troisième noun F (*in a French school*) the equivalent of Year 10. noun M **au troisième** on the third floor. adjective third.

trombone noun M **1** trombone; **2** paperclip (*because of its shape*).

trompe noun F trunk (*elephant's*).

tromper verb [1] **1** to deceive; **2 se tromper** to make a mistake; **il s'est trompé** he made a mistake; **je me suis trompé de train** I got the wrong train; **vous vous êtes trompé de numéro** you've got the wrong number.

trompette noun F trumpet; **jouer de la trompette** to play the trumpet.

tronc noun M trunk (*of a tree*).

tronçonneuse noun F chain saw.

trop adverb **1** too; **c'est trop loin** it's too far; **c'est beaucoup trop cher** it's much too expensive; **2** too much; **j'ai trop mangé** I've eaten too much; **tu m'en as donné trop** you've given me too much; **3 trop de** too much; too many; **trop de pain** too much bread; **trop de tomates** too many tomatoes; **trop de monde** too many people; **4 de trop** too many; too much; **il y a une chaise de trop** there's one chair too many; **il y a dix francs de trop** that's ten francs too much.

tropique noun M tropic.

trottoir noun M pavement.

trou noun M hole.

troublant *adjective* disturbing.

trouer *verb* [1] to make a hole in; **des chaussettes trouées** socks with holes in them.

trouille *noun* F **avoir la trouille** (*informal*) to be scared.

troupe *noun* F **1 une troupe de théâtre** a theatre company; **2** flock (*of birds*); **3** troop (*of tourists or children*).

troupeau (*plural* **troupeaux**) *noun* M herd (*of cattle*); flock (*of sheep*).

trousse *noun* F pencil case.

trousseau (*plural* **trousseaux**) *noun* M **un trousseau de clés** a bunch of keys.

trousse de maquillage *noun* F make-up bag.

trousse de toilette *noun* F toilet bag.

trouver *verb* [1] **1** to find; **as-tu trouvé ton passeport?** did you find your passport?; **2** to think; **j'ai trouvé le film passionnant** I thought the film was wonderful; **3 se trouver** to be (*in a place*); **les gens qui se trouvaient autour de moi** the people who were around me; **savez-vous où se trouve la gare routière?** do you know where the bus station is?

truc *noun* M (*informal*) **1** thing; **un petit truc en bois** a little thing made of wood; **il y a un truc qui ne va pas** something's wrong; **le jazz, ce n'est pas mon truc** jazz just isn't my thing; **2** trick; **il doit y avoir un truc** there must be a trick to it.

truite *noun* F trout.

TSVP SHORT FOR **tournez s'il vous plaît** PTO (*please turn over*).

TTC SHORT FOR **toutes taxes comprises** inclusive of tax.

tu *pronoun* you (*'tu' is used when talking to family members, people you know well, and people of your own age; otherwise 'vous' is used for 'you'*).

tube *noun* M **1** tube; **2** (*informal*) hit (*a pop song*).

tuer *verb* [1] **1** to kill; **2 se tuer** to be killed (*accidentally*); **elle s'est tuée dans un accident de voiture** she was killed in a car accident.

tue-tête *in phrase* **crier à tue-tête** to shout at the top of your voice.

tuile *noun* F **1** tile; **2** thin almond biscuit.

tulipe *noun* F tulip.

Tunisie *noun* F Tunisia.

tunisien (F **tunisienne**) *adjective* Tunisian.

tunnel *noun* M tunnel; **le tunnel sous la Manche** the Channel Tunnel.

turc *noun* M, *adjective* Turkish.

Turquie *noun* F Turkey.

tutoyer *verb* [39] to address somebody as 'tu' (*rather than 'vous'*); **il ne faut pas tutoyer ton professeur** you mustn't address your teacher as 'tu'; **et si on se tutoyait?** shall we say 'tu' to each other?

tuyau (*plural* **tuyaux**) *noun* M
1 pipe; **2** (*informal*) tip (*a helpful hint*).

tuyau d'arrosage *noun* M
hosepipe.

TVA *noun* F SHORT FOR **taxe à la valeur ajoutée** VAT.

type *noun* M **1** kind; **quel type de papier?** what type of paper?;
2 (*informal*) guy; **le type qui a ouvert la porte** the guy who opened the door.

typique *adjective* typical.

tyranniser *verb* [1] to bully.

tzigane *noun* M & F,
adjective gypsy.

U u

un, une (*plural* **des**) *article, pronoun, number* **1** a, an; **un lion** a lion; **une fraise** a strawberry; **des cerises** (some) cherries; **2** one; **un pour moi** one for me; **un par un** one by one; **trente et une personnes** thirty-one people; **les uns pensent que…** some think that…; **un jour sur deux** every other day; **3** l'**un(e) et l'autre** the one and the other; **l'un est français et l'autre est allemand** one's French and the other's German;
4 l'**un(e) ou l'autre** either of them; **tu peux prendre l'un ou l'autre, ça n'a pas d'importance** you can take either of them, it doesn't matter.

uni *adjective* **1** close-knit (*family or group*); **2** plain (*not patterned*); **un tissu uni** a plain fabric.

uniforme *noun* M uniform.

union *noun* F union; **l'ex-Union soviétique** the former Soviet Union.

Union européenne *noun* F
European Union.

unique *adjective* **1** only; **elle est fille unique** she's an only child; **il est fils unique** he's an only child; **l'unique raison** the only reason; **2** single;
'prix unique' 'all one price';
3 unique.

uniquement *adverb* only.

unité *noun* F **1** unity; **2** unit (*of currency, measurement, etc*).

univers *noun* M universe.

universitaire *adjective* university
(*degree, town*); academic (*work*).

université *noun* F university.

urbanisme *noun* M town
planning.

urgence *noun* F **1** urgency; **il y a urgence!** it's urgent!; **il faut téléphoner d'urgence** you must phone at once; **2** emergency; **les urgences, le service des urgences** the casualty department.

urgent *adjective* urgent.

USA *plural noun* M USA; **aux USA** in (or to) the USA.

usage *noun* M **1** use; **à l'usage** with use; **en usage** in use; **à usage externe** for external use only;
2 'hors d'usage' 'not in service'.

usagé *adjective* **1** worn; **2** used.

usager *noun* M user.

usé *adjective* worn.

user verb [1] to wear out (*shoes, clothing*).

usine noun F factory.

ustensile noun M utensil.

utile adjective useful.

utiliser verb [1] to use.

utilité noun F usefulness; **un livre d'une grande utilité** a very useful book.

V v

va verb SEE **aller**.

vacances plural noun F holidays; **les vacances scolaires** the school holidays; **les grandes vacances** the summer holidays; **être en vacances** to be on holiday; **bonnes vacances!** have a good holiday!

vacancier, vacancière noun M, F holiday-maker.

vacarme noun M din; **ils faisaient un vacarme pas possible!** they were making an amazing din!

vaccination noun F vaccination.

vacciner verb [1] to vaccinate; **se faire vacciner** to be vaccinated.

vache noun F cow.
adjective mean.

vachement adverb (*informal*) really; **c'était vachement bien!** it was really good!

va-et-vient noun M coming and going.

vagabond noun M tramp.

vagin noun M vagina.

vague[1] noun F wave (*in the sea*).

vague[2] adjective vague.

vaguement adverb vaguely.

vain adjective **1** useless; **2 en vain** in vain.

vaincre verb [79] **1** to defeat; **2** to overcome.

vainqueur noun M winner.

vais verb SEE **aller**.

vaisseau (*plural* **vaisseaux**) noun M vessel.

vaisselle noun F dishes; **faire la vaisselle** to do the washing-up.

valable adjective valid.

valet noun M jack; **le valet de pique** the jack of spades.

valeur noun F value; **des objets de valeur** valuables; **c'est sans valeur** it's of no value.

valider verb [1] to stamp (*a ticket*).

valise noun F suitcase; **faire ses valises** to pack.

vallée noun F valley.

valoir verb [80] **1** to be worth; **ça vaut combien?** how much is it worth?; **ce tableau vaut cher** that painting's worth a lot; **2 valoir la peine** to be worth it; **ça ne vaut pas la peine d'y aller s'il pleut** it's not worth going if it's raining; **ça vaudrait la peine d'essayer** it would be worth a try; **3 il vaut mieux faire** it would be better to do; **il vaut mieux**

téléphoner avant it would be better to phone first.

valse *noun* F waltz.

vampire *noun* M vampire.

vandalisme *noun* M vandalism.

vanille *noun* F vanilla; **une glace à la vanille** a vanilla ice-cream.

vanter *verb* [1] **se vanter** to boast.

vapeur *noun* F steam; **faire cuire des légumes à la vapeur** to steam vegetables.

vaporisateur *noun* M (perfume) spray.

variable *adjective* variable, changeable.

varicelle *noun* F chickenpox; **avoir la varicelle** to have chickenpox.

varié *adjective* varied, various; **'sandwichs variés'** 'a selection of sandwiches'.

varier *verb* [1] to vary.

variété *noun* F **1** variety; **2 un spectacle de variétés** a variety show.

vas *verb* SEE **aller**.

vase[1] *noun* M vase.

vase[2] *noun* F mud.

vaste *adjective* large, enormous.

va-vite *adverb* **à la va-vite** in a rush.

veau (*plural* **veaux**) *noun* M **1** calf; **2** veal.

vécu *verb* SEE **vivre**.

vedette *noun* F star; **une vedette de cinéma** a film star.

végétal *adjective* vegetable; **l'huile végétale** vegetable oil.

végétarien, végétarienne *noun* M, F, *adjective* vegetarian.

véhicule *noun* M vehicle.

veille *noun* F **la veille** the day before; **je l'ai rencontrée la veille** I met her the day before; **elle est arrivée la veille au soir** she arrived the evening before; **la veille de Noël** Christmas Eve; **la veille du jour de l'an** New Year's Eve.

veilleuse *noun* F **1** night-light; **2** pilot light.

veinard *noun* M (*informal*) **petit veinard!** you lucky little devil!

veine *noun* F **1 avoir de la veine** (*informal*) to be lucky; **2** vein.

vélo *noun* M bike; **je suis venu à vélo** I came by bike; **faire du vélo** to go cycling.

vélomoteur *noun* M moped.

vélo tout-terrain *noun* M mountain bike.

velours *noun* M **1** velvet; **2** corduroy.

velouté *noun* M cream soup; **velouté de champignons** cream of mushroom soup.

vendanges *plural noun* F grape harvest.

vendeur, vendeuse *noun* M, F shop assistant.

vendre *verb* [3] to sell; **vendre quelque chose à quelqu'un** to sell somebody something; **j'ai vendu**

mon ordinateur à Colette I've sold my computer to Colette; **'à vendre'** 'for sale'; **'vendu'** 'sold'.

vendredi *noun* M **1** Friday; **nous sommes vendredi aujourd'hui** it's Friday today; **vendredi dernier** last Friday; **vendredi prochain** next Friday; **2** on Friday; **je l'ai vu vendredi soir** I saw him on Friday evening; **3** on Fridays; **fermé le vendredi** closed on Fridays; **4 tous les vendredis** every Friday; **le vendredi saint** Good Friday.

vénéneux (F **vénéneuse**) *adjective* poisonous (*plant*).

vengeance *noun* F revenge.

venger *verb* [52] **se venger** to have your revenge.

venimeux (F **venimeuse**) *adjective* poisonous (*snake, spider*).

venir *verb* [81] **1** to come; **il vient de Provence** he comes from Provence; **elles sont venues mardi** they came on Tuesday; **viens voir!** come and see!; **2 faire venir** to send for; **il faut faire venir le médecin** we must send for the doctor; **3 venir de faire** to have just done; **ils viennent d'arriver** they have just arrived; **elle venait de partir** she had just left.

vent *noun* M wind; **un vent du sud** a south wind.

vente *noun* F sale; **être en vente** to be on sale.

vente aux enchères *noun* F auction sale.

ventilateur *noun* M fan.

ventre *noun* M stomach; **avoir mal au ventre** to have stomachache.

venu *verb* SEE **venir**.

ver *noun* M worm.

verbe *noun* M verb.

verdict *noun* M verdict.

verger *noun* M orchard.

verglas *noun* M black ice.

vérifier *verb* [1] to check.

véritable *adjective* real.

vérité *noun* F truth.

vernir *verb* [2] to varnish.

vernis à ongles *noun* M nail varnish.

verre *noun* M **1** glass; **un verre de vin** a glass of wine; **2** glass; **un vase en verre** a glass vase; **3** lens (*of spectacles*).

verrou *noun* M bolt (*on a door*).

verrouiller *verb* [1] to bolt (*a door*).

verrue *noun* F wart.

vers[1] *preposition* **1** towards; **il montait vers l'église** he was going up towards the church; **2** about (*a time*); **vers midi** about twelve; **vers la fin du mois** around the end of the month.

vers[2] *noun* M line of poetry; **des vers** poetry.

Verseau *noun* M Aquarius (*sign of the Zodiac*).

versement *noun* M payment.

verser *verb* [1] to pour; **Sylvie m'a versé une tasse de thé** Sylvie poured me a cup of tea.

ersion *noun* F **1** version; **2** translation (*into your own language*).

erso *noun* M back (*of a piece of paper*); **voir au verso** see overleaf.

ert *adjective* green; ★ **avoir la main verte** to have green fingers.

ertical (M *plural* **verticaux**) *adjective* vertical, upright.

ertige *noun* M vertigo.

erveine *noun* F verbena tea.

este *noun* F jacket.

estiaire *noun* M **1** cloakroom (*in a theatre, restaurant, etc*); **2** changing room (*in a gym, sports ground*).

êtement *noun* M garment; **les vêtements** clothes; **'vêtements pour enfants'** 'children's wear'.

étérinaire *noun* M & F vet.

euf, veuve *noun* M, F widower, widow.

exer *verb* [1] to annoy; to offend.

iande *noun* F meat.

ibrer *verb* [1] to vibrate.

ictime *noun* F victim.

ictoire *noun* F victory.

ide *adjective* empty. *noun* M **1** space; **dans le vide** in(to) space; **2** vacuum; **emballé sous vide** vacuum-packed.

idéo *noun* F video; **une cassette vidéo** a video cassette; **une caméra vidéo** a video camera; **un jeu vidéo** a video game.

idéoclip *noun* M music video.

vidéoclub *noun* M video shop.

vidéothèque *noun* F video library.

vider *verb* [1] to empty.

vie *noun* F life; **toute ma vie** all my life; **il est encore en vie** he's still alive; **ton mode de vie** your lifestyle; ★ **c'est la vie** that's life, that's the way it goes.

vieil *adjective* SEE **vieux**.

vieillard, vieillarde *noun* M, F old man, old woman.

vieille *adjective* SEE **vieux**.

vieillesse *noun* F old age.

vieillir *verb* [2] to age; **il a beaucoup vieilli récemment** he's aged a lot recently.

vierge *noun* F virgin; **la Sainte Vierge** the Virgin Mary. *adjective* **1** blank; **une cassette vierge** a blank cassette; **2 laine vierge** pure new wool; **l'huile d'olive vierge** virgin olive oil.

Vierge *noun* F Virgo (*sign of the Zodiac*).

vieux, vieil (*before a vowel or silent 'h'*) (F **vieille**) (M *plural* **vieux**) *adjective* old; **une vieille ville** an old town; **un vieil arbre** an old tree. *noun* M, F **un vieux** an old man; **une vieille** an old woman.

vieux garçon *noun* M bachelor.

vif (F **vive**) *adjective* **1** bright; **rose vif** bright pink; **2** lively; **une vive discussion** a lively discussion; **3 avoir l'esprit vif** to be quick-witted.

vigne *noun* F vine; vineyard.

vigneron, vigneronne *noun* M, F wine-grower.

vignette *noun* F **1** label; **2** tax disc.

vignoble *noun* M vineyard.

vilain *adjective* **1** ugly; **2** naughty; **c'est vilain, ça!** that's naughty!

villa *noun* F detached house; villa.

village *noun* M village.

ville *noun* F town, city; **une grande ville** a city; **en ville** in (or into) town.

vin *noun* M wine.

vinaigre *noun* M vinegar.

vinaigrette *noun* F French dressing.

vingt *number* twenty; **Marion a vingt ans** Marion's twenty; **le vingt juillet** the twentieth of July; **à vingt heures** at 8 p.m.; **vingt et un** twenty-one.

vingtaine *noun* F about twenty; **une vingtaine de personnes** about twenty people.

vingtième *adjective* twentieth.

viol *noun* M rape.

violemment *adjective* violently.

violence *noun* F violence.

violent *adjective* violent.

violer *verb* [1] to rape.

violet (F **violette**[1]) *adjective* purple.

violette[2] *noun* F violet (*the flower*).

violon *noun* M violin; **jouer du violon** to play the violin.

violoncelle *noun* M cello; **jouer du violoncelle** to play the cello.

vipère *noun* F adder, viper.

virage *noun* M bend (*in the road*).

virgule *noun* F **1** comma; **2** decimal point; **sept virgule trois** seven point three.

virus *noun* M virus.

vis[1] *verb* SEE **vivre**.

vis[2] *noun* F screw.

visa *noun* M visa.

visage *noun* M face.

viser *verb* [1] **1** to aim; **2** to aim at (*a target*).

visibilité *noun* F visibility.

visible *adjective* visible, obvious.

visite *noun* F visite; **une visite chez nos cousins** a visit to our cousins; **rendre visite à quelqu'un** to visit somebody; **elle a de la visite** she's got visitors.

visiter *verb* [1] to visit (*a place*); **on peut visiter l'appartement?** can we see round the flat?

visiteur, visiteuse *noun* M, F visitor.

vit *verb* SEE **vivre**.

vitamine *noun* F vitamin.

vite *adverb* **1** fast; **tu conduis trop vite** you drive too fast; **parle moins vite** speak more slowly; **2** quick; **vite! le bus arrive!** quick! here's the bus!; **ce sera vite fait** it won't take long; **3** soon; **on sera vite arrivé** we'll soon be there; **elle a vite compris** she understood immediately.

vitesse noun F **1** speed; **elle est partie à toute vitesse** she rushed off; **2** gear; **en deuxième vitesse** in second gear.

vitrail (plural **vitraux**) noun M stained glass window.

vitre noun F window.

vitrine noun F shop window.

vivant adjective **1** living; **2** lively.

vive[1] adjective SEE **vif**.

vive[2] exclamation **Vive le roi!** Long live the king!

vivement adverb **1** **réagir vivement** to react strongly; **2 vivement les vacances!** roll on the holidays!

vivre verb [82] to live; **ils vivent ensemble** they live together; **ils ont vécu dans plusieurs pays différents** they've lived in several different countries.

vocabulaire noun M vocabulary.

vœu (plural **vœux**) noun M **1** wish; **faire un vœu** to make a wish; **meilleurs vœux!** best wishes! (especially at the New Year); **2** vow.

vogue noun F fashion; **en vogue** in fashion.

voici preposition **1** here is, here are; **voici l'addition** here's the bill; **voici les clés** here are the keys; **me voici!** here I am!; **2** this is; **voici ma sœur** this is my sister.

voie noun F **1** way; **être sur la bonne voie** to be on the right track; **2** track (for trains); **la voie ferrée** the railway track; **le train de Bourges entre en gare voie dix** the

train from Bourges is now arriving at platform ten; **3** lane (on a main road); **une route à trois voies** a three-lane road.

voilà preposition **1** there is, there are; **voilà tes lunettes, là-bas sur la table** there are your glasses, over there on the table; **la voilà devant la boulangerie** there she is outside the baker's; **2** here is, here are; **voilà Anna qui arrive** here's Anna coming now; **voilà ton café** here's your coffee; **voilà, c'est tout** right, that's all; **3** that is; **voilà ma fille** that's my daughter; **et voilà pourquoi** and that's why.

voile[1] noun M veil.

voile[2] noun F sail; **des cours de voile** sailing lessons.

voilier noun M sailing boat.

voir verb [13] **1** to see; **je ne vois rien** I can't see anything; **je viendrai te voir un de ces jours** I'll come and see you one of these days; **oui, je vois, tu veux dire que...** yes, I see, you mean that...; **un film à voir** a film worth seeing; **peut-être, on verra** perhaps, we'll see; **2 se voir** to be noticeable; **ça ne se verra pas** nobody will notice; **3 se voir** to see each other; **ils se voient à Noël** they see each other at Christmas; **4 faire voir quelque chose à quelqu'un** to show somebody something; **je te ferai voir mes photos de vacances** I'll show you my holiday photos; **fais voir!** let's have a look!; **5 ça n'a rien à voir avec mon problème** that's got nothing to do with my problem; ★ **il ne voit pas plus loin que le bout de son nez** he can't see any further than the end of his nose; ★ **elle ne peut pas le voir (en peinture)** she can't stand him (*literally: she can't bear to see him (in a painting)*); ★ **j'en ai vu d'autres** I've seen worse.

voisin, voisine *noun* M, F neighbour; **Claire est chez les voisins** Claire's round at the neighbours'; **ma voisine de table** the girl sitting next to me at table.

voisinage *noun* M neighbourhood.

voiture *noun* F **1** car; **en voiture** by car; **2** carriage (*on a train*).

voix *noun* F **1** voice; **à haute voix** aloud; **à voix basse** softly; **2** vote.

vol *noun* M **1** flight; **le vol pour Milan** the Milan flight; **2** theft; ★ **à vol d'oiseau** as the crow flies (*literally: by bird flight*).

volaille *noun* F poultry; **les foies de volaille** chicken livers.

volant *noun* M **1** steering wheel; **qui était au volant?** who was driving?; **2** shuttlecock. *adjective* flying.

volcan *noun* M volcano.

volée *noun* F volley.

voler *verb* [1] **1** to fly; **2** to steal; **voler quelque chose à quelqu'un** to steal something from someone; **on leur a volé leur voiture** their car's been stolen; **3 voler quelqu'un** to rob somebody.

volet *noun* M shutter.

voleur, voleuse *noun* M, F thief.

volley *noun* M volleyball; **jouer au volley** to play volleyball.

volontaire *noun* M & F volunteer.

volonté *noun* F **1** will; **la bonne volonté** goodwill; **2 à volonté** unlimited; **'pizza à volonté'** 'as much pizza as you want'.

volontiers *adverb* gladly; **'tu viens avec nous?' – 'volontiers'** 'will you come too?' – 'I'd love to'; **'tu me le prêtes?' – 'volontiers'** 'will you lend it to me?' – 'of course'.

volume *noun* M volume.

vomir *verb* [2] to be sick, to vomit.

vos *adjective* SEE **votre**.

voter *verb* [1] to vote.

votre (*plural* **vos**) *adjective* your; **nous connaissons votre fils** we know your son; **vos billets, monsieur** your tickets, sir.

vôtre *pronoun* **le vôtre, la vôtre, les vôtres** yours; **une maison comme la vôtre** a house like yours; **mes parents et les vôtres** my parents and yours; ★ **à la vôtre!** cheers!

vouloir *verb* [14] **1** to want; **elle ne veut rien** she doesn't want anything; **veux-tu venir avec nous?** do you want to come with us?; **je n'ai pas voulu arriver trop tôt** I didn't want to arrive too early; **il veut qu'elle l'appelle** he wants her to phone him; **il m'a vexé sans le vouloir** he annoyed me without meaning to; **2** to like; **si tu veux** if you like; **je voudrais visiter Versailles** I'd like to go to Versailles; **'encore du café?' – 'oui, je veux bien'** 'more coffee?' – 'yes, I'd love some'; **3 voulez-vous m'excuser?** would you excuse me?; **veux-tu fermer la porte?** would you shut the door?; **veux-tu te taire!** will you be quiet!; **4 vouloir dire** to mean; **qu'est-ce que tu veux dire?** what do you mean?; **si tu vois ce que je veux dire** if you see what I mean; **qu'est-ce que ce mot veut dire?** what does this word mean?; **5 en vouloir à quelqu'un** to bear a grudge against someone; **elle leur en veut** she's never forgiven them; ★ **vouloir c'est pouvoir** where there's a will there's a way (*literally: to want is to be able*).

voulu *verb* SEE **vouloir.**

vous *pronoun* **1** you; **avec vous** with you; **est-ce que ce sac est à vous?** is this your bag?; **à vous de jouer!** your turn to play!; **2** to you; **je vous écrirai** I'll write to you; **3** yourself; **ne vous coupez pas!** don't cut yourself!

vous-même(s) *pronoun* yourself, yourselves; **vous me l'avez dit vous-même** you told me yourself; **est-ce que vous l'avez fait vous-mêmes?** did you do it by yourselves?

voûte *noun* F vault, arch.

vouvoyer *verb* [39] to use 'vous' to mean 'you' (*rather than 'tu' which you would use only when talking to intimate friends, family, and people of your own age*); **ils se connaissent depuis des années mais ils continuent à se vouvoyer** they've known each other for years but they still address each other as 'vous'.

voyage *noun* M journey; **bon voyage! have a good trip!**

voyage organisé *noun* M package tour.

voyager *verb* [52] to travel.

voyageur, voyageuse *noun* M, F passenger.

voyelle *noun* F vowel.

voyou *noun* M hooligan.

vrac *adverb* **acheter des olives en vrac** to buy olives loose (*as opposed to pre-packaged*).

vrai *adjective* **1** true; **c'est une histoire vraie** it's a true story; **2** real; **c'est un vrai problème** it's a real problem; **c'est vrai?** really?; **pour de vrai** for real; **3 à vrai dire** to tell the truth.

vraiment *adverb* really.

vraisemblable *adjective* likely; **peu vraisemblable** unlikely.

vraisemblablement *adverb* probably.

VTT *noun* M SHORT FOR **vélo tout-terrain** mountain bike.

vu *verb* SEE **voir.**
adjective **1 vu que** seeing that; **vu qu'il pleut, ce n'est pas la peine d'y aller** seeing it's raining, there's no point in going; **2 être mal vu** to be disapproved of; **il est plutôt mal vu** people don't think much of him; **c'est mal vu de faire beaucoup de bruit** they don't like people making a lot of noise; **cette critique a été mal vue** this criticism didn't go down well; **3 être bien vu** to be well thought of; **elle est très bien vue dans la société** people in the company think highly of her.

vue *noun* F **1** eyesight; **perdre la vue** to lose your eyesight; **2** sight; **je le connais de vue** I know him by sight; **rien qu'à la vue de la viande** at the very sight of meat; **3** view; **une chambre avec vue sur le lac** a room with a view of the lake.

vulgaire *adjective* vulgar.

W w

wagon *noun* M **1** railway carriage; **2** waggon.

wagon-lit *noun* M sleeper (*on a train*).

wagon-restaurant *noun* M restaurant car.

wallon *noun* M, *adjective* (F **wallonne**) Walloon (*French-speaking Belgian*); **les Wallons** the Walloon.

WC (*pronounced 'vaysay'*) *plural noun* M toilet; **aller aux WC** to go to the toilet; **il est aux WC** he's in the loo.

X x

xylophone *noun* M xylophone; **jouer du xylophone** to play the xylophone.

Y y

y *pronoun, adverb* **1** there; **j'y vais demain** I'm going there tomorrow;

2 il y a there is, there are; **il y a un café à côté** there's a café next door; **il y a des tomates dans le frigo** there are some tomatoes in the fridge; **3 j'y pensais** I was thinking of it; **tu n'y peux rien** you can't do anything about it.

yaourt *noun* M yoghurt.

yeux *plural noun* M SEE **œil**.

yougoslave *adjective* Yugoslavian.

Yougoslavie *noun* F Yugoslavia; **l'ex-Yougoslavie** the former Yugoslavia.

Z z

zapper *verb* [1] to channel hop.

zèbre *noun* M zebra.

zéro *noun* M zero; nil; love (*in tennis*); **trois à zéro** three-nil; **zéro heure** midnight; ★ **il faut tout reprendre à zéro** we'll have to start again from scratch.

zézayer *verb* [59] to lisp.

zigzag *noun* M zigzag; **une route en zigzag** a winding road.

zodiaque *noun* M zodiac.

zone *noun* F **1** zone, area; **2 la zone** the slums.

zone industrielle *noun* F industrial estate.

zoo *noun* M zoo.

zut *exclamation* (*informal*) damn!

VERB TABLES
AND FORMS

aimer
to like *or* to love

Imperative	Past participle
aim**e**	aim**é**
aim**ons**	
aim**ez**	

Present

j' aim**e**
tu aim**es**
il aim**e**
nous aim**ons**
vous aim**ez**
ils aim**ent**

Present subjunctive

j' aim**e**
tu aim**es**
il aim**e**
nous aim**ions**
vous aim**iez**
ils aim**ent**

Perfect

j' ai aim**é**
tu as aim**é**
il a aim**é**
nous avons aim**é**
vous avez aim**é**
ils ont aim**é**

Imperfect

j' aim**ais**
tu aim**ais**
il aim**ait**
nous aim**ions**
vous aim**iez**
ils aim**aient**

Future

j' aimer**ai**
tu aimer**as**
il aimer**a**
nous aimer**ons**
vous aimer**ez**
ils aimer**ont**

Conditional

j' aimer**ais**
tu aimer**ais**
il aimer**ait**
nous aimer**ions**
vous aimer**iez**
ils aimer**aient**

finir
to finish

Imperative	Past participle
fin**is** fin**issons** fin**issez**	fin**i**

Present

je fin**is**
tu fin**is**
il fin**it**
nous fin**issons**
vous fin**issez**
ils fin**issent**

Perfect

j' ai fin**i**
tu as fin**i**
il a fin**i**
nous avons fin**i**
vous avez fin**i**
ils ont fin**i**

Future

je finir**ai**
tu finir**as**
il finir**a**
nous finir**ons**
vous finir**ez**
ils finir**ont**

Present subjunctive

je fin**isse**
tu fin**isses**
il fin**isse**
nous fin**issions**
vous fin**issiez**
ils fin**issent**

Imperfect

je fin**issais**
tu fin**issais**
il fin**issait**
nous fin**issions**
vous fin**issiez**
ils fin**issaient**

Conditional

je finir**ais**
tu finir**ais**
il finir**ait**
nous finir**ions**
vous finir**iez**
ils finir**aient**

attendre
to wait

Imperative	Past participle
atten**ds**	attend**u**
attend**ons**	
attend**ez**	

Present

j'	attend**s**
tu	attend**s**
il	attend
nous	attend**ons**
vous	attend**ez**
ils	attend**ent**

Present subjunctive

j'	attend**e**
tu	attend**es**
il	attend**e**
nous	attend**ions**
vous	attend**iez**
ils	attend**ent**

Perfect

j'	ai attend**u**
tu	as attend**u**
il	a attend**u**
nous	avons attend**u**
vous	avez attend**u**
ils	ont attend**u**

Imperfect

j'	attend**ais**
tu	attend**ais**
il	attend**ait**
nous	attend**ions**
vous	attend**iez**
ils	attend**aient**

Future

j'	attendr**ai**
tu	attendr**as**
il	attendr**a**
nous	attendr**ons**
vous	attendr**ez**
ils	attendr**ont**

Conditional

j'	attendr**ais**
tu	attendr**ais**
il	attendr**ait**
nous	attendr**ions**
vous	attendr**iez**
ils	attendr**aient**

se laver
to wash
(oneself)

Imperative	Past participle
lav**e**–toi	lav**é**
lav**ons**–nous	
lav**ez**–vous	

Present

je me lav**e**
tu te lav**es**
il se lav**e**
nous nous lav**ons**
vous vous lav**ez**
ils se lav**ent**

Perfect

je me suis lav**é**
tu t'es lav**é**
il s'est lav**é**
nous nous sommes lav**é(s)**
vous vous êtes lav**é(s)**
ils se sont lav**é(s)**

Future

je me laver**ai**
tu te laver**as**
il se laver**a**
nous nous laver**ons**
vous vous laver**ez**
ils se laver**ont**

Present subjunctive

je me lav**e**
tu te lav**es**
il se lav**e**
nous nous lav**ions**
vous vous lav**iez**
ils se lav**ent**

Imperfect

je me lav**ais**
tu te lav**ais**
il se lav**ait**
nous nous lav**ions**
vous vous lav**iez**
ils se lav**aient**

Conditional

je me laver**ais**
tu te laver**ais**
il se laver**ait**
nous nous laver**ions**
vous vous laver**iez**
ils se laver**aient**

avoir
to have

Imperative	Past participle
aie	eu
ayons	
ayez	

Present

j' **ai**
tu **as**
il **a**
nous av**ons**
vous av**ez**
ils **ont**

Perfect

j' ai **eu**
tu as **eu**
il a **eu**
nous avons **eu**
vous avez **eu**
ils ont **eu**

Future

j' **aurai**
tu **auras**
il **aura**
nous **aurons**
vous **aurez**
ils **auront**

Present subjunctive

j' **aie**
tu **aies**
il **ait**
nous **ayons**
vous **ayez**
ils **aient**

Imperfect

j' av**ais**
tu av**ais**
il av**ait**
nous av**ions**
vous av**iez**
ils av**aient**

Conditional

j' **aurais**
tu **aurais**
il **aurait**
nous **aurions**
vous **auriez**
ils **auraient**

être
to be

Imperative	Past participle
sois	été
soyons	
soyez	

Present

je	**suis**
tu	**es**
il	**est**
nous	**sommes**
vous	**êtes**
ils	**sont**

Present subjunctive

je	**sois**
tu	**sois**
il	**soit**
nous	**soyons**
vous	**soyez**
ils	**soient**

Perfect

j'	ai **été**
tu	as **été**
il	a **été**
nous	avons **été**
vous	avez **été**
ils	ont **été**

Imperfect

j'	**étais**
tu	**étais**
il	**était**
nous	**étions**
vous	**étiez**
ils	**étaient**

Future

je	**serai**
tu	**seras**
il	**sera**
nous	**serons**
vous	**serez**
ils	**seront**

Conditional

je	**serais**
tu	**serais**
il	**serait**
nous	**serions**
vous	**seriez**
ils	**seraient**

aller
to go

Imperative	Past participle
va	all**é**
all**ons**	
all**ez**	

Present		Present subjunctive	
je	**vais**	j'	**aille**
tu	**vas**	tu	**ailles**
il	**va**	il	**aille**
nous	all**ons**	nous	all**ions**
vous	all**ez**	vous	all**iez**
ils	**vont**	ils	**aillent**

Perfect		Imperfect	
je	suis all**é**	j'	all**ais**
tu	es all**é**	tu	all**ais**
il	est all**é**	il	all**ait**
nous	sommes all**és**	nous	all**ions**
vous	êtes all**é(s)**	vous	all**iez**
ils	sont all**és**	ils	all**aient**

Future		Conditional	
j'	**irai**	j'	**irais**
tu	**iras**	tu	**irais**
il	**ira**	il	**irait**
nous	**irons**	nous	**irions**
vous	**irez**	vous	**iriez**
ils	**iront**	ils	**iraient**

devoir
to have to

Imperative	Past participle
dois	dû
dev**ons**	
dev**ez**	

Present

je **dois**
tu **dois**
il **doit**
nous dev**ons**
vous dev**ez**
ils **doivent**

Present subjunctive

je **doive**
tu **doives**
il **doive**
nous dev**ions**
vous dev**iez**
ils **doivent**

Perfect

j' ai **dû**
tu as **dû**
il a **dû**
nous avons **dû**
vous avez **dû**
ils ont **dû**

Imperfect

je dev**ais**
tu dev**ais**
il dev**ait**
nous dev**ions**
vous dev**iez**
ils dev**aient**

Future

je dev**rai**
tu dev**ras**
il dev**ra**
nous dev**rons**
vous dev**rez**
ils dev**ront**

Conditional

je dev**rais**
tu dev**rais**
il dev**rait**
nous dev**rions**
vous dev**riez**
ils dev**raient**

dire
to say

Imperative	Past participle
dis	dit
disons	
dites	

Present

je **dis**
tu **dis**
il **dit**
nous **disons**
vous **dites**
ils **disent**

Perfect

j' ai **dit**
tu as **dit**
il a **dit**
nous avons **dit**
vous avez **dit**
ils ont **dit**

Future

je dir**ai**
tu dir**as**
il dir**a**
nous dir**ons**
vous dir**ez**
ils dir**ont**

Present subjunctive

je **dise**
tu **dises**
il **dise**
nous **disions**
vous **disiez**
ils **disent**

Imperfect

je **disais**
tu **disais**
il **disait**
nous **disions**
vous **disiez**
ils **disaient**

Conditional

je dir**ais**
tu dir**ais**
il dir**ait**
nous dir**ions**
vous dir**iez**
ils dir**aient**

faire
to do
or to make

Imperative	Past participle
fais	fait
faisons	
faites	

Present

je	**fais**
tu	**fais**
il	**fait**
nous	**faisons**
vous	**faites**
ils	**font**

Present subjunctive

je	**fasse**
tu	**fasses**
il	**fasse**
nous	**fassions**
vous	**fassiez**
ils	**fassent**

Perfect

j'	ai **fait**
tu	as **fait**
il	a **fait**
nous	avons **fait**
vous	avez **fait**
ils	ont **fait**

Imperfect

je	**faisais**
tu	**faisais**
il	**faisait**
nous	**faisions**
vous	**faisiez**
ils	**faisaient**

Future

je	**ferai**
tu	**feras**
il	**fera**
nous	**ferons**
vous	**ferez**
ils	**feront**

Conditional

je	**ferais**
tu	**ferais**
il	**ferait**
nous	**ferions**
vous	**feriez**
ils	**feraient**

mettre
to put

Imperative	Past participle
mets	mis
mettons	
mettez	

Present

je **mets**
tu **mets**
il **met**
nous mett**ons**
vous mett**ez**
ils mett**ent**

Perfect

j' ai **mis**
tu as **mis**
il a **mis**
nous avons **mis**
vous avez **mis**
ils ont **mis**

Future

je mettr**ai**
tu mettr**as**
il mettr**a**
nous mettr**ons**
vous mettr**ez**
ils mettr**ont**

Present subjunctive

je mett**e**
tu mett**es**
il mett**e**
nous mett**ions**
vous mett**iez**
ils mett**ent**

Imperfect

je mett**ais**
tu mett**ais**
il mett**ait**
nous mett**ions**
vous mett**iez**
ils mett**aient**

Conditional

je mettr**ais**
tu mettr**ais**
il mettr**ait**
nous mettr**ions**
vous mettr**iez**
ils mettr**aient**

pouvoir
to be able

Imperative

the imperative
of **pouvoir** is
not used

Past participle

pu

Present

je **peux**
tu **peux**
il **peut**
nous pouv**ons**
vous pouv**ez**
ils **peuvent**

Present subjunctive

je **puisse**
tu **puisses**
il **puisse**
nous **puissions**
vous **puissiez**
ils **puissent**

Perfect

j' ai **pu**
tu as **pu**
il a **pu**
nous avons **pu**
vous avez **pu**
ils ont **pu**

Imperfect

je pouv**ais**
tu pouv**ais**
il pouv**ait**
nous pouv**ions**
vous pouv**iez**
ils pouv**aient**

Future

je **pourrai**
tu **pourras**
il **pourra**
nous **pourrons**
vous **pourrez**
ils **pourront**

Conditional

je **pourrais**
tu **pourrais**
il **pourrait**
nous **pourrions**
vous **pourriez**
ils **pourraient**

voir
to see

Imperative	Past participle
vois	vu
voyons	
voyez	

Present

| je vois |
| tu vois |
| il voit |
| nous voyons |
| vous voyez |
| ils voient |

Present subjunctive

| je voie |
| tu voies |
| il voie |
| nous voyions |
| vous voyiez |
| ils voient |

Perfect

| j' ai vu |
| tu as vu |
| il a vu |
| nous avons vu |
| vous avez vu |
| ils ont vu |

Imperfect

| je voyais |
| tu voyais |
| il voyait |
| nous voyions |
| vous voyiez |
| ils voyaient |

Future

| je verrai |
| tu verras |
| il verra |
| nous verrons |
| vous verrez |
| ils verront |

Conditional

| je verrais |
| tu verrais |
| il verrait |
| nous verrions |
| vous verriez |
| ils verraient |

vouloir
to want

Imperative	Past participle
veuille	voul**u**
veuillons	
veuillez	

Present

je	**veux**
tu	**veux**
il	**veut**
nous	voul**ons**
vous	voul**ez**
ils	**veulent**

Perfect

j'	ai voul**u**
tu	as voul**u**
il	a voul**u**
nous	avons voul**u**
vous	avez voul**u**
ils	ont voul**u**

Future

je	**voudrai**
tu	**voudras**
il	**voudra**
nous	**voudrons**
vous	**voudrez**
ils	**voudront**

Present subjunctive

je	**veuille**
tu	**veuilles**
il	**veuille**
nous	voul**ions**
vous	voul**iez**
ils	**veuillent**

Imperfect

je	voul**ais**
tu	voul**ais**
il	voul**ait**
nous	voul**ions**
vous	voul**iez**
ils	voul**aient**

Conditional

je	**voudrais**
tu	**voudrais**
il	**voudrait**
nous	**voudrions**
vous	**voudriez**
ils	**voudraient**

French irregular verb forms

This list shows the main forms of other irregular verbs. The number before the infinitive is the number given after verbs in the dictionary which follow this pattern.

(1) = Present   (3) = Imperfect
(2) = Past participle   (4) = Future

15 **abréger** (1) j'abrège, nous abrégeons, ils abrègent (2) abrégé (3) j'abrégeais (4) j'abrégerai

16 **acheter** (1) j'achète, nous achetons, ils achètent (2) acheté (3) j'achetais (4) j'achèterai

17 **acquérir** (1) j'acquiers, il acquiert, nous acquérons, vous acquérez ils acquièrent (2) acquis (3) j'acquérais (4) j'acquerrai

18 **appeler** (1) j'appelle, nous appelons (2) appelé (3) j'appelais (4) j'appellerai

19 **apprendre** (1) j'apprends, nous apprenons, vous apprenez, ils apprennent (2) appris (3) j'apprenais (4) j'apprendrai

20 **s'asseoir** (1) je m'assieds, nous nous asseyons, vous vous asseyez, ils s'asseyent (2) assis (3) je m'asseyais (4) je m'assiérai

21 **battre** (1) je bats, il bat, nous battons (2) battu (3) je battais (4) je battrai

22 **boire** (1) je bois, nous buvons, ils boivent (2) bu (3) je buvais (4) je boirai

23 **bouillir** (1) je bous, nous bouillons, (2) bouilli (3) je bouillais (4) je bouillirai

24 **céder** (1) je cède, nous cédons, ils cèdent (2) cédé (3) je cédais (4) je céderai

25 **conclure** (1) je conclus, nous concluons (2) conclu (3) je concluais (4) je conclurai

26 **conduire** (1) je conduis, nous conduisons (2) conduit (3) je conduisais (4) je conduirai

27 **connaître** (1) je connais, nous connaissons (2) connu (3) je connaissais (4) je connaîtrai

28 **coudre** (1) je couds, nous cousons, vous cousez, ils cousent (2) cousu (3) je cousais (4) je coudrai

29 **courir** (1) je cours, nous courons (2) couru (3) je courais (4) je courrai

30 **couvrir** (1) je couvre, nous couvrons (2) couvert (3) je couvrais (4) je couvrirai

31 **craindre** (1) je crains, nous craignons (2) craint (3) je craignais (4) je craindrai

32 **créer** (1) je crée, nous créons (2) créé (3) je créais (4) je créerai

33 **croire** (1) je crois, nous croyons ils croient (2) cru (3) je croyais (4) je croirai

34 **croître** (1) je croîs, nous croissons (2) crû, crue (3) je croissais (4) je croîtrai

35 **cueillir** (1) je cueille, nous cueillons (2) cueilli (3) je cueillais (4) je cueillerai

36 **cuire** (1) je cuis, nous cuisons, ils cuisent (2) cuit (3) je cuisais (4) je cuirai

37 **dormir** (1) je dors, nous dormons (2) dormi (3) je dormais (4) je dormirai

38 **écrire** (1) j'écris, nous écrivons (2) écrit (3) j'écrivais (4) j'écrirai

39 **employer** (1) j'emploie, nous employons, vous employez, ils emploient (2) employé (3) j'employais (4) j'emploierai

40 **envoyer** (1) j'envoie, nous envoyons, vous envoyez, ils envoient (2) envoyé (3) j'envoyais (4) j'enverrai

41 **essuyer** (1) j'essuie, nous essuyons, vous essuyez, ils essuient (2) essuyé (3) j'essuyais (4) j'essuierai

42 **faillir** (1) je faille (2) failli

43 **falloir** (1) il faut (2) fallu (3) il fallait (4) il faudra

44 **fuir** (1) je fuis, nous fuyons, ils, fuient (2) fui (3) je fuyais (4) je fuirai

45 **geler** (1) je gèle, nous gelons, vous gelez, ils gèlent (2) gelé (3) je gelais (4) je gèlerai

46 **haïr** (1) je hais, nous haïssons, ils haïssent (2) haï (3) je haïssais (4) je haïrai

47 **interdire** (1) j'interdis, nous interdisons, vous interdisez (2) interdit (3) j'interdisais (4) j'interdirai

48 **jeter** (1) je jette, nous jetons, ils jettent (2) jeté (3) je jetais (4) je jetterai

49 **joindre** (1) je joins, nous joignons (2) joint (3) je joignais (4) je joindrai

50 **lever** (1) je lève, nous levons, ils lèvent (2) levé (3) je levais (4) je lèverai

51 **lire** (1) je lis, nous lisons (2) lu (3) je lisais (4) je lirai

52 **manger** (1) je mange, nous mangeons (2) mangé (3) je mangeais (4) je mangerai

53 **mentir** (1) je mens, nous mentons (2) menti (3) je mentais (4) je mentirai

54 **mourir** (1) je meurs, nous mourons, ils meurent (2) mort (3) je mourais (4) je mourrai

55 **naître** (1) je nais, il naît, nous naissons (2) né (3) je naissais (4) je naîtrai

56 **offrir** (1) j'offre, nous offrons (2) offert (3) j'offrais (4) j'offrirai

57 **paraître** (1) je parais, il paraît, nous paraissons (2) paru (3) je paraissais (4) je paraîtrai

58 **partir** (1) je pars, nous partons (2) parti (3) je partais (4) je partirai

59 **payer** (1) je paie/je paye, nous payons, vous payez, ils paient/ils payent (2) payé (3) je payais (4) je paierai/je payerai

60 **peindre** (1) je peins, nous peignons (2) peint (3) je peignais (4) je peindrai

61 **placer** (1) je place, nous plaçons (2) placé (3) je plaçais (4) je placerai

62 **plaire** (1) je plais, il plaît, nous plaisons (2) plu (3) je plaisais (4) je plairai

63 **pleuvoir** (1) il pleut (2) plu (3) il pleuvait (4) il pleuvra

64 **prendre** (1) je prends, nous prenons, ils prennent (2) pris (3) je prenais (4) je prendrai

65 **prévoir** (1) je prévois, nous prévoyons, vous prévoyez, ils prévoient (2) prévu (3) je prévoyais (4) je prévoirai

66 **recevoir** (1) je reçois, il reçoit, ils reçoivent (2) reçu (3) je recevais (4) je recevrai

67 **résoudre** (1) je résous, nous résolvons, vous résolvez, ils résolvent (2) résolu (3) je résolvais (4) je résoudrai

68 **rire** (1) je ris, nous rions (2) ri (3) je riais (4) je rirai

69 **rompre** (1) je romps, il rompt, nous rompons (2) rompu (3) je rompais (4) je romprai

70 **savoir** (1) je sais, nous savons, ils savent (2) su (3) je savais (4) je saurai

71 **servir** (1) je sers, nous servons (2) servi (3) je servais (4) je servirai

72 **sortir** (1) je sors, nous sortons (2) sorti (3) je sortais (4) je sortirai

73 **souffrir** (1) je souffre, nous souffrons (2) souffert (3) je souffrais (4) je souffrirai

74 **suffire** (1) je suffis, nous suffisons (2) suffi (3) je suffisais (4) je suffirai

75 **suivre** (1) je suis, nous suivons (2) suivi (3) je suivais (4) je suivrai

76 **taire** (1) je me tais, nous nous taisons (2) tu (3) je me taisais (4) je me tairai

77 **tenir** (1) je tiens, nous tenons, ils tiennent (2) tenu (3) je tenais (4) je tiendrai

78 **traire** (1) je trais, nous trayons, ils traient (2) trait (3) je trayais (4) je trairai

79 **vaincre** (1) je vaincs, il vainc, nous vainquons (2) vaincu (3) je vainquais

80 **valoir** (1) je vaux, il vaut, nous valons (2) valu (3) je valais (4) je vaudrai

81 **venir** (1) je viens, nous venons, ils viennent (2) venu (3) je venais (4) je viendrai

82 **vivre** (1) je vis, nous vivons (2) vécu (3) je vivais (4) je vivrai

A a

a *indefinite article* **1** (*before a noun which is masculine in French*) un; **a tree** un arbre; **2** (*before a noun which is feminine in French*) une; **a table** une table; **3 ten francs a kilo** dix francs le kilo; **4 fifty kilometres an hour** cinquante kilomètres l'heure; **5 three times a day** trois fois par jour.

abandon *verb* abandonner [1].

abbey *noun* abbaye F; **Westminster Abbey** l'Abbaye de Westminster.

abbreviation *noun* abréviation F.

abide *verb* **I can't abide...** je ne supporte pas...

ability *noun* capacité F; **the ability to do** la capacité de faire.

able *adjective* **to be able to do** pouvoir [12] faire; **she wasn't able to come** elle n'a pas pu venir.

abnormal *adjective* anormal (M *plural* anormaux).

about *preposition* **1** (*on the subject of*) sur; **a film about Picasso** un film sur Picasso; **2 what's it about?** de quoi s'agit-il?; **3** (*concerning or in relation to*) au sujet de; **he wants to talk to you about your exam** il veut te parler au sujet de ton examen; **4 to talk about something** parler de quelque chose; **what is she talking about?** de quoi parle-t-elle?; **5 to think about something/somebody** penser à quelque chose/quelqu'un; **I'm thinking about you** je pense à toi.

adverb **1** (*approximately*) environ, à peu près; **there are about sixty people** il y a environ soixante personnes, il y a à peu près soixante personnes; **2** (*when talking about the time*) vers; **about three o'clock** vers trois heures; ★ **to be about to do** être sur le point de faire; **I'm (just) about to leave** je suis sur le point de partir.

above *preposition* **1** au dessus de; **above the table** au dessus de la table; **2 above all** surtout.

abroad *adverb* à l'étranger; **to go abroad** aller à l'étranger; **to live abroad** vivre à l'étranger.

abscess *noun* abcès M.

abseiling *noun* descente F en rappel.

absent *adjective* absent; **to be absent from** être absent de.

absent-minded *adjective* distrait.

absolute *adjective* complet (F complète); **an absolute disaster** un désastre complet.

absolutely *adverb* **1** absolument; **it's absolutely dreadful** c'est absolument affreux; **2** tout à fait; **you're absolutely right** tu as tout à fait raison.

absorb *verb* absorber [1].

abuse *noun* **1 alcohol abuse** abus M d'alcool; **drug abuse** usage M des stupéfiants; **2** (*violent treatment of a person*) mauvais traitement M; **3** (*insults*) injures F *plural*.

verb **to abuse somebody**
maltraiter [1] quelqu'un.

academic *adjective* **the academic
year** l'année universitaire.

accelerate *verb* accélérer [24].

accelerator *noun* accélérateur M.

accent *noun* accent M; **she has a
French accent** elle a un accent
français.

accept *verb* accepter [1].

acceptable *adjective* acceptable.

acceptance *noun* acceptation F.

access *noun* accès M.
verb **to access something** accéder
[24] à quelque chose.

accessory *noun* accessoire M.

accident *noun* 1 accident M; **to
have an accident** avoir un accident;
a road accident un accident de la
route; **a car accident** un accident
de voiture; 2 (*chance*) hasard M;
by accident par hasard; **I found it
by accident** je l'ai trouvé par hasard.

accidental *adjective* fortuit; **an
accidental discovery** une
découverte fortuite.

accidentally *adverb* 1 (*without
meaning to*) accidentellement; **I
accidentally knocked over his
glass** j'ai accidentellement
renversé son verre; 2 (*by chance*)
par hasard; **I accidentally
discovered that...** j'ai découvert
par hasard que...

accommodate *verb* recevoir [66];
**the centre can accommodate sixty
people** le centre peut recevoir
soixante personnes.

accommodation *noun* logement
M; **I'm looking for
accommodation** je cherche un
logement.

accompany *verb* **to accompany
somebody** accompagner [1]
quelqu'un.

according *in phrase* **according to**
selon; **according to Sophie** selon
Sophie.

accordion *noun* accordéon M.

account *noun* 1 (*in a bank, shop, o
post office*) compte M; **a bank
account** un compte bancaire; **to
open an account** ouvrir un compte
I have fifty pounds in my account
j'ai cinquante livres sur mon
compte; 2 (*a description of an
experience or event*) compte rendu
M; 3 **on account of** à cause de; **th
station is closed on account of the
strike** la gare est fermée à cause de
la grève; 4 **to take something into
account** tenir compte de quelque
chose; **we will take his illness into
account** nous tiendrons compte de
sa maladie.

accountant *noun* comptable M &
F; **she is an accountant** elle est
comptable.

accuracy *noun* précision F.

accurate *adjective* précis.

accurately *adverb* avec précision.

accuse *verb* accuser [1]; **to accuse
somebody of something** accuser
quelqu'un de quelque chose; **to
accuse someone of doing
something** accuser quelqu'un
d'avoir fait quelque chose; **she**

accused me of stealing her pen elle m'a accusé d'avoir volé son stylo.

ace *noun* as M; **the ace of hearts** l'as de cœur.
adjective super (*informal*); **he's an ace drummer** c'est un super batteur.

ache *verb* **my arm aches** j'ai mal au bras; **my head aches** j'ai mal à la tête.

achieve *verb* **1** accomplir [2]; **she's achieved a great deal** elle a beaucoup accompli; **2 to achieve an ambition** réaliser [1] une ambition; **3 to achieve an aim** atteindre [60] un objectif; **4 to achieve success** réussir [2].

achievement *noun* **1** réussite F; **it's a great achievement** c'est une grande réussite; **2 a sense of achievement** un sentiment de satisfaction.

acid *noun* acide M.

acid rain *noun* pluies F *plural* acides.

acne *noun* acné F.

acorn *noun* gland M.

acrobat *noun* acrobate M & F.

across *preposition* **1** (*over to the other side of*) **to walk across something** traverser [1] quelque chose; **we walked across the park** nous avons traversé le parc; **to run across the road** traverser la route en courant; **2** (*on the other side of*) de l'autre côté de; **the house across the street** la maison de l'autre côté de la rue; **3 across from** en face de;

she was sitting across from me elle était assise en face de moi.

acrylic *noun* acrylique M.

act *noun* acte M.
verb **1** (*in a play or film*) jouer [1]; **to act the part of** jouer le rôle de; **2** (*to take action*) agir [2].

action *noun* action F.

active *adjective* actif (F active).

activity *noun* activité F.

activity holiday *noun* vacances F *plural* sportives.

actor *noun* acteur M; **who's your favourite actor?** qui est votre acteur préféré?

actress *noun* actrice F; **she's my favourite actress** c'est mon actrice préférée.

actual *adjective* **his actual words** ses paroles précises; ★ **in actual fact** en fait.

actually *adverb* **1** (*in fact, as it happens*) en fait; **actually, I've changed my mind** en fait, j'ai changé d'avis; **he's not actually here at the moment** en fait il n'est pas là en ce moment; **2** (*really and truly*) vraiment; **did she actually say that?** est-ce qu'elle a vraiment dit ça?

acupuncture *noun* acupuncture F.

acute *adjective* **1** (*pain*) vif (F vive); **2 an acute accent** un accent aigu.

ad *noun* **1** pub F (*informal*); **2** (*in a newspaper*) annonce F; **to put an ad in the paper** mettre une annonce dans le journal; **the small ads** les petites annonces.

AD après Jésus-Christ, apr. J-C; **in 400 AD** en quatre cents après Jésus-Christ.

adapt *verb* **1 to adapt something** adapter [1] quelque chose (*a book or film*); **2 to adapt to something** s'adapter [1] à quelque chose; **she's adapted to the new system** elle s'est adaptée au nouveau système.

adaptor *noun* adaptateur M.

add *verb* ajouter [1]; **add three eggs** ajoutez trois œufs.
●**to add something up** additionner [1] quelque chose.

addict *noun* **1** (*drug addict*) drogué, droguée M , F; **2** accro M & F (*informal*); **she's a telly addict** c'est une accro de la télé; **he's a football addict** c'est un accro du foot.

addicted *adjective* **1 to become addicted to heroin** former une dépendance à l'héroïne; **2 I'm addicted to tomatoes** je suis obsédé par les tomates.

addition *noun* **1** (*adding up*) addition F; **2 in addition** en plus; **3 in addition to** en plus de.

additional *adjective* supplémentaire; **additional costs** les frais supplémentaires.

additive *noun* additif M.

address *noun* adresse F; **what's your address?** quelle est ton adresse?; **to change address** changer d'adresse.

address book *noun* carnet M d'adresses.

adequate *adjective* suffisant.

adhesive *noun* colle F.
adjective collant; **adhesive tape** du papier collant.

adjective *noun* adjectif M.

adjust *verb* **1 to adjust something** régler [24] quelque chose; **to adjust the height** régler la hauteur; **2 to adjust to something** s'adapter [1] à quelque chose.

adjustable *adjective* réglable.

administration *noun* administration F.

admiral *noun* amiral M.

admiration *noun* admiration F.

admire *verb* admirer [1].

admission *noun* entrée F; **'no admission'** 'entrée interdite'; **'admission free'** 'entrée gratuite'.

admit *verb* **1** (*confess*) reconnaître [27]; **she admits she lied** elle reconnaît qu'elle a menti; **2** (*concede*) admettre [11]; **I must admit that…** j'admets que…; **3** (*allow to enter*) laisser [1] entrer; **to admit somebody to a restaurant** laisser entrer quelqu'un dans un restaurant; **4 to be admitted to hospital** être [6] hospitalisé.

adolescence *noun* adolescence F

adolescent *noun* adolescent M adolescente F.

adopt *verb* adopter [1].

adopted *adjective* adoptif (F adoptive).

adoption *noun* adoption F.

adore *verb* adorer [1].

Adriatic Sea *noun* **the Adriatic Sea** la mer Adriatique.

adult *noun* adulte M & F. *adjective* adulte; **the adult population** la population adulte.

Adult Education *noun* enseignement M pour adultes.

advance *noun* progrès M; **advances in technology** des progrès dans le domaine de la technologie. *verb* 1 (*make progress*) progresser [1]; 2 (*move forward*) avancer [61].

advanced *adjective* avancé.

advantage *noun* 1 avantage M; **there are several advantages** il y a plusieurs avantages; 2 **to take advantage of something** profiter de quelque chose; **I took advantage of the sales to buy myself some shoes** j'ai profité des soldes pour m'acheter des chaussures; 3 **to take advantage of somebody** (*unfairly*) exploiter quelqu'un.

Advent *noun* Avent M.

adventure *noun* aventure F.

adventurous *adjective* aventureux (F aventureuse).

adverb *noun* adverbe M.

advert, advertisement *noun* 1 (*at the cinema or on television*) publicité F; 2 (*commercial advertisement in a newspaper*) annonce F; 3 (*small ad in a newspaper advertising a job, an*

article for sale, etc) petite annonce F.

advertise *verb* 1 **to advertise something in the newspaper** (*in the small ads*) mettre [11] une annonce pour quelque chose dans le journal; **I saw a bike advertised in the paper** j'ai vu une annonce pour un vélo dans le journal; 2 **to advertise a product** faire [10] de la publicité pour un produit.

advertising *noun* publicité F.

advice *noun* conseils M *plural*; **to ask for advice about something** demander des conseils à propos de quelque chose; **a piece of advice** un conseil.

advise *verb* conseiller [1]; **to advise somebody to do** conseiller à quelqu'un de faire; **I advised him to stop** je lui ai conseillé d'arrêter; **I advised her not to wait** je lui ai conseillé de ne pas attendre.

aerial *noun* antenne F.

aerobics *noun* aérobic M; **to do aerobics** faire de l'aérobic.

aeroplane *noun* avion M.

aerosol *noun* **an aerosol can** une bombe.

affair *noun* 1 (*event*) affaire F; **international affairs** les affaires internationales; 2 **a love affair** une aventure amoureuse.

affect *verb* affecter [1].

affectionate *adjective* affectueux (F affectueuse).

afford *verb* **to be able to afford to do** avoir [5] les moyens de faire; **we**

can't afford to go out much nous n'avons pas les moyens de sortir beaucoup; **I can't afford a new bike** je n'ai pas les moyens de m'acheter un nouveau vélo.

afraid *adjective* **1 to be afraid of something** avoir peur de quelque chose; **she's afraid of dogs** elle a peur des chiens; **2 I'm afraid there's no milk left** je suis désolé mais il ne reste plus de lait; **I'm afraid so** hélas oui; **I'm afraid not** hélas non.

Africa *noun* Afrique F; **in Africa** en Afrique; **to Africa** en Afrique.

African *noun* Africain M, Africaine F.
adjective africain (F africaine).

after *preposition, adverb, conjunction* après; **after 10 o'clock** après dix heures; **after lunch** après le déjeuner; **after school** après l'école; **the day after tomorrow** après-demain; **soon after** peu après; **after I've finished my homework** après que j'aurai fini mes devoirs; **to run after somebody** courir après quelqu'un.

after all *adverb* après tout; **after all, she's only six** elle n'a que six ans après tout.

afternoon *noun* après-midi M or F; **this afternoon** cet après-midi; **tomorrow afternoon** demain après-midi; **yesterday afternoon** hier après-midi; **on Saturday afternoon** samedi après-midi; **on Saturday afternoons** le samedi après-midi; **at four o'clock in the afternoon** à quatre heures de l'après-midi; **every afternoon** tous les après-midi.

afters *noun* dessert M.

after-shave *noun* après-rasage M.

afterwards *adverb* après; **shortly afterwards** peu de temps après.

again *adverb* **1** (*one more time*) encore une fois; **try again** essaie encore une fois; **I've forgotten it again** je l'ai oublié encore une fois; **2** (*once more*) de nouveau; **she's ill again** elle est de nouveau malade; **3 I saw her again yesterday** je l'ai revue hier; **you should ask again** tu devrais redemander; **4 I don't want to see her again** je ne veux plus la revoir; **never again!** jamais plus!

against *preposition* contre; **against the wall** contre le mur; **to lean against the wall** s'appuyer contre le mur; **I'm against the idea** je suis contre l'idée; **the fight against racism** la lutte contre le racisme.

age *noun* âge M; **1 at the age of fifteen** à l'âge de quinze ans; **she's the same age as me** elle a le même âge que moi; **to be under age** être mineur; **2 I haven't seen Johnny for ages** ça fait une éternité que je n'ai pas vu Johnny; **I haven't been to London for ages** ça fait une éternité que je ne suis pas allé à Londres.

aged *adjective* âgé de; **a woman aged thirty** une femme âgée de trente ans.

agenda *noun* ordre M du jour.

agent *noun* agent M; **an estate agent** un agent immobilier; **a travel agent's** une agence de voyage.

aggressive *adjective* agressif (F agressive).

ago *adverb* **an hour ago** il y a une heure; **three days ago** il y a trois jours; **five years ago** il y a cinq ans; **a long time ago** il y a longtemps; **not long ago** il n'y a pas longtemps; **how long ago was it?** c'était il y a combien de temps?

agree *verb* **1 to agree with somebody** être [6] d'accord avec quelqu'un; **I agree with Laura** je suis d'accord avec Laura; **I don't agree** je ne suis pas d'accord; **2 I agree that. . .** je suis d'accord sur le fait que. . .; **I agree that it's too late now** je suis d'accord sur le fait qu'il est maintenant trop tard; **3 to agree to do** accepter [1] de faire; **Steve's agreed to help me** Steve a accepté de m'aider; **4 coffee doesn't agree with me** je ne supporte pas le café.

agreement *noun* accord M.

agricultural *adjective* agricole.

agriculture *noun* agriculture F.

ahead *adverb* **1 go ahead!** allez-y!; **2 straight ahead** tout droit; **go straight ahead until you get to the crossroads** allez tout droit jusqu'au carrefour; **3 our team was ten points ahead** notre équipe avait dix points d'avance; **4 to be ahead of time** être en avance.

aid *noun* **1** aide F; **aid to developing countries** l'aide aux pays en voie de développement; **2 in aid of** au profit de; **in aid of the homeless** au profit des sans-abri.

AIDS *noun* sida M (*short for:*

syndrome immunodéficitaire acquis); **to have AIDS** avoir le sida.

aim *noun* objectif M; **their aim is to control pollution** leur objectif est de contrôler la pollution.
verb **1 to aim to do** avoir [5] l'intention de faire; **we're aiming to finish it today** nous avons l'intention de le finir aujourd'hui; **2 a campaign aimed at young people** une campagne qui vise les jeunes; **3 to aim a gun at somebody** braquer [1] un révolver sur quelqu'un.

air *noun* **1** air M; **in the open air** en plein air; **to go out for a breath of air** sortir prendre l'air; **2 to travel by air** voyager en avion.

airbag *noun* (*in a car*) airbag M.

air-conditioned *adjective* climatisé.

air conditioning *noun* climatisation F.

Air Force *noun* Armée F de l'air.

air hostess *noun* hôtesse F de l'air; **she's an air hostess** elle est hôtesse de l'air.

airline *noun* compagnie F aérienne.

airmail *noun* **by airmail** par avion.

airport *noun* aéroport M.

aisle *noun* allée F centrale.

alarm *noun* alarme F; **a fire alarm** une alarme incendie; **a burglar alarm** une alarme contre le vol.

alarm clock *noun* réveil M.

album *noun* album M.

alcohol *noun* alcool M.

alcoholic *noun* alcoolique M & F. *adjective* alcoolisé; **alcoholic drinks** les boissons alcoolisées.

A levels *plural noun* bac M; baccalauréat M (*Students take 'le bac' at the same age as A levels are taken in Britain. However, they are examined in many more subjects, usually around 7, and are given one overall mark out of 20*).

Algeria *noun* Algérie F; **to Algeria** en Algérie; **in Algeria** en Algérie.

alike *adjective* pareil (F pareille); **1 they're all alike** ils sont tous pareils; **2 to look alike** se ressembler; **the two brothers look alike** les deux frères se ressemblent.

alive *adjective* vivant.

all *adjective, adverb, pronoun* **1** tout (M *plural* tous); **all the knives** tous les couteaux; **all the forks** toutes les fourchettes; **all the time** tout le temps; **all day** toute la journée; **2 they've eaten it all** ils ont tout mangé; **after all** après tout; **not at all** pas du tout; **they're all there** ils sont tous là; **3 all alone** tout seul; **she's all alone at the moment** elle est toute seule en ce moment; **4 it's all I have** c'est tout ce que j'ai; **5 three all** trois partout.

all along *adverb* depuis le début; **I knew it all along** je le savais depuis le début.

allergic *adjective* allergique; **to be allergic to something** être allergique à quelque chose.

allow *verb* **1 to allow somebody to do** permettre [11] à quelqu'un de faire; **the teacher allowed them to go out** le prof leur a permis de sortir; **2 to be allowed to do** avoir [5] le droit de faire; **I'm not allowed to go out during the week** je n'ai pas le droit de sortir en semaine.

all right *adverb* **1** (*yes*) d'accord; **'come round to my house around six' – 'all right'** 'passe chez moi vers six heures' – 'd'accord'; **2** (*fine*) bien; **is everything all right?** est-ce que tout va bien?; **she's all right now** elle va bien maintenant; **it's all right by me** ça ne me dérange pas; **3** (*not bad*) pas mal; **the meal was all right** le repas n'était pas mal; **4 are you all right?** ça va?; **5 is it all right to…?** est-ce qu'on peut…?; **is it all right to leave the door open?** est-ce qu'on peut laisser la porte ouverte?

almond *noun* amande F.

almost *adverb* presque; **almost every day** presque tous les jours; **almost everybody** presque tout le monde; **she's almost five** elle a presque cinq ans.

alone *adjective* **1** seul; **he lives alone** il habite seul; **2 leave me alone!** laisse-moi tranquille!; **3 leave these papers alone!** ne touche pas à ces papiers!

along *preposition* **1** le long de; **there are trees all along the road** il y a des arbres tout le long de la route; **2** (*there is often no direct translation for 'along' so the sentence has to be expressed differently*) **she lives along the road from me** elle habite dans la même rue que moi; **to go for a walk along the beach** aller se promener sur la plage.

aloud *adverb* à haute voix; **to read something aloud** lire quelque chose à haute voix.

alphabet *noun* alphabet M.

Alps *plural noun* **the Alps** les Alpes.

already *adverb* déjà; **they've already left** ils sont déjà partis; **it's six o'clock already!** il est déjà six heures!

Alsation *noun* (*dog*) berger M allemand.

also *adverb* aussi; **I've also invited Karen** j'ai aussi invité Karen.

alter *verb* changer [52].

alternate *adjective* **on alternate days** un jour sur deux.

alternative *noun* **1** possibilité F; **there are several alternatives** il y a plusieurs possibilités; **2 we have no alternative** nous n'avons pas le choix.
adjective autre; **to find an alternative solution** trouver une autre solution.

alternatively *adverb* sinon; **alternatively, we could go together on Saturday** sinon, on pourrait y aller ensemble samedi.

alternative medicine *noun* médecine F douce.

although *conjunction* bien que (*followed by subjunctive*); **although she's ill, she's willing to help us** bien qu'elle soit malade, elle est prête à nous aider.

altogether *adverb* **1** en tout; **I've spent thirty pounds altogether** j'ai dépensé trente livres en tout;

2 (*completely*) complètement; **I'm not altogether convinced** je ne suis pas complètement convaincu.

aluminium *noun* aluminium M.

always *adverb* toujours; **I always leave at five** je pars toujours à cinq heures.

am *verb* SEE be.

a.m. *abbreviation* du matin; **at 8 a.m.** à huit heures du matin.

amateur *noun* amateur M; **amateur dramatics** théâtre M amateur.

amaze *verb* surprendre [64]; **what amazes me is...** ce qui me surprend c'est...

amazed *adjective* stupéfait; **I was amazed to see her** j'étais stupéfait de la voir.

amazing *adjective* **1** (*terrific*) fantastique; **your dress is amazing!** ta robe est fantastique!; **they've got an amazing house** ils ont une maison fantastique; **2** (*extraordinary*) extraordinaire; **she has an amazing number of friends** elle a un nombre extraordinaire d'amis; **he told me an amazing story** il m'a raconté une histoire extraordinaire.

ambassador *noun* ambassadeur M, ambassadrice F.

ambition *noun* ambition F.

ambitious *adjective* ambitieux (F ambitieuse).

ambulance *noun* ambulance F.

ambulance driver *noun* ambulancier M, ambulancière F.

amenities *plural noun*
équipements M *plural*.

America *noun* Amérique F; **in America** en Amérique; **to America** en Amérique.

American *noun* Américain M, Américaine F.
adjective américain (F américaine).

among, amongst *preposition* **1** parmi; **I found it amongst my books** je l'ai trouvé parmi mes livres; **2** (*between*) entre; **you can decide amongst yourselves** vous pouvez décider entre vous.

amount *noun* **1** quantité F; **an enormous amount of bread** une énorme quantité de pain; **a huge amount of work** un travail énorme; **2** (*of money*) somme F; **a large amount of money** une grosse somme d'argent.

amp *noun* **1** (*electricity*) ampère M; **2** (*amplifier*) ampli M (*informal*).

amplifier *noun* amplificateur M.

amuse *verb* amuser [1].

amusement arcade *noun* salle F de jeux électroniques.

amusing *adjective* amusant.

an *article* SEE **a**.

anaesthetic *noun* anesthésie F.

analyse *verb* analyser [1].

analysis *noun* analyse F.

ancestor *noun* ancêtre M & F.

anchovy *noun* anchois M.

ancient *adjective* **1** (*historic*) ancien (F ancienne); **an ancient**

abbey une abbaye ancienne; **2** (*very old*) très vieux (F très vieille); **an ancient pair of jeans** un très vieux jean; **3 ancient Greece** la Grèce antique.

and *conjunction* **1** et; **Sean and Anna** Sean et Anna; **Rosie and I** Rosie et moi; **your shoes and socks** tes chaussures et tes chaussettes; **2 louder and louder** de plus en plus fort.

angel *noun* ange M.

anger *noun* colère F.

angle *noun* angle M.

angrily *adverb* avec colère.

angry *adjective* **to be angry** être en colère; **she was angry with me** elle était en colère contre moi; **to get angry** se fâcher [1].

animal *noun* animal M (*plural* animaux).

ankle *noun* cheville F; **to break your ankle** se casser la cheville.

anniversary *noun* anniversaire M; **a wedding anniversary** un anniversaire de mariage.

announce *verb* annoncer [61].

announcement *noun* annonce F.

annoy *verb* agacer [61]; **to be annoyed** être [6] agacé; **to get annoyed** se fâcher [1]; **she got annoyed** elle s'est fâchée.

annoying *adjective* agaçant.

annual *adjective* annuel (F annuelle).

anorak *noun* anorak M.

anorexia *noun* anorexie F.

another *adjective* **1** un autre (F une autre); **would you like another cup of tea?** voulez-vous une autre tasse de thé?; **2** encore; **another two years** encore deux ans; **we need another three chairs** il nous faut encore trois chaises.

answer *noun* **1** réponse F; **the right answer** la bonne réponse; **the wrong answer** la mauvaise réponse; **2 the answer to a problem** la solution à un problème. *verb* **1** répondre à [3]; **he hasn't answered our letter** il n'a pas répondu à notre lettre; **2 to answer the door** aller [5] ouvrir la porte.

answering machine *noun* répondeur M; **to leave a message on the answering machine** laisser un message au répondeur.

ant *noun* fourmi F.

Antarctic *noun* Antarctique M.

anthem *noun* **the national anthem** l'hymne national.

antibiotic *noun* antibiotique F.

antique *noun* **antiques** les antiquités F. *adjective* ancien (F ancienne); **an antique table** une table ancienne.

antique shop *noun* magasin d'antiquités M.

antiseptic *noun* antiseptique M.

anxious *adjective* inquiet (F inquiète).

anxiously *adverb* avec inquiétude.

any *adjective, adverb, pronoun* **1** du, de l', de la, des; **is there any butter?** y a-t-il du beurre?; **is there any oil?** y a-t-il de l'huile?; **is there any flour?** y a-t-il de la farine?; **are there any eggs?** y a-t-il des œufs?; **2** de (*used in negative sentences*) **there isn't any flour** il n'y a pas de farine; **there aren't any eggs** il n'y a pas d'œufs; **3** en (*when 'any' is used on its own without a noun*) **I don't want any** je n'en veux pas; **4** not...any **more** ne...plus; **there isn't any more butter** il n'y a plus de beurre; **I don't go there any more** je n'y vais plus.

anybody, anyone *pronoun* **1** (*in questions and after 'if'*) quelqu'un; **is anybody in?** est-ce qu'il y a quelqu'un?; **if anybody wants some beer, it's in the fridge** si quelqu'un veut de la bière, elle est au frigo; **does anybody want some tea?** qui veut du thé?; **2** not...anybody ne...personne; **there isn't anybody in her office** il n'y a personne dans son bureau; **3** (*absolutely anybody*) n'importe qui; **anybody can go** n'importe qui peut y aller.

anyhow *adverb* SEE **anyway**.

anyone *pronoun* SEE **anybody**.

anything *pronoun* **1** (*in questions*) quelque chose; **is there anything I can do to help?** est-ce que je peux faire quelque chose pour t'aider?; **2** not...anything ne...rien; **there isn't anything on the table** il n'y a rien sur la table; **3** (*anything at all*) n'importe quoi; **anything could happen** il pourrait arriver n'importe quoi.

anyway, anyhow *adverb* de toute façon; **anyway, I'll ring you before I**

leave de toute façon, je t'appellerai avant de partir.

anywhere *adverb* **1** (*in questions*) quelque part; **have you seen my keys anywhere?** est-ce que tu as vu mes clés quelque part?; **are you going anywhere tomorrow?** est-ce que tu vas quelque part demain?; **2** not...**anywhere** ne...nulle part; **I can't find my keys anywhere** je ne trouve nulle part mes clés; **3** (*absolutely anywhere*) n'importe où; **put your cases down anywhere** pose tes valises n'importe où.

apart *adjective, adverb* **1** (*separate*) séparé; **we don't like being apart** nous n'aimons pas être séparés; **2 to be two metres apart** être à deux mètres l'un de l'autre; **3** apart from à part; **apart from Judy everybody was there** à part Judy tout le monde y était.

apartheid *noun* apartheid M.

apartment *noun* appartement M.

apologize *verb* s'excuser [1]; **he apologizes for his behaviour** il s'excuse de son comportement; **he apologized to Tanya** il s'est excusé auprès de Tanya.

apology *noun* excuses F *plural*.

apostrophe *noun* apostrophe F.

apparatus *noun* **1** (*in a gym*) agrès M *plural*; **2** (*in a lab*) matériel M.

apparent *adjective* apparent.

apparently *adverb* apparemment.

appeal *noun* appel M.
verb **1 to appeal for** lancer [61] un appel pour; **2 to appeal to somebody** tenter [1] quelqu'un;

horror films don't appeal to me les films d'épouvante ne me tentent pas.

appear *verb* **1** apparaître [57]; **Mick appeared at the door** Mick est apparu à la porte; **2 to appear on television** passer [1] à la télévision; **3** (*seem*) paraître [57]; **it appears that somebody has stolen the key** il paraît que quelqu'un a volé la clé.

appendicitis *noun* appendicite F.

appetite *noun* appétit M; **it'll spoil your appetite** ça te coupera l'appétit.

applaud *verb* applaudir [2].

applause *noun* applaudissements M *plural*.

apple *noun* pomme F.

apple core *noun* trognon M de pomme.

apple tree *noun* pommier M.

applicant *noun* candidat M, candidate F.

application *noun* **a job application** une candidature.

application form *noun* (*for a job*) dossier M de candidature.

apply *verb* **1 to apply for a job** poser [1] sa candidature à un poste; **2 to apply for a course** faire [10] une demande d'inscription à un cours; **3 to apply to** s'appliquer [1] à; **that doesn't apply to students** cela ne s'applique pas aux étudiants.

appointment *noun* rendez-vous M; **to make a dental appointment** prendre rendez-vous chez le dentiste; **I've got a hair**

appointment at four j'ai rendez-vous chez le coiffeur à seize heures.

appreciate *verb* **I appreciate your advice** je vous suis reconnaissant de vos conseils; **I'd appreciate it if you could tidy up afterwards** je te serais reconnaissant de ranger après.

apprentice *noun* apprenti M, apprentie F.

apprenticeship *noun* apprentissage M.

approach *verb* (*come near to*) **1** s'approcher de [1]; **we were approaching Paris** nous nous approchions de Paris; **2** (*tackle*) aborder [1] (*a task or problem*).

appropriate *adjective* approprié.

approval *noun* approbation F.

approve *verb* **to approve of** apprécier [1]; **they don't approve of her friends** ils n'apprécient pas ses amis.

approximate *adjective* approximatif (F approximative).

approximately *adverb* environ; **approximately fifty people** environ cinquante personnes.

apricot *noun* abricot M.

apricot tree *noun* abricotier M.

April *noun* avril M; **in April** en avril.

April Fool *noun* poisson M d'avril.

April Fool's Day *noun* le premier avril.

apron *noun* tablier M.

Aquarius *noun* Verseau M; **Sharon's Aquarius** Sharon est Verseau.

Arab *noun* Arabe M & F. *adjective* arabe; **the Arab countries** les pays arabes.

arch *noun* arc M.

archaeologist *noun* archéologue M & F; **she's an archaeologist** elle est archéologue.

archaeology *noun* archéologie F.

archbishop *noun* archevêque M.

architect *noun* architecte M & F; **he's an architect** il est architecte.

architecture *noun* architecture F.

Arctic *noun* Arctique M.

are *verb* SEE **be**.

area *noun* **1** (*part of a town*) quartier; **a nice area** un quartier bien; **a rough area** un quartier mal fréquenté; **2** (*region*) région F; **in the Leeds area** dans la région de Leeds.

argue *verb* se disputer [1]; **1 there's no point in arguing** ce n'est pas la peine de se disputer; **2 to argue about something** discuter [1] de quelque chose; **they're arguing about the result** ils sont en train de discuter du résultat.

argument *noun* dispute F; **to have an argument** se disputer.

Aries *noun* Bélier M; **Pauline's Aries** Pauline est Bélier.

arm *noun* bras M; **to fold your arms** se croiser les bras; **arm in arm** bras dessus bras dessous; **to break your arm** se casser le bras.

armchair *noun* fauteuil M.

armed *adjective* armé.

army *noun* armée F; **to join the army** s'engager dans l'armée.

around *preposition, adverb* 1 (*with time*) vers; **we'll be there around ten** on va arriver vers dix heures; 2 (*with ages or amounts*) environ; **she's around fifteen** elle a environ quinze ans; **we need around six kilos** il nous faut environ six kilos; 3 (*surounding*) autour de; **the countryside around Edinburgh** le paysage autour d'Édimbourg; 4 (*near*) **is there a post office around here?** est-ce qu'il y a un bureau de poste près d'ici?; **is Phil around?** est-ce que Phil est là?; 5 (*wrapped around*) autour de; **she had a scarf around her neck** elle avait une écharpe autour du cou.

arrange *verb* **to arrange to do** prévoir [65] de faire; **we've arranged to see a film on Saturday** nous avons prévu de voir un film samedi.

arrest *noun* **to be under arrest** être en état d'arrestation.
verb arrêter [1].

arrival *noun* arrivée F.

arrive *verb* arriver [1]; **they arrived at 3 p.m.** ils sont arrivés à quinze heures.

arrow *noun* flèche F.

art *noun* 1 art M; **modern art** l'art moderne; 2 (*school subject*) dessin M; **the art class** le cours de dessin.

artery *noun* artère F.

art gallery *noun* (*public*) musée M des beaux arts.

article *noun* article M.

artichoke *noun* artichaut M.

artificial *adjective* artificiel (F artificielle).

artist *noun* artiste M & F; **he's an artist** c'est un artiste.

artistic *adjective* artistique.

art school *noun* école F de beaux arts.

as *conjunction, adverb* 1 comme; **as you know** comme vous le savez; **as usual** comme d'habitude; **as I told you** comme je t'avais dit; 2 (*because*) puisque; **as there were no trains, we took the bus** puisqu'il n'y avait pas de trains, nous avons pris le bus; 3 **as...as** aussi...que; **he's as tall as his brother** il est aussi grand que son frère; **you must be as tired as I am** tu dois être aussi fatigué que moi; 4 **as much...as** autant de...que; **you have as much time as I do** tu as autant de temps que moi; 5 **as many...as** autant de...que; **we have as many problems as he does** nous avons autant de problèmes que lui; 6 **as long as** pourvu que (*with subjunctive*); **we'll go tomorrow, as long as it's a nice day** on va y aller demain, pourvu qu'il fasse beau; 7 **for as long as** aussi longtemps que; **you can stay for as long as you like** tu peux rester aussi longtemps que tu veux; 8 **as soon as possible** dès que possible; 9 **to work as** travailler comme; **he works as a taxi driver in the evenings** il travaille comme chauffeur de taxi le soir.

asbestos *noun* amiante F.

ash *noun* cendre F.

ashamed *adjective* **to be ashamed**

avoir honte; **you should be ashamed of yourself!** tu devrais avoir honte!

ashtray noun cendrier M.

Asia noun Asie F; **in Asia** en Asie.

Asian noun Asiatique M & F. adjective asiatique.

ask verb **1** demander [1]; **you can ask at reception** tu peux demander à l'accueil; **to ask somebody something** demander quelque chose à quelqu'un; **I asked him where he lives** je lui ai demandé où il habite; **to ask for something** demander quelque chose; **I asked for three coffees** j'ai demandé trois cafés; **to ask somebody to do** demander à quelqu'un de faire; **ask Danny to give you a hand** demande à Danny de te donner un coup de main; **2 to ask somebody a question** poser [1] une question à quelqu'un; **I asked you a question!** je t'ai posé une question!; **3** inviter [1]; **they've asked us to a party at their house** ils nous ont invité à une soirée chez eux; **4 Paul's asked Janie out on Friday** Paul a invité Janie à sortir avec lui vendredi.

asleep adjective **to be asleep** dormir [37]; **the baby's asleep** le bébé dort; **to fall asleep** s'endormir [37].

asparagus noun asperges F plural.

aspirin noun aspirine F.

assembly noun (at school) rassemblement M.

assess verb évaluer [1].

assignment noun (at school) devoir M.

assist verb aider [1].

assistance noun aide F.

assistant noun **1** assistant M, assistante F; **2 a shop assistant** un vendeur, une vendeuse.

association noun association F.

assorted adjective variés (F variées).

assortment noun mélange M.

assume verb supposer [1].

assure verb assurer [1].

asthma noun asthme M; **she has asthma** elle souffre de l'asthme.

astrology noun astrologie F.

astronaut noun astronaute M & F.

astronomy noun astronomie F.

at preposition **1** à (note that 'à + le' always becomes 'au' and 'à + les' always becomes 'aux') **at home** à la maison; **at school** à l'école; **at my office** à mon bureau; **at the market** au marché; **at meetings** aux réunions; **2** (talking about the time) à; **at eight o'clock** à huit heures; **3 at night** la nuit; **at the weekend** le weekend; **4 at Emma's house** chez Emma; **she's at her brother's this evening** elle est chez son frère ce soir; **at the hairdresser's** chez le coiffeur; **5 at last** enfin; **he's found a job at last** il a enfin trouvé un emploi.

athlete noun athlète M & F.

athletic adjective athlétique.

athletics noun athlétisme M.

Atlantic *noun* Atlantique M.

atlas *noun* atlas M.

atmosphere *noun* atmosphère F.

atom *noun* atome M.

atomic *adjective* atomique.

attach *verb* attacher [1].

attached *adjective* **to be attached to** être [6] attaché à.

attack *noun* attaque F.
verb attaquer [1].

attempt *noun* tentative F; **at the first attempt** à la première tentative.
verb **to attempt to do** essayer [59] de faire.

attend *verb* assister à [1]; **to attend a class** assister à un cours.

attention *noun* attention F; **to pay attention to** faire attention à; **I wasn't paying atttention** je ne faisais pas attention.

attic *noun* grenier M; **in the attic** au grenier.

attitude *noun* attitude F.

attract *verb* attirer [1].

attraction *noun* attraction F.

attractive *adjective* séduisant.

aubergine *noun* aubergine F.

auction *noun* vente F aux enchères.

audience *noun* public M.

August *noun* août M; **in August** en août.

aunt, auntie *noun* tante F.

au pair *noun* jeune fille F au pair; **I'm looking for a job as an au pair** je cherche un emploi de jeune fille au pair.

Australia *noun* Australie F; **in Australia** en Australie; **to Australia** en Australie.

Australian *noun* Australien M, Australienne F.
adjective australien (F australienne).

Austria *noun* Autriche F; **in Austria** en Autriche; **to Austria** en Autriche.

Austrian *noun* Autrichien M, Autrichienne F.
adjective autrichien (F autrichienne).

author *noun* auteur M.

autobiography *noun* autobiographie F.

autograph *noun* autographe M.

automatic *adjective* automatique.

automatically *adverb* automatiquement.

autumn *noun* automne M; **in autumn** en automne.

availability *noun* disponibilité F.

available *adjective* disponible.

avenue *noun* avenue F.

average *noun* moyenne F; **on average** en moyenne; **above average** au-dessus de la moyenne.
adjective moyen (F moyenne); **the average height** la hauteur moyenne.

avocado *noun* avocat M.

avoid *verb* éviter [1]; **she avoided me** elle m'a évité; **to avoid doing**

éviter de faire; **I avoid speaking to him** j'évite de lui parler.

awake *adjective* **to be awake** être réveillé; **is Lola awake?** est-ce que Lola est réveillée?; **are you still awake?** tu ne dors pas?

award *noun* prix M; **to win an award** remporter un prix.

aware *adjective* **to be aware of a noise** être conscient d'un bruit; **to be aware of a problem** être au courant d'un problème; **as far as I'm aware** à ma connaissance.

away *adverb* **1 to be away** être absent; **I'll be away next week** je serai absent la semaine prochaine; **2 to go away** partir; **Laura's gone away for a week** Laura est partie pour une semaine; **go away!** va-t-en!; **3 to run away** partir en courant; **the thieves ran away** les voleurs sont partis en courant; **4 the school is two kilometres away** l'école est à deux kilomètres; **how far away is it?** c'est à quelle distance d'ici?; **not far away** pas loin d'ici; **5 to put something away** ranger quelque chose; **I'll just put my books away** je vais juste ranger mes livres; **6 to give something away** donner quelque chose; **she's given away all her tapes** elle a donné toutes ses cassettes.

away match *noun* match M à l'extérieur.

awful *adjective* **1** affreux (F affreuse); **the film was awful!** le film était affreux!; **2 I feel awful** (*ill*) je ne me sens pas bien du tout; **3 I feel awful about it** ça m'ennuie

vraiment; **4 an awful lot of** énormément de.

awkward *adjective* **1** difficile; **it's an awkward situation** c'est une situation difficile; **it's a bit awkward** c'est un peu difficile; **an awkward child** un enfant difficile; **2 an awkward question** une question gênante.

axe *noun* hache F.

B b

baby *noun* bébé M.

babysit *verb* faire [10] du babysitting.

babysitter *noun* babysitter M & F.

babysitting *noun* babysitting M.

back *noun* **1** (*of a person or animal*) dos M; **to do something behind someone's back** faire quelque chose dans le dos de quelqu'un; **2** (*of a piece of paper, your hand, or a garment*) dos M; **on the back** au dos; **3** (*of a car, a plane, or a building*) arrière M; **we have seats at the back** nous avons des places à l'arrière; **a garden at the back of the house** un jardin à l'arrière de la maison; **4 the children at the back of the room** les enfants au fond de la salle; **5** (*of a chair or sofa*) dossier M; **6** (*in football or hockey*) arrière M; **left back** arrière gauche. *adjective* **1** arrière (*a wheel or seat*); **the back seat of the car** le siège arrière de la voiture; **2 the back gate** la porte de derrière; **the back**

garden le jardin de derrière.
adverb **1 to go back** rentrer; **to go back to school** rentrer à l'école; **Lisa's gone back to London** Lisa est rentrée à Londres; **2 to come back** rentrer; **they've come back from Italy** ils sont rentrés d'Italie; **she's back at work** elle a repris le travail; **Sue's not back yet** Sue n'est pas encore rentrée; **we went by bus and walked back** nous avons pris le bus pour y aller et nous sommes rentrés à pied; **3 to phone back** rappeler; **I'll ring back later** je rappellerai plus tard; **4 to give something back to somebody** rendre quelque chose à quelqu'un; **I gave him back his cassettes** je lui ai rendu ses cassettes; **give it back!** rends-le-moi!
verb **1** (*to support*) soutenir [81] (*a candidate, for example*); **2** (*to bet on*) parier [1] sur (*a horse*).
● **to back up** (*computing*) **to back up a file** sauvegarder [1] un fichier sur disquette.
● **to back somebody up** soutenir [77] quelqu'un.

backache *noun* mal M de dos.

backbone *noun* colonne F vertébrale.

back door *noun* **1** (*of a building*) porte F de derrière; **2** (*of a car*) porte F arrière.

backfire *verb* (*turn out badly*) échouer [1].

background *noun* **1** (*of a person*)(*social*) milieu M; **2** (*of events or a situation*) contexte M; **3** (*in a picture or view*) arrière-plan M; **the trees in the background** les

arbres à l'arrière-plan;
4 background music la musique d'ambiance; **5 background noise** les bruits M *plural* de fond.

backhand *noun* revers M.

backing *noun* **1** (*on sticky-back plastic, for example*) revêtement M intérieur. **2** (*moral support*) soutien M; **3** (*in music*) **a backing group** un groupe d'accompagnement.

backpack *noun* sac M à dos.
verb **to go backpacking** partir [58] en voyage avec son sac à dos.

back seat *noun* siège M arrière.

backside *noun* derrière M.

backstage *adverb* **to go backstage** aller dans les coulisses.

backstroke *noun* dos M crawlé.

back to front *adverb* à l'envers; **your jumper's back to front** ton pull est à l'envers.

backup *noun* **1** (*support*) soutien M; **2** (*in computing*) **a backup disk** un disque de sauvegarde.

backwards *adverb* (*to lean or fall*) en arrière.

bacon *noun* **1** (*French streaky bacon*) lard M; **2** (*thin-sliced British type*) bacon M; **bacon and eggs** œufs au bacon.

bad *adjective* **1** (*not good*) mauvais (*goes before the noun*); **bad work** du mauvais travail; **a bad meal** un mauvais repas; **his new film's not bad** son nouveau film n'est pas mauvais; **it's bad for your health** c'est mauvais pour la santé; **I'm bad at physics** je suis mauvais en

physique; **2** (*serious*) grave; **a bad accident** un accident grave; **a bad cold** un gros rhume; **3** (*rotten*) pourri; **a bad apple** une pomme pourrie; **to go bad** se gâter.
4 (*rude*) **bad language** du langage grossier; **5** (*naughty*) vilain; **bad dog!** vilain!; **bad girl!** vilaine!;
★ **too bad!** (*I'm sorry for you*) pas de chance!; (*I don't care*) tant pis!

badge *noun* badge M.

badly *adverb* **1** mal; **he writes badly** il écrit mal; **I slept badly** j'ai mal dormi; **the exam went badly** l'examen s'est mal passé;
2 (*seriously*) (*to hurt or damage*) gravement; **la voiture a été gravement endommagée** the car was badly damaged; **badly hurt** grièvement blessé.

bad-mannered *adjective* mal élevé.

badminton *noun* badminton M; **to play badminton** jouer au badminton.

bad-tempered *adjective* **1** (*for a little while*) irrité; **2** (*always*) **she's very bad-tempered** elle a très mauvais caractère.

bag *noun* sac M.

baggage *noun* bagages M *plural*.

baggage allowance *noun* franchise F de baggages.

baggage reclaim *noun* réception F des bagages.

bagpipes *plural noun* cornemuse F; **to play the bagpipes** jouer de la cornemuse.

bags *plural noun* bagages M *plural*;

to pack your bags faire ses bagages; ★ **to have bags under your eyes** avoir des valises sous les yeux (*informal*).

bake *verb* **to bake a cake** faire [10] un gâteau; **to bake vegetables** faire [10] cuire des légumes au four.

baked *adjective* **1** (*fish or fruit*) au four; **baked apples** les pommes au four; **2 a baked potato** une pomme de terre au four.

baked beans *plural noun* les haricots blancs à la sauce tomate.

baker *noun* boulanger M, boulangère F; **to go to the baker's** aller à la boulangerie.

bakery *noun* boulangerie F.

balance *noun* **1** équilibre M; **to lose your balance** perdre l'équilibre; **2** (*money in your bank account*) solde M.

balanced *adjective* équilibré.

balcony *noun* balcon M.

bald *adjective* chauve.

ball *noun* **1** (*for tennis or golf*) balle F; **2** (*for football or volleyball*) ballon M; **3** (*of string or wool*) pelote F.

ballet *noun* ballet M.

ballet dancer *noun* danseur M de ballet, danseuse de ballet.

ballet shoe *noun* chausson M de danse.

balloon *noun* **1** ballon M; **2** (*hot air*) montgolfière F.

ballot *noun* scrutin M.

ballpoint (pen) *noun* stylo M à bille.

ban *noun* interdiction F; **a ban on smoking** une interdiction de fumer. *verb* interdire [47].

banana *noun* banane F; **a banana yoghurt** un yaourt à la banane.

band *noun* 1 (*playing music*) groupe M; **a rock band** un groupe de rock; 2 **a jazz band** un orchestre de jazz; 3 **a brass band** une fanfare; 4 **a rubber band** un élastique.

bandage *noun* bandage M. *verb* mettre [11] un bandage à.

bang *noun* 1 (*noise*) boum M; 2 (*of a door or window*) claquement M. *verb* 1 (*to hit*) taper [1] sur (*a drum, for example*); **he banged his fist on the table** il a tapé du poing sur la table; 2 (*to knock*) cogner [1]; **to bang on the door** cogner à la porte; **I banged my head on the door** je me suis cogné la tête contre la porte; **I banged into the table** j'ai heurté la table; 3 **to bang the door** claquer [1] la porte. *exclamation* (*like a gun*) pan!

banister(s), bannister(s) (*plural*) *noun* rampe F (d'escalier).

bank *noun* 1 (*for money*) banque F; **I'm going to the bank** je vais à la banque; 2 (*of a river or lake*) bord M.

bank account *noun* compte M bancaire.

bank balance *noun* solde M bancaire.

bank card *noun* carte F bancaire.

bank holiday *noun* jour M férié.

banknote *noun* billet M de banque.

bank statement *noun* relevé M de compte.

bar *noun* 1 (*selling drinks*) bar M; **Janet works in a bar** Janet travaille dans un bar; 2 (*the counter*) comptoir M; **on the bar** sur le bar; 3 **a bar of chocolate** une tablette de chocolat; 4 **a bar of soap** une savonnette; 5 (*made of wood or metal*) barre F; **a metal bar** une barre en métal; 6 (*in music*) mesure F. *verb* 1 (*to block physically*) barrer [1]; **to bar someone's way** barrer le passage à quelqu'un; 2 (*to ban from an activity*) exclure [25].

barbecue *noun* barbecue M; **there's a barbecue tonight** il y a un barbecue ce soir. *verb* **to barbecue a chicken** faire [10] griller un poulet au barbecue; **barbecued chicken** du poulet grillé au barbecue.

barbed wire *noun* barbelé M.

bare *adjective* nu.

barefoot *adjective* **to be barefoot** être nu-pieds; **to walk barefoot** marcher pieds nus.

bargain *noun* (*a good buy*) affaire F; **I got a bargain** j'ai fait une affaire; **it's a bargain!** c'est une bonne affaire!

barge *noun* péniche F.

bark *noun* 1 (*of a tree*) écorce F; 2 (*of a dog*) aboiement M. *verb* aboyer [39].

barmaid noun barmaid F.

barman noun barman M.

barn noun grange F.

barrel noun tonneau M (plural tonneaux).

barrier noun barrière F.

base noun base F.

baseball noun base-ball M; **a baseball cap** une casquette de base-ball.

based adjective **1 to be based on** être fondé sur; **the film is based on a true story** le film est fondé sur une histoire vraie; **2 to be based in** être basé à; **he's based in Bristol** il est basé à Bristol.

basement noun sous-sol M; **in the basement** au sous-sol.

bash noun **1** bosse F; **it's got a bash on the wing** il y a une bosse à l'aile; **2 I'll have a bash** je vais essayer un coup.
verb cogner [1]; **I bashed my head** je me suis cogné la tête.

basic adjective **1** de base; **basic knowledge** des connaissances de base; **her basic salary** son salaire de base; **2 the basic facts** les faits essentiels; **3** (not luxurious) rudimentaire; **the flat's a bit basic** l'appartement est un peu rudimentaire.

basically adverb **1** au fond; **it's basically all right** au fond ça va; **2** à vrai dire; **basically, I don't really want to go** à vrai dire, je ne veux pas vraiment y aller.

basics noun rudiments M plural.

basin noun (washbasin) lavabo M.

basis noun **1** base F; **2 on the basis of** sur la base de; **on a regular basis** régulièrement.

basket noun **1** (for shopping) panier M; **2** (other) corbeille F; **a waste-paper basket** une corbeille à papier; **a linen basket** une corbeille à linge.

basketball noun basketball M; **to play basketball** jouer au basketball.

bass noun **1** basse F; **to play bass** jouer de la basse; **2 a double bass** une contrebasse.

bass drum noun grosse caisse F.

bass guitar noun guitare F basse.

bassoon noun basson M; **to play the bassoon** jouer du basson.

bat noun **1** (for cricket or baseball) batte F; **2** (for table tennis) raquette F; **3** (animal) chauve-souris F.

bath noun **1** bain M; **to have a bath** prendre un bain; **I was in the bath** j'étais dans mon bain; **2** (bathtub) baignoire F; **the bath's pink** la baignoire est rose.

bathe verb **1** laver [1] (a wound); **2** (go swimming) se baigner [1].

bathroom noun salle F de bains (plural salles de bains).

baths plural noun piscine F.

bath towel noun serviette F de bain.

batter noun (for frying) pâte F à frire; **fish in batter** des beignets de poisson; **pancake batter** la pâte à crèpes.

battery noun 1 (*for a torch or radio for example*) pile F; 2 (*for a car*) batterie F.

battle noun bataillle F.

bay noun baie F.

B.C. (*short for: before Christ*) av. J.-C.

be verb 1 être [6]; **Melanie is in the kitchen** Melanie est dans la cuisine; **where is the butter?** où est le beurre?; **I'm tired** je suis fatigué; **when we were in France** quand nous étions en France; 2 (*with jobs and professions*) être; **she's a teacher** elle est professeur (*note that 'a' is not translated*); **he's a taxi driver** il est chauffeur de taxi; 3 (*in clock times*) être; **it's three o'clock** il est trois heures; **it's half past five** il est cinq heures et demie; 4 (*days of the week and dates*) **what day is it today?** nous sommes quel jour aujourd'hui?; **it's Tuesday today** nous sommes mardi aujourd'hui; **it's the twentieth of May** nous sommes le vingt mai; 5 (*talking about age*) avoir [5]; **how old are you?** quel âge as-tu?; **I'm fifteen** j'ai quinze ans; **Harry's twenty** Harry a vingt ans; 6 (*cold, hot, hungry*) avoir [5]; **I'm hot** j'ai chaud; **I'm cold** j'ai froid; **I'm hungry** j'ai faim; 7 (*weather*) faire [10]; **it's cold today** il fait froid aujourd'hui; **it's a nice day** il fait beau; 8 **I've never been to Paris** je ne suis jamais allé à Paris; **have you been to Britain before?** est-ce que tu es déjà venu en Grande Bretagne?; 9 **to be loved** être aimé; **he has been killed** il a été tué.

beach noun plage F; **to go to the beach** aller à la plage; **on the beach** sur la plage.

bead noun perle F.

beak noun bec M.

beam noun 1 (*of light*) rayon M; 2 (*for a roof*) poutre F.

bean noun haricot M; **baked beans** les haricots à la sauce tomate; **green beans** les haricots verts.

bear noun ours M.
verb 1 supporter [1]; **I can't bear him** je ne peux pas le supporter; **I can't bear the idea** je ne supporte pas l'idée; 2 **to bear something in mind** tenir [77] compte de quelque chose; **I'll bear it in mind** je ne l'oublierai pas.
●**to bear up** tenir [77] le coup.

beard noun barbe F.

bearded adjective barbu.

bearings plural noun **to get one's bearings** se repérer [24].

beast noun 1 (*animal*) bête F; 2 **you beast!** chameau!

beat noun rythme M.
verb 1 (*defeat*) battre [21]; **we beat them!** on les a battus!; 2 **to beat the eggs** battre les œufs; 3 **you can't beat a good meal** rien ne vaut un bon repas.
●**to beat somebody up** tabasser [1] quelqu'un (*informal*).

beautiful adjective beau (F belle) (M plural beaux) (*goes before the noun*); **a beautiful day** un beau jour; **a beautiful girl** une belle fille; **beautiful pictures** de beaux tableaux; **a beautiful place** un bel endroit (*'bel' for masculine nouns beginning with a vowel or silent 'h'*).

beautifully *adverb* admirablement.

beauty *noun* beauté F.

beauty spot *noun* (*for tourists*) beau site M.

because *conjunction* 1 parce que; **because it's you** parce que c'est toi; **because it's cold** parce qu'il fait froid; 2 **because of** à cause de; **because of the accident** à cause de l'accident.

become *verb* devenir [81].

bed *noun* 1 lit M; **a double bed** un grand lit; **in bed** au lit; **to go to bed** aller se coucher; 2 (*flower bed*) parterre M.

bedclothes *plural noun* couvertures F *plural*.

bedding *noun* literie F.

bedroom *noun* chambre F; **bedroom furniture** les meubles de chambre; **my bedroom window** la fenêtre de ma chambre.

bedside *noun* **a bedside table** une table de chevet.

bedsit, bedsitter *noun* chambre F meublée.

bedspread *noun* dessus-de-lit M.

bedtime *noun* **it's bedtime** c'est l'heure d'aller se coucher.

bee *noun* abeille F.

beech *noun* hêtre M.

beef *noun* bœuf M; **we had roast beef** on a mangé du rôti de bœuf.

beefburger *noun* hamburger M.

beer *noun* bière F; **two beers please** deux bières s'il vous plaît; **a beer can** une canette de bière.

beetle *noun* scarabée M.

beetroot *noun* betterave F.

before *preposition, adverb* 1 avant; **before Monday** avant lundi; **he left before me** il est parti avant moi; 2 **the day before** la veille; **the day before the wedding** la veille du mariage; **the day before yesterday** avant-hier; **the week before** la semaine d'avant; 3 (*already*) déjà; **I've seen him before somewhere** je l'ai déjà vu quelque part; **I had seen the film before** j'avais déjà vu le film. *conjunction* 1 avant de; **before doing** avant de faire; **I closed the windows before leaving** (or **before I left**) j'ai fermé les fenêtres avant de partir; 2 avant que; **phone me before they leave** appelle-moi avant qu'ils s'en aillent; **oh, before I forget …** avant que j'oublie …

beforehand *adverb* (*ahead of time*) à l'avance; **phone beforehand** appelle à l'avance.

beg *verb* 1 (*ask for money*) mendier [1]; 2 (*ask*) supplier [1]; **she begged me not to leave** elle m'a supplié de ne pas partir; **I beg your pardon** je vous demande pardon.

begin *verb* 1 commencer [61]; **the meeting begins at ten** la réunion commence à dix heures; **the words beginning with P** les mots qui commencent par un P; 2 **to begin to do** commencer à faire; **I'm beginning to understand** je commence à comprendre.

beginner noun débutant M, débutante F.

beginning noun début M; **at the beginning** au début; **at the beginning of the holidays** au début des vacances.

behalf noun **on behalf of** pour.

behave verb 1 se comporter [1]; **he behaved badly** il s'est mal comporté; 2 **to behave yourself** être sage; **behave yourselves!** soyez sages!

behaviour noun comportement M.

behind noun derrière M. preposition, adverb 1 derrière; **behind the sofa** derrière le canapé; **behind them** derrière eux; **the car behind** la voiture de derrière; 2 (not making progress) **he's behind in class** il a du retard en classe; 3 **to leave something behind** oublier quelque chose; **I've left my keys behind** j'ai oublié mes clés.

beige adjective beige.

Belgian noun Belge M & F. adjective belge.

Belgium noun Belgique F; **to Belgium** en Belgique; **in Belgium** en Belgique.

belief noun conviction F; **his political beliefs** ses convictions politiques.

believe verb 1 croire [33]; **I believe you** je te crois; **they believed what I said** ils ont cru ce que j'ai dit; **I don't believe you!** ce n'est pas vrai!; 2 **to believe in** croire à; **to believe in**

ghosts croire aux fantômes; **to believe in God** croire en Dieu.

bell noun 1 (in a church) cloche F; 2 (on a door) sonnette F; **ring the bell!** appuyez sur la sonnette!; 3 (for a cat or toy) grelot M; ★ **tha name rings a bell** ce nom me dit quelque chose (literally: says something to me).

belong verb 1 **to belong to** appartenir [81] à; **that belongs to Richard** cela appartient à Richard; 2 **to belong to a club** faire [10] partie d'un club; 3 (go) aller [5]; **tha chair belongs in the study** cette chaise va dans le bureau; **where doe this vase belong?** ce vase va où?

belongings plural noun affaires F plural; **all my belongings are in London** toutes mes affaires sont à Londres.

below preposition au-dessous de; **below the window** au-dessous de l fenêtre; **the flat below yours** l'appartement au-dessous du tien. adverb 1 (further down) en bas; **shouts came from below** des cris venaient d'en bas; 2 **the flat below** l'appartement de dessous.

belt noun ceinture F.

bench noun banc M.

bend noun 1 (in a road) virage M; 2 (in a river) courbe F. verb 1 (to make a bend in) plier [1] (your arm or leg, or a wire); 2 (to curve) (a road or path) tourner [1]; 3 **to bend down** or **forwards** se pencher [1]; **she bent down to look** elle s'est penchée pour regarder.

beneath preposition sous.

enefit *noun* **1** avantage M;
2 unemployment benefit les
allocations F *plural* de chômage.

ent *adjective* tordu.

eret *noun* béret M.

erth *noun* couchette F.

eside *preposition* (*next to*) à côté
de; **she was sitting beside me** elle
était assise à côté de moi; ★ **that's
beside the point** ça n'a rien à voir.

esides *adverb* **1** (*anyway*)
d'ailleurs; **besides, it's too late**
d'ailleurs, il est trop tard; **2** (*as well*)
en plus; **four dogs, and six cats
besides** quatre chiens et six chats en
plus.

est *adjective* **1** meilleur; **it's the
best** c'est le meilleur; **that's the
best car** cette voiture-là est la
meilleure; **she's my best friend**
c'est ma meilleure amie; **2 she's the
best at tennis** c'est elle la meilleure
en tennis; **the best thing to do is to
phone them** la meilleure chose à
faire, c'est de les appeler.
adverb le mieux; **he plays best** il
joue le mieux; **I like Paris best** c'est
Paris que j'aime le mieux; **best of all**
mieux que tout; ★ **all the best!**
(*good luck*) bonne chance!; (*cheers*)
à ta santé!; ★ **it's the best I can do**
je ne peux pas faire mieux; ★ **to do
your best to do** faire de son mieux
pour faire; **I did my best to help her**
j'ai fait de mon mieux pour l'aider.

est man *noun* garçon d'honneur
M.

et *noun* pari M.
verb parier [1]; **to bet on a horse**

parier sur un cheval; **I bet you he'll
forget!** je te parie qu'il va oublier!

better *adjective* **1** meilleur; **she's
found a better flat** elle a trouvé un
meilleur appartement; **this road's
better than the other one** cette
route est meilleure que l'autre;
2 mieux; **this pen writes better** ce
stylo écrit mieux; **it works better
than the other one** ça fonctionne
mieux que l'autre; **3 even better**
encore mieux; **it's even better than
before** c'est encore mieux
qu'avant; **4** (*less ill*) **to be better**
aller mieux; **he's a bit better today**
il va un peu mieux aujourd'hui; **to
feel better** se sentir mieux; **I feel
better** je me sens mieux; **5 to get
better** s'améliorer; **my French is
getting better** mon français
s'améliore; **6 so much the better**
tant mieux; **the sooner the better**
le plus vite possible.
adverb **you had better phone at
once** tu ferais mieux d'appeler tout
de suite; **he'd better not go** il ferait
mieux de ne pas y aller; **I'd better go
now** je dois partir maintenant.

better off *adjective* **1** (*richer*) plus
riche; **they're better off than us** ils
sont plus riches que nous; **2** (*more
comfortable*) mieux; **you'd be better
off in bed** tu serais mieux au lit.

between *preposition* entre;
between London and Dover entre
Londres et Douvres; **between
Monday and Friday** entre lundi et
vendredi; **between the two** entre les
deux.

beyond *preposition* **1** (*in space and
time*) au-delà de; **beyond the**

border au-delà de la frontière;
2 it's beyond me! ça me dépasse!

Bible *noun* **the Bible** la Bible.

bicycle *noun* vélo M; **by bicycle** à vélo.

bicycle lane *noun* piste F cyclable.

big *adjective* **1** grand (*goes before the noun*); **a big house** une grande maison; **a big city** une grande ville; **my big sister** ma grande sœur; **it's too big for me** c'est trop grand pour moi; **2** gros (F grosse) (*before the noun*); **a big dog** un gros chien; **a big car** une grosse voiture; **a big mistake** une grosse erreur.

bigheaded *adjective* **to be bigheaded** avoir la grosse tête.

big screen *noun* grand écran M.

big toe *noun* gros orteil M.

bike *noun* vélo M; **by bike** à vélo.

bikini *noun* bikini M.

bilingual *adjective* bilingue.

bill *noun* **1** (*in a restaurant*) addition F; **can we have the bill, please** l'addition, s'il vous plaît; **2** (*for gas, electricity, etc*) facture F.

billiards *noun* billard M; **to play billiards** jouer au billard.

billion *noun* milliard M.

bin *noun* poubelle F.

binoculars *noun* jumelles F *plural*.

biochemistry *noun* biochimie F.

biography *noun* biographie F.

biology *noun* biologie F.

bird *noun* oiseau M (*plural* oiseaux).

bird sanctuary *noun* réserve F ornithologique.

birdwatching *noun* **to go birdwatching** observer les oiseaux.

Biro™ *noun* bic™ M.

birth *noun* naissance F.

birth certificate *noun* acte M de naissance.

birthday *noun* **1** anniversaire M; **happy birthday!** joyeux anniversaire!; **2 a birthday present** un cadeau d'anniversaire.

birthday party *noun* **1** (*for a child*) goûter M d'anniversaire; **2** (*for an adult*) soirée F d'anniversaire.

biscuit *noun* biscuit M.

bishop *noun* évêque M.

bit *noun* **1** (*of bread, cheese, wood*) morceau M; **a bit of chocolate** un morceau de chocolat; **2** (*of string, paper, garden*) bout M; **a bit of string** un bout de ficelle; **with a little bit of garden** avec un petit bout de jardin; **3** (*a small amount*) **a bit of** un peu de; **a bit of sugar** un peu de sucre; **with a bit of luck** avec un peu de chance; **wait a bit!** attends un peu!; **a bit of news** une nouvelle; **to have a bit of trouble with** avoir un petit problème avec; **4** (*in a book or film, for example*) passage M; **this bit is brilliant!** ce passage est génial!; **5 to fall to bits** tomber en morceaux; **6 a bit** un peu; **a bit hot** un peu chaud; **a bit early** un peu

trop tôt; **7** (*for a horse*) mors M;
★ **bit by bit** petit à petit.

ite *noun* **1** (*snack*) morceau M; **I'll
just have a bite before I go** je vais
juste manger un morceau avant de
partir; **2** (*from an insect*) piqûre F;
a mosquito bite une piqûre de
moustique; **3** (*from a dog*) morsure
F.
verb **1** (*a person or a dog*) mordre
[3]; **2** (*an insect*) piquer [1]; ★ **to
bite one's nails** se ronger [52] les
ongles.

itter *adjective* (*taste*) amer (F
amère).

lack *adjective* **1** noir; **my black
jacket** ma veste noire; **to turn
black** noircir [2]; **2 a Black man** un
Noir; **a Black woman** une Noire;
3 a black coffee un café noir.

lackberry *noun* mûre F.

lackbird *noun* merle M.

lackboard *noun* tableau M noir.

lackcurrant *noun* cassis M.

lack eye *noun* œil M au beurre
noir.

lade *noun* lame F.

lame *noun* responsabilité F; **to
take the blame for something**
prendre la responsabilité de quelque
chose.
verb **to blame someone for
something** tenir [77] quelqu'un
responsable de quelque chose; **they
blamed him for the accident** ils l'ont
tenu reponsable de l'accident; **she is
to blame for it** elle en est
responsable; **I blame the parents!** à
mon avis c'est la faute des parents!;

I don't blame you! je te comprends!

blank *noun* blanc M.
adjective **1** (*a page or piece of paper,
or a cheque*) blanc (F blanche); (*a
tape or disk*) vierge; (*a screen*) vide;
2 my mind went blank j'ai eu un
trou de mémoire.

blanket *noun* couverture F.

blast *noun* **1** (*an explosion*)
explosion F; **2** (*of air*) souffle M;
3 to play music at full blast jouer
de la musique à plein volume.

blaze *noun* incendie M.
verb brûler [1].

blazer *noun* blazer M.

bleach *noun* eau F de javel.

bleed *verb* saigner [1]; **my nose is
bleeding** je saigne du nez.

blend *noun* mélange M.

blender *noun* mixer M.

bless *verb* bénir [2]; **bless you!**
(*after a sneeze*) à tes souhaits!

blind *noun* (*in a window*) store M.
adjective aveugle; **to go blind**
perdre la vue.

blink *verb* (*your eyes*) cligner [1] des
yeux.

blister *noun* ampoule F.

blizzard *noun* tempête F de neige.

blob *noun* goutte F.

block *noun* **1 a block of flats** un
immeuble; **an office block** un
immeuble de bureaux; **2** (*a square
group of buildings*) **to go round the
block** faire le tour du pâté de
maisons.
verb **1** bloquer [1] (*an exit or a*

road); **2** boucher [1] (*a drain or a hole*); **the sink's blocked** l'évier est bouché.

blonde *adjective* blond.

blood *noun* sang M.

blood test *noun* prise F de sang.

blotchy *adjective* (*skin*) marbré.

blouse *noun* chemisier M.

blow *noun* coup M.
verb **1** (*the wind or a person*) souffler [1]; **2** (*in an explosion*) **the bomb blew a hole in the wall** la bombe a fait un trou dans le mur; **3 to blow your nose** se moucher [1].
● **to blow something out** souffler [1] (*a candle*); éteindre [60] (*flames*).
● **to blow up** (*explode*) exploser [1].
● **to blow something up** gonfler [1] (*a balloon or tyre*); faire [10] sauter (*a building*); **they blew up the president's residence** ils ont fait sauter la résidence du président.

blow-dry *noun* brushing M; **a cut and blow-dry** une coupe brushing.

blue *adjective* bleu; **blue eyes** les yeux bleus.

bluebell *noun* jacinthe F des bois.

blues *plural noun* le blues M singular.

blunder *noun* gaffe F.

blunt *adjective* **1** (*a knife or scissors*) émoussé; **2** (*a pencil*) mal taillé; **3** (*person*) brusque.

blurred *adjective* **1** indistinct; **2** (*photo*) flou.

blush *verb* rougir [2].

board *noun* **1** (*plank*) planche F; **2** (*blackboard*) tableau M noir; **3** (*notice board*) panneau M d'affichage; **4** (*for a board game*) je M; **5 a chess board** un échiquier M; **6** (*accommodation in a hotel*) **full board** pension F complète; **half board** demi-pension F; **7 on board** à bord; **they were o board the ferry** ils étaient à bord d ferry.

boarder *noun* (*in a school*) interne M & F.

board game *noun* jeu M de sociét (*plural* jeux de société).

boarding *noun* embarquement M.

boarding card *noun* carte F d'embarquement.

boarding school *noun* école F privée avec internat.

boast *verb* se vanter [1]; **he was boasting about his new bike** il se vantait de son nouveau vélo.

boat *noun* **1** (*in general*) bateau M; **2** (*sailing boat*) voilier M; **3** (*rowing boat*) barque F.

body *noun* **1** corps M; **2** (*corpse*) cadavre M.

bodybuilding *noun* culturisme M

bodyguard *noun* garde M du corp

boil *noun* **1 bring the water to the boil** portez l'eau à ébullition; **2** (*swelling*) furoncle M.
verb **1** bouillir [23]; **the water's boiling** l'eau bout; **2** faire [10] bouillir; **I'm going to boil some water** je vais faire bouillir de l'eau; **to boil vegetables** faire [10] cuire

des légumes à l'eau bouillante; **to boil an egg** faire cuire un œuf.
to boil over déborder [1].

oiled egg *noun* œuf M à la coque.

oiler *noun* (*for central heating*) chaudière F.

oiling *adjective* 1 (*water*) bouillant; 2 **it's boiling hot today!** il fait une chaleur infernale aujourd'hui!

olt *noun* (*on a door*) verrou M. *verb* (*to lock*) verrouiller [1] (*a door*).

omb *noun* bombe F. *verb* bombarder [1].

ombing *noun* 1 (*in a war*) bombardement M; 2 (*a terrorist attack*) attentat M à la bombe.

one *noun* 1 os M; 2 (*of a fish*) arête F.

onfire *noun* 1 (*for rubbish*) feu M de jardin; 2 (*for a celebration*) feu M de joie.

onnet *noun* capot M (*of a car*).

ook *noun* 1 (*that you read*) livre M; **a book about dinosaurs** un livre sur les dinosaures; **a biology book** un livre de biologie; 2 **an exercise book** un cahier; 3 (*of cheques, stamps, tickets, etc*) carnet M; **a cheque book** un carnet de chèques.
verb réserver [1]; **I booked a table for 8 p.m.** j'ai réservé une table pour vingt heures.

ookcase *noun* bibliothèque F.

ooking *noun* (*for a theatre or a holiday, for example*) réservation F.

booking office *noun* bureau M de location.

booklet *noun* brochure F.

bookshelf *noun* étagère F.

bookshop *noun* librairie F.

boot *noun* 1 (*for football, walking, climbing, or skiing*) chaussure F; **walking boots** des chaussures de randonnée; 2 (*short fashion boot*) bottine F; 3 (*knee-high boot or wellington*) botte F; 4 (*of a car*) coffre M.

border *noun* (*between countries*) frontière F; **at the border** à la frontière.

bore *noun* 1 (*a boring person*) raseur M, raseuse F (*informal*); 2 (*a nuisance*) **what a bore!** quelle barbe!

bored *adjective* **to be bored** s'ennuyer; **I'm bored** je m'ennuie; **to get bored** s'ennuyer.

boring *adjective* ennuyeux (F ennuyeuse).

born *verb* né; **to be born** naître [55]; **she was born in June** elle est née en juin.

borrow *verb* emprunter [1]; **can I borrow your bike?** puis-je t'emprunter ton vélo?; **to borrow something from someone** emprunter quelque chose à quelqu'un; **I'll borrow some money from Dad** je vais emprunter de l'argent à Papa.

Bosnia *noun* Bosnie F.

boss *noun* patron M, patronne F.

bossy *adjective* autoritaire.

both *pronoun* **1** (*of people*) tous les deux (F toutes les deux); **they both came** ils sont venus tous les deux; **both my sisters were there** mes sœurs y étaient toutes les deux; **2** (*of things*) les deux; **they are both sold** les deux sont vendus; **both my feet** mes deux pieds; **3 both at home and at school** à la maison comme à l'école; **both in summer and in winter** en été comme en hiver.

bother *noun* ennui M; **I've had a lot of bother with the car** j'ai eu beaucoup d'ennuis avec la voiture; **it's too much bother** c'est trop de tracas; **it's no bother** ce n'est pas un problème; **without any bother** sans aucune difficulté.
verb **1** (*to disturb*) déranger [52]; **I'm sorry to bother you** je suis désolé de vous déranger; **2** (*to worry*) inquiéter [24]; **that doesn't bother me at all** ça ne m'inquiète pas du tout; **don't bother about dinner** ne t'inquiète pas pour le dîner; **3 she didn't even bother to come** elle n'a même pas pris la peine de venir; **don't bother!** ce n'est pas la peine !

bottle *noun* bouteille F.

bottle bank *noun* conteneur M à verre.

bottle opener *noun* ouvre-bouteille M.

bottom *noun* **1** (*of a hill, a wall, or steps*) pied M; **at the bottom of the ladder** au pied de l'échelle; **2** (*of a bag or a bottle, a hole, a stretch of water, or a garden*) fond M; **at the bottom of the lake** au fond du lac; **3 at the bottom of the page** en bas de la page; **4** (*buttocks*) derrière M.

adjective **1** inférieur; **the bottom shelf** le rayon inférieur; **2** (*a division, team, or place*) dernier (F dernière); **3 the bottom sheet** le drap de dessous; **the bottom flat** l'appartement du rez-de-chaussée.

bounce *verb* rebondir [2].

bouncer *noun* videur M.

bound *adjective* (*certain*) **he's bound to be late** il va sûrement être en retard; **that was bound to happen** cela devait arriver.

boundary *noun* limite F; (*for sports*) limites F *plural* du terrain.

bow *noun* **1** (*in a shoelace or ribbon*) nœud M; **2** (*for a violin*) archet M; **3 a bow and arrow** un arc et une flèche.

bowels *plural noun* intestins M *plural*.

bowl *noun* **1** (*for cereal, for example*) bol M; **2** (*larger, for salad or mixing*) saladier M; **3** (*for washing up*) cuvette F.
verb lancer [61] (*a ball*).

bowler *noun* (*in cricket*) lanceur M.

bowling *noun* (*tenpin*) bowling M; **to go bowling** jouer au bowling.

bow tie *noun* nœud M papillon.

box *noun* **1** boîte F; **a box of chocolates** une boîte de chocolats; **2 a cardboard box** un carton; **3** (*on an application form*) case F.

boxer *noun* **1** (*fighter*) boxeur M; **2** (*dog*) boxer M.

boxer shorts *plural noun* caleçon M singular.

boxing *noun* **1** boxe F; **2 a boxing match** un match de boxe.

Boxing Day *noun* le lendemain de Noël.

box office *noun* guichet M.

boy *noun* garçon M; **a little boy** un petit garçon.

boyfriend *noun* copain M.

bra *noun* soutien-gorge M.

brace *noun* (*for teeth*) appareil M.

bracelet *noun* bracelet M.

bracket *noun* **in brackets** entre parenthèses.

brain *noun* cerveau M (*plural* cerveaux).

brainwave *noun* idée F géniale.

brake *noun* frein M.
verb freiner [1].

bramble *noun* ronce F.

branch *noun* **1** (*of a tree*) branche F; **2** (*of a shop*) succursale F; **our Oxford branch** notre succursale à Oxford; **3** (*of a bank*) agence F.

brand *noun* marque F.

brand new *adjective* tout neuf (F toute neuve).

brandy *noun* cognac M.

brass *noun* **1** (*the metal*) laiton M; **2** (*in an orchestra*) **the brass** les cuivres M *plural*.

brass band *noun* fanfare F.

brave *adjective* courageux (F courageuse).

bread *noun* pain M; **a slice of bread** une tranche de pain.

break *noun* **1** (*a short rest*) pause F; **fifteen minutes' break** une pause de quinze minutes; **to take a break** faire une pause; **2** (*in school*) récréation F; **3 the Christmas break** les vacances de Noël.
verb **1** casser [1]; **he broke a glass** il a cassé un verre; **I broke a tooth/my arm** je me suis cassé une dent/le bras; **2** se casser [1]; **the eggs broke** les œufs se sont cassés; **3 to break your arm** se casser le bras; **4 to break your promise** manquer [1] à sa promesse; **he broke the rules** il n'a pas respecté les règlements; **you mustn't break the rules** il faut respecter les règlements; **5 to break a record** battre [21] un record; **6 to break the news** annoncer [61] la nouvelle.
● **to break down** tomber [1] en panne; **the car broke down** la voiture est tombée en panne.
● **to break in** (*a thief*) entrer [1] par effraction.
● **to break out 1** (*a fire*) se déclarer [1]; **2** (*a fight or a storm*) éclater [1]; **3** (*a prisoner*) s'évader [1].
● **to break up 1** (*a family or couple*) se séparer [1]; **2** (*a crowd or clouds*) se disperser [1]; **3** (*for the holidays*) **we break up on Thursday** les cours finissent jeudi.

breakdown *noun* **1** (*of a vehicle*) panne F; **we had a breakdown on the motorway** nous sommes tombés en panne sur l'autoroute; **2** (*in talks or negotiations*) rupture F; **3** (*a nervous collapse*) dépression F; **to have a (nervous) breakdown** faire une dépression.

breakdown truck *noun* camion M de dépannage.

breakfast *noun* petit déjeuner M; **we have breakfast at eight** nous prenons le petit déjeuner à huit heures.

break-in *noun* cambriolage M.

breast *noun* **1** (*a woman's*) sein M; **2** (*of a chicken or other fowl*) blanc M.

breaststroke *noun* brasse F.

breath *noun* **1** (*when you breathe in*) souffle M; **out of breath** à bout de souffle; **to get one's breath** reprendre son souffle; **to take a deep breath** respirer profondément; **2** (*when you breathe out*) haleine F; **to have bad breath** avoir mauvaise haleine.

breathe *verb* respirer [1].

breathing *noun* respiration F.

breed *noun* (*of dog, for example*) race F.
verb **1** élever [50] (*animals*); **2** (*to have babies*) se reproduire [26]; **rabbits breed fast** les lapins se reproduisent vite.

breeze *noun* brise F.

brew *verb* **1** préparer [1] (*tea*); **2** brasser [1] (*beer*).

brick *noun* brique F; **a brick wall** un mur de briques.

bride *noun* mariée F; **the bride and groom** les mariés M *plural*.

bridegroom *noun* marié M.

bridesmaid *noun* demoiselle F d'honneur.

bridge *noun* **1** (*over a river*) pont M; **a bridge over the Thames** un pont sur la Tamise; **2** (*card game*) bridge M; **to play bridge** jouer au bridge.

bridle *noun* bride F.

brief *adjective* bref (F brève).

briefcase *noun* serviette F.

briefly *adjective* brièvement.

briefs *plural noun* slip M.

bright *adjective* **1** (*colour, light*) vif (F vive); **bright green socks** des chaussettes vert vif; **2 bright sunshine** un soleil éclatant; **3** (*clever*) intelligent; **she's not very bright** elle n'est pas très intelligente; ★ **to look on the bright side** voir le bon côté des choses.

brighten up *verb* **the weather's brightening up** le temps s'éclaircit.

brilliant *adjective* **1** (*very clever*) brillant; **a brilliant surgeon** un chirurgien brillant; **he's brilliant at maths** il est très doué en maths; **2** (*wonderful*) génial (M *plural* géniaux) (*informal*); **the party was brilliant!** le boum était génial!

bring *verb* **1** apporter [1] (*something you carry*); **they brought a present** ils ont apporté un cadeau; **bring your camera!** apporte ton appareil-photo!; **it brings good luck** ça porte bonheur; **2** amener [50] (*a person or an animal*); **she's bringing all the children** elle va amener tous les enfants; **3 to bring something back** rapporter [1] quelque chose; **4 to bring up** élever [50] (*children*); **he was brought up by his aunt** il a été élevé par sa tante.

bristle *noun* poil M.

Britain, Great Britain *noun* Grande-Bretagne F; **in Britain** en Grande-Bretagne; **to Britain** en Grande-Bretagne; **Britain is sending aid** la Grande-Bretagne envoie de l'aide.

British *plural noun* **the British** les Britanniques; **the British love animals** les Britanniques adorent les animaux.
adjective britannique; **the British army** l'armée britannique; **the British Isles** les îles Britanniques.

Brittany *noun* Bretagne F; **in Brittany** en Bretagne; **to Brittany** en Bretagne.

broad *adjective* (*wide*) large.

broad bean *noun* fève F.

broadcast *noun* émission F.
verb diffuser [1] (*a programme*).

broccoli *noun* brocolis M *plural*; **to eat broccoli** manger des brocolis.

brochure *noun* brochure F.

broke *adjective* **to be broke** (*no money*) être fauché (*informal*).

broken *adjective* cassé; **the window's broken** la vitre est cassée; **to have a broken leg** avoir la jambe cassée.

bronchitis *noun* bronchite F; **to have bronchitis** avoir une bronchite.

brooch *noun* broche F.

broom *noun* **1** (*for sweeping*) balai M; **2** (*bush*) genêt M.

brother *noun* frére M; **my little**

brother mon petit frère; **my mother's brother** le frère de ma mère.

brother-in-law *noun* beau-frère M (*plural* beaux-frères).

brown *adjective* **1** marron (*does not change in the feminine or plural*); **my brown jacket** ma veste marron; **your brown shoes** tes chaussures marron; **light brown** marron clair; **dark brown** marron foncé; **2** châtain (*hair*); **3** (*tanned in the sun*) bronzé; **to go brown** bronzer.

brown bread *noun* pain M complet.

brown sugar *noun* sucre M brun.

bruise *noun* **1** (*on a person*) bleu M; **2** (*on fruit*) tache F.

brush *noun* **1** (*for your hair, clothes, nails, or shoes*) brosse F; **my hair brush** ma brosse à cheveux; **2** (*for sweeping*) balai M; **3** (*paintbrush*) pinceau M.
verb brosser [1]; **to brush your hair** se brosser les cheveux; **she brushed her hair** elle s'est brossé les cheveux; **to brush your teeth** se brosser les dents.

Brussels *noun* Bruxelles.

Brussels sprout *noun* chou M de Bruxelles.

bubble *noun* bulle F.

bubble bath *noun* bain M moussant.

bucket *noun* seau M (*plural* seaux).

buckle *noun* boucle F.

Buddhism *noun* bouddhisme M.

Buddhist *noun* bouddhiste M & F.

budget *noun* budget M.

budgie *noun* perruche F.

buffet *noun* buffet M.

buffet car *noun* voiture F bar.

bug *noun* **1** (*insect*) bestiole F (*informal*); **2** (*germ*) microbe F; **a stomach bug** une gastroentérite; **3** (*in a computer*) bug M.

build *verb* construire [26]; **they are building three houses over there** ils construisent trois maisons là-bas.

builder *noun* maçon M.

building *noun* bâtiment M; (*with offices or flats*) immeuble M.

building site *noun* chantier M.

built-up *adjective* urbanisé; **a built-up area** une agglomération.

bulb *noun* **1** (*for a light*) ampoule F; **2** (*that you plant*) bulbe M.

bull *noun* taureau M (*plural* taureaux).

bulldozer *noun* bulldozer M.

bullet *noun* balle F.

bulletin *noun* bulletin M; **a news bulletin** un bulletin d'informations.

bully *noun* brute F; **he's a bully** c'est une brute. *verb* tyranniser [1].

bum *noun* (*bottom*) derrière M.

bump *noun* **1** (*that sticks up*) bosse F; **a bump on the head** une bosse à la tête; **a bump in the road** une bosse sur la route; **2** (*jolt*) secousse F; **3** (*noise*) bruit M sourd. *verb* **1** (*to bang*) cogner [1]; **I bumped my head** je me suis cogné la tête; **2 to bump into something** rentrer [1] dans quelque chose; **3 to bump into somebody** (*meet by chance*) croiser [1] quelqu'un.

bumper *noun* pare-chocs M.

bumpy *adjective* **1** accidenté (*road*); **2** agité (*plane landing*).

bun *noun* **1** (*for a burger*) petit pain M; **2** (*sugary*) petit cake M.

bunch *noun* **1** (*of flowers*) bouquet M; **2** (*of carrots or radishes*) botte F; **3** (*of keys*) trousseau M; **4 a bunch of grapes** une grappe de raisin.

bundle *noun* tas M.

bungalow *noun* pavillon M.

bunk *noun* **1** (*on a train or boat*) couchette F; **2 bunk beds** des lits superposés.

bureau *noun* agence F.

burger *noun* hamburger M.

burglar *noun* cambrioleur M.

burglar alarm *noun* sonnerie F d'alarme.

burglary *noun* cambriolage M.

burn *noun* brûlure F. *verb* **1** brûler [1]; **I've burned the rubbish** j'ai brûlé les ordures; **the fire's burning well** le feu brûle bien; **she burnt herself on the grill** elle s'est brûlée au grill; **you'll burn your finger!** tu vas te brûler le doigt!; **2** laisser [1] brûler (*something you're cooking*); **Mum's burnt her cake** maman a laissé brûler son gâteau;

3 (*through sunburn*) **I burn easily** j'attrape facilement des coups de soleil.

burnt *adjective* brûlé.

burst *verb* **1** crever [50] (*a balloon or tyre, for example*); **a burst tyre** un pneu crevé; **2 to burst out laughing** éclater [1] de rire; **3 to burst into tears** fondre [3] en larmes; **4 to burst into flames** prendre [64] feu.

bury *verb* enterrer [1].

bus *noun* **1** (*public transport*) autobus M, bus M; **we'll take the bus** on va prendre le bus; **on the bus** dans le bus; **a bus ticket** un ticket de bus; **a bus stop** un arrêt de bus; **2** (*coach*) car M; **to go to London by bus** aller à Londres en car.

bus driver *noun* conducteur de bus M, conductrice de bus F.

bush *noun* buisson M.

business *noun* **1** (*commercial dealings*) affaires F *plural*; **to be in business** être dans les affaires; **he's in Leeds on business** il est à Leeds en voyage d'affaires; **he's in the insurance business** il travaille dans l'assurance; **a business letter** une lettre d'affaires; **2** (*firm or company*) entreprise F; **small businesses** les petites entreprises; **3 mind your own business!** occupe-toi de tes affaires!; **that's my business!** ça me regarde!

business class *noun* classe F affaires.

businessman *noun* homme M d'affaires.

business trip *noun* voyage M d'affaires.

businesswoman *noun* femme F d'affaires.

bus pass *noun* carte F de bus.

bus route *noun* ligne F d'autobus.

bus shelter *noun* abribus™ M.

bus station *noun* gare F routière.

bust *noun* **bust size** tour M de poitrine.

busy *adjective* **1** occupé (*a person*); chargé (*a day or week*); **don't disturb him, he's busy** ne le dérange pas, il est occupé; **2 a busy day** une journée chargée; **3** (*full of cars or people*) très fréquenté (*a road*); **the shops were busy** il y avait beaucoup de monde dans les magasins; **4** (*phone*) **the line's busy** la ligne est occupée.

but *conjunction* mais; **small but strong** petit mais fort; **not Thursday but Friday** pas jeudi mais vendredi; **I'll try, but it's difficult** j'essaierai, mais c'est difficile. *preposition* sauf; **anything but that** tout, sauf ça; **everyone but Roger** tout le monde sauf Roger; **the last but one** l'avant-dernier.

butcher *noun* boucher M; **he's a butcher** il est boucher; **the butcher's** la boucherie.

butter *noun* beurre M. *verb* beurrer [1].

buttercup *noun* bouton M d'or.

butterfly *noun* papillon M.

button *noun* bouton M.

buttonhole *noun* boutonnière F.

buy *noun* **a good buy** une bonne affaire; **a bad buy** une mauvaise affaire.
verb acheter [16]; **I bought the tickets** j'ai acheté les billets; **to buy something for somebody** acheter quelque chose à quelqu'un; **Sarah bought him a sweater** Sarah lui a acheté un pull; **to buy something from someone** acheter quelque chose à quelqu'un; **I bought a bike from Tim** j'ai acheté un vélo à Tim.

buzz *verb* (*a fly or bee*) bourdonner [1].

buzzer *noun* sonnerie F.

by *preposition* **1** par; **by telephone** par téléphone; **to take somebody by the hand** prendre quelqu'un par la main; **eaten by a dog** mangé par un chien; **by mistake** par erreur; **2** (*travel*) en; **to come by bus** venir en bus; **to leave by train** partir en train; **by bike** en vélo; **3** (*near*) à côté de; **by the fire** à côté du feu; **by the sea** au bord de la mer; **close by** tout près; **4** (*before*) avant; **ready by Monday** prêt avant lundi; **Kevin was back by four** Kevin est rentré avant quatre heures; **5** by **yourself** tout seul; **I was by myself in the house** j'étais tout seul chez moi; **she did it by herself** elle l'a fait toute seule; **6 by the way** au fait; **7 to go by** passer.

bye *exclamation* au revoir; **bye for now!** à bientôt!

bypass *noun* rocade F.

C c

cab *noun* **1** taxi M; **to call a cab** appeler un taxi; **2** (*on a lorry*) cabine F.

cabbage *noun* chou M (*plural* choux).

cable *noun* câble M.

cable car *noun* téléférique M.

cable television *noun* télévision F par câble.

cactus *noun* cactus M.

café *noun* café M.

cage *noun* cage F.

cagoule *noun* K-way™ M.

cake *noun* gâteau M (*plural* gâteaux); **would you like a piece of cake?** veux-tu un morceau de gâteau?

calculate *verb* calculer [1].

calculation *noun* calcul M.

calculator *noun* calculatrice F.

calendar *noun* calendrier M.

calf *noun* **1** (*animal*) veau M; **2** (*o your leg*) mollet.

call *noun* (*telephone*) appel M; **I had several calls this morning;** j'ai eu plusieurs appels ce matin; **thank you for your call** merci de votre appel; **a phone call** un coup de téléphone.
verb **1** appeler [18]; **to call a taxi** appeler un taxi; **to call the doctor**

appeler le médecin; **they called the police** ils ont appelé la police; **call this number** appelez ce numéro; **thank you for calling** merci de votre appel; **I'll call you back later** je te rappellerai plus tard; **2** appeler [18]; **they've called the baby Julie** ils ont appelé le bébé Julie; **3 to be called** s'appeler [18]; **she has a brother called Dan** elle a un frère qui s'appelle Dan; **what's he called?** il s'appelle comment?

call box noun cabine F téléphonique.

calm adjective calme.
verb calmer [1];
● **to calm down** se calmer; **he's calmed down a bit** il s'est calmé un peu;
● **to calm somebody down** calmer quelqu'un; **I tried to calm her down** j'ai essayé de la calmer.

calmly adverb calmement.

calorie noun calorie F.

camcorder noun caméscope M.

camel noun chameau M.

camera noun **1** appareil M photo (plural appareils photo); **2** (film or TV camera) caméra.

cameraman noun caméraman M.

camp noun camp M.
verb camper [1].

campaign noun campagne F.

camper van noun camping-car M.

camping noun camping M; **to go camping** faire du camping; **we're going camping in Brittany this summer** nous allons faire du camping en Bretagne cet été.

campsite noun terrain M de camping.

can[1] noun **1** boîte F; **a can of tomatoes** une boîte de tomates; **2** (for petrol or oil) bidon M.

can[2] verb **1** pouvoir [12]; **I can't be there before ten** je ne peux pas y être avant dix heures; **you can leave your bag here** to peux laisser ton sac ici; **can you open the door, please?** peux-tu ouvrir la porte, s'il te plaît?; **can I help you?** est-ce que je peux vous aider?; **they couldn't come** ils n'ont pas pu venir; **you could ring back tomorrow** tu pourrais rappeler demain; **you could have told me** tu aurais pu me le dire; **2** (not translated) **can you hear me?** est-ce que tu m'entends?; **I can't see him** je ne le vois pas; **I can't remember** je ne me souviens pas; **I can't find my keys** je ne trouve pas mes clés; **3** (know how to) savoir [70]; **she can't drive** elle ne sait pas conduire; **can you play the piano?** est-ce que tu sais jouer du piano?

Canada noun Canada M; **to Canada** au Canada; **in Canada** au Canada.

Canadian noun Canadien M, Canadienne F.
adjective canadien (F canadienne).

canal noun canal M (plural canaux).

cancel verb annuler [1]; **the concert's been cancelled** le concert a été annulé.

cancer noun cancer M; **to have lung cancer** avoir un cancer du poumon.

Cancer noun Cancer M; **I'm Cancer** je suis Cancer.

candidate noun candidat M, candidate F.

candle noun bougie F.

candlestick noun bougeoir M.

candyfloss noun barbe F à papa.

canned adjective en conserve; **canned tomatoes** les tomates en conserve.

cannot verb SEE **can²**

canoe noun canoë M.

canoeing noun **to go canoeing** faire du canoë; **I like canoeing** j'aime faire du canoë.

can-opener noun ouvre-boîte M.

canteen noun cantine F.

canvas noun toile F.

cap noun 1 (*hat*) casquette F; **a baseball cap** une casquette de baseball; 2 (*on a bottle or tube*) bouchon M.

capable adjective capable.

capacity noun capacité F.

capital noun 1 (*city*) capital F; **Paris is the capital of France** Paris est la capitale de la France; 2 (*letter*) majuscule F; **in capitals** en majuscules.

capitalism noun capitalisme M.

Capricorn noun Capricorne M; **Linda's Capricorn** Linda est Capricorne.

capsize verb chavirer [1].

captain noun capitaine M.

capture verb capturer [1].

car noun voiture F; **in the car** dans la voiture; **to park the car** garer la voiture; **we're going by car** nous y allons en voiture; **a car crash** un accident de voiture.

caramel noun caramel M.

caravan noun caravane F.

card noun carte F; **un jeu de cartes** a card game; a pack of cards; **faire une partie de cartes** to have a game of cards.

cardboard noun carton M.

cardigan noun cardigan M.

cardphone noun téléphone M à carte.

care noun 1 soin M; **to take care to do** prendre soin de faire; 2 **to take care of somebody** s'occuper de quelqu'un; 3 **take care!** (*be careful*) fais attention!; (*when saying goodbye*) à bientôt!
verb 1 **to care about** se soucier de; **to care about pollution** se soucier de la pollution; 2 **she doesn't care** ça lui est égal; **I couldn't care less!** ça m'est complètement égal!

career noun carrière F.

careful adjective prudent; 1 **a careful driver** un conducteur prudent; 2 **be careful!** fais attention!

carefully adverb 1 **read the instructions carefully** lisez attentivement les instructions; **listen carefully** écoutez bien; 2 (*handle*) avec précaution; **she put the vase down carefully** elle a posé le vase avec précaution; 3 **to copy**

something carefully recopier soigneusement quelque chose; **4 drive carefully!** sois prudent!

careless *adjective* **1 he's very careless** il ne fait pas du tout attention à ce qu'il fait; **2 this is careless work** c'est du travail peu soigné; **a careless mistake** une faute d'inattention; **3 careless driving** la conduite imprudente.

caretaker *noun* gardien M, gardienne F.

car ferry *noun* ferry M.

car hire *noun* location F de voitures.

Caribbean *noun* **1 the Caribbean (islands)** les Caraïbes; **2 the Caribbean** (*sea*) la mer des Caraïbes.

carnation *noun* œillet M.

carnival *noun* carnaval M.

car park *noun* parking M.

carpenter *noun* menuisier M.

carpentry *noun* menuiserie F.

carpet *noun* **1** (*fitted*) moquette F; **2** (*loose*) tapis M.

car phone *noun* téléphone F de voiture.

car radio *noun* autoradio M.

carriage *noun* (*of a train*) voiture F.

carrier bag *noun* sac M en plastique.

carrot *noun* carotte F.

carry *verb* **1** porter [1]; **she was carrying a parcel** elle portait un paquet; **2** (*vehicle, plane*)

transporter [1]; **the coach was carrying schoolchildren** le car transportait des écoliers.

● **to carry on** continuer [1]; **they carried on talking** ils ont continué à parler.

carrycot *noun* porte-bébé M.

carsick *adjective* **to be carsick** avoir le mal de la route.

carton *noun* **1** (*of cream or yoghurt*) pot M; **2** (*of milk or orange*) brique F.

cartoon *noun* **1** (*a film*) dessin M animé; **2** (*a comic strip*) bande F dessinée; **3** (*an amusing drawing*) dessin M humoristique.

cartridge *noun* (*for a pen or a video*) cartouche F.

carve *verb* découper [1] (*meat*).

case[1] *noun* **1** (*suitcase*) valise F; **to pack a case** faire une valise; **2** (*a large wooden box, for wine for example*) caisse F; **3** (*for spectacles or small things*) étui M.

case[2] *noun* **1** cas M; **in that case** en ce cas; **that's not the case** ce n'est pas le cas; **a case of flu** un cas de grippe; **2 in case** au cas où; **in case he's late** au cas où il serait en retard; **check first, just in case** vérifie d'abord, au cas où; **3 in any case** de toute façon; **in any case, it's too late** de toute façon, c'est trop tard.

cash *noun* **1** (*money in general*) argent M; **I haven't any cash on me** je n'ai pas d'argent sur moi; **2** (*money rather than a cheque*) espèces F *plural*; **to pay in cash**

payer en espèces; **£50 in cash** cinquante livres en espèces.

cash card *noun* carte F de retrait.

cash desk *noun* caisse F; **pay at the cash desk** payez à la caisse.

cash dispenser *noun* guichet M automatique.

cashew *noun* cajou M.

cashier *noun* caissier M, caissière F.

cash point *noun* = cash dispenser.

cassette *noun* cassette F.

cassette recorder *noun* magnétophone M à cassettes.

cast *noun* les acteurs M *plural*; **the cast were on stage** les acteurs étaient sur scène.

castle *noun* **1** château M (*plural* châteaux); **2** (*in chess*) tour F.

casual *adjective* décontracté.

casualty *noun* **1** (*in an accident*) victime F; **there are 17 casualties** il y a dix-sept victimes; **2** (*hospital department*) urgences F *plural*; **he's in casualty** il est aux urgences.

cat *noun* chat M; (*female*) chatte F; **a big black cat** un gros chat noir; ★ **it's raining cats and dogs** il pleut des cordes (*literally: it's raining in ropes*).

catalogue *noun* catalogue M.

catastrophe *noun* catastrophe F.

catch *noun* **1** (*on a door*) fermeture F; **2** (*a drawback*) piège M; **what's the catch?** où est le piège? *verb* **1** attraper [1]; **Tom caught the**

ball Tom a attrapé le ballon; **you can't catch me!** vous ne m'attraperez pas!; **can you catch hold of the branch?** peux-tu attraper la branche?; **2 to catch somebody doing** attraper quelqu'un en train de faire; **he was caught stealing money** il a été attrapé en train de voler de l'argent; **3** prendre [64] (*a bus or plane*); **did Tim catch his plane?** est-ce que Tim a pris son avion?; **4** attraper [1] (*an illness*); **he's caught chickenpox** il a attrapé la varicelle; **I've caught a cold** j'ai attrapé un rhume; **5** saisir [2] (*what somebody says*); **I didn't catch your name** je n'ai pas saisi votre nom.

● **to catch up with somebody** rattraper [1] quelqu'un.

category *noun* catégorie F.

catering *noun* restauration F.

caterpillar *noun* chenille F.

cathedral *noun* cathédrale F; **Winchester cathedral** la cathédrale de Winchester.

Catholic *noun, adjective* catholique M & F.

cattle *plural noun* bétail M singular.

cauliflower *noun* chou-fleur M (*plural* choux-fleurs); **cauliflower cheese** un gratin de chou-fleur.

cause *noun* cause F; **the cause of the accident** la cause de l'accident; **for a good cause** pour une bonne cause. *verb* **1** causer [1] (*damage or problems*); **to cause problems** causer des problèmes; **2** provoquer

[1] (*chaos or disease*); **the strike caused delays** la grève a provoqué des retards.

caution *noun* prudence F.

cautious *adjective* prudent.

cave *noun* grotte F.

caving *noun* spéléologie F; **to go caving** faire de la spéléologie.

CD *noun* CD M.

CD player *noun* platine F laser.

CD-ROM *noun* CD-ROM M.

ceiling *noun* plafond M; **on the ceiling** au plafond.

celebrate *verb* fêter [1]; **I'm celebrating my birthday** je fête mon anniversaire.

celebrity *noun* célébrité F.

celery *noun* céleri M.

cell *noun* cellule F.

cellar *noun* cave F.

cello *noun* violoncelle M; **to play the cello** jouer du violoncelle.

cement *noun* ciment M.

cemetery *noun* cimetière M.

centenary *noun* centenaire M.

centigrade *adjective* centigrade; **ten degrees centigrade** dix degrés centigrade.

centimetre *noun* centimètre M.

central *adjective* central (M *plural* centraux); **central London** le centre de Londres; **the office is very central** le bureau est en plein centre-ville.

central heating *noun* chauffage M central.

centre *noun* centre M; **in the centre of** au centre de; **in the town centre** en centre-ville; **a shopping centre** un centre commercial.

century *noun* siècle M; **in the twentieth century** au vingtième siècle; **the twenty-first century** le vingt-et-unième siècle.

cereal *noun* **breakfast cereal** céréales F *plural* pour le petit déjeuner; **to have cereal for breakfast** prendre des céréales au petit déjeuner.

ceremony *noun* cérémonie F.

certain *adjective* certain; **a certain number of** un certain nombre de; **are you certain of the address?** es-tu certain de l'adresse?; **I'm certain of it** j'en suis certain; **to be certain that** être sûr que; **Nicola's certain you're wrong** Nicola est sûre que tu as tort; **nobody knows for certain** personne ne sait au juste.

certainly *adverb* certainement; **certainly not** certainement pas.

certificate *noun* **1** certificat M; **2 a birth certificate** un acte de naissance.

chain *noun* chaîne F.

chair *noun* **1** (*upright*) chaise F; **a kitchen chair** une chaise de cuisine; **2** (*with arms*) fauteuil M.

chair lift *noun* télésiège M.

chalet *noun* **1** (*in the mountains*) chalet M; **2** (*in a holiday camp*) bungalow M.

chalk noun craie F.

challenge noun 1 (*that excites you*) challenge M; **the challenge of new ideas** le challenge des nouvelles idées; 2 (*that is difficult*) épreuve F; **the exam was a real challenge** l'examen était une vraie épreuve.

champion noun champion M, championne F; **world champion** champion du monde.

chance noun 1 (*an opportunity*) occasion F; **to have the chance to do** avoir l'occasion de faire; **if you have the chance to go to New York** si tu as l'occasion d'aller à New York; **I haven't had the chance to write to him** je n'ai pas eu l'occasion de lui écrire; 2 (*likelihood*) chance F; **there's little chance of winning** il y a peu de chance de gagner; 3 (*luck*) **by chance** par hasard; **do you have her address, by any chance?** aurais-tu par hasard son adresse?

change noun 1 changement M; **a change of plan** un changement de programme; **they've made some changes to the house** ils ont fait des changements dans la maison; **for a change, let's eat out** mangeons au restaurant pour changer; **it makes a change from hamburgers** cela change un peu des hamburgers; 2 **a change of clothes** des vêtements de rechange; 3 (*cash*) monnaie F; **I haven't any change** je n'ai pas de monnaie.
verb 1 (*transform completely*) changer [52]; **it changed my life** cela m'a changé la vie; **Liz never changes** Liz ne change jamais; 2 (*to switch from one thing to another*) changer de [52]; **we changed trains at Crewe** nous avons changé de train à Crewe; **I must change my shirt** je dois changer de chemise; **they changed places** ils ont changé de place; **to change your mind** changer d'avis; 3 (*to exchange in a shop*) échanger [52]; **can I change it for the larger size?** puis-je l'échanger contre la taille au-dessus?; 4 (*to change your clothes*) se changer [52]; **Mike's gone up to change** Mike est monté se changer.

changing room noun (*for sport or swimming*) 1 vestiaire M; 2 (*in a shop*) salon M d'essayage.

channel noun 1 (*on TV*) chaîne F; **to change channels** changer de chaîne; 2 **the Channel** la Manche.

Channel Islands plural noun îles F plural Anglo-Normandes.

Channel Tunnel noun tunnel M sous la Manche.

chaos noun pagaille F (*informal*); **it was chaos!** c'était la pagaille!

chapel noun chapelle F.

chapter noun chapitre M; **in chapter two** au chapitre deux.

character noun 1 (*personality*) caractère M; **a house with a lot of character** une maison qui a du caractère; 2 (*somebody in a book, play, or film*) personnage M; **the main character** le personnage principal.

characteristic adjective caractéristique.

charcoal noun 1 (*for burning*)

charbon M de bois; **2** (*for drawing*) fusain M.

charge *noun* **1** (*what you pay*) frais M *plural*; **a booking charge** des frais de réservation; **an extra or additional charge** un supplément; **there's no charge** c'est gratuit; **2 to be in charge** être responsable; **who's in charge of these children?** qui est responsable de ces enfants?; **3 to be on a charge of theft** être inculpé de vol.
verb **1** (*to ask a specific sum*) prendre [64]; **they charge fifteen pounds an hour** ils prennent quinze livres de l'heure; **how much do you charge for one day?** combien prenez-vous pour une journée?; **2** (*to ask people to pay*) faire [10] payer; **we don't charge, it's free** nous ne faisons pas payer les gens, c'est gratuit; **3 to charge somebody with** inculper [1] quelqu'un de (*a crime*).

charity *noun* organisation F caritative.

charm *noun* charme M.

charming *adjective* charmant.

chart *noun* **1** (*table*) tableau M; **2 the weather chart** la carte du temps; **3 the charts** le hit-parade; **number one in the charts** numéro un au hit-parade.

charter flight *noun* vol M charter.

chase *noun* poursuite F; **a car chase** une poursuite en voiture.
verb pourchasser [1] (*a person or animal*).

chat *noun* conversation F; **to have a chat with somebody** bavarder avec quelqu'un.

chat show *noun* talk-show M.

chatter *verb* **1** (*gossip*) bavarder [1]; **2 my teeth are chattering** je claque des dents.

cheap *adjective* pas cher (F pas chère); **cheap shoes** des chaussures pas chères; **that's very cheap!** ce n'est vraiment pas cher!

cheaper *adjective* moins cher (F moins chère).

cheaply *adverb* pas cher; **to eat cheaply** manger pas cher.

cheap rate *adjective* à tarif réduit; **a cheap rate phone call** un appel à tarif réduit.

cheat *noun* tricheur M, tricheuse F. *verb* tricher [1].

check *noun* **1** (*in a factory or at border controls*) contrôle M; **passport check** contrôle des passeports; **2** (*by a doctor*) examen M; **3** (*in chess*) **check!** échec au roi!
verb (*to make sure*) vérifier [1]; **he checked the time** il a vérifié l'heure; **check they're all back** vérifiez qu'ils sont tous rentrés; **check with your father** demande à ton père.
●**to check in** enregistrer [1] (*for a flight*).

check-in *noun* enregistrement M.

checkout *noun* caisse F; **at the checkout** à la caisse.

check-up *noun* examen M médical.

cheek *noun* **1** (*part of face*) joue

F; **2** (*nerve*) **what a cheek!** quel culot! (*informal*).

cheeky *adjective* **1** coquin; **2** (*rude*) impoli.

cheer *noun* **1 three cheers for Tom!** faisons un ban à Tom! **2** (*when you have a drink*) **cheers!** à la vôtre!
verb (*to shout hurray*) applaudir [2].
● **to cheer up: cheer up!** courage!
● **to cheer somebody up** remonter [1] le moral à quelqu'un; **your visit's cheered me up** ta visite m'a remonté le moral.

cheerful *adjective* gai.

cheese *noun* fromage M; **blue cheese** le fromage bleu; **a cheese sandwich** un sandwich au fromage.

chef *noun* chef M cuisinier.

chemical *noun* chimie F.

chemist *noun* **1** pharmacien M, pharmacienne F; **2 chemist's** pharmacie F; **at the chemist's** à la pharmacie; **3** (*scientist*) chimiste M & F.

chemistry *noun* chimie F.

cheque *noun* chèque M; **to pay by cheque** payer par chèque; **to write a cheque** faire un chèque.

chequebook *noun* carnet M de chèques.

cherry *noun* cerise F.

chess *noun* échecs M *plural*; **to play chess** jouer aux échecs.

chessboard *noun* échiquier M.

chest *noun* **1** (*part of the body*) poitrine F; **2** (*box*) coffre M; **3 a chest of drawers** une commode.

chestnut *noun* marrron M.

chestnut tree *noun* **1** (*horse-chestnut*) marronnier M; **2** (*sweet chestnut*) châtaignier M.

chew *verb* mâcher [1] (*food*).

chewing gum *noun* chewing-gum M.

chick *noun* (*of a hen*) poussin M.

chicken *noun* poulet M; **roast chicken** du poulet rôti; **chicken thighs** des cuisses de poulet; **a chicken sandwich** un sandwich au poulet.

chickenpox *noun* varicelle F.

chicory *noun* endive F.

child *noun* enfant M & F; **Jenny's children** les enfants de Jenny.

childish *adjective* puéril.

child-minder *noun* nourrice F.

chill *noun* fraîcheur F.

chilled *adjective* (*wine*) bien frais.

chilli *noun* piment M.

chilly *adjective* frisquet (F frisquette); **it's chilly today** il fait frisquet aujourd'hui.

chimney *noun* cheminée F.

chimpanzee *noun* chimpanzé M.

chin *noun* menton M.

china *noun* porcelaine F; **a china plate** une assiette en porcelaine.

China *noun* Chine F; **in China** en Chine.

Chinese noun **1 the Chinese**
(*people*) les Chinois; **2** (*language*)
chinois M.
adjective chinois; **a Chinese man**
un Chinois; **a Chinese woman** un
Chinoise; **a Chinese meal** un repas
chinois.

chip noun **1** (*fried potato*) frite F;
I'd like some chips j'aimerais des
frites; **2** (*microchip*) puce F; **3** (*in
glass or china*) ébréchure F.

chipped *adjective* ébréché.

chives *plural noun* ciboulette F
singular.

chocolate noun chocolat M; **a
chocolate ice-cream** une glace au
chocolat; **hot chocolate** chocolat
M chaud; **a box of chocolates** une
boîte de chocolats.

choice noun choix M; **you have a
choice of two flights** vous avez le
choix entre deux vols.

choir noun **1** (*in a school*) chorale
F; **I sing in the choir** je fais partie
de la chorale; **2** (*professional*)
chœur M.

choke noun (*on a car*) starter M.
verb **1** (*by yourself*) s'étouffer [1];
she was choking on a bone elle
s'étouffait avec une arête; **2** (*smoke
or fumes*) étouffer [1].

choose *verb* choisir [2]; **you chose
well** tu as bien choisi; **Cathy chose
the red one** Cathy a choisi le rouge;
**it's hard to choose from all these
colours** il est difficile de choisir
parmi toutes ces couleurs.

chop noun côtelette F; **a lamb
chop** une côtelette d'agneau.
verb hacher [1].

chopstick noun baguette F.

chord noun accord M.

chorus noun **1** (*when you all join in
the song*) refrain M; **2** (*a group of
singers*) chœur M.

Christ noun le Christ.

christening noun baptême M.

Christian noun, *adjective* chrétien
M, chrétienne F.

Christian name noun prénom M.

Christmas noun Noël M; **at
Christmas** à Noël; **Happy
Christmas!** Joyeux Noël !

Christmas card noun carte F de
Noël.

Christmas carol noun chant M
de Noël.

Christmas cracker noun
diablotin M.

Christmas Day noun jour M de
Noël.

Christmas dinner noun repas M
de Noël.

Christmas Eve noun veille F de
Noël; **on Christmas Eve** la veille de
Noël.

Christmas present noun cadeau
M de Noël.

Christmas tree noun sapin M de
Noël.

chunk noun morceau M.

church noun église F; **to go to
church** aller à l'église.

churchyard noun cimetière M.

chute noun (in a swimming pool or playground) toboggan M.

cider noun cidre M.

cigar noun cigare M.

cigarette noun cigarette F; **to light a cigarette** allumer une cigarette.

cinema noun cinéma M; **to go to the cinema** aller au cinéma.

circle noun cercle M; **to sit in a circle** s'asseoir en cercle; **to go round in circles** tourner en rond.

circuit noun 1 (for athletes) piste F; 2 (for cars) circuit M.

circumflex noun accent M circonflexe.

circumstances plural noun **under the circumstances** dans ces circonstances.

circus noun cirque M.

citizen noun citoyen M, citoyenne F.

city noun (grande) ville F; **the city of Paris** la ville de Paris.

city centre noun centre-ville M; **in the city centre** au centre-ville.

civilization noun civilisation F.

civil servant noun fonctionnaire M & F; **he's a civil servant** il est fonctionnaire.

civil war noun guerre civile F.

claim verb prétendre [3]; **he claimed to know** il prétendait savoir.

clap verb 1 applaudir [2]; **everyone clapped** tout le monde a applaudi; 2 **to clap your hands** battre [21] des mains.

clapping noun applaudissements M plural.

clarinet noun clarinette F; **to play the clarinet** jouer de la clarinette.

clash noun (for example, between police and demonstrators) affrontement M. verb 1 (rival groups) s'affronter [1]; 2 (colours) jurer [1]; **the curtains clash with the wallpaper** les rideaux jurent avec le papier peint.

clasp noun (of a necklace) fermoir M.

class noun 1 (a group of students or pupils) classe F; **she's in the same class as me** elle est dans la même classe que moi; 2 (a lesson) cours M; **an art class** un cours de dessin; **in class** en cours; 3 (division) classe F; **a social class** une classe sociale.

classic adjective classique.

classical adjective classique; **classical music** la musique classique.

classroom noun classe F.

claw noun 1 (of a cat or dog) griffe F; 2 (of a crab) pince F.

clay noun 1 (for modelling) argile F; 2 **a clay court** (in tennis) un terrain en terre battue.

clean adjective 1 propre; **a clean shirt** une chemise propre; **my hands are clean** j'ai les mains propres; 2 (germ-free) pur (air or water). verb nettoyer [39]; 1 **I cleaned the whole house** j'ai nettoyé toute la maison; 2 **to clean your teeth** se laver [1] les dents; **I'm going to clean my teeth** je vais me laver les dents.

cleaner *noun* **1** (*in a public place*) agent M de nettoyage; **2** (*cleaning lady*) femme F de ménage; **3 a dry cleaner's** un pressing.

cleaning *noun* **to do the cleaning** faire le ménage.

cleanser *noun* **1** (*for the house*) produit d'entretien; **2** (*for your face*) démaquillant M.

clear *adjective* **1** (*that you can see through*) transparent; **clear glass** du verre transparent; **2** (*cloudless*) clair; **3** (*easy to understand*) clair; **clear instructions** des instructions claires; **is that clear?** est-ce que c'est clair?; **it's clear that …** il est clair que …
verb **1** enlever [50] (*papers, rubbish, or clothes*); **have you cleared your stuff out of your room?** as-tu enlevé tes affaires de ta chambre?; **2** débarrasser [1] (*a table or a room*); **can I clear the table?** puis-je débarrasser la table?; **3** dégager [52] (*a road or path*); **4** (*fog or snow*) se dissiper [1]; **and then the fog cleared** et puis le brouillard s'est dissipé; **5 to clear your throat** se racler [1] la gorge.
to clear something up ranger [52] quelque chose; **I'll just clear up my books** je vais juste ranger mes livres.

clearly *adjective* **1** (*to think, speak, or hear*) clairement; **2** (*obviously*) manifestement; **she was clearly worried** manifestement, elle était inquiète.

clementine *noun* clémentine F.

clever *adjective* **1** intelligent; **their children are all very clever** leurs enfants sont tous très intelligents; **2** (*ingenious*) astucieux (F astucieuse); **a clever idea** une idée astucieuse.

client *noun* client M, cliente F.

cliff *noun* falaise F.

climate *noun* climat M.

climb *verb* **1** monter [1] (*a hill, stairs*); **2** faire [10] l'escalade de (*a mountain*); **we climbed Mont Blanc** nous avons fait l'escalade du Mont Blanc.

climber *noun* alpiniste M & F.

climbing *noun* escalade F; **they go climbing in Italy** ils font de l'escalade en Italie.

clinic *noun* centre M médical (*plural* centres médicaux).

clip *noun* **1** (*from a film*) extrait M; **2** (*for your hair*) barrette F.
verb **1** (*to cut*) couper [1]; **2** (*to fasten*) attacher [1].

cloakroom *noun* (*for coats*) vestiaire M.

clock *noun* (*large*) horloge F; (*smaller*) pendule F; **an alarm clock** un réveil; **to put the clocks forward an hour** avancer les pendules d'une heure; **to put the clocks back** reculer les pendules.

clock radio *noun* radio-réveil M.

close[1] *adjective, adverb* **1** (*result*) serré; **2** (*friend or relation*) proche; **3** (*near*) près; **the station's very close** la gare est tout près; **she lives close by** elle habite tout près;

close to the cinema près du cinéma; **not very close** pas très près.

close² noun fin F; **at the close** à la fin.
verb fermer [1]; **close your eyes!** ferme les yeux!; **she closed the door** elle a fermé la porte; **the post office closes at six** la poste ferme à six heures.

closed *adjective* fermé; **'closed on Mondays'** 'fermé le lundi'.

closely *adverb* de près; **to examine something closely** regarder quelque chose de près.

closing date *noun* date F limite; **the closing date for entries** la date limite pour les inscriptions.

closing-down sale *noun* liquidation F.

closing time *noun* heure F de fermeture.

cloth *noun*
1 (*for the floor*) serpillière F;
2 (*for polishing*) chiffon M;
3 (*for drying up*) torchon M;
4 (*fabric by the metre*) tissu M.

clothes *plural noun* vêtements M *plural*; **to put your clothes on** s'habiller; **to take your clothes off** se déshabiller; **to change your clothes** se changer.

clothes hanger *noun* cintre M.

clothes line *noun* corde F à linge.

clothes peg *noun* pince F à linge.

clothing *noun* vêtements M *plural*.

cloud *noun* nuage M.

cloudy *adjective* nuageux (F nuageuse).

clove *noun* 1 clou M de girofle; **2 a clove of garlic** une gousse d'ail.

clown *noun* clown M.

club *noun* 1 (*association*) club M; **he's in the football club** il fait partie du club de foot; **2** (*in cards*) trèfle M; **the four of clubs** le quatre de trèfle; **3** (*golfing iron*) crosse F.

clue *noun* 1 indice M; **they have a few clues** ils ont quelques indices; **2** (*in a crossword*) définition F; ★ **haven't a clue** je n'ai aucune idée.

clumsy *adjective* maladroit.

clutch *noun* (*in a car*) embrayage M.
verb **to clutch something** tenir [77] quelque chose fermement.

coach *noun* 1 (*bus*) car M; **by coach** en car; **on the coach** dans le car; **to travel by coach** voyager en car; **2** (*sports trainer*) entraîneur M, entraîneuse F; **3** (*railway carriage*) wagon M.

coach station *noun* gare F routière.

coach trip *noun* excursion F en car; **to go on a coach trip** faire une excursion en car.

coal *noun* charbon M.

coal mine *noun* mine F de charbon.

coal miner *noun* mineur M.

coarse *adjective* grossier (F grossière).

coast *noun* côte F; **on the east coast** sur la côte est.

coat *noun* **1** manteau M (*plural* manteaux); **2 a coat of paint** une couche de peinture.

coat hanger *noun* cintre M.

cobweb *noun* toile F d'araignée.

cockerel *noun* coq M.

cocoa *noun* (*drink*) chocolat M (chaud); (*powder*) cacao M.

coconut *noun* noix F de coco.

cod *noun* cabillaud M.

code *noun* **1** code M; **the highway code** le code de la route; **2 the dialling code for Cambridge** l'indicatif pour Cambridge.

coffee *noun* café M; **a cup of coffee** un café; **a black coffee, please** un café, s'il vous plaît; **a white coffee** un café au lait.

coffee break *noun* pause-café F.

coffee cup *noun* tasse F à café.

coffee machine *noun* cafetière F; (*electric*) cafetière F électrique.

coffee table *noun* table basse F.

coffin *noun* cercueil M.

coin *noun* pièce F de monnaie; **a pound coin** une pièce d'une livre.

coincidence *noun* coïncidence F.

Coke™ *noun* coca M; **two Cokes™ please** deux cocas s'il vous plaît.

colander *noun* passoire F.

cold *noun* **1** (*cold weather*) froid M; **to be out in the cold** être dehors dans le froid; **2** (*illness*) rhume M; **to have a cold** être enrhumé; **Carol's got a cold** Carol est enrhumée; **a bad cold** un gros rhume.
adjective **1** froid; **your hands are cold** tu as les mains froides; **cold milk** du lait froid; **2** (*weather, temperature*) **it's cold today** il fait froid aujourd'hui; **it's cold in the kitchen** il fait froid dans la cuisine; **3** (*feeling*) **I'm cold** j'ai froid.

cold sore *noun* bouton M de fièvre.

collapse *verb* **1** (*a roof or a wall*) s'écrouler [1]; **2** (*a person*) **he collapsed in his office** il a eu un malaise dans son bureau.

collar *noun* **1** (*on a garment*) col M; **2** (*for a dog*) collier M.

collarbone *noun* clavicule F.

colleague *noun* collègue M & F.

collect *verb* **1** (*as a hobby*) collectionner [1]; **I collect stamps** je collectionne les timbres; **2** aller [7] chercher (*a person*); **she collects the children from school** elle va chercher les enfants à la sortie de l'école; **3** passer [64] prendre (*thing*); **I have to collect a book at the library** je dois passer prendre un livre à la bibliothèque; **4** encaisser [1] (*fares or money*); **5 to collect in the exercise books** ramasser [1] les cahiers.

collection *noun* **1** (*of stamps, CDs, etc*) collection F; **2** (*of money*) collecte F.

college *noun* **1** (*for higher education*) établissement M d'études supérieures; **to go to college** faire des études supérieures; **2** (*a school*) collège M.

collie *noun* colley M.

collision noun collision F.

colour noun couleur F; **what colour is your car?** de quelle couleur est ta voiture?; **what colour is it?** c'est de quelle couleur?; **do you have it in a different colour?** est-ce que vous l'avez dans une autre couleur?
verb (with paints or crayons) colorier [1]; **to colour something red** colorier quelque chose en rouge.

colour blind adjective daltonien (F daltonienne).

colour film noun pellicule F couleur (plural pellicules couleur).

colourful adjective en couleurs vives.

colouring book noun album M à colorier.

colour scheme noun couleurs F plural.

colour supplement noun supplément M illustré.

column noun colonne F.

comb noun peigne M.
verb **to comb your hair** se peigner [1]; **I'll just comb my hair** je vais juste me peigner.

combine verb combiner [1] (two separate things); **they don't combine well** ils ne se combinent pas bien.

come verb 1 venir [81]; **come quick!** viens vite!; **come and see!** venez voir!; **Nick came by bike** Nick est venu à vélo; **did Jess come to school yesterday?** est-ce que Jess est venue à l'école hier?; **Alan comes from Scotland** Alan vient de l'Écosse; **can you come over for a coffee?** peux-tu venir prendre un café?; 2 arriver [1]; **coming!** j'arrive! **the bus is coming** le bus arrive; 3 **to come down** descendre [3] (the stairs or the street); 4 **to come up** monter [1]; **can you come up a moment?** peux-tu monter un instant?; 5 **to come in** entrer [1]; **come in!** entrez!; **she came into the kitchen** elle est entrée dans la cuisine; 6 **to come for** passer [1] prendre (a person); **my father's coming for me** mon père passe me prendre; 7 **come along!** dépêche-toi!

● **to come back** revenir [81]; **he's coming back to collect us** il revient nous chercher.

● **to come off** (a button or handle, for example) se détacher [1]; (a lid) s'enlever [50].

● **to come out** 1 sortir [72]; **they came out when I called** ils sont sortis quand j'ai appelé; **the CD's coming out soon** le CD sort bientôt; 2 (the sun or moon) se montrer [1].

● **to come up to somebody** aborder [1] quelqu'un.

comedian noun comique M.

comedy noun comédie F.

comfortable adjective 1 confortable; **this chair's really comfortable** ce fauteuil est très confortable; 2 **to feel comfortable** (a person) se sentir à l'aise; **are you comfortable there?** êtes-vous bien là?

comfortably adverb confortablement.

comic noun (magazine) illustré M.

omic strip *noun* bande F dessinée.

omma *noun* virgule F.

ommand *noun* ordre M.

omment *noun* (*in a conversation*) remarque F; **he made some rude comments about my friends** il a fait des remarques impolies sur mes amis.

ommentary *noun* reportage M en direct; **the commentary of the match** le reportage du match.

ommentator *noun* commentateur M, commentatrice F; **a sports commentator** un commentateur sportif.

ommercial *noun* spot M publicitaire.
adjective commercial (M *plural* commerciaux).

ommit *verb* **1** commettre [11] (*a crime*); **2 to commit yourself** s'engager [52].

ommittee *noun* comité M.

ommon *adjective* **1** courant; **it's a common problem** c'est un problème courant; **2 in common** en commun; **they have nothing in common** ils n'ont rien en commun.

ommon sense *noun* bon sens M.

ommunicate *verb* communiquer [1].

ommunication *noun* communication F.

ommunion *noun* communion F.

communism *noun* communisme M.

communist *noun* communiste M & F.

community *noun* communauté F; **the European Community** la Communauté Européenne.

commute *verb* **to commute between Oxford and London** faire [10] le trajet entre Oxford et Londres tous les jours.

commuter *noun* navetteur M, navetteuse F.

compact disc *noun* disque compact M.

compact disc player *noun* platine F laser.

company *noun* **1** (*business*) société F; **an insurance company** une société d'assurances; **she's set up a company** elle a monté une société; **2** compagnie F; **an airline company** une compagnie aérienne; **a theatre company** une compagnie théâtrale; **3 to keep somebody company** tenir compagnie à quelqu'un; **the dog keeps me company** le chien me tient compagnie.

comparatively *adverb* relativement.

compare *verb* comparer [1]; **if you compare the French with the English** si on compare les Français aux Anglais; **our house is small compared with yours** notre maison est petite par rapport à la vôtre.

comparison *noun* comparaison F; **in comparison with** par rapport à.

compartment *noun*
compartiment M.

compass *noun* boussole F.

compatible *adjective* (*computing*)
compatible.

compete *verb* **1 to compete in
something** participer [1] à quelque
chose (*race, event*); **2 to compete
for something** se disputer [1]
quelque chose (*jobs, places*); **thirty
people competing for one job**
trente personnes qui se disputent un
seul emploi.

competent *adjective* compétent.

competition *noun* concours M; **a
fishing competition** un concours de
pêche.

competitor *noun* concurrent M,
concurrente F.

complain *verb* se plaindre [31]; **we
complained about the hotel and the
meals** nous nous sommes plaints de
l'hôtel et des repas.

complete *adjective* complet (F
complète); **the complete
collection** la collection complète.
verb (*to finish*) compléter [24].

completely *adverb* complètement.

complexion *noun* teint M.

complicated *adjective* compliqué.

compliment *noun* compliment M;
to pay somebody a compliment
faire un compliment à quelqu'un.

compose *verb* composer [1];
composed of composé de.

composer *noun* compositeur M,
compositrice F.

compromise *noun* compromis M.

compulsory *adjective* obligatoire.

computer *noun* ordinateur M; **to
work on a computer** travailler sur
ordinateur; **to have something on
computer** avoir quelque chose sur
ordinateur.

computer engineer *noun*
technicien M en informatique,
technicienne F en informatique.

computer game *noun* jeu M
électronique (*plural* jeux
électroniques).

computer programmer *noun*
programmeur M, programmeuse F.

computer science *noun*
informatique F.

computing *noun* informatique F.

conceited *adjective* vaniteux (F
vaniteuse).

concentrate *verb* se concentrer [1
I can't concentrate je n'arrive pas
me concentrer; **I was concentratin
on the film** je me concentrais sur le
film.

concentration *noun*
concentration F.

concern *noun* (*worry*) inquiétude
F; **there is no cause for concern**
n'y a pas lieu de s'inquiéter.
verb **1** (*to affect*) concerner [1]; **thi
doesn't concern you** ceci ne te
concerne pas; **2 as far as I'm
concerned** en ce qui me concerne.

concert *noun* **1** concert M; **to go
to a concert** aller à un concert; **2
concert ticket** un billet de concert

conclusion *noun* conclusion F.

concrete *noun* béton M; **a concrete floor** un sol en béton.

condemn *verb* condamner [1].

condition *noun* **1** condition F; **in good condition** en bonne condition; **weather conditions** les conditions météorologiques; **2** (*something you agree to*) condition F; **the conditions of sale** les conditions de vente; **on condition that you let me pay** à condition que tu me laisses payer.

conditional *noun* conditionnel M.

conditioner *noun* (*for your hair*) après-shampooing M.

condom *noun* préservatif M.

conduct *noun* conduite F.
verb diriger [52] (*an orchestra or a piece of music*).

conductor *noun* (*of an orchestra*) chef M d'orchestre.

cone *noun* **1** (*for ice cream*) cornet M; **2** (*for traffic*) balise F.

conference *noun* conférence F.

confess *verb* avouer [1].

confession *noun* confession F.

confidence *noun* **1** (*self-confidence*) assurance F; **to be lacking in confidence** manquer d'assurance; **2** (*faith in somebody else*) confiance F; **to have confidence in somebody** avoir confiance en quelqu'un.

confident *adjective* **1** (*sure of yourself*) assuré; **2** (*sure that something will happen*) sûr.

confirm *verb* confirmer [1]; **we'll confirm the date** nous confirmerons la date.

confuse *verb* **1** troubler [1] (*a person*); **2** confondre [69]; **I confuse him with his brother** je le confonds avec son frère.

confused *adjective* **1** confus; **he gave us a confused story** il nous a raconté une histoire confuse; **2 I'm confused about the holiday dates** je ne comprends pas bien les dates des vacances; **now I'm completely confused!** là je ne comprends plus rien!

confusing *adjective* pas clair; **the instructions are confusing** les instructions ne sont pas claires.

confusion *noun* confusion F.

congratulate *verb* féliciter [1]; **I congratulated Tim on his success** j'ai félicité Tim de son succès; **we congratulate you on winning** nous vous félicitons d'avoir gagné.

congratulations *plural noun* félicitations F *plural*; **congratulations on the baby!** félicitations pour le bébé!

conjurer *noun* prestidigitateur M.

connect *verb* (*to plug in to the mains*) brancher [1] (*a dishwasher or TV, for example*).

connection *noun* **1** (*between two ideas or events*) rapport M; **there's no connection between his letter and my decision** il n'y a aucun rapport entre sa lettre et ma décision; **2** (*between trains or planes*) correspondance F; **Sally missed her connection** Sally a raté sa correspondance; **3** (*electrical*) contact M; **a faulty connection** un mauvais contact.

conscience *noun* conscience F; **to have a guilty conscience** avoir mauvaise conscience.

conscious *adjective* conscient.

consequence *noun* conséquence F.

consequently *adverb* par conséquent.

conservation *noun* (*of nature*) protection F.

conservative *noun, adjective* conservateur M, conservatrice F.

conservatory *noun* jardin M d'hiver.

consider *verb* 1 (*to give thought to*) considérer [24] (*a suggestion or idea*); 2 (*to think you might do*) envisager [52]; **we are considering buying a flat** nous envisageons d'acheter un appartement; 3 **all things considered** tout compte fait.

considerate *adjective* attentionné (*a person*).

consideration *noun* considération F.

considering *preposition* étant donné; **considering her age** étant donné son âge; **considering he did it all himself** étant donné qu'il a tout fait lui-même.

consist *verb* **to consist of** être [6] composé de.

consonant *noun* consonne F.

constant *adjective* permanent.

constipated *adjective* constipé.

construct *verb* construire [26].

construction *noun* construction F.

consult *verb* consulter [1].

consumer *noun* consommateur M, consommatrice F.

contact *noun* 1 (*touch*) contact M; **to be in contact with somebody** être en contact avec quelqu'un; **we've lost contact** nous avons perdu contact; 2 (*people you know*) connaissance F; **Rob has contacts in the music business** Rob a des connaissances dans le monde de la musique.
verb contacter [1]; **I'll contact you tomorrow** je te contacterai demain.

contact lens *noun* lentille F de contact (*plural* lentilles de contact).

contain *verb* contenir [77].

container *noun* récipient M.

contemporary *adjective* 1 (*around today*) contemporain; 2 (*modern*) moderne.

contents *plural noun* contenu M; **the contents of my suitcase** le contenu de ma valise.

contest *noun* concours M.

contestant *noun* concurrent M, concurrente F.

continent *noun* continent M; **on the Continent** en Europe continentale.

continental *adjective* **a continent**

holiday des vacances en Europe continentale.

continue *verb* continuer [1]; **we continued (with) our journey** nous avons continué notre voyage; **Jill continued chatting** Jill a continué de bavarder; **'to be continued'** 'à suivre'.

continuous *adjective* continu; **continuous assessment** le contrôle continu.

contraceptive *noun* contraceptif M.

contract *noun* contrat M.

contradict *verb* contredire [47].

contradiction *noun* contradiction F.

contrary *noun* contraire M; **on the contrary** au contraire.

contrast *noun* contraste M.

contribute *verb* donner [1] (*money*).

contribution *noun* (*to charity or an appeal*) don M.

control *noun* (*of a crowd or animals*) contrôle M; **the police have lost control** la police a perdu le contrôle; **keep your dogs under control** maîtrisez vos chiens; **everything's under control** tout va bien; **the fire was out of control** on ne maîtrisait plus l'incendie. *verb* **1** maîtriser [1] (*a crowd, animals, or a fire, for example*); **2 to control oneself** se contrôler [1].

convenient *adjective* **1** commode; **frozen vegetables are very convenient** les légumes congelés sont très commodes; **2 to be convenient for somebody** convenir à quelqu'un; **if that's convenient for you** si cela vous convient; **3 the house is convenient for shops and schools** la maison est bien située par rapport aux magasins et aux écoles.

conventional *adjective* **1** conventionnel (F conventionnelle); **2** (*person*) conformiste.

conversation *noun* conversation F.

convert *verb* transformer [1]; **we're going to convert the garage into a workshop** nous allons transformer le garage en atelier.

convince *verb* convaincre [79]; **I'm convinced you're wrong** je suis convaincu que tu as tort.

convincing *adjective* convaincant.

cook *noun* cuisinier M, cuisinière F. *verb* **1** faire [10] la cuisine; **who's cooking tonight?** qui fait la cuisine ce soir?; **I like cooking** j'aime faire la cuisine; **2** faire [10] cuire (*vegetables, pasta, etc*); **cook the carrots for five minutes** faites cuire les carottes pendant cinq minutes; **3** préparer [1] (*a meal*); **Fran's busy cooking supper** Fran est en train de préparer le dîner; **4** (*food*) cuire [36]; **the sausages are cooking** les saucisses sont en train de cuire; **is the chicken cooked?** est-ce que le poulet est cuit?

cooker *noun* cuisinière F; **an electric cooker** une cuisinière électrique; **a gas cooker** une cuisinière à gaz.

cookery *noun* cuisine F.

cookery book *noun* livre M de cuisine.

cooking *noun* cuisine F; **to do the cooking** faire la cuisine; **Italian cooking** la cuisine italienne.

cool *noun* 1 (*coldness*) fraîcheur F; **stay in the cool** reste à la fraîcheur; 2 (*calm*) **to lose one's cool** perdre son sang-froid; **he kept his cool** il a gardé son sang-froid.
adjective 1 (*cold*) frais (F fraîche); **a cool drink** une boisson fraîche; **it's cool inside** il fait frais dans la maison; 2 (*laid-back*) décontracté; 3 (*sophisticated*) branché (*informal*).
verb refroidir [2]; **while the engine was cooling (down)** pendant que le moteur refroidissait.

cop *noun* flic M (*informal*).

cope *verb* 1 (*to manage*) se débrouiller [1]; **she copes well** elle se débrouille bien; 2 **to cope with** s'occuper [1] de (*children or work*); **I'll cope with the dishes** je m'occuperai de la vaisselle; 3 faire [10] face à (*problems*); **she's had a lot to cope with** elle a été obligée de faire face à beaucoup de choses; **he can't cope any more** il n'arrive plus à faire face.

copy *noun* 1 copie F; **make ten copies of this letter** faites dix copies de cette lettre; 2 (*of a book*) exemplaire M.
verb copier [1]; **I copied (down) the address** j'ai copié l'adresse.

cord *noun* (*for a blind, for example*) cordon M.

cordless telephone *noun* téléphone M sans fil.

core *noun* (*of an apple or a pear*) trognon M.

cork *noun* 1 (*in a bottle*) bouchon M; 2 (*material*) liège M.

corkscrew *noun* tire-bouchon M.

corn *noun* 1 (*wheat*) blé M; 2 (*sweetcorn*) maïs M.

corner *noun* coin M; **in a corner of the kitchen** dans un coin de la cuisine; **at the corner of the street** au coin de la rue; **out of the corner of your eye** du coin de l'œil; **it's just round the corner** c'est tout près.

cornflakes *noun* corn-flakes M *plural*.

Cornwall *noun* Cornouailles F; **in Cornwall** en Cornouailles.

corpse *noun* cadavre M.

correct *adjective* 1 exact; **yes, that's correct** oui, c'est exact; 2 bon (F bonne); **the correct sum** la bonne somme; **the correct answer** la bonne réponse; **the correct choice** le bon choix.
verb corriger [52].

correction *noun* correction F.

correspond *verb* correspondre [3].

corridor *noun* couloir M.

Corsica *noun* Corse F; **to Corsica** en Corse.

cosmetics *plural noun* produits M *plural* de beauté.

cost *noun* prix M; **the cost of a new**

computer le prix d'un nouvel ordinateur; **the cost of living** le coût de la vie.
verb coûter [1]; **how much does it cost?** combien est-ce que ça coûte?; **the tickets cost £10** les billets coûtent dix livres; **it costs too much** cela coûte trop cher.

costume *noun* costume M.

cosy *adjective* (*a bed or room*) douillet (F douillette); **it's cosy by the fire** on est bien à côté du feu.

cot *noun* lit M d'enfant.

cottage *noun* petite maison F.

cotton *noun* 1 (*fabric*) coton M; **a cotton shirt** une chemise en coton; 2 (*thread*) fil M de coton.

cotton wool *noun* ouate F de coton.

couch *noun* canapé M.

cough *noun* toux F; **a nasty cough** une mauvaise toux; **to have a cough** tousser.
verb tousser [1].

could *verb* 1 **if he could pay** s'il pouvait payer; **I couldn't open it** je ne pouvais pas l'ouvrir; **they couldn't smoke there** ils ne pouvaient pas fumer là; **she did all she could** elle a fait tout ce qu'elle pouvait; 2 (*knew how to*) **he couldn't drive** il ne savait pas conduire; **I couldn't swim** je ne savais pas nager; 3 (*with seeing, hearing, or smelling*) **I could hear the police car** j'entendais la voiture de police; **she couldn't see anything** elle ne voyait rien; 4 (*might*) **could I speak to David?** pourrais-je parler à David?;

you could try telephoning tu pourrais téléphoner.

council *noun* conseil M.

count *verb* 1 (*reckon up*) compter [1]; **I counted my money** j'ai compté mon argent; **thirty-five not counting the children** trente-cinq sans compter les enfants; 2 **to count as** être [6] considéré comme; **children over twelve count as adults** les enfants au-dessus de douze ans sont considérés comme adultes.

counter *noun* 1 (*in a shop or café*) comptoir M; 2 (*in a post office or bank*) guichet M; 3 (*in a big store*) rayon M; **on the cheese counter** au rayon fromagerie; 4 (*for board games*) jeton M.

country *noun* 1 (*France, England, etc*) pays M; **a foreign country** un pays étranger; **from another country** d'un autre pays; 2 (*not town*) campagne F; **to live in the country** vivre à la campagne; **a country walk** une promenade à la campagne; **a country road** une route de campagne.

country dancing *noun* danse F folklorique.

countryside *noun* campagne F.

county *noun* comté M.

couple *noun* 1 (*a pair*) couple M; 2 **a couple of** deux ou trois; **a couple of times** deux ou trois fois; **I've got a couple of things to do** j'ai deux ou trois choses à faire.

courage *noun* courage M.

courier *noun* 1 (*on a package holiday*) accompagnateur M, accompagnatrice F; **2** (*delivery service*) coursier M; **by courier** par coursier.

course *noun* **1** (*lessons*) cours M; **a beginners' course** un cours pour débutants; **a computer course** un cours d'informatique; **to go on a course** suivre un cours; **2** (*part of a meal*) plat M; **the main course** le plat principal; **a golf course** un golf; **3 of course** bien sûr; **yes, of course!** oui, bien sûr!; **he's forgotten, of course** il a oublié, bien sûr.

court *noun* **1** (*for tennis or squash*) court M; **2** (*for basketball*) terrain M.

courtyard *noun* cour F.

cousin *noun* cousin M, cousine F; **my cousin Sonia** ma cousine Sonia.

cover *noun* **1** (*for a book*) couverture F; **2** (*for a duvet or cushion*) housse F; **a duvet cover** une housse de couette. *verb* **1** (*to protect or cover up*) couvrir [30]; **cover the wound** couvrez la blessure; **he was covered in spots** il était couvert de boutons; **2** (*with leaves, snow, or fabric*) recouvrir [30]; **the ground was covered with snow** le sol était recouvert de neige.

cow *noun* vache F; **mad cow disease** maladie F de la vache folle.

coward *noun* lâche M & F.

cowboy *noun* cowboy M.

crab *noun* crabe M.

crack *noun* **1** (*in a wall or cup*) fêlure F; **2** (*a cracking noise*) craquement M. *verb* **1** (*to make a crack in*) fêler [1] (*a cup, a chair, or a bone*); **2** (*to break*) casser [1] (*a nut or an egg*); **3** (*to split by itself: ice, for example*) se fêler [1]; **4** (*to make a noise*) (*a twig*) craquer [1].

cracker *noun* **1** (*biscuit*) cracker M; **2** (*Christmas cracker*) diablotin M.

crackle *verb* crépiter [1].

craft *noun* (*at school*) travaux manuels M *plural*.

cramp *noun* crampe F; **to have cramp in your leg** avoir une cramp à la jambe.

crane *noun* grue F.

crash *noun* **1** (*an accident*) accident M; **a car crash** un accident de voiture; **2** (*smashing noise*) fracas M; **a crash of broken glass** un fracas de verre brisé. *verb* **1** (*a car or plane*) s'écraser [1] **the plane crashed** l'avion s'est écrasé; **2 to crash into something** rentrer [1] dans quelque chose; **the car crashed into a tree** la voiture e rentrée dans un arbre.

crash course *noun* cours M intensif.

crash helmet *noun* casque M.

crate *noun* **1** (*for bottles or china*) caisse F; **2** (*for fruit*) cageot M.

crawl *noun* (*in swimming*) crawl M. *verb* **1** (*a person, a baby*) marcher [1] à quatre pattes; **2** (*cars in a jan*) rouler [1] au pas; **we were crawlin along** nous roulions au pas.

crayon *noun* **1** (*wax*) crayon M gras; **2** (*coloured pencil*) crayon M de couleur.

craze *noun* vogue F; **the craze for rollerblades** la vogue des rollers.

crazy *adjective* fou (F folle).

creak *verb* (*a hinge*) grincer [61]; (*a floorboard*) craquer [1].

cream *noun* crème F; **strawberries and cream** des fraises à la crème.

cream cheese *noun* fromage M à tartiner.

crease *noun* pli M.

creased *adjective* froissé.

create *verb* créer [32].

creative *adjective* créatif (F créative) (*a person*).

creature *noun* créature F.

crèche *noun* crèche F.

credit *noun* crédit M; **to buy something on credit** acheter quelque chose à crédit.

credit card *noun* carte F de crédit.

cress *noun* cresson M.

crew *noun* **1** (*on a ship or plane*) équipage M; **2** (*rowing or filming*) équipe F.

crew cut *noun* cheveux M *plural* en brosse.

cricket *noun* **1** (*game*) cricket M; **to play cricket** jouer au cricket; **2** (*insect*) grillon M.

cricket bat *noun* batte F de cricket.

crime *noun* **1** crime M; **murder is a crime** le meurtre est un crime;

2 (*within society*) criminalité F; **the fight against crime** la lutte contre la criminalité.

criminal *noun, adjective* criminel M, criminelle F.

crimson *adjective* pourpre.

crisis *noun* crise F.

crisp *noun* chips F; **a packet of (potato) crisps** un sachet de chips. *adjective* **1** (*biscuit*) croustillant; **2** (*apple*) croquant.

critical *adjective* **1** critique (*a remark or somebody's condition*); **2** décisif (F décisive) (*a moment*).

criticism *noun* critique F.

criticize *verb* critiquer [1].

Croatia *noun* Croatie F.

crockery *noun* vaisselle F.

crocodile *noun* crocodile M.

crook *noun* (*criminal*) escroc M.

crop *noun* récolte F.

cross *noun* croix F.
adjective fâché; **she's very cross** elle est très fâchée; **I'm cross with you** je suis fâché contre toi.
verb **1** (*to cross over*) traverser [1]; **to cross the road** traverser la rue; **2 to cross your legs** croiser [1] les jambes; **3 to cross into Italy** passer [1] en Italie; **4** (*to cross each other*) se croiser [1]; **the two roads cross here** les deux routes se croisent ici.

● **to cross out** rayer [59] (*a mistake, for example*).

cross-Channel *adjective* trans-Manche; **a cross-Channel ferry** un ferry trans-Manche.

cross-country noun **1** cross M; **2 cross-country skiing** le ski de fond.

crossing noun **1** (*from one place to another*) traversée F; **a Channel crossing** une traversée trans-Manche; **2 a pedestrian crossing** un passage piétons; **a level crossing** un passage à niveau.

cross-legged adjective **to sit cross-legged** être assis en tailleur.

crossroads noun carrefour M; **at the crossroads** au carrefour.

crossword noun mots M plural croisés; **to do the crossword** faire les mots croisés.

crouch verb s'accroupir [2].

crow noun corbeau M; ★ **ten kilometres as the crow flies** dix kilomètres à vol d'oiseau.
verb (*a cock*) chanter [1].

crowd noun foule F; **in the crowd** dans la foule; **a crowd of 5,000** une foule de cinq mille.
verb **to crowd into** s'entasser [1] dans (*a room or bus, for example*); **we all crowded into the train** nous nous sommes tous entassés dans le train.

crowded adjective bondé.

crown noun couronne F.

crude adjective **1** (*rough and ready*) rudimentaire; **2** (*vulgar*) grossier (F grossière).

cruel adjective cruel (F cruelle).

cruise noun croisière F; **to go on a cruise** faire une croisière.

crumb noun miette F.

crumple verb froisser [1].

crunch verb croquer [1] (*an apple*).

crunchy adjective croquant.

crush verb écraser [1].

crust noun croûte F.

crusty adjective croustillant (*bread*).

crutch noun béquille F; **to be on crutches** marcher avec des béquilles.

cry noun cri M.
verb **1** (*weep*) pleurer [1]; **2** (*call out*) crier [1].

crystal noun cristal M.

cub noun **1** (*animal*) petit M; **2** (*scout*) louveteau M.

cube noun cube M; **an ice cube** u glaçon.

cubic adjective (*for measurements*) cube; **three cubic metres** trois mètres cube.

cubicle noun **1** (*in a changing room*) cabine F; **2** (*in a public lavatory*) cabinet M.

cuckoo noun coucou M.

cucumber noun concombre M.

cuddle noun **to give somebody a cuddle** faire un câlin à quelqu'un.
verb câliner [1].

cue noun (*billiards, pool, snooker*) queue F de billard.

cuff noun (*on a shirt*) manchette F.

cul-de-sac noun impasse F.

culture noun culture F.

cunning *adjective* rusé.

cup *noun* **1** (*for drinking*) tasse F; **a cup of tea** une tasse de thé; **2** (*a trophy*) coupe F.

cupboard *noun* placard M; **in the kitchen cupboard** dans le placard de la cuisine.

cup tie *noun* match M de coupe.

cure *noun* remède M.
verb guérir [2].

curiosity *noun* curiosité F.

curious *adjective* curieux (F curieuse).

curl *noun* boucle F.
verb friser [1] (*hair*).

currant *noun* raisin M de Corinthe.

currency *noun* **foreign currency** les devises étrangères.

current *noun* (*of electricity or water*) courant M.
adjective actuel (F actuelle) (*a situation, for example*).

current affairs *noun* actualité F.

curriculum *noun* programme M.

curry *noun* curry M; **chicken curry** le curry de poulet.

curtain *noun* rideau M (*plural* rideaux).

cushion *noun* coussin M.

custard *noun* **1** (*runny*) crème F anglaise; **2** (*baked*) flan M.

custom *noun* coutume F.

customer *noun* client M, cliente F.

customs *plural noun* douane F singular; **to go through customs** passer à la douane.

customs hall *noun* douane F.

customs officer *noun* douanier M, douanière F.

cut *noun* **1** (*injury*) coupure F; **2** (*haircut*) coupe F.
verb **1** couper [1]; **I've cut the bread** j'ai coupé le pain; **you'll cut yourself!** tu vas te couper!; **Kevin's cut his finger** Kevin s'est coupé le doigt; **2 to cut the grass** tondre [3] le gazon; **3 to get your hair cut** se faire [10] couper les cheveux; **Anne's had her hair cut** Anne s'est fait couper les cheveux; **4 to cut prices** baisser les prix.
● **to cut down something** abattre [21] (*a tree*).
● **to cut out something 1** découper [1] (*a shape, a newspaper article*); **2** supprimer (*sugar, fatty food, etc*).
● **to cut up something** couper [1] (*food*).

cutlery *noun* couverts M *plural*.

CV *noun* CV M.

cycle *noun* (*bike*) vélo M.
verb faire [10] du vélo; **do you like cycling?** est-ce que tu aimes faire du vélo?; **we cycle to school** nous allons à l'école en vélo.

cycle lane *noun* piste F cyclable.

cycle race *noun* course F cycliste.

cycling *noun* cyclisme M.

cycling holiday *noun* vacances F *plural* à vélo.

cyclist *noun* cycliste M & F.

D d

dad noun **1** père M; **Anna's dad** le père d'Anna; **my dad works in a bank** mon père travaille dans une banque; **2** (*within the family*) papa M; **Dad's not home yet** Papa n'est pas encore rentré.

daffodil noun jonquille F.

daily adjective quotidien (F quotidienne).

dairy products plural noun les produits laitiers M plural.

daisy noun pâquerette F.

dam noun barrage M.

damage noun dégâts M plural; **there's no damage** il n'y a pas de dégâts.
verb endommager [52].

damn noun **he doesn't give a damn** il s'en fiche complètement (*informal*).
exclamation **damn!** zut! (*informal*).

damp adjective humide.
noun humidité F; **because of the damp** à cause de l'humidité.

dance noun danse F; **a folk dance** une danse traditionnelle.
verb danser [1]; **I like dancing** j'aime danser.

dancer noun danseur M, danseuse F.

dancing noun danse F.

dancing class noun cours M de danse; **to go to dancing classes** suivre des cours de danse.

dandruff noun pellicules F plural.

danger noun danger M; **to be in danger** être en danger.

dangerous adjective dangereux (F dangereuse); **it's dangerous to drive too fast** il est dangereux de conduire trop vite.

Danish noun danois M.
adjective danois.

dare verb **1** oser [1]; **to dare to do** oser faire; **I didn't dare suggest it** je n'ai pas osé le suggérer; **2** **don't you dare tell her I'm here!** je t'interdis de lui dire que je suis là!; **3** **I dare you!** chiche que tu y vas! (*informal*); **I dare you to tell him!** chiche que tu le lui dises! (*informal*).

daring adjective osé; **that was a bit daring!** c'était un peu osé!

dark noun **in the dark** dans l'obscurité; **after dark** après la tombée de la nuit; **to be afraid of the dark** avoir peur du noir.
adjective **1** (*colour*) foncé; **a dark blue skirt** une jupe bleu foncé; **2** **she has dark brown hair** elle est brune; **3** **it's dark already** il fait nuit déjà; **it gets dark around five** nuit commence à tomber vers cinq heures; **4** (*room*) sombre; **the kitchen's a bit dark** la cuisine est plutôt sombre; **it's dark in here** il fait sombre ici.

darkness noun obscurité F; **in darkness** dans l'obscurité.

darling noun chéri M, chérie F;

see you later, darling! à tout à l'heure, chéri!

dart *noun* fléchette F; **to play darts** jouer aux fléchettes.

data *plural noun* données F *plural*.

database *noun* base F de données.

date *noun* 1 date F; **the date of the meeting** la date de la réunion; **to fix a date for** fixer une date pour; **2 what's the date today?** nous sommes le combien aujourd'hui?; **3 out of date** (*passport, driving licence, etc*) périmé; (*technology, method, information, etc*) dépassé; **my passport's out of date** mon passeport est périmé; **4** (*fruit*) datte F.

date of birth *noun* date F de naissance.

daughter *noun* fille F; **Tina's daughter** la fille de Tina.

daughter-in-law *noun* belle-fille F (*plural* belles-filles).

dawn *noun* aube F.

day *noun* 1 jour M; **three days later** trois jours plus tard; **the day I went to London** le jour où je suis allé à Londres; **2** (*just from morning until evening*) journée F; **we spent the day in London** nous avons passé la journée à Londres; **it rained all day** il a plu pendant toute la journée; **3 it's going to be a nice day tomorrow** il va faire beau demain; **4 the day after** le lendemain; **the day after the wedding** le lendemain du mariage; **the day after tomorrow** après-demain; **my sister's arriving the day after tomorrow** ma sœur arrive

après-demain; **5 the day before** la veille; **the day before the wedding** la veille du mariage; **the day before yesterday** avant-hier; **my sister arrived the day before yesterday** ma sœur est arrivée avant-hier.

dead *adjective, adverb* 1 **her father's dead** son père est mort; **2** (*really*) vachement (*informal*); **he's dead nice** il est vachement gentil; **it was dead good** c'était vachement bien; **it's dead easy** c'est vachement facile; **you're dead right** tu as absolument raison; **she arrived dead on time** elle est arrivée à l'heure pile.

dead end *noun* impasse F.

deadline *noun* date F limite.

deaf *adjective* sourd.

deafening *adjective* assourdissant.

deal *noun* 1 (*involving money*) affaire; **it's a good deal** c'est une bonne affaire; **2** marché M; **I'll make a deal with you** je ferai un marché avec toi; **it's a deal!** marché conclu!; **3 a great deal of** beaucoup de; **I don't have a great deal of time** je n'ai pas beaucoup de temps.
verb (*in cards*) donner [1]; **it's you to deal** c'est à toi de donner.
● **to deal with something** s'occuper [1] de quelque chose; **Linda deals with the accounts** Linda s'occupe de la comptabilité; **I'll deal with it as soon as possible** je m'en occuperai dès que possible.

dear *adjective* 1 cher (F chère); **Dear Sylvie** Chère Sylvie; **2** (*expensive*) cher (F chère).

death noun mort F; **after his father's death** après la mort de son père; ★ **you'll frighten him to death** tu lui feras une peur bleue; ★ **I'm bored to death** je m'ennuie à mourir; ★ **I'm sick to death of it** j'en ai marre (informal).

death penalty noun peine F de mort.

debate noun débat M. verb débattre [21].

debt noun dette F; **to get into debt** s'endetter.

decade noun décennie F.

decaffeinated adjective décaféiné.

deceive verb tromper [1].

December noun décembre M; **in December** en décembre.

decent adjective **1** convenable; **a decent salary** un salaire convenable; **2 a decent meal** un bon repas; **3 he seems a decent enough guy** il semble être un type plutôt bien (informal).

decide verb décider [1]; **to decide to do** décider de faire; **she's decided to buy a car** elle a décidé d'acheter une voiture; **she's decided not to buy a car** elle a décidé de ne pas acheter une voiture.

decimal adjective décimal (M plural décimaux).

decimal point noun virgule F.

decision noun décision F; **the right decision** la bonne décision; **the wrong decision** la mauvaise

décision; **to make a decision** prendre une décision.

deck noun (on a ship) pont M.

deckchair noun transat M.

declare verb déclarer [1].

decorate verb **1** décorer [1]; **to decorate the Christmas tree** décorer le sapin de Noël; **2** peindre; **we're decorating the kitchen this weekend** on va peindre la cuisine ce weekend.

decoration noun décoration F.

decrease noun diminution F; **a decrease in the number of** une diminution du nombre de. verb diminuer [1].

deduct verb déduire [26].

deep adjective profond; **a deep feeling of gratitude** un profond sentiment de reconnaissance; **the river is very deep here** la rivière est très profonde ici; **how deep is the swimming pool?** quelle est la profondeur de la piscine?; **a hole two metres deep** un trou de deux mètres de profondeur.

deep end noun **the deep end** (of a swimming pool) le grand bassin.

deep freeze noun congélateur M.

deeply adverb profondément.

deer noun **1** (red deer) cerf M; **2** (roe deer) chevreuil M; **3** (fallow deer) daim M.

defeat noun défaite F. verb battre [21].

defect noun défaut M.

defence noun défense F.

defend *verb* défendre [3].

defender *noun* défenseur.

define *verb* définir [2].

definite *adjective* 1 net (F nette) (*before the noun*) **a definite change** un net changement; **a definite improvement** une nette amélioration; 2 (*certain*) sûr; **it's not definite yet** ce n'est pas encore sûr; 3 (*exact*) précis; **a definite answer** une réponse précise; **I don't have a definite idea of what I want** je n'ai pas une idée précise de ce que je veux.

definitely *adverb* 1 (*when giving your opinion about something*) sans aucun doute; **the blue one is definitely the biggest** le bleu est sans aucun doute le plus grand; **your French is definitely better than mine** ton français est sans aucun doute meilleur que le mien; **'are you sure you like this one better?'** – **'definitely!'** 'tu es sûr que tu préfères celui-ci?' – 'sans aucun doute!'; 2 **she's definitely going to be there** elle va y être, c'est sûr; **I'm definitely not going** c'est décidé, je n'y vais pas.

definition *noun* définition F.

degree *noun* 1 degré M; **thirty degrees** trente degrés; 2 **a university degree** un diplôme universitaire.

delay *noun* retard M; **a two-hour delay** un retard de deux heures. *verb* 1 (*make late*) retarder [1]; **the flight was delayed by bad weather** le vol a été retardé pas le mauvais temps; 2 (*postpone*) différer [24];

the decision has been delayed until Thursday la décision a été différée jusqu'à jeudi.

delete *verb* effacer [61].

deliberate *adjective* délibéré.

deliberately *adverb* exprès; **you did it deliberately** tu l'as fait exprès; **he left it there deliberately** il a fait exprès de le laisser là.

delicate *adjective* délicat.

delicatessen *noun* épicerie F fine.

delicious *adjective* délicieux (F délicieuse).

delighted *adjective* ravi; **they're delighted with their new flat** ils sont ravis de leur nouvel appartement; **I'm delighted to hear you can come** je suis ravi d'apprendre que vous pouvez venir.

deliver *verb* 1 livrer [1]; **they're delivering the washing machine tomorrow** ils vont livrer la machine à laver demain; 2 distribuer [1] (*mail*).

delivery *noun* livraison F.

demand *noun* demande F. *verb* exiger [52].

demo *noun* (*protest*) manif F (*informal*).

democracy *noun* démocratie F.

democratic *adjective* démocratique.

demolish *verb* démolir [2].

demonstrate *verb* 1 faire [10] la démonstration de (*a machine, product, or technique*); 2 (*protest*) manifester [1]; **to demonstrate**

against something manifester contre quelque chose.

demonstration noun 1 (of machine, product, technique) démonstration F; 2 (protest) manifestation.

demonstrator noun (in protest) manifestant M, manifestante F.

denim noun jean M; **a denim jacket** un blouson en jean.

Denmark noun Danemark M; **in Denmark** au Danemark; **to Denmark** au Danemark.

dense adjective dense.

dent noun bosse F.
verb cabosser [1].

dental adjective 1 dentaire; **dental floss** du fil dentaire; **dental hygiene** l'hygiène dentaire; 2 **a dental appointment** un rendez-vous chez le dentiste.

dental surgeon noun chirurgien-dentiste M.

dentist noun dentiste M & F; **my mum's a dentist** ma mère est dentiste.

deny verb nier [1].

deodorant noun déodorant M.

depart verb partir [58].

department noun 1 (in school, university) département M; **the language department** le département de langues; 2 (in a shop) rayon M; **the men's department** le rayon hommes.

department store noun grand magasin M.

departure noun départ M.

departure lounge noun salle F d'embarquement.

depend verb **to depend on** dépendre [3] de; **it depends on the price** ça dépend du prix; **it depends on what you want** ça dépend de ce que tu veux; **it depends** ça dépend.

deposit noun 1 (when renting or hiring) caution F; 2 (when booking a holiday or hotel room) arrhes F plural; **to pay a deposit** verser des arrhes; 3 (on a bottle) consigne F.

depressed adjective déprimé.

depressing adjective déprimant.

depth noun profondeur F.

deputy noun adjoint M, adjointe F.

deputy head noun directeur adjoint M, directrice adjointe F.

descend verb descendre [3].

describe verb décrire [38].

description noun description F.

desert noun désert M; **in the desert** dans le désert.

desert island noun île F déserte.

deserve verb mériter [1].

design noun 1 conception F; **the design of the plane** la conception de l'avion; 2 (artistic design) design M; **fashion design** le stylisme; 3 (pattern) motif M; **a floral design** un motif floral.
verb 1 concevoir [66] (a machine, plane, system); 2 créer [32] (costumes, clothes, fabric, scenery).

designer noun 1 (fashion designer

styliste M & F; **2** (*graphic designer*)
graphiste M & F.

desire *noun* désir M.
verb désirer [1].

desk *noun* **1** (*in office or at home*)
bureau M; **2** (*pupil's*) table F;
3 the reception desk la réception;
the information desk le bureau des
renseignements.

despair *noun* désespoir M.
verb **to despair of doing** désespérer
[24] de faire.

desperate *adjective* **1** désespéré; **a
desperate attempt** une tentative
désespérée; **2 to be desperate to
do** avoir très envie de faire; **I'm
desperate to see you** j'ai très envie
de te voir.

despise *verb* mépriser [1].

dessert *noun* dessert M; **what's for
dessert?** qu'est-ce qu'il y a comme
dessert?

destination *noun* destination F.

destroy *verb* détruire [26].

destruction *noun* destruction F.

detached house *noun* maison F
individuelle.

detail *noun* détail M.

detailed *adjective* détaillé.

detective *noun* **1** (*police*)
inspecteur de police M; **2 a
private detective** un détective.

detective story *noun* roman M
policier.

detention *noun* retenue F.

detergent *noun* détergent M.

determined *adjective* résolu; **he's
determined to leave** il est résolu de
partir.

detour *noun* détour M.

develop *verb* **1** développer [1]; **to
get a film developed** faire
développer une pellicule; **2** se
développer; **how children develop**
comment les enfants se
développent.

developing country *noun* pays
M en voie de développement.

development *noun*
développement M.

devil *noun* diable M.

devoted *adjective* dévoué.

diabetes *noun* diabète M.

diabetic *noun, adjective* diabète
M & F; **to be (a) diabetic** être
diabète.

diagonal *adjective* diagonal (M
plural diagonaux).

diagram *noun* schéma M.

dial *verb* composer [1] le numéro; **lift
the receiver and dial 142** décrochez
et composez le 142.

dialling tone *noun* tonalité F.

dialogue *noun* dialogue M.

diamond *noun* **1** diamant M;
2 (*in cards*) carreau; **the jack of
diamonds** le valet de carreau;
3 (*shape*) losange M.

diarrhoea *noun* diarrhée F; **to
have diarrhoea** avoir la diarrhée.

diary *noun* **1** agenda M; **j'ai
marqué la date de la réunion dans
mon agenda** I've noted the date of

the meeting in my diary; **2** journal intime; **to keep a diary** tenir un journal (intime).

dice *noun* dé M; **to throw the dice** jeter le dé.

dictation *noun* dictée F.

dictionary *noun* dictionnaire M; **to look up a word in the dictionary** chercher un mot dans le dictionnaire.

did *verb* SEE **do**.

die *verb* **1** mourir [54]; **my grannie died in January** ma grand-mère est morte en janvier; **2 to be dying to do** mourir d'envie de faire; **I'm dying to see them!** je meurs d'envie de les voir!

diesel *noun* **1** gazole M; **2 a diesel engine** un moteur diesel; **a diesel car** une voiture diesel.

diet *noun* **1** alimentation F; **to have a healthy diet** avoir une alimentation saine; **2** (*slimming or special*) régime M; **to be on a diet** être au régime; **a salt-free diet** un régime sans sel.

difference *noun* **1** différence F; **I can't see any difference between the two** je ne vois pas la différence entre les deux; **what's the difference between...?** quelle est la différence entre...?; **2 it makes a difference** ça change quelque chose; **it makes no difference** ça ne change rien; **it makes no difference what I say** je peux dire ce que je veux, ça ne change rien.

different *adjective* différent; **the two sisters are very different** les deux sœurs sont très différentes;

she's very different from her sister elle est très différente de sa sœur.

difficult *adjective* difficile; **it's really difficult** c'est vraiment difficile; **it's difficult to decide** il est difficile de décider.

difficulty *noun* **1** difficulté F; **2 to have difficulty doing** avoir du mal à faire; **I had difficulty finding your house** j'ai eu du mal à trouver ta maison.

dig *verb* **to dig a hole** creuser [1] un trou.

digestion *noun* digestion F.

digital *adjective* numérique; **a digital recording** un enregistrement numérique; **a digital watch** une montre à affichage numérique.

dim *adjective* **1 a dim light** une lumière faible; **2 she's a bit dim** elle est un peu bouchée (*informal*).

dimension *noun* dimension F.

din *noun* vacarme M; **they were making a dreadful din** ils faisaient un vacarme pas possible; **stop making such a din!** arrêtez de faire ce vacarme!

dinghy *noun* **1 a sailing dinghy** un dériveur; **2 a rubber dinghy** un canot pneumatique.

dining room *noun* salle à manger F; **in the dining room** dans la salle à manger.

dinner *noun* **1** (*evening*) dîner M; **to invite somebody to dinner** inviter quelqu'un à dîner; **2** (*midday*) déjeuner M; **to have school dinner** manger à la cantine

dinner party *noun* dîner M.

dinner time *noun* **1** (*evening*) l'heure du dîner; **2** (*midday*) l'heure du déjeuner.

dinosaur *noun* dinosaure M.

diploma *noun* diplôme M.

direct *adjective* direct. *verb* **1** réaliser [1] (*programme, film*); **2** mettre en scène (*play*); **3** régler (*traffic*).

direction *noun* **1** direction F; **in the other direction** dans l'autre direction; **2 to ask somebody for directions** demander son chemin à quelqu'un; **3 directions for use** mode M d'emploi.

directly *adverb* **1** directement; **2 directly afterwards** immédiatement après.

director *noun* **1** (*of a company*) directeur M, directrice F; **2** (*of a programme or film*) réalisateur M, réalisatrice F; **3** (*of a play*) metteur M en scène.

directory *noun* annuaire M; **to be ex-directory** être sur la liste rouge.

dirt *noun* saleté F.

dirty *adjective* sale; **my hands are dirty** j'ai les mains sales; **to get something dirty** salir quelque chose; **you'll get your dress dirty** tu vas salir ta robe; **to get dirty** se salir; **the curtains get dirty quickly** les rideaux se salissent vite.

disabled *adjective* handicapé; **disabled people** les handicapés.

disadvantage *noun*
1 désavantage M; **2 to be at a disadvantage** être désavantagé.

disagree *verb* **I disagree** je ne suis pas d'accord; **I disagree with James** je ne suis pas d'accord avec James.

disappear *verb* disparaître [27].

disappearance *noun* disparition F.

disappointed *adjective* déçu; **I was disappointed with my marks** j'ai été déçu par mes notes.

disappointment *noun* déception F.

disaster *noun* désastre M; **it was a complete disaster** ça a été un désastre complet.

disastrous *adjective* désastreux (F désastreuse).

discipline *noun* discipline F.

disc *noun* **1 a compact disc** un disque compact; **2 a slipped disc** une hernie discale; **3 a tax disc** (*for a vehicle*) une vignette.

disc-jockey *noun* disc-jockey M.

disco *noun* **1** soirée F disco; **they're having a disco** ils font une soirée disco; **2** (*club*) discothèque.

discount *noun* réduction F.

discourage *verb* décourager [52].

discover *verb* découvrir [30].

discovery *noun* découverte F.

discreet *adjective* discret (F discrète).

discrimination *noun* discrimination F; **racial**

discrimination la discrimination raciale.

discuss *verb* **to discuss something** discuter [1] de quelque chose; **we'll discuss the problem tomorrow** nous allons discuter du problème demain; **I'm going to discuss it with Phil** je vais en discuter avec Phil.

discussion *noun* discussion F.

disease *noun* maladie F.

disgraceful *adjective* scandaleux (F scandaleuse).

disguise *noun* déguisement M; **to be in disguise** être déguisé. *verb* déguiser [1]; **disguised as a woman** déguisé en femme.

disgust *noun* dégoût M.

disgusted *adjective* dégoûté.

disgusting *adjective* dégoûtant.

dish *noun* **1** plat M; **a large white dish** un grand plat blanc; **he cooked my favourite dish** il a préparé mon plat favori; **2 to do the dishes** faire la vaisselle.

dishcloth *noun* (*for drying up*) torchon M.

dishonest *adjective* malhonnête.

dishonesty *noun* malhonnêteté F.

dish towel *noun* torchon M.

dishwasher *noun* lave-vaisselle M.

disinfect *verb* désinfecter [1].

disinfectant *noun* désinfectant M.

disk *noun* disque M; **a floppy disk** une disquette; **the hard disk** le disque dur.

diskette *noun* disquette F.

dislike *verb* ne pas aimer [1]; **I dislike sport** je n'aime pas le sport.

dismay *noun* consternation F.

dismiss *verb* licencier [1] (*an employee*).

disobedient *adjective* désobéissant.

display *noun* **1** exposition F; **a handicrafts display** une exposition d'artisanat; **to be on display** être exposé; **2 a window display** une vitrine; **3 a firework display** un feu d'artifice. *verb* exposer [1].

disposable *adjective* jetable.

disqualify *verb* disqualifier [1].

disrupt *verb* perturber [1].

dissolve *verb* dissoudre [67].

distance *noun* distance F; **from a distance** de loin; **in the distance** au loin; **it's within walking distance** on peut y aller à pied.

distant *adjective* lointain.

distinct *adjective* net (F nette).

distinctly *adverb* **1** distinctement; **2 it's distinctly odd** c'est vraiment bizarre.

distract *verb* distraire [78].

distribute *verb* distribuer [1].

district *noun* **1** (*in town*) quartier M; **a poor district of Paris** un quartier pauvre de Paris; **2** (*in the country*) région F.

disturb verb déranger [52]; **sorry to disturb you** je suis désolé de vous déranger.

ditch noun fossé M.
verb **to ditch somebody** plaquer [1] quelqu'un (informal).

dive noun plongeon M.
verb plonger [52].

diver noun plongeur M, plongeuse F.

diversion noun (traffic) déviation F.

divide verb diviser [1].

diving noun plongée F.

diving board noun plongeoir M.

division noun division F.

divorce noun divorce M.

divorced adjective divorcé.

DIY noun bricolage M; **to do DIY** faire du bricolage; **a DIY shop** un magasin de bricolage.

dizzy adjective **I feel dizzy** j'ai la tête qui tourne.

DJ noun disc-jockey M.

do verb 1 faire [10]; **what are you doing?** qu'est-ce que tu fais?; **I'm doing my homework** je fais mes devoirs; **what have you done with the hammer?** qu'est-ce que tu as fait du marteau?; 2 (questions in French are formed either with 'est-ce que' or by putting the subject after the verb and a hyphen between them) **do you want some strawberries?** est-ce que tu veux des fraises?, veux-tu des fraises?; **when does it start?** quand est-ce que ça commence?; **how did**

you open the door? comment as-tu ouvert la porte?; 3 (in negative sentences) **don't, doesn't, didn't** ne…pas; **I don't like mushrooms** je n'aime pas les champignons; **Rosie doesn't like spinach** Rosie n'aime pas les épinards; **you didn't shut the door** tu n'as pas fermé la porte; **it doesn't matter** ça ne fait rien; 4 (when it refers back to another verb, 'do' is not translated) **'do you live here?'** – **'yes, I do'** 'est-ce que tu habites ici?' – 'oui'; **she has more money than I do** elle a plus d'argent que moi; **'I live in Oxford'** – **'so do I'** 'j'habite à Oxford' – 'moi aussi'; **'I didn't phone Gemma'** – **'neither did I'** 'je n'ai pas appelé Gemma' – 'ni moi non plus'; 5 **don't you?, doesn't he? etc.** n'est-ce pas? **you know Helen, don't you?** tu connais Helen, n'est-ce pas?; **she left on Thursday, didn't she?** elle est partie jeudi, n'est-ce pas?; 6 **that'll do** ça ira; **it'll do like that** ça ira comme ça.
● **to do something up** 1 lacer [61] (shoes); 2 boutonner [1] (cardigan, jacket); 3 retaper [1] (house).
● **to do without** se passer [1] de; **we can do without knives** on peut se passer de couteaux.

doctor noun médecin M; **her mother's a doctor** sa mère est médecin.

document noun document M.

documentary noun documentaire M.

dodgems plural noun **the dodgems** les autos F plural tamponneuses.

dog *noun* chien M; (*female*) chienne F.

do-it-yourself *noun* bricolage M.

dole *noun* allocations chômage F *plural*; **to be on the dole** être au chômage.

doll *noun* poupée F.

dollar *noun* dollar M.

dolphin *noun* dauphin M.

domino *noun* domino M; **to play dominoes** jouer aux dominos.

donkey *noun* âne M.

don't SEE **do**.

door *noun* **1** porte F; **to open the door** ouvrir la porte; **to shut the door** fermer la porte; **2** (*of a vehicle or train*) portière F.

doorbell *noun* sonnerie F; **to ring the doorbell** sonner à la porte; **there's the doorbell!** on sonne!

doorstep *noun* pas M de la porte.

dot *noun* **1** (*written*) point M; **2** (*on fabric*) pois M; **3 at ten on the dot** à dix heures pile.

double *adjective, adverb* **1** double; **a double helping** une double portion; **a double whisky** un double whisky; **2** le double; **double the time** le double du temps; **double the price** le double du prix; **3 a double room** une chambre pour deux personnes; **4 a double bed** un grand lit.

double bass *noun* contrebasse F; **to play the double bass** jouer de la contrebasse.

double-breasted *adjective* **a**

double-breasted jacket une veste croisée.

double-decker bus *noun* autobus M à impériale.

double glazing *noun* double vitrage M.

doubles *noun* (*in tennis*) double M; **to play a game of doubles** faire un double.

doubt *noun* doute M; **there's no doubt about it** il n'y a aucun doute là-dessus; **I have my doubts** j'ai des doutes.
verb **to doubt something** douter [1] de quelque chose; **I doubt it** j'en doute; **to doubt that** douter que (+ *subjunctive*); **I doubt they'll do it** je doute qu'ils le fassent.

doubtful *adjective* **1** pas sûr; **it's doubtful** ce n'est pas sûr; **2 to be doubtful about doing** hésiter à faire; **I'm doubtful about inviting them together** j'hésite à les inviter ensemble.

dough *noun* pâte F.

doughnut *noun* beignet M.

Dover *noun* Douvres; **to Dover** à Douvres.

down *adverb, preposition* **1** en bas; **he's down in the cellar** il est en bas dans la cave; **2 down the road** (*nearby*) à côté; **there's a chemist's just down the road** il y a une pharmacie juste à côté; **3 to go down** descendre; **I went down to the kitchen** je suis descendu dans la cuisine; **to walk down the street** descendre la rue; **to run down the stairs** descendre les escaliers en courant; **4 to come down**

descendre; **she came down from her bedroom** elle est descendue de sa chambre; **5 to sit down** s'asseoir; **she sat down on the sofa** elle s'est assise sur le canapé.

downstairs *adverb* **1** en bas; **she's downstairs in the sitting-room** elle est en bas dans le salon; **the dog sleeps downstairs** le chien dort en bas; **2** du dessous; **the flat downstairs** l'appartement du dessous; **the people downstairs** les voisins du dessous.

doze *verb* sommeiller [1].

dozen *noun* douzaine F; **a dozen eggs** une douzaine d'œufs.

drag *noun* **what a drag!** quelle barbe! (*informal*); **she's a bit of a drag** elle n'est pas marrante (*informal*).
verb traîner [1].

dragon *noun* dragon M.

drain *noun* égout M.
verb égoutter [1] (*vegetables*).

drama *noun* **1** (*subject*) art M dramatique; **2 he made a big drama about it** il en a fait tout un cinéma (*informal*).

dramatic *adjective* spectaculaire.

draught *noun* courant d'air M.

draughts *noun* dames F *plural*; **to play draughts** jouer aux dames.

draw *noun* **1** (*in a match*) match nul M; **it was a draw** ils ont fait match nul; **2** (*lottery*) tirage M au sort.
verb **1** dessiner [1]; **I can't draw horses** je ne sais pas dessiner les chevaux; **she can draw really well** elle dessine vraiment bien; **2 to**

draw a picture faire [10] un dessin; **3 to draw the curtains** tirer [1] les rideaux; **4 to draw a crowd** attirer [1] une foule de spectateurs; **5** (*in a match*) faire [10] match nul; **we drew three all** nous avons fait match nul trois à trois; **6 to draw lots** tirer [1] au sort.

drawback *noun* inconvénient M.

drawer *noun* tiroir M.

drawing *noun* dessin M.

drawing pin *noun* punaise F.

dreadful *adjective* affreux (F affreuse).

dreadfully *adverb* terriblement; **I'm dreadfully late** je suis terriblement en retard; **I'm dreadfully sorry** je suis vraiment navré.

dream *noun* rêve M; **to have a dream** faire un rêve; **I had a horrible dream last night** j'ai fait un rêve horrible cette nuit.
verb rêver [1]; **to dream about something** rêver de quelque chose.

drenched *adjective* trempé; **to get drenched** se faire tremper; **we got drenched on the way home** on s'est fait tremper en rentrant.

dress *noun* robe F.
verb **to dress a child** habiller [1] un enfant.
● **to dress up** se déguiser [1]; **to dress up as a vampire** se déguiser en vampire.

dressed *adjective* **1** habillé; **is Tom dressed yet?** est-ce que Tom est habillé?; **she was dressed in black trousers and a yellow shirt** elle était habillée d'un pantalon noir et une chemise jaune; **2 to get dressed** s'habiller; **I got dressed quickly** je me suis vite habillé.

dresser *noun* (*for dishes*) vaisselier M.

dressing gown *noun* robe de chambre F.

dressing table *noun* coiffeuse F.

drier *noun* **a hair drier** un sèche-cheveux; **a tumble drier** un sèche-linge.

drift *noun* **a snow drift** une congère.

drill *noun* perceuse F.

drink *noun* **1** boisson F; **a hot drink** une boisson chaude; **a cold drink** une boisson fraîche; **2 would you like a drink?** tu veux boire quelque chose?; **3 to go out for a drink** aller prendre un pot (*informal*).
verb boire [22]; **he drank a glass of water** il a bu un verre d'eau.

drive *noun* **1 to go for a drive** faire un tour en voiture; **2** (*up to a house*) allée F.
verb **1** conduire [26]; **she drives very fast** elle conduit très vite; **to drive a car** conduire une voiture; **I'd like to learn to drive** j'aimerais apprendre à conduire; **can you drive?** tu sais conduire?; **2** aller en voiture; **we drove to Paris** nous sommes allés à Paris en voiture; **3 to drive somebody (to a place)** emmener [50] quelqu'un en voiture; **Mum drove me to the station** Maman m'a emmené en voiture à la gare; **to drive somebody home** raccompagner [1] quelqu'un;

★ **she drives me mad!** elle me rend folle!

driver *noun* **1** conducteur M, conductrice F; **2** (*of a taxi or bus*) chauffeur M.

driving instructor *noun* moniteur M d'auto-école.

driving lesson *noun* leçon F de conduite.

driving licence *noun* permis M de conduire.

driving test *noun* permis M de conduire; **to take your driving test** passer son permis; **Jenny's passed her driving test** Jenny a eu son permis.

drop *noun* goutte F.
verb **1 to drop something** laisser [1] tomber quelque chose; **I dropped my glasses** j'ai laissé tomber mes lunettes; **I'm going to drop history next year** je vais laisser tomber l'histoire l'année prochaine; **drop it!** laisse tomber!; **2** déposer [1] (*a person*); **could you drop me at the station?** est-ce que tu peux me déposer à la gare?

drown *verb* se noyer [39]; **she drowned in the lake** elle s'est noyée dans le lac.

drug *noun* **1** (*medicine*) médicament M; **2** (*illegal*) **drugs** la drogue.

drug abuse *noun* usage M des stupéfiants.

drug addict *noun* toxicomane M & F.

drug addiction *noun* toxicomanie F.

drum *noun* **1** tambour M;
2 drums la batterie; **to play drums**
jouer de la batterie.

drum kit *noun* batterie F.

drummer *noun* batteur M,
batteuse F.

drunk *noun* ivrogne M & F.
adjective ivre.

dry *adjective* sec (F sèche).
verb **1** sécher [1]; **to let something
dry** laisser [1] sécher quelque
chose; **2 to dry your hair** se sécher
les cheveux; **3 to dry your hands**
essuyer [41] les mains; **to dry the
dishes** s'essuyer [41] la vaisselle;
4 to dry the washing faire [10]
sécher le linge.

dry cleaner's *noun* pressing M.

dryer *noun* SEE **drier**.

dubbed *adjective* **a dubbed film** un
film doublé.

duck *noun* canard M.

due *adjective, adverb* **1 to be due to
do** devoir faire; **we're due to leave
on Thursday** nous devons partir
jeudi; **Paul's due back soon** Paul
doit bietôt revenir; **2 due to** en
raison de; **the match has been
cancelled due to bad weather** le
match a été annulé en raison du
mauvais temps.

duke *noun* duc M.

dull *adjective* **1 dull weather** un
temps maussade; **it's a dull day
today** il fait un temps maussade
aujourd'hui; **2** (*boring*) ennuyeux
(F ennuyeuse).

dumb *adjective* **1** muet (F muette);

to be deaf and dumb être sourd-
muet; **2** (*stupid*) bête; **he asked
some dumb questions** il a posé des
questions bêtes.

dummy *noun* (*for a baby*) tétine F.

dump *verb* **1** jeter [48] (*rubbish*);
2 plaquer [1] (*a person*) (*informal*);
she's dumped her boyfriend elle a
plaqué son copain.

dungarees *plural noun* salopette F
singular.

dungeon *noun* cachot M.

Dunkirk *noun* Dunkerque.

during *preposition* pendant; **during
the night** pendant la nuit; **I saw her
during the holidays** je l'ai vue
pendant les vacances.

dusk *noun* **at dusk** à la nuit
tombante.

dust *noun* poussière F.
verb épousseter [48].

dustbin *noun* poubelle F; **to put
something in the dustbin** jeter
quelque chose à la poubelle.

dustman *noun* éboueur M.

dusty *adjective* poussiéreux (F
poussiéreuse).

Dutch *noun* **1** (*language*)
hollandais M; **2 the Dutch**
(*people*) les Hollandais M *plural*.
adjective hollandais.

duty *noun* **1** devoir M; **to have a
duty to do** avoir le devoir de faire;
you have a duty to inform us vous
avez le devoir de nous informer;
2 to be on duty être de service; **to
be on night duty** être de service de

nuit; **I'm off duty tonight** je ne suis pas de service ce soir.

duty-free *adjective* hors taxes; **the duty-free shops** les boutiques hors taxes; **duty-free purcheses** les achats hors taxes.

duvet *noun* couette F.

duvet cover *noun* housse F de couette.

dwarf *noun* nain M, naine F.

dye *noun* teinture F.
verb teindre [60]; **to dye your hair** se teindre les cheveux; **I'm going to dye my hair pink** je vais me teindre les cheveux en rose.

dynamic *adjective* dynamique.

dyslexia *noun* dyslexie F.

dyslexic *adjective* dyslexique.

E e

each *adjective* chaque; **each time** chaque fois; **curtains for each window** des rideaux pour chaque fenêtre.
pronoun chacun (F chacune); **my sisters each have a computer** mes sœurs ont chacune un ordinateur; **she gave us an apple each** elle nous a donné une pomme à chacun; **each of you** chacun de vous, chacune de vous; **we each got a present** chacun de nous a reçu un cadeau; **the tickets cost ten pounds each** les billets coûtent dix livres chacun.

each other *pronoun* ('each other' is usually translated using a reflexive pronoun) **they love each other** ils s'aiment; **we know each other** nous nous connaissons; **do you often see each other?** est-ce que vous vous voyez souvent?

eagle *noun* aigle M.

ear *noun* oreille F.

earache *noun* **to have earache** avoir une otite.

earlier *adverb* **1** (*a while ago*) tout à l'heure; **your brother phoned earlier** ton frère a appelé tout à l'heure; **2** (*not as late*) plus tôt; **we should have started earlier** nous aurions dû commencer plus tôt; **earlier in the morning** plus tôt le matin.

early *adverb* **1** (*in the morning*) tôt; **to get up early** se lever tôt; **it's too early** il est trop tôt; **2** (*for an appointment*) en avance; **we're early, the train doesn't leave until ten** nous sommes en avance, le train ne part qu'à dix heures; **Grandma likes to be early** Grand-mère aime être en avance.
adjective **1** (*one of the first*) premier (F première); **in the early months** pendant les premiers mois; **I'm getting the early train** je prends le premier train; **2 to have an early lunch** déjeuner tôt; **Jan's having an early night** Jan va se coucher tôt; **we're making an early start** nous partons tôt; **3 in the early afternoon** en début d'après-midi; **in the early hours** au petit matin.

earn *verb* gagner [1] (*money*); **Richard earns four pounds an**

hour Richard gagne quatre livres de l'heure.

earnings *plural noun* salaire M.

earring *noun* boucle F d'oreille.

earth *noun* terre F; **life on earth** la vie sur terre; ★ **what on earth are you doing?** mais qu'est-ce que tu fais là?

earthquake *noun* tremblement M de terre.

easily *adverb* **1** (*to do something*) facilement; **2** (*by far*) de loin; **he's easily the best** il est de loin le meilleur.

east *noun* est M; **in the east** à l'est. *adjective, adverb* est; **the east side** le côté est; **an east wind** un vent d'est; **east of Paris** à l'est de Paris.

Easter *noun* Pâques M; **they're coming at Easter** ils viennent à Pâques; **Happy Easter** Joyeuses Pâques.

Easter Day *noun* dimanche M de Pâques.

Easter egg *noun* œuf M de Pâques.

Eastern Europe *noun* Europe F de l'Est.

easy *adjective* facile; **it's easy!** c'est facile!; **it was easy to decide** c'était facile à décider.

eat *verb* **1** manger [52]; **he was eating a banana** il mangeait une banane; **we're going to have something to eat** nous allons manger quelque chose; **2** prendre [64] (*a meal*); **we were eating**

breakfast nous prenions le petit déjeuner; **3 to eat out** manger au restaurant.

EC *noun* (*short for European Community*) CE F, Communauté F européenne.

echo *noun* écho M. *verb* retentir [2].

ecological *adjective* écologique.

ecology *noun* écologie F.

economical *adjective* **1** économe (*a person*); **2** économique (*way of doing something*); **it's more economical to buy a big one** c'est plus économique d'acheter un grand.

economics *noun* économie F.

economy *noun* économie F.

eczema *noun* eczéma M.

edge *noun* **1** bord M; **the edge of the table** le bord de la table; **at the edge of the lake** au bord du lac; **2 to be on edge** être énervé.

edible *adjective* comestible.

Edinburgh *noun* Édimbourg.

edit *verb* éditer [1].

editor *noun* (*of a newspaper*) rédacteur en chef M, rédactrice en chef F.

educate *verb* (*a teacher*) instruire [26].

education *noun* éducation F.

educational *adjective* éducatif (F éducative).

effect *noun* effet M; **the effect of the accident** l'effet de l'accident; **to**

have an effect on avoir un effet sur; **it had a good effect on the whole family** ça a eu un bon effet sur toute la famille; **special effects** les effets spéciaux.

effective *adjective* efficace.

efficient *adjective* efficace.

effort *noun* effort M; **to make an effort** faire un effort; **David made an effort to help us** David a fait un effort pour nous aider; **he didn't even make the effort to apologize** il n'a même pas fait l'effort pour s'excuser.

e.g. par ex.

egg *noun* œuf M; **a dozen eggs** une douzaine d'œufs; **a fried egg** un œuf au plat; **two boiled eggs** deux œufs à la coque; **a hard-boiled egg** un œuf dur; **scrambled eggs** les œufs brouillés.

egg-cup *noun* coquetier M.

eggshell *noun* coquille F d'œuf.

egg-white *noun* blanc M d'œuf.

egg-yolk *noun* jaune M d'œuf.

eight *number* huit M; **Maya's eight** Maya a huit ans; **at eight o'clock** à huit heures.

eighteen *number* dix-huit M; **Jason's eighteen** Jason a dix-huit ans.

eighth *number* **1** huitième; **2 the eighth of July** le huit juillet; **on the eighth floor** au huitième étage.

eighty *number* quatre-vingts; **eighty-five** quatre-vingt-cinq (*note that the 's' disappears when another number follows*).

Eire *noun* la République d'Irlande; **in Eire** en République d'Irlande.

either *pronoun* **1** (*one or the other*) l'un ou l'autre; **choose either (of them)** choisis l'un ou l'autre; **I don't like either (of them)** je n'aime ni l'un ni l'autre; **2** (*both*) les deux; **either is possible** tous les deux sont possibles.
conjunction **1 either … or** ou … ou; **either Thursday or Friday** ou jeudi ou vendredi; **either Susie or Judy** ou Susie ou Judy; **he either wrote or phoned** il a ou écrit ou appelé; **2** (*with a negative*) non plus; **he doesn't want to either** il ne veut pas non plus; **I don't know them either** je ne les connais pas non plus.

elastic *noun, adjective* élastique M.

elastic band *noun* élastique M.

elbow *noun* coude M.

elder *adjective* aîné; **her elder brother** son frère aîné.

elderly *adjective* âgé; **the elderly** les personnes F *plural* âgées.

eldest *adjective* aîné; **her eldest brother** son frère aîné.

elect *verb* élire [51]; **she has been elected** elle a été élue.

election *noun* élection F; **in the election** aux élections.

electric *adjective* électrique.

electrical *adjective* électrique.

electrician *noun* électricien M, électricienne F.

electricity *noun* électricité F; **to**

turn off the electricity couper le courant.

electronic *adjective* électronique.

electronics *noun* électronique F.

elegant *adjective* élégant.

elephant *noun* éléphant M.

eleven *number* onze M; **Josh is eleven** Josh a onze ans; **at eleven o'clock** à onze heures; **a football eleven** une équipe de football.

eleventh *number* onzième; **the eleventh of May** le onze mai; **on the eleventh floor** à l'onzième étage.

eliminate *verb* éliminer [1].

else *adverb* **1** d'autre; **somebody else** quelqu'un d'autre; **did you see anyone else?** as-tu vu quelqu'un d'autre?; **nothing else** rien d'autre; **I don't want anything else** je ne veux rien d'autre; **2 something else** autre chose; **would you like something else?** désirez-vous autre chose?; **3 somewhere else** ailleurs; **4 or else** sinon; **hurry up, or else we'll be late** dépêche-toi, sinon nous serons en retard.

e-mail *noun* courrier électronique M.

embankment *noun* **1** (*by a river*) quai M; **2** (*by a railway*) remblai M.

embarrassed *adjective* gêné; **I was terribly embarrassed** j'étais très gêné.

embarrassing *adjective* gênant.

embassy *noun* ambassade F; **the**

French Embassy l'ambassade de France.

embroider *verb* broder [1].

embroidery *noun* broderie F.

emergency *noun* cas M d'urgence; **in an emergency, break the glass** en cas d'urgence, cassez la vitre; **it's an emergency!** c'est urgent!

emergency exit *noun* sortie F de secours.

emergency landing *noun* atterrissage M d'urgence.

emotion *noun* émotion F.

emotional *adjective* **1** ému (*a person*); **she was quite emotional** elle était tout émue; **2** (*a speech or an occasion*) chargé d'émotion.

emperor *noun* empereur M.

emphasize *verb* **he emphasized that it wasn't compulsory** il a insisté [1] sur le fait que ce n'était pas obligatoire.

empire *noun* empire M; **the Roman Empire** l'Empire Romain.

employ *verb* employer [39].

employee *noun* salarié M, salariée F.

employer *noun* employeur M, employeuse F.

employment *noun* travail M.

empty *adjective* vide; **an empty bottle** une bouteille vide; **the room was empty** la pièce était vide. *verb* vider [1]; **I emptied the teapot into the sink** j'ai vidé la théière dans l'évier.

enchanting *adjective* ravissant.

enclose *verb* (*in a letter*) joindre [49]; **please find enclosed a cheque** veuillez trouver ci-joint un chèque.

encore *noun* bis M; **to give an encore** jouer un bis.

encourage *verb* encourager [52]; **to encourage somebody to do something** encourager quelqu'un à faire quelque chose; **Mum encouraged me to try again** Maman m'a encouragé à essayer encore une fois.

encouragement *noun* encouragement M.

encouraging *adjective* encourageant.

encyclopedia *noun* encyclopédie F.

end *noun* 1 (*last part*) fin F; **'The End'** 'Fin'; **at the end of the film** à la fin du film; **by the end of the day** à la fin de la journée; **in the end I went home** finalement je suis rentré chez moi; **Sally's coming at the end of June** Sally viendra fin juin; 2 (*of a table, garden, stick, or road, for example*) bout M; **hold the other end** tiens l'autre bout; **at the end of the street** au bout de la rue; 3 (*in tennis or football*) côté M; **to change ends** changer de côté. *verb* 1 (*to put an end to*) mettre [11] fin à (*an arrangement*); **they've ended the strike** ils ont mis fin à la grève; 2 (*to come to an end*) se terminer [1]; **the day ended with a dinner** la journée s'est terminée par un dîner.

●**to end up** 1 **to end up doing** finir [2] par faire; **we ended up taking a taxi** nous avons fini par prendre un taxi; 2 **to end up somewhere** se retrouver [1] quelque part; **Rob ended up in San Francisco** Rob s'est retrouvé à San Francisco.

ending *noun* fin F.

endless *adjective* interminable (*a day or a journey, for example*).

enemy *noun* ennemi M, ennemie F; **to make enemies** se faire des ennemis.

energetic *adjective* énergique.

energy *noun* énergie F.

engaged *adjective* 1 (*to be married*) fiancé; **they're engaged** ils sont fiancés; **to get engaged** se fiancer [61]; 2 (*a phone or toilet*) occupé; **it's engaged, I'll ring later** c'est occupé, j'appellerai plus tard.

engagement *noun* (*to marry*) fiançailles F *plural*.

engagement ring *noun* bague F de fiançailles.

engine *noun* 1 (*in a car*) moteur M; 2 (*pulling a train*) locomotive F.

engineer *noun* 1 (*who comes for repairs*) technicien M; 2 (*who builds roads and bridges*) ingénieur M.

England *noun* Angleterre F; **in England** en Angleterre; **to England** en Angleterre; **I am from England** j suis anglais.

English *noun* 1 (*the language*) anglais M; **do you speak English?** parlez-vous anglais?; **he answered**

English il a répondu en anglais;
2 (*English people*) **the English** les
Anglais M *plural*.
adjective **1** (*of or from England*)
anglais; **the English team** l'équipe
anglaise; **2 an English lesson** un
cours d'anglais; **our English
teacher** notre professeur d'anglais.

English Channel *noun* **the
English Channel** la Manche.

Englishman *noun* Anglais M.

Englishwoman *noun* Anglaise F.

enjoy *verb* **1** aimer [1]; **did you enjoy
the party?** as-tu aimé la soirée?; **we
really enjoyed the concert** nous
avons beaucoup aimé le concert;
2 to enjoy doing aimer faire; **I enjoy
swimming** j'aime nager; **do you
enjoy living in York?** aimez-vous
vivre à York?; **3 to enjoy oneself**
s'amuser [1]; **we really enjoyed
ourselves** nous nous sommes très
bien amusés; **enjoy yourselves!**
amusez-vous bien!; **did you enjoy
yourself?** tu t'es bien amusé?

enjoyable *adjective* agréable.

enlarge *verb* agrandir [2] (*a photo,
for example*).

enlargement *noun* (*of a photo*)
agrandissement M.

enormous *adjective* énorme.

enough *adverb, pronoun* **1** assez;
there's enough for everyone il y en
a assez pour tout le monde;
2 (*followed by a noun*) assez de; **is
there enough bread?** est-ce qu'il y a
assez de pain?; **3** (*followed by an
adjective or adverb*) suffisamment;
big enough suffisamment grand;
slowly enough suffisamment

lentement; **4 that's enough** ça
suffit.

enquire *verb* se renseigner [1]; **I'm
going to enquire about the trains**
je vais me renseigner sur les
trains.

enquiry *noun* demande F de
renseignements; **to make enquiries
about something** demander des
renseignements sur quelque chose.

enrol *verb* s'inscrire [38]; **I want to
enrol on the course** je veux
m'inscrire au cours.

enter *verb* **1** (*to go inside*) entrer [1]
dans (*a room or building*); **we all
entered the church** nous sommes
tous entrés dans l'église; **2 to enter
for** s'inscrire [38] à (*an exam or
competition*); s'inscrire pour (*a
race*).

entertain *verb* **1** (*to keep amused*)
divertir [2]; **something to entertain
the children** quelque chose pour
divertir les enfants; **2** (*to have
people round*) recevoir [66]; **they
don't entertain much** ils reçoivent
peu.

entertaining *noun* **they do a lot of
entertaining** ils reçoivent
beaucoup.
adjective amusant.

entertainment *noun* (*fun*)
distractions F *plural*; **there wasn't
much entertainment in the
evenings** il n'y avait pas beaucoup
de distractions le soir.

enthusiasm *noun* enthousiasme
M.

enthusiast *noun* passionné M,
passionnée F; **he's a rugby**

enthusiast c'est un passionné de rugby.

enthusiastic *adjective* enthousiaste.

entire *adjective* entier (F entière); **the entire class** la classe entière.

entirely *adverb* complètement.

entrance *noun* entrée F.

entry *noun* (*the way in*) entrée F; **'no entry'** 'défense d'entrer'.

entry phone *noun* interphone M.

envelope *noun* enveloppe F.

environment *noun* environnement M.

environmental *adjective* écologique.

environment-friendly *adjective* écologique.

envy *noun* envie F.

epidemic *noun* épidémie F.

epileptic *noun* épileptique M & F.

episode *noun* épisode M.

equal *adjective* égal (M *plural* égaux); **in equal quantities** en quantités égales.
verb égaler [1].

equally *adjective* (*to share*) en parts égales; **we divided it equally** nous l'avons divisé en parts égales.

equality *noun* égalité F.

equator *noun* équateur M.

equip *verb* équiper [1]; **well equipped for the hike** bien équipé pour la randonnée; **equipped with rucksacks** équipés de sacs à dos.

equipment *noun* **1** (*for sport*) équipement M; **2** matériel M; **laboratory equipment** le matériel de laboratoire; **3** (*for sports*) équipement M.

equivalent *adjective* **to be equivalent to** être équivalent à.

error *noun* **1** (*in spelling or typing*) faute F; **a spelling error** une faute d'orthographe; **2** (*in maths or on a computer*) erreur F.

error message *noun* message M d'erreur.

escalator *noun* escalier M mécanique.

escape *noun* (*from prison*) évasion F.
verb **1** (*a person*) s'évader [1]; **2** (*an animal*) s'échapper [1].

escort *noun* escorte F; **a police escort** une escorte de police.

especially *adjective* **1** (*above all*) surtout; **there are lots of tourists, especially in August** il y a beaucoup de touristes, surtout en août; **2** (*unusually*) particulièrement; **'is he rich?'** – **'not especially'** 'est-il riche?' – 'pas particulièrement'.

essay *noun* rédaction F; **an essay on pollution** une rédaction sur la pollution.

essential *adjective* essentiel (F essentielle); **it's essential to reply quickly** il est essentiel de répondre vite.

establishment *noun* (*an organization*) établissement M.

estate *noun* **1** (*a housing estate*)

cité F; **2** (*a big house and grounds*)
domaine M.

state agent's *noun* agence F
immobilière.

state car *noun* break M.

stimate *noun* **1** (*a quote for work*)
devis M; **2** (*a rough guess*)
estimation F.
verb évaluer [1].

tc etc.

thnic *adjective* ethnique; **an ethnic
minority** une minorité ethnique.

U *noun* (SHORT FOR **European
Union**); Union européenne F.

urope *noun* Europe F; **in Europe**
en Europe; **to Europe** en Europe.

uropean *noun* Européen M,
Européennne F.
adjective européen (F européenne).

uropean Union *noun* Union F
européenne.

ve *noun* **Christmas Eve** la veille de
Noël; **New year's Eve** la Saint-
Sylvestre.

ven[1] *adverb* **1** même; **even Lisa
didn't like it** même Lisa, elle ne l'a
pas aimé; **without even asking** sans
même demander; **2 even if** même
si; **even if they arrive** même s'ils
arrivent; **3 not even** même pas; **I
don't like animals, not even dogs**
je n'aime pas les animaux, même pas
les chiens; **4 even bigger** encore
plus grand; **even more
embarrassing** encore plus gênant;
even faster encore plus vite;
5 even more than encore plus que;
**I liked the song even more than
their last one** j'ai aimé la chanson

encore plus que leur dernière;
6 even so quand même; **even so,
we had a good time** nous nous
sommes bien amusés quand même.

even[2] *adjective* **1** (*a surface or layer*)
régulier (F régulière); **2** (*a number*)
pair; **six is an even number** six est
un numéro pair; **3** (*with the same
score*) à égalité (*competitors*); **Lee
and Blair are even** Lee et Blair sont
à égalité.

evening *noun* **1** soir M; **this
evening** ce soir; **at six o'clock in the
evening** à six heures du soir;
tomorrow evening demain soir; **on
Thursday evening** jeudi soir; **the
evening before** la veille au soir;
every evening tous les soirs; **I work
in the evening(s)** je travaille le soir;
the evening meal le repas du soir;
2 (*from beginning to end*) soirée F;
during the evening pendant la
soirée; **an evening with Pavarotti**
une soirée avec Pavarotti.

evening class *noun* cours M du
soir.

event *noun* **1** (*a happening*)
événement M; **2** (*in athletics*)
épreuve F; **track events** les
épreuves de vitesse; **3 in any
event, at all events** de toute façon.

eventful *adjective* mouvementé (*a
day or an outing*).

eventually *adverb* finalement.

ever *adverb* **1** (*at any time*) jamais;
hardly ever presque jamais; **have
you ever noticed that?** as-tu jamais
remarqué ça?; **no-one ever came**
personne n'est jamais venu; **hotter
than ever** plus chaud que jamais;

more slowly than ever plus lentement que jamais; **2** (*always*) toujours; **as cheerful as ever** toujours aussi gai; **the same as ever** toujours le même; **3 ever since** depuis; **and it's been raining ever since** et depuis il pleut tout le temps.

every *adjective* **1** tous (F toutes); **every house has a garden** toutes les maisons ont un jardin; **every day** tous les jours; **every Monday** tous les lundis; **every ten kilometres** tous les dix kilomètres; **I've seen every one of his films** j'ai vu tous ses films; **2** (*each*) chaque; **every time** chaque fois; **3 every now and then** de temps en temps.

everybody, everyone *pronoun* tout le monde; **everybody knows that …** tout le monde sait que …; **everyone else** tous les autres.

everything *pronoun* tout; **everything is ready** tout est prêt; **everything's fine** tout va bien; **everything else** tout le reste; **everything you said** tout ce que tu as dit.

everywhere *adverb* partout; **there was mud everywhere** il y avait de la boue partout; **everywhere she went** partout où elle allait; **everywhere else** partout ailleurs.

evidently *adverb* manifestement.

evil *noun* mal M. *adjective* mauvais.

exact *adjective* exact; **the exact amount** la somme exacte; **it's the exact opposite** c'est exactement le contraire.

exactly *adverb* exactement; **they're exactly the same age** ils ont exactement le même âge; **yes, exactly** oui, exactement.

exaggerate *verb* exagérer [24].

exaggeration *noun* exagération F.

exam *noun* examen M; **a history exam** un examen d'histoire; **to sit an exam** passer un examen; **to pass an exam** réussir un examen; **to fail an exam** échouer à un examen.

examination *noun* examen M.

examine *verb* examiner [1].

examiner *noun* examinateur M, examinatrice F.

example *noun* exemple M; **for example** par exemple; **to set a good example** donner l'exemple.

excellent *adjective* excellent.

except *preposition* **1** sauf; **except March** sauf au mois de mars; **every day except Tuesday** tous les jours sauf le mardi; **except when it rains** sauf quand il pleut; **2 except for** sauf; **except for the children** sauf les enfants.

exception *noun* exception F; **without exception** sans exception; **with the exception of** à l'exception de.

exchange *noun* échange M; **in exchange for his help** en échange de son aide; **an exchange visit** un voyage d'échange. *verb* échanger [52]; **can I exchange this shirt for a smaller one?** puis-échanger cette chemise contre une plus petite?

xchange rate *noun* taux M d'échange.

xcite *verb* exciter [1].

xcited *adjective* **1** excité (*a person or animal*); **the children are excited** les enfants sont excités; **2 to get excited** s'exciter; **the dogs get excited when they hear the car** les chiens s'excitent quand ils entendent la voiture.

xciting *adjective* passionnant; **a really exciting film** un film vraiment passionnant.

xclamation mark *noun* point M d'exclamation.

xcursion *noun* excursion F.

xcuse *noun* excuse F; **Gary has a good excuse** Gary a une bonne excuse; **that's no excuse** ce n'est pas une excuse.
verb (*apologizing*) **excuse me!** excusez-moi!

xercise *noun* exercice M; **a maths exercise** un exercice de maths; **physical exercise** l'exercice physique.

xercise bicycle *noun* vélo M d'appartement.

xercise book *noun* cahier M; **my French exercise book** mon cahier de français.

xhausted *adjective* épuisé.

xhaust fumes *plural noun* gaz M *plural* d'échappement.

xhaust (pipe) *noun* pot M l'échappement.

xhibition *noun* exposition F; **the**

Cézanne exhibition l'exposition Cézanne.

exist *verb* exister [1].

exit *noun* sortie F.

expect *verb* **1** attendre [3] (*guests or a baby*); **we're expecting thirty people** nous attendons trente personnes; **2** s'attendre à [3] (*something to happen*); **I didn't expect that** je ne m'attendais pas à ça; **I didn't expect it at all** je ne m'y attendais pas du tout; **3** (*as a supposition*) imaginer [1]; **I expect you're tired** j'imagine que tu es fatigué; **I expect she'll bring her boyfriend** j'imagine qu'elle amènera son copain; **yes, I expect so** oui, j'imagine.

expedition *noun* expédition F.

expel *verb* **to be expelled** (*from school*) se faire [10] renvoyer.

expenses *noun* frais M *plural*.

expensive *adjective* cher (F chère); **those shoes are too expensive for me** ces chaussures sont trop chères pour moi; **the most expensive CDs** les CDs les plus chers.

experience *noun* expérience F.

experienced *adjective* expérimenté.

experiment *noun* expérience F; **to do an experiment** faire une expérience.

expert *noun* spécialiste M & F; **he's a computer expert** c'est un spécialiste en informatique.

expire *verb* expirer [1].

expiry date *noun* date F
d'expiration.

explain *verb* expliquer [1].

explanation *noun* explication F.

explode *verb* exploser [1].

explore *verb* explorer [1].

explosion *noun* explosion F.

exposure *noun* (*of a film*) pose F;
a 24-exposure film une pellicule de
vingt-quatre poses.

express *noun* (*a train*) rapide M.
verb 1 exprimer [1]; 2 **to express
yourself** s'exprimer.

expression *noun* expression F.

extend *verb* agrandir [2] (*a
building*).

extension *noun* 1 (*to a house*)
addition F; 2 (*telephone*) poste
M; **can I have extension 2347
please?** est-ce que je peux avoir le
poste vingt-trois quarante-sept, s'il
vous plaît? (*note that in spoken
French telephone numbers are
usually broken down into groups of
two figures; this applies to longer
numbers as well*); 3 (*electrical*)
rallonge F.

extension lead *noun* rallonge F.

extension number *noun* numéro
M de poste.

exterior *adjective* extérieur.

extinguish *verb* éteindre [60].

extinguisher *noun* (*fire
extinguisher*) extincteur M.

extra *adjective* supplémentaire;
extra homework des devoirs
supplémentaires; **wine is extra** le
vin est en supplément; **you have to
pay extra** il faut payer un
supplément; **at no extra charge**
sans supplément.
adverb **extra hot** extra-chaud;
extra large extra-grand.

extraordinary *adjective*
extraordinaire.

extra-special *adjective*
exceptionnel (F exceptionnelle).

extra time *noun* (*in football*)
prolongation F; **to go into extra
time** jouer les prolongations.

extravagant *adjective* dépensier
dépensière) (*a person*).

extreme *noun* extrême M; **to go
extremes** pousser les choses à
l'extrême.
adjective extrême.

extremely *adverb* extrêmement;
extremely fast extrêmement vite.

eye *noun* œil M (*plural* yeux); **my
left eye** mon œil gauche; **a girl with
blue eyes** la fille aux yeux bleus;
shut your eyes! ferme les yeux!;
★ **to keep an eye on something**
surveiller quelque chose; ★ **to
make eyes at somebody** faire des
yeux doux à quelqu'un.

eyebrow *noun* sourcil M.

eyelash *noun* cil M.

eyelid *noun* paupière F.

eyeliner *noun* eye-liner M.

eye make-up *noun* maquillage M
pour les yeux.

eyesight *noun* vue F.

F f

fabric noun (*cloth*) tissu M.

fabulous adjective sensationnel (F sensationnelle).

face noun **1** (*of a person*) visage M; **you've got chocolate on your face** tu as du chocolat sur le visage; **2 to pull a face** faire une grimace; **3** (*of a clock or watch*) cadran M.
verb **1** (*a person*) faire [10] face à; **she faced her attacker** elle a fait face à son agresseur; **2 the house faces the park** la maison donne sur le jardin public; **3** (*to stand the idea of*) avoir [5] le courage de; **I can't face going back** je n'ai pas le courage de rentrer; **4 to face up to something** faire face à quelque chose.

facilities plural noun **1 the school has good sport facilities** l'école dispose d'un bon ensemble sportif; **2 the flat has cooking facilities** l'appartement a une cuisine équipée.

fact noun fait M; **the fact is that …** le fait est que …; **in fact** en fait; **is that a fact?** vraiment?

factory noun usine F.

fade verb **1** (*fabric*) se décolorer [1]; **faded jeans** un jean délavé; **2 the colours have faded** les couleurs ont passé.

fail verb **1** rater [1] (*a test or exam*); **I failed my driving test** j'ai raté

mon permis; **2** échouer [1]; **three students failed** trois étudiants ont échoué; **3** (*not to do*) **to fail to do** manquer [1] de faire; **he failed to contact us** il a manqué de nous contacter; ★ **without fail** sans faute; **ring me without fail** appelle-moi sans faute.

failure noun **1** échec M; **it was a terrible failure** c'était un échec terrible; **2** (*a breakdown in a machine*) panne F; **a power failure** une panne de courant.

faint adjective **1 to feel faint** se sentir mal; **2** (*slight*) léger (F légère); **a faint smell of gas** une légère odeur de gaz; **I haven't the faintest idea** je n'en ai pas la moindre idée; **3** (*a voice or sound*) faible.
verb s'évanouir [2]; **Lisa fainted** Lisa s'est évanouie.

fair noun foire F.
adjective **1** (*not unfair*) juste; **it's not fair!** ce n'est pas juste!; **2** (*hair*) blond; **he's fair-haired** il a les cheveux blonds; **3** (*skin*) clair; **people with fair skin** les gens qui ont la peau claire; **4** (*fairly good*) assez bon (F assez bonne) (*a chance, condition, or performance*); **her history is fair** son histoire est assez bonne; **5** (*weather*) **if it's fair tomorrow** s'il ne pleut pas demain.

fairground noun champ M de foire.

fairly adverb (*quite*) assez; **she's fairly happy** elle est assez contente.

fairy noun fée F.

fairy tale noun conte M de fées.

faith noun **1** (*trust*) confiance F; **to**

have faith in somebody avoir confiance en quelqu'un;
2 (*religious belief*) foi F.

faithful *adjective* fidèle.

faithfully *adverb* **yours faithfully** veuillez agréer, Monsieur (or Madame) mes salutations distinguées.

fake *noun* faux M; **the diamonds were fakes** les diamants étaient des faux.
adjective faux (F fausse) (*goes before the noun*); **a fake passport** un faux passeport.

fall *noun* chute F; **to have a fall** tomber.
verb **1** tomber [1]; **mind, you'll fall attention, tu vas tomber; Tony fell off his bike** Tony est tombé de son vélo; **she fell downstairs** elle est tombée dans l'escalier; **my jacket fell on the floor** ma veste est tombée par terre; **2** (*the temperature*) descendre [3]; **it fell to minus eleven last night** il est descendu à moins onze cette nuit; **3** (*prices*) baisser [1].

false *adjective* faux (F fausse) (*goes before the noun*); **a false alarm** une fausse alerte.

false teeth *plural noun* dentier M.

fame *noun* renommée F.

familiar *adjective* familier (F familière); **your face is familiar** votre visage m'est familier.

family *noun* famille F; **a family of six** une famille de six personnes; **Ben's one of the family** Ben fait partie de la famille; **the Barnes family** la famille Barnes.

famous *adjective* célèbre.

fan *noun* **1** fan M & F (*informal*); **Diana's an Oasis fan** Diana est une fan de Oasis; **2** (*of a team*) supporter M; **Brian's a Chelsea fan** Brian est un supporter de Chelsea; **3** (*electric, for cooling*) ventilateur M; **4** (*that you hold in your hand*) éventail M.

fanatic *noun* fanatique M & F.

fancy *noun* **to take someone's fancy** faire envie à quelqu'un; **the picture took his fancy** le tableau lu a fait envie.
adjective (*equipment*) sophistiqué.
verb **1** (*to want*) **do you fancy a coffee?** tu veux un café?; **do you fancy going to the new film?** ça te dirait d'aller voir le nouveau film?; **2 I really fancy him** il me plaît beaucoup; **3** (*just*) **fancy that!** pas possible!; **fancy you being here!** tiens donc, toi ici!

fancy dress *noun* **in fancy dress** déguisé; **a fancy-dress party** une soirée déguisée.

fantastic *adjective* génial (M *plure* géniaux) (*informal*); **really? that's fantastic!** vraiment? c'est génial!; **fantastic holiday** des vacances géniales.

far *adverb, adjective* **1** loin; **it's not far** ce n'est pas loin; **is it far to Carlisle?** est-ce que Carlisle est lo d'ici?; **how far is it to Bristol?** Bris est à quelle distance d'ici?; **he took us as far as Newport** il nous a accompagnés jusqu'à Newport; **2 by far** de loin; **the prettiest by far** de loin le plus joli; **3** (*much*) beaucoup; **far better** beaucoup mieux; **far faster** beaucoup plus vite; **far too many people** beaucoup trop de gens; **4 so far** jusqu'ici; **so far everything's going well** jusqu'ici tout va bien; ★ **as far as I know** pour autant que je sache.

fare noun **1** (*on a bus or the underground*) prix M du ticket; **2** (*on a train or plane*) prix M du billet; **half fare** demi-tarif M; **full fare** plein tarif M; **the return fare to Cardiff** le prix d'un aller-retour à Cardiff.

Far East noun Extrême-Orient M.

farm noun ferme F.

farmer noun agriculteur M, agricultrice F.

farmhouse noun ferme F.

farming noun agriculture F.

fascinating adjective fascinant.

fashion noun mode F; **in fashion** à la mode; **out of fashion** démodé.

fashionable adjective à la mode.

fashion model noun mannequin M.

fashion show noun présentation de collection.

fast adjective **1** rapide; **a fast car** une voiture rapide; **2 my watch is fast** ma montre avance; **you're ten minutes fast** ta montre avance de dix minutes.
adverb **1** vite; **he swims fast** il nage vite; **2 to be fast asleep** être profondément endormi.

fast forward noun avance F rapide.

fat noun **1** (*butter, cream, etc*) matières F plural grasses; **2** (*on meat*) gras M; **3** (*on your body*) graisse F.
adjective gros (F grosse) (*goes before the noun*); **a fat man** un gros monsieur; **to get fat** grossir.

fatal adjective (*accident*) mortel (F mortelle).

father noun père M; **my father's office** le bureau de mon père.

Father Christmas noun le père Noël.

father-in-law noun beau-père M.

fault noun **1** (*when you are responsible*) faute F; **it's Stephen's fault** c'est la faute de Stephen; **it's not my fault** ce n'est pas ma faute; **2** (*a defect*) défaut M; **there's a fault in this sweater** il y a un défaut dans ce pull; **3** (*in tennis*) faute F.

favour noun **1** (*a kindness*) service M; **to do somebody a favour** rendre service à quelqu'un; **can you do me a favour?** peux-tu me rendre service?; **to ask a favour of somebody** demander un service à quelqu'un; **2 to be in favour of something** être pour quelque chose.

favourite adjective préféré; **my favourite band** mon groupe préféré.

fear noun peur F.
verb craindre [31]; **to fear the worst** craindre le pire.

feather noun plume F.

feature noun **1** (*of your face*) trait M; **to have delicate features** avoir des traits délicats; **2** (*of a car or a machine*) caractéristique F.

February *noun* février M; **in February** en février.

fed up *adjective* **I'm fed up** j'en ai marre (*informal*); **I'm fed up with working every day** j'en ai marre de travailler tous les jours.

feed *verb* donner [1] à manger à; **have you fed the dog?** est-ce que tu as donné à manger au chien?

feel *verb* **1** se sentir [58]; **I feel tired** je me sens fatigué; **I don't feel well** je ne me sens pas bien; **2** sentir [58]; **I didn't feel a thing** je n'ai rien senti; **3 to feel afraid** avoir [5] peur; **to feel cold** avoir froid; **to feel thirsty** avoir soif; **4 to feel like doing** avoir envie de faire; **I feel like going to the cinema** j'ai envie d'aller au cinéma; **5** (*touch*) toucher [1].

feeling *noun* **1** (*in your mind*) sentiment M; **a feeling of embarrassment** un sentiment de gêne; **to show your feelings** montrer ses sentiments; **to hurt somebody's feelings** blesser quelqu'un; **2** (*in your body*) sensation F; **a dizzy feeling** une sensation de vertige; **3** (*an impression or intuition*) impression F; **I have the feeling James doesn't like me** j'ai l'impression que James ne m'aime pas.

felt-tip (pen) *noun* feutre M.

female *noun* (*animal*) femelle F. *adjective* **1** féminin (*person, population*); **2** femelle (*animal, insect*).

feminine *adjective* féminin.

feminist *noun, adjective* féministe M & F.

fence *noun* (*round a field*) clôture F.

fern *noun* fougère F.

ferry *noun* ferry M.

fertilizer *noun* engrais M.

festival *noun* (*for films, art, or music*) festival M.

fetch *verb* aller [7] chercher; **Tom's fetching the children** Tom est allé chercher les enfants; **fetch me the other knife!** va me chercher l'autre couteau!

fever *adjective* fièvre F.

few *adjective, pronoun* **1** peu de; **few people think that ...** peu de gens pensent que ...; **very few houses have a swimming-pool** très peu de maisons ont une piscine; **2 a few** (*followed by a noun*) quelques; **a few weeks earlier** quelques semaines plus tôt; **in a few minutes** dans quelques minutes; **3 a few** (*itself*) quelques-uns (F quelques-unes); **have you any tomatoes? we want a few for the salad** avez-vous des tomates? nous en voulons quelques-unes pour la salade; **4 quite a few** pas mal de; **there were quite a few questions** il y avait pas mal de questions.

fewer *adjective* moins de; **there are fewer tourists this year** il y a moins de touristes cette année.

fiction *noun* **I read a lot of fiction** je lis beacoup de romans.

field *noun* **1** (*with grass or crops*) champ M; **a field of wheat** un champ de blé; **2** (*for sport*) terrain M; **3** (*the kind of work you do*) domaine M.

fierce *adjective* **1** féroce (*an animal or person*); **2** violent (*a storm or a battle*).

fifteen *number* quinze; **Lara's fifteen** Lara a quinze ans.

fifth *number* cinquième; **the fifth of January** le cinq janvier; **on the fifth floor** au cinquième étage.

fifty *number* cinquante M; **my uncle's fifty** mon oncle a cinquante ans.

fig *noun* figue F.

fight *noun* **1** (*a scuffle*) bagarre F; **2** (*in boxing*) combat M; **3** (*against illness*) lutte F.
verb **1** (*to have a fight*) se battre [21]; **they were fighting** ils se battaient; **2** (*to quarrel*) se disputer [1]; **they're always fighting** ils sont toujours en train de se disputer; **3** (*struggle against*) lutter [1] contre (*poverty or a disease*).

fighting *noun* **1** (*in the streets or a pub, for example*) bagarre F; **2** (*in war*) combat M.

figure *noun* **1** (*number*) chiffre M; **a four-figure number** un nombre de quatre chiffres; **2** (*body shape*) ligne F; **good for your figure** bon pour la ligne; **3** (*a person*) personnage M; **a familiar figure** un personnage familier; **4** (*diagram*) figure F.

file *noun* **1** (*for records of a person or case*) dossier M; **2** (*ring binder*) classeur M; **3** (*cardboard folder*) chemise F; **4** (*on a computer*) fichier M; **5 a nail file** une lime. *verb* **1** classer [1] (*documents*); **2 to file your nails** se limer [1] les ongles.

fill *verb* remplir [2] (*a container*); **she filled my glass** elle a rempli mon verre; **a smoke-filled room** une pièce remplie de fumée.
● **to fill in** remplir [2] (*a form*).
● **to fill in for someone** remplacer [61] quelqu'un.

film *noun* **1** (*in a cinema*) film M; **shall we go and see a film?** si on allait voir un film?; **the new film about Picasso** le nouveau film au sujet de Picasso; **2** (*for a camera*) pellicule F; **a 24-exposure colour film** une pellicule couleur de 24 poses.

film star *noun* vedette F de cinéma.

filter *noun* filtre M.

filthy *adjective* dégoûtant.

fin *noun* nageoire F.

final *noun* (*in sport*) finale F. *adjective* dernier (F dernière); **the final instalment** le dernier épisode; **the final result** le résultat final.

finally *adverb* finalement.

find *verb* trouver [1]; **did you find your passport?** as-tu trouvé ton passeport?; **I can't find my keys** je ne trouve pas mes clefs.
● **to find out** **1** (*to enquire*) se renseigner [1]; **I don't know, I'll find out** je ne sais pas, je me renseignerai; **2 to find something out** découvrir [30] (*the facts or an answer*); **when Lucy found out the truth** quand Lucy a découvert la vérité.

fine *noun* amende F; (*for parking or speeding*) contravention F.
adjective **1** (*in good health*) bien; **'how are you?' – 'fine, thanks'** 'comment ça va?' – 'très bien merci'; **2** (*very good*) excellent; **she's a fine athlete** c'est une excellente athlète; **3** (*convenient*) très bien; **ten o'clock? yes, that's fine** dix heures? oui, très bien; **Friday will be fine** vendredi sera très bien; **4** (*sunny*) beau (F belle) (*weather or a day*); **if it's fine** s'il fait beau; **5** (*not coarse or thick*) fin; **in fine wool** en laine fine.

finely *adjective* (*chopped or grated*) finement.

finger *noun* doigt M; ★ **I'll keep my fingers crossed for you** je croise les doigts pour toi.

fingernail *noun* ongle M.

finish *noun* **1** (*end*) fin F; **2** (*in a race*) arrivée F.
verb **1** finir [2]; **wait, I haven't finished** attends, je n'ai pas fini; **when does school finish?** à quelle heure finit l'école?; **2** (*to finish off*) terminer [1] (*work or a project*); **have you finished the book?** est-ce que tu as terminé le livre?; **3 to finish doing** finir de faire; **have you finished telephoning?** as-tu fini de téléphoner?
to finish with finir avec; **have you finished with the computer?** as-tu fini avec l'ordinateur?

Finland *noun* Finlande F; **in Finland** en Finlande; **to Finland** en Finlande.

Finnish *noun* finnois M (*the language*).
adjective finlandais.

fir tree *noun* sapin M.

fire *noun* **1** (*in a grate*) feu M; **to light a fire** allumer un feu; **sitting by the fire** assis près du feu; **2 to catch fire** prendre feu; **3** (*accidental*) incendie M; **a fire in a factory** un incendie dans une usine.
verb **1** (*to shoot*) tirer [1]; **the soldiers were firing** les soldats tiraient; **to fire at somebody** tirer sur quelqu'un; **2** décharger (*a gun*).

fire alarm *noun* alarme F incendie

fire brigade *noun* pompiers M *plural*.

fire engine *noun* voiture F des pompiers.

fire escape *noun* escalier M de secours.

fire extinguisher *noun* extincteur M.

fire fighter *noun* pompier M.

fireplace *noun* cheminée F.

fire station *noun* caserne F de pompiers.

firework *noun* feu M d'artifice (*plural* feux d'artifice); **there will be a firework display** il y aura un feu d'artifice.

firm *noun* (*business*) entreprise F.
adjective ferme.

first *adjective, adverb* **1** premier (F première); **Susan's the first** Susan est la première; **the first of May** le premier mai; **for the first time** pour la première fois; **I came first in the**

200 metres je suis arrivé premier aux 200 mètres; **2** (*to begin with*) d'abord; **first, I'm going to make some tea** d'abord je vais faire du thé; **3 at first** au début; **at first he was shy** au début il était timide.

first aid *noun* premiers secours M *plural*.

first class *adjective* **1** de première classe (*a ticket, carriage, or hotel*); **a first-class compartment** un compartiment de première classe; **he always travels first class** il voyage toujours en première; **2** au tarif rapide (*a letter or stamp*); **six first-class stamps** six timbres au tarif rapide.

first floor *noun* premier étage M; **on the first floor** au premier étage.

firstly *adverb* premièrement.

first name *noun* prénom M.

fish *noun* poisson M; **do you like fish?** aimez-vous le poisson? *verb* pêcher [1]; **Dad was fishing for trout** Papa pêchait la truite.

fish and chips *noun* poisson M frit avec des frites.

fisherman *noun* pêcheur M.

fishing *noun* pêche F; **I love fishing** j'adore la pêche; **to go fishing** aller à la pêche.

fishing rod *noun* canne F à pêche.

fishing tackle *noun* matériel M de pêche.

fist *noun* poing M.

fit *noun* **1** (*of rage*) **to have a fit** piquer une crise; **your dad'll have a**

fit when he sees your hair! ton père va piquer une crise quand il va voir tes cheveux!; **2 an epileptic fit** une crise d'épilepsie.
adjective (*healthy*) en forme; **I feel really fit** je me sens vraiment en forme; **to keep fit** se maintenir en forme.
verb **1** (*to be the right size for*) (*a garment*) être [6] de la taille de (*a person*); (*shoes*) être à la pointure de; **this skirt doesn't fit me** cette jupe n'est pas à ma taille; **2** (*be able to be put into*) aller [7] dans; **will my cases all fit in the car?** est-ce que mes valises iront dans la voiture?; **the key doesn't fit in the lock** la clé ne va pas dans la serrure; **3** (*install*) installer [1]; **they've fitted an alarm** ils ont installé une alarme.

fitted carpet *noun* moquette F.

fitted kitchen *noun* cuisine F intégrée.

fitting room *noun* cabine F d'essayage.

five *number* cinq M; **Belinda's five** Belinda a cinq ans; **it's five o'clock** il est cinq heures.

fix *verb* **1** (*repair*) réparer [1]; **Mum's fixed the computer** Maman a réparé l'ordinateur; **2** (*to decide on*) fixer [1]; **to fix a date** fixer une date; **at a fixed price** à prix fixe; **3** préparer [1] (*a meal*); **I'll fix supper** c'est moi qui vais préparer le repas du soir.

fizzy *adjective* gazeux (F gazeuse); **fizzy water** eau F gazeuse.

flag *noun* drapeau M (*plural* drapeaux).

flame *noun* flamme F.

flamingo *noun* flamant M rose.

flan *noun* tarte F; **an onion flan** une tarte à l'oignon.

flap *verb* battre [21]; **the bird flapped its wings** l'oiseau battait des ailes.

flash *noun* 1 **a flash of lightning** un éclair; 2 **to do something in a flash** faire quelque chose en un clin d'œil; 3 (*on a camera*) flash M.
verb 1 (*a light*) clignoter [1]; 2 **to flash by or past** passer [1] comme un éclair; 3 **to flash your headlights** faire [10] un appel de phares.

flashback *noun* flash-back M.

flat *noun* appartement M; **a third-floor flat** un appartement au troisième étage.
adjective 1 plat; **flat shoes** des chaussures plates; **a flat landscape** un paysage plat; 2 **a flat tyre** un pneu crevé.

flatmate *noun* colocataire M & F.

flatter *verb* flatter [1].

flattering *adjective* flatteur (F flatteuse).

flavour *noun* 1 (*taste*) goût M; **the sauce had no flavour** la sauce n'avait aucun goût; 2 (*of drink, ice cream, etc*) parfum M; **what flavour of ice cream would you like?** tu veux quel parfum de glace?
verb parfumer [1]; **vanilla-flavoured** parfumé à la vanille.

flea *noun* puce F.

flea market *noun* marché M aux puces.

flesh *noun* chair F.

flex *noun* fil M.

flexible *adjective* flexible (*an arrangement*).

flight *noun* 1 vol M; **a charter flight** un vol charter; **the flight from Moscow is delayed** le vol de Moscou est retardé; 2 **a flight of stairs** un escalier; **four flights of stairs** quatre étages.

fling *verb* lancer [61].

flipper *noun* (*for a swimmer*) palme F.

flirt *verb* flirter [1].

float *verb* flotter [1].

flood *noun* 1 (*of water*) inondation F; **the floods in the south** les inondations au sud; **to be in floods of tears** verser des torrents de larmes; 2 (*of letters or complaints*) déluge M.
verb inonder [1]

floodlight *noun* projecteur M.

floor *noun* 1 (*wooden*) plancher M; (*concrete*) sol M; **to sweep the floor** balayer; **to sweep the kitchen floor** balayer la cuisine; **your glasses are on the floor** tes lunettes sont par terre; 2 (*a storey*) étage M **on the second floor** au deuxième étage.

floppy disk *noun* disquette F.

florist *noun* fleuriste M & F.

flour *noun* farine F.

flow *verb* couler [1].

flower *noun* fleur F; **a bunch of**

flowers un bouquet.
verb fleurir [2].

flu *noun* grippe F: **to have flu** avoir
la grippe.

fluent *adjective* **she speaks fluent
Italian** elle parle couramment
l'italien.

fluently *adverb* couramment.

flush *verb* **1** (*to go red*) rougir [2];
2 to flush the lavatory tirer [1] la
chasse.

flute *noun* flûte F; **to play the flute**
jouer de la flûte.

fly *noun* mouche F.
verb **1** (*a bird, a bee, or a plane*)
voler [1]; **2** (*in a plane*) prendre [64]
l'avion; **we flew to Edinburgh** nous
sommes allés à Édimbourg en avion;
we flew from Gatwick nous
sommes partis de Gatwick; **3** faire
[10] voler (*a kite*); **4** (*to pass
quickly*) (*time*) passer [1] très vite.

fly spray *noun* bombe F insecticide.

foam *noun* **1** (*foam rubber*) mousse
F; **a foam mattress** un matelas
mousse; **2** (*on a drink*) mousse F.

focus *noun* **to be in focus** être au
point; **to be out of focus** être flou.
verb mettre [11] au point (*a camera*).

fog *noun* brouillard M.

foggy *adjective* brumeux (F
brumeuse) (*weather*); **it was foggy**
il y avait du brouillard.

foil *noun* (*kitchen foil*) papier M
aluminium.

fold *noun* pli M.
verb **1** plier [1]; **to fold something**

up plier quelque chose; **2 to fold
your arms** croiser [1] les bras.

folder *noun* chemise F.

folding *adjective* pliant; **a folding
table** une table pliante.

follow *verb* suivre [75]; **follow me!**
suivez-moi!; **followed by a dinner**
suivi d'un dîner; **do you follow me?**
vous me suivez?

following *adjective* suivant; **the
following year** l'année suivante.

fond *adjective* **to be fond of
somebody** aimer beaucoup
quelqu'un; **I'm very fond of him** je
l'aime beaucoup.

food *noun* **1** nourriture F; **to buy
food** acheter à manger; **I like French
food** j'aime la cuisine française;
2 (*stocks*) provisions F *plural*; **we
bought food for the holiday** nous
avons acheté des provisions pour les
vacances.

fool *noun* idiot M, idiote F.

foot *noun* **1** pied M; **Lucy came on
foot** Lucy est venue à pied; **2** (*the
bottom*) **at the foot of the stairs** en
bas de l'escalier.

football *noun* **1** (*the game*) football
M; **to play football** jouer au
football; **2** (*ball*) ballon M de
football.

footballer *noun* joueur de football
M, joueuse de football F.

footpath *noun* sentier M.

footprint *noun* empreinte F.

footstep *noun* pas M.

for *preposition* **1** pour; **a present for**

my mother un cadeau pour ma mère; **petrol for the car** de l'essence pour la voiture; **sausages for lunch** des saucisses pour le déjeuner; **it's for cleaning** c'est pour nettoyer; **what's it for?** c'est pour quoi faire?; **2** (*time expressions in the past or future*) pendant; **I studied French for six years** (*but I no longer do*) j'ai étudié le français pendant six ans; **I'll be away for four days** je serai absent pendant quatre jours; **3** (*time expressions in the past but continuing in the present*) depuis; **I've been waiting here for an hour** (*and I'm still waiting*) j'attends ici depuis une heure; **my brother's been living in Paris for three years** (*and he still lives there*) mon frère habite à Paris depuis trois ans; **4 I sold my bike for fifty pounds** j'ai vendu mon vélo cinquante livres; **5 what's the French for 'bee'?** comment dit-on 'bee' en français?

forbid *verb* défendre [3]; **to forbid somebody to do something** défendre à quelqu'un de faire quelque chose; **I forbid you to go out** je te défends de sortir.

forbidden *adjective* défendu.

force *noun* force F.
verb forcer [61]; **to force somebody to do** forcer quelqu'un à faire.

forecast *noun* (*weather forecast*) météo F.

forefinger *noun* index M.

foreground *noun* premier plan M; **in the foreground** au premier plan.

forehead *noun* front M.

foreign *adjective* étranger (F étrangère); **in a foreign country** dans un pays étranger.

foreigner *noun* étranger M, étrangère F.

foresee *verb* prévoir [65].

forest *noun* forêt F.

forever *adverb* **1** pour toujours; **I'd like to stay here forever** j'aimerais rester là pour toujours; **2** (*nonstop*) sans arrêt; **he's forever asking questions** il pose sans arrêt des questions.

forget *verb* oublier [1]; **I forget his name** j'oublie son nom; **we've forgotten the bread!** nous avons oublié le pain!; **to forget to do** oublier de faire; **I forgot to phone** j'ai oublié d'appeler; **to forget about something** oublier quelque chose.

forgive *verb* pardonner [1] à; **to forgive somebody** pardonner à quelqu'un; **I forgave him** je lui ai pardonné; **to forgive somebody for doing** pardonner à quelqu'un d'avoir fait; **I forgave her for losing my ring** je lui ai pardonné d'avoir perdu ma bague.

fork *noun* fourchette F.

form *noun* **1** formulaire M; **to fill in a form** remplir un formulaire; **2** (*shape or kind*) forme F; **in the form of** sous forme de; **3 to be on form** être en forme; **4** (*in school*) classe F.
verb former [1].

formal *adjective* officiel (F officielle) (*invitation, event, complaint, etc*).

format *noun* format M.

former *adjective* ancien (F

ancienne) (*goes before the noun*); **a former pupil** un ancien élève.

fortnight *noun* quinze jours M *plural*; **we're going to Spain for a fortnight** nous allons passer quinze jours en Espagne.

fortunately *adverb* heureusement.

forty *number* quarante; **my aunt's forty** ma tante a quarante ans.

forward *noun* (*in sport*) avant M. *adverb* **to move forward** avancer; **a seat further forward** une place plus en avant.

foster child *noun* enfant adoptif M, enfant adoptive F.

foul *noun* (*in sport*) faute F. *adjective* infect; **the weather's foul** il fait un temps infect.

fountain *noun* fontaine F.

fountain pen *noun* stylo M à encre.

four *number* quatre M; **Simon's four** Simon a quatre ans; **it's four o'clock** il est quatre heures; ★ **on all fours** à quatre pattes.

fourteen *number* quatorze M; **Susie's fourteen** Susie a quatorze ans.

fourth *number* quatrième; **the fourth of July** le quatre juillet; **on the fourth floor** au quatrième étage.

fox *noun* renard M.

fragile *adjective* fragile.

frame *noun* cadre M.

franc *noun* franc M; **a fifty-franc note** un billet de cinquante francs.

France *noun* France F; **in France** en France; **to France** en France; **I like France** j'aime la France; **Nadine's from France** Nadine est française.

frantic *adjective* **1** (*very upset*) fou (F folle); **Mum was frantic with worry** Maman était folle d'inquiétude; **2** (*desperate*) désespéré (*efforts or a search*).

freckle *noun* tache F de rousseur.

free *adjective* **1** (*when you don't pay*) gratuit; **the bus is free** le bus est gratuit; **a free ticket** un billet gratuit; **2** (*not occupied*) libre; **are you free on Thursday?** es-tu libre jeudi?; **3 sugar-free** sans sucre; **lead-free** sans plomb. *verb* libérer [24].

freedom *noun* liberté F.

free gift *noun* cadeau M (*plural* cadeaux).

freeze *verb* **1** (*in a freezer*) congeler [45]; **frozen peas** des petits pois congelés; **2** (*in cold weather*) geler [45]; **it's freezing outside** il gèle dehors.

freezer *noun* congélateur M.

freezing *noun* zéro M; **three degrees below freezing** trois degrés en-dessous de zéro. *adjective* **I'm freezing** je suis gelé (*informal*); **it's freezing outside** il fait très froid dehors.

French *noun* **1** (*the language*) français M; **to speak French** parler français; **say it in French** dis-le en français; **to learn French** apprendre le français; **2** (*the people*) **the French** les Français M *plural*; **most**

of the French la plupart des
Français.
adjective 1 français; **Jean-Marc is
French** Jean-Marc est français;
2 de français (*a teacher or a lesson*);
the French class le cours de
français.

French bean *noun* haricot M vert.

French dressing *noun* vinaigrette
F.

French fries *plural noun* frites F
plural.

Frenchman *noun* Français M.

French window *noun* porte-
fenêtre F (*plural* portes-fenêtres).

Frenchwoman *noun* Française F.

frequent *adjective* fréquent.

fresh *adjective* frais (F fraîche); **fresh
eggs** des œufs frais; **I'm going out
for some fresh air** je vais prendre de
l'air.

Friday *noun* vendredi M; **next
Friday** vendredi prochain; **last
Friday** vendredi dernier; **on Friday**
vendredi; **I'll phone you on Friday
evening** je t'appellerai vendredi
soir; **on Fridays** le vendredi; **closed
on Fridays** fermé le vendredi; **every
Friday** tous les vendredis; **Good
Friday** le Vendredi saint.

fridge *noun* frigo M (*informal*); **put
it in the fridge** mets-le au frigo.

friend *noun* ami M, amie F; **a
friend of mine** un ami (or une amie)
à moi; **to make friends** (*in a general
way*) se faire des amis; **he made
friends with Danny** il est devenu ami
avec Danny.

friendly *adjective* sympathique.

friendship *noun* amitié F.

fries *plural noun* frites F *plural*.

fright *noun* peur F; **get a fright**
avoir peur; **you gave me a fright!** tu
m'as fait peur!

frighten *verb* effrayer [59].

frightened *adjective* **to be
frightened** avoir peur; **Martin's
frightened of snakes** Martin a peur
des serpents.

frightening *adjective* effrayant.

fringe *noun* frange F.

frog *noun* grenouille F.

from *preposition* de; **a letter from
Tom** une lettre de Tom; **100 metres
from the cinema** à cent mètres du
cinéma; **from Monday to Friday** du
lundi jusqu'au vendredi; **he comes
from Dublin** il vient de Dublin; **two
years from now** d'ici deux ans; **from
seven o'clock onwards** à partir de
sept heures.

front *noun* 1 (*of a building, a
garment, or a cupboard*) devant M;
2 (*of a car*) avant M; **sitting in the
front** assis à l'avant; 3 (*of a train or
a queue*) tête F; **there are seats at
the front of the train** il y a des places
en tête du train; 4 (*of a card or
envelope*) recto M; **the address is
on the front** l'adresse est au recto;
5 (*in a theatre, cinema, or class*)
premier rang M; **seats at the front**
des places au premier rang; 6 **in
front of** devant; **in front of the TV**
devant la télé; **in front of me** devant
moi.
adjective 1 de devant; **his front**

paw sa patte de devant; **in the front row** au premier rang; **2** avant; **the front seat** (*of a car*) le siège avant; **the front wheel** la roue avant.

front door *noun* porte F d'entrée.

frontier *noun* frontière F.

frost *noun* gel M.

frosty *adjective* **1** **it's frosty this morning** il gèle ce matin; **2** couvert de givre (*windscreen, grass, etc*).

frown *verb* froncer [61] les sourcils; **he frowned at us** il nous a regardés en fronçant les sourcils.

frozen *adjective* (*in a freezer*) surgelé; **a frozen pizza** une pizza surgelée.

fruit *noun* fruits M *plural* (*note that in French 'un fruit' is a piece of fruit, whereas 'fruit' in English meaning several pieces of fruit always has to be 'fruits' in the plural in French*); **we bought cheese and fruit** nous avons acheté du fromage et des fruits; **fruit juice** le jus de fruits.

fruit machine *noun* machine F à sous.

fruit salad *noun* salade F de fruits.

frustrated *adjective* frustré.

fry *verb* faire [10] frire; **we fried the fish** nous avons fait frire les poissons; **a fried egg** un œuf au plat.

frying pan *noun* poêle F.

fuel *noun* (*for a vehicle or plane*) carburant M.

full *adjective* **1** plein; **this glass is full** ce verre est plein; **the train was full of tourists** le train était plein de touristes; **2** complet (F complète) (*a hotel or flight*); **3** (*top*) **at full speed** à toute vitesse; **at full volume** à plein volume; **4** **I'm full** j'ai assez mangé; **5** **to write something out in full** écrire quelque chose en toutes lettres.

full stop *noun* point M.

full-time *noun* **a full-time job** un travail à plein temps.

fully *adjective* entièrement.

fun *noun* plaisir M; **to have fun** s'amuser; **have fun!** amusez-vous bien!; **we had fun catching the ponies** nous nous sommes beaucoup amusés en attrapant les poneys; **skiing is fun** c'est amusant de faire du ski; **I do it for fun** je le fais pour m'amuser; ★ **to make fun of somebody** se moquer de quelqu'un.

funds *plural noun* fonds M *plural*.

funeral *noun* enterrement M.

funfair *noun* fête F foraine.

funny *adjective* **1** (*when you laugh*) drôle; **how funny you are!** que tu es drôle!; **a funny story** une histoire drôle; **2** (*strange*) bizarre; **that's funny, I'm sure I paid** c'est bizarre, je suis certain que j'ai payé; **a funny noise** un bruit bizarre.

fur *noun* **1** (*on an animal*) poils M *plural*; **2** (*for a coat*) fourrure F; **a fur coat** un manteau de fourrure.

furious *adjective* furieux (F furieuse); **she was furious with Steve** elle était furieuse contre Steve.

furniture *noun* meubles M *plural*;
to buy some furniture acheter des
meubles; **a piece of furniture** un
meuble.

further *adverb* plus loin; **further
than the station** plus loin que la
gare; **ten kilometres further on** dix
kilomètres plus loin; **further
forward** plus en avant; **further
back** plus en arrière.

fuse *noun* fusible M.

fuss *noun* histoires F *plural*; **to
make a fuss** faire des histoires; **to
make a fuss about the bill** faire
toute une histoire à propos de
l'addition.

fussy *adjective* **to be fussy about
something** être difficile sur quelque
chose (*food, for example*).

future *noun* 1 avenir M; **in future**
à l'avenir; **in the future** dans
l'avenir; 2 (*in grammar*) futur M; **a
verb in the future** un verbe au futur.

G g

gadget *noun* gadget M.

gain *verb* 1 gagner [1]; **in order to
gain time** pour gagner du temps; **we
have nothing to gain** nous n'avons
rien à gagner; 2 **to gain speed**
prendre de la vitesse; **to gain weight**
prendre du poids.

gale *noun* vent M violent.

gallery *noun* **an art gallery** (*public*)
un musée; (*private*) une galerie.

gamble *verb* jouer [1].

game *noun* 1 jeu M; **children's
games** les jeux d'enfant; **a game of
chance** un jeu de hasard; **a board
game** un jeu de société; 2 **a game
of** une partie de; **to have a game of
cards** faire une partie de cartes;
3 match M; **a game of football** un
match de foot.

gang *noun* bande F; **all the gang
were there** toute la bande y était.

gangster *noun* gangster M.

gap *noun* 1 (*hole*) trou M; 2 (*in
time*) intervalle M; **a two-year gap**
un intervalle de deux ans; 3 **an age
gap** une différence d'âge.

garage *noun* garage M.

garden *noun* jardin M.

gardener *noun* jardinier M; **he
wants to be a gardener** il veut être
jardinier.

gardening *noun* jardinage M.

garlic *noun* ail M.

garlic mayonnaise *noun* aïoli M.

garment *noun* vêtement M.

gas *noun* gaz M.

gas cooker *noun* cuisinière F à
gaz.

gas fire *noun* radiateur M à gaz.

gas meter *noun* compteur M à gaz.

gate *noun* 1 (*garden*) portail M;
2 (*field*) barrière F; 3 (*at the
airport*) porte F.

gather *verb* 1 (*people*) se
rassembler [1]; **a crowd gathered**
une foule s'est rassemblée;

2 cueillir [35] (*fruit, vegetables, flowers*); **3 as far as I can gather** autant que je sache.

gay *adjective* homosexuel (F homosexuelle).

gaze *verb* **to gaze at something** regarder [1] quelque chose.

gear *noun* **1** (*in a car*) vitesse F; **to change gear** changer de vitesse; **2** (*equipment*) matériel M; **camping gear** du matériel de camping; **3** (*things*) affaires; **I've left all my gear at Gary's** j'ai laissé toutes mes affaires chez Gary.

gear lever *noun* levier M de vitesses.

gel *noun* **hair gel** le gel pour les cheveux.

Gemini *noun* Gémeaux M *plural*; **Steph's Gemini** Steph est Gémeaux.

gender *noun* (*of a word*) genre M; **what is the gender of 'maison'?** quel est le genre de 'maison'?

general *noun* général M (*plural* généraux). *adjective* général (M *plural* généraux); **in general** en général.

general election *noun* élections législatives F *plural*.

general knowledge *noun* connaissances générales F *plural*.

generally *adverb* généralement.

generation *noun* génération F.

generator *noun* générateur M.

generous *adjective* généreux (F généreuse).

genetics *noun* génétique F.

Geneva *noun* Genève; **to Geneva** à Genève; **in Geneva** à Genève; **Lake Geneva** le lac Léman.

genius *noun* génie M; **Lisa, you're a genius!** Lisa, tu es un génie !

gentle *adjective* doux (F douce).

gentleman *noun* monsieur M (*plural* messieurs); **ladies and gentlemen** mesdames et messieurs.

gently *adverb* doucement.

gents *noun* toilettes F *plural*; (*marked on the door*) 'Messieurs'; **where's the gents?** où sont les toilettes?

genuine *adjective* **1** (*real*) véritable; **a genuine diamond** un véritable diamant; **2** (*authentic*) authentique; **a genuine signature** une signature authentique; **3** sincère (*person*); **she's very genuine** elle est très sincère.

geography *noun* géographie F.

germ *noun* microbe M.

German *noun* **1** Allemand M, Allemande F; **2** (*language*) allemand. *adjective* allemand.

Germany *noun* Allemagne F; **to Germany** en Allemagne; **in Germany** en Allemagne.

get *verb* **1** (*have, receive*) avoir [5]; **he's got lots of money** il a beaucoup d'argent; **she's got long hair** elle a les cheveux longs; **I got a bike for my birthday** j'ai eu un vélo pour mon anniversaire; **I got your letter yesterday** j'ai eu ta lettre hier; **I got fifteen for my French homework** j'ai eu quinze pour mon devoir français; **2** (*fetch*) chercher [1]; **I'll go and get some bread** j'irai chercher du pain; **I'll get your bag for you** je te chercherai ton sac; **3** (*obtain*) trouver [1]; **Fred's got a job** Fred a trouvé un emploi; **where did you get that jacket?** où est-ce que tu as trouvé cette veste?; **4 to have got to do** devoir [8] faire; **I've got to phone before midday** je dois appeler avant midi; **5 to get to somewhere** arriver [1] quelque part; **when we got to London** quand nous sommes arrivés à Londres; **to get here** (or **there**) arriver; **we got here this morning** nous sommes arrivés ce matin; **what time did they get there?** ils sont arrivés à quelle heure?; **6** (*become*) commencer [61] à être; **I'm getting tired** je commence à être fatigué; **it's getting late** il commence à être tard; **it's getting dark** il commence à faire nuit; **I'm getting hungry** je commence à avoir faim; **7 to get something done** faire [10] faire quelque chose; **I'm getting my hair cut this afternoon** je vais me faire couper les cheveux cet après-midi.

● **to get back** rentrer [1]; **Mum gets back at six** Maman rentre à six heures.

● **to get something back** récupérer [24] quelque chose; **did you get your books back?** est-ce que tu as récupéré tes livres?

● **to get into something** monter [1] dans quelque chose (*a vehicle*); **he got into the car** il est monté dans la voiture.

● **to get off something** descendre [3] de quelque chose; **I got off the train at Banbury** je suis descendu du train à Banbury.

● **to get on** aller [7]; **how's Amanda getting on?** comment va Amanda?

● **to get on something** monter [1] dans quelque chose (*vehicle*); **she got on the train at Reading** elle est montée dans le train à Reading.

● **to get on with somebody** s'entendre [3] avec quelqu'un; **she doesn't get on with her brother** elle ne s'entend pas avec son frère.

● **to get out of something** descendre [3] de quelque chose (*vehicle*); **Laura got out of the car** Laura est descendue de la voiture.

● **to get something out** sortir [72] quelque chose; **Robert got his guitar out** Robert a sorti sa guitare.

● **to get together** se voir; [13] **we must get together soon** il faut qu'on se voie bientôt.

● **to get up** se lever; [50] **I get up at seven** je me lève à sept heures.

ghost *noun* fantôme M.

giant *noun* géant M, géante F. *adjective* énorme; **a giant lorry** un énorme camion.

gift *noun* **1** cadeau M (*plural* cadeaux); **a Christmas gift** un cadeau de Noël; **2 to have a gift for something** être doué pour quelque chose; **Jo has a real gift for languages** Jo est vraiment douée pour les langues.

gifted *adjective* doué.

gigantic *adjective* gigantesque.

gin *noun* gin M.

ginger *noun* gingembre M.

giraffe *noun* giraffe F.

girl *noun* **1** fille F; **three boys and four girls** trois garçons et quatre

filles; **a little girl** une petite fille;
when I was a little girl quand j'étais
petite; **2** (*a teenager or young
woman*) jeune fille F; **an eighteen-
year-old girl** une jeune fille de dix-
huit ans.

girlfriend *noun* copine F; **Darren's
gone out with his girlfriend** Darren
est sorti avec sa copine; **Lizzie and
her girlfriends have gone to the
cinema** Lizzie et ses copines sont
allées au cinéma.

give *verb* donner [1]; **to give
something to somebody** donner
quelque chose à quelqu'un; **I'll give
you my address** je te donnerai mon
adresse; **give me the key** donne-moi
la clé; **Yasmin's dad gave her the
money** le père de Yasmin lui a donné
l'argent.

to give something away donner
quelque chose; **she's given away all
her books** elle a donné tous ses
livres.

to give something back to somebody
rendre [3] quelque chose à
quelqu'un; **I gave her back the keys**
je lui ai rendu les clés.

to give in céder [24]; **my mum said
no but she gave in in the end** maman
a dit non, mais elle a fini par céder.

to give up abandonner [1] **I give up!**
j'abandonne!

to give up doing arrêter [1] de faire;
she's given up smoking elle a arrêté
de fumer.

glad *adjective* content; **I'm glad to
hear he's better** je suis content
d'apprendre qu'il va mieux; **I'm glad
to be back** je suis content d'être de
retour.

glance *noun* coup d'œil M.

verb **to glance at something** jeter
[48] un coup d'œil à quelque chose;
Sara glanced at the envelope Sara
a jeté un coup d'œil à l'enveloppe.

glass *noun* verre M; **a glass of
water** un verre d'eau; **a glass table**
une table en verre.

glasses *plural noun* lunettes F
plural; **to wear glasses** porter des
lunettes.

glider *noun* planeur M.

global *adjective* mondial (M *plural*
mondiaux).

global warming *noun* le
réchauffement de la planète.

globe *noun* globe M.

glove *noun* gant M; **a pair of
gloves** une paire de gants.

glove compartment *noun* boîte
F à gants.

glue *noun* colle F.

go *noun* **1** (*in a game*) **whose go is
it?** c'est à qui de jouer?; **it's my go**
c'est à moi de jouer; **2 to have a go
at doing** essayer de faire; **I'll have a
go at mending it for you** j'essaierai
de le réparer pour toi.
verb **1** aller [7]; **we're going to
London tomorrow** nous allons à
Londres demain; **Mark's gone to the
dentist's** Mark est allé chez le
dentiste; **to go for a walk** aller se
promener; **2** (*with another verb*)
aller; **I'm going to make some tea**
je vais faire du thé; **he was going to
phone me** il allait m'appeler;
3 (*leave*) partir [58]; **Pauline's
already gone** Pauline est déjà
partie; **we're going on holiday**

tomorrow nous partons en vacances demain; **4** (*an event*) se passer [1]; **did the party go well?** est-ce que la soirée s'est bien passée?

- **to go away** s'en aller [7]; **go away!** va-t-en!

- **to go back 1** retourner [1]; **I'm going back to France in March** je retourne en France en mars; **I'm not going back there again!** je n'y retourne plus! **2** (*to home, school, office*) rentrer [1]; **I went back home** je suis rentré chez moi.

- **to go down 1** descendre [3]; **she's gone down to the kitchen** elle est descendue dans la cuisine; **to go down the stairs** descendre l'escalier; **2** (*price, temperature*) baisser [1]; **prices have gone down** les prix ont baissé; **3** (*tyre, balloon, airbed*) se dégonfler [1].

- **to go in** entrer [1]; **he went in and shut the door** il est entré et il a fermé la porte.

- **to go into 1** (*person*) entrer dans; **Fran went into the kitchen** Fran est entrée dans la cuisine; **2** (*object*) rentrer [1] dans; **this file won't go into my bag** ce classeur ne rentre pas dans mon sac.

- **to go off 1** (*bomb*) exploser [1]; **2** (*alarm clock*) sonner [1]; **my alarm clock went off at six** mon réveil a sonné à six heures; **3** (*fire or burglar alarm*) se déclencher [1]; **the fire alarm went off** l'alarme d'incendie s'est déclenchée.

- **to go on 1** se passer [1]; **what's going on?** qu'est-ce qui se passe?; **2 to go on doing** continuer [1] à faire; **she went on talking** elle a continué à parler. **3 to go on about something** ne pas arrêter [1] de

parler de quelque chose; **he's always going on about his dog** il n'arrête pas de parler de son chien.

- **to go out 1** sortir [72]; **I'm going out tonight** je sors ce soir; **she went out of the kitchen** elle est sortie de la cuisine; **2 to be going out with somebody** sortir avec quelqu'un; **she's going out with my brother** elle sort avec mon frère; **3** (*light, fire*) s'éteindre [60]; **the light went out** la lumière s'est éteinte.

- **to go past something** passer [1] devant quelque chose; **we went past your house** nous sommes passés devant chez toi.

- **to go round to: go round to somebody's house** aller [7] chez quelqu'un; **I went round to Fred's last night** je suis allé chez Fred hier soir.

- **to go round something 1** faire [10] le tour de (*building, park, garden*); **2** visiter [1] (*museum, monument*).

- **to go through** passer [1] par; **the train went through Dijon** le train est passé par Dijon; **you can go through my office** tu peux passer par mon bureau.

- **to go up 1** (*person*) monter [1]; **she's gone up to her room** elle est montée dans sa chambre; **to go up the stairs** monter l'escalier; **2** (*prices*) augmenter [1]; **the price of petrol has gone up** le prix de l'essence a augmenté.

goal *noun* but M; **to score a goal** marquer un but.

goalkeeper *noun* gardien M de but.

goat *noun* chèvre F; **goat's cheese** le fromage de chèvre.

god *noun* dieu M (*plural* dieux).

God *noun* Dieu M; **to believe in God** croire en Dieu.

godchild *noun* filleul M, filleule F.

goddaughter *noun* filleule F.

goddess *noun* déesse F.

godfather *noun* parrain M.

godmother *noun* marraine F.

godson *noun* filleul M.

goggles *plural noun* lunettes F *plural*; **swimming goggles** les lunettes de plongée; **skiing goggles** les lunettes de ski.

go-karting *noun* karting M; **to go go-karting** faire du karting.

gold *noun* or M; **a gold bracelet** un bracelet en or.

goldfish *noun* poisson rouge M.

golf *noun* golf M; **to play golf** jouer au golf.

golf club *noun* **1** (*place*) club M de golf; **2** (*iron*) crosse F de golf.

golf course *noun* terrain M de golf.

good *adjective* **1** bon (F bonne); **she's a good teacher** c'est un bon professeur; **the cherries are very good** les cerises sont très bonnes; **2 to be good for you** être bon pour la santé; **tomatoes are good for you** les tomates sont bonnes pour la santé; **3 to be good at** être bon en; **she's good at art** elle est bonne en dessin; **4** (*well-behaved*) sage; **be good!** sois sage!; **5** (*kind*) gentil (F gentille); **she's been very good to me** elle a été très gentille avec moi; **6 for good** pour de bon; **I've**

stopped smoking for good j'ai arrêté de fumer pour de bon.

good afternoon *exclamation* bonjour.

goodbye *exclamation* au revoir.

good evening *exclamation* bonsoir.

Good Friday *noun* le Vendredi saint.

good-looking *adjective* beau (F belle) (M *plural* beaux); **Maya's boyfriend's really good-looking** le copain de Maya est très beau.

good morning *exclamation* bonjour.

goodness *exclamation* mon Dieu!; **for goodness sake!** au nom du ciel!

goodnight *exclamation* bonne nuit.

goods *plural noun* marchandises F *plural*.

goods train *noun* train M de marchandises.

goose *noun* oie F.

goose pimples *noun* chair F de poule.

gorgeous *adjective* superbe; **a gorgeous dress** une robe superbe; **it's a gorgeous day** il fait un temps superbe.

gorilla *noun* gorille M.

gorse *noun* ajoncs M *plural*.

gosh *exclamation* ça alors!

gossip *noun* **1** (*person*) bavard M, bavarde F; **2** (*news*) nouvelles F *plural*; **what's the latest gossip?**

quoi de neuf?
verb bavarder [1].

government *noun* gouvernement
M.

grab *verb* **1** saisir [2]; **she grabbed
my arm** elle m'a saisi par le bras;
**2 to grab something from
somebody** arracher [1] quelque
chose à quelqu'un; **he grabbed the
book from me** il m'a arraché le livre.

graceful *adjective* élégant.

grade *noun* (*mark*) note F; **to get
good grades** avoir de bonnes notes.

gradual *adjective* progressif (F
progressive).

gradually *adverb* petit à petit; **the
weather got gradually better** le
temps s'est amélioré petit à petit.

graffiti *plural noun* graffiti M
plural.

grain *noun* grain M.

grammar *noun* grammaire F.

grammar school *noun* (*from age
11 to 15*) collège M; (*from age 15 to
18*) lycée M.

grammatical *adjective* **a
grammatical error** une faute de
grammaire.

gramme *noun* gramme M.

gran *noun* mamie F (*informal*).

grandchildren *plural noun* petits-
enfants M *plural*.

granddad *noun* papy M
(*informal*).

granddaughter *noun* petite-fille
F.

grandfather *noun* grand-père M.

grandma *noun* mamie F
(*informal*).

grandmother *noun* grand-mère F.

grandpa *noun* papi M (*informal*).

grandparents *plural noun*
grandparents M *plural*.

grandson *noun* petit-fils M.

granny *noun* mamie F (*informal*).

grape *noun* **a grape** un grain de
raisin; **to buy some grapes** acheter
du raisin; **do you like grapes?** est-
ce que tu aimes le raisin?; **a bunch of
grapes** une grappe de raisin.

grapefruit *noun* pamplemousse
M.

graph *noun* graphique M.

grasp *verb* saisir [2].

grass *noun* **1** herbe F; **sitting on
the grass** assis sur l'herbe;
2 (*lawn*) pelouse F; **to cut the
grass** tondre la pelouse.

grasshopper *noun* sauterelle F.

grate *verb* râper [1]; **grated cheese**
du fromage râpé.

grateful *adjective* reconnaissant.

grater *noun* râpe F.

grave *noun* tombe F.

gravel *noun* gravillons M *plural*.

graveyard *noun* cimetière M.

gravy *noun* sauce F au jus de rôti.

grease *noun* graisse F.

greasy *adjective* gras (F grasse); **to
have greasy skin** avoir la peau

grasse; **I hate greasy food** je déteste la nourriture grasse.

great *adjective* **1** grand; **a great poet** un grand poète; **2** (*terrific*) génial (M *plural* géniaux); **it was a great party!** ça a été une soirée géniale!; **great!** génial!; **3 a great deal of** beaucoup de; **a great many** beaucoup de; **there are a great many things still to be done** il reste beaucoup de choses à faire.

Great Britain *noun* Grande-Bretagne F; **in Great Britain** en Grande-Bretagne; **to Great Britain** en Grande-Bretagne; **to be from Great Britain** être britannique.

Greece *noun* Grèce F; **to Greece** en Grèce; **in Greece** en Grèce.

greedy *adjective* (*with food*) gourmand.

Greek *noun* **1** (*person*) Grec M, Grecque F; **2** (*language*) grec M. *adjective* grec (F grecque).

green *noun* **1** (*colour*) vert M; **a pale green** un vert pâle; **2 greens** (*vegetables*) les légumes verts; **3 the Greens** (*ecologists*) les Verts M *plural*.
adjective **1** vert; **a green door** une porte verte; **2** écologiste; **the Green Party** le parti écologiste.

greengrocer *noun* marchand M de fruits et légumes.

greenhouse *noun* serre F.

greenhouse effect *noun* effet M de serre.

greetings *plural noun* **Season's Greetings** meilleurs vœux M *plural*.

greetings card *noun* carte F de vœux.

grey *adjective* gris; **a grey skirt** une jupe grise; **to have grey hair** avoir les cheveux gris.

greyhound *noun* lévrier M.

grid *noun* **1** (*grating*) grille F; **2** (*network*) réseau M (*plural* réseaux).

grief *noun* chagrin M.

grill *noun* (*of a cooker*) gril M. *verb* **to grill something** faire [10] griller quelque chose; **I grilled the sausages** j'ai fait griller les saucisses.

grim *adjective* sinistre.

grin *noun* sourire M. *verb* sourire [68].

grip *noun* prise F. *verb* serrer [1].

grit *noun* (*for roads*) gravillons M *plural*.

groan *noun* **1** (*of pain*) gémissement M; **2** (*of disgust, boredom*) grognement M. *verb* **1** (*in pain*) gémir [2]; **2** (*in disgust, boredom*) grogner [1].

grocer *noun* épicier M; **my dad's a grocer** mon père est épicier.

groceries *plural noun* provisions F *plural*; **to buy some groceries** acheter des provisions.

grocer's *noun* épicerie F; **I met Jake in the grocer's** j'ai rencontré Jake à l'épicerie.

groom *noun* (*bridegroom*) marié

M; **the bride and groom** les jeunes mariés.

gross *adjective* **1 a gross injustice** une injustice flagrante; **2 a gross error** une erreur grossière; **3** (*disgusting*) dégoûtant; **the food was gross!** la nourriture était dégoûtante!

ground *noun* **1** terre F; **to sit on the ground** s'asseoir par terre; **to throw something on the ground** jeter quelque chose par terre; **2** (*for sport*) terrain M; **a football ground** un terrain de foot.
adjective moulu; **ground coffee** du café moulu.

ground floor *noun* rez-de-chaussée M; **they live on the ground floor** ils habitent au rez-de-chaussée.

group *noun* groupe M.

grow *verb* **1** (*plant, hair*) pousser [1]; **you hair's grown!** tes cheveux ont poussé!; **2** (*person*) grandir [2]; **my little sister's grown a lot this year** ma petite sœur a beaucoup grandi cette année; **3** (*number*) augmenter [1]; **the number of students has grown** le nombre d'étudiants a augmenté; **4** faire [10] pousser (*fruit, vegetables*); **our neighbours grow strawberries** nos voisins font pousser des fraises; **5 to grow a beard** se laisser [1] pousser la barbe; **6 to grow old** vieillir [2].
● **to grow up** grandir [2]; **the children are growing up** les enfants grandissent; **she grew up in Scotland** elle a grandi en Écosse.

growl *verb* grogner [1].

grown-up *noun* adulte M & F.

growth *noun* croissance F.

grudge *noun* **to bear a grudge against somebody** en vouloir à quelqu'un; **she bears me a grudge** elle m'en veut.

gruesome *adjective* horrible.

grumble *verb* se plaindre [31]; **she's always grumbling** elle est toujours en train de se plaindre; **to grumble about something** se plaindre de quelque chose.

guarantee *noun* garantie F; **a year's guarantee** une garantie d'un an.
verb garantir [2].

guard *noun* **1 a prison guard** un gardien de prison; **2** (*on a train*) chef M de train; **3 a security guard** un vigile.
verb surveiller [1].

guard dog *noun* chien M de garde.

guess *noun* **have a guess!** devine!; **it's a good guess** tu as deviné.
verb deviner [1]; **guess who I saw last night!** devine qui j'ai vu hier soir!; **you'll never guess!** tu ne devineras jamais!

guest *noun* **1** invité M, invitée F; **we've got guests coming tonight** nous avons des invités ce soir; **2** (*in a hotel*) client M, cliente F; **3 a paying guest** un hôte payant.

guide *noun* **1** (*person or book*) guide M; **2** (*girl guide*) guide F; (*belonging to a church company of girl guides*) éclaireuse F.

guidebook *noun* guide M.

guide dog *noun* chien M d'aveugle.

guideline *noun* indication F.

guilty *adjective* coupable; **to feel guilty** se sentir coupable.

guinea pig *noun* (*pet*) cochon M d'Inde; (*in an experiment*) cobaye M; **they want me to be a guinea pig** ils veulent que je serve de cobaye.

guitar *noun* guitare F; **to play the guitar** jouer de la guitare; **on the guitar** à la guitare.

gum *noun* **1** (*in mouth*) gencive F; **2** (*chewing gum*) chewing-gum M.

gun *noun* **1** revolver M; **2** (*rifle*) fusil M.

gust *noun* **a gust of wind** une rafale de vent.

gutter *noun* (*in the street*) caniveau M (*plural* caniveaux).

guy *noun* type M (*informal*); **he's a nice guy** c'est un type sympa; **a guy from Newcastle** un type qui vient de Newcastle.

gym *noun* gym F; **to go to the gym** aller à la gym.

gymnasium *noun* gymnase M.

gymnast *noun* gymnaste M & F.

gymnastics *noun* gymnastique F.

gym shoe *noun* tennis M.

H h

habit *noun* habitude F; **to have a habit of doing** avoir l'habitude de faire; **it's a bad habit** c'est une mauvaise habitude.

haddock *noun* églefin M; **smoked haddock** haddock M.

hail *noun* grêle F.

hailstone *noun* grêlon M.

hailstorm *noun* averse F de grêle.

hair *noun* **1** cheveux M *plural*; **to have short hair** avoir les cheveux courts; **to brush your hair** se brosser les cheveux; **to wash your hair** se laver les cheveux; **to have your hair cut** se faire couper les cheveux; **she's had her hair cut** elle s'est fait couper les cheveux; **2 a hair** (*from the head*) un cheveu; (*from the body*) un poil.

hairbrush *noun* brosse F à cheveux.

haircut *noun* **1** coupe F; **I like your new haircut** j'aime bien ta nouvelle coupe; **2 to have a haircut** se faire couper les cheveux.

hairdresser *noun* coiffeur M, coiffeuse F; **she's a hairdresser** elle est coiffeuse; **at the hairdresser's** chez le coiffeur.

hair drier *noun* sèche-cheveux M.

hair gel *noun* gel M pour les cheveux.

hairgrip *noun* pince F à cheveux.

hair remover *noun* crème F dépilatoire.

hairslide *noun* barrette F.

hairspray *noun* laque F.

hairstyle *noun* coiffure F.

hairy *adjective* poilu.

half *noun* **1** moitié F; **half of** la moitié de; **I gave him half of the money** je lui ai donné la moitié de l'argent; **half an apple** la moitié d'une pomme; **you've only eaten half of it** tu n'en as mangé que la moitié; **half the people** la moitié des gens; **2 to cut something in half** couper quelque chose en deux; **3** (*as a fraction*) demi; **three and a half** trois et demi; **she's five and a half** elle a cinq ans et demi; **4** (*in time*) demi, demie; **half an hour** une demi-heure; **an hour and a half** une heure et demie; **it's half past three** il est trois heures et demie; **5** (*in weights and measures*) demi, demie; **half a litre** un demi-litre; **half a cup** une demi-tasse.

half hour *noun* demi-heure F; **every half hour** toutes les demi-heures.

half price *adjective, adverb* à moité prix; **half-price CDs** des CD à moitié prix; **I bought it half price** je l'ai acheté à moitié prix.

half-time *noun* mi-temps F; **at half-time** à la mi-temps.

halfway *adverb* **1** à mi-chemin; **halfway between Paris and Dijon** à mi-chemin entre Paris et Dijon; **2 to be halfway through doing** avoir à moitié fini de faire; **I'm halfway through my homework** j'ai à moitié fini mes devoirs.

hall *noun* **1** (*in a house*) entrée F; **2** (*public*) salle F; **the village hall** la salle des fêtes; **a concert hall** une salle de concert.

Hallowe'en *noun* la veille de la Toussaint (*the French do not have any particular customs for this date*).

ham *noun* jambon M; **a slice of ham** une tranche de jambon; **a ham sandwich** un sandwich au jambon.

hamburger *noun* hamburger M.

hammer *noun* marteau M (*plural* marteaux).

hamster *noun* hamster M.

hand *noun* **1** main F; **to have something in your hand** avoir quelque chose à la main; **to hold somebody's hand** tenir quelqu'un par la main; **2 to give somebody a hand** donner un coup de main à quelqu'un; **can you give me a hand to move the table?** est-ce que tu peux me donner un coup de main pour déplacer la table?; **do you need a hand?** est-ce que tu as besoin d'un coup de main?; **3 on the other hand...** par contre...; **4** (*of a watch or clock*) aiguille F; **the hour hand** l'aiguille des heures.
verb **to hand something to somebody** passer [1] quelque chose à quelqu'un; **I handed him the keys** je lui ai passé les clés.

● **to hand something in** rendre [3] quelque chose; **I've handed in my homework** j'ai rendu mon devoir.

● **to hand something out** distribuer [1] quelque chose; **Claire handed out the exercise books** Claire a distribué les cahiers.

handbag *noun* sac M à main (*plural* sacs à main).

handcuffs *plural noun* menottes F *plural*.

handful *noun* **a handful of** une poignée de.

andkerchief *noun* mouchoir M.

andicapped *adjective* handicapé.

andle *noun* **1** (*of a door or drawer*) poignée F; **2** (*on a cup or basket*) anse F; **3** (*of a knife, tool, or saucepan*) manche M; **4** (*of a frying pan*) queue F.
verb **1** s'occuper [1] de; **Gina handles the accounts** Gina s'occupe de la comptabilité; **2 she's good at handling people** elle a un bon contact avec les gens; **3 I can't handle any more problems!** j'en ai assez de problèmes comme ça!

andlebars *plural noun* guidon M.

and luggage *noun* bagages M *plural* à main.

andmade *adjective* fait à la main.

andsome *adjective* beau (F belle); **he's a handsome guy** c'est un beau type.

andwriting *noun* écriture F.

andy *adjective* **1** pratique; **this little knife's very handy** ce petit couteau est très pratique; **2** sous la main; **I always keep a notebook handy** je garde toujours un calepin sous la main.

ang *verb* **1** être [6] accroché; **there was a mirror hanging on the wall** il y avait un miroir accroché au mur; **2 to hang something** accrocher [1] quelque chose; **we hung the mirror on the wall** nous avons accroché le miroir au mur.

to hang around traîner [1]; **we were hanging around outside the cinema** on traînait devant le cinéma.

- **to hang down** pendre [3].
- **to hang on** attendre [3]; **hang on a second!** attends une seconde!
- **to hang up** (*on the phone*) raccrocher [1]; **she hung up on me** elle m'a raccroché au nez (*literally: she hung up on my nose*).
- **to hang something up** accrocher [1] quelque chose; **you can hang your coat up in the hall** tu peux accrocher ton manteau dans l'entrée.

hang-gliding *noun* deltaplane M; **to go hang-gliding** faire du deltaplane.

hangover *noun* gueule F de bois; **to have a hangover** avoir la gueule de bois.

happen *verb* **1** se passer [1]; **what's happening?** qu'est-ce qui se passe?; **it happened in June** ça s'est passé en juin; **2 what's happened to the can-opener?** où est l'ouvre-boîte?; **3 if you happen to see Jill** si par hasard tu vois Jill.

happily *adverb* **1** joyeusement; **she smiled happily** elle a souri jouyeusement; **2** (*willingly*) volontiers; **I'll happily do it for you** je le ferai pour toi volontiers.

happiness *noun* bonheur M.

happy *adjective* heureux (F heureuse); **a happy child** un enfant heureux; **Happy Birthday!** Bon anniversaire!

harbour *noun* port M.

hard *adjective* **1** dur; **to go hard** durcir; **2** (*difficult*) difficile; **a hard question** une question difficile; **it's hard to know...** il est difficile de savoir...

adverb **1 to work hard** travailler dur; **2 to try hard** faire beaucoup d'efforts.

hard disk *noun* (*in a computer*) disque dur M.

hardly *adverb* **1** à peine; **I can hardly hear him** je l'entends à peine; **2 hardly any** presque pas de; **there's hardly any milk** il n'y a presque pas de lait; **3 hardly ever** presque jamais; **I hardly ever see them** je ne les vois presque jamais; **4 there was hardly anybody** il n'y avait presque personne.

hard up *adjective* fauché (*informal*).

hare *noun* lièvre M.

harm *noun* **it won't do you any harm** ça ne te fera pas de mal. *verb* **to harm somebody** faire [10] du mal à quelqu'un; **they did not harm him** ils ne lui ont pas fait de mal; **a cup of coffee won't harm you** une tasse de café ne te fera pas de mal.

harmful *adjective* nuisible.

harmless *adjective* inoffensif (F inoffensive).

hat *noun* chapeau M (*plural* chapeaux).

hate *verb* détester [1]; **I hate geography** je déteste la géographie.

hatred *noun* haine F.

have *verb* **1** avoir [5]; **Anna has three brothers** Anna a trois frères; **how many sisters do you have?** tu as combien de sœurs?; **2 to have got** avoir [5]; **we've got a dog** nous avons un chien; **what have you got**

in your hand? qu'est-ce que tu as à la main?; **3** (*to form past tenses, som* verbs in French take 'avoir' and som 'être'*) **I've finished** j'ai fini; **have yo seen the film?** est-ce que tu as vu l film?; **Rosie hasn't arrived yet** Rosie n'est pas encore arrivée; **he ha left** il était parti; **4 to have to do** devoir [8] faire; **I have to phone my mum** je dois appeler ma mère; **5** prendre [64] (*food, drink, a shower*); **we had a coffee** nous avons pris un café; **what will you have?** qu'est-ce que tu prends?; **I'l have an omelette** je prends une omelette; **I'm going to have a shower** je vais prendre une douche; **6 to have lunch** déjeuner [1]; **to have dinner** (*in the evening*) dîner [1]; **7 to have something done** faire [10] faire quelque chose **I'm going to have my hair cut** je va me faire couper les cheveux.

hay *noun* foin M.

hay fever *noun* rhume M des foin

hazelnut *noun* noisette F.

he *pronoun* il; **he lives in Manchester** il habite à Mancheste

head *noun* **1** tête F; **he had a cap on his head** il avait une casquette sur la tête; **at the head of the queu** à la tête de la queue; **2** (*of school*) directeur M, directrice F; **3** (*whe tossing a coin*) **'heads or tails?'** – **'heads'** 'pile ou face?' – 'face'. (*n that it is in fact 'tails or heads' in French*).

● **to head for something** se diriger [5 vers quelque chose; **Liz headed fo the door** Liz s'est dirigée vers la porte.

headache *noun* **I've got a headache** j'ai mal à la tête.

headlight *noun* phare M.

headline *noun* gros titre M; **to hit the headlines** faire la une.

headmaster *noun* directeur M.

headmistress *noun* directrice F.

headphones *plural noun* casque M singular.

headteacher *noun* directeur M, directrice F.

health *noun* santé F.

health centre *noun* centre médico-social M

healthy *adjective* **1** (*person*) **to be healthy** être en bonne santé; **2 a healthy diet** une alimentation saine.

heap *noun* tas M; **I've got heaps of things to do** j'ai un tas de choses à faire.

hear *verb* **1** entendre [3]; **I can't hear you** je ne t'entends pas; **I can't hear anything** je n'entends rien; **2** apprendre [64] (*news*); **I hear you've bought a dog** j'apprends que tu as acheté un chien.
to hear about something entendre [3] parler de quelque chose; **have you heard about the concert?** as-tu entendu parler du concert?
to hear from somebody avoir [5] des nouvelles de quelqu'un; **have you heard from Amanda?** as-tu des nouvelles d'Amanda?

heart *noun* **1** cœur M; **to learn something by heart** apprendre quelque chose par cœur; **2** (*in*

cards) cœur; **the jack of hearts** le valet de cœur.

heart attack *noun* crise cardiaque F.

heat *noun* chaleur F.
verb **1** chauffer [1]; **the soup's heating** la soupe est en train de chauffer; **2 to heat something** faire [10] chauffer quelque chose; **I'll go and heat the soup** je vais faire chauffer la soupe.
● **to heat something up** faire [10] réchauffer quelque chose; **I'm heating up the sauce** je fais réchauffer la sauce.

heater *noun* radiateur M.

heather *noun* bruyère F.

heating *noun* chauffage M.

heatwave *noun* vague F de chaleur.

heaven *noun* paradis M.

heavy *adjective* **1** lourd; **my rucksack's really heavy** mon sac à dos est très lourd; **2** (*busy*) chargé; **I've got a heavy day tomorrow** j'ai une journée chargée demain; **3 heavy rain** des pluies fortes.

heavy metal *noun* (*music*) hard rock M.

hectic *adjective* **a hectic day** une journée mouvementée.

hedge *noun* haie F.

hedgehog *noun* hérisson M.

heel *noun* talon M.

height *noun* **1** (*of a person*) taille F; **2** (*of a building*) hauteur F; **3** (*of a mountain*) altitude F.

helicopter *noun* hélicoptère M.

hell *noun* enfer M; **it's hell here!** c'est infernal ici!

hello *exclamation* **1** (*polite*) bonjour!; **2** (*informal*) salut!; **3** (*on the telephone*) allô!

helmet *noun* casque M.

help *noun* aide F; **do you need any help?** est-ce que tu as besoin d'aide?
verb **1** aider [1]; **to help somebody to do** aider quelqu'un à faire; **can you help me move the table?** peux-tu m'aider à déplacer la table?; **2 to help yourself to something** se servir [71] de quelque chose; **help yourselves to vegetables** servez-vous de légumes; **help yourself!** sers-toi!; **3 help!** au secours!

helpful *adjective* (*person*) serviable.

hem *noun* ourlet M.

hen *noun* poule F.

her *pronoun* **1** la, l' (*before a vowel or silent 'h'*); **I know her** je la connais; **I can hear her** je l'entends; **listen to her!** écoute-la!; **I saw her last week** je l'ai vue la semaine dernière; **2** (*to her*) lui; **I gave her my address** je lui ai donné mon adresse; **3** (*after a preposition*) elle; **with her** avec elle; **without her** sans elle; (*in comparisons*) **he's older than her** il est plus âgé qu'elle.
adjective **1** (*before a masculine noun*) son; **her brother** son frère; **her book** son livre; **2** (*before a feminine noun*) sa; **her sister** sa sœur; **her house** sa maison (*but 'sa' becomes 'son' before a feminine noun beginning with a vowel or silent 'h'*); **her address** son adresse; **3** (*before*

a plural noun) ses; **her children** ses enfants; **4** (*with parts of the body*) le, la, les; **she had a glass in her hand** elle avait un verre à la main; **she's washing her hands** elle se lave les mains.

herb *noun* herbe F.

here *adverb* **1** ici; **not far from here** pas loin d'ici; **2** là; **Tom isn't here at the moment** Tom n'est pas là en ce moment; **3 here is** voilà; **here's my address** voilà mon adresse; **4 here are** voilà; **here are the photos** voilà les photos; **and here they are!** et les voilà!

hero *noun* héros M.

heroin *noun* héroïne F.

heroine *noun* héroïne F.

herring *noun* hareng M.

hers *pronoun* **1** (*for a masculine noun*) le sien; **I took my hat and she took hers** j'ai pris mon chapeau et elle a pris le sien; **2** (*for a feminine noun*) la sienne; **I gave her my address and she gave me hers** je lui ai donné mon adresse et elle m'a donné la sienne; **3** (*for a masculine plural noun*) les siens; **I've invited my parents and Karen's invited hers** j'ai invité mes parents et Karen a invité les siens; **4** (*for a feminine plural noun*) les siennes; **I showed her my photos and she showed me hers** je lui ai montré mes photos et elle m'a montré les siennes; **5** à elle; **the green one's hers** le vert est à elle; **it's hers** c'est à elle.

herself *pronoun* **1 she's hurt herself** elle s'est blessée; **2 she said it herself** elle l'a dit elle-même; **3 she did it by herself** elle l'a fait toute seule.

esitate *verb* hésiter [1]; **to hesitate to do** hésiter à faire.

eterosexual *noun* hétérosexuel M, hétérosexuelle F.

i *exclamation* salut!

iccups *plural noun* **to have the hiccups** avoir le hoquet.

idden *adjective* caché.

ide *verb* (*person*) se cacher [1]; **1 she hid behind the door** elle s'est cachée derrière la porte; **2 to hide something** cacher [1] quelque chose; **who's hidden the chocolate?** qui a caché le chocolat?

ide-and-seek *noun* **to play hide-and-seek** jouer à cache-cache.

i-fi *noun* chaîne F hi-fi.

igh *adjective* **1** haut; **on a high shelf** sur une étagère haute; **the wall is very high** le mur est très haut; **how high is the wall?** quelle est la hauteur du mur?; **the wall is two metres high** le mur fait deux mètres de hauteur; **2** (*number, price, temperature*) élevé; **food prices are very high** les prix de la nourriture sont très élevés; **3 at high speed** à grande vitesse; **4 high winds** des vents violents; **5 a high voice** une voix aiguë.

igh-heeled *adjective* à hauts talons; **high-heeled shoes** des chaussures à hauts talons.

igh jump *noun* saut M en hauteur.

ighly *adverb* extrêmement.

hijack *verb* **to hijack a plane** détourner [1] un avion.

hijacker *noun* pirate M de l'air.

hike *noun* randonnée F; **to go on a hike** faire une randonnée.

hilarious *adjective* hilarant.

hill *noun* **1** (*in landscape*) colline F; **you can see the hills** on voit les collines; **2** (*hillside*) coteau M (*plural* coteaux); **the houses on the hill** les maisons sur le coteau; **3** (*sloping street or road*) **to go up the hill** monter; **you go up the hill to the church and then turn right** vous montez jusqu'à l'église et vous tournez à droite.

him *pronoun* **1** le, l' (*before a vowel or silent 'h'*); **I know him** je le connais; **I can hear him** je l'entends; **listen to him!** écoute-le!; **I saw him last week** je l'ai vu la semaine dernière; **2** (*to him*) lui; **I gave him my address** je lui ai donné mon adresse; **3** (*after a preposition*) lui; **with him** avec lui; **without him** sans lui; (*in comparisons*) **she's older than him** elle est plus âgée que lui.

himself *pronoun* **1 he's hurt himself** il s'est blessé; **2 he said it himself** il l'a dit lui-même; **3 he did it by himself** il l'a fait tout seul.

Hindu *adjective* hindou.

hip *noun* hanche F.

hippie *noun* hippie M & F.

hippopotamus *noun* hippopotame M.

hire *noun* location F; **car hire** location de voitures; **for hire** à louer.

verb louer [1]; **we're going to hire a car** nous allons louer une voiture.

his *adjective* **1** (*before a masculine noun*) son; **his brother** son frère; **his book** son livre; **2** (*before a feminine noun*) sa; **his sister** sa sœur; **his house** sa maison (*but 'sa' becomes 'son' before a feminine noun beginning with a vowel or silent 'h'*); **his address** son adresse; **3** (*before a plural noun*) ses; **his children** ses enfants; **4** (*with parts of the body*) le, la, les; **he had a glass in his hand** il avait un verre à la main; **he's washing his hands** il se lave les mains.
pronoun **1** (*for a masculine noun*) le sien; **I took my hat and he took his** j'ai pris mon chapeau et il a pris le sien; **2** (*for a feminine noun*) la sienne; **I gave him my address and he gave me his** je lui ai donné mon adresse et il m'a donné la sienne; **3** (*for a masculine plural noun*) les siens; **I've invited my parents and Steve's invited his** j'ai invité mes parents et Steve a invité les siens; **4** (*for a feminine plural noun*) les siennes; **I showed him my photos and he showed me his** je lui ai montré mes photos et il m'a montré les siennes; **5** à lui; **the green car's his** la voiture verte est à lui; **it's his** c'est à lui.

history *noun* histoire F.

hit *noun* **1** (*song*) tube M (*informal*); **their latest hit** leur dernier tube; **2** (*success*) succès M; **the film is a huge hit** le film a un succès fou.
verb **1** frapper [1]; **to hit the ball** frapper la balle; **2 to hit your head**

on something se cogner [1] la tête contre quelque chose; **3** heurter [1] **the car hit a tree** la voiture a heurté un arbre; **4 to be hit by a car** (*person*) être [6] renversé par une voiture.

hitch *noun* problème M; **there's been a slight hitch** il y a eu un petit problème.
verb **to hitch a lift** faire [10] du stop (*informal*).

hitchhike *verb* faire [10] du stop (*informal*); **we hitchhiked to Dijon** nous sommes allés à Dijon en stop.

hitchhiker *noun* autostoppeur M, autostoppeuse F.

HIV-negative *adjective* séronégatif (F séronégative).

HIV-positive *adjective* séropositif (F séropositive).

hobby *noun* passe-temps M.

hockey *noun* hockey M; **to play hockey** jouer au hockey.

hockey stick *noun* crosse F de hockey.

hold *verb* **1** tenir [77]; **to hold something in your hand** tenir quelque chose à la main; **can you hold the torch?** est-ce que tu peux tenir la lampe?; **2** (*contain*) contenir [77]; **a jug which holds a litre** un pichet qui contient un litre; **3 to hold a meeting** organiser [1] une réunion; **4 can you hold the line, please** ne quittez pas, s'il vous plaît; **5 hold on!** (*wait*) attends!; (*on telephone*) ne quittez pas!
● **to hold somebody up** (*delay*) retenir [77] quelqu'un; **I was held up at the**

dentist's j'ai été retenu chez le dentiste.

to hold something up (*raise*) lever [50] quelque chose; **he held up his glass** il a levé son verre.

old-up *noun* **1** retard M; **2** (*traffic jam*) bouchon M; **3** (*robbery*) hold-up M.

ole *noun* trou M.

oliday *noun* **1** vacances F *plural*; **where are you going for your holiday?** où est-ce que vous partez en vacances?; **have a good holiday!** bonnes vacances!; **to be away on holiday** être en vacances; **to go on holiday** partir en vacances; **the school holidays** les vacances scolaires; **2** (*from work*) congé M; **I'm taking two days' holiday next week** je prends deux jours de congé la semaine prochaine; **3 a public holiday** un jour férié; **Monday's a holiday** lundi est férié.

oliday home *noun* résidence F secondaire.

olland *noun* Hollande F; **to Holland** en Hollande; **in Holland** en Hollande.

ollow *adjective* creux (F creuse).

oly *adjective* saint.

ome *noun* maison F; **I was at home** j'étais à la maison; **to stay at home** rester à la maison; **make yourself at home** fais comme chez toi.
adverb **1** chez soi; **Susie's gone home** Susie est rentrée chez elle; **I'll call in and see you on my way home** je passerai te voir en rentrant chez moi; **2 to get home** rentrer;

we got home at midnight nous sommes rentrés à minuit.

homeless *adjective* sans abri; **the homeless** les sans-abri M *plural*.

homemade *adjective* fait maison; **homemade cakes** des gâteaux faits maison.

home match *noun* match M à domicile.

homeopathic *adjective* homéopathique.

homesick *adjective* **to be homesick** avoir le mal du pays.

homework *noun* devoirs M *plural*; **I did my homework** j'ai fait mes devoirs; **my French homework** mes devoirs de français; (*written*) mon devoir de français.

homosexual *adjective, noun* homosexuel (F homosexuelle).

honest *adjective* honnête.

honestly *adverb* franchement.

honesty *noun* honnêteté F.

honey *noun* miel M.

honeymoon *noun* voyage M de noces; **they're going to Paris on their honeymoon** ils partent à Paris en voyage de noces.

honeysuckle *noun* chèvrefeuille M.

honour *noun* honneur M.

hood *noun* capuchon M.

hook *noun* **1** crochet M; **2 to take the phone of the hook** décrocher le téléphone.

hooligan *noun* voyou M.

hooray *exclamation* hourra!

hoover *verb* passer [1] l'aspirateur; **I hoovered my bedroom** j'ai passé l'aspirateur dans ma chambre.

Hoover™ *noun* aspirateur M.

hope *noun* espoir M; **to give up hope** perdre espoir.
verb espérer [24]; **we hope you'll be able to come** nous espérons que vous allez pouvoir venir; **hoping to see you on Friday** en espérant de te voir vendredi; **here's hoping!** espérons que ça marche!; **I hope so** je l'espère; **I hope not** j'espère que non.

hopefully *adverb* avec un peu de chance; **hopefully, the film won't have started** avec un peu de chance, le film n'aura pas commencé.

hopeless *adjective* nul (F nulle) (*informal*); **I'm completely hopeless at geography** je suis complètement nul en géographie.

horizontal *adjective* horizontal (M *plural* horizontaux).

horn *noun* 1 (*of an animal*) corne F; 2 (*of a car*) klaxon M; **to sound your horn** klaxonner; 3 (*musical instrument*) cor M; **to play the horn** jouer du cor.

horoscope *noun* horoscope M.

horrible *adjective* 1 affreux (F affreuse); **the weather was horrible** il a fait un temps affreux; 2 (*person*) désagréable; **she's really horrible!** elle est vraiment désagréable; **he was really horrible to me** il a été vraiment désagréable avec moi.

horror *noun* horreur F.

horror film *noun* film M d'épouvante.

horse *noun* cheval M (*plural* chevaux).

horse chestnut *noun* 1 (*tree*) marronnier M; 2 (*nut*) marron M.

horseshoe *noun* fer M à cheval.

hose *noun* tuyau M (*plural* tuyaux).

hosepipe *noun* tuyau M d'arrosage.

hospital *noun* hôpital M (*plural* hôpitaux); **to be in hospital** être à l'hôpital; **to be taken into hospital** être hospitalisé.

hospitality *noun* hospitalité F.

hostage *noun* otage M.

hostel *noun* **youth hostel** auberge F de jeunesse.

hostess *noun* hôtesse F; **an air hostess** une hôtesse de l'air.

hot *adjective* 1 chaud; **a hot drink** une boisson chaude; **be careful, the plates are hot!** fais attention, les assiettes sont très chaudes!; 2 (*a person*) **to be hot** avoir chaud; **I'm hot** j'ai chaud; **I'm very hot** j'ai très chaud; **I'm too hot** j'ai trop chaud; 3 (*the weather or temperature in a room*) **it's hot today** il fait chaud aujourd'hui; **it's very hot in the kitchen** il fait très chaud dans la cuisine; 4 (*food: spicy*) épicé; **the curry's too hot for me** le curry est trop épicé pour moi.

hot dog *noun* hot-dog M.

hotel *noun* hôtel M.

hour *noun* heure F; **two hours later** deux heures plus tard; **we waited for two hours** nous avons attendu pendant deux heures; **two hours ago** il y a deux heures; **to be paid by the hour** être payé à l'heure; **every hour** toutes les heures; **half an hour** une demi-heure; **a quarter of an hour** un quart d'heure; **an hour and a half** une heure et demie.

house *noun* 1 maison F; **to buy a house** acheter une maison; 2 **at somebody's house** chez quelqu'un; **I'm at Judy's house** je suis chez Judy; **I'm going to Judy's house tonight** je vais chez Judy ce soir; **I phoned from Judy's house** j'ai téléphoné de chez Judy.

housewife *noun* femme F au foyer.

housework *noun* ménage M; **to do the housework** faire le ménage.

hovercraft *noun* aéroglisseur M.

how *adverb* 1 comment; **how did you do it?** comment l'as-tu fait?; **how are you?** comment allez-vous?; 2 **how much?** combien?; **how much money do you have?** tu as combien d'argent?; **how much is it?** (*price*) ça coûte combien?; 3 **how many?** combien?; **how many brothers do you have?** tu as combien de frères?; 4 **how old are you?** quel âge as-tu?; 5 **how far is it?** c'est à quelle distance?; **how far is it to Paris?** Paris est à quelle distance d'ici?; 6 **how long will it take?** ça va prendre combien de temps?; **how long have you known**

her? tu la connais depuis combien de temps?

however *adverb* cependant.

hug *noun* **to give somebody a hug** serrer quelqu'un dans ses bras; **she gave me a hug** elle m'a serré dans ses bras.

huge *adjective* immense.

hum *verb* fredonner [1].

human *adjective* humain.

human being *noun* être humain M.

humour *noun* humour M; **to have a sense of humour** avoir le sens de l'humour.

hundred *number* 1 cent; **two hundred** deux cents; **two hundred and ten** deux cent dix (*note that there is no 's' on 'cent' when it is followed by another number*); **a hundred people** cent personnes; 2 **about a hundred** une centaine; **about a hundred people** une centaine de personnes; **hundreds of people** des centaines de personnes.

Hungary *noun* Hongrie F.

hunger *noun* faim F.

hungry *adjective* **to be hungry** avoir faim; **I'm hungry** j'ai faim.

hunt *verb* 1 chasser [1] (*an animal*); 2 rechercher [1] (*person*).

hunting *noun* chasse F; **fox-hunting** la chasse au renard.

hurry *noun* **to be in a hurry** être pressé; **I'm in a hurry** je suis pressé. *verb* se dépêcher [50]; **I must hurry** je dois me dépêcher; **he hurried**

home il s'est dépêché de rentrer chez lui; **hurry up!** dépêche-toi!

hurt *verb* **1 to hurt somebody** faire [10] mal à quelqu'un; **you're hurting me!** tu me fais mal!; **that hurts!** ça fait mal!; **2 my back hurts** j'ai mal au dos; **3 to hurt yourself** se faire [10] mal; **did you hurt yourself?** est-ce que tu t'es fait mal?
adjective **1** (*in an accident*) blessé; **three people were hurt** trois personnes ont été blessées; **2** (*in feelings*) blessé; **she felt hurt** elle était blessée.

husband *noun* mari M.

hutch *noun* clapier M.

hymn *noun* cantique M.

hypermarket *noun* hypermarché M.

hyphen *noun* trait M d'union.

I i

I *pronoun* **1** je, j' (*before a vowel or a silent 'h'*); **I am Scottish** je suis écossais; **I have two sisters** j'ai deux sœurs; **2** moi; **Robert and I** Robert et moi; **Tony and I left before you** Tony et moi sommes partis avant vous.

ice *noun* **1** glace F; **2** (*on the roads*) verglas M; **3** (*in a drink*) glaçons M *plural*.

ice cream *noun* glace F; **a chocolate ice cream** une glace au chocolat.

ice-cube *noun* glaçon M.

ice hockey *noun* hockey M sur glace.

ice rink *noun* patinoire F.

ice-skating *noun* **to go ice-skating** faire [10] du patin à glace.

icy *adjective* **1** verglacé (*a road*); **2** (*very cold*) glacial; **an icy wind** un vent glacial.

idea *noun* idée F; **what a good idea!** quelle bonne idée!; **I've no idea** je n'ai aucune idée.

ideal *adjective* idéal (M *plural* idéaux).

identical *adjective* identique.

identification *noun* identification F.

identify *verb* identifier [1].

identity card *noun* carte F d'identité.

idiom *noun* idiome M.

idiot *noun* idiot M, idiote F.

idiotic *adjective* bête.

idyllic *adjective* idyllique.

i.e. c-à-d (*short for: c'est-à-dire*).

if *conjunction* **1** si, s' (*before 'il' and 'ils'*); **if Sue's there** si Sue est là; **if it rains** s'il pleut; **if I won the lottery** si je gagnais la loterie; **if not** sinon; **2 if only ...** si seulement ...; **if only you'd told me** si seulement tu me l'avais dit; **3 even if** même si; **even if it snows** même s'il neige; **4 if I were you...** à ta place ...; **if I were you, I'd forget it** à ta place je l'oublierais.

ignore *verb* **1** ignorer [1] (*a person*); **2** ne pas écouter [1] (*what somebody says*); **3 just ignore it** ne fais pas attention.

ill *adjective* malade; **to fall ill, to be taken ill** tomber malade; **I feel ill** je ne me sens pas bien.

illegal *adjective* illégal (M *plural* illégaux).

illegible *adjective* illisible.

illness *noun* maladie F.

illusion *noun* illusion F.

illustrated *adjective* illustré.

illustration *noun* illustration F.

image *noun* image F; ★ **he's the spitting image of his father** c'est son père tout craché.

imagination *noun* imagination F; **to show imagination** faire preuve d'imagination.

imaginative *adjective* plein d'imagination.

imagine *verb* imaginer [1]; **imagine that you're very rich** imagine que tu es très riche; **you can't imagine how hard it was!** tu ne peux pas t'imaginer combien c'était difficile !

imitate *verb* imiter [1].

imitation *noun* imitation F.

immediate *adjective* immédiat.

immediately *adverb* immédiatement; **I rang them immediately** je les ai appelés immédiatement; **immediately before** juste avant; **immediately after** juste après.

immigrant *noun* immigré M, immigrée F.

immigration *noun* immigration F.

impatience *noun* impatience F.

impatient *adjective* **1** impatient; **2 to get impatient with somebody** s'impatienter contre quelqu'un.

impatiently *adverb* avec impatience.

imperfect *noun* (*of a verb*) imparfait M; **in the imperfect** à l'imparfait.

importance *noun* importance F.

important *adjective* important.

impossible *adjective* impossible; **it's impossible to find a telephone** il est impossible de trouver un téléphone.

impressed *adjective* impressionné.

impression *noun* impression F; **to make a good impression on somebody** faire bonne impression sur quelqu'un; **I got the impression he was hiding something** j'avais l'impression qu'il cachait quelque chose.

impressive *adjective* impressionnant.

improve *verb* **1 to improve something** améliorer [1] quelque chose; **2** (*get better*) s'améliorer [1]; **the weather is improving** le temps s'améliore.

improvement *noun* **1** (*a clear change for the better*) amélioration F. **2** (*gradual progress*) progrès M *plural* (*in schoolwork, for example*).

in *preposition, adverb* **1** dans; **in my pocket** dans ma poche; **in the newspaper** dans le journal; **in the kitchen** dans la cuisine; **in my class** dans ma classe; **I was in the bath** j'étais dans mon bain; **2** à; **in Oxford** à Oxford; **a house in the country** une maison à la campagne; **in school** à l'école; **in the sun** au soleil; **the girl in the pink shirt** la fille à la chemise rose; **3** en; **in France** en France (*BUT*) **in Portugal** au Portugal (*'en' for feminine countries, 'au' for most masculine countries*); **in town** en ville; **in French** en français; **4** (*time expressions*) **in May** en mai; **in '94** en quatre-vingt-quatorze; **in winter** en hiver; **in summer** en été; (*BUT*) **in spring** au printemps; **in the morning** le matin; **at eight in the morning** à huit heures du matin; **in the night** pendant la nuit; **I'll phone you in ten minutes** je t'appellerai dans dix minutes; **she did it in five minutes** elle l'a fait en cinq minutes; **5** (*talking about a group*) de; **the tallest boy in the class** le garçon le plus grand de la classe; **the biggest city in the world** la ville la plus grande du monde; **6 in time** à temps; **7 in the photo** sur la photo; **8 in the rain** sous la pluie; **9 dressed in white** habillé en blanc; **10 to come in** entrer; **to go in** entrer; **we went into the cinema** nous sommes entrés dans le cinéma; **to run in** entrer en courant; **11 to be in** être là; **Mick's not in at the moment** Mick n'est pas là en ce moment.

incident *noun* incident M.

include *verb* comprendre [64]; **dinner is included in the price** le dîner est compris dans le prix; **service included** service compris.

including *preposition* (y) compris; **£50 including VAT** cinquante livres TVA comprise; **everyone, including children** tout le monde, y compris les enfants; **including Sundays** y compris les dimanches; **not including Sundays** sans compter les dimanches.

income *noun* revenu M.

income tax *noun* impôt M sur le revenu.

inconvenient *adjective* **1** incommode (*a place or an arrangement*); **2** inopportun (*a time*).

increase *noun* augmentation F (*in price, for example*).
verb augmenter [1]; **the price has increased by £10** le prix a augment de dix livres.

incredible *adjective* incroyable.

incredibly *adverb* (*very*) extrêmement; **the film's incredibly boring** le film est extrêmement ennuyeux.

indeed *adverb* **1** (*to emphasize*) vraiment; **she's very pleased indeed** elle est vraiment très contente; **I'm very hungry indeed** j'ai vraiment très faim; **thank you very much indeed** merci beaucoup; **2** (*certainly*) bien sûr; **'can you hear his radio?' – 'indeed I can!'** 'entends-tu sa radio?' – 'bien sûr que oui!'

indefinite article *noun* (*in grammar*) article indéfini M.

independence *noun* indépendance F.

independent *adjective* indépendant; **an independent school** une école privée.

index *noun* index M.

India *noun* Inde F; **in India** en Inde; **to India** en Inde.

Indian *noun* Indien M, Indienne F. *adjective* indien (F indienne).

indicate *verb* indiquer [1].

indication *noun* indication F.

indigestion *noun* indigestion F; **to have indigestion** avoir une indigestion.

individual *noun* individu M. *adjective* 1 individuel (F individuelle) (*a serving or a contribution, for example*); 2 **individual tuition** des cours particuliers.

indoor *adjective* couvert; **an indoor swimming pool** une piscine couverte.

indoors *adverb* à l'intérieur; **it's cooler indoors** il fait plus frais à l'intérieur; **to go indoors** rentrer.

industrial *adjective* industriel (F industrielle).

industrial estate *noun* zone industrielle F.

industry *noun* industrie F; **the advertising industry** l'industrie de la publicité.

inefficient *adjective* inefficace.

inevitable *adjective* inévitable.

inevitably *adverb* inévitablement.

inexperienced *adjective* inexpérimenté.

infant school *noun* école F maternelle.

infection *noun* infection F; **an eye infection** une infection de l'œil; **a throat infection** une angine.

infectious *adjective* contagieux (F contagieuse).

infinitive *noun* infinitif M; **in the infinitive** à l'infinitif.

inflammable *adjective* inflammable.

inflatable *adjective* pneumatique (*a mattress or a boat*).

inflate *verb* gonfler [1] (*a mattress or boat*).

inflation *noun* inflation F.

influence *noun* influence F; **to be a good influence on somebody** avoir une bonne influence sur quelqu'un. *verb* influencer [61].

inform *verb* informer [1]; **to inform somebody that** informer quelqu'un du fait que; **they informed us that there was a problem** ils nous ont informés du fait qu'il y avait un problème; **to inform somebody of something** informer quelqu'un de quelque chose.

informal *adjective* 1 simple (*a meal or event, for example*); 2 (*language*) familier (F familière); **an informal expression** une expression familière.

information *noun* renseignements M *plural*; **I need some information**

about flights to Paris j'ai besoin de quelques renseignements sur les vols vers Paris; **a piece of information** un renseignement.

information desk, information office *noun* bureau M des renseignements.

information technology, IT *noun* informatique F.

infuriating *adjective* exaspérant.

ingredient *noun* ingrédient M.

inhabitant *noun* habitant M, habitante F.

initials *plural noun* initiales F *plural*; **put your initials here** marquez vos initiales ici.

initiative *noun* initiative F.

injection *noun* piqûre F; **to give somebody an injection** faire une piqûre à quelqu'un.

injure *verb* blesser [1].

injured *adjective* blessé.

injury *noun* blessure F.

ink *noun* encre F.

in-laws *plural noun* beaux-parents M *plural*.

inner *adjective* intérieur.

innocent *adjective* innocent.

insane *adjective* fou (F folle).

inscription *noun* inscription F.

insect *noun* insecte M; **an insect bite** une piqûre d'insecte.

insect repellent *noun* insectifuge M.

inside *noun* intérieur M; **the inside**

of the oven l'intérieur du four. *preposition* à l'intérieur de; **inside the cinema** à l'intérieur du cinéma. *adverb* à l'intérieur; **she's inside, I think** elle est à l'intérieur, je crois; **to go inside** rentrer.

inside out *adjective, adverb* à l'envers.

insincere *adjective* peu sincère.

insist *verb* **1** insister [1]; **if you insist** puisque tu insistes; **to insist on doing** insister pour faire; **he insisted on paying** il a insisté pour payer; **2 to insist that** affirmer [1] que; **Ruth insisted I was wrong** Ruth a affirmé que j'avais tort.

insomnia *noun* insomnie F.

inspector *noun* inspecteur M, inspectrice F.

install *verb* installer [1].

instalment *noun* (*of a story or serial*) épisode M.

instance *noun* **for instance** par exemple.

instant *noun* instant M; **come here this instant!** viens ici tout de suite! *adjective* **1** instantané (*coffee or soup*); **2** (*immediate*) immédiat (*an effect or a success, for example*).

instantly *adverb* immédiatement.

instead *adverb* **1 Ted couldn't go, so I went instead** Ted ne pouvait pas y aller, donc je suis allé à sa place; **we didn't go to the concert, we went to Lucy's instead** au lieu d'aller au concert, nous sommes allés chez Lucy; **2 instead of** au lieu de; **instead of pudding I had cheese** j'ai pris le fromage au lieu d'un dessert; **instead of playing tennis we went swimming** au lieu de jouer au tennis nous sommes allés à la piscine.

instinct *noun* instinct M.

institute *noun* institut M.

institution *noun* institution F.

instruct *verb* **to instruct somebody to do** donner [1] l'ordre à quelqu'un de faire; **the teacher instructed us to stay together** le professeur nous a donné l'ordre de rester en groupe.

instructions *plural noun* instructions F *plural*; **follow the instructions on the packet** suivez les instructions sur l'emballage; **'instructions for use'** 'mode d'emploi'.

instructor *noun* moniteur M, monitrice F; **my skiing instructor** mon moniteur de ski.

instrument *noun* instrument M; **to play an instrument** jouer d'un instrument.

insulin *noun* insuline F.

insult *noun* insulte F. *verb* insulter [1].

insurance *noun* assurance F; **travel insurance** l'assurance voyage.

intelligence *noun* intelligence F.

intelligent *adjective* intelligent.

intend *verb* **1** vouloir [14]; **as I intended** comme je le voulais; **2 to intend to do** avoir [5] l'intention de faire; **we intend to spend the night in Rome** nous avons l'intention de passer la nuit à Rome.

intensive care *noun* **in intensive care** en réanimation.

intention *noun* intention F; **I have no intention of paying** je n'ai aucune intention de payer.

interest *noun* **1** (*hobby*) centre M d'intérêt; **what are your interests?** quels sont vos centres d'intérêts?; **2** (*keenness*) intérêt M; **he has an interest in jazz** il a un intérêt pour le jazz.
verb intéresser [1]; **that doesn't interest me** ça ne m'intéresse pas.

interested *adjective* **to be interested in** s'intéresser à; **Sean's very interested in cooking** Sean s'intéresse beaucoup à la cuisine.

interesting *adjective* intéressant.

interfere *verb* **1 to interfere with something** (*to fiddle with it*) toucher [1] quelque chose; **don't interfere with my computer!** ne touche pas mon ordinateur; **2 to interfere in** se mêler [1] à (*someone else's affairs*).

interior designer *noun* designer M & F.

international *adjective* international (M *plural* internationaux).

Internet *noun* Internet M; **on the Internet** sur Internet.

interpret *verb* (*act as an interpreter*) faire [10] l'interprète.

interpreter *noun* interprète M & F.

interrupt *verb* interrompre [69].

interruption *noun* interruption F.

interval *noun* entracte M (*in a play or concert*).

interview *noun* **1** (*for a job*) entretien M; **a job interview** un entretien; **2** (*in a newspaper, on TV or radio*) interview F.
verb interviewer [1] (*on TV, radio*).

interviewer *noun* interviewer M.

into *preposition* **1** dans; **he's gone into the bank** il est entré dans la banque; **I put the cat into his basket** j'ai mis le chat dans son panier; **we all got into the car** nous sommes tous montés dans la voiture; **2 to go into town** aller en ville; **Mum's gone into the office** Maman est allée au bureau; **to get into bed** se mettre au lit; **to translate into French** traduire en français; **to change pounds into francs** changer des livres sterling en francs; **3 to be into jazz** être fana du jazz (*informal*).

introduce *verb* présenter [1]; **she introduced me to her brother** elle m'a présenté à son frère; **can I introduce you to my mother?** je te présente ma mère.

introduction *noun* (*in a book*) introduction F.

intuition *noun* intuition F.

invade *verb* envahir [2].

invalid *noun* malade M & F.

invent *verb* inventer [1].

invention *noun* invention F.

inventor *noun* inventeur M, inventrice F.

inverted commas *plural noun*

guillemets M *plural*; **in inverted commas** entre guillemets.

investigation *noun* (*by police*) enquête F; **an investigation into the fire** une enquête sur l'incendie.

invisible *adjective* invisible.

invitation *noun* invitation F; **an invitation to dinner** une invitation à dîner.

invite *verb* inviter [1]; **Kirsty invited me to lunch** Kirsty m'a invité à déjeuner; **he's invited me out on Tuesday** il m'a invitée à sortir avec lui mardi.

inviting *adjective* **1** appétissant (*a meal*); **2** accueillant (*a room*).

involve *verb* **1** nécessiter [1]; **it involves a lot of work** cela nécessite beaucoup de travail; **2** (*to affect*) concerner [1]; **the play will involve everybody** le spectacle va concerner tout le monde; **two cars were involved** deux voitures ont été concernées; **3 to be involved in** participer [1] à; **I am involved in the new project** je participe au nouveau projet.

Iran *noun* Iran M.

Iraq *noun* Iraq M.

Ireland *noun* Irlande F; **in Ireland** en Irlande; **to Ireland** en Irlande; **the Republic of Ireland** la République d'Irlande.

Irish *noun* **1** (*the language*) irlandais M; **2** (*the people*) **the Irish** les Irlandais M *plural*.
adjective irlandais.

Irishman *noun* Irlandais M.

ish Sea *noun* mer F d'Irlande.

ishwoman *noun* Irlandaise F.

on *noun* 1 (*for clothes*) fer M à repasser; 2 (*the metal*) fer M.
verb repasser [1].

oning *noun* repassage M; **to do the ironing** faire le repassage.

oning board *noun* planche F à repasser.

onmonger's *noun* quincaillerie F.

regular *adjective* irrégulier (F irrégulière).

ritable *adjective* irritable.

ritate *verb* irriter [1].

ritating *adjective* irritant.

lam *noun* Islam M.

lamic *adjective* islamique.

land *noun* île F.

olated *adjective* isolé.

rael *noun* Israël M.

raeli *noun* Israélien M, sraélienne F.
djective israélien (F israélienne).

sue *noun* 1 (*something you iscuss*) question F; **a political ssue** une question politique; 2 (*of magazine*) numéro M.
erb (*hand out*) distribuer [1].

ronoun 1 (*as the subject*) il (*when t stands for a masculine noun*); elle (*when it stands for a feminine noun*); **where is my bag?'** – **'it's in the itchen'** 'où est mon sac?' – 'il est ans la cuisine'; **'how old is your ar?'** – **'it's five years old'** 'quel

âge a ta voiture?' – 'elle a cinq ans'; 2 (*as the object*) le (*when it stands for a masculine noun*); la (*when it stands for a feminine noun*); l' (*before a vowel or silent 'h'*); **his new book? I know it** son nouveau livre? je le connais; **his address? I know it** son addresse? je le connais; **where's my book? I've lost it** où est mon livre? je l'ai perdu; 3 **yes, it's true** oui, c'est vrai; **it doesn't matter** ça ne fait rien; 4 **who is it?** qui c'est?; **it's me** c'est moi; **what is it?** qu'est-ce que c'est?; 5 **it's raining** il pleut; **it's a nice day** il fait beau; **it's two o'clock** il est deux heures.

IT *noun* (*short for information technology*) informatique F.

Italian *noun* 1 (*the language*) italien M; 2 (*person*) Italien M, Italienne F.
adjective 1 italien (F italienne); **Italian food** la cuisine italienne; 2 d'italien (*a teacher or a lesson*); **my Italian class** mon cours d'italien.

italics *noun* italique M; **in italics** en italique.

Italy *noun* Italie F; **in Italy** en Italie; **to Italy** en Italie.

itch *verb* **my back is itching** j'ai le dos qui me démange; **this sweater itches** ce pull me gratte.

item *noun* article M.

its *determiner* son (*before a masculine noun or a feminine noun beginning with a vowel or silent 'h'*); sa (*before a feminine noun*); ses (*before a plural noun*); **the dog has lost its collar** le chien a perdu son collier; **the dog's in its kennel** le chien est dans sa niche; **its ear** son oreille; **its toys** ses jouets.

itself *pronoun* **1** se, s' (*before a vowel or silent 'h'*); **the cat is washing itself** le chat se lave; **2 he left the dog by itself** il a laissé le chien tout seul.

ivy *noun* lierre M.

J j

jack *noun* **1** (*in cards*) valet M; **the jack of clubs** le valet de trèfle; **2** (*for a car*) cric M.

jacket *noun* veste F.

jacket potato *noun* pomme F de terre en robe des champs.

jackpot *noun* gros lot M; **to win the jackpot** gagner le gros lot.

jail *noun* prison F.
verb emprisonner.

jam *noun* **1** (*that you eat*) confiture F; **raspberry jam** la confiture de framboises; **2 a traffic jam** un embouteillage.

jammed *adjective* coincé.

January *noun* janvier M; **in January** en janvier.

Japan *noun* Japon M; **in Japan** au Japon.

Japanese *noun* **1** (*the language*) japonais M; **2** (*person*) Japonais M, Japonaise F; **the Japanese** les Japonais M *plural*.
adjective japonais.

jar *noun* (*small*) pot M; (*large*) bocal M (*plural* bocaux); **a jar of jam** un pot de confiture.

javelin *noun* javelot M.

jaw *noun* mâchoire F.

jazz *noun* jazz M.

jealous *adjective* jaloux (F jalouse).

jeans *noun* jean M; **my jeans** mo⟩ jean; **a pair of jeans** un jean.

jelly *noun* gelée F.

jellyfish *noun* méduse F.

jersey *noun* **1** (*a pullover*) pull-ov⟩ M; **2** (*for football*) maillot M.

Jersey *noun* Jersey F.

Jesus *noun* Jésus M; **Jesus Chris⟩** Jésus-Christ.

jet *noun* jet M.

jet lag *noun* décalage M horaire.

jetty *noun* jetée F.

Jew *noun* Juif M, Juive F.

jewel *noun* bijou M (*plural* bijoux).

jeweller *noun* bijoutier M, bijoutière F.

jeweller's *noun* bijouterie F.

jewellery *noun* bijoux M *plural*.

Jewish *adjective* juif (F juive).

jigsaw *noun* puzzle M.

job *noun* **1** (*paid work*) emploi M; **job as a secretary** un emploi comme secrétaire; **he's got a job** trouvé un emploi; **out of a job** sa⟩ emploi; **what's your job?** qu'est-c⟩ que vous faites comme travail?; **a j⟩**

offer une offre d'emploi; **2** (*a task*) travail M; **it's not an easy job** ce n'est pas un travail facile; **she made a good job of it** elle a fait un bon travail.

bless *adjective* sans emploi.

ckey *noun* jockey M.

g *verb* **to go jogging** faire [10] du ogging.

in *verb* **1** (*become a member of*) 'inscrire [38] à; **I've joined the judo club** je me suis inscrit au club de udo; **2** (*to meet up with*) rejoindre 49]; **I'll join you later** je vous ejoindrai plus tard.

o join in 1 participer [1]; **Ruth never oins in** Ruth ne participe jamais; **: to join in something** participer [1] ı quelque chose; **won't you join in he game?** veux-tu participer au eu?

iner *noun* menuisier M.

int *noun* **1** (*of meat*) rôti M; **a oint of beef** un rôti de bœuf; **2** (*in our body*) articulation F.

ke *noun* (*a funny story*) ›laisanterie F; **to tell a joke** aconter une plaisanterie. *erb* plaisanter [1]; **you must be ›king!** tu plaisantes!

ker *noun* (*in cards*) joker M.

rdan *noun* Jordanie F.

ırnalism *noun* journalisme M.

ırnalist *noun* journaliste M & F; **ean's a journalist** Sean est ›urnaliste.

ırney *noun* **1** (*a long one*) voyage 1; **our journey to Turkey** notre

voyage en Turquie; **2** (*shorter: to work or school*) trajet M; **a bus journey** un trajet en bus.

joy *noun* joie F.

joy-riding *noun* rodéo M à la voiture volée.

joystick *noun* (*for computer games*) manette F de jeu.

judge *noun* juge M. *verb* estimer [1] (*a time or distance*).

judo *noun* judo M; **he does judo** il fait du judo.

jug *noun* pot M.

juice *noun* jus M; **two orange juices please** deux jus d'orange s'il vous plaît.

juicy *adjective* juteux (F juteuse).

jukebox *noun* jukebox M.

July *noun* juillet M; **in July** en juillet.

jumble sale *noun* vente F de charité.

jumbo jet *noun* gros-porteur M.

jump *noun* saut M; **a parachute jump** un saut en parachute. *verb* sauter [1].

jumper *noun* pull M.

June *noun* juin M; **in June** en juin.

jungle *noun* jungle F.

junior *adjective* primaire; **a junior school** une école primaire; **the juniors** les élèves du primaire.

junk *noun* (*real rubbish*) bric-à-brac M.

junk food *noun* **you shouldn't eat**

junk food tu devrais manger correctement (*there is no word for junk food in French, so you will need to express it differently, according to the context*).

junk shop *noun* magasin M de brocante.

jury *noun* jury M.

just *adverb* 1 juste; **just before midday** juste avant midi; **just after the church** juste après l'église; **just for fun** juste pour rire; 2 **to have just done** venir de faire; **Tom has just arrived** Tom vient d'arriver; **Helen had just called** Helen venait d'appeler; 3 **to be just doing** être en train de faire; **I'm just finishing the ironing** je suis en train de finir le repassage; 4 (*only*) ne...que; **he's just a child** il n'est qu'un enfant; **there's just me and Justine** il n'y a que moi et Justine; 5 **just coming!** j'arrive!

justice *noun* justice F.

justify *verb* justifier [1].

K k

kangaroo *noun* kangourou M.

karaoke *noun* karaoké M.

karate *noun* karaté M.

kebab *noun* brochette F.

keen *adjective* 1 (*enthusiastic*) enthousiaste; **you don't look too keen** tu n'as pas l'air très enthousiaste; 2 (*committed*)

passionné; **he's a keen photographer** c'est un photographe passionné; 3 **I'm not keen on fish** je n'aime pas trop le poisson; 4 **to be keen on doing** (o **to do**) avoir très envie de faire; **I'm not keen on camping** je n'ai pas tr envie de faire du camping.

keep *verb* 1 garder [1]; **I kept the letter** j'ai gardé la lettre; **will you keep my seat?** veux-tu garder ma place?; **they kept her in hospital** il l'ont gardée à l'hôpital; **to keep a secret** garder un secret; 2 **to keep somebody waiting** faire [10] attendre quelqu'un; 3 (*to store*) ranger [52]; **I keep my bike in the garage** je range mon vélo dans le garage; **where do you keep saucepans?** où rangez-vous les casseroles?; 4 **to keep on doing** continuer [1] à faire; **she kept on talking** elle a continué à parler; **ke straight on** continuez tout droit; 5 **to keep on doing** (*time after tim* he keeps on ringing me up; 6 il n'arrête pas de m'appeler; 7 (*stay* rester [1]; **keep calm!** restez calme **keep out of the sun** reste à l'abri soleil; 8 **to keep a promise** tenir [77] sa promesse.

keep fit *noun* gymnastique F d'entretien.

kennel *noun* 1 (*for one dog*) nich F; 2 (*for boarding*) **kennels** che M.

kerb *noun* bord M du trottoir.

kettle *noun* bouilloire F; **to put t kettle on** mettre l'eau à chauffer.

key *noun* 1 (*for a lock*) clé F; **a bunch of keys** un trousseau de clés; **2** (*on a piano or typewriter*) touche F.

eyboard noun (*for a piano or a computer*) clavier M.

eyring noun porte-clés M.

ick noun **1** (*from a person or a horse*) coup M de pied; **to give somebody a kick** donner un coup de pied à quelqu'un; **2** (*in football*) tir M; ★ **to get a kick out of doing** prendre plaisir à faire.
verb **to kick somebody** donner [1] un coup de pied à quelqu'un; **to kick the ball** donner un coup de pied dans le ballon.
o kick off donner [1] le coup d'envoi.

ck-off noun coup M d'envoi.

d noun gosse M & F (*child*); **Dad's ooking after the kids** Papa 'occupe des gosses.

dnap verb enlever [50].

dney noun **1** (*part of your body*) ein M; **2** (*for eating*) rognon M.

ll verb tuer [1]; **she was killed in an ccident** elle a été tuée dans un ccident.

ler noun (*murderer*) meurtrier M, meurtrière F.

o noun kilo M; **a kilo of sugar** un ilo de sucre; **fifteen francs a kilo** uinze francs le kilo.

ogramme noun kilogramme M.

ometre noun kilomètre M.

t noun kilt M.

d noun sorte F; **all kinds of eople** toutes sortes de gens.
djective gentil (F gentille); **Marion**

was very kind to me Marion a été très gentille avec moi.

kindness noun gentillesse F.

king noun roi M; **King George** le roi Georges; **the king of hearts** le roi de cœur.

kingdom noun royaume M; **the United Kingdom** le Royaume-Uni.

kiosk noun **1** (*for newspapers or snacks*) kiosque M; **2** (*for a phone*) cabine F.

kipper noun hareng fumé M.

kiss noun baiser M; **to give somebody a kiss** embrasser quelqu'un.
verb embrasser [1]; **kiss me!** embrasse-moi!; **we kissed each other** nous nous sommes embrassés.

kit noun **1** (*of tools*) trousse F; **a tool kit** une trousse à outils; **2** (*clothes*) affaires F *plural*; **where's my football kit?** où sont mes affaires de foot?; **3** (*for making a model, a piece of furniture, etc*) kit M.

kitchen noun cuisine F; **the kitchen table** la table de la cuisine.

kitchen foil noun papier M d'aluminium.

kitchen garden noun jardin M potager.

kitchen roll noun essuie-tout M.

kite noun (*toy*) cerf-volant M; **to fly a kite** faire voler un cerf-volant.

kitten noun chaton M.

kiwi fruit noun kiwi M.

knee noun genou M

(*plural* genoux); **on (your) hands and knees** à quatre pattes.

kneel *verb* se mettre [11] à genoux.

knickers *plural noun* petite culotte F.

knife *noun* couteau M (*plural* couteaux).

knight *noun* (*in chess*) cavalier M.

knit *verb* tricoter [1].

knitting *noun* tricot M.

knob *noun* bouton M.

knock *noun* coup M; **a knock on the head** un coup à la tête; **a knock at the door** un coup à la porte. *verb* **1** (*to bang*) cogner [1]; **I knocked my arm on the table** je me suis cogné le bras contre la table; **2 to knock on something** (*a person*) frapper [1] à (*the door*).
● **to knock down 1** (*in a traffic accident*) renverser [1] (*a person*); **2** (*to demolish*) démolir [2] (*an old building*).
● **to knock out 1** (*to make unconscious*) assommer [1]; **2** (*in sport, to eliminate*) éliminer [1].

knot *noun* nœud M; **to tie a knot in something** nouer quelque chose.

know *verb* **1** (*know a fact*) savoir [70]; **do you know where Tim is?** sais-tu où est Tim?; **I know they've moved house** je sais qu'ils ont déménagé; **he knows it by heart** il le sait par cœur; **yes, I know** oui, je sais; **you never know!** on ne sait jamais!; **2** (*be personally acquainted with*) connaître [27] (*a person, place, book, or music, for example*); **do you know the**

Jacksons? est-ce que tu connais le Jackson?; **all the people I know** tou les gens que je connais; **I don't kno** **his mother** je ne connais pas sa mère; **3 to know how to do** savoi [70] faire; **Steve knows how to mal couscous** Steve sait faire du couscous; **Liz knows how to mend** **it** Liz sait le réparer; **4 to know about** être [6] au courant de (*the latest news*); **5 to know about** s'y connaître [27] en (*machines, cooking, etc*); **Lindy knows about computers** Lindy s'y connaît en informatique.

knowledge *noun* connaissance F.

Koran *noun* Coran M.

kosher *adjective* kascher.

L l

lab *noun* labo M.

label *noun* étiquette F.

laboratory *noun* laboratoire M.

Labour *noun* les travaillistes M *plural*; **to vote for the Labour party** voter pour les travaillistes; **t Labour Party** le parti travailliste.

lace *noun* **1** (*for a shoe*) lacet M; **2** (*for curtains, for example*) dentelle F.

lad *noun* gars M.

ladder *noun* (*for climbing, or in y tights*) échelle F.

ladies *noun* (*lavatory*) toilettes F

plural; (on a sign) **'Ladies'** 'Dames'.

lady noun dame F; **ladies and gentlemen** mesdames et messieurs.

ladybird noun coccinelle F.

lager noun bière F blonde.

laid-back adjective relaxe.

lake noun lac M; **Lake Geneva** le lac Léman.

lamb noun agneau M (plural agneaux); **a leg of lamb** un gigot.

lame adjective boiteux (F boiteuse); **he is lame** il boite.

lamp noun lampe F.

lamp-post noun réverbère M.

lampshade noun abat-jour M (plural abat-jour).

land noun 1 terre F; **I can see land** je vois la terre; 2 (property) terrain M; **a piece of land** un terrain. verb 1 (plane, passenger) atterrir [2]; 2 (leave a ship) débarquer [1].

landing noun 1 (on the stairs) palier M; 2 (of a plane) atterrissage M; 3 (from a boat) débarquement M.

landlady noun propriétaire F.

landlord noun propriétaire M.

landscape noun paysage M.

lane noun 1 (a country path) chemin M; 2 (of a motorway) voie F.

language noun 1 (French, Italian, etc) langue F; **a foreign language** une langue étrangère; 2 (way of

speaking) langage M; **bad language** un langage grossier.

language lab noun laboratoire M de langues.

lap noun 1 (your knees) genoux M plural; **on my lap** sur mes genoux; 2 (in races) tour M de piste.

laptop noun portable M.

larder noun garde-manger M.

large adjective 1 grand (goes before the noun); **a large number** un grand nombre; **a large house** une grande maison; 2 gros (F grosse) (a piece, part, animal) (goes before the noun); **a large piece of cake** un gros morceau de gâteau; 3 nombreux (F nombreuse) (crowd or family); **I come from a large family** je viens d'une famille nombreuse.

laser noun laser M.

last adjective dernier (F dernière); **the last time** la dernière fois; **last week** la semaine dernière; **last night** (in the evening) hier soir; (in the night) cette nuit. adverb 1 (in final position) (to arrive or leave) en dernier; **Rob arrived last** Rob est arrivé en dernier; **at last!** enfin!; 2 (most recently) **I last saw him in May** la dernière fois que je l'ai vu était en mai. verb durer [1]; **the play lasted two hours** le spectacle a duré deux heures.

late adjective, adverb 1 en retard; **we're late** nous sommes en retard; **they arrived late** ils sont arrivés en retard; **to be late for something** être en retard pour quelque chose; **we were late for the film** nous étions en retard pour le film; **2 to be late** (*a bus or train*) avoir du retard; **the train was an hour late** le train a eu une heure de retard; **3** (*late in the day*) tard; **we got up late** nous nous sommes levés tard; **the chemist is open late** la pharmacie est ouverte tard; **late last night** tard hier soir; **too late!** trop tard!

lately *adverb* ces derniers temps.

later *adverb* plus tard; **I'll explain later** j'expliquerai plus tard; **see you later!** à tout à l'heure!

latest *adjective* **1** dernier (F dernière); **the latest news** les dernières nouvelles; **2 at the latest** au plus tard.

Latin *noun* latin M.

laugh *noun* rire M; **to do something for a laugh** faire quelque chose pour rigoler (*informal*).
verb **1** rire [68]; **everybody laughed** tout le monde a ri; **2 to laugh at** se moquer [1] de; **I tried to explain but they laughed at me** j'ai essayé d'expliquer mais ils se sont moqués de moi.

launderette *noun* laverie F automatique.

lavatory *noun* toilettes F *plural*; **to go to the lavatory** aller aux toilettes.

lavender *noun* lavande F.

law *noun* **1** loi F; **it's against the law** c'est interdit; **2** (*subject of study*) droit M.

lawn *noun* pelouse F.

lawnmower *noun* tondeuse F à gazon.

lawyer *noun* avocat M, avocate F.

lay *verb* **1** (*put*) poser [1]; **she laid the card on the table** elle a posé la carte sur la table; **2** (*spread out*) étaler [1]; **we laid newspaper on the floor** nous avons étalé du papier journal sur le parquet; **3 to lay the table** mettre [11] la table.

lay-by *noun* aire F de stationnement.

layer *noun* couche F.

lazy *adjective* paresseux (F paresseuse).

lead[1] *noun* **1** (*when you are ahead*) **to be in the lead** être en tête; **Baxter's in the lead** Baxter est en tête; **we have a lead of three points** nous avons trois points d'avance; **2** (*electric*) fil M; **3** (*for a dog*) laisse F; **on a lead** en laisse. *adjective* (*a role or a singer*) principal (M *plural* principaux). *verb* **1** mener [50]; **the path leads to the sea** le chemin mène à la mer; **2 to lead the way** montrer [1] le chemin; **3 to lead to something** entraîner [1] quelque chose (*an accident or problems, for example*).

lead[2] *noun* (*the metal*) plomb M.

leader *noun* **1** (*of a gang*) chef M; **2** (*of a political party*) dirigeant M, dirigeante F; **3** (*in a competition*) premier M, première F.

lead-free petrol *noun* essence F sans plomb.

lead singer *noun* chanteur

principal M,   chanteuse principale F.

leaf *noun* feuille F.

leaflet *noun* dépliant M.

league *noun* (*in sport*) championnat M.

leak *noun* fuite F;   **a gas leak** une fuite de gaz.
verb (*a bottle or a roof*) fuir [44].

lean *adjective* (*meat*) maigre.
verb **1 to lean on something** s'appuyer [41] contre quelque chose; **2** (*prop*) appuyer [41]; **lean the ladder against the tree!** appuie l'échelle contre l'arbre!; **3** (*a person*) se pencher [1]; **to lean out of the window** se pencher par la fenêtre; **lean forward a bit** penche-toi un peu en avant.

leap *verb* sauter [1].

leap year *noun* année F bissextile.

learn *verb* apprendre [64]; **to learn Russian** apprendre le russe; **to learn (how) to drive** apprendre à conduire.

learner *noun* apprenant M, apprenante F;   **to be a fast learner** apprendre vite.

learner driver *noun* élève M & F d'auto-école.

least *adverb, adjective, pronoun* **1** le moins; **I like the blue shirt least** c'est la chemise bleue que j'aime le moins; **2** (*followed by a noun*) le moins de; **Tony has the least money** c'est Tony qui a le moins d'argent; **3** (*followed by an adjective*) le moins, la moins, les moins (*according to the gender and number of the noun going with the adjective*) **the least expensive hotel** l'hôtel le moins cher; **the least expensive car** la voiture la moins chère; **the least expensive shoes** les chaussures les moins chères; **4 the least** (*the slightest*) le moindre, la moindre (*according to the gender of the noun that follows*); **I haven't the least idea** je n'ai pas la moindre idée; **5 at least** (*at a minimum*) au moins; **at least twenty people** au moins vingt personnes; **6 at least** (*at any rate*) du moins; **at least, I think she's a teacher** du moins, je crois qu'elle est professeur.

leather *noun* cuir M;   **a leather jacket** un blouson en cuir.

leave *noun* congé M;   **three days' leave** trois jours de congé.
verb **1** (*go away*) partir [58]; **they're leaving tomorrow** ils vont partir demain; **we left at six** nous sommes partis à six heures; **2** (*go away from*) quitter [1]; **I left the office at five** j'ai quitté le bureau à cinq heures; **Guy left school at sixteen** Guy a quitté l'école à seize ans; **3** (*go out of*) sortir [72] de; **she left the cinema at ten** elle est sortie du cinéma à dix heures; **4** (*deposit*) laisser [1]; **you can leave your coats in the hall** vous pouvez laisser vos manteaux dans l'entrée; **5** (*not do*) laisser [1]; **let's leave the washing up!** laissons la vaisselle!; **6** (*forget*) oublier [1]; **he left his umbrella on the train** il a oublié son parapluie dans le train; **7 be left** rester [1]; **there are two pancakes left** il reste deux crêpes; **we have ten minutes left** il nous reste dix minutes; **I don't**

have any money left il ne me reste plus d'argent.

lecture *noun* **1** (*at university*) cours magistral M (*plural* cours magistraux); **2** (*public*) conférence F.

lecturer *noun* professeur M à l'université.

leek *noun* poireau M (*plural* poireaux).

left *noun* gauche F; **to drive on the left** conduire à gauche; **turn left at the church** tournez à gauche à l'église; **on my left** à ma gauche. *adjective* gauche; **his left foot** son pied gauche.

left-hand *noun* **the left-hand side** la gauche.

left-handed *adjective* gaucher M, gauchère F.

left luggage office *noun* consigne F.

leftovers *plural noun* restes M *plural*.

leg *noun* **1** (*of a person or a horse*) jambe F; **my left leg** ma jambe gauche; **to break your leg** se casser la jambe; **2** (*of other animals*) patte F; **3** (*of a table or chair*) pied M; **4** (*in cooking*) **a leg of chicken** une cuisse de poulet; **a leg of lamb** un gigot; ★ **to pull somebody's leg** faire [10] marcher quelqu'un.

legal *adjective* légal (M *plural* légaux).

leggings *plural noun* caleçon M.

leisure *noun* loisirs M *plural*; **in my leisure time** pendant mes loisirs.

lemon *noun* citron M; **a lemon yoghurt** un yaourt au citron.

lemonade *noun* limonade F.

lemon juice *noun* jus M de citron.

lend *verb* prêter [1]; **to lend something to somebody** prêter quelque chose à quelqu'un; **I lent Judy my bike** j'ai prêté mon vélo à Judy; **will you lend it to me?** veux-tu me le prêter?

length *noun* longueur F.

lens *noun* **1** (*in a camera*) objectif M; **2** (*in spectacles*) verre M; **3 contact lenses** les lentilles F *plural* de contact.

Lent *noun* Carême M.

lentil *noun* lentille F.

Leo *noun* Lion M; **I'm Leo** je suis Lion.

leotard *noun* justaucorps M.

lesbian *noun* lesbienne F.

less *pronoun, adjective, adverb* **1** moins; **Richard eats less** Richard mange moins; **2** (*before a noun*) moins de; **less traffic** moins de circulation; **less time** moins de temps; **3** (*before an adjective or adverb*) moins; **less interesting** moins intéressant; **less quickly than us** moins vite que nous; **4 less than** moins de; **less than three hours** moins de trois heures; **less than a kilo** moins d'un kilo; **5 less than** (*in comparisons*) moins que; **you spent less than me** tu as dépensé moins que moi.

lesson *noun* **1** (*class*) cours M; **th**

history lesson le cours d'histoire; **to take tennis lessons** prendre des cours de tennis; **2** (*one in a planned series*) leçon F; **a driving lesson** une leçon de conduite.

let¹ *verb* **1** (*allow*) **to let somebody do** laisser [1] quelqu'un faire; **she lets me borrow her bike** elle me laisse emprunter son vélo, **will you let me go alone?** veux-tu me laisser y aller toute seule?; **the police let us through** la police nous a laissés passer; **let me see** (*show me*) laisse-moi voir; **2** (*as a suggestion or a command*) **let's go!** allons-y!; **let's not talk about it** n'en parlons pas; **let's see, if Tuesday is the third ...** voyons, si mardi est le trois ...; **let's eat out** si on mangeait au restaurant!

to let off 1 tirer [1] (*fireworks*); **2** faire [10] exploser (*a bomb*); **3** (*to excuse from*) dispenser [1] de (*homework*).

let² *verb* (*to rent out*) louer [1]; **'flat to let'** 'appartement à louer'.

letter *noun* lettre F; **a letter for you from Delia** une lettre pour toi de Delia; **G is the letter after F** G est la lettre après F.

letter box *noun* boîte F à lettres.

lettuce *noun* salade F; **two lettuces** deux salades.

leukaemia *noun* leucémie F.

level *noun* niveau M (*plural* niveaux); **at street level** au niveau de la rue.
adjective **1** droit (*a shelf or floor*); **2** plat (*ground*).

level crossing *noun* passage M à niveau.

lever *noun* levier M.

liar *noun* menteur M, menteuse F.

liberal *adjective* libéral (M *plural* libéraux); **the Liberal Democrats** le parti libéral-démocrate.

Libra *noun* Balance F; **Sean's Libra** Sean est Balance.

librarian *noun* bibliothécaire M & F; **Mark's a librarian** Mark est bibliothécaire.

library *noun* bibliothèque F; **the public library** la bibliothèque municipale.

licence *noun* **1** (*for driving or fishing*) permis M; **a driving licence** un permis de conduire; **2** (*for a TV*) redevance F.

lick *verb* lécher [1].

lid *noun* couvercle M; **she took the lid off** elle a enlevé le couvercle.

lie *noun* mensonge M; **to tell a lie** (or **lies**) mentir.
verb **1** (*to be stretched out*) être [6] allongé; **Jimmy was lying on the bed** Jimmy était allongé sur le lit; **my coat lay on the bed** mon manteau était sur le lit; **2 to lie down** se coucher [1]; (*for a little while*) s'allonger [52]; **come and lie down in the sun** viens t'allonger au soleil; **3** (*not to tell the truth*) mentir [53].

lie-in *noun* **to have a lie-in** faire la grasse matinée.

life *noun* vie F; **all her life** toute sa vie; **full of life** plein de vie; **that's life!** c'est la vie!

lifebelt *noun* bouée F de sauvetage.

lifeboat *noun* canot M de sauvetage.

life jacket *noun* gilet M de sauvetage.

life-style *noun* style M de vie.

lift *noun* 1 ascenseur M; **let's take the lift** prenons l'ascenseur; 2 (*a ride*) **to give somebody a lift to the station** déposer quelqu'un à la gare; **Tom gave me a lift home** Tom m'a déposé chez moi; **can I give you a lift?** puis-je vous déposer quelque part?
verb soulever [50]; **he lifted the box** il a soulevé le carton.

light *noun* 1 (*electric*) lumière F; **will you turn the light on?** veux-tu allumer la lumière?; **to turn off the light** éteindre la lumière; 2 (*streetlight*) réverbère M; 3 (*a headlight for a car*) phare M; **are your lights on?** as-tu allumé tes phares?; 4 (*an indicator on a machine*) voyant M; 5 **traffic lights** les feux M *plural*; **the lights were green** le feu était au vert; 6 **have you got a light?** tu as du feu?
adjective 1 (*in colour*) clair; **light blue eyes** des yeux bleu clair; 2 (*not night*) **it gets light at six** il fait jour à six heures; 3 (*not heavy*) léger (F légère); **a light sweater** un pull léger; **a light breeze** une brise légère.
verb 1 allumer [1] (*the oven, the fire, or a cigarette*); **we lit a fire** nous avons fait un feu; 2 craquer [1] (*a match*).

light bulb *noun* ampoule F.

lighter *noun* briquet M.

lighthouse *noun* phare M.

lightning *noun* éclairs M *plural*; **a flash of lightning** un éclair; **to be struck by lightning** être frappé par la foudre.

light switch *noun* interrupteur M.

like[1] *preposition, conjunction* 1 comme; **like me** comme moi; **like this** comme ça; **like a duck** comme un canard; **like I said** comme j'ai dit; **what's it like?** c'est comment?; **what was the weather like?** quel temps faisait-il?; 2 **to look like** ressembler [1] à; **Cindy looks like her father** Cindy ressemble à son père.

like[2] *verb* 1 aimer [1] (bien); **I like fish** j'aime bien le poisson; **I don't like snakes** je n'aime pas les serpents; **Mum likes travelling** Maman aime bien voyager; **I like Renoir best** je préfère Renoir; 2 **I would like** je voudrais; **would you like a coffee?** est-ce que tu voudrais un café?; **what would you like to eat?** qu'est-ce que tu veux manger?; **yes, if you like** oui, si tu veux.

likely *adjective* probable; **it's not very likely** ce n'est pas très probable; **she's likely to phone** elle va probablement appeler.

lilac *noun* lilas M.

lily *noun* lys M.

lily of the valley *noun* muguet M.

lime *noun* citron vert M.

limit *noun* limitation F; **the speed limit** la limitation de vitesse.

limp *noun* **to have a limp** boiter [1].

line *noun* **1** ligne F; **a straight line** une ligne droite; **six lines of text** six lignes de texte; **to draw a line** tirer un trait; **2 a railway line** (*from one place to another*) une ligne de chemin de fer; **on the railway line** (*the track*) sur la voie ferrée; **3** (*a queue of people or cars*) file F; **to stand in line** faire la queue; **4** (*telephone*) ligne F; **the line's bad** la ligne est mauvaise; **hold the line, please** ne quittez pas. *verb* doubler [1] (*a coat*).

linen *noun* lin M; **a linen jacket** une veste en lin.

lining *noun* doublure F.

link *noun* rapport M; **what's the link between the two?** quel est le rapport entre les deux? *verb* relier [1] (*two places*); **the terminals are linked by a shuttle service** les terminaux sont reliés par une navette.

lion *noun* lion M.

lino *noun* linoléum M.

lip *noun* lèvre F.

lip-read *verb* lire [51] sur les lèvres.

lipstick *noun* rouge M à lèvres.

liquid *noun, adjective* liquide M.

liquidizer *noun* mixer M.

list *noun* liste F.

listen *verb* **1** écouter [1]; **I wasn't listening** je n'écoutais pas; **2 to listen to** écouter [1]; **listen to the music** écoutez la musique; **you're**

not listening to me tu ne m'écoutes pas.

listener *noun* (*to the radio*) auditeur M, auditrice F.

literally *adverb* littéralement.

literature *noun* littérature F.

litre *noun* litre M; **a litre of milk** un litre de lait.

litter *noun* (*rubbish*) détritus M *plural*.

litter bin *noun* poubelle F.

little *adjective, pronoun* **1** (*small*) petit (*goes before the noun*); **a little boy** un petit garçon; **a little break** une petite pause; **2** (*not much*) peu (de); **they have little money** ils ont peu d'argent; **we have very little time** nous avons très peu de temps; **3 a little** un peu (de); **4 we have a little money** nous avons un peu d'argent; **just a little, please** juste un peu, s'il vous plaît; **it's a little late** c'est un peu tard; **a little more** un peu plus; **a little less** un peu moins; ★ **little by little** petit à petit.

little finger *noun* petit doigt M.

live¹ *verb* **1** (*in a house or town*) habiter [1]; **Susan lives in York** Susan habite à York; **we live in a flat** nous habitons dans un appartement; **they live at number 57** ils habitent au numéro cinquante-sept; **we're living in the country now** nous habitons à la campagne maintenant; **2** (*be or stay alive, spend one's life*) vivre [82]; **lions live in Africa** les lions vivent en Afrique; **they live on fruit** ils vivent de fruits; **they live together** ils vivent ensemble.

live² *adjective* **1** en direct (*a broadcast*); **a live concert** un concert en direct; **a broadcast live from Wembley** une émission en direct de Wembley; **2** (*alive*) vivant.

lively *adjective* animé (*a party or restaurant, for example*).

liver *noun* foie M.

living *noun* vie F; **to earn a living** gagner sa vie.

living room *noun* salle F de séjour.

lizard *noun* lézard M.

load *noun* **1** (*on a lorry*) chargement M; **a (lorry-) load of bricks** un camion de briques; **2 a bus-load of tourists** un autobus plein de touristes; **3 loads of** des tas de (*informal*); **loads of people** des tas de gens; **they've got loads of money** ils sont bourrés de fric (*informal*).
verb charger [52]; **a lorry loaded with wood** un camion chargé de bois.

loaf *noun* pain M; **a loaf of wholemeal bread** un pain complet.

loan *noun* prêt M.
verb prêter.

loathe *verb* détester [1]; **I loathe getting up early** je déteste me lever tôt.

lobster *noun* homard M.

local *noun* **1** (*a pub*) pub M du coin; **2 the locals** (*people*) les gens du coin.
adjective **the local library** la

bibliothèque du coin; **the local newspaper** le journal local.

lock *noun* **1** (*with a key*) serrure F; **2** (*on a canal*) écluse F.
verb **to lock the door** fermer [1] la porte à clé; **the door was locked** la porte était fermée à clé.

locker *noun* casier M.

locker room *noun* vestiaire M.

lodger *noun* locataire M & F.

loft *noun* grenier M.

log *noun* bûche F; **a log fire** un feu de bois.

logical *adjective* logique.

lollipop *noun* sucette F.

London *noun* Londres; **to London** à Londres; **a day in London** une journée à Londres; **the London streets** les rues de Londres.

Londoner *noun* Londonien M, Londonienne F.

lonely *adjective* **1** seul; **to feel lonely** se sentir seul; **2** (*a place*) isolé.

long *adjective, adverb* **1** long (F longue); **a long film** un film long; **a long day** une longue journée; **it's an hour long** ça dure une heure; **2 a long time** longtemps; **he stayed for a long time** il est resté longtemps; **I've been here for a long time** je suis là depuis longtemps; **a long time ago** il y a longtemps; **this won't take long** ça ne prendra pas longtemps; **3 how long?** combien de temps?; **how long have you been here?** tu es là depuis combien de temps?; **long ago** il y a longtemps; **4 a long way**

loin; **it's a long way to the cinema** le cinéma est loin d'ici; **5 all night long** toute la nuit; **6 he doesn't work here any longer** il ne travaille plus ici.
verb **to long to do** avoir [5] très envie de faire; **I'm longing to see you** j'ai très envie de te voir.

long-distance call *noun* (*within the country*) appel M interurbain.

longer *adverb* **no longer** ne...plus; **I no longer know** je ne sais plus; **they no longer live here** ils n'habitent plus ici.

long jump *noun* saut M en longueur.

longlife milk *noun* lait M longue conservation.

loo *noun* toilettes F *plural*.

look *noun* **1** (*a glance*) coup M d'œil; **to have a look at something** jeter un coup d'œil à quelque chose; **2** (*a tour*) **to have a look round the town** faire un tour dans la ville; **to have a look round the shops** faire les magasins; **3 to have a look for** chercher (*something you've lost*).
verb **1** regarder [1]; **I wasn't looking** je ne regardais pas; **to look out of the window** regarder par la fenêtre; **2 to look at** regarder [1]; **Andy was looking at the photos** Andy regardait les photos; **3** (*to seem*) avoir [5] l'air; **Melanie looks pleased** Melanie a l'air contente; **the salad looks delicious** la salade a l'air délicieuse; **4 to look like** ressembler [1] à; **Sally looks like her aunt** Sally ressemble à sa tante; **they look like each other** ils se

ressemblent; **what does the house look like?** comment est la maison?

● **to look after 1** s'occuper [1] de; **Dad's looking after the baby** Papa s'occupe du bébé; **2** surveiller [1] (*luggage*).

● **to look for** chercher [1]; **I'm looking for the keys** je cherche les clés.

● **to look forward to something** attendre [3] quelque chose avec impatience (*a party or a trip, for example*).

● **to look out** (*to be careful*) faire [10] attention; **look out, it's hot!** (fais) attention, c'est chaud !

● **to look something up** chercher [1] quelque chose (*in a dictionary or directory*); **you can look it up in the dictionary** tu peux le chercher dans le dictionnaire.

loose *adjective* **1** (*a screw or knot*) desserré; **2** (*a garment*) ample; **3 loose change** la petite monnaie; ★ **I'm at a loose end** je ne sais pas trop quoi faire.

lorry *noun* camion M.

lorry driver *noun* routier M.

lose *verb* **1** perdre [3]; **we lost** nous avons perdu; **we lost the match** nous avons perdu le match; **Sam's lost his watch** Sam a perdu sa montre; **2 to get lost** se perdre [3]; **we got lost in the woods** nous nous sommes perdus dans les bois.

loss *noun* perte F.

lost *adjective* perdu.

lost property *noun* objets M *plural* trouvés.

lot *noun* **1 a lot** beaucoup; **Jason eats a lot** Jason mange beaucoup;

I spent a lot j'ai beaucoup dépensé; **he's a lot better** il va beaucoup mieux; **2 a lot of** beaucoup de; **a lot of coffee** beaucoup de café; **lots of people** beaucoup de gens; **'what are you doing tonight?' – 'not a lot'** 'qu'est-ce que tu fais ce soir?' – 'pas grand-chose'.

lottery noun loterie F; **to win the lottery** gagner à la loterie.

loud adjective **1** fort; **in a loud voice** d'une voix forte; **2 to say something out loud** dire quelque chose à haute voix.

loudly adverb fort.

loudspeaker noun haut-parleur M (plural haut-parleurs).

lounge noun **1** (in a house or hotel) salon M; **2** (in an airport) **the departure lounge** la salle d'embarquement.

love noun **1** amour M; **to be in love with somebody** être amoureux de quelqu'un; **she's in love with Jake** elle est amoureuse de Jake; **Gina sends her love** Gina t'embrasse; **with love from Charlie** amitiés, Charlie; **2** (in tennis) zéro M.
verb **1** aimer [1] (a person); **I love you** je t'aime; **2** aimer beaucoup (place, suggestion); **she loves London** elle aime beaucoup Londres; **I'd love to come** j'aimerais beaucoup venir; **3** adorer [1] (activity, thing); **I love dancing** j'adore danser; **Wayne loves seafood** Wayne adore les fruits de mer.

lovely adjective **1** (to look at) joli; **a lovely dress** une jolie robe; **their garden is lovely** leur jardin est très joli; **a lovely house** une belle maison; **2 it's a lovely day** il fait très beau; **we had lovely weather** il a fait très beau; **3** (food, meal) délicieux (F délicieuse).

low adjective bas (F basse); **a low table** une table basse; **at a low price** à prix bas; **in a low voice** à voix basse.

lower adjective (not as high) inférieur.
verb baisser [1].

low-fat milk noun lait écrémé M.

luck noun chance F; **good luck!** bonne chance!; **bad luck!** pas de chance!; **with a bit of luck** avec un peu de chance.

luckily adverb heureusement; **luckily for them** heureusement pour eux.

lucky adjective **1 to be lucky** (a person) avoir de la chance; **we were lucky** nous avons eu de la chance; **2 to be lucky** (bringing luck) porter bonheur; **it's supposed to be lucky** c'est censé porter bonheur; **my lucky number** mon numéro porte-bonheur.

luggage noun bagages M plural; **my luggage is in the boot** mes bagages sont dans le coffre.

lump noun morceau M (plural morceaux).

lunch noun déjeuner M; **to have lunch** déjeuner [1]; **we had lunch in Oxford** nous avons déjeuné à Oxford.

lunch break *noun* pause-déjeuner F.

lunch hour, lunch time *noun* heure F du déjeuner.

lung *noun* poumon M.

Luxembourg *noun* 1 (*country*) Luxembourg M; **to Luxembourg** au Luxembourg; **in Luxembourg** au Luxembourg; 2 (*city*) Luxembourg; **in Luxembourg** à Luxembourg.

luxurious *adjective* luxueux (F luxueuse).

luxury *noun* luxe M.

lyrics *plural noun* paroles F *plural*.

M m

mac *noun* imper M (*informal*).

macaroni *noun* macaronis M *plural*; **we had macaroni** nous avons mangé des macaronis.

machine *noun* machine F.

machinery *noun* machines F *plural*.

mackerel *noun* maquereau M (*plural* maquereaux).

mad *adjective* 1 fou (F folle); **she's completely mad!** elle est complètement folle!; 2 (*angry*) furieux (F furieuse); **my mum will be mad!** ma mère sera furieuse!; 3 **to be mad about something** adorer quelque chose; **she's mad about horses** elle adore les chevaux.

madam *noun* madame F.

madman *noun* fou M.

madness *noun* folie F.

magazine *noun* magazine M.

maggot *noun* asticot M.

magic *noun* magie F.
adjective 1 magique; **a magic wand** une baguette magique; 2 (*great*) super.

magician *noun* 1 (*wizard*) magicien M; 2 (*conjurer*) prestidigitateur M.

magnificent *adjective* magnifique.

magnifying glass *noun* loupe F.

magnolia *noun* magnolia M.

mahogany *noun* acajou M.

maiden name *noun* nom M de jeune fille.

mail *noun* courrier M; **e-mail** (*electronic mail*) courrier M électronique.

mail order *noun* **to buy something by mail order** acheter quelque chose par correspondance; **a mail order catalogue** un catalogue de vente par correspondance.

main *adjective* principal (M *plural* principaux); **the main entrance** l'entrée principale.

mainly *adverb* principalement.

main road *noun* route F principale.

maize *noun* maïs M.

major *adjective* majeur.

Majorca *noun* Majorque F.

majority *noun* majorité F.

make *noun* marque F; **what make is your bike?** de quelle marque est ton vélo?
verb 1 faire [10]; **I made an omelette** j'ai fait unc omclette; **she made her bed** elle a fait son lit; **he made me wait** il m'a fait attendre; **she makes me laugh** elle me fait rire; **two and three make five** deux et trois font cinq; 2 fabriquer [1]; **they make computers** ils fabriquent des ordinateurs; **'made in France'** 'fabriqué en France'; 3 rendre [3]; **to make somebody happy** rendre quelqu'un heureux; **that makes me hungry** ça me donne faim; 4 gagner [1] (*money*); **he makes forty pounds a day** il gagne quarante livres par jour; **to make a living** gagner sa vie; 5 (*force*) **to make somebody do something** obliger [52] quelqu'un à faire quelque chose; **she made him give the money back** elle l'a obligé à rendre l'argent; 6 **to make a meal** préparer [1] un repas; 7 **to make a phone call** passer [1] un coup de fil; **I have to make a few phone calls** je dois passer quelques coups de fil; 8 **I can't make it tonight** je ne peux pas venir ce soir.
● **to make something up** 1 inventer [1] quelque chose; **she made up an excuse** elle a inventé une excuse; 2 **to make it up** (*after a quarrel*) se réconcilier [1]; **they've made it up now** il se sont maintenant réconciliés.

make-up *noun* maquillage M; **to put on your make-up** se maquiller; **Jo's putting on her make-up** Jo est en train de se maquiller; **I don't wear make-up** je ne me maquille pas.

male *adjective* 1 mâle (*animal*); **a male rat** un rat mâle; 2 (*sex : on a form*) masculin; 3 **a male rôle** un rôle pour homme; **a male voice** une voix d'homme; **a male student** un étudiant.

male chauvinist *noun* macho M.

Malta *noun* Malte F.

man *noun* homme M.

manage *verb* 1 diriger [52] (*business, team*); **she manages a travel agency** elle dirige une agence de voyages; 2 (*cope*) se débrouiller [1]; **I can manage** je me débrouille; 3 **to manage to do** réussir [2] à faire; **he managed to open the door** il a réussi à ouvrir la porte; **I didn't manage to get in touch with her** je n'ai pas réussi à la contacter.

management *noun* 1 gestion F; **a management course** un cours de gestion; 2 direction; **a meeting with management** une réunion avec la direction.

manager *noun* 1 (*of a company or a bank*) directeur M, directrice F; 2 (*of a shop or restaurant*) gérant M, gérante F; 3 (*in sport and entertainment*) manager M.

manageress *noun* gérante F.

mandarin (orange) *noun* mandarine F.

mango *noun* mangue F.

mania *noun* manie F.

maniac *noun* fou M, folle F; **she drives like a maniac!** elle conduit comme une folle!

mankind *noun* humanité F.

man-made *adjective* (*fibre*) synthétique.

manner *noun* **1 in a manner of speaking** pour ainsi dire; **2 to have good manners** être poli; **it's bad manners to talk like that** ce n'est pas poli de parler comme ça.

manpower *noun* main-d'œuvre F.

mantelpiece *noun* cheminée F.

manual *noun* manuel M.

manufacture *verb* fabriquer [1].

manufacturer *noun* fabricant M.

manure *noun* fumier M.

many *adjective, pronoun*
1 beaucoup de; **does she have many friends?** est-ce qu'elle a beaucoup d'amis?; **we didn't see many people** nous n'avons pas vu beaucoup de gens; **there aren't many onions left** il ne reste pas beaucoup d'oignons; **not many** pas beaucoup; **many of them forgot** beaucoup d'entre eux ont oublié; **2 very many** beaucoup; **there aren't very many glasses** il n'y a pas beaucoup de verres; **3 so many** tant; **I have so many things to do!** j'ai tant de choses à faire!; **4 so many** autant de; **I've never eaten so many strawberries** je n'ai jamais mangé autant de fraises; **5 as many as** autant que; **you can take as many as you like** tu peux en prendre autant que tu veux; **6 too many** trop (de); **I've got too many things to do** j'ai trop de choses à faire; **there were too many people** il y avait trop de monde; **that's far too many!** c'est beaucoup trop! **7 how many?**
combien?; **how many are there?** il y en a combien?; **how many sisters have you got?** tu as combien de sœurs?; **how many are there left?** il en reste combien?

map *noun* **1** carte F; **a road map** une carte routière; **2** (*of a town*) plan M.

marathon *noun* marathon M.

marble *noun* **1** marbre M; **a marble fireplace** une cheminée en marbre; **2** bille F; **to play marbles** jouer aux billes.

March *noun* mars M; **in March** en mars.

march *noun* (*demonstration*) manifestation F.
verb (*demonstrators*) défiler [1].

mare *noun* jument F.

margarine *noun* margarine F.

margin *noun* marge F.

marijuana *noun* marijuana F.

mark *noun* **1** (*at school*) note F; **I got a good mark for my French homework** j'ai eu une bonne note pour mon devoir de français; **what mark did you get for French?** tu as eu combien en français?; **2** (*stain*) tache F.
verb corriger [52]; **the teacher marks our homework** le professeur corrige nos devoirs.

market *noun* marché M.

marketing *noun* marketing M.

marmalade *noun* confiture F d'oranges amères.

maroon *adjective* bordeaux; **a maroon jumper** un pull bordeaux.

marriage *noun* mariage M.

married *adjective* marié; **a married couple** un couple marié; **they've been married for twenty years** ils sont mariés depuis vingt ans.

marry *verb* **1 to marry somebody** épouser [1] quelqu'un; **she married a Frenchman** elle a épousé un Français; **2 to get married** se marier [1]; **they got married in July** ils se sont mariés en juillet.

marvellous *adjective* merveilleux (F merveilleuse); **the weather's marvellous** il fait un temps merveilleux.

marzipan *noun* pâte F d'amandes.

mascara *noun* mascara M.

masculine *noun* (*in French and other grammars*) masculin M; **in the masculine** au masculin.

mash *verb* écraser [1] (*vegetables*).

mashed potatoes *plural noun* purée F de pommes de terre.

mask *noun* masque M.

mass *noun* **1 a mass of** une masse de; **2 masses of** beaucoup de; **they've got masses of money** ils ont beaucoup d'argent; **there's masses left over** il en reste beaucoup; **3** (*religious*) messe F; **to go to mass** aller à la messe.

massage *noun* massage M.

massive *adjective* énorme.

master *verb* maîtriser [1].

masterpiece *noun* chef-d'œuvre M (*plural* chefs-d'œuvre).

mat *noun* **1** (*doormat*) paillasson M; **2** (*to put under a hot dish*) dessous-de-plat M; **3 a table mat** un set de table.

match *noun* **1** allumette F; **a box of matches** une boîte d'allumettes; **2** (*sports*) match M (*plural* matchs); **a football match** un match de foot; **to watch the match** regarder le match; **to win the match** gagner le match; **to lose the match** perdre le match.
verb être [6] assorti à; **the jacket matches the skirt** la veste est assortie à la jupe.

matching *adjective* **matching curtains and cushions** des rideaux et des coussins assortis.

mate *noun* copain M, copine F (*informal*); **I'm going out with my mates tonight** je sors avec mes copains ce soir.

material *noun* **1** (*fabric*) tissu M; **2** (*information*) documentation F; **3** (*substance*) matière F; **raw materials** les matières premières F *plural*.

mathematics *noun* mathématiques F *plural*.

maths *noun* maths F *plural*; **I like maths** j'aime bien les maths; **Anna's good at maths** Anna est forte en maths.

matter *noun* **what's the matter?** qu'est-ce qu'il y a?
verb **1 the things that matter** les choses importantes; **it matters a lot to me** c'est très important pour

moi; **2 it doesn't matter** ça ne fait rien; **it doesn't matter if it rains** ça ne fait rien s'il pleut; **3 it doesn't matter** (*whether one thing or another*) ça n'a pas d'importance; **you can write it in French or English, it doesn't matter** tu peux l'écrire en français ou en anglais, ça n'a pas d'importance.

mattress *noun* matelas M.

mature *adjective* mûr.

maximum *noun* maximum M; **the maximum possible** le maximum possible.
adjective maximum (*does not change in the feminine or plural*); **the maximum temperature** la température maximum; **maximum profits** les bénéfices maximum.

May *noun* mai M; **in May** en mai.

May Day *noun* le Premier Mai.

may *verb* **1 she may be ill** elle est peut-être malade; **we may go to Spain** nous irons peut-être en Espagne; **2** (*asking permission*) **may I close the door?** est-ce que je peux fermer la porte?

maybe *adverb* peut-être; **maybe not** peut-être pas; **maybe he's forgotten** il a peut-être oublié; **maybe they've got lost** ils se sont peut-être perdus.

mayonnaise *noun* mayonnaise F.

mayor *noun* maire M.

me *pronoun* **1** me, m' (*before a vowel or silent 'h'*); **she knows me** elle me connaît; **can you help me, please?** est-ce que tu peux m'aider, s'il te plaît?; **can you lend me a pen?** peux-tu me prêter un stylo?; **can you give me your address?** peux-tu me donner ton adresse?; **2** (*after a preposition*) moi; **I took her with me** je l'ai emmenée avec moi; **they left without me** ils sont partis sans moi; **3** (*in commands*) moi; **listen to me!** écoute-moi!; **wait for me!** attends-moi! **excuse me!** excusez-moi!; **4** (*in comparisons*) **than me** que moi; **she's older than me** elle est plus âgée que moi; **5 me too!** moi aussi!

meal *noun* repas M.

mean *verb* **1** vouloir [14] dire; **what do you mean?** qu'est-ce que tu veux dire?; **what does that mean?** qu'est-ce que ça veut dire?; **that's not what I meant** ce n'est pas ce que je voulais dire; **2 to mean to do** avoir [5] l'intention de faire; **I meant to phone my mother** j'avais l'intention d'appeler ma mère; **3 to be meant to do** être [6] censé faire; **she was meant to be here at six** elle était censée être là à six heures.
adjective **1** (*with money*) radin (*informal*); **2** (*unkind*) méchant; **she's really mean to her brother** elle est vraiment méchante avec son frère; **what a mean thing to do!** c'est vraiment méchant!

meaning *noun* sens M.

means *noun* moyen M; **a means of transport** un moyen de transport; **a means of doing** un moyen de faire; **we have no means of contacting him** nous n'avons aucun moyen de le contacter; **by means of** au moyen de; **by all means** certainement.

meantime *adverb* **for the**

meantime pour le moment; **in the meantime** pendant ce temps.

measles *noun* rougeole F.

measure *verb* mesurer [1].

measurements *plural noun* **1** (*of a room or an object*) dimensions F *plural*; **the measurements of the room** les dimensions de la pièce; **2** (*of a person*) mensurations F *plural*; **my chest measurement** mon tour de poitrine; **my waist measurement** mon tour de taille.

meat *noun* viande F.

Mecca *noun* Mecque F.

mechanic *noun* mécanicien M; **he's a mechanic** il est mécanicien.

mechanical *adjective* mécanique.

medal *noun* médaille F; **the gold medal** la médaille d'or.

media *noun* **the media** les médias M *plural*.

medical *noun* visite F médicale; **to have a medical** passer une visite médicale.
adjective médical (M *plural* médicaux).

medicine *noun* **1** médicament M; **I'd like some cough medicine** je voudrais un médicament pour la toux; **2** (*subject of study*) médecine F; **she's studying medicine** elle fait des études de médecine; **3 alternative medicine** la médecine douce.

Mediterranean *noun* **the Mediterranean** la Méditerranée.

medium *adjective* moyen (F moyenne).

medium-sized *noun* de taille moyenne.

meet *verb* **1** (*by chance*) rencontrer [1]; **I met Rosie outside the baker's** j'ai rencontré Rosie devant la boulangerie; **2** (*by appointment*) retrouver [1]; **I'll meet you outside the cinema at six** je te retrouverai devant le cinéma à six heures; **3** se retrouver [1]; **we're meeting at six** nous allons nous retrouver à six heures; **4** (*get to know*) faire [10] la connaissance de; **I met a French girl last week** j'ai fait la connaissance d'une Française la semaine dernière; **5 Tom, have you met Oskar?** Tom, est-ce que tu connais Oskar?; **6** (*off a train, bus, etc*) venir [81] chercher; **my dad's meeting me at the station** mon père vient me chercher à la gare.

meeting *noun* réunion F; **there's a meeting at ten o'clock** il y a une réunion à dix heures; **she's in a meeting** elle est en réunion.

megabyte *noun* mégaoctet M.

melody *noun* mélodie F.

melon *noun* melon M.

melt *verb* **1** fondre [3]; **it melts in your mouth** ça fond dans la bouche; **2 to melt something** faire [10] fondre quelque chose; **melt the butter in a saucepan** faites fondre le beurre dans une casserole.

member *noun* membre M; **she's a member of the Labour Party** elle est membre du parti travailliste.

Member of Parliament *noun* député M.

membership *noun* adhésion F.

membership card *noun* carte F de membre.

membership fee *noun* cotisation F.

memorial *noun* **a war memorial** un monument aux morts.

memorial service *noun* messe F commémorative.

memorize *verb* **to memorize something** apprendre [64] quelque chose par cœur.

memory *noun* **1** (*of a person or computer*) mémoire F; **you have a good memory!** tu as bonne mémoire!; **I have a bad memory** je n'ai pas de mémoire; **2** (*of the past*) souvenir M; **I have good memories of my stay in France** j'ai de bons souvenirs de mon séjour en France.

mend *verb* réparer [1].

meningitis *noun* méningite F.

mental *adjective* mental (M *plural* mentaux); **a mental illness** une maladie mentale; **a mental hospital** un hôpital psychiatrique.

mention *verb* mentionner [1].

menu *noun* menu M; **on the menu** au menu.

mercy *noun* pitié F.

meringue *noun* meringue F.

merit *noun* mérite M.

mermaid *noun* sirène F.

merry *adjective* **1** joyeux (F joyeuse); **Merry Christmas** Joyeux Noël; **2** (*from drinking*) éméché (*informal*).

merry-go-round *noun* manège M.

mess *noun* désordre M; **my papers are in a mess** mes papiers sont dans le désordre; **to make a mess** mettre du désordre; **to clear up the mess** mettre de l'ordre; **what a mess!** quelle pagaille! (*informal*).
● **to mess about** faire [10] l'imbécile; **stop messing about!** arrête de faire l'imbécile!
● **to mess about with something** jouer [1] avec quelque chose; **it's dangerous to mess about with matches** il est dangereux de jouer avec les allumettes.
● **to mess something up** mettre [11] la pagaille dans quelque chose (*informal*); **you've messed up all my papers** tu as mis la pagaille dans toutes mes papiers.

message *noun* message M; **a telephone message** un message téléphonique.

messenger *noun* messager M.

messy *adjective* **1** **it's a messy job** c'est un travail salissant; **2** **he's a messy eater** il mange n'importe comment; **her writing's really messy** elle écrit n'importe comment.

metal *noun* métal M (*plural* métaux).

meter *noun* **1** (*electricity, gas, taxi*) compteur M; **to read the meter** relever le compteur; **2** **a parking meter** un parcmètre.

method *noun* méthode F.

Methodist *noun* méthodiste M &

F; **I'm a Methodist** je suis méthodiste.

metre *noun* mètre M.

metric *adjective* métrique.

Mexico *noun* Mexique M; **in Mexico** au Mexique; **to Mexico** au Mexique.

microchip *noun* puce F.

microphone *noun* microphone M.

microscope *noun* microscope M.

microwave oven *noun* four M à micro-ondes.

midday *noun* midi M; **at midday** à midi.

middle *noun* **1** milieu M; **in the middle of the room** au milieu de la pièce; **in the middle of the night** au milieu de la nuit; **2 to be in the middle of doing** être en train de faire; **when she phoned I was in the middle of washing my hair** quand elle a appelé j'étais en train de me laver les cheveux.

middle-aged *adjective* d'un certain âge; **a middle-aged lady** une dame d'un certain âge.

middle-class *adjective* de la classe moyenne; **a middle-class family** une famille de la classe moyenne.

Middle-East *noun* Moyen-Orient M; **in the Middle East** au Moyen-Orient.

midge *noun* moucheron M.

midnight *noun* minuit M; **at midnight** à minuit.

Midsummer's Day *noun* la Saint Jean.

might *verb* **'are you going to phone him?'** – **'I might'** 'est-ce que tu vas l'appeler? – 'peut-être'; **I might invite Jo** j'inviterai peut-être Jo; **Amanda might know** Amanda le saurait peut-être; **he might have forgotten** il a peut-être oublié.

migraine *noun* migraine F.

mike *noun* micro M (*informal*).

mild *adjective* doux (F douce); **it's quite mild today** il fait plutôt doux aujourd'hui.

mile *noun* **1** mille M (*the French use kilometres for distances; to convert miles roughly to kilometres, multiply by 8 and divide by 5*); **the village is ten miles from Oxford** le village est à seize kilomètres d'Oxford; **2 it's miles better!** c'est dix fois meilleur!

military *adjective* militaire.

milk *noun* lait M; **full-cream milk** le lait entier; **skimmed milk** le lait écrémé; **semi-skimmed milk** le lait demi-écrémé.
verb traire [78].

milk chocolate *noun* chocolat M au lait.

milk jug *noun* pot M à lait.

milkman *noun* laitier M.

milk shake *noun* milk-shake M.

millimetre *noun* millimètre M.

million *noun* million M; **a million people** un million de personnes; **two million people** deux millions de personnes.

millionaire *noun* millionnaire M.

mimic *verb* imiter [1].

mince *noun* viande hachée F.

mind *noun* 1 esprit M; **it crossed my mind that...** il m'est venu à l'esprit que...; 2 **to change your mind...** changer d'avis; **I've changed my mind** j'ai changé d'avis; 3 **to make up your mind** se décider; **I can't make up my mind** je n'arrive pas à me décider.
verb 1 surveiller [1]; **can you mind my bag for me?** est-ce que tu peux surveiller mon sac?; 2 s'occuper [1] de (*baby*); **could you mind the baby for ten minutes?** est-ce que tu peux t'occuper du bébé pendant dix minutes?; 3 **do you mind if...?** est-ce que cela vous dérange si...?; **do you mind if I close the door?** est-ce que cela vous dérange si je ferme la porte?; **I don't mind** cela ne me dérange pas; **I don't mind the heat** la chaleur ne me dérange pas; 4 **mind the step!** attention à la marche!; 5 **never mind!** tant pis!

mine[1] *noun* mine F; **a coal mine** une mine de charbon.

mine[2] *pronoun* 1 (*for a masculine noun*) le mien; **she took her hat and I took mine** elle a pris son chapeau et j'ai pris le mien; 2 (*for a feminine noun*) la mienne; **she gave me her address and I gave her mine** elle m'a donné son adresse et je lui ai donné la mienne; 3 (*for a masculine plural noun*) les miens; **Karen's invited her parents and I've invited mine** Karen a invité ses parents et j'ai invité les miens; 4 (*for a feminine plural noun*) les miennes;

she showed me her photos and I showed her mine elle m'a montré ses photos et je lui ai montré les miennes; 5 à moi; **the green one's mine** le vert est à moi; **it's mine** c'est à moi.

miner *noun* mineur M.

mineral water *noun* eau minérale F.

miniature *noun, adjective* miniature F.

minibus *noun* minibus M.

minimum *noun* minimum M; **a minimum of** un minimum de. *adjective* minimum (*does not change in the feminine or plural*); **the minimum age** l'âge minimum; **minimum safety measures** des mesures de sécurité minimum; **the minimum amount** le minimum.

miniskirt *noun* mini-jupe F.

minister *noun* 1 (*in government*) ministre M; 2 (*of a church*) pasteur M.

ministry *noun* ministère M.

minor *adjective* mineur.

minority *noun* minorité F.

mint *noun* 1 (*herb*) menthe F; 2 (*sweet*) bonbon M à la menthe.

minus *preposition* moins; **seven minus three is four** sept moins trois égale quatre; **it was minus ten this morning** il a fait moins dix ce matin.

minute[1] *noun* minute F; **just a minute!** une minute!; **I'll be ready in two minutes** je serai prêt dans deux minutes; **it's five minutes' walk from**

here c'est à cinq minutes à pied d'ici.

minute² *adjective* minuscule; **the bedrooms are minute** les chambres sont minuscules.

miracle *noun* miracle M.

mirror *noun* **1** glace F; **I looked at myself in the mirror** je me suis regardé dans la glace; **2** (*rearview mirror in a car*) rétroviseur M.

misbehave *verb* se conduire [26] mal.

mischief *noun* **to get up to mischief** faire des bêtises.

mischievous *adjective* coquin.

miser *noun* avare M & F.

miserable *adjective* **1** malheureux (F malheureuse); **he was miserable without her** il était malheureux sans elle; **I feel really miserable today** je n'ai vraiment pas le moral aujourd'hui; **2 it's miserable weather** il fait un sale temps; **3 she gets paid a miserable wage** elle gagne un salaire de misère.

misfire *verb* tomber [1] à plat; **our plans misfired** nos projets sont tombés à plat.

misfortune *noun* malheur M.

misjudge *verb* **1** mal évaluer [1]; **she misjudged the distance** elle a mal évalué la distance; **2** mal juger [52] (*a person*); **everybody had misjudged her** tout le monde l'avait mal jugée.

mislay *verb* égarer [1]; **I've mislaid my keys** j'ai égaré mes clés.

misleading *adjective* trompeur (F trompeuse); **it's a misleading advertisement** c'est une publicité trompeuse.

miss *verb* **1** rater [1]; **she missed her train** elle a raté son train; **I missed the film** j'ai raté le film; **the ball missed the goal** le ballon a raté le but; **missed!** raté!; **2** manquer [1]; **he's missed several classes** il a manqué plusieurs cours; **to miss an opportunity** manquer une occasion; **3 I miss you** tu me manques; **she's missing her sister** sa sœur lui manque; **I miss France** la France me manque.

Miss *noun* Mademoiselle; **Miss Jones** Mademoiselle Jones; (*written as*) Mlle Jones.

missing *adjective* **1** manquant; **she's found the missing pieces** ell a trouvé les pièces manquantes; **the missing link** le chaînon manquant; **2 there's a plate missing** il manque une assiette; **there are three forks missing** il manque trois fourchettes; **3 to go missing** disparaître; **several things have gone missing lately** plusieurs choses ont disparu récemment; **three people are missing** trois personnes ont disparu.

missionary *noun* missionnaire M F.

mist *noun* brume F.

mistake *noun* **1** erreur F; **by mistake** par erreur; **it was my mistake** c'était une erreur de ma part; **2** faute F; **a spelling mistake** une faute d'orthographe; **you've made lots of mistakes** tu as fait beaucoup de fautes; **3 to make**

a mistake (*be mistaken*) se tromper; **sorry, I made a mistake** je suis désolé, je me suis trompé. *verb* **I mistook you for your brother** je vous ai pris pour votre frère.

mistaken *adjective* **to be mistaken** se tromper; **you're mistaken** tu te trompes.

mistletoe *noun* gui M.

misty *adjective* brumeux (F brumeuse); **a misty morning** un matin brumeux; **it's misty this morning** il y a de la brume ce matin.

misunderstand *verb* mal comprendre [64]; **I misunderstood** j'ai mal compris.

misunderstanding *noun* malentendu M; **there's been a misunderstanding** il y a eu un malentendu.

mix *noun* 1 mélange M; **a good mix of people** un bon mélange de gens; 2 **a cake mix** une préparation pour gâteau. *verb* 1 mélanger [52]; **mix all the ingredients together** mélangez tous les ingrédients; 2 **to mix with** fréquenter [1]; **she mixes with lots of interesting people** elle fréquente beaucoup de gens intéressants. **to mix up** 1 mélanger [52]; **you've mixed up all my papers** tu as mélangé tous mes papiers; **you've got it all mixed up!** tu mélanges tout! (*story*); 2 (*confuse*) confondre [69]; **I get him mixed up with his brother** je le confonds avec son frère.

mixed *adjective* varié; **a mixed programme** un programme varié.

mixed salad *noun* salade composée F.

mixed school *noun* école mixte F.

mixture *noun* mélange M; **it's a mixture of jazz and rock** c'est un mélange de jazz et de rock.

moan *verb* râler [1] (*informal*); **stop moaning!** arrête de râler!

mobile home *noun* mobile home M.

mobile phone *noun* téléphone portatif M.

mock *noun* (*mock exam*) examen blanc M. *verb* se moquer [1] de; **stop mocking me!** arrête de te moquer de moi!

model *noun* 1 (*type*) modèle M; **the latest model** le dernier modèle; 2 (*fashion model*) mannequin M; **she's a model** elle est mannequin de luxe; 3 (*of a plane, car, etc*) modèle réduit M; **he makes models** il fait des modèles réduits; 4 (*of a building*) maquette F; **a model of Westminster Abbey** une maquette de l'Abbaye de Westminster.

model aeroplane *noun* modèle réduit d'avion M.

model railway *noun* chemin de fer miniature M.

model village *noun* village miniature M.

modem *noun* modem M.

moderate *adjective* modéré.

modern *adjective* moderne.

modern languages *noun* langues vivantes F *plural*.

modernize *verb* moderniser [1].

modest *adjective* modeste.

modify *verb* modifier [1].

moisture *noun* humidité F.

moisturizer *noun* 1 (*lotion*) lait hydratant M; 2 (*cream*) crème hydratante F.

mole *noun* 1 (*animal*) taupe F; 2 (*on skin*) graine F de beauté.

molecule *noun* molécule F.

molehill *noun* taupinière F.

moment *noun* 1 instant M; **he'll be here in a moment** il sera là dans un instant; **at any moment** à tout instant; 2 **at the moment** en ce moment; **at the right moment** au bon moment.

Monaco *noun* Monaco.

monarchy *noun* monarchie F.

monastery *noun* monastère M.

Monday *noun* lundi M; **on Monday** lundi; **I'm going out on Monday** je sors lundi; **see you on Monday!** à lundi!; **on Mondays** le lundi; **the museum is closed on Mondays** le musée est fermé le lundi; **every Monday** tous les lundis; **last Monday** lundi dernier; **next Monday** lundi prochain.

money *noun* argent M; **I don't have enough money** je n'ai pas assez d'argent; **to make money** gagner de l'argent; **they gave me my money back** (*in a shop*) ils m'ont remboursé.

money box *noun* tirelire F.

mongrel *noun* chien bâtard M.

monitor *noun* (*on computer*) moniteur M.

monk *noun* moine M.

monkey *noun* 1 singe M; 2 **you little monkey!** petit galopin! (*informal*).

monotonous *adjective* monotone.

monster *noun* monstre M.

month *noun* mois M; **in the month of May** au mois de mai; **this month** ce mois-ci; **next month** le mois prochain; **we're leaving next month** nous allons partir le mois prochain; **last month** le mois dernier; **every month** tous les mois; **in two months' time** dans deux mois; **at the end of the month** à la fin du mois.

monthly *adjective* mensuel (F mensuelle); **a monthly payment** une mensualité.

monument *noun* monument M.

mood *noun* humeur F; **to be in a good mood** être de bonne humeur; **to be in a bad mood** être de mauvaise humeur; **I'm not in the mood** ça ne me dit rien.

moody *adjective* lunatique.

moon *noun* lune F; **by the light of the moon** au clair de lune; ★ **to be over the moon** être aux anges (*literally: to be at the level of the angels*).

moonlight *noun* clair M de lune; **by moonlight** au clair de lune.

moor *noun* lande F; **the Yorkshire moors** les landes du Yorkshire.
verb amarrer [1] (*a boat*).

moped *noun* mobylette™ F.

moral *noun* morale F; **the moral of the story** la morale de l'histoire.
adjective moral (M *plural* moraux).

morals *plural noun* moralité F.

morale *noun* moral M; **to boost somebody's morale** remonter le moral à quelqu'un; **he's been trying to boost their morale** il essaie de leur remonter le moral.

more *adverb* 1 plus; **more interesting** plus intéressant; **more difficult** plus difficile; **more slowly** plus lentement; **more easily** plus facilement; 2 **more...than** plus...que; **the book's more interesting than the film** le livre est plus intéressant que le film.
adjective 1 plus de; **they have more money than we do** ils ont plus d'argent que nous; **I'll have a little more milk** je prendrai un peu plus de lait; 2 (*of something you have already*) encore de; **would you like some more cake?** voulez-vous encore du gâteau?; **a few more glasses** encore quelques verres.
pronoun 1 plus; **he eats more than me** il mange plus que moi; **I'll have a little more** je prendrai un peu plus; **I don't want any more** je n'en veux plus; 2 (*of something you have already*) encore; **we need three more** il nous en faut encore trois; 3 **more and more** de plus en plus; **books are getting more and more expensive** les livres coûtent de plus en plus cher; **it takes more and more**

time ça prend de plus en plus de temps; 4 **more or less** plus ou moins; **it's more or less finished** c'est plus ou moins fini.

morning *noun* 1 matin M; **this morning** ce matin; **tomorrow morning** demain matin; **yesterday morning** hier matin; **in the morning** le matin; **she doesn't work in the morning** elle ne travaille pas le matin; **on Friday mornings** le vendredi matin; **at six o'clock in the morning** à six heures du matin; 2 (*as a period of time spent doing something*) matinée F; **I spent the whole morning doing the washing-up** j'ai passé toute la matinée à faire la vaisselle.

Morocco *noun* Maroc M; **to Morocco** au Maroc; **in Morocco** au Maroc.

Moscow *noun* Moscou; **in Moscow** à Moscou.

Moslem *noun* musulman M, musulmane F.

mosque *noun* mosquée F.

mosquito *noun* moustique M; **a mosquito bite** une piqûre de moustique.

most *adjective, adverb, pronoun* 1 (*followed by a plural noun*) la plupart de; **most children like chocolate** la plupart des enfants aiment le chocolat; **most of my friends** la plupart de mes amis; 2 (*followed by a singular noun*) presque tout; **they've eaten most of the chocolate** ils ont mangé presque tout le chocolat; 3 **most of**

the time la plupart du temps; **4 the most** (*followed by adjective*) le plus, la plus, les plus; **the most interesting film** le film le plus intéressant; **the most exciting story** l'histoire la plus passionnante; **the most boring books** les livres les plus ennuyeux; **5 the most** (*followed by noun*) le plus de; **I've got the most time** c'est moi qui ai le plus de temps; **6 the most** (*after verb*) le plus; **what I hate most is the noise** ce que je déteste le plus, c'est le bruit.

moth *noun* **1** (*butterfly*) papillon M de nuit; **2** (*clothes moth*) mite F.

mother *noun* mère F; **my mother** ma mère; **Kate's mother** la mère de Kate.

mother-in-law *noun* belle-mère F (*plural* belles-mères).

Mother's Day *noun* la fête des Mères (*in France the last Sunday in May*).

motion *noun* mouvement M.

motivated *adjective* motivé.

motivation *noun* motivation F.

motor *noun* moteur M.

motorbike *noun* moto F.

motorcyclist *noun* motocycliste M & F.

motorist *noun* automobiliste M & F.

motor racing *noun* course F automobile.

motorway *noun* autoroute F.

mouldy *adjective* moisi.

mountain *noun* montagne F; **in the mountains** à la montagne.

mountain bike *noun* VTT M (*short for 'vélo tout-terrain'*).

mountaineer *noun* alpiniste M & F.

mountaineering *noun* alpinisme M; **to go mountaineering** faire de l'alpinisme.

mountainous *adjective* montagneux (F montagneuse).

mouse *noun* souris F (*both the animal and for a computer*).

mousse *noun* mousse F; **chocolate mousse** la mousse au chocolat.

moustache *noun* moustache F; **a man with a moustache** un moustachu.

mouth *noun* bouche F.

mouthful *noun* bouchée F.

mouth organ *noun* harmonica M; **to play the mouth organ** jouer de l'harmonica.

move *noun* **1** (*to a different house*) déménagement M; **2** (*in a game*) **your move!** à toi de jouer! *verb* **1** bouger [52]; **she didn't move** elle n'a pas bougé; **2 move up a bit** pousse-toi un peu; **3** enlever [50] (*an object*); **can you move your bag, please?** peux-tu enlever ton sac, s'il te plaît?; **4** (*car, traffic*) avancer [61]; **the traffic was moving slowly** la circulation avançait lentement; **5 to move forward** avancer [61]; **he moved forward a step** il s'est avancé d'un pas; **6** (*move house*) déménager [52];

we're moving on Tuesday nous déménageons mardi; **they've moved to France** ils se sont installés en France.

movement *noun* mouvement M.

movie *noun* film M; **to go to the movies** aller au cinéma.

moving *adjective* **1** en marche; **a moving vehicle** un véhicule en marche; **2** (*emotionally*) émouvant; **it's a very moving film** c'est un film très émouvant.

mow *verb* tondre [3]; **to mow the grass** tondre la pelouse.

mower *noun* tondeuse F à gazon.

MP *noun* député M; **she is an MP** elle est député.

Mr *noun* Monsieur (*usually abbreviated to 'M.'*); **Mr Angus Brown** M. Angus Brown.

Mrs *noun* Madame (*usually abbreviated to 'Mme'*); **Mrs Mary Hendry** Mme Mary Hendry.

Ms *noun* Madame (*usually abbreviated to 'Mme'; note that there is no direct equivalent to 'Ms' in French, but 'Madame' may be used whether the woman is married or not*).

much *adjective, adverb, pronoun* **1** beaucoup; **she doesn't eat much** elle ne mange pas beaucoup; **we don't go out much** nous ne sortons pas beaucoup; **much more** beaucoup plus; **much shorter** beaucoup plus court; **2** (*followed by a noun*) beaucoup de; **we don't have much time** nous n'avons pas beaucoup de temps; **there isn't much**

butter left il ne reste pas beaucoup de beurre; **3 very much** beaucoup; **thank you very much** merci beaucoup; **I don't watch television very much** je ne regarde pas beaucoup la télé; **4 very much** (*followed by a noun*) beaucoup de; **there isn't very much milk** il n'y a pas beaucoup de lait; **5 not much** pas beaucoup; **'do you have a lot of homework?' – 'no, not much'** 'est-ce que tu as beaucoup de devoirs?' – 'non, pas beaucoup'; **6 so much** tellement; **we liked it so much!** nous l'avons tellement aimé!; **I have so much to do!** j'ai tellement de choses à faire!; **7 so much** autant; **you shouldn't have given me so much** tu n'aurais pas dû m'en donner autant; **8 as much as** autant que; **you can take as much as you like** tu peux en prendre autant que tu veux; **9 too much** trop (de); **her parents give her too much money** ses parents lui donnent trop d'argent; **that's far too much!** c'est beaucoup trop!; **10 how much?** combien (de)?; **how much is it?** ça coûte combien?; **how much do you want?** tu en veux combien?; **how much sugar do you want?** tu veux combien de sucre?

mud *noun* boue F.

muddle *noun* désordre M; **to be in a muddle** être en désordre.

muddy *adjective* **1** (*path, road*) boueux (F boueuse); **2** (*shoes, clothes*) couverts de boue; **your boots are all muddy** tes bottes sont couvertes de boue.

mug *noun* grande tasse F; **a mug of coffee** une grande tasse de café. *verb* **to mug somebody** agresser [1] quelqu'un; **to be mugged** se faire [10] agresser; **my brother was mugged in the park** mon frère s'est fait agresser au parc.

mugging *noun* agression F.

multiplication *noun* multiplication F.

multiply *verb* mulitplier [1]; **to multiply six by four** multiplier six par quatre.

mum, mummy *noun* 1 mère F; **Tom's mum** la mère de Tom; **I'll ask my mum** je vais demander à ma mère; 2 (*within the family or as a name*) maman F; **mum's not back yet** maman n'est pas encore rentrée.

mumps *noun* oreillons M *plural*.

murder *noun* meurtre M. *verb* assassiner [1].

murderer *noun* assassin M.

muscle *noun* muscle M.

muscular *adjective* musclé.

museum *noun* musée M; **to go to the museum** aller au musée.

mushroom *noun* champignon M; **a mushroom salad** une salade aux champignons.

music *noun* musique F; **pop music** la musique pop; **classical music** la musique classique.

musical *noun* comédie musicale F. *adjective* 1 **a musical instrument** un instrument de musique; 2 **they're a very musical family** ils sont très musiciens dans la famille.

musician *noun* musicien M, musicienne F.

Muslim *noun* musulman M, musulmane F.

mussel *noun* moule F.

must *verb* 1 falloir [43] (*to express obligation 'falloir' is used as an impersonal verb*); **we must leave now** il faut partir maintenant; (*the construction 'il faut que' is followed by a verb in the subjunctive*) **I must tell you something** il faut que je te dise quelque chose; **you must be there at eight** il faut que tu sois là à huit heures; **you must learn the vocabulary** il faut que tu apprennes le vocabulaire; 2 (*expressing probability*) devoir [8]; **you must be tired** tu dois être fatigué; **it must be five o'clock** il doit être cinq heures; **he must have forgotten** il a dû oublier.

mustard *noun* moutarde F.

mutter *verb* marmonner [1].

my *adjective* 1 (*before a masculine noun*) mon; **my brother** mon frère; **my book** mon livre; 2 (*before a feminine noun*) ma; **my sister** ma sœur; **my house** ma maison (*but 'ma' becomes 'mon' before a feminine noun beginning with a vowel or silent 'h'*); **my address** mon adresse; 3 (*before a plural noun*) mes; **my children** mes enfants; 4 (*with parts of the body*) le, la, les; **I had a glass in my hand** j'avais un verre à la main; **I'm washing my hands** je me lave les mains.

myself *pronoun* 1 **I've hurt myself** je me suis blessé; 2 **I said it myself**

je l'ai dit moi-même; **3 by myself**
tout seul; **I did it by myself** je l'ai fait
tout seul.

mysterious *adjective* mystérieux
(F mystérieuse).

mystery *noun* **1** mystère M;
2 (*book*) roman policier M.

myth *noun* mythe M.

mythology *noun* mythologie F.

N n

nail *noun* **1** (*on finger or toe*) ongle
M; **to bite your nails** se ronger les
ongles; **2** (*metal*) clou M.
verb clouer [1].

nailbrush *noun* brosse F à ongles.

nailfile *noun* lime F à ongles.

nail scissors *noun* ciseaux M
plural à ongles.

nail varnish *noun* vernis M à
ongles.

nail varnish remover *noun*
dissolvant M.

naked *adjective* nu.

name *noun* **1** nom M; **I've
forgotten her name** j'ai oublié son
nom; **what's your name?** comment
vous appelez-vous?; **my name is
Joy** je m'appelle Joy; **2** (*of a book or
film*) titre M.

nap *noun* petit somme M; **to have a
nap** faire un petit somme.

napkin *noun* serviette F.

nappy *noun* couche F.

narrow *adjective* étroit; **a narrow
street** une rue étroite.

nasty *adjective* **1** (*mean*) méchant;
that was a nasty thing to do c'était
méchant; **2** (*unpleasant*)
désagréable; **that's a nasty job** c'est
une tâche désagréable; **3** (*bad*)
mauvais; **a nasty smell** une
mauvaise odeur.

nation *noun* nation F.

national *adjective* national (M
plural nationaux).

national anthem *noun* hymne M
national.

nationality *noun* nationalité F.

national park *noun* parc national
M (*plural* parcs nationaux).

natural *adjective* naturel (F
naturelle).

naturally *adverb* naturellement.

nature *noun* nature F.

nature reserve *noun* réserve F
naturelle.

naughty *adjective* vilain.

navy *noun* marine F; **my uncle's in
the navy** mon oncle est dans la
marine.

navy-blue *adjective* bleu marine;
navy-blue gloves des gants bleu
marine.

near *adjective* proche; **the nearest
shop** le magasin le plus proche.
adverb, preposition **1** près; **they live
quite near** ils habitent tout près; **to
come nearer** s'approcher; **2 near**

(to) près de; **near the station** près de la gare.

nearby *adverb* tout près; **there's a park nearby** il y a un parc tout près.

nearly *adverb* presque; **nearly empty** presque vide; **we're nearly there** nous sommes presque arrivés.

neat *adjective* 1 (*well-organized*) bien rangé; **a neat desk** un bureau bien rangé; 2 soigné (*a garden, your clothes, or the way you look*).

neatly *adverb* avec soin.

necessarily *adverb* **not necessarily** pas forcément.

necessary *adjective* nécessaire; **if necessary** si besoin est.

neck *noun* 1 (*of a person*) cou M; 2 (*of a garment*) encolure F.

necklace *noun* collier M.

need *noun* **there's no need, I've done it already** inutile, c'est fait; **there's no need to wait** inutile d'attendre.
verb 1 avoir [5] besoin de; **we need bread** nous avons besoin de pain; **they need help** ils ont besoin d'aide; **everything you need** tout ce qu'il vous faut; 2 (*to have to*) devoir [8]; **I need to drop in at the bank** je dois passer à la banque; 3 **you needn't decide today** tu n'es pas obligé de décider aujourd'hui; **you needn't wait** tu n'es pas obligé d'attendre.

needle *noun* aiguille F.

negative *noun* (*of a photo*) négatif M.

neglected *adjective* mal entretenu.

neighbour *noun* voisin M, voisine F; **we're going round to the neighbours'** on va chez les voisins.

neighbourhood *noun* quartier M; **a nice neighbourhood** un quartier agréable.

neither *conjunction* 1 **neither... nor** ni...ni; **I have neither the time nor the money** je n'ai ni le temps ni l'argent; 2 **neither do I** moi non plus; **'I don't like fish'** – **'neither do I'** 'je n'aime pas le poisson' – 'moi non plus'; (*translations using 'non plus' can be used for many similar replies*) **'I wasn't invited'** – **'neither was I'** 'je n'ai pas été invité' – 'moi non plus'; **'I didn't like the film'** – **'neither did Kirsty'** 'je n'ai pas aimé le film' – 'Kirsty non plus'; 3 **'which do you like?'** – **'neither'** 'lequel aimes-tu?' – 'ni l'un ni l'autre'.

nephew *noun* neveu M (*plural* neveux).

nerve *noun* 1 (*in the body*) nerf M; 2 **to lose one's nerve** perdre son courage; 3 **you've got a nerve!** tu as un sacré culot! (*informal*); ★ **he gets on my nerves** il me tape sur les nerfs (*informal*).

nervous *adjective* nerveux (F nerveuse); **to feel nervous** (*before a performance or an exam*) avoir le trac (*informal*).

nest *noun* nid M.

net *noun* 1 (*for fishing or in tennis*) filet M; 2 (*in football*) filets M *plural*.

Netherlands *noun* Pays-Bas M *plural*; **in the Netherlands** aux Pays-Bas.

nettle *noun* ortie F.

network *noun* réseau M
(*plural* réseaux).

neutral *noun* (*in a gearbox*) point
mort M; **to be in neutral** être au
point mort.
adjective neutre.

never *adjective* **1** ne ... jamais; **Ben
never smokes** Ben ne fume jamais;
I've never seen the film je n'ai
jamais vu le film; **2** jamais; **'have
you ever been to Spain?' – 'no,
never'** 'est-ce que tu es déjà allé en
Espagne?' – 'non, jamais'; **3** **never
again** plus jamais; **4** **never mind**
ça ne fait rien.

nevertheless *adverb* néanmoins.

new *adjective* **1** (*different or
unknown to you*) nouveau (F
nouvelle); **have you seen their new
house?** as-tu vu leur nouvelle
maison?; **Debbie's new boyfriend** le
nouveau copain de Debbie;
2 (*brand new*) neuf (F neuve); **it's a
new car** c'est une voiture neuve.

newcomer *noun* nouveau venu M
(*plural* nouveaux venus), nouvelle
venue F (*plural* nouvelles venues).

news *plural noun* **1** (*everyday
gossip*) nouvelle F, nouvelles F
plural; **a piece of good news** une
bonne nouvelle; **I've got good news**
j'ai de bonnes nouvelles; **any news?**
y a-t-il des nouvelles?; **2** (*on TV*)
journal M; **the midday news** le
journal de midi; **3** (*on the radio*)
the news les informations.

newsagent *noun* marchand M de
journaux; **at the newsagent's** chez
le marchand de journaux.

newspaper *noun* journal M
(*plural* journaux).

newsreader *noun* présentateur
M, présentatrice F.

New Year *noun* le Nouvel An;
Happy New Year! Bonne Année!

New Year's Day *noun* le jour de
l'An.

New Year's Eve *noun* la Saint-
Sylvestre.

New Zealand *noun* Nouvelle-
Zélande F.

next *adjective* **1** prochain; **the next
train is at ten** le prochain train est à
dix heures; **next week** la semaine
prochaine; **next Thursday** jeudi
prochain; **next year** l'année
prochaine; **the next time I see you**
la prochaine fois que je te verrai;
2 (*following*) suivant; **I saw her the
next week** je l'ai vue la semaine
suivante; **the next day** le lendemain;
the letter arrived the next day la
lettre est arrivée le lendemain;
3 (*next-door*) voisin; **in the next
room** dans la pièce voisine.
adverb **1** (*afterwards*) ensuite;
what did he say next? qu'est-ce
qu'il a dit ensuite?; **2** (*now*)
maintenant; **what shall we do
next?** qu'est-ce qu'on fait
maintenant?; **3** **next to** à côté de;
the girl next to Pat la fille à côté de
Pat; **it's next to the baker's** c'est à
côté de la boulangerie.

next door *adverb* à côté; **they live
next door** ils habitent à côté; **the girl
next door** la fille d'à côté.

nice *adjective* **1** (*pleasant*) agréable;
we had a nice evening nous avons

passé une soirée agréable;
Brighton's a nice town Brighton est une ville agréable; **have a nice time!** amusez-vous bien!; **2** (*attractive to look at*) joli; **that's a nice dress** elle est jolie, cette robe; **3** (*kind, friendly*) sympathique (*a person*); **she's really nice** elle est vraiment sympathique; **4 to be nice to somebody** être gentil avec quelqu'un; **she's been very nice to me** elle a été très gentille avec moi; **5** (*tasting good*) bon (F bonne); **let's have a nice cup of tea** si on prenait une bonne tasse de thé; **6** (*weather*) **it's a nice day** il fait beau; **we had nice weather** il a fait beau.

nick *verb* (*steal*) piquer [1] (*informal*).

nickname *noun* surnom M.

niece *noun* nièce F.

night *noun* **1** (*before you go to bed*) soir M; **what did you do last night?** qu'est-ce que tu as fait hier soir?; **see you tomorrow night!** à demain soir!; **I saw Greg last night** j'ai vu Greg hier soir; **2** (*after bedtime*) nuit F; **it's cold at night** il fait froid la nuit; **to stay the night with somebody** coucher chez quelqu'un.

night club *noun* boîte F de nuit.

nightie *noun* chemise F de nuit.

nightingale *noun* rossignol M.

nightmare *noun* cauchemar M; **to have a nightmare** faire un cauchemar.

night-time *noun* nuit F.

nil *noun* zéro M; **they won four-nil** ils ont gagné quatre à zéro.

nine *number* neuf M; **Jake's nine** Jake a neuf ans.

nineteen *number* dix-neuf M; **Kate's nineteen** Kate a dix-neuf ans

ninety *number* quatre-vingt-dix M.

ninth *number* neuvième; **on the ninth floor** au neuvième étage; **the ninth of June** le neuf juin.

no *adverb* non; **I said no** j'ai dit non; **no thank you** non merci.
adjective **1** pas de; **we've got no bread** nous n'avons pas de pain; **no problem!** pas de problème!; **2** (*on a notice*) **'no smoking'** 'défense de fumer'; **'no parking'** 'stationnement interdit'.

nobody *pronoun* personne; **'who's there?' – 'nobody'** 'qui est là?' – 'personne'; **there's nobody in the kitchen** il n'y a personne dans la cuisine; **nobody knows me** personne ne me connaît; **nobody answered** personne n'a répondu.

nod *verb* (*to say yes*) faire [10] oui de la tête; **he nodded** il a fait oui de la tête.

noise *noun* bruit M; **to make a noise** faire du bruit.

noisy *adjective* bruyant.

none *pronoun* **1** (*not one*) aucun (F aucune); **'how many students failed the exam?' – 'none'** 'combien d'étudiants ont raté l'examen?' – 'aucun'; **none of the girls knows him** aucune des filles ne le connaît; **2 there's none left** il n'y en a plus; **there are none left** il n'y en a plus.

nonsense *noun* bêtises F *plural*; **to talk nonsense** dire des bêtises; **nonsense! she's at least thirty!** tu dis des bêtises! elle a au moins trente ans!

non-smoker *noun* non-fumeur M.

non-stop *adjective* direct (*a train or flight*).
adverb sans arrêt; **she talks non-stop** elle parle sans arrêt.

noodles *plural noun* nouilles F *plural*.

noon *noun* midi M; **at (twelve) noon** à midi.

no-one *pronoun* personne; **'who's there?' – 'no-one'** 'qui est là?' – 'personne'; **there's no-one in the kitchen** il n'y a personne dans la cuisine; **no-one knows me** personne ne me connaît; **no-one answered** personne n'a répondu.

nor *conjunction* **1 neither...nor** ni...ni; **I have neither the time nor the money** je n'ai ni le temps ni l'argent; **2 nor do I** moi non plus; **'I don't like fish' – 'nor do I'** 'je n'aime pas le poisson' – 'moi non plus'; (*translations using 'non plus' can be used for many similar replies*) **'I wasn't invited' – 'nor was I'** 'je n'ai pas été invité' – 'ni moi non plus'.

normal *adjective* **1** normal (M *plural* normaux); **2** (*usual*) habituel (F habituelle).

normally *adverb* normalement.

Normandy *noun* Normandie F; **in Normandy** en Normandie.

north *noun* nord M; **in the north** au nord.
adjective, adverb nord (*never agrees*); **the north side** le côté nord; **a north wind** un vent du nord; **north of Paris** au nord de Paris.

North America *noun* Amérique F du Nord.

northeast *noun* nord-est M.
adjective **in northeast England** au nord-est de l'Angleterre.

Northern Ireland *noun* Irlande F du Nord.

North Pole *noun* pôle Nord M.

North Sea *noun* **the North Sea** la mer du Nord.

northwest *noun* nord-ouest M.
adjective **in northwest England** au nord-ouest de l'Angleterre.

Norway *noun* Norvège F; **in Norway** en Norvège.

Norwegian *noun* **1** (*person*) Norvégien M, Norvégienne F; **2** (*language*) norvégien M.
adjective norvégien (F norvégienne).

nose *noun* nez M; **to blow your nose** se moucher.

nosebleed *noun* **to have a nosebleed** saigner du nez.

not *adverb* **1** pas; **not on Saturdays** pas le samedi; **not all alone!** pas tout seul!; **not bad** pas mal; **not at all** pas du tout; **not yet** pas encore; **2** (*when used with a verb*) ne...pas; **it's not my car** ce n'est pas ma voiture; **I don't know** je ne sais pas; **Sam didn't phone** Sam n'a pas appelé; **we decided not to wait** nous avons décidé de ne pas attendre; **3 I hope not** j'espère que non.

note *noun* **1** (*a short letter*) mot M; **she left me a note** elle m'a laissé un mot; **2 to take notes** prendre [64] des notes; **3** (*a banknote*) billet M; **a ten-pound note** un billet de dix livres; **4** (*in music*) note F; (*on the keyboard*) touche F.

notebook *noun* carnet M.

notepad *noun* bloc-notes M (*plural* blocs-notes).

nothing *pronoun* **1** rien; **'what did you say?' – 'nothing'** 'qu'est-ce que tu as dit?' – 'rien'; **2** (*with an adjective*) **nothing new** rien de nouveau; **nothing special** rien de particulier; **3** (*when used with a verb*) ne…rien; **she knows nothing** elle ne sait rien; **but there was nothing there** mais il n'y avait rien; **I saw nothing** je n'ai rien vu; **there's nothing happening** il ne se passe rien; **4 there's nothing new** il n'y a rien de nouveau.

notice *noun* **1** (*a sign*) panneau M (*plural* panneaux); **2** (*an advertisement*) annonce F; **3 don't take any notice of her!** ne fais pas attention à elle!; **4 to do something at short notice** faire quelque chose à la dernière minute.
verb remarquer [1]; **I didn't notice anything** je n'ai rien remarqué.

noticeable *adjective* visible.

notice board *noun* panneau M d'affichage.

nought *noun* zéro M.

noun *noun* nom M.

novel *noun* roman M.

novelist *noun* romancier M, romancière F.

November *noun* novembre M; **in November** en novembre.

now *adverb* **1** maintenant; **where is he now?** il est où maintenant?; **they've got six children now** ils ont six enfants maintenant; **2 he's busy just now** il est occupé en ce moment; **I saw her just now in the corridor** je viens de la voir dans le couloir; **3 do it right now!** fais-le tout de suite!; **4 now and then** de temps en temps.

nowhere *adjective* **1** nulle part; **nowhere in France** nulle part en France; **2 there's nowhere to park** il n'y a pas d'endroit pour se garer.

nuclear *adjective* nucléaire; **a nuclear power station** une centrale nucléaire.

nude *noun* **in the nude** nu. *adjective* nu.

nuisance *noun* **it's a nuisance** c'est embêtant.

numb *adjective* **1** (*with cold*) engourdi; **2** (*with an anaesthetic*) insensible.

number *noun* **1** (*of a house, telephone, or account*) numéro M; **I live at number thirty-one** j'habite au numéro trente-et-un; **my new phone number** mon nouveau numéro de téléphone; **2** (*a written figure*) chiffre M; **the third number is a 7** le troisième chiffre est un 7; **3** (*an amount*) nombre M; **a large number of visitors** un grand nombre de visiteurs.

number plate *noun* plaque F d'immatriculation.

nun *noun* religieuse F.

nurse *noun* infirmier M, infirmière F; **Janet's a nurse** Janet est infirmière.

nursery *noun* **1** (*for children*) crèche F; **2** (*for plants*) pépinière F.

nursery school *noun* école F maternelle.

nut *noun* **1** (*walnut*) noix F; **2** (*almond*) amande F; **3** (*peanut*) cacahuète F; **4** (*for a bolt*) écrou M.

nutmeg *noun* noix F de muscade.

nylon *noun* nylon M.

O o

oak *noun* chêne M.

oar *noun* rame F.

oats *noun* avoine F; **porridge oats** les flocons d'avoine.

obedient *adjective* obéissant.

obey *verb* obéir [2] à (*a person*); **to obey the rules** respecter [1] les règlements.

object *noun* objet M.
verb soulever [50] des objections; **if you don't object** si vous n'avez pas d'objection.

objection *noun* objection F.

oblong *adjective* rectangulaire.

oboe *noun* hautbois M; **to play the oboe** jouer du hautbois.

obscene *adjective* obscène.

observe *verb* observer [1].

obsessed *adjective* obsédé; **she's obsessed with her diet** elle est obsédée par son régime.

obstacle *noun* obstacle M.

obstinate *adjective* têtu.

obstruct *verb* gêner [1] (*people or the traffic*).

obtain *verb* obtenir [77].

obvious *adjective* évident.

obviously *adverb* **1** (*of course*) évidemment; **'do you want to come too?'** – **'obviously, but it's a bit difficult'** 'veux-tu nous accompagner?' – 'évidemment, mais c'est un peu difficile'; **2** (*looking at something*) manifestement; **the house is obviously empty** la maison est manifestement vide.

occasion *noun* occasion F; **a special occasion** une grande occasion.

occasionally *adverb* de temps en temps.

occupation *noun* profession F.

occupied *adjective* occupé.

occur *verb* **1** **it occurs to me that my cousins live nearby** il me vient à l'esprit que mes cousins habitent tout près; **it never occurred to me** cela ne m'est pas venu à l'idée; **2** (*happen*) avoir [5] lieu; **the**

accident occurred on Monday
l'accident a eu lieu lundi.

ocean *noun* océan M.

o'clock *adverb* **at ten o'clock** à dix
heures; **it's three o'clock** il est trois
heures.

October *noun* octobre M; **in
October** en octobre.

octopus *noun* pieuvre F.

odd *adjective* 1 (*strange*) bizarre;
**that's odd, I'm sure I heard the
phone** c'est bizarre, je suis sûr
d'avoir entendu le téléphone;
2 (*number*) impair; **three is an odd
number** trois est un chiffre impair;
3 **to be the odd one out** être
l'exception.

odds and ends *plural noun*
bricoles F *plural*.

of *preposition* 1 de; **a kilo of
tomatoes** un kilo de tomates; **the
end of my work** la fin de mon
travail; 2 (*note that 'de le' becomes
'du' and 'de les' becomes 'des'*) **the
beginning of the concert** le début
du concert; **the name of the flower**
le nom de la fleur; **the parents of the
children** les parents des enfants;
3 **Ray has four horses but he's
selling three of them** Ray a trois
chevaux mais il en vend trois; **we ate
a lot of it** nous en avons mangé
beaucoup; 4 **two of us** deux d'entre
nous; 5 **the sixth of June** le six
juin; 6 **made of** en; **a bracelet
made of silver** un bracelet en
argent.

off *adverb, adjective, preposition*
1 (*switched off*) éteint; **is the telly**

off? est-ce que la télé est éteinte?; **to
turn off the lights** éteindre la
lumière; 2 (*tap, water, gas*) fermé;
to turn off the tap fermer le
robinet; 3 (*turned off at the meter*)
coupé; **the gas and electricity were
off** le gaz et l'électricité étaient
coupés; 4 **to be off** (*to leave*) s'en
aller [7]; **I'm off** je m'en vais; 5 **a day
off** un jour de congé; **Caroline took
three days off work** Caroline a pris
trois jours de congé; **to be off sick**
être malade; **Maya's off school
today** Maya n'est pas à l'école
aujourd'hui; 6 (*cancelled*) annulé;
the match is off le match est
annulé; 7 '**20% off shoes**' '20% de
remise sur les chaussures'.

offence *noun* 1 (*crime*) délit M;
2 **to take offence** s'offenser [1]; **he
takes offence easily** il s'offense
facilement.

offer *noun* 1 offre F; **a job offer**
une offre d'emploi; 2 '**on (special)
offer**' 'en promotion'.
verb 1 offrir [56] (*a present, a
reward, or a job*); **he offered her a
chair** il lui a offert une chaise; 2 **to
offer to do** proposer [1] de faire;
**Blake offered to drive me to the
station** Blake m'a proposé de me
conduire à la gare.

office *noun* bureau M
(*plural* bureaux); **he's still at the
office** il est toujours au bureau; **Sue
works in the same office** Sue
travaille dans le même bureau.

office block, office building
noun immeuble M de bureaux.

official *adjective* officiel (F

officielle); **the official version** la version officielle.

off-licence *noun* magasin M de vins et de spiritueux.

often *adverb* souvent; **he's often late** il est souvent en retard; **how often do you see Rosie?** est-ce que tu vois Rosie souvent?; **I'd like to see Eric more often** j'aimerais voir Eric plus souvent.

oil *noun* **1** olive oil l'huile d'olive; **suntan oil** l'huile solaire; **2** (*crude oil*) pétrole M.

oil painting *noun* peinture F à l'huile (*both the activity and the object*).

oil rig *noun* plateforme pétrolière F.

ointment *noun* pommade F.

okay *adjective* **1** d'accord; **okay, tomorrow at ten** d'accord, demain à dix heures; **is it okay with you if I don't come till Friday?** tu es d'accord si je ne viens que vendredi?; **2** (*person*) sympa (*informal*); **Daisy's okay** Daisy est sympa; **3** (*nothing special*) pas mal; **the film was okay** le film n'était pas mal; **4** (*not ill*) **are you okay?** ça va?; **I've been ill but I'm okay now** j'ai été malade, mais ça va mieux maintenant.

old *adjective* **1** (*not young, not new*) vieux, vieil (*before a vowel or silent 'h'*) (F vieille); **an old man** un vieux monsieur; **an old lady** une vieille dame; **an old tree** un vieil arbre; **old people** les personnes âgées; **bring some old clothes** apporte de vieux vêtements; **2** (*previous*) ancien (F ancienne); **our old car was a Rover**

notre ancienne voiture était une Rover; **I've only got their old address** je n'ai que leur ancienne adresse; **3** (*talking about age*) **how old are you?** tu as quel âge?; **James is ten years old** James a dix ans; **a two-year-old child** un enfant de deux ans; **4** my older sister ma sœur aînée; **she's older than me** elle est plus âgée que moi; **he's a year older than me** il a un an de plus que moi.

old age *noun* vieillesse F.

old age pensioner *noun* retraité M, retraitée F.

old-fashioned *noun* **1** (*clothes, music, style*) démodé; **2** (*a person*) vieux jeu (*never agrees*); **my parents are so old-fashioned** mes parents sont si vieux jeu.

olive *noun* olive F.

olive oil *noun* huile F d'olive.

Olympic Games, Olympics *plural noun* Jeux Olympiques M *plural*.

omelette *noun* omelette F; **a cheese omelette** une omelette au fromage.

on *preposition* **1** sur; **on the desk** sur le bureau; **on the road** sur la route; **on the beach** sur la plage; **2** (*in expressions of time*) **on March 21st** le 21 mars; **he's arriving on Tuesday** il arrive mardi; **it's shut on Saturdays** c'est fermé le samedi; **on rainy days** quand il pleut; **3** (*for buses, trains, etc*) **she arrived on the bus** elle est arrivée en bus; **I met Jackie on the bus** j'ai vu Jackie dans le bus; **I slept on the plane** j'ai

dormi dans l'avion; **let's go on our bikes!** allons-y à vélo!; **4 on TV** à la télé; **on the radio** à la radio; **on video** en vidéo; **5 on holiday** en vacances; **on strike** en grève.
adjective **1** (*switched on*) **to be on** (*TV, light, oven*) être [6] allumé; (*radio, machine*) être en marche; **all the lights were on** toutes les lumières étaient allumées; **is the radio on?** est-ce que la radio est en marche?; **I've put the oven on** j'ai allumé le four; **2** (*happening*) **what's on on TV?** qu'est-ce qu'il y a à la télé?; **what's on this week at the cinema?** qu'est-ce qui passe cette semaine au cinéma?

once *adverb* **1** une fois; **I've tried once already** j'ai déjà essayé une fois; **try once more** essaie encore une fois; **once a day** une fois par jour; **more than once** plus d'une fois; **2 at once** (*immediately*) tout de suite; **the doctor came at once** le médecin est venu tout de suite; **3 at once** (*at the same time*) à la fois; **I can't do two things at once** je ne peux pas faire deux choses à la fois.

one *number* un (F une); **one son** un fils; **one apple** une pomme; **if you want a pen I've got one** si tu veux un stylo j'en ai un; **at one o'clock** à une heure.
pronoun **1** on; **one never knows** on ne sait jamais; **2 this one** celui-ci (F celle-ci); **I like that bike, but this one's cheaper** j'aime bien ce vélo-là, mais celui-ci est moins cher; **do you want the red tie or this one?** veux-tu la cravate rouge ou celle-ci?; **3 that one** celui-là (F celle-là); **'which video?'** – **'that one'** (quelle

vidéo?' – 'celle-là'; **4 which one?** lequel? (F laquelle?); **'my foot's hurting'** – **'which one?'** 'j'ai mal au pied' – 'lequel?' **'she borrowed a skirt from me'** – **'which one?'** 'elle m'a emprunté une jupe' – 'laquelle?'

one's *determiner* son, sa, ses; **one does one's best** on fait de son mieux; **to pay for one's car** pour payer sa voiture; **to love one's children** aimer ses enfants; **to wash one's hands** se laver les mains.

oneself *noun* **1 to wash oneself** se laver; **to hurt oneself** se blesser; **2** (*for emphasis*) soi-même; **one has to do everything oneself** il faut tout faire soi-même; **3 (all) by oneself** tout seul (F toute seule).

one-way street *noun* sens unique M.

onion *noun* oignon M; **onion soup** la soupe à l'oignon.

only *adjective* **1** seul; **the only free seat** la seule place libre; **the only thing to do** la seule chose à faire; **2 an only child** un enfant unique.
adverb
conjunction **1** (*with a verb*) ne...que; **they've only got two bedrooms** ils n'ont que deux chambres; **Anne's only free on Fridays** Anne n'est libre que le vendredi; **there are only three left** il n'en reste que trois; **2** seulement; **'how long did they stay?'** – **'only two days'** 'ils sont restés combien de temps?' – 'deux jours seulement'; **3** (*but*) mais; **I'd walk, only it's raining** j'irais à pied, mais il pleut.

onto *preposition* sur.

open *noun* **in the open** en plein air.
adjective **1** (*not shut*) ouvert; **the door's open** la porte est ouverte; **the baker's is not open** la boulangerie n'est pas ouverte; **2 in the open air** en plein air.
verb **1** ouvrir [30]; **can you open the door for me?** est-ce que tu peux ouvrir la porte?; **Sam opened his eyes** Sam a ouvert les yeux; **the bank opens at nine** la banque ouvre à neuf heures; **2 the door opened slowly** la porte s'est ouverte lentement.

open-air *adjective* en plein air; **an open-air swimming pool** une piscine en plein air.

opera *noun* opéra M.

operation *noun* opération F; **to have an operation** se faire opérer; **she's had an operation** elle s'est fait opérer.

opinion *noun* avis M; **in my opinion** à mon avis.

opinion poll *noun* sondage M.

opponent *noun* adversaire M & F.

opportunity *noun* occasion F; **to have the opportunity of doing** avoir l'occasion de faire; **I took the opportunity to visit the museum** j'ai profité de l'occasion pour visiter le musée.

opposite *noun* contraire M; **no, quite the opposite** non, tout le contraire.
adjective **1** opposé (*a direction, side, or view, for example*); **she went off in the opposite direction** elle est partie dans la direction opposée;
2 (*facing*) d'en face; **in the house opposite** dans la maison d'en face.
adverb en face; **they live opposite** ils habitent en face.
preposition en face de; **opposite the station** en face de la gare.

optician *noun* opticien M, opticienne F.

optimistic *adjective* optimiste.

option *noun* choix M; **we have no option** nous n'avons pas le choix.

optional *adjective* facultatif (F facultative).

or *conjunction* **1** ou; **English or French?** anglais ou français?; **today or Tuesday?** aujourd'hui ou mardi?; **2** (*in negatives*) **I don't have a cat or a dog** je n'ai ni un chat ni un chien; **not in June or July** ni en juin ni en juillet; **3** (*or else*) sinon; **phone Mum, or she'll worry** appelle maman, sinon elle va s'inquiéter.

oral *noun* (*an exam*) oral M (*plural* oraux); **the French oral** l'oral de français.

orange *noun* (*the fruit*) orange F; **an orange juice** un jus d'orange.
adjective orange (*never changes*); **my orange socks** mes chaussettes orange.

orchestra *noun* orchestre M.

order *noun* **1** (*arrangement*) ordre M; **in the right order** dans le bon ordre; **in the wrong order** dans le mauvais ordre; **in alphabetical order** dans l'ordre alphabétique; **2** (*in a restaurant or café*) commande F; **can I take your orders?** puis-je prendre vos commandes?; **3 'out of order'** 'en

panne'; **4 in order to do** pour faire;
we hurried in order to be on time
nous nous sommes dépêchés pour
arriver à l'heure.
verb **1** (*in a restaurant or a shop*)
commander [1]; **we ordered steaks**
nous avons commandé des steaks;
2 réserver [1] (*a taxi*).

ordinary *adjective* ordinaire.

organ *noun* (*the instrument*) orgue
M; **to play the organ** jouer de
l'orgue.

organic *adjective* biologique
(*food*).

organization *noun* organisation
F.

organize *verb* organiser [1].

orienteering *noun* course F
d'orientation.

original *adjective* original
(M *plural* originaux); **the original
version was better** la version
originale était meilleure; **it's a really
original novel** c'est un roman très
original.

originally *adverb* à l'origine;
**originally we wanted to take the
car** à l'origine nous voulions
prendre la voiture.

Orkneys *plural noun* **the Orkneys**
les Orcades F *plural*.

ornament *noun* bibelot M.

orphan *noun* orphelin M, orpheline
F.

ostrich *noun* autruche F.

other *adjective* **1** autre; **the other
day** l'autre jour; **we took the other
road** nous avons pris l'autre route;

give me the other one donne-moi
l'autre; **where are the others?** où
sont les autres?; **the other two cars**
les deux autres voitures; **2 every
other week** une semaine sur deux;
3 somebody or other quelqu'un;
something or other quelque chose;
somewhere or other quelque part.

otherwise *adverb* (*in other ways*) à
part ça; **the flat's a bit small but
otherwise it's lovely** l'appartement
n'est pas très grand mais à part ça il
est très bien.
conjunction (*or else*) sinon; **I'll
phone home, otherwise they'll
worry** je vais appeler chez moi,
sinon ils vont s'inquiéter.

ought *verb* ('*ought*' *is translated by
the conditional tense of* '*devoir*' [8]) **I
ought to go now** je devrais partir
maintenant; **they ought to know the
address** ils devraient savoir
l'adresse; **you oughtn't to have any
problems** vous ne devriez pas avoir
des problèmes.

our *adjective* **1** notre; **our house**
notre maison; **2** (*before a plural
noun*) nos; **our parents** nos
parents; **3** (*with parts of the body*)
le, la, les; **we'll go and wash our
hands** on va se laver les mains.

ours *pronoun* **1** (*for a masculine
noun*) le nôtre; **their garden's
bigger than ours** leur jardin est plus
grand que le nôtre; **2** (*for a
feminine noun*) la nôtre; **their house
is smaller than ours** leur maison est
plus petite que la nôtre; **3** (*for a
plural noun*) les nôtres; **they've
invited their friends and we've
invited ours** ils ont invité leurs amis
et nous avons invité les nôtres; **4** à

nous; **the green one's ours** le vert est à nous; **it's ours** c'est à nous; **a friend of ours** un ami à nous.

ourselves *pronoun* 1 nous; **we introduced ourselves** nous nous sommes présentés; 2 (*for emphasis*) nous-mêmes; **in the end we did it ourselves** finalement nous l'avons fait nous-mêmes.

out *adverb* 1 (*outside*) dehors; **it's cold out there** il fait froid dehors; **out in the rain** sous la pluie; **they're out in the garden** ils sont dans le jardin; 2 **to go out** sortir [72]; **she went out an hour ago** elle est sortie il y a une heure; **Mr. Barnes is out** Monsieur Barnes est sorti; **are you going out this evening?** est-ce que tu sors ce soir?; **Alison's going out with Danny at the moment** Alison sort avec Danny en ce moment; **he's asked me out** il m'a invitée à sortir avec lui; 3 (*light, fire*) éteint; **are all the lights out?** est-ce que toutes les lumières sont éteintes?; **the fire was out** le feu était éteint; 4 **to go out of the room** sortir de la pièce; **he threw it out of the window** il l'a jeté par la fenêtre; **to drink out of a glass** boire dans un verre; **she took the photo out of her bag** elle a pris la photo dans son sac.

outdoor *adjective* (*an activity or sport*) de plein air; **an outdoor restaurant** un restaurant en plein air.

outdoors *adverb* en plein air.

outing *noun* sortie F; **to go on an outing** faire une sortie.

outline *noun* (*of an object*) contour M.

out-of-date *noun* 1 (*no longer valid*) périmé; **my passport's out of date** mon passeport est périmé; 2 (*old-fashioned*) démodé; **they played out-of-date music** ils ont joué la musique démodée.

outside *noun* extérieur M; **it's blue on the outside** c'est bleu à l'extérieur.
adjective extérieur.
adverb dehors; **it's cold outside** il fait froid dehors.
preposition devant (*a building*); **I'll meet you outside the cinema** on se retrouve devant le cinéma.

outskirts *noun* périphérie F; **on the outskirts of York** à la périphérie de York.

oval *adjective* ovale.

oven *noun* four M; **I've put it in the oven** je l'ai mis au four.

over *preposition* 1 (*above*) au-dessus de; **there's a mirror over the sideboard** il y a un miroir au-dessus du buffet; 2 (*involving movement*) par-dessus; **she jumped over the fence** elle a sauté par-dessus la clôture; **he threw the ball over the wall** il a jeté la balle par-dessus le mur; 3 **over here** par ici; **the drinks are over here** les boissons sont par ici; 4 **over there** là-bas; **she's over there talking to Julian** elle est là-bas en train de discuter avec Julian; 5 (*more than*) plus de; **it will cost over a hundred pounds** ça coûtera plus de cent livres; **he's over sixty** il a plus de soixante ans; 6 (*during*) pendant; **over the weekend** pendant le weekend; **over Christmas** à Noël; 7 (*finished*) terminé; **when the meeting's over** quand la réunion sera terminée; **it's all over now** c'est terminé maintenant; **8 over the phone** par téléphone; **to ask someone over** inviter quelqu'un; **can you come over on Saturday?** peux-tu venir chez moi samedi?; **9 all over the place** partout; **all over the house** partout dans la maison.

overseas *adverb* à l'étranger; **Dave works overseas** Dave travaille à l'étranger.

oversleep *verb* se réveiller [1] trop tard.

overtake *verb* doubler [1] (*another car*).

overtime *noun* **to work overtime** faire [10] des heures supplémentaires.

overweight *adjective* (*a person*) trop gros (F trop grosse).

owe *verb* devoir [8]; **I owe Rick ten pounds** je dois dix livres à Rick.

owing *adjective* **1** (*to pay*) à payer; **there's five pounds owing** il y a cinq livres à payer; **2 owing to** en raison de; **owing to the snow** en raison de la neige.

owl *noun* hibou M (*plural* hiboux).

own *adjective* **1** propre (*goes before the noun*); **my own computer** mon propre ordinateur; **I've got my own room** j'ai une chambre à moi; **2 on your own** tout seul (F toute seule); **Annie did it on her own** Annie l'a fait toute seule.
verb posséder [24].

owner *noun* propriétaire M & F.

oxygen *noun* oxygène M.

oyster *noun* huître F.

ozone layer *noun* couche F d'ozone.

P p

pace *noun* **1** (*a step*) pas M; **2** (*the speed you walk at*) allure F; **at a brisk pace** à vive allure.

Pacific *noun* **the Pacific ocean** l'océan M Pacifique.

pack *noun* **1** paquet M; **2 a pack of cards** un jeu de cartes.
verb **1** faire [10] ses bagages; **I haven't packed yet** je n'ai pas encore fait mes bagages; **2 I'll pack my case tonight** je ferai ma valise ce soir; **have you packed my red shirt?** as-tu mis ma chemise rouge dans la valise?

package *noun* paquet M.

package holiday, package tour *noun* voyage M organisé.

packed lunch *noun* panier-repas M.

packet *noun* **1** paquet M; **a packet of biscuits** un paquet de biscuits; **2** (*bag*) sachet M; **a packet of crisps** un sachet de chips.

packing *noun* **to do your packing** faire ses bagages.

pad *noun* (*of paper*) bloc-notes M.

paddle *noun* (*for a canoe*) pagaie F.
verb (*at the seaside*) **to go paddling** faire [10] trempette.

padlock *noun* cadenas M.

page *noun* page F; **on page seven** à la page sept.

pain *noun* douleur F; **I've got a pain in my leg** j'ai mal à la jambe; **to be in pain** souffrir [73]; ★ **Eric's a real pain (in the neck)** Eric est vraiment pénible.

painful *adjective* douloureux (F douloureuse).

paint *noun* peinture F; **'wet paint'** 'peinture fraîche'.
verb peindre [60]; **to paint something pink** peindre quelque chose en rose.

paintbrush *noun* pinceau M (*plural* pinceaux).

painter *noun* peintre M.

painting *noun* (*picture*) tableau M (*plural* tableaux); **a painting by Monet** un tableau de Monet.

pair *noun* **1** paire F; **a pair of socks** une paire de chaussettes; **a pair of scissors** une paire de ciseaux; **2 a pair of jeans** un jean; **a pair of trousers** un pantalon; **a pair of knickers** un slip; **3 to work in pairs** travailler en groupes de deux.

Pakistan *noun* Pakistan M; **in Pakistan** au Pakistan; **to Pakistan** au Pakistan.

Pakistani *noun* Pakistanais M, Pakistanaise F.
adjective pakistanais.

palace *noun* palais M.

pale *adjective* pâle; **pale green** vert pâle (*never changes*); **pale green**

curtains des rideaux vert pâle; **to turn pale** pâlir [2].

palm *noun* **1** (*of your hand*) paume F; **2** (*a palm tree*) palmier M.

pan *noun* **1** (*saucepan*) casserole F; **a pan of water** une casserole d'eau; **2** (*frying-pan*) poêle F.

pancake *noun* crêpe F.

panel *noun* **1** (*on radio or TV*) (*for a discussion*) invités M *plural* (*i.e. guests*); (*for a quiz show*) jury M; **2** (*for a wall or a bath, for example*) panneau M (*plural* panneaux).

panel game *noun* jeu M (*plural* jeux).

panic *noun* panique F.
verb s'affoler [1]; **don't panic!** pas de panique!

panther *noun* panthère F.

pannier *noun* (*on a bike*) sacoche F.

pantomime *noun* spectacle M pour enfants.

pants *plural noun* slip M.

paper *noun* **1** papier M; **a sheet of paper** une feuille de papier; **2 a paper cup** un gobelet en carton; **a paper hanky** un mouchoir en papier; **3** (*newspaper*) journal M (*plural* journaux); **it was in the paper** c'était dans le journal.

paperback *noun* livre M de poche.

paperclip *noun* trombone M (*because of its shape*).

paper shop *noun* magasin M de journaux.

paper towel *noun* essuie-tout M.

parachute *noun* parachute M.

parachuting *noun* parachutisme M; **to go parachuting** faire du parachutisme.

parade *noun* défilé M.

paradise *noun* paradis M.

paraffin *noun* pétrole M.

paragraph *noun* paragraphe M; **'new paragraph'** 'à la ligne'.

parallel *adjective* parallèle.

paralysed *adjective* paralysé.

parcel *noun* paquet M.

pardon *noun* **I beg your pardon** pardon; **pardon?** pardon?

parent *noun* parent M; **my parents are Scottish** mes parents sont écossais; **a parents' evening** une réunion pour les parents d'élèves.

Paris *noun* Paris; **Marie lives in Paris** Marie habite à Paris.

Parisian *noun* Parisien M, Parisienne F.
adjective parisien (F parisienne).

park *noun* **1** parc M; **a theme park** un parc à thème; **2 a car park** un parking.
verb **1** se garer [1]; **you can park outside the house** vous pouvez vous garer devant la maison; **2 to park a car** garer [1] une voiture; **where did you park the car?** où as-tu garé la voiture?

parking *noun* stationnement M; **'no parking'** 'stationnement interdit'.

parking meter *noun* parcmètre M.

parking space *noun* place F.

parking ticket *noun* PV M (*informal*).

parliament *noun* parlement M.

parrot *noun* perroquet M.

parsley *noun* persil M.

part *noun* **1** partie F; **part of the garden** une partie du jardin; **the last part of the concert** la dernière partie du concert; **that's part of your job** ça fait partie de votre travail; **2 to take part in something** participer à quelque chose; **3** (*a role in a play*) rôle M; **4 spare parts** pièces F *plural* détachées.

particular *adjective* particulier (F particulière); **nothing in particular** rien de particulier.

particularly *adverb* **1** (*unusually*) spécialement; **not particularly interesting** pas spécialement intéressant; **2** (*in particular*) surtout; **particularly since it's our last day** surtout que c'est notre dernier jour.

parting *noun* (*in your hair*) raie F.

partly *adverb* en partie.

partner *noun* **1** (*in a game*) partenaire M; **2** (*the person you live with*) partenaire M & F; **3** (*in business*) associé M, associée F.

part-time *adjective, adverb* à temps partiel; **part-time work** du travail à temps partiel; **to work part-time** travailler à temps partiel.

party *noun* **1** fête F; **a Christmas party** une fête de Noël; **to have a**

birthday party faire une fête d'anniversaire; **2** (*more formal, in the evening*) soirée F; **we've been invited to a party at the Smiths' house** nous sommes invités à une soirée chez les Smith; **3** (*group*) groupe M; **a party of schoolchildren** un groupe d'élèves; **a rescue party** une équipe de secouristes; **4** (*in politics*) parti M; **the Labour party** le parti travailliste.

party game *noun* jeu M de société (*plural* jeux de société).

pass *noun* **1** (*to let you in*) laisser-passer M (*plural* laisser-passer); **2 a bus pass** une carte de bus; **3** (*a mountain pass*) col M; **4** (*in an exam*) **to get a pass in history** être reçu en histoire.
verb **1** (*go past*) passer [1] devant (*a place or building*); **we passed your house** nous sommes passés devant chez toi; **2** (*to overtake*) doubler [1] (*a car*); **3** (*give*) passer [1]; **could you pass me the paper please?** peux-tu me passer le journal s'il te plaît?; **4** (*time*) passer [1]; **the time passed slowly** le temps passait lentement; **5** (*in an exam*) être [6] reçu; **did you pass?** as-tu été reçu?; **to pass an exam** être reçu à un examen.

passage *noun* **1** (*a corridor*) couloir M; **2** (*a piece of text*) passage M.

passenger *noun* **1** (*in a car, plane, or ship*) passager M, passagère F; **2** (*in a train, bus, or underground*) voyageur M, voyageuse F.

passerby *noun* passant M, passante F.

passion *noun* passion F.

passionate *adjective* passionné.

passive *noun* passif M.
adjective passif (F passive).

Passover *noun* Pâque juive F.

passport *noun* passeport M; **an EU passport** un passeport de l'UE.

password *noun* mot M de passe.

past *noun* passé M; **in the past** dans le passé.
adjective **1** (*recent*) dernier (F dernière) (*goes before the noun*); **in the past few weeks** pendant les dernières semaines; **2** (*over*) fini; **winter is past** l'hiver est fini.
preposition, adverb **1 to walk or drive past something** passer devant quelque chose; **we went past the school** nous sommes passés devant l'école; **Ray went past in his new car** Ray est passé dans sa nouvelle voiture; **2** (*the other side of*) après; **it's just past the post office** c'est juste après la poste; **3** (*talking about time*) **ten past six** six heures dix; **half past four** quatre heures et demie; **a quarter past two** deux heures et quart.

pasta *noun* pâtes F *plural*; **I don't like pasta** je n'aime pas les pâtes.

pasteurized *adjective* pasteurisé.

pastry *noun* pâte F.

patch *noun* **1** (*fabric, for mending*) pièce F; **2** (*of snow or ice*) plaque F; **3** (*of blue sky*) coin M.

path *noun* chemin M; (*very narrow*) sentier M.

pathetic *adjective* (*useless, hopeless*) lamentable.

patience *noun* **1** patience F; **2** (*card game*) réussite F.

patient *noun* patient M, patiente F. *adjective* patient.

patiently *adverb* avec patience.

patio *noun* terrasse F.

patrol car *noun* voiture F de police.

pattern *noun* **1** (*on wallpaper or fabric*) motif M; **2** (*dressmaking*) patron M; **3** (*knittting*) modèle M.

pause *noun* pause F.

pavement *noun* trottoir M; **on the pavement** sur le trottoir.

paw *noun* patte F.

pawn *noun* pion M.

pay *noun* salaire M.
verb **1** payer [59]; **I'm paying** c'est moi qui paie; **to pay cash** payer comptant; **2 to pay for something** payer [59] quelque chose; **Tony paid for the drinks** Tony a payé les boissons; **it's all paid for** c'est tout payé; **3 to pay by credit card** régler [24] par carte de crédit; **to pay by cheque** régler par chèque; **4 to pay somebody back** (*money*) rembourser [1] quelqu'un; **5 to pay attention** faire [10] attention; **6 to pay a visit to somebody** rendre [3] visite à quelqu'un.

paydesk *noun* caisse F.

payment *noun* paiement M; (*of a bill*) règlement M.

pay phone *noun* téléphone public M.

PC *noun* (*computer*) PC M.

pea *noun* petit pois M.

peace *noun* paix F.

peaceful *adjective* paisible (*day, scene*).

peach *noun* pêche F.

peacock *noun* paon M.

peak *noun* (*of a mountain*) pic M.

peak period (*for holidays*) période F de pointe.

peak rate *noun* (*for phoning*) tarif rouge M.

peak time *noun* (*for traffic*) heures F *plural* de pointe.

peanut *noun* cacahuète F.

peanut butter *noun* beurre M de cacahuètes.

pear *noun* poire F.

pearl *noun* perle F.

pebble *noun* **1** (*on the road*) caillou M (*plural* cailloux); **2** (*on a beach*) galet M.

peculiar *adjective* bizarre.

pedal *noun* pédale F.
verb pédaler [1].

pedal boat *noun* pédalo™ M.

pedestrian *noun* piéton M.

pedestrian crossing *noun* passage M pour piétons.

pedestrian precinct *noun* zone F piétonne.

pee *noun* **to have a pee** faire [10] pipi (*informal*).

peel *noun* **1** (*of an apple*) peau F; **2** (*of an orange*) écorce F. *verb* éplucher [1] (*fruit, vegetables*).

peer *verb* **to peer at something** regarder [1] quelque chose attentivement.

peg *noun* **1** (*hook*) patère F; **2 a clothes peg** une pince à linge; **3 a tent peg** un piquet.

pen *noun* stylo M; **a felt pen** un stylo-feutre.

penalty *noun* **1** (*a fine*) amende F; **2** (*in football*) penalty M; **3** (*in rugby*) pénalité F.

pence *plural noun* pence M *plural*.

pencil *noun* crayon M; **to write in pencil** écrire au crayon.

pencil case *noun* trousse F.

pencil sharpener *noun* taille-crayon M.

pendant *noun* pendentif M.

penfriend *noun* correspondant M, correspondante F; **my French pen-friend is called Christelle** ma correspondante française s'appelle Christelle.

penguin *noun* pingouin M.

penis *noun* pénis M.

penknife *noun* canif M.

penny *noun* penny M.

pension *noun* retraite F.

pensioner *noun* retraité M, retraitée F.

people *plural noun* **1** gens M *plural*: **people round here** les gens d'ici; **nice people** des gens sympathiques; **2** (*when you're counting them*) personnes F *plural*; **ten people** dix personnes; **several people** plusieurs personnes; **how many people have you asked?** tu as invité combien de personnes?; **3 people say he's very rich** on dit qu'il est très riche.

pepper *noun* **1** (*spice*) poivre M; **2** poivron M; **a green pepper** un poivron vert.

peppermill *noun* moulin M à poivre.

peppermint *noun* menthe F; **peppermint tea** le thé à la menthe.

per *preposition* par; **ten pounds per person** dix livres par personne.

per cent *adverb* pour cent; **sixty per cent of students** soixante pour cent des étudiants.

percentage *noun* pourcentage M.

percussion *noun* percussion F; **to play percussion** jouer des percussions.

perfect *adjective* **1** parfait; **she speaks perfect English** elle parle un anglais parfait; **2** (*ideal*) idéal (M *plural* idéaux); **the perfect place for a picnic** l'endroit idéal pour un pique-nique.

perfectly *adverb* parfaitement.

perform *verb* **1** jouer [1] (*a piece of music or a play*); **2** chanter [1] (*a song*).

performance *noun* **1** (*playing or acting*) interprétation F; **a wonderful performance of**

Macbeth une superbe
interprétation de Macbeth;
2 (*show*) spectacle M; **the
performance starts at eight** le
spectacle commence à huit heures;
3 (*the results of a team or company*)
performance F.

performer *noun* artiste M & F.

perfume *noun* parfum M.

perhaps *adverb* peut-être; **perhaps
it's in the drawer?** c'est peut-être
dans le tiroir?; **perhaps he's missed
the train** il a peut-être raté le train.

period *noun* **1** période F; **a two-
year period** une période de deux
ans; **2** (*in school*) cours M; **a forty-
five-minute period** un cours de
quarante-cinq minutes;
3 (*menstruation*) règles F *plural*;
during your period pendant vos
règles.

perm *noun* permanente F.

permanent *adjective* permanent.

permanently *adverb* en
permanence.

permission *noun* permission F; **to
get permission to do** obtenir la
permission de faire.

permit *noun* permis M.
verb permettre [11]; **to permit
somebody to do** permettre à
quelqu'un de faire; **smoking is not
permitted** il est interdit de fumer;
weather permitting si le temps le
permet.

person *noun* personne F; **there's
room for one more person** il y a de
la place pour une autre personne; **in
person** en personne.

personal *adjective* personnel (F
personnelle).

personality *noun* personnalité F.

personally *adverb*
personnellement; **personally, I'm
against it** personnellement, je suis
contre.

perspiration *noun* transpiration
F.

persuade *verb* persuader [1]; **to
persuade somebody to do**
persuader quelqu'un de faire; **we
persuaded Tim to wait a bit** nous
avons persuadé Tim d'attendre un
peu.

pessimistic *adjective* pessimiste.

pest *noun* **1** (*greenfly for example*)
insecte M nuisible; **2** (*annoying
person*) casse-pieds M & F.

pet *noun* **1** animal M de compagnie
(*plural* animaux de compagnie); **do
you have a pet?** avez-vous un
animal de compagnie?; **a pet dog**
un chien; **2** (*favourite person*)
chouchou M, chouchoute F; **Julie
is teacher's pet** Julie est la
chouchoute du prof.

petal *noun* pétale M.

pet name *noun* petit nom M.

petrol *noun* essence F; **to fill up
with petrol** faire le plein d'essence;
to run out of petrol tomber en
panne d'essence.

petrol station *noun* station F
d'essence.

pharmacy *noun* pharmacie F.

pheasant *noun* faisan M.

philosophy *noun* philosophie F.

phone *noun* téléphone M; **she's on the phone** elle est au téléphone; **I was on the phone to Sophie** j'étais au téléphone avec Sophie; **you can book by phone** on peut réserver par téléphone.
verb 1 téléphoner [1]; **while I was phoning** pendant que je téléphonais; **2 to phone somebody** appeler [18] quelqu'un; **I'll phone you tonight** je t'appellerai ce soir.

phone book *noun* annuaire M.

phone box *noun* cabine F téléphonique.

phone call *noun* appel M; **phone calls are free** les appels sont gratuits; **to make a phone call** téléphoner.

phone card *noun* télécarte F.

phone number *noun* numéro M de téléphone.

photo *noun* photo F; **to take a photo** prendre une photo; **to take a photo of somebody** prendre quelqu'un en photo; **I took a photo of their house** j'ai pris leur maison en photo.

photocopier *noun* photocopieuse F.

photocopy *noun* photocopie F.
verb photocopier [1].

photograph *noun* photo F; **to take a photograph** prendre une photo; **to take a photograph of somebody** prendre quelqu'un en photo.
verb photographier [1].

photographer *noun* photographe M & F.

photography *noun* photographie F.

phrase *noun* expression F.

phrase-book *noun* manuel M de conversation.

physical *adjective* physique.

physicist *noun* physicien M, physicienne F.

physics *noun* physique F.

physiotherapist *noun* kinésithérapeute M & F.

physiotherapy *noun* kinésithérapie F.

pianist *noun* pianiste M & F.

piano *noun* piano M; **to play the piano** jouer du piano; **Steve played it on the piano** Steve l'a joué au piano; **a piano lesson** une leçon de piano.

pick *noun* **take your pick!** choisis!
verb 1 (*to choose*) choisir [2]; **pick a card** choisis une carte; **2** (*for a team*) sélectionner [1]; **I've been picked for Saturday** j'ai été sélectionné pour samedi; **3** cueillir [35] (*fruit or flowers*).
● **to pick up 1** (*lift*) prendre [64]; **he picked up the papers and went out** il a pris les papiers et il est sorti; **2** (*collect together*) ramasser [1]; **I'll pick up the toys** je ramasserai les jouets; **3** (*to collect*) venir [81] chercher; **I'll pick you up at six** je viendrai te chercher à six heures; **I'll pick up the keys tomorrow** je viendrai chercher les clés demain;

4 (*learn*) apprendre [64]; **you'll soon pick it up** tu vas vite l'apprendre.

picnic *noun* pique-nique M; **to have a picnic** pique-niquer.

pickpocket *noun* pickpocket M.

picture *noun* 1 (*a painting*) tableau M (*plural* tableaux); **a picture by Renoir** une tableau de Renoir; **he painted a picture of a horse** il a peint un cheval; 2 (*a drawing*) dessin M; **draw me a picture of your little sister** dessine-moi ta petite sœur; 3 (*in a book*) illustration F; **a book with lots of pictures** un livre avec beaucoup d'illustrations; 4 (*the cinema*) **the pictures** le cinéma; **to go to the pictures** aller au cinéma.

pie *noun* 1 (*sweet*) tarte F; **an apple pie** une tarte aux pommes; 2 (*savoury*) tourte F; **a meat pie** une tourte à la viande.

piece *noun* 1 (*a bit*) morceau M (*plural* morceaux); **a big piece of cheese** un gros morceau de fromage; 2 (*that you fit together*) pièce F; **the pieces of a jigsaw** les pièces d'un puzzle; **to take something to pieces** démonter [1] quelque chose; 3 **a piece of furniture** un meuble; **four pieces of luggage** quatre valises; **a piece of information** un renseignement; **that's a piece of luck!** c'est un coup de chance!; 4 (*coin*) pièce F; **a five-franc piece** une pièce de cinq francs.

pier *noun* jetée F.

pierced *adjective* percé; **to have**

pierced ears avoir les oreilles percées.

pig *noun* cochon M.

pigeon *noun* pigeon M.

piggy bank *noun* tirelire F.

pigtail *noun* natte F.

pile *noun* 1 (*a neat stack*) pile F; **a pile of plates** une pile d'assiettes; 2 (*a heap*) tas M; **a pile of dirty shirts** un tas de chemises sales.
●**to pile something up** (*neatly*) empiler [1] quelque chose; (*in a heap*) entasser [1] quelque chose.

pill *noun* comprimé M; **the pill** (*contraceptive*) la pilule.

pillar *noun* pilier M.

pillar box *noun* boîte F aux lettres.

pillow *noun* oreiller M.

pilot *noun* pilote M.

pimple *noun* bouton M.

pin *noun* 1 (*for sewing*) épingle F; 2 **a three-pin plug** une prise à trois fiches.
●**to pin up** 1 épingler [1] (*a hem*); 2 accrocher [1] (*a notice*).

PIN *noun* (*personal identification number*) code confidentiel M.

pinball *noun* flipper M; **to play pinball** jouer au flipper; **a pinball machine** un flipper.

pinch *noun* (*of salt, for example*) pincée F.
verb 1 (*steal*) piquer [1]; **somebody's pinched my bike** on m'a piqué mon vélo; 2 **to pinch somebody** pincer [61] quelqu'un.

pine *noun* pin M; **a pine table** une table en pin.

pineapple *noun* ananas M.

pine cone *noun* pomme F de pin.

ping-pong *noun* ping-pong M; **to play ping-pong** jouer au ping-pong.

pink *adjective* rose.

pip *noun* (*in a fruit*) pépin M.

pipe *noun* 1 (*for gas or water*) tuyau M (*plural* tuyaux); 2 (*to smoke*) pipe F; **he smokes a pipe** il fume la pipe.

pirate *noun* pirate M.

pirated *adjective* piraté; **a pirated video** une vidéo piratée.

Pisces *noun* Poissons M *plural*; **Amanda is Pisces** Amanda est Poissons.

pit *noun* fosse F.

pitch *noun* terrain M; **a football pitch** un terrain de foot.
verb **to pitch a tent** dresser [1] une tente.

pity *noun* 1 **what a pity!** quel dommage!; **it would be a pity to miss the beginning** ce serait dommage de rater le début; 2 (*feeling sorry for somebody*) pitié F.
verb **to pity somebody** plaindre [31] quelqu'un.

pizza *noun* pizza F.

place *noun* 1 endroit M; **in a warm place** dans un endroit chaud; **Rome is a wonderful place** Rome est un endroit merveilleux; **all over the place** partout; 2 (*a space*) place F;

a place for the car une place pour la voiture; **is there a place for me?** y a-t-il une place pour moi?; **will you keep my place?** veux-tu me garder ma place?; **to change places** changer de place; 3 (*in a race*) place F; **in first place** à la première place; 4 **at your place** chez toi; **we'll go round to Zafir's place** on ira chez Zafir; 5 **to take place** avoir [5] lieu; **the competition will take place at four** le concours aura lieu à quatre heures.
verb mettre [11]; **he placed his cup on the table** il a mis sa tasse sur la table.

plain *noun* plaine F.
adjective 1 simple; **plain cooking** une cuisine simple; 2 (*unflavoured*) nature; **a plain yoghurt** un yaourt nature; 3 (*not patterned*) uni; **plain curtains** des rideaux unis.

plait *noun* natte F.

plan *noun* 1 projet M; **what are your plans for this summer?** quels sont vos projets pour cet été?; **to go according to plan** se passer comme prévu; **everything went according to plan** tout s'est passé comme prévu; 2 (*a map*) plan M.
verb 1 **to plan to do** avoir [5] l'intention de faire; **we're planning to leave at eight** nous avons l'intention de partir à huit heures; 2 (*make plans for*) préparer [1]; **Ricky's planning a trip to Italy** Ricky prépare un voyage en Italie; 3 (*organize*) organiser [1]; **I'm planning my day** j'organise ma journée; 4 (*to design*) concevoir [66] (*a house or garden*); **a well-**

planned kitchen une cuisine bien conçue.

plane *noun* avion M; **we went by plane** nous avons pris l'avion.

planet *noun* planète F.

plank *noun* planche F.

plant *noun* plante F; **a house plant** une plante d'intérieur.
verb planter [1].

plaster *noun* **1** (*sticking plaster*) pansement adhésif M; **2** (*for walls*) plâtre M; **3 to have your leg in plaster** avoir la jambe dans le plâtre.

plastic *noun* plastique M; **a plastic bag** un sac en plastique.

plate *noun* assiette F.

platform *noun* **1** (*in a station*) quai M; **the train arriving at platform six** le train qui entre en gare quai numéro six; **2** (*for lecturing or performing*) estrade F.

play *noun* pièce F; **a play by Molière** une pièce de Molière; **our school is putting on a play** notre école monte une pièce.
verb **1** jouer [1]; **the children were playing with a ball** les enfants jouaient avec un ballon; **they play all kinds of music** ils jouent toutes sortes de musique; **who's playing Hamlet?** qui est-ce qui joue Hamlet?; **2** jouer [1] à (*a game*); **to play tennis** jouer au tennis; **they were playing cards** ils jouaient aux cartes; **3** jouer [1] de (*a musical instrument*); **Helen plays the violin** Helen joue du violon; **4** mettre [11] (*a tape, CD, or record*); **play me your new CD** mets-moi ton nouveau CD.

player *noun* **1** (*in sport*) joueur M, joueuse F; **a football player** un joueur de foot; **2** (*musician*) musicien M, musicienne F.

playground *noun* cour F de récréation.

playgroup *noun* halte-garderie F.

playing field *noun* terrain M de sport.

playroom *noun* salle F de jeux.

plaza *noun* **a shopping plaza** un centre commercial.

pleasant *adjective* agréable.

please *adverb* s'il vous plaît; (*less formal*), s'il te plaît; **two coffees, please** deux cafés, s'il vous plaît; **could you turn the TV off, please?** est-ce que tu peux éteindre la télé s' te plaît?

pleased *adjective* content; **I was really pleased!** j'étais très content! **she was pleased with her present** elle était contente de son cadeau; **pleased to meet you!** enchanté!

pleasure *noun* plaisir M.

plenty *pronoun* **1** (*lots*) beaucoup; **there's plenty of bread** il y a beaucoup de pain; **he's got plenty money** il a beaucoup d'argent; **2** (*quite enough*) **we've got plenty time for a coffee** nous avons largement le temps de prendre un café; **thank you, that's plenty!** merci, ça suffit largement!

plot *noun* (*of a film or novel*) intrigue F.

plough *verb* labourer [1].

plug *noun* **1** (*electrical*) prise F;

2 (*in a bath or sink*) bonde F; **to pull out the plug** retirer la bonde.

plum *noun* prune F; **a plum tart** une tarte aux prunes.

plumber *noun* plombier M; **he's a plumber** il est plombier.

plump *adjective* potelé.

plunge *verb* plonger [52].

plural *noun* pluriel M; **in the plural** au pluriel.

plus *preposition* plus; **three children plus the baby** trois enfants plus le bébé.

p.m. *adverb* (*French people usually express times after midday in terms of the 24-hour clock*) **1 at two p.m.** à quatorze heures; **at nine p.m.** à vingt-et-une heures; **2** (*however, you can also use 'de l'après-midi', for times up to 6 p.m. and 'du soir' for times after that*) **at two p.m.** à deux heures de l'après-midi; **at nine p.m.** à neuf heures du soir.

poached egg *noun* œuf M poché.

pocket *noun* poche F.

pocket money *noun* argent M de poche.

poem *noun* poème M.

poet *noun* poète M.

poetry *noun* poésie F.

point *noun* **1** (*tip*) pointe F; **the point of a nail** la pointe d'un clou; **2** (*in time*) moment M; **at that point the police arrived** à ce moment là, la police est arrivée; **3 to get the point** comprendre; **I don't get the point** je ne comprends pas;

what's the point of waiting? à quoi bon attendre?; **there's no point phoning, he's out** ça ne sert à rien d'appeler, il est sorti; **that's not the point** il ne s'agit pas de ça; **4 that's a good point!** c'est vrai!; **5 from my point of view** de mon point de vue; **6 her strong point** son point fort; **7** (*in scoring*) point M; **fifteen points to eleven** quinze points à onze; **8** (*in decimals*) (*in French, a comma is used for the decimal point, so 6,75*) **6 point 4** 6 virgule 4 (*this is how you say it aloud*).
verb **1** indiquer [1]; **a notice pointing to the station** un panneau qui indiquait la gare; **James pointed out the cathedral** James nous a montré la cathédrale; **2** (*with finger*) montrer [1] du doigt; **he pointed at one of the children** il a montré l'un des enfants du doigt; **3 I'd like to point out that I'm paying** je vous signale que c'est moi qui paie.

pointless *adjective* inutile; **it's pointless to keep on ringing** c'est inutile de continuer de sonner.

poison *noun* poison M.
verb empoisonner [1].

poisonous *adjective* **1** toxique (*chemical or gas*); **2** vénéneux (F vénéneuse) (*toadstools or berries*); **3** venimeux (F venimeuse) (*snake or insect*).

Poland *noun* Pologne F; **in Poland** en Pologne.

polar bear *noun* ours M polaire.

pole *noun* **1** (*for a tent*) mât M; **2** (*for skiing*) bâton M; **3 the North Pole** le pôle Nord.

Pole noun (*a Polish person*) Polonais M, Polonaise F.

police noun **the police** la police; **the police are coming** la police arrive (*note that a singular verb is used after 'la police'*).
verb surveiller [1].

police car noun voiture F de police.

policeman noun agent M de police.

police station noun commissariat M de police.

policewoman noun femme F policier.

polish noun 1 (*for furniture*) cire F; 2 (*for shoes*) cirage M.
verb cirer [1] (*shoes or furniture*).

Polish noun, adjective polonais M.

polite adjective poli; **to be polite to somebody** être poli avec quelqu'un.

political adjective politique.

politician noun homme politique M, femme politique F.

politics noun politique F.

polluted adjective pollué.

pollution noun pollution F.

polo-necked adjective à col roulé; **a polo-necked jumper** un pull à col roulé.

polythene bag noun sac M en plastique.

pond noun 1 (*large*) étang M; 2 (*smaller*) mare F; 3 (*in a garden*) bassin M.

pony noun poney M.

ponytail noun queue F de cheval.

poodle noun caniche M.

pool noun 1 (*swimming pool*) piscine F; 2 (*in the country*) étang M; 3 (*puddle*) flaque F; 4 (*game*) billard M américain; **to have a game of pool** jouer au billard américain; **5 the football pools** le loto sportif; **to do the pools** jouer au loto sportif.

poor adjective 1 pauvre; **a poor area** un quartier pauvre; **a poor family** une famille pauvre; **poor Tanya's failed her exam** la pauvre Tanya a raté son examen; 2 (*bad*) mauvais; **this is poor work** c'est du mauvais travail; **the weather was pretty poor** le temps était assez mauvais.

pop noun pop M; **a pop concert** un concert de pop; **a pop star** un pop star; **a pop song** une chanson pop.
● **to pop into** faire [10] un saut à; **I'll just pop into the bank** je vais juste faire un saut à la banque.

popcorn noun pop-corn M.

pope noun pape M.

poppy noun coquelicot M.

popular adjective populaire.

population noun population F.

porch noun porche M.

pork noun porc M; **a pork chop** une côtelette de porc.

porridge noun porridge M.

port noun 1 port M; **the ferry was in port** le ferry était au port; 2 (*wine*) porto M.

porter noun 1 (*at a station or airport*) porteur M; 2 (*in a hotel*) portier M.

portion *noun* (*of food*) portion F.

portrait *noun* portrait M.

Portugal *noun* Portugal M; **to Portugal** au Portugal; **in Portugal** au Portugal.

Portuguese *noun* 1 (*language*) portugais M; 2 (*a person*) Portugais M, Portugaise F. *adjective* portugais.

posh *adjective* chic (*never changes*); **a posh house** une maison chic.

position *noun* position F.

positive *adjective* 1 (*sure*) sûr; **I'm positive he's left** je suis sûr qu'il est parti; 2 (*enthusiastic*) positif (F positive); **her reaction was very positive** sa réaction était très positive; **try to be more positive** essaie d'être plus positif.

possess *verb* posséder [24].

possessions *plural noun* affaires F *plural*; **all my possessions are in the flat** toutes mes affaires sont dans l'appartement.

possibility *noun* possibilité F.

possible *adjective* possible; **it's possible** c'est possible; **if possible** si possible; **as quickly as possible** le plus vite possible.

possibly *adverb* 1 (*maybe*) peut-être; **'will you be at home at midday?' – 'possibly'** 'est-ce que tu seras chez toi à midi?' – 'peut-être'; 2 (*for emphasis*) **how can you possibly believe that?** mais comment donc peux-tu croire ça?; **I can't possibly arrive before Thursday** je ne peux vraiment pas arriver avant jeudi.

post *noun* 1 poste F; **to send something by post** envoyer quelque chose par la poste; 2 (*letters*) courrier M; **is there any post for me?** y a-t-il du courrier pour moi?; 3 (*a pole*) poteau M (*plural* poteaux); 4 (*a job*) poste M. *verb* **to post a letter** mettre [11] une lettre à la poste.

postbox *noun* boîte F à lettres.

postcard *noun* carte postale F.

postcode *noun* code postal M.

poster *noun* 1 (*for decoration*) poster M; **I've bought an Oasis poster** j'ai acheté un poster d'Oasis; 2 (*advertising*) affiche F; **I saw a poster for the concert** j'ai vu une affiche pour le concert.

postman *noun* facteur M; **has the postman been?** est-ce que le facteur est passé?

post office *noun* poste F; **the post office is on the right** la poste est à droite.

postpone *verb* **to postpone something** remettre [11] quelque chose à plus tard.

postwoman *noun* factrice F.

pot *noun* 1 (*jar*) pot M; **a pot of honey** un pot de miel; 2 (*teapot*) théière F; **I'll make a pot of tea** je vais faire du thé; 3 **the pots and pans** les casseroles F *plural*; ★ **to take pot luck** manger à la fortune du pot.

potato *noun* pomme F de terre; **fried**

potatoes des pommes de terre sautées; **mashed potatoes** de la purée.

potato crisps *plural noun* chips M *plural*.

pottery *noun* poterie F.

pound *noun* **1** (*money*) livre F; **fourteen pounds** quatorze livres; **how much is that in pounds?** c'est combien en livres sterling?; **2** (*in weight*) livre F; **a pound of apples** une livre de pommes.

pour *verb* **1** verser [1] (*liquid*); **he poured the milk into the pan** il a versé le lait dans la casserole; **2** servir [71] (*a drink*); **to pour the tea** servir le thé; **I poured him a drink** je lui ai servi à boire; **3** (*with rain*) **it's pouring** il pleut à verse.

poverty *noun* pauvreté F.

powder *noun* poudre F.

power *noun* **1** (*electricity*) courant M; **a power cut** une coupure de courant; **2** (*energy*) énergie F; **nuclear power** l'énergie nucléaire; **3** (*over other people*) pouvoir M; **to be in power** être au pouvoir.

powerful *adjective* puissant.

power point *noun* prise F de courant.

power station *noun* centrale F électrique.

practical *adjective* pratique.

practically *adverb* pratiquement.

practice *noun* **1** (*for sport*) entraînement M; **hockey practice** l'entraînement de hockey; **2** (*for an instrument*) **to do your piano**

practice travailler [1] son piano; **3 to be out of practice** être rouillé; **4 in practice** en pratique.

practise *verb* **1** travailler [1] (*music, language, etc*); **a week in Berlin to practise my German** une semaine à Berlin pour travailler mon allemand; **2** (*in a sport*) s'entraîner [1]; **the team practises on Wednesdays** l'équipe s'entraîne le mercredi.

praise *verb* **to praise somebody for something** féliciter [1] quelqu'un de quelque chose.

pram *noun* landau M.

prawn *noun* crevette F.

pray *verb* prier [1].

prayer *noun* prière F.

precaution *noun* précaution F; **to take precautions** prendre ses précautions.

precinct *noun* **a shopping precinct** un quartier commerçant; **a pedestrian precinct** une zone piétonne.

precious *adjective* précieux (F précieuse).

precisely *adverb* précisément; **at eleven o'clock precisely** à onze heures précises.

preface *noun* préface F.

prefer *verb* préférer [24]; **I prefer coffee to tea** je préfère le café au thé.

pregnant *adjective* enceinte.

prejudice *noun* préjugé M; **a prejudice** un préjugé; **to fight**

against racial prejudice lutter contre les préjugés raciaux.

prejudiced *adjective* **to be prejudiced** avoir des préjugés.

preliminary *adjective* préliminaire.

première *noun* première F (*of a play or film*).

prep *noun* devoirs M *plural*; **my English prep** mes devoirs d'anglais.

preparation *noun* 1 préparation F; 2 **the preparations for** les préparatifs M *plural* pour; **our preparations for Christmas** nos préparatifs pour Noël.

prepare *verb* préparer [1]; **to prepare somebody for** préparer quelqu'un à (*a surprise or shock*); **to be prepared for the worst** s'attendre [3] au pire.

prepared *adjective* prêt; **I'm prepared to pay half** je suis prêt à en payer la moitié.

preposition *noun* préposition F.

prep school *noun* école primaire privée F.

prescription *noun* ordonnance F; **on prescription** sur ordonnance.

presence *noun* présence F; **in my presence** en ma présence.

presence of mind *noun* présence F d'esprit.

present *noun* 1 (*a gift*) cadeau M (*plural* cadeaux); **to give somebody a present** offrir un cadeau à quelqu'un; 2 (*the time now*) présent M; **in the present (tense)** au présent; **that's all for the present** c'est tout pour le moment.

adjective 1 (*attending*) présent; **is Tracy present?** est-ce que Tracy est présente?; **to be present at** assister [1] à; **fifty people were present at the funeral** cinquante personnes ont assisté à l'enterrement; 2 (*existing now*) actuel (F actuelle); **the present situation** la situation actuelle; 3 **at the present time** actuellement.
verb 1 remettre [11] (*a prize*); 2 (*introduce*) présenter [1].

presenter *noun* (*on TV*) présentateur M, présentatrice F.

presently *adverb* (*soon*) bientôt.

president *noun* président M, présidente F.

press *noun* **the press** la presse. *verb* 1 (*to push*) appuyer [41]; **press here to open** appuyez ici pour ouvrir; 2 appuyer [41] sur (*a button, switch, or pedal*); **he pressed the button** il a appuyé sur le bouton.

press conference *noun* conférence F de presse.

pressure *noun* pression F.

pressure group *noun* groupe M de pression.

pretend *verb* **to pretend to do** faire [10] semblant de faire; **he's pretending not to hear** il fait semblant de ne pas entendre.

pretty *adjective* joli (*goes before the noun*); **a pretty dress** une jolie robe. *adverb* plutôt; **it was pretty silly** c'était plutôt bête.

prevent *verb* **to prevent somebody from doing** empêcher [1] quelqu'un de faire; **there's nothing to prevent**

you from leaving rien ne vous empêche de partir.

previous *adjective* précédent.

previously *adverb* auparavant.

price *noun* prix M; **the price per kilo** le prix du kilo; **CDs have gone up in price** les CD ont augmenté.

price list *noun* liste F des prix.

price ticket *noun* étiquette F.

prick *verb* piquer [1]; **to prick your finger** se piquer le doigt.

pride *noun* fierté F.

priest *noun* prêtre M.

primary school *noun* école F primaire.

primary (school) teacher *noun* instituteur M, institutrice F.

prime minister *noun* Premier ministre M.

primrose *noun* primevère F.

prince *noun* prince M; **Prince Charles** le prince Charles.

princess *noun* princesse F; **Princess Anne** la princesse Anne.

principal *noun* (*of a college*) directeur M, directrice F. *adjective* (*main*) principal (M *plural* principaux).

principle *noun* principe M; **on principle** par principe; **that's true in principle** cela est vrai en principe.

print *noun* **1** (*letters*) caractères M *plural*; **in small print** en petits caractères; **2** (*a photo*) tirage M; **a colour print** un tirage en couleur.

printer *noun* imprimante F.

print-out *noun* copie F papier.

prison *noun* prison F; **in prison** en prison.

prisoner *noun* prisonnier M, prisonnière F.

private *adjective* **1** privé; **a private school** une école privée; **'private property'** 'propriété privée'; **2** particulier (F particulière) (*lesson*); **to have private lessons** prendre des cours particuliers.

privately *adverb* en privé.

prize *noun* prix M; **to win a prize** gagner un prix.

prize-giving *noun* distribution F des prix.

prizewinner *noun* gagnant M, gagnante F.

probable *adjective* probable.

probably *adverb* probablement.

problem *noun* problème M; **it's a serious problem** c'est un grave problème; **no problem!** pas de problème!

process *noun* **1** processus M; **2 to be in the process of doing** être en train de faire.

produce *noun* (*food*) produits M *plural*. *verb* produire [26]; **I produced my passport** j'ai produit mon passeport; **it produces a lot of heat** ça produit beaucoup de chaleur.

producer *noun* (*of a film or programme*) metteur M en scène.

product *noun* produit M.

production *noun* **1** (*of a film or*

opera) production F; **2** (*of a play*) mise F en scène; **a new production of Hamlet** une nouvelle mise en scène de Hamlet; **3** (*by a factory*) production F.

profession *noun* profession F.

professional *noun* professionnel M, professionnelle F; **he's a professional** c'est un professionnel. *adjective* professionnel (F professionnelle); **she's a professional singer** c'est une chanteuse professionnelle.

professor *noun* professeur M.

profile *noun* profil M.

profit *noun* bénéfice M.

profitable *adjective* rentable.

program *noun* **a computer program** un programme informatique.

programme *noun* **1** (*for a play or an event*) programme M; **2** (*on TV or radio*) émission F.

progress *noun* **1** progrès M; **to make progress** faire des progrès; **2 to be in progress** être en cours.

project *noun* **1** (*at school*) dossier M; **2** (*a plan*) projet M; **a project to build a bridge** un projet pour construire un pont.

projector *noun* projecteur M.

promise *noun* promesse F; **to make a promise** faire une promesse; **to break a promise** manquer à sa promesse; **it's a promise!** c'est promis! *verb* **to promise to do** promettre [11] de faire; **I've promised to be**

home by ten j'ai promis de rentrer avant dix heures.

promote *verb* **to be promoted** être [6] promu.

promotion *noun* promotion F.

promptly *adjective* **1** (*at once*) immédiatement; **he promptly fell off again** il est retombé immédiatement; **2** (*quickly*) rapidement; **please reply promptly** répondez rapidement s'il vous plaît; **3 promptly at five o'clock** à cinq heures précises.

pronoun *noun* pronom M.

pronounce *verb* prononcer [61]; **it's hard to pronounce** c'est difficile à prononcer.

pronunciation *noun* prononciation F.

proof *noun* preuve F; **there's no proof that ...** rien ne prouve que ...

propaganda *noun* propagande F.

propeller *noun* hélice F.

proper *adjective* **1** (*real, genuine*) vrai; **a proper doctor** un vrai médecin; **I need a proper meal** j'ai besoin d'un vrai repas; **2** (*correct*) bon (F bonne); **the proper answer** la bonne réponse; **the proper tool** le bon outil; **in its proper place** à sa place.

properly *adverb* comme il faut; **hold it properly** tiens-le comme il faut; **is it properly wrapped?** est-ce que c'est emballé comme il faut?

property *noun* (*your belongings*) affaires F *plural*; propriété F; **'private property'** 'propriété privée'.

proposal *noun* proposition F.

propose *verb* **1** (*suggest*) proposer [1]; **2** (*marriage*) **he proposed to her** il l'a demandée en mariage.

protect *verb* protéger [15].

protection *noun* protection F.

protein *noun* protéine F.

protest *noun* protestation F; **in spite of their protests** malgré leurs protestations.
verb **1** (*to grumble*) protester [1]; **he protested, but …** il a protesté, mais …; **2** (*demonstrate*) manifester [1].

Protestant *noun, adjective* protestant M, protestante F.

protester *noun* manifestant M, manifestante F.

protest march *noun* manifestation F.

proud *adjective* fier (F fière).

prove *verb* prouver [1].

proverb *noun* proverbe M.

provide *verb* fournir [2].

provided *conjunction* à condition que; **provided you do it now** à condition que tu le fasses maintenant (*note that a verb in the subjunctive is needed*).

prune *noun* pruneau M (*plural* pruneaux).

psychiatrist *noun* psychiatre M & F; **he's a psychiatrist** il est psychiatre.

psychological *adjective* psychologique.

psychologist *noun* psychologue M & F; **she's a psychologist** elle est psychologue.

psychology *noun* psychologie F.

PTO TSVP (= *tournez s'il vous plaît*).

pub *noun* pub M.

public *noun* **the public** le public; **in public** en public.
adjective **1** public (F publique); **2** **the public library** la bibliothèque municipale.

public address system *noun* sonorisation F.

public holiday *noun* jour M férié; **January 1 is a public holiday** le premier janvier est férié.

publicity *noun* publicité F.

public school *noun* école F privée.

public transport *noun* transports M *plural* en commun.

publish *verb* publier [1].

publisher *noun* éditeur M.

pudding *noun* (*dessert*) dessert M; **for pudding we've got strawberries** comme dessert nous avons des fraises.

puddle *noun* flaque F.

puff *noun* (*of smoke*) bouffée F.

puff pastry *noun* pâte feuilletée F.

pull *verb* tirer [1]; **pull hard!** tire fort!; **to pull a rope** tirer sur une corde; **he pulled a letter out of his pocket** il a tiré une lettre de sa poche; ★ **you're pulling my leg!** tu me fais marcher.
● **to pull down** baisser [1] (*a blind*).
● **to pull in** (*at the roadside*) s'arrêter [1].

pullover *noun* pull-over M.

pump *noun* pompe F; **a bicycle pump** une pompe à vélo.
verb 1 pomper [1]; **they were pumping the water out of the cellar** ils pompaient l'eau de la cave.
●**to pump up** gonfler [1] (*a tyre*).

pumpkin *noun* citrouille F.

punch *noun* 1 (*in boxing*) coup M de poing; 2 (*drink*) punch M.
verb 1 **to punch somebody** donner [1] un coup de poing à quelqu'un; **he punched me** il m'a donné un coup de poing; 2 composter [1] (*a ticket*).

punctual *adjective* ponctuel (F ponctuelle).

punctuation *noun* ponctuation F.

punctuation mark *noun* signe M de ponctuation.

puncture *noun* crevaison F; **we had a puncture on the way** nous avons crevé en route.

punish *verb* punir [2].

punishment *noun* punition F.

pupil *noun* élève M & F.

puppet *noun* marionnette F.

puppy *noun* chiot M; **a labrador puppy** un chiot labrador.

pure *adjective* pur.

purple *adjective* violet (F violette).

purpose *noun* 1 but M; **what was the purpose of her call?** quel était le but de son appel?; 2 **on purpose** exprès; **she did it on purpose** elle l'a fait exprès; **he closed the door on purpose** il a fait exprès de fermer la porte.

purr *verb* ronronner [1].

purse *noun* porte-monnaie M (*plural* porte-monnaie).

push *noun* **to give something a push** pousser [1] quelque chose.
verb 1 pousser [1]; **he pushed me** il m'a poussé; 2 (*to press*) appuyer [41] sur (*a bell or button*); 3 **to push somebody to do** pousser [1] quelqu'un à faire; **his teacher is pushing him to sit the exam** son prof le pousse à passer l'examen.
●**to push something away** repousser [1] quelque chose; **she pushed her plate away** elle a repoussé son assiette.

pushchair *noun* poussette F.

put *verb* 1 mettre [11]; **you can put the cream in the fridge** tu peux mettre la crème au frigo; **where did you put my bag?** où est-ce que tu as mis mon sac?; **put your suitcase here** mets ta valise ici; 2 (*write*) écrire [38]; **put your address here** écris ton adresse ici.
●**to put away** ranger [52]; **I'll put the shopping away** je vais ranger les courses.
●**to put back** 1 remettre [11]; **I put it back in the drawer** je l'ai remis dans le tiroir; 2 (*postpone*) remettre [11]; **the meeting has been put back until Thursday** la réunion a été remise à jeudi.
●**to put down** poser [1]; **she put the vase down on the table** elle a posé le vase sur la table.
●**to put off** 1 (*postpone*) remettre [11]; **he's put off my lesson till Thursday** il a remis ma leçon à jeudi; 2 (*turn off*) éteindre [60] (*a light or TV*); **don't forget to put off**

the lights n'oublie pas d'éteindre la lumière; **3 to put somebody off something** dégoûter [1] quelqu'un de quelque chose; **it really put me off Chinese food!** ça m'a vraiment dégoûté de la nourriture chinoise! **4 to be put off** (*doing something*) se décourager [52]; **don't be put off!** ne te décourage pas!

● **to put on 1** mettre [11] (*clothing, make-up, CD*); **I'll just put my shoes on** je vais juste mettre mes chaussures; **he's put on Oasis** il a mis Oasis; **2** (*switch on*) allumer [1] (*a light or heating*); **could you put the lamp on?** est-ce que tu peux allumer la lampe?; **3** monter [1] (*a play*); **we're putting on a French play** nous sommes en train de monter une pièce française.

● **to put out 1** (*put outside*) sortir [72]; **have you put the rubbish out?** as-tu sorti les ordures?; **2** éteindre [60] (*a fire, light, or cigarette*); **I've put the lights out** j'ai éteint la lumière; **3 to put out your hand** tendre [3] la main.

● **to put up 1** lever [50] (*your hand*); **I put up my hand** j'ai levé la main; **2** mettre [11] (*picture*); **I've put up some photos in my room** j'ai mis des photos dans ma chambre; **3** afficher [1] (*a notice*); **4** augmenter [1] (*the price*); **they've put up the price of the tickets** ils ont augmenté le prix des billets; **5** (*for the night*) héberger [52]; **can you put me up on Friday?** est-ce que tu peux m'héberger vendredi?

● **to put up with something** supporter [1]; **I don't know how she puts up with it** je ne sais pas comment elle le supporte.

puzzle *noun* (*jigsaw*) puzzle M.

puzzled *adjective* perplexe.

pyjamas *plural noun* pyjama M singular; **a pair of pyjamas** un pyjama; **where are my pyjamas?** où est mon pyjama?

Pyrenees *noun* les Pyrénées F *plural*; **in the Pyrenees** dans les Pyrénées.

Q q

qualification *noun* **1** diplôme M (*certificate, exam, degree*); **2 qualifications** qualifications F *plural*; **vocational qualifications** les qualifications professionnelles.

qualify *verb* **1** (*to be eligible*) avoir [5] droit à; **we don't qualify for a reduction** nous n'avons pas droit à une réduction; **2** (*in sport*) se qualifier [1].

qualified *adjective* **1** qualifié; **she's a qualified ski instructor** c'est une monitrice de ski qualifiée; **2** (*having a degree or a diploma*) diplômé; **a qualified architect** un architecte diplômé.

quality *noun* qualité F; **good quality vegetables** des légumes de bonne qualité.

quantity *noun* quantité F.

quarantine *noun* quarantaine F.

quarrel *noun* dispute F; **to have a quarrel** se disputer [1]. *verb* se disputer [1]; **they're always**

quarrelling ils sont tout le temps en train de se disputer.

quarter *noun* 1 quart M; **a quarter of the class** le quart de la classe; **three quarters of the class** les trois quarts de la classe; 2 **a quarter past ten** dix heures et quart; **a quarter to ten** dix heures moins le quart; **a quarter of an hour** un quart d'heure; **three quarters of an hour** trois quarts d'heure; **an hour and a quarter** une heure et quart.

quartet *noun* quatuor M; **a jazz quartet** un quatuor de jazz.

quay *noun* quai M.

queen *noun* reine F; **Queen Elizabeth** la reine Elizabeth; **the Queen Mother** la reine mère.

query *noun* question F; **are there any queries?** y a-t-il des questions?

question *noun* question F; **to ask a question** poser une question; **I asked her a question** je lui ai posé une question; **it's a question of time** c'est une question de temps; **it's out of the question!** c'est hors de question!
verb interroger [52].

question mark *noun* point M d'interrogation.

questionnaire *noun* questionnaire M; **to fill in a questionnaire** remplir un questionnaire.

queue *noun* 1 (*of people*) queue F; **to stand in a queue** faire la queue; 2 (*of cars*) file F.
verb faire [10] la queue; **we were queueing for check-in** nous

faisions la queue pour l'enregistrement.

quick *adjective* 1 rapide; **a quick lunch** un déjeuner rapide; **it's quicker on the motorway** c'est plus rapide par l'autoroute; **to have a quick look at something** jeter un coup d'œil rapide à quelque chose; 2 **quick! there's the bus!** vite! voilà le bus!; **be quick!** dépêche-toi!

quickly *adverb* vite; **I'll just quickly phone my mother** je vais vite appeler ma mère.

quiet *adjective* 1 (*silent*) silencieux (F silencieuse); **the children are very quiet** les enfants sont très silencieux; 2 **to keep quiet** se taire [76]; **please keep quiet** taisez-vous, s'il vous plaît; 3 (*gentle*) doux (F douce); **some quiet music** de la musique douce; **in a quiet voice** à voix basse; 4 (*peaceful*) tranquille; **a quiet street** une rue tranquille; **a quiet day at home** une journée tranquille à la maison.

quietly *adverb* 1 (*to move*) sans bruit; **he got up quietly** il s'est levé sans bruit; 2 (*speak*) doucement; 3 (*read or play*) en silence.

quilt *noun* couette F.

quite *adverb* 1 assez; **it's quite cold outside** il fait assez froid dehors; **that's quite a good idea** c'est une assez bonne idée; **he sings quite well** il chante assez bien; **quite often** assez souvent; 2 **not quite** pas tout à fait; **the meat's not quite cooked** la viande n'est pas tout à fait cuite; 3 **quite a lot of** pas mal de; **we've got quite a lot of friends here** nous avons pas mal d'amis ici;

quite a few people pas mal de gens.

quiz *noun* quiz M.

quotation *noun* (*from a book*) citation F.

quotation marks *plural noun* guillemets M *plural*; **in quotation marks** entre guillemets.

quote *noun* 1 (*from a book*) citation F; 2 (*estimate*) devis M; 3 **in quotes** entre guillemets. *verb* citer [1].

R r

rabbi *noun* rabbin M.

rabbit *noun* lapin M.

rabbit hutch *noun* clapier M.

rabies *noun* rage F.

race *noun* 1 (*a sports event*) course F; **a cycle race** une course cycliste; **to have a race** faire la course; 2 (*an ethnic group*) race F.

racer *noun* (*bike*) vélo M de course.

racetrack *noun* 1 (*for horses*) champ M de course; 2 (*for cars*) circuit M; 3 (*for cycles*) piste F.

racing *noun* courses F *plural*.

racing car *noun* voiture F de course.

racing driver *noun* pilote M de course.

racial *adjective* racial (M *plural* raciaux); **racial discrimination** la discrimination raciale.

racism *noun* racisme M.

racist *noun, adjective* raciste M & F.

rack *noun* (*for luggage*) porte-bagages M.

racket *noun* 1 (*for tennis*) raquette F; **here's your tennis racket** voici ta raquette de tennis; 2 (*noise*) vacarme M.

radiation *noun* radiation F.

radiator *noun* radiateur M.

radio *noun* radio F; **to listen to the radio** écouter la radio; **to hear something on the radio** entendre quelque chose à la radio.

radioactive *adjective* radioactif (F radioactive).

radio-controlled *adjective* téléguidé.

radio station *noun* station F de radio.

radish *noun* radis M.

rag *noun* chiffon M.

rage *noun* colère F; **she's in a rage** elle est furieuse; ★ **it's all the rage** ça fait fureur.

raid *noun* 1 hold-up M; 2 (*by the police*) rafle F.

rail *noun* 1 (*the railway*) **to go by rail** prendre le train; 2 (*on a balcony or bridge*) balustrade F; 3 (*on stairs*) rampe F; 4 (*for a train*) rail M.

rail strike *noun* grève F des cheminots.

railing(s) (*plural*) *noun* grille F.

railway noun **1** (the system) chemin M de fer; **the railways** les chemins de fer; **2 a railway line** une ligne de chemin de fer (from one place to another); **3 on the railway line** sur la voie ferée (the rails).

railway carriage noun wagon M.

railway station noun gare F; **opposite the railway station** en face de la gare.

rain noun pluie F; **in the rain** sous la pluie.
verb pleuvoir [63]; **it's raining** il pleut; **it's going to rain** il va pleuvoir.

rainbow noun arc-en-ciel M (plural arcs-en-ciel).

raincoat noun imperméable M.

raindrop noun goutte F de pluie.

rainy adjective pluvieux (F pluvieuse).

raise verb **1** (lift up) lever [50]; **she raised her head** elle a levé la tête; **2** (increase) augmenter [1] (a price or a salary); **3 to raise money for something** collecter [1] des fonds pour quelque chose; **4 to raise the alarm** donner [1] l'alarme; **5 to raise somebody's spirits** remonter [1] le moral à quelqu'un.

raisin noun raisin M sec.

rake noun rateau M (plural rateaux).

rally noun **1** (a meeting) rassemblement M; **2** (for sport) rallye M; **3** (in tennis) échange M.

rambler noun randonneur M, randonneuse F.

rambling noun randonnée F.

ramp noun (for a wheelchair, for example) rampe F.

ranch noun ranch M.

range noun **1** (a choice) gamme F; **we offer a range of sports** nous vous proposons une gamme de sports; **in a wide range of colours** dans un grand choix de coloris; **a top-of-the-range computer** un ordinateur haut de gamme; **2** (of mountains) chaîne F.

rap noun rap M (music).

rape noun viol M.
verb violer [1].

rare adjective **1** rare; **a rare bird** un oiseau rare; **2** saignant (a steak); **medium-rare** à point.

rarely adverb rarement.

rash noun rougeurs F plural; **I've got a rash on my arms** j'ai des rougeurs sur les bras.
adjective irréfléchi; **a rash decision** une décision irréfléchie.

raspberry noun framboise F; **raspberry jam** la confiture de framboises; **a raspberry tart** une tarte aux framboises.

rat noun rat M.

rate noun **1** (a charge) tarif M; **what are the rates for children?** quels sont les tarifs pour les enfants?; **reduced rates** les tarifs réduits; **2** (a level) taux M; **a high cancellation rate** un taux élevé d'annulation; **3 at any rate** en tout cas.

rather adverb **1** plutôt; **I'm rather**

busy je suis plutôt occupé;
2 rather than plutôt que; **in
summer rather than winter** en été
plutôt qu'en hiver; **3 I'd rather
wait** je préfère attendre; **they'd
rather come on Thursday** ils
préfèrent venir jeudi; **4 rather a lot
of** pas mal de; **I've got rather a lot
of shopping to do** j'ai pas mal de
courses à faire.

rave *noun* rave M (*a party*).

raw *adjective* cru.

razor *noun* rasoir M.

razor blade *noun* lame F de rasoir.

RE *noun* éducation religieuse F.

reach *noun* portée F; **out of reach**
hors de portée; **within reach** (*of
your hand*) à portée de main; **within
easy reach of the sea** à proximité
de la mer.
verb **1** arriver [1] à; **when you reach
the church** quand vous arrivez à
l'église; **to reach a decision** arriver
à une décision; **2 to reach the final**
arriver [1] à la finale.

react *verb* réagir [2].

reaction *noun* réaction F.

read *verb* lire [51]; **what are you
reading at the moment?** qu'est-ce
que tu lis en ce moment? **I'm reading
a detective novel** je lis un roman
policier; **he read out the list** il a lu la
liste à haute voix.

reading *noun* lecture F; **I don't
much like reading** je n'aime pas
beaucoup la lecture; **some easy
reading for the beach** de la lecture
facile pour la plage.

ready *adjective* prêt; **supper's not

ready yet le dîner n'est pas encore
prêt; **are you ready to leave?** est-ce
que tu es prêt à partir?; **to get ready**
se préparer [1]; **I'm getting ready to
go out** je me prépare pour sortir; **I
was getting ready for bed** je me
préparais pour me coucher; **I'll get
your room ready** je vais préparer ta
chambre.

real *adjective* vrai; **it's a real
diamond** c'est un vrai diamant; **he's
a real bore** c'est un vrai casse-pieds
is that his real name? est-ce que
c'est son vrai nom?; **her real father is
dead** son vrai père est mort.

realistic *adjective* réaliste.

reality *noun* réalité F.

realize *verb* se rendre [3] compte; **I
hadn't realized** je ne m'en étais pas
rendu compte; **I didn't realize he
was French** je ne me suis pas rendu
compte qu'il était français; **do you
realize what time it is?** tu te rends
compte de l'heure qu'il est?

really *adverb* vraiment; **not really**
pas vraiment; **is it really midnight?**
est-il vraiment minuit?; **the film was
really good** le film était vraiment
très bon; **really?** c'est vrai?

rear *noun* arrière M.
adjective arrière; **the rear door** la
porte arrière.

reason *noun* raison F; **the reason
for the delay** la raison du retard; **the
reason why I phoned** la raison pour
laquelle j'ai appelé.

reasonable *adjective* raisonnable.

reassure *verb* rassurer [1].

reassuring *adjective* rassurant.

rebuild *verb* reconstruire [26].

receipt *noun* reçu M.

receive *verb* recevoir [66].

receiver *noun* combiné M; **to pick up the receiver** décrocher [1].

recent *adjective* récent.

recently *adverb* récemment.

reception *noun* 1 réception F; **he's waiting at reception** il attend à la réception; **a big wedding reception** une grande réception de mariage; 2 **to get a good reception** avoir un bon accueil.

receptionist *noun* réceptionniste M & F.

recipe *noun* recette F; **can I have the recipe for your salad?** est-ce que je peux prendre la recette de ta salade?

reckon *verb* penser [1]; **I reckon it's a good idea** je pense que c'est une bonne idée.

recognize *verb* reconnaître [27].

recommend *verb* conseiller [1]; **can you recommend a dentist?** est-ce que vous pouvez me conseiller un dentiste?; **I recommend the fish soup** je vous conseille la soupe de poisson.

record *noun* 1 record M; **it's a world record** c'est le record mondial; **record sales for the CD** des ventes record pour le CD; **the hottest summer on record** l'été le plus chaud qu'on ait jamais enregistré; 2 **to keep a record of something** noter quelque chose; 3 (*music*) disque M; **a Miles Davis record** un disque de Miles Davis; 4 (*office files*) dossier M; **I'll just check your records** je vais juste vérifier votre dossier. *verb* (*on tape or CD*) enregistrer [1]; **they're recording a new album** ils sont en train d'enregistrer un nouvel album.

recorder *noun* 1 flûte F à bec; **to play the recorder** jouer de la flûte à bec; 2 **a cassette recorder** un magnétophone à cassettes; **a video recorder** un magnétoscope.

recording *noun* enregistrement M.

record player *noun* tourne-disque M.

recover *verb* se remettre [11]; **she's recovered now** elle s'est maintenant remise.

recovery *noun* (*from an illness*) rétablissement M.

recovery vehicle *noun* camion M de dépannage.

rectangle *noun* rectangle M.

rectangular *adjective* rectangulaire.

recycle *verb* recycler [1].

red *adjective* 1 rouge; **a red shirt** une chemise rouge; **a bright red car** une voiture rouge vif; **to go red** rougir [2]; 2 roux (F rousse) (*hair*); **to have red hair** avoir les cheveux roux.

Red Cross *noun* **the Red Cross** la Croix-Rouge.

redcurrant *noun* groseille F;

redcurrant jelly la gelée de groseilles.

redecorate verb refaire [10]; **they've redecorated the kitchen** ils ont refait la cuisine.

redo verb refaire [10].

reduce verb réduire [68]; **they've reduced the price** ils ont réduit le prix; **to reduce speed** ralentir [2].

reduction noun réduction F.

redundant adjective **to be made redundant** être licencié.

reel noun (of cotton) bobine F.

referee noun (in sport) arbitre M.

reference noun références F plural (for a job); **she gave me a good reference** elle m'a fourni de bonnes références.

reference book noun ouvrage M de référence.

refill noun recharge F.

reflect verb refléter [24].

reflection noun **1** (in a mirror) image F; **2** (thought) réflexion F; **on reflection** à la réflexion.

reflexive adjective **a reflexive verb** un verbe réfléchi.

refreshing adjective rafraîchissant.

refrigerator noun réfrigérateur M.

refugee noun refugié M, refugiée F.

refund noun remboursement M. verb rembourser [1].

refusal noun refus M.

refuse noun (rubbish) ordures F plural. verb refuser [1]; **I refused** j'ai refusé; **he refuses to help** il refuse de nous aider.

regards plural noun amitiés F plural; **'regards to your parents'** 'mes amitiés à vos parents'; **Nat sends his regards** tu as le bonjour de Nat.

reggae noun reggae M.

region noun région F.

regional adjective régional (M plural régionaux).

register noun (in school) cahier M des absences. verb s'inscrire [38].

registered letter noun lettre F recommandée.

registration number noun numéro M d'immatriculation (of a vehicle).

regret verb regretter [1].

regular adjective régulier (F régulière); **regular visits** des visites régulières.

regularly adverb régulièrement.

regulation noun règlement M.

rehearsal noun répétition F.

rehearse verb répéter [24].

reheat verb réchauffer [1].

rein noun rêne F.

reject verb rejeter [48].

related adjective apparenté; **we're not related** nous ne sommes pas apparentés.

relation *noun* **my relations** ma famille; **there were just relations and close friends** il n'y avait que la famille et des amis proches; **she's got relations in France** elle a de la famille en France.

relationship *noun* relations F *plural*; **we have a good relationship** nous avons de bonnes relations.

relative *noun* membre M de la famille; **there were a few relatives at the funeral** il y avait quelques membres de la famille à l'enterrement; **all my relatives** toute ma famille.

relatively *adverb* relativement.

relax *verb* se détendre [3]; **I'm going to relax and watch telly tonight** je vais me détendre en regardant la télé ce soir.

relaxed *adjective* détendu.

relaxing *adjective* reposant.

relay race *noun* course F de relais.

release *noun* **1** nouveauté F; **this week's new releases** les nouveautés de la semaine; **2** (*of a prisoner or hostage*) libération F. *verb* **1** sortir [72] (*a record or a video*); **2** libérer [24] (*a person*).

relevant *adjective* pertinent.

reliable *adjective* fiable.

relief *noun* soulagement M; **what a relief!** quel soulagement!

relieve *verb* soulager [52] (*pain*).

relieved *adjective* soulagé; **I was relieved to hear you'd arrived** j'ai été soulagé d'apprendre que tu étais arrivé.

religion *noun* religion F.

religious *adjective* **1** croyant (*a person*); **Jane's not religious** Jane n'est pas croyante; **2** religieux (F religieuse) (*art or music, for example*).

rely *verb* **to rely on somebody** compter [1] sur quelqu'un; **I'm relying on you for Saturday** je compte sur toi pour samedi.

remain *verb* rester [1].

remains *plural noun* restes M *plural*; **the remains of the chicken** les restes du poulet; **the remains of a castle** les restes d'un château.

remark *noun* remarque F; **to make remarks about** faire des remarques sur.

remarkable *adjective* remarquable.

remarkably *adverb* remarquablement.

remember *verb* **1** se souvenir [81]; **I don't remember** je ne me souviens plus; **2 to remember something** se souvenir [81] de quelque chose; **I can't remember the number** je ne me souviens pas du numéro; **3 to remember to do** ne pas oublier [1] de faire; **remember to shut the door** n'oublie pas de fermer la porte; **I remembered to bring the CDs** je n'ai pas oublié d'apporter les CD.

remind *verb* **1** rappeler [18]; **to remind somebody to do** rappeler à quelqu'un de faire; **remind your mother to pick me up** rappelle à ta mère de venir me chercher; **2 it reminds me of Paris** ça me fait penser [1] à Paris; **he reminds me of Frank** il me fait penser à Frank; **oh, that reminds me…** oh, ça me fait penser…

remote *adjective* isolé.

remote control *noun* télécommande F.

remove *verb* enlever [50]; **he removed his jacket** il a enlevé sa veste; **the chairs had all been removed** quelqu'un avait enlevé toutes les chaises.

renew *verb* renouveler [18] (*a passport or licence*).

rent *noun* loyer M.
verb louer [1]; **Simon's rented a flat** Simon a loué un appartement.

rental *noun* location F.

reorganize *verb* réorganiser [1].

repair *noun* réparation F.
verb réparer [1]; **to get something repaired** faire [10] réparer quelque chose; **we've had the television repaired** nous avons fait réparer la télévision.

repay *verb* rembourser [1]; **he repaid me the money he owed me** il m'a remboursé l'argent qu'il me devait.

repeat *noun* reprise F (*of a programme*).
verb répéter [24].

repeatedly *adverb* à plusieurs reprises.

repertoire *noun* répertoire M.

repetitive *adjective* répétitif (F répétitive).

replace *verb* remplacer [61].

reply *noun* réponse F; **I didn't get a reply to my letter** je n'ai pas reçu de réponse à ma lettre; **there's no reply** ça ne répond pas (*on the telephone*).
verb répondre [3]; **I still haven't replied to the letter** je n'ai toujours pas répondu à la lettre.

report *noun* **1** (*of an event*) compte rendu M; **2** (*school report*) bulletin M scolaire.
verb **1** signaler [1] (*a problem or accident*); **we've reported the theft** nous avons signalé le vol; **2** se présenter [1]; **I had to report to reception** je devais me présenter à la réception.

reporter *noun* journaliste M & F.

represent *verb* représenter [1].

representative *noun* représentant M, représentante F.

reproach *noun* reproche M.
verb reprocher [1].

reproduction *noun* reproduction F.

reptile *noun* reptile M.

republic *noun* république F.

reputation *noun* réputation F; **a good reputation** une bonne réputation; **she has a reputation for honesty** elle a la réputation d'être honnête.

request *noun* demande F; **on request** sur demande.
verb demander [1].

rescue *noun* secours M; **to come to somebody's rescue** venir au secours de quelqu'un.

verb sauver [1]; **they rescued the dog** ils ont sauvé le chien.

rescue party *noun* équipe F de secours.

rescue worker *noun* secouriste M & F.

research *noun* recherche F; **for research into Aids** pour la recherche sur le Sida; **to do research** faire des recherches. *verb* **to research into** faire [10] des recherches sur; **a well-researched programme** un programme bien documenté.

resemblance *noun* ressemblance F.

reservation *noun* (*a booking*) réservation F; **to make a reservation** faire une réservation.

reserve *noun* **1** réserve F; **we have some in reserve** nous en avons en réserve; **2 a nature reserve** une réserve naturelle; **3** (*for a match*) remplaçant M, remplaçante F. *verb* réserver [1]; **this table is reserved** cette table est réservée.

reservoir *noun* réservoir M.

resident *noun* résident M, résidente F.

residential *adjective* résidentiel (F résidentielle); **a residential area** un quartier résidentiel.

resign *verb* démissionner [1].

resignation *noun* (*from a post*) démission F.

resist *verb* résister [1] à (*an offer or temptation*); **I can't resist!** je ne peux pas résister!

resit *verb* repasser [1] (*an exam*).

resort *noun* **1** (*for holidays*) **a holiday resort** un lieu de villégiature; **a ski resort** une station de ski; **a seaside resort** une station balnéaire; **2 as a last resort** en dernier recours.

respect *noun* respect M. *verb* respecter [1].

respectable *adjective* respectable.

respectful *adjective* respectueux (F respectueuse).

responsibility *noun* responsabilité F.

responsible *adjective* **1** (*to blame*) responsable; **he's responsible for the delay** il est responsable du retard; **2** (*in charge*) responsable; **I'm responsible for booking the rooms** je suis responsable de la réservation des chambres; **3** (*reliable*) sérieux (F sérieuse); **he's not very responsible** il n'est pas très sérieux.

rest *noun* **1 the rest** le reste; **the rest of the day** le reste du jour; **the rest of the bread** le reste du pain; **2** (*the others*) les autres; **the rest have gone home** les autres sont rentrés; **3** repos M; **ten days' complete rest** dix jours de repos total; **to have a rest** se reposer [1]; **4** (*a short break*) pause F; **to stop for a rest** faire une pause. *verb* (*have a rest*) se reposer [1].

restaurant *noun* restaurant M.

restful *adjective* reposant.

restless *adjective* nerveux (F nerveuse).

restrain *verb* retenir [77].

restrict *verb* limiter [1].

restriction *noun* limitation F.

result *noun* **1** résultat M; **the exam results** les résultats des examens; **2 as a result** par conséquent; **as a result we missed the ferry** par conséquent nous avons raté le ferry.

retire *verb* (*from work*) prendre [64] sa retraite; **she retires in June** elle prend sa retraite en juin; **for retired people** pour les retraités.

retirement *noun* retraite F.

return *noun* **1** retour M; **the return journey** le voyage de retour; **by return of post** par retour de courrier; **2 in return** en échange; **in return for his help** en échange de son aide; ★ **many happy returns!** bon anniversaire! *verb* **1** (*come back*) revenir [81]; **he returned ten minutes later** il est revenu dix minutes plus tard; **2** (*get home*) rentrer [1]; **to return from holiday** rentrer de vacances; **I'll ask her to phone as soon as she returns** je lui demanderai de vous appeler dès qu'elle rentre; **3** (*to give back*) rendre [3]; **Gemma's never returned the video** Gemma n'a jamais rendu la vidéo.

return fare *noun* prix M d'un billet aller-retour.

return ticket *noun* billet M aller-retour.

reveal *verb* révéler [24].

reverse *verb* **1** (*in a car*) faire [10] marche arrière; **2 to reverse the charges** faire [10] un appel en PCV.

review *noun* (*of a book, play, or film*) critique F. *verb* faire [10] la critique de (*a play or concert*); **the film was well reviewed** le film a eu une bonne critique.

revise *verb* réviser [1]; **Tessa's busy revising for her exams** Tessa est en train de réviser pour ses examens.

revision *noun* révision F.

revive *verb* ranimer [1].

revolting *adjective* infect; **the sausages are revolting** les saucisses sont infectes.

revolution *noun* révolution F; **the Fench Revolution** la Révolution française.

revolving door *noun* porte F à tambour.

reward *noun* récompense F; **a £100 reward** cent livres de récompense. *verb* récompenser [1].

rewarding *adjective* enrichissant.

rewind *verb* rembobiner [1] (*a cassette or video*).

rhinoceros *noun* rhinocéros M.

rhubarb *noun* rhubarbe F.

rhyme *noun* rime F.

rhythm *noun* rythme M.

rib *noun* côte F.

ribbon *noun* ruban M.

rice *noun* riz M; **chicken and rice** du poulet au riz; **rice pudding** le riz au lait.

rich *adjective* riche; **we're not very rich** nous ne sommes pas très riches; **the rich and the poor** les riches et les pauvres.

rid *adjective* **to get rid of something** se débarrasser de quelque chose; **we got rid of the car** nous nous sommes débarrassés de la voiture.

riddle *noun* devinette F.

ride *noun* tour M; **to go for a ride (on a bike)** faire un tour à vélo; **to go for a ride (on a horse)** faire une promenade à cheval.
verb **1 to learn to ride a bike** apprendre [64] à faire du vélo; **can you ride a bike?** sais-tu faire [10] du vélo?; **2 to learn to ride (a horse)** apprendre [3] à monter à cheval; **I've never ridden a horse** je ne suis jamais monté à cheval.

rider *noun* **1** (*on a horse*) cavalier M, cavalière F; **2** (*on a bike*) cycliste M & F.

ridiculous *adjective* ridicule.

riding *noun* équitation F; **to go riding** faire [10] de l'équitation.

riding school *noun* école F d'équitation.

rifle *noun* fusil M.

right *noun* **1** (*not left*) droite F; **on the right** à droite; **on my right** à ma droite; **2** (*to do something*) droit M; **the right to strike** le droit de grève; **you have no right to say that** tu n'as pas le droit de dire ça.
adjective, adverb **1** (*not left*) droit; **my right hand** ma main droite; **2** (*correct*) bon (F bonne); **the right answer** la bonne réponse; **the right telephone number** le bon numéro de téléphone; **the right amount of** la bonne quantité de; **is this the right address?** est-ce que c'est la bonne adresse?; **3 to be right** (*a person*) avoir raison; **you see, I was right** tu vois, j'avais raison; **4 you were right to stay at home** tu as bien fait de rester chez toi; **he was right not to say anything** il a bien fait de ne rien dire; **5** (*moral*) bien; **it's not right to talk like that** ce n'est pas bien de parler comme ça.
adverb **1** (*direction*) à droite; **turn right at the lights** tournez à droite aux feux; **2** (*correctly*) comme il faut; **you're not doing it right** tu ne le fais pas comme il faut; **3** (*completely*) tout; **right at the bottom** tout au fond; **right at the beginning** tout au début; **right now** tout de suite; **right in the middle** en plein milieu; **4** (*okay*) bon; **right, let's go** bon, allons-y.

right-hand *adjective* **on the right-hand side** à droite.

right-handed *adjective* droitier (F droitière).

rind *noun* **1** (*on fruit*) peau F; **2** (*on cheese*) croûte F.

ring *noun* **1** (*on the phone*) **to give somebody a ring** appeler [18] quelqu'un; **2** (*for your finger*) bague F; **3** (*circle*) cercle M; **4 there was a ring at the door** on a sonné à la porte.
verb **1** (*a bell or phone*) sonner [1]; **the phone rang** le téléphone a sonné; **2** (*phone*) appeler [18]; **I'll ring you tomorrow** je t'appellerai demain; **could you ring for a taxi?** est-ce que tu peux appeler un taxi?
● **to ring back** rappeler [18]; **I'll ring**

you back later je te rappellerai tout
à l'heure.
● **to ring off** raccrocher [1].

ring road *noun* rocade F.

rinse *verb* rincer [61].

riot *noun* émeute F.

rioting *noun* émeutes F *plural*.

rip *verb* déchirer [1].

ripe *adjective* mûr; **are the tomatoes
ripe?** est-ce que les tomates sont
mûres?

rip-off *noun* **it's a rip-off!** c'est de
l'arnaque!

rise *noun* **1** hausse F; **a rise in
price** une hausse de prix; **2 a pay
rise** une augmentation.
verb **1** (*the sun*) se lever [50]; **when
the sun rose** quand le soleil s'est
levé; **2** (*prices*) augmenter [1].

risk *noun* risque F; **to take risks**
prendre des risques.
verb risquer [1]; **he risks losing his
job** il risque de perdre son emploi.

river *noun* **1** rivière F; **we
picnicked on the edge of a river**
nous avons pique-niqué au bord
d'une rivière; **2** fleuve M; **the
rivers of Europe** les fleuves de
l'Europe (*'fleuve' is only used for a
river which flows directly into the sea
like the Thames in Britain or the Seine
in France*).

Riviera *noun* **the French Riviera** la
Côte d'Azur.

road *noun* **1** route F; **the road to
London** la route de Londres; **2** (*in
a town*) rue F; **the butcher's is on
the other side of the road** la

boucherie est de l'autre côté de la
rue; **3 across the road** en face;
they live across the road from us
ils habitent en face de chez nous.

road accident *noun* accident M
de la route.

road map *noun* carte F routière.

roadside *noun* **by the roadside** au
bord de la route.

road sign *noun* panneau M de
signalisation (*plural* panneaux de
signalisation).

roadworks *plural noun* travaux M
plural.

roast *noun* rôti M.
adjective rôti; **roast potatoes** les
pommes de terre rôties; **roast beef**
le rôti de bœuf.

rob *verb* **1** voler [1] (*a person*);
2 dévaliser [1] (*a bank*).

robber *noun* voleur M, voleuse F.

robbery *noun* vol M; **a bank
robbery** un hold-up.

robot *noun* robot M.

rock *noun* **1** (*a big stone*) rocher M;
she was sitting on a rock elle était
assise sur un rocher; **2** (*the
material*) roche F; **3** (*music*) rock
M; **a rock band** un groupe de rock;
to dance rock and roll danser le
rock.

rock climbing *noun* escalade F; **to
go rock climbing** faire de
l'escalade.

rock star *noun* rock-star F.

rocket *noun* fusée F.

rocking horse *noun* cheval M à bascule.

rocky *adjective* rocailleux (F rocailleuse).

rod *noun* **a fishing rod** une canne à pêche.

role *noun* rôle M; **to play the role of** jouer le rôle de.

roll *noun* **1** rouleau M (*plural* rouleaux); **a roll of fabric** un rouleau de tissu; **a roll of sellotape™** un rouleau de scotch™; **a toilet roll** un rouleau de papier hygiénique; **2 a bread roll** un petit pain.
verb rouler [1].

roller *noun* rouleau M (*plural* rouleaux).

rollerblades *plural noun* rollers M *plural*.

rollercoaster *noun* montagnes russes F *plural* (*literally: Russian mountains*).

roller skates *plural noun* patins M *plural* à roulettes.

Roman Catholic *noun, adjective* catholique M & F.

romantic *adjective* romantique.

roof *noun* toit M.

roof rack *noun* galerie F.

room *noun* **1** pièce F; **she's in the other room** elle est dans l'autre pièce; **it's the biggest room in the house** c'est la pièce la plus grande de la maison; **a three-room flat** un appartement à trois pièces; **2** (*a bedroom*) chambre F; **Freda's in her room** Freda est dans sa chambre; **I**

tidied my room last night j'ai rangé ma chambre hier soir; **3** (*space*) place F; **enough room for two** assez de place pour deux; **very little room** très peu de place.

roommate *noun* camarade M & F de chambre.

root *noun* racine F.

rope *noun* corde F.

rose *noun* rose F.

rosebush *noun* rosier M.

rot *verb* pourrir [2].

rota *noun* tableau M de service.

rotten *adjective* pourri.

rough *adjective* **1** (*scratchy*) rugueux (F rugueuse); **2** (*vague*) approximatif (F approximative); **a rough idea** une idée approximative; **3** (*stormy*) agité; **a rough sea** une mer agitée; **in rough weather** par gros temps; **4** (*difficult*) **to have a rough time** passer par une période dificile; **5 to sleep rough** dormir à la dure.

roughly *adjective* (*approximately*) **roughly ten per cent** à peu près dix pour cent; **it takes roughly three hours** ça prend à peu près trois heures.

round *noun* **1** (*in a tournament*) manche F; **2** (*of cards*) partie F; **3 a round of drinks** une tournée; **it's my round** c'est ma tournée.
adjective rond; **a round table** une table ronde.
preposition **1** autour de; **round the city** autour de la ville; **round my arm** autour de mon bras; **they were sitting round the table** ils étaient

assis autour de la table; **2 to go round the shops** faire les magasins; **to go round a museum** visiter un musée; **it's just round the corner** c'est tout près.
adverb **1 to go round to somebody's house** aller chez quelqu'un; **we invited Sally round for lunch** nous avons invité Sally à déjeuner; **2 all the year round** toute l'année.

roundabout *noun* **1** (*for traffic*) rond-point M; **2** (*in a fairground*) manège M.

route *noun* **1** (*that you plan*) itinéraire M; **the best route is via Calais** le meilleur itinéraire est par Calais; **2 a bus route** un parcours de bus.

routine *noun* routine F.

row¹ *noun* **1** rang M; **in the front row** au premier rang; **in the back row** au dernier rang; **2** rangée F; **a row of books** une rangée de livres; **3 four times in a row** quatre fois de suite.

row² *verb* (*in a boat*) ramer [1]; **it's your turn to row** c'est à toi de ramer; **we rowed across the lake** nous avons traversé le lac à la rame.

row³ *noun* **1** (*a quarrel*) dispute F; **to have a row** se disputer; **they've had a row** ils se sont disputés; **I had a row with my parents** je me suis disputé avec mes parents; **2** (*noise*) vacarme M; **they were making a terrible row!** ils faisaient un vacarme pas possible!

rowing *noun* aviron M; **to go rowing** faire de l'aviron.

rowing boat *noun* barque F.

royal *adjective* royal (M *plural* royaux); **the royal family** la famille royale.

rub *verb* frotter [1]; **to rub your eyes** se frotter les yeux.
● **to rub something out** effacer [61] quelque chose.

rubber *noun* **1** (*an eraser*) gomme F; **2** (*material*) caoutchouc M; **rubber soles** des semelles en caoutchouc.

rubbish *noun* **1** (*for the bin*) ordures F *plural*; **2** (*nonsense*) bêtises F *plural*; **you're talking rubbish!** tu dis des bêtises! *adjective* nul (F nulle); **the film was rubbish** le film était nul; **they're a rubbish band** c'est un groupe nul.

rubbish bin *noun* poubelle F.

rucksack *noun* sac M à dos.

rude *adjective* **1** impoli; **that's rude** c'est impoli; **2 a rude joke** une plaisanterie grossière; **a rude word** un gros mot.

rug *noun* **1** tapis M; **2** (*a blanket*) couverture F.

rugby *noun* rugby M; **to play rugby** jouer au rugby; **a rugby match** un match de rugby.

ruin *noun* ruine F; **in ruins** en ruines.
verb **1** abîmer [1]; **you'll ruin your jacket** tu vas abîmer ta veste; **2** gâcher [1] (*day, holiday*); **it ruined my evening** ça m'a gâché la soirée.

rule *noun* **1** règle F; **the rules of the game** les règles du jeu; **2 the**

school rules le règlement de l'école; **3 as a rule** en général.

ruler *noun* règle F; **I've lost my ruler** j'ai perdu ma règle.

rum *noun* rhum F.

rumour *noun* rumeur F.

run *noun* **1 to go for a run** courir; **2** (*in cricket*) point M; **to score fifteen runs** marquer quinze points; **3 in the long run** à long terme.
verb **1** courir [29]; **I ran ten kilometres** j'ai couru dix kilomètres; **he ran across the pitch** il a traversé le terrain en courant; **Kitty ran for the bus** Kitty a couru pour attraper le bus; **2** (*organize*) organiser [1]; **who's running this concert?** qui est-ce qui organise ce concert?; **3** diriger [52] (*a business*); **he ran the firm for forty years** il a dirigé l'entreprise pendant quarante ans; **4** (*a train or bus*) circuler [1]; **the buses don't run on Sundays** les bus ne circulent pas le dimanche; **5 to run a bath** faire [10] couler un bain.
● **to run away** s'enfuir [44].
● **to run into** rentrer [1] dans; **the car ran into a lamp-post** la voiture est rentrée dans un réverbère.
● **to run out of something: we've run out of bread** il ne reste plus de pain; **I'm running out of money** je n'ai presque plus d'argent.
● **to run somebody over** écraser [1] quelqu'un; **you'll get run over!** tu vas te faire écraser!

runner *noun* coureur M, coureuse F.

runner-up *noun* second M, seconde F.

running *noun* (*for exercise*) course F.
adjective **1 running water** l'eau courante; **2 three days running** trois jours de suite; **six times running** six fois de suite.

runway *noun* piste F.

rush *noun* (*a hurry*) **to be in a rush** être pressé; **sorry, I'm in a rush** désolé, je suis pressé.
verb **1** (*hurry*) se dépêcher [50]; **I must rush!** il faut que je me dépêche!; **2** (*run*) se précipiter [1]; **she rushed into the street** elle s'est précipitée dans la rue; **3 Louise was rushed to hospital** on a emmené Louise d'urgence à l'hôpital.

rush hour *noun* heures F *plural* de pointe; **in the rush hour** aux heures de pointe.

Russia *noun* Russie F; **in Russia** en Russie.

Russian *noun* **1** (*a person*) Russe M & F; **2** (*the language*) russe M.
adjective russe.

rust *noun* rouille F.

rusty *adjective* rouillé.

rye *noun* seigle M.

S s

Sabbath *noun* **1** (*Jewish*) sabbat M; **2** (*Christian*) dimanche M.

sack *noun* **1** sac M; **2 to get the**

sack être mis à la porte.
verb **to sack somebody** mettre [11] quelqu'un à la porte.

sad *adjective* triste.

saddle *noun* selle F.

saddlebag *noun* sacoche F.

sadly *adverb* **1** tristement; **she looked at me sadly** elle m'a regardé tristement; **2** (*unfortunately*) malheureusement.

safe *adjective* **1** (*out of danger*) hors de danger; **to feel safe** se sentir en sécurité; **2** (*not dangerous*) pas dangereux (F pas dangereuse); **the path is safe** le sentier n'est pas dangereux; **it's not safe** c'est dangereux.

safety *noun* sécurité F.

safety belt *noun* ceinture F de sécurité.

safety pin *noun* épingle F de nourrice.

Sagittarius *noun* Sagittaire M; **Kylie's Sagittarius** Kylie est Sagittaire.

sail *noun* voile F.

sailing *noun* voile F; **to go sailing** faire de la voile; **she's does a lot of sailing** elle fait beaucoup de voile.

sailing boat *noun* voilier M.

sailor *noun* marin M.

saint *noun* saint M, sainte F.

sake *noun* **1 for your mother's sake** par égard pour ta mère; **2 for heaven's sake!** nom de Dieu!

salad *noun* salade F; **a tomato salad** une salade de tomates.

salad dressing *noun* vinaigrette F.

salami *noun* saucisson M.

salary *noun* salaire M.

sale *noun* **1** (*selling*) vente F; **the sale of the house** la vente de la maison; **'for sale'** 'à vendre'; **2 the sales** les soldes F *plural*; **I bought it in the sales** je l'ai acheté en solde.

sales assistant *noun* vendeur M, vendeuse F.

salesman *noun* représentant M; **he's a salesman** il est représentant.

saleswoman *noun* représentante F.

salmon *noun* saumon M.

salt *noun* sel M.

salty *adjective* salé.

Salvation Army *noun* armée F du Salut.

same *adjective* **1** même; **she said the same thing** elle a dit la même chose; **her birthday's the same day as mine** son anniversaire est le même jour que le mien; **at the same time** en même temps; **their car's the same as ours** ils ont la même voiture que nous; **2 the same** (*after verb*) pareil; **the two bikes are not the same** les deux vélos ne sont pas pareils; **it's not the same** ce n'est pas pareil.

sample *noun* échantillon M; **a free sample** un échantillon gratuit.

sand *noun* sable M.

sandal *noun* sandale F; **a pair of sandals** une paire de sandales.

sand castle *noun* château M de sable (*plural* châteaux de sable).

sandpaper *noun* papier M de verre.

sandwich *noun* sandwich M; **a ham sandwich** un sandwich au jambon.

sanitary towel *noun* serviette hygiénique F.

Santa Claus *noun* le père Noël.

sarcastic *adjective* sarcastique.

sardine *noun* sardine F.

satchel *noun* cartable M.

satellite *noun* satellite M.

satellite dish *noun* antenne parabolique F.

satellite television *noun* télévision F par satellite.

satisfactory *adjective* satisfaisant.

satisfied *adjective* satisfait.

satisfy *verb* satisfaire [10].

satisfying *adjective* **1** (*pleasing*) satisfaisant; **2 a satisfying meal** un repas consistant.

Saturday *noun* samedi M; **on Saturday** samedi; **I'm going out on Saturday** je sors samedi; **see you on Saturday!** à samedi!; **on Saturdays** le samedi; **the museum is closed on Saturdays** le musée est fermé le samedi; **every Saturday** tous les samedis; **last Saturday** samedi dernier; **next Saturday** samedi prochain; **to have a Saturday job** travailler le samedi.

sauce *noun* sauce F.

saucepan *noun* casserole F.

saucer *noun* soucoupe F.

sausage *noun* **1** saucisse F; **2** (*salami*) saucisson M.

save *verb* **1** (*rescue*) sauver [1]; **to save somebody's life** sauver la vie à quelqu'un; **the doctors saved his life** les médecins lui ont sauvé la vie; **2** mettre [11] de côté (*money, food*); **I've saved £60** j'ai mis soixante livres de côté; **3** (*avoid spending*) économiser [1]; **I walk to school to save money** je vais à l'école à pied pour économiser de l'argent; **4 to save time** gagner [1] du temps; **we'll take a taxi to save time** on va prendre un taxi pour gagner du temps; **5** (*on a computer*) sauvegarder [1].

● **to save up** mettre [11] de l'argent à côté; **I'm saving up to go to Spain** je mets de l'argent à côté pour aller en Espagne.

savings *plural noun* économies F *plural*; **I've spent all my savings** j'ai dépensé toutes mes économies.

savoury *adjective* salé; **I prefer savoury things to sweet things** j'aime mieux les choses salées que les choses sucrées.

saw *noun* scie F.

sawdust *noun* sciure F.

sax *noun* saxo M (*informal*); **to play the sax** jouer du saxo.

saxophone *noun* saxophone M; **to play the saxophone** jouer du saxophone.

say *verb* **1** dire [9]; **what did you say?** qu'est-ce que tu as dit?; **she says she's tired** elle dit qu'elle est fatiguée; **he said to wait here** il a dit d'attendre ici; **as they say** comme on dit; **that goes without saying** cela va sans dire; **2 to say something again** répéter [24] quelque chose.

saying *noun* dicton M; **as the saying goes** comme on dit.

scale *noun* **1** (*of a map or model*) échelle F; **large-scale** à grande échelle; **2** (*extent*) ampleur F; **the scale of the disaster** l'ampleur du désastre; **3** (*in music*) gamme F; **4** (*of a fish*) écaille F.

scales *noun* **1** balance F singular; **kitchen scales** une balance de cuisine; **2 bathroom scales** un pèse-personne M singular.

scallop *noun* coquille F Saint-Jacques.

scandal *noun* **1** scandale M; **2** (*gossip*) ragots M *plural*.

Scandinavia *noun* Scandinavie F.

Scandinavian *adjective* scandinave.

scar *noun* cicatrice F.

scarce *adjective* rare.

scare *noun* **1** panique F; **it caused a scare** cela a provoqué une panique; **2 a bomb scare** une alerte à la bombe.
verb **to scare somebody** faire [10] peur à quelqu'un; **you scared me!** tu m'as fait peur!

scarecrow *noun* épouvantail M.

scared *adjective* **to be scared** avoir [5] peur; **I'm scared!** j'ai peur; **to be scared of** avoir [5] peur de; **he's scared of dogs** il a peur des chiens;

I'm scared of falling j'ai peur de tomber.

scarf *noun* **1** (*silky*) foulard M; **2** (*long, warm*) écharpe F.

scary *adjective* effrayant.

scene *noun* **1** (*of an incident or a crime*) lieux M *plural*; **to be on the scene** être sur les lieux; **the scene of the crime** le lieu du crime; **2** (*world*) monde M; **on the music scene** dans le monde de la musique; **3 scenes of violence** des incidents violents; **4 to make a scene** faire une scène.

scenery *noun* **1** (*landscape*) paysage M; **2** (*theatrical*) décors M *plural*.

scent *noun* parfum M.

scented *adjective* parfumé.

schedule *noun* programme M.

scheduled flight *noun* vol régulier M.

scheme *noun* projet M.

scholarship *noun* bourse F.

school *noun* école F; **at school** à l'école; **to go to school** aller à l'école.

schoolbook *noun* livre scolaire M.

schoolboy *noun* écolier M.

schoolchildren *plural noun* écoliers M *plural*.

schoolfriend *noun* camarade M & F de classe.

schoolgirl *noun* écolière F.

science *noun* science F; **I like science** j'aime la science; **the**

science teacher le prof de sciences.

science fiction *noun* science-fiction F.

scientific *adjective* scientifique.

scientist *noun* scientifique M & F.

scissors *plural noun* ciseaux M *plural*; **a pair of scissors** une paire de ciseaux.

scoff *verb* (*eat*) bouffer [1] (*informal*).

scooter *noun* **1** (*motor scooter*) scooter M; **2** (*for a child*) trottinette F.

score *noun* score M; **the score was three two** le score était trois à deux. *verb* **1** marquer [1]; **Lenny scored a goal** Lenny a marqué un but; **I scored three points** j'ai marqué trois points; **2** (*keep score*) compter [1] les points.

Scorpio *noun* Scorpion M; **Jess is Scorpio** Jess est Scorpion.

Scot *noun* Écossais M, Écossaise F; **the Scots** les Écossais M *plural*.

Scotland *noun* Écosse F; **in Scotland** en Écosse; **to Scotland** en Écosse; **Pauline's from Scotland** Pauline est écossaise.

Scots *adjective* écossais; **a Scots accent** un accent écossais.

Scotsman *noun* Écossais M.

Scotswoman *noun* Écossaise F.

Scottish *adjective* écossais; **a Scottish accent** un accent écossais.

scout *noun* scout M.

scrambled eggs *plural noun* œufs brouillés M *plural*.

scrap *noun* **a scrap of paper** un bout de papier.

scrapbook *noun* album M.

scrape *verb* gratter [1].

scratch *noun* **1** (*on your skin*) égratignure F; **2** (*on a surface*) rayure F; ★ **to start from scratch** partir de zéro. *verb* (*scratch yourself*) se gratter [1]; **to scratch your head** se gratter la tête.

scream *noun* cri M. *verb* crier [1].

screen *noun* écran M; **on the screen** à l'écran.

screw *noun* vis F. *verb* visser [1].

screwdriver *noun* tournevis M.

scribble *verb* griffonner [1].

scrub *verb* récurer [1] (*a saucepan*); **to scrub your nails** se brosser [1] les ongles.

sculpture *noun* sculpture F.

sculptor *noun* sculpteur M; **Rebecca's a sculptor** Rebecca est sculpteur.

sea *noun* mer F.

seafood *noun* fruits M *plural* de mer; **I love seafood** j'adore les fruits de mer.

seagull *noun* mouette F.

seal *noun* (*animal*) phoque M. *verb* coller [1] (*envelope*).

seaman *noun* marin M.

search *verb* **1** fouiller [1]; **I've searched my desk but I can't find the letter** j'ai fouillé dans mon bureau mais je ne trouve pas la lettre; **2 to search for** chercher [1]; **I've been searching everywhere for the scissors** j'ai chercher les ciseaux partout.

seashell *noun* coquillage M.

seasick *adjective* **to be seasick** avoir le mal de mer.

seaside *noun* **at the seaside** au bord de la mer.

season *noun* saison F; **the rugby season** la saison de rugby; **strawberries are not in season at the moment** ce n'est pas la saison des fraises en ce moment; **off-season prices** des prix hors saison.

season ticket *noun* carte F d'abonnement.

seat *noun* **1** siège M; **the front seat** (*in a car*) le siège avant; **the back seat** le siège arrière; **take a seat** assieds-toi; **2** (*in a cinema, theatre, etc*) place F; **to book a seat** réserver une place; **can you keep my seat?** est-ce que tu peux garder ma place?

seatbelt *noun* ceinture F de sécurité.

seaweed *noun* algues F *plural*.

second *noun* seconde F; **can you wait a second?** est-ce que tu peux attendre une seconde? *adjective* **1** deuxième; **for the second time** pour la deuxième fois; **2 the second of July** le deux juillet.

secondary school *noun* **1** collège M (*up to the end of the equivalent of Year 10*); **2** lycée M (*for the equivalent of Years 11 to 13*).

secondhand *adjective, adverb* d'occasion; **a secondhand bike** un vélo d'occasion; **I bought it secondhand** je l'ai acheté d'occasion.

secondly *adverb* deuxièmement.

secret *noun* secret M; **to keep a secret** garder un secret; **in secret** en secret. *adjective* secret (F secrète); **a secret plan** un projet secret.

secretarial college *noun* école F de secrétariat.

secretary *noun* secrétaire M & F; **she's a secretary** elle est secrétaire; **the secretary's office** le secrétariat.

secretly *adverb* secrètement.

sect *noun* secte F.

section *noun* section F.

security *noun* sécurité F.

security guard *noun* vigile M; **he's a security guard** il est vigile.

see *verb* **1** voir [13]; **I saw Lindy yesterday** j'ai vu Lindy hier; **have you seen the film?** est-ce que tu as vu le film?; **I haven't see her for ages** ça fait une éternité que je l'ai pas vue; **I'll see what I can do** je vais voir ce que je peux faire; **2 to be able to see** voir [13]; **I can't see anything** je ne vois rien; **3 see you!** salut! **see you on Saturday!** à samedi!; **see you soon!** à bientôt!
● **to see to something** s'occuper [1] d

quelque chose; **Jo's seeing to the drinks** Jo s'occupe des boissons.

seed *noun* graine F; **to plant seeds** semer des graines.

seem *verb* **1** paraître [57]; **it seems odd to me** ça me paraît bizarre; **it seems he's left** il paraît qu'il est parti; **2** (*look, appear to be*) avoir [5] l'air; **he seems a bit shy** il a l'air un peu timide; **the museum seems to be closed** le musée a l'air d'être fermé.

seesaw *noun* tapecul M.

select *verb* sélectionner [1].

self-confidence *noun* confiance F en soi; **she doesn't have much self-confidence** elle n'a pas beaucoup de confiance en elle.

self-contained *noun* **a self-contained flat** un appartement indépendant.

self-employed *noun* **the self-employed** les travailleurs indépendants M *plural*. *adjective* **to be self-employed** travailler à son compte; **my parents are self-employed** mes parents travaillent à leur compte.

selfish *adjective* égoïste.

self-service *adjective* **a self-service restaurant** un self (*informal*).

sell *verb* vendre [3]; **to sell something to somebody** vendre quelque chose à quelqu'un; **I sold him my bike** je lui ai vendu mon vélo; **the house has been sold** la maison a été vendue; **the concert's sold out** il ne reste plus de billets pour le concert.

sell-by date *noun* date F limite de vente.

Sellotape™ *noun* Scotch™ M. *verb* **to sellotape something** scotcher [1] quelque chose (*informal*).

semi *noun* maison jumelée F (*literally: a twinned house*); **we live in a semi** nous habitons dans une maison jumelée.

semicircle *noun* demi-cercle M.

semicolon *noun* point-virgule M.

semi-detached house *noun* maison jumelée F (*literally: a twinned house*); **we live in a semi-detached house** nous habitons dans une maison jumelée.

semi-final *noun* demi-finale F.

semi-skimmed milk *noun* lait demi-écrémé M.

send *verb* envoyer [40]; **to send something to somebody** envoyer quelque chose à quelqu'un; **I sent her a present for her birthday** je lui ai envoyé un cadeau pour son anniversaire.
- **to send somebody back** renvoyer [40] quelqu'un.
- **to send something back** renvoyer [40] quelque chose.

sender *noun* expéditeur M, expéditrice F.

senior citizen *noun* personne F du troisième âge.

sensational *adjective* sensationnel (F sensationnelle).

sense *noun* **1** sens M; **common sense** le bon sens; **it doesn't make sense** ça n'a pas de sens; **it makes sense** ça paraît logique; **to have a sense of humour** avoir le sens de l'humour; **she has no sense of humour** elle n'a aucun sens de l'humour; **2 the sense of smell** l'odorat M; **the sense of touch** le toucher.

sensible *adjective* raisonnable; **she's very sensible** elle est très raisonnable; **it's a sensible decision** c'est une décision raisonnable.

sensitive *adjective* sensible; **for sensitive skin** pour peaux sensibles.

sentence *noun* **1** phrase F; **write a sentence in French** écris une phrase en français; **2 the death sentence** la peine de mort. *verb* condamner [1]; **to be sentenced to death** être condamné à mort.

sentimental *adjective* sentimental (M *plural* sentimentaux).

separate *adjective* **1** à part; **in a separate pile** dans une pile à part; **on a separate sheet of paper** sur une feuille à part; **2** (*different*) autre; **that's a separate problem** c'est un autre problème; **3 they have separate rooms** ils ont chacun leur chambre. *verb* **1** séparer [1]; **2** (*a couple*) se séparer [1].

separately *adverb* séparément.

separation *noun* séparation F.

September *noun* septembre M; **in September** en septembre.

sequel *noun* suite F.

sequence *noun* **1** série F; **a sequence of events** une série d'événements; **2 in sequence** dans l'ordre; **3** (*in a film*) séquence F.

sergeant *noun* **1** (*in the police*) brigadier M; **2** (*in the army*) sergent M.

serial *noun* feuilleton M.

series *noun* série F; **a television series** une série télévisée.

serious *adjective* **1** sérieux (F sérieuse); **a serious discussion** une discussion sérieuse; **are you serious?** sérieusement?; **2** grave (*illness, injury, mistake, problem*); **we have a serious problem** nous avons un grave problème.

seriously *adverb* **1** sérieusement; **seriously, I have to go now** sérieusement je dois partir maintenant; **seriously?** vraiment?; **2 to take somebody seriously** prendre quelqu'un au sérieux; **3** gravement (*ill, injured*); **she is seriously ill** elle est gravement malade.

servant *noun* domestique M & F.

serve *noun* (*in tennis*) service M; **it's my serve** c'est à moi de servir. *verb* **1** (*in tennis*) servir [71]; **2 can you serve the vegetables, please?** est-ce que tu peux servir les légumes s'il te plaît?; **they served the fish with a lemon sauce** ils ont servi le poisson accompagné d'une sauce a citron; ★ **it serves him right** c'est bien fait pour lui.

service *noun* **1** (*in a restaurant, from a company, etc*) service M; **the service is very slow** le service est très lent; **service is included** le service est compris; **2 the emergency services** les services des urgences; **3** (*church service*) office M; **4** (*of a car or machine*) révision F.
verb réviser [1] (*a car or a machine*).

service area *noun* aire F de services.

service charge *noun* service M; **what is the service charge?** le service est de combien?; **there is no service charge** le service est compris.

service station *noun* station-service F (*plural* stations-service).

serviette *noun* serviette F.

session *noun* séance F.

set *noun* **1** (*for playing a game*) jeu M (*plural* jeux); **a chess set** un jeu d'échecs; **2 a train set** un petit train; **3** (*in tennis*) set M.
adjective fixe; **at a set time** à une heure fixe; **a set menu** un menu fixe.
verb **1** fixer [1] (*date, time*); **2** établir [2] (*record*); **3 to set the table** mettre [11] la table; **to set an alarm clock** mettre [11] un réveil; **I've set my alarm for seven** j'ai mis mon réveil à sept heures; **4 to set a watch** régler [24] une montre; **5** (*sun*) se coucher [1].
to set off partir [58]; **we're setting off at ten** nous allons partir à dix heures; **they set off for Paris**

yesterday ils sont partis pour Paris hier.
●**to set off something 1** faire [10] partir (*firework*); **2** faire [10] exploser (*bomb*); **3** déclencher [1] (*alarm*).
●**to set out** partir [58]; **they set out for Paris yesterday** ils sont partis pour Paris hier.

settee *noun* canapé M.

settle *verb* régler [24] (*a bill or a problem*).

seven *number* sept; **Rosie's seven** Rosie a sept ans.

seventeen *number* dix-sept; **Jonny's seventeen** Jonny a dix-sept ans.

seventh *adjective* septième; **on the seventh floor** au septième étage; **the seventh of July** le sept juillet.

seventies *plural noun* **the seventies** les années soixante-dix; **in the seventies** aux années soixante-dix.

seventieth *adjective* soixant-dixième; **it's her seventieth birthday** elle fête ses soixante-dix ans.

seventy *number* soixante-dix; **my grandma's seventy** ma grand-mère a soixante-dix ans.

several *adjective, pronoun* plusieurs; **I've seen her several times** je l'ai vue plusieurs fois; **I've read several of her novels** j'ai lu plusieurs de ses romans; **he took several** il en a pris plusieurs.

sew *verb* coudre [28].

sewing *noun* couture F; **I like sewing** j'aime la couture.

sewing machine *noun* machine F à coudre.

sex *noun* sexe M.

sex education *noun* éducation sexuelle F.

sexism *noun* sexisme M.

sexist *adjective* sexiste; **sexist remarks** des propos sexistes.

sexual *adjective* sexuel (F sexuelle).

sexual harassment *noun* harcèlement sexuel M.

sexuality *noun* sexualité F.

sexy *adjective* sexy.

shabby *adjective* miteux (F miteuse).

shade *noun* **1** (*of a colour*) ton M; **a pretty shade of green** un joli vert; **2 in the shade** à l'ombre.

shadow *noun* ombre F.

shake *verb* **1** (*tremble*) trembler [1]; **my hands are shaking** j'ai les mains qui tremblent; **2 to shake something** secouer [1] quelque chose; **3 to shake hands with somebody** serrer [1] la main à quelqu'un; **she shook hands with me** elle m'a serré la main; **we shook hands** nous nous sommes serré la main; **4 to shake your head** (*meaning no*) faire [10] non de la tête.

shaken *adjective* bouleversé; **I was shaken by the news** j'ai été bouleversé par la nouvelle.

shall *verb* **shall I come with you?**

est-ce que tu veux que je t'accompagne?; **shall we stop now?** si on s'arrêtait maintenant?

shallow *adjective* peu profond; **the water's very shallow here** l'eau est très peu profonde ici.

shambles *noun* pagaille F (*informal*); **it was a total shambles!** ça a été la pagaille complète!

shame *noun* **1** honte F; **shame on you!** tu devrais avoir honte!; **2 what a shame!** quel dommage!; **it's a shame she can't come** c'est dommage qu'elle ne puisse pas venir (*note that 'c'est dommage que' is followed by a verb in the subjunctive*).

shameful *adjective* honteux (F honteuse).

shampoo *noun* shampooing M; **I bought some shampoo** j'ai acheté du shampooing.

shamrock *noun* trèfle M.

shandy *noun* panaché M; **a half of shandy** un demi panaché.

shape *noun* forme F.

share *noun* **1** part F; **your share of the money** ta part de l'argent; **he paid his fair share** il a payé sa part; **2** (*in a company*) action F. *verb* partager [52]; **I'm sharing a room with Emma** je partage une chambre avec Emma.

shark *noun* requin M.

sharp *adjective* **1** (*knife*) bien aiguisé; **this knife isn't very sharp** ce couteau ne coupe pas très bien; **2 a sharp pencil** un crayon bien taillé; **3 a sharp bend** un virage brusque; **4** (*clever*) intelligent.

shave *verb* **1** (*have a shave*) se raser [1]; **he's just shaving** il est en train de se raser; **2 to shave your legs** se raser [1] les jambes; **to shave off your beard** se raser la barbe.

shaver *noun* **an electric shaver** un rasoir électrique.

shaving cream *noun* crème F à raser.

shaving foam *noun* mousse F à raser.

she *pronoun* elle; **she's in her room** elle est dans sa chambre; **she's a student** elle est étudiante; **she's a very good teacher** c'est un très bon prof; **here she is!** la voici!; **there she is!** la voilà!

shed *noun* remise F.

sheep *noun* mouton M.

sheepdog *noun* chien M de berger (*plural* chiens de berger).

sheer *adjective* **1** pur; **it's sheer stupidity!** c'est de la pure bêtise!; **2** (*tights*) extra-fin.

sheet *noun* **1** (*for a bed*) drap M; **2 a sheet of paper** une feuille de papier; **a blank sheet** une feuille blanche; **3** (*of glass or metal*) plaque; ★ **to be as white as a sheet** être blanc comme un linge; **she was as white as a sheet** elle était blanche comme un linge.

shelf *noun* **1** (*in the home*) étagère F; **a set of shelves** une étagère; **2** (*in a shop, in a fridge*) rayon M.

shell *noun* **1** (*of an egg or a nut*)

coquille F; **2** (*seashell*) coquillage M; **3** (*explosive*) obus M.

shellfish *noun* fruits M *plural* de mer.

shelter *noun* **1** abri M; **in the shelter of** à l'abri de; **to take shelter from the rain** se mettre à l'abri de la pluie; **2 a bus shelter** un abribus™.

shepherd *noun* berger M.

sheriff *noun* shérif M.

sherry *noun* sherry M.

Shetland Islands *plural noun* îles Shetland F *plural*.

shield *noun* bouclier M.

shift *noun* service M; **the night shift** le service de nuit; **to be on night shift** être de nuit.
verb **to shift something** déplacer [61] quelque chose; **can you help me shift this table?** est-ce que tu peux m'aider à déplacer cette table?

shifty *adjective* louche; **he looks a bit shifty** il a l'air un peu louche; **a shifty-looking guy** un type un peu louche.

shin *noun* tibia M.

shine *verb* briller [1].

shiny *adjective* brillant.

ship *noun* **1** bateau M; **2 a passenger ship** un paquebot; **3** (*large naval vessel*) navire M.

shipbuilding *noun* construction navale F.

shipyard *noun* chantier naval M.

shirt *noun* **1** (*man's*) chemise F; **2** (*woman's*) chemisier M.

shiver *verb* frissonner [1].

shock *noun* **1** choc M; **it was a shock** ça a été un choc; **it gave me a shock** j'ai eu un choc; **2 an electric shock** une décharge; **to get an electric shock** prendre une décharge.
verb choquer [1].

shocked *adjective* choqué.

shocking *adjective* choquant.

shoe *noun* chaussure F; **a pair of shoes** une paire de chaussures.

shoelace *noun* lacet M.

shoe polish *noun* cirage M.

shoe shop *noun* magasin M de chaussures.

shoot *verb* **1** (*fire*) tirer [1]; **to shoot at somebody** tirer sur quelqu'un; **she shot him in the leg** elle lui a tiré une balle dans la jambe; **he was shot in the arm** il a reçu une balle dans le bras; **2** (*kill*) abattre [21]; **he was shot by terrorists** il a été abattu par des terroristes; **3** (*execute*) fusiller [1]; **4** (*in football, hockey*) shooter [1]; **5 to shoot a film** tourner [1] un film.

shop *noun* magasin M; **a shoe shop** un magasin de chaussures; **to go round the shops** faire les magasins.

shop assistant *noun* vendeur M, vendeuse F; **Brad's a shop assistant** Brad est vendeur.

shopkeeper *noun* commerçant M, commerçante F.

shoplifter *noun* voleur à l'étalage M, voleuse à l'étalage F.

shoplifting *noun* vol M à l'étalage.

shopping *noun* courses F *plural*; **can you put the shopping away?** est-ce que tu peux ranger les courses?; **I've got a lot of shopping to do** j'ai beaucoup de courses à faire; **to go shopping** (*for food*) faire des courses; (*for fun, to buy clothes or presents*) faire du shopping.

shopping bag *noun* sac M à provisions.

shopping trolley *noun* **1** (*in a supermarket*) chariot M; **2** (*personal*) caddie™ M.

shop window *noun* vitrine F.

short *adjective* **1** court; **a short dress** une robe courte; **she has short hair** elle a les cheveux courts; **2 a short break** une petite pause; **t go for a short walk** faire une petite promenade; **it's a short walk from the station** c'est à quelques minute à pied de la gare; **3 to be short of something** ne pas avoir beaucoup de quelque chose; **we're a bit short of money at the moment** nous n'avons pas beaucoup d'argent en c moment; **we're getting short of time** il ne nous reste pas beaucoup de temps.

shortage *noun* pénurie F.

shortbread *noun* sablé M.

shortcrust pastry *noun* pâte brisée F.

short cut *noun* raccourci M; **we took a short cut** nous avons pris u raccourci.

shortly *adverb* bientôt.

shorts *plural noun* short M singula

a pair of shorts un short; **my red shorts** mon short rouge.

short-sighted *adjective* myope; **I'm short-sighted** je suis myope.

short story *noun* nouvelle F.

shot *noun* 1 (*from a gun*) coup M de feu (*plural* coups de feu); 2 (*a photo*) photo F; **I took several shots of the garden** j'ai pris plusieurs photos du jardin.

shotgun *noun* fusil M de chasse (*plural* fusils de chasse).

should *verb* 1 (*'should' is translated by the conditional tense of 'devoir'*) devoir [8]; **you should ask Simon** tu devrais demander à Simon; **the potatoes should be cooked now** les pommes de terre devraient être cuites maintenant; 2 (*'should have' is translated by the past conditional tense of 'devoir'*) **you should have told me** tu aurais dû me le dire; **I shouldn't have stayed** je n'aurais pas dû rester; 3 (*'should' meaning 'would' is translated by the conditional tense of the verb*) **I should forget it if I were you** à ta place je l'oublierais; 4 **I should think** à mon avis; **I should think he's forgotten** à mon avis, il a oublié.

shoulder *noun* épaule F.

shoulder bag *noun* sac M à bandoulière.

shout *noun* cri M.
verb crier [1]; **stop shouting!** arrêtez de crier!; **they shouted at us to come back** ils nous ont crié de revenir.

shovel *noun* pelle F.

show *noun* 1 (*on stage*) spectacle M; **we went to see a show** nous sommes allés voir un spectacle; 2 (*on TV*) émission F; **he has a TV show** il a une émission à la télé; 3 (*exhibition*) salon M; **the motor show** le salon des automobiles.
verb 1 montrer [1]; **to show something to somebody** montrer quelque chose à quelqu'un; **I'll show you my photos** je te montrerai mes photos; **to show somebody how to do** montrer à quelqu'un comment on fait; **he showed me how to make pancakes** il m'a montré comment on fait les crêpes; 2 **it shows!** ça se voit!

● **to show off** frimer [1] (*informal*).

shower *noun* 1 (*in a bathroom*) douche F; **to have a shower** prendre une douche; 2 (*of rain*) averse F.

show-jumping *noun* saut M d'obstacles.

show-off *noun* frimeur M, frimeuse F (*informal*).

shriek *verb* hurler [1].

shrimp *noun* crevette F.

shrink *verb* rétrécir [2].

Shrove Tuesday *noun* mardi gras M.

shrug *verb* **to shrug your shoulders** hausser [1] les épaules.

shuffle *verb* **to shuffle the cards** battre [21] les cartes.

shut *adjective* fermé; **the shops are shut** les magasins sont fermés.
verb fermer [1]; **can you shut the door please?** est-ce que tu peux

fermer la porte, s'il te plaît?; **the shops shut at six** les magasins ferment à six heures.
● **to shut up** (*be quiet*) se taire [76]; **shut up!** tais-toi!

shutter *noun* volet M.

shuttle *noun* navette F; **there's a shuttle service from the airport** il y a une navette de l'aéroport.

shuttlecock *noun* volant M.

shy *adjective* timide.

shyness *noun* timidité F.

Sicily *noun* Sicile F; **to Sicily** en Sicile; **in Sicily** en Sicile.

sick *adjective* 1 (*ill*) malade; 2 **to be sick** (*vomit*) vomir [2]; **I was sick several times** j'ai vomi plusieurs fois; **to feel sick** avoir envie de vomir; 3 **a sick joke** une plaisanterie malsaine; 4 **to be sick of something** en avoir assez de quelque chose; **I'm sick of staying at home every night** j'en ai assez de rester à la maison tous les soirs.

sickness *noun* maladie F.

side *noun* 1 côté M; **on the other side of the street** de l'autre côté de la rue; **on the wrong side** du mauvais côté; **I'm on your side** (*I agree with you*) je suis de ton côté; 2 (*edge*) bord M; **at the side of the road** au bord de la route; **by the side of the pool** au bord de la piscine; 3 (*team*) équipe F; **she plays on our side** elle joue dans notre équipe; 4 **to take sides** prendre parti; 5 **side by side** côte à côte.

sideboard *noun* buffet M.

sideburns *noun* pattes F *plural*.

side-effect *noun* effet secondaire M.

side street *noun* petite rue F.

sieve *noun* passoire F.

sigh *noun* soupir M.
verb pousser [1] un soupir.

sight *noun* 1 spectacle M; **it was a marvellous sight** c'était un spectacle merveilleux; 2 **at the sight of** à la vue de; 3 (*eyesight*) vue F; **to have poor sight** avoir une mauvaise vue; **to know somebody by sight** connaître quelqu'un de vue; **out of sight** caché; 4 **to see the sights** visiter les attractions touristiques.

sightseeing *noun* tourisme M; **to do some sightseeing** faire du tourisme.

sign *noun* 1 (*notice*) panneau M (*plural* panneaux); **there's a sign on the door** il y a un panneau sur la porte; 2 (*trace, indication*) signe M; 3 (*of the Zodiac*) signe M; **what sign are you?** tu es de quel signe? *verb* 1 signer [1]; **to sign a cheque** signer un chèque; 2 (*using sign language*) communiquer [1] en langage par signes.
● **to sign on** (*as unemployed*) s'inscrire [38] au chômage.

signal *noun* signal M (*plural* signaux).

signature *noun* signature F.

significance *noun* importance F.

significant *adjective* important.

sign language *noun* langage M par signes.

signpost *noun* poteau indicateur M (*plural* poteaux indicateurs).

silence *noun* silence M.

silent *adjective* silencieux (F silencieuse).

silicon chip *noun* puce électronique F.

silk *noun* soie F. *adjective* en soie; **a silk shirt** une chemise en soie.

silky *adjective* soyeux (F soyeuse).

silly *adjective* idiot; **it was a really silly thing to do** c'était vraiment idiot.

silver *noun* argent M. *adjective* **a silver spoon** une cuillère en argent; **a silver medal** une médaille d'argent.

similar *adjective* semblable.

similarity *noun* ressemblance F.

simmer *verb* **to simmer something** faire [10] mijoter quelque chose.

simple *adjective* facile.

simply *adverb* simplement.

sin *noun* péché M.

since *preposition, adverb, conjunction* **1** depuis (*notice that French uses the present tense where English uses 'have done' or 'have been doing'*) **I have been in Paris since Saturday** je suis à Paris depuis samedi; **I've been learning French since last year** j'apprends le français depuis l'année dernière; **2** depuis que (*the same thing happens with tenses here as above*)

since I have known him depuis que je le connais; **since I've been learning French** depuis que j'apprends le français; **3 I haven't seen her since** je ne l'ai pas revue depuis; **I haven't seen her since Monday** je ne l'ai pas revue depuis lundi; **since when?** depuis quand?; **4** (*because*) puisque; **since it was raining, the match was cancelled** puisqu'il pleuvait le match a été annulé.

sincere *adjective* sincère.

sincerely *adverb* **Yours sincerely** (*in a business letter*) Veuillez agréer Madame (or Monsieur) l'expression de mes sentiments distingués; (*to somebody you know*) Cordialement (*in French there are very formal and rigid formulae for signing letters*).

sing *verb* chanter [1].

singer *noun* chanteur M, chanteuse F.

singing *noun* **1** chant M; **a singing lesson** une leçon de chant; **2 I like singing** j'aime chanter.

single *noun* aller simple M; **a single to Lyons, please** un aller simple pour Lyon, s'il vous plaît. *adjective* **1** (*not married*) célibataire; **2 a single room** une chambre pour une personne; **a single bed** un lit pour une personne; **3 not a single** pas un seul, pas une seule; **I haven't had a single reply** je n'ai pas reçu une seule réponse.

single parent *noun* **she's a single parent** elle élève ses enfants toute seule; **a single-parent family** une famille monoparentale.

singles *plural noun* (*in tennis*) simple M singular; **the women's singles** le simple dames; **the men's singles** le simple messieurs.

singular *noun* singulier M; **in the singular** au singulier.

sink *noun* évier M.
verb couler [1].

sir *noun* monsieur M; **yes, sir** oui, Monsieur.

siren *noun* sirène F.

sister *noun* sœur F; **my sister's ten** ma sœur a dix ans.

sister-in-law *noun* belle-sœur F (*plural* belles-sœurs).

sit *verb* 1 s'asseoir [20]; **you can sit on the sofa** tu peux t'asseoir sur le canapé; **I can sit on the floor** je peux m'asseoir par terre; 2 **to be sitting** être [6] assis; **Leila was sitting on the sofa** Leila était assise sur le canapé; 3 **to sit an exam** passer [1] un examen; **she's sitting her driving test on Thursday** elle passe son permis jeudi.
● **to sit down** s'asseoir [20]; **he sat down on a chair** il s'est assis sur une chaise; **do sit down** asseyez-vous.

sitcom *noun* comédie F de situation (*plural* comédies de situation).

site *noun* 1 **a building site** un chantier; 2 **a camping site** un camping; 3 **an archaeolological site** un site archéologique.

sitting room *noun* salon M.

situated *adjective* **to be situated**

être situé; **the house is situated in a small village** la maison est située dans un petit village.

situation *noun* situation F.

six *number* six; **Harry's six** Harry a six ans.

sixteen *number* seize; **Alice is sixteen** Alice a seize ans.

sixth *adjective* sixième; **on the sixth floor** au sixième étage; **the sixth of July** le six juillet.

sixty *number* soixante; **she's sixty** elle a soixante ans.

size *noun* 1 grandeur F; **it depends on the size of the house** ça dépend de la grandeur de la maison; 2 (*precise measurements*) dimensions F *plural*; **what size is the window?** quelles sont les dimensions de la fenêtre?; 3 (*in clothes*) taille F; **what size do you take?** quelle taille est-ce que vous faites?; 4 (*of shoes*) pointure F; **I take a size thirty-eight** je fais du trente-huit.

skate *noun* 1 **an ice skate** un patin à glace; 2 **a roller skate** un patin à roulettes.
verb 1 (*ice-skate*) faire [10] du patin à glace; 2 (*roller-skate*) faire [10] du patin à roulettes.

skateboard *noun* skateboard M.

skateboarding *noun* skateboard M; **to go skateboarding** faire du skateboard.

skating *noun* 1 (*ice*) patin M à glace; **to go skating** faire du patin à glace; 2 **roller-skating** le patin à roulettes; **to go roller-skating** faire du patin à roulettes.

skating rink noun patinoire F.

skeleton noun squelette M.

sketch noun **1** (drawing) croquis M; **2** (comedy routine) sketch M.

ski noun ski M.
verb faire [10] du ski; **he can ski** il sait faire du ski.

ski boot noun chaussure F de ski.

skid verb déraper [1]; **the car skidded** la voiture a dérapé.

skiing noun ski M; **to go skiing** faire du ski.

ski lift noun remonte-pente M.

skimmed milk noun lait écrémé M.

skin noun peau F (plural peaux).

skinhead noun skinhead M & F.

skinny adjective maigre.

skip noun (for rubbish) benne F.
verb **1** sauter [1] (a meal, part of a book); **I skipped a few chapters** j'ai sauté quelques chapitres; **2 to skip a lesson** sécher un cours (informal).

ski pants noun fuseau M singular; **I bought some ski pants** j'ai acheté un fuseau.

ski suit noun combinaison F de ski.

skirt noun jupe F; **a long skirt** une jupe longue; **a straight skirt** une jupe droite; **a mini-skirt** une mini-jupe.

skittles plural noun quilles F

plural; **to play skittles** jouer aux quilles.

skull noun crâne M.

sky noun ciel M.

skyscraper noun gratte-ciel M (plural gratte-ciel).

slam verb claquer [1]; **she slammed the door** elle a claqué la porte.

slang noun argot M.

slap noun claque F.
verb **to slap somebody** donner [1] une claque à quelqu'un.

slate noun ardoise F.

sledge noun luge F.

sledging noun **to go sledging** faire [10] de la luge.

sleep noun sommeil M; **I had a good sleep** j'ai bien dormi; **to go to sleep** s'endormir [37].
verb dormir [37]; **she's sleeping** elle dort.

sleeping bag noun sac M de couchage.

sleeping pill noun somnifère M.

sleepy adjective **to be sleepy** avoir sommeil; **I feel sleepy** j'ai sommeil; **he was getting sleepy** il commençait à avoir sommeil.

sleet noun neige fondue F.

sleeve noun manche F; **a long-sleeved jumper** un pull à manches longues; **a short-sleeved shirt** une chemise à manches courtes; **to roll up your sleeves** retrousser ses manches.

slice noun tranche F; **a slice of ham** une tranche de jambon.

verb **to slice something** couper [1] quelque chose en tranches.

slide *noun* **1** (*photo*) diapositive F; **2** (*hairslide*) barrette F; **3** (*for sliding down*) toboggan M.

slight *adjective* léger (F légère); **there is a slight problem** il y a un léger problème.

slightly *adverb* légèrement.

slim *adjective* mince.
verb **I'm slimming** je fais un régime.

sling *noun* écharpe F; **to have your arm in a sling** avoir le bras en écharpe.

slip *noun* **1** (*mistake*) erreur F; **2** (*petticoat*)(*from waist*) jupon M; (*full-length*) combinaison F.
verb **1** (*slide*) glisser [1]; **2 it had slipped my mind** j'avais oublié.

slipper *noun* pantoufle F.

slippery *adjective* glissant.

slope *noun* pente F.

slot *noun* fente F.

slot machine *noun* **1** (*games machine*) machine F à sous; **2** (*vending machine*) distributeur automatique M.

slow *adjective* **1** lent; **the service is a bit slow** le service est un peu lent; **2 my watch is slow** ma montre retarde.
● **to slow down** ralentir [2].

slowly *adverb* **1** lentement; **he got up slowly** il s'est levé lentement; **2** (*speak, drive*) doucement; **can you speak more slowly, please?** est-ce que vous pouvez parler plus doucement, s'il vous plaît?

slug *noun* limace F.

slush *noun* neige fondue F.

sly *adjective* (*person*) rusé; ★ **on the sly** en douce.

smack *noun* claque F.
verb **to smack somebody** donner [1] une claque à quelqu'un.

small *adjective* petit (*goes before the noun*); **a small dog** un petit chien.

smart *adjective* **1** (*well-dressed, posh*) chic; **a smart restaurant** un restaurant chic; **2** (*clever*) intelligent.

smash *noun* **a car smash** un accident de voiture.
verb casser [1]; **they smashed a window** ils ont cassé une vitre.

smashing *adjective* formidable.

smell *noun* odeur F; **a nasty smell** une mauvaise odeur; **there's a smell of burning** ça sent le brûlé.
verb **1** sentir [58]; **I can't smell anything** je ne sens rien; **I can smell lavender** ça sent la lavande; **2** (*smell bad*) sentir [58] mauvais; **the drains smell** les égouts sentent mauvais.

smelly *adjective* qui sent mauvais; **her smelly dog** son chien qui sent mauvais.

smile *noun* sourire M.
verb sourire [68].

smoke *noun* fumée F.
verb fumer [1]; **she doesn't smoke** elle ne fume pas; **he smokes a pipe** il fume la pipe.

smoker *noun* fumeur M, fumeuse F.

smoking *noun* 'no smoking'
'défense de fumer'; **to give up
smoking** arrêter de fumer.

smooth *adjective* 1 lisse; **a smooth
surface** une surface lisse;
2 (*person*) mielleux (F mielleuse).

smug *adjective* suffisant.

smuggle *verb* **to smuggle
something** faire [10] passer quelque
chose en contrebande.

smuggler *noun* 1 contrebandier
M, contrebandière F; 2 **a drugs
smuggler** un passeur de drogue.

smuggling *noun* 1 contrebande
F; 2 (*of drugs or arms*) trafic M.

snack *noun* casse-croûte M.

snail *noun* escargot M.

snake *noun* serpent M.

snap *noun* (*card game*) bataille F.
verb 1 (*break*) casser [1]; 2 **to snap
your fingers** faire [10] claquer ses
doigts.

snapshot *noun* photo F.

snarl *verb* gronder [1].

snatch *verb* arracher [1]; **to snatch
something from somebody**
arracher quelque chose à quelqu'un;
he snatched my book il m'a arraché
mon livre; **she had her bag
snatched** on lui a arraché son sac.

sneak *verb* **to sneak in** entrer [1]
furtivement; **to sneak out** sortir [72]
furtivement; **he sneaked up on me**
il s'est approché de moi sans faire de
bruit.

sneeze *verb* éternuer [1].

sniff *verb* renifler [1].

snob *noun* snob M & F.

snobbery *noun* snobisme M.

snooker *noun* snooker M; **to play
snooker** jouer au snooker.

snooze *noun* somme M; **to have a
snooze** faire un petit somme.

snore *verb* ronfler [1].

snow *noun* neige F.
verb neiger [52]; **it's snowing** il
neige; **it's going to snow** il va
neiger.

snowball *noun* boule F de neige
(*plural* boules de neige).

snowman *noun* bonhomme M de
neige (*plural* bonshommes de
neige).

so *conjunction, adverb* 1 tellement;
he's so lazy il est tellement
paresseux; **the coffee's so hot I can't
drink it** le café est tellement chaud
que je n'arrive pas à le boire; 2 **not
so** moins; **our house is a bit like
yours, but not so big** notre maison
est un peu comme la vôtre, mais
moins grande; 3 **so much**
tellement; **I hate it so much!** je le
déteste tellement!; 4 **so much, so
many** tellement de; **I have so much
work to do** j'ai tellement de travail à
faire; **we've got so many problems**
nous avons tellement de
problèmes; 5 (*therefore*) donc; **he
got up late, so he missed his train**
il s'est levé tard, donc il a raté son
train; 6 (*starting a sentence*) alors;
so what's your name? alors, tu
t'appelles comment?; **so what shall
we do?** alors, qu'est-ce qu'on fait?;
so what? et alors?; 7 **so do I, so
did I** moi aussi; **'I live in Leeds'** –

'so do I' 'j'habite à Leeds' – 'moi aussi'; **'I hated the film'** – **'so did I'** 'j'ai détesté le film' – 'moi aussi'; **so am I** moi aussi; **so do we** nous aussi; **8 I think so** je crois; **I hope so** j'espère.

soak *verb* tremper [1].

soaked *adjective* trempé; ★ **to be soaked to the skin** être trempé jusqu'aux os (*literally: to be soaked to the bones*).

soaking *adjective* trempé; **soaking wet** trempé.

soap *noun* **1** savon M; **a cake of soap** un savon; **2** (*soap opera: on TV*) feuilleton M.

soap powder *noun* lessive F.

sober *adjective* **to be sober** ne pas avoir bu; **he's sober** il n'a pas bu; **are you sure she's sober?** tu es sûr qu'elle n'a pas bu?

soccer *noun* football M; **to play soccer** jouer au football.

social *adjective* social (M *plural* sociaux).

socialism *noun* socialisme M.

socialist *noun, adjective* socialiste M & F.

social security *noun* **1** aide sociale F; **to be on social security** recevoir de l'aide sociale; **2 the social security** (*the system*) sécurité sociale F.

social worker *noun* travailleur social M (*plural* travailleurs sociaux), travailleuse sociale F; **she's a social worker** elle est travailleuse sociale.

society *noun* société F.

sociology *noun* sociologie F.

sock *noun* chaussette F; **a pair of socks** une paire de chaussettes.

socket *noun* (*power point*) prise F de courant (*plural* prises de courant).

sofa *noun* canapé M.

sofa bed *noun* canapé-lit M.

soft *adjective* doux (F douce); ★ **to have a soft spot for somebody** avoir un faible pour quelqu'un.

soft drink *noun* boisson non alcoolisée F.

software *noun* logiciel M.

soft toy *noun* peluche F.

soil *noun* terre F.

solar energy *noun* énergie solaire F.

soldier *noun* soldat M.

solicitor *noun* **1** (*dealing with property or documents*) notaire M; **she's a solicitor** elle est notaire; **2** (*dealing with lawsuits*) avocat M, avocate F; **she's a solicitor** elle est avocate.

solid *adjective* **1** massif (F massive); **a table made of solid pine** une table en pin massif; **a solid gold ring** une bague en or massif; **solid silver** argent massif; **2** (*not flimsy*) solide; **a solid structure** une structure solide.

solo *noun* solo M; **a guitar solo** un solo de guitare.
adjective, adverb en solo; **a solo**

album un album en solo; **to play solo** jouer en solo.

soloist *noun* soliste M & F.

solution *noun* solution F.

solve *verb* résoudre [67].

some *adjective, adverb* **1** (*followed by a singular noun*) du (*with a masculine noun*), de la (*with a feminine noun*), de l'* (*with a noun beginning with a vowel or silent 'h'*); **would you like some butter?** voulez-vous du beurre?; **may I have some salad?** puis-je avoir de la salade?; **can you lend me some money?** est-ce que tu peux me prêter de l'argent?; **2** (*followed by a plural noun*) des; **I've bought some apples** j'ai acheté des pommes; **3** (*referring to something that has been mentioned*) en; **'would you like butter?' – 'thanks, I've got some'** 'veux-tu du beurre?' – 'merci, j'en ai'; **he's eaten some of it** il en a mangé un peu; **4 some people think he's wrong** il y a des gens qui pensent qu'il a tort; **5 some day** un de ces jours.

somebody, someone *pronoun* quelqu'un; **there's somebody in the garden** il y a quelqu'un dans le jardin.

somehow *adverb* **1** d'une manière ou d'une autre; **I've got to finish this essay somehow** je dois finir cette rédaction d'une manière ou d'une autre; **2 I somehow think they won't come** quelque chose me dit qu'ils ne viendront pas.

something *pronoun* quelque chose; **I've got something to tell you** j'ai quelque chose à te dire; **something pretty** quelque chose de joli; **something interesting** quelque chose d'intéressant; **there's something wrong** il y a quelque chose qui ne va pas; **their house is really something!** leur maison c'est vraiment quelque chose!; **! a guy called Colin something or other** un type qui s'appelle Colin quelque chose.

sometime *adverb* un de ces jours; **give me a ring sometime** appelle-moi un de ces jours; **I'll ring you sometime next week** je t'appellerai dans le courant de la semaine prochaine.

sometimes *adverb* quelquefois; **I sometimes take the train** quelquefois je prends le train.

somewhere *adverb* quelque part; **I've put my bag down somewhere** j'ai posé mon sac quelque part; **I've met you somewhere before** je vous ai déjà vu quelque part.

son *noun* fils M.

song *noun* chanson F.

son-in-law *noun* gendre M.

soon *adverb* **1** bientôt!; **it will soon be the holidays** c'est bientôt les vacances; **see you soon!** à bientôt!; **2 as soon as** dès que; **as soon as she arrives** dès qu'elle arrive; **as soon as possible** dès que possible; **3 it's too soon** c'est trop tôt.

sooner *adverb* **1** plus tôt; **we should have started sooner** nous aurions dû commencer plus tôt; **2 I'd sooner wait** je préfère attendre; **★ sooner or later** tôt ou tard.

soprano *noun* soprano M & F.

sore *noun* plaie F.
adjective **to have a sore leg** avoir mal à la jambe; **to have a sore throat** avoir mal à la gorge; **my arm's sore** j'ai mal au bras; ★ **it's a sore point** c'est un sujet délicat.

sorry *adjective* **1** désolé; **I'm really sorry** je suis vraiment désolé; **sorry to disturb you** je suis désolé de vous déranger; **I'm sorry I forgot your birthday** je suis désolé d'avoir oublié ton anniversaire; **2 sorry!** excusez-moi! **3 sorry?** comment? **4 to feel sorry for somebody** plaindre [31] quelqu'un.

sort *noun* sorte F; **what sort of music do you like?** tu aimes quelle sorte de musique?; **all sorts of** toutes sortes de; **for all sorts of reasons** pour toutes sortes de raisons.
● **to sort something out 1** mettre [11] de l'ordre dans (*room, desk, papers, possessions*); **I must sort out my room tonight** je dois mettre de l'ordre dans ma chambre ce soir; **2** s'occuper [1] de (*problem, arrangement*); **Liz is sorting it out** Liz s'en occupe.

so-so *adjective* moyen (F moyenne); **'how was the film?' – 'so-so'** 'c'était comment le film?' – 'moyen'.

soul *noun* **1** âme F; **2** (*music*) soul M.

sound *noun* **1** (*noise*) bruit; **the sound of voices** le bruit des voix; **2** (*volume*) volume M; **to turn down the sound** baisser le volume.
verb **it sounds easy** ça a l'air facile; **it sounds as if she's happy** elle a l'air d'être heureuse.

sound asleep *adjective* profondément endormi.

sound effect *noun* effet sonore M.

soundtrack *noun* bande sonore F.

soup *noun* soupe F; **mushroom soup** la soupe aux champignons.

soup plate *noun* assiette creuse F.

soup spoon *noun* cuillère F à soupe.

sour *adjective* **1** (*taste*) aigre; **2 the milk has gone sour** le lait a tourné.

south *noun* sud M; **in the south** au sud.
adjective, adverb sud (*never agrees*); **the south side** le côté sud; **a south wind** un vent du sud; **south of Paris** au sud de Paris.

South Africa *noun* Afrique F du Sud.

South America *noun* Amérique F du Sud.

southeast *noun* sud-est M.
adjective **in southeast England** au sud-est de l'Angleterre.

South Pole *noun* pôle Sud M.

southwest *noun* sud-ouest M.
adjective **in southwest England** au sud-ouest de l'Angleterre.

souvenir *noun* souvenir M.

soya *noun* soja M.

soy sauce *noun* sauce F de soja.

space *noun* **1** (*room*) place F; **is**

there enough space? est-ce qu'il y a de la place?; **there's enough space for two** il y a de la place pour deux; **2** (*gap*) espace M; **leave a space** laissez un espace; **3** (*outer space*) espace M; **in space** dans l'espace.

spacecraft *noun* engin spatial M.

spade *noun* **1** pelle F; **2** (*in cards*) pique M; **the queen of spades** la reine de pique.

Spain *noun* Espagne F; **in Spain** en Espagne; **to Spain** en Espagne.

Spaniard *noun* Espagnol M, Espagnole F.

spaniel *noun* épagneul M.

Spanish *noun* **1** (*language*) espagnol M; **I'm learning Spanish** j'apprends l'espagnol; **2 the Spanish** (*people*) les Espagnols M *plural*; *adjective* espagnol; **Pedro is Spanish** Pedro est espagnol.

spank *verb* **to spank somebody** donner [1] une fessée à quelqu'un.

spanner *noun* clé anglaise F.

spare *adjective* (*part, battery*) de rechange; **we have a spare ticket** nous avons un billet de trop. *verb* **I can't spare the time** je n'ai pas le temps; **can you spare a moment?** est-ce que tu as un instant?

spare part *noun* pièce F de rechange.

spare room *noun* chambre F d'amis.

spare time *noun* temps libre M; **in**

my spare time dans mon temps libre.

spare wheel *noun* roue F de secours.

sparkling *adjective* **sparkling (mineral) water** l'eau (minérale) pétillante; **sparkling wine** le vin mousseux.

sparrow *noun* moineau M (*plural* moineaux).

speak *verb* **1** parler [1]; **do you speak French?** est-ce que vous parlez français?; **spoken French** le français parlé; **2 to speak to somebody** parler [1] à quelqu'un; **she's speaking to Mike** elle parle à Mike; **I've never spoken to her** je ne lui ai jamais parlé; **I'll speak to him about it** je vais lui en parler; **3 who's speaking?** (*on the phone*) c'est qui à l'appareil?

speaker *noun* **1** (*on a music system*) enceinte F; **2** (*at a public lecture*) conférencier M, conférencière F; **3** (*of a language*) **a French speaker** un/une francophone; **an English speaker** un/une anglophone.

special *adjective* spécial (M *plural* spéciaux).

specialist *noun* spécialiste M & F.

specialize *verb* **to specialize in** être [6] spécialisé dans; **we specialize in French cars** nous sommes spécialisés dans les voitures françaises.

specially *adverb* **1** spécialement; **not specially** pas spécialement; **the poems have been specially chosen for small children** les poèmes ont été spécialement choisis pour les petits enfants; **2** (*specifically*) exprès; **I came specially in order to see you** je suis venu exprès pour te voir; **I made this cake specially for you** j'ai fait ce gâteau exprès pour toi.

species *noun* espèce F.

specific *adjective* précis.

spectacles *plural noun* lunettes F *plural*.

spectacular *adjective* spectaculaire.

spectator *noun* spectateur M, spectatrice F.

speech *noun* discours M; **to make a speech** faire un discours.

speechless *adjective* muet (F muette); **to be speechless with rage** rester muet de colère; **I was speechless** j'étais stupéfait.

speed *noun* vitesse F; **at top speed** à toute vitesse; **what speed was he doing?** il roulait à quelle vitesse?; **a twelve-speed bike** un vélo à douze vitesses.
● **to speed up** accélérer [24].

speeding *noun* excès M de vitesse; **he was fined for speeding** il a reçu une contravention pour excès de vitesse.

speed limit *noun* limitation F de vitesse.

spell *noun* (*of time*) période F; **a cold spell** une période de temps froid; **sunny spells** des éclaircies F *plural*.
verb **1** (*in writing*) écrire [38]; **how do you spell it?** ça s'écrit

comment?; **how do you spell your surname?** ça s'écrit comment, ton nom de famille?; **2** (*out loud*) épeler [18].

spelling *noun* orthographe F; **a spelling mistake** une faute d'orthographe.

spend *verb* **1** dépenser [1] (*money*); **I've spent all my money** j'ai dépensé tout mon argent; **2** passer [1] (*time*); **we spent three days in Paris** nous avons passé trois jours à Paris; **she spends her time writing letters** elle passe son temps à écrire des lettres.

spice *noun* épice F.

spicy *adjective* épicé; **he doesn't like spicy food** il n'aime pas les choses épicées.

spider *noun* araignée F.

spill *verb* renverser [1]; **I've spilled my wine on the carpet** j'ai renversé mon vin sur la moquette.

spinach *noun* épinards F *plural*; **do you like spinach?** est-ce que tu aimes les épinards?

spine *noun* colonne vertébrale F.

spiral *noun* spirale F.

spiral staircase *noun* escalier M en colimaçon.

spire *noun* flèche F.

spirit *noun* **1** (*energy*) énergie F; **2 to get into the spirit of the occasion** se mettre dans l'ambiance.

spirits *noun* **1** (*alcohol*) alcools forts M *plural*; **2 to be in good spirits** être de bonne humeur.

spit *verb* cracher [1]; **to spit something out** cracher quelque chose.

spite *noun* **1 in spite of** malgré; **we decided to go in spite of the rain** nous avons décidé d'y aller malgré la pluie; **2** (*nastiness*) méchanceté F; **to do something out of spite** faire quelque chose par méchanceté.

spiteful *adjective* méchant.

splash *noun* **1** (*noise*) plouf M; **2 a splash of colour** une touche de couleur.
verb éclabousser [1].

splendid *adjective* splendide.

splinter *noun* écharde F.

split *verb* **1** (*with an axe or a knife*) fendre [3]; **to split a piece of wood** fendre un morceau de bois; **2** (*come apart*) se fendre [3]; **the lining has split** la doublure s'est fendue; **3** (*divide up*) partager [52]; **they split the money between them** ils ont partagé l'argent entre eux.
● **to split up 1** (*a couple or group*) se séparer [1]; **2 she's split up with her boyfriend** elle a rompu avec son copain.

spoil *verb* **1** gâcher [1]; **it completely spoiled the evening** ça a complètement gâché la soirée; **to spoil the surprise** gâcher la surprise; **2** gâter [1] (*a child*).

spoiled *adjective* gâté; **a spoiled child** un enfant gâté.

spoilsport *noun* trouble-fête M & F.

spoke *noun* (*of a wheel*) rayon M.

spokesman *noun* porte-parole M (*plural* porte-parole).

spokeswoman *noun* porte-parole M (*plural* porte-parole).

sponge *noun* éponge F.

sponge bag *noun* trousse F de toilette.

sponge cake *noun* génoise F.

sponsor *noun* sponsor M.
verb sponsoriser [1].

spontaneous *adjective* spontané.

spooky *adjective* **1** (*atmosphere*) sinistre; **2 a spooky story** une histoire qui fait froid dans le dos.

spoon *noun* cuillère F; **a soup spoon** une cuillère à soupe; **a teaspoon** une petite cuillère.

spoonful *noun* cuillère F.

sport *noun* sport M; **to be good at sport** être bon en sport; **my favourite sport** mon sport préféré.

sports bag *noun* sac M de sport.

sports car *noun* voiture F de sport.

sports centre *noun* centre sportif M.

sports club *noun* club M sportif.

sportsman *noun* sportif M.

sportswear *noun* vêtements M *plural* de sport.

sportswoman *noun* sportive F.

sporty *adjective* sportif (F sportive); **she's very sporty** elle est très sportive.

spot *noun* **1** (*in fabric*) pois M; **a red tie with black spots** une cravate rouge aux pois noirs; **2** (*on your skin*) bouton M; **I've got spots** j'ai des boutons; **to be covered in spots** être couvert de boutons; **3** (*stain*) tache F; **you've got a spot on your tie** tu as une tache sur ta cravate; **4** (*spotlight*) projecteur M; (*in the home*) spot M; **5 on the spot** (*immediately*) sur-le-champ; **we'll do it for you on the spot** nous le ferons sur-le-champ; **6** (*at hand*) sur place; **they have experts on the spot** ils ont des experts sur place. *verb* repérer [24]; **I spotted her in the crowd** je l'ai repérée dans la foule.

spotless *adjective* impeccable.

spotlight *noun* **1** projecteur M; **2** (*in the home*) spot M.

spotty *adjective* (*pimply*) boutonneux (F boutonneuse).

spouse *noun* époux M, épouse F.

sprain *noun* entorse F. *verb* **to sprain your ankle** se faire [10] une entorse à la cheville.

spray *noun* (*spray can*) bombe F. *verb* vaporiser [1] (*liquid*).

spread *noun* pâte à tartiner F; **cheese spread** le fromage à tartiner. *verb* **1** (*news or a disease*) se propager [52]; **2** étaler [1] (*butter, jam, cement, glue, etc*).

spreadsheet *noun* (*on a computer*) tableur M.

spring *noun* **1** (*the season*) printemps M; **in the spring** au printemps; **spring flowers** les fleurs du printemps; **2** (*made of metal*) ressort M; **3** (*providing water*) source F.

spring-cleaning *noun* grand nettoyage M de printemps.

springtime *noun* printemps M; **in springtime** au printemps.

spring water *noun* eau F de source.

sprint *noun* sprint M. *verb* courir [2] à toute vitesse.

sprinter *noun* sprinteur M, sprinteuse F.

sprout *noun* (*Brussels sprout*) chou M de Bruxelles (*plural* choux de Bruxelles).

spy *noun* espion M, espionne F. *verb* **to spy on somebody** espionner [1] quelqu'un.

spying *noun* espionnage M.

squabble *verb* se disputer [1].

square *noun* **1** (*shape*) carré; **2** (*in a town or village*) place F; **the village square** la place du village; ★ **to go back to square one** retourner à la case départ. *adjective* carré; **a square box** une boîte carrée; **three square metres** trois mètres carrés; **the room is four metres square** la pièce fait quatre mètres carrés.

squash *noun* **1** (*drink*) sirop M; **orange squash** le sirop d'orange; **2** (*sport*) squash M; **to play squash** jouer au squash.

squeak *verb* **1** (*door, hinge*) grincer [61]; **2** (*person, animal*) pousser [1] un petit cri.

squeeze *verb* **1** serrer [1] (*somebody's arm, hand, etc*); **2** presser [1] (*toothpaste*).

squirrel *noun* écureil M.

stab *verb* poignarder [1].

stable *noun* écurie F.
adjective stable.

stack *noun* 1 (*pile*) pile F;
2 **stacks of** plein de; **she's got stacks of CDs** elle a plein de CD.

stadium *noun* stade M.

staff *noun* 1 (*of a company*) personnel M; 2 (*in a school*) professeurs M *plural*.

stage *noun* 1 (*for a performance*) scène F; **on stage** sur scène;
2 (*phase*) stade M; **at this stage of the project** à ce stade du projet; **at this stage it's hard to know** pour l'instant il est difficile de savoir.

staggered *adjective* (*amazed*) stupéfié.

stain *noun* tache F.
verb tacher [1].

stainless steel *noun* inox M; **a stainless steel sink** un évier en inox.

stair *noun* 1 (*step*) marche F;
2 **stairs** escalier M; **I met her on the stairs** je l'ai croisée dans l'escalier.

staircase *noun* escalier M.

stale *adjective* (*bread*) rassis.

stalemate *noun* (*in chess*) pat M.

stall *noun* 1 (*at a market or fair*) stand M; 2 **the stalls** (*in a theatre*) l'orchestre M singular.

stammer *noun* **to have a stammer** bégayer [59].
verb bégayer [59].

stamp *noun* timbre M.

verb 1 affranchir [2] (*a letter*); 2 **to stamp your foot** taper [1] du pied.

stamp album *noun* album M de timbres.

stamp collection *noun* collection F de timbres.

stand *verb* 1 être [6] debout; **several people were standing** plusieurs personnes étaient debout; 2 (*when you say somebody is standing somewhere 'standing' is not usually translated*) **we were standing outside the cinema** nous étions devant le cinéma; **I'm standing here waiting for you** je suis là en train de t'attendre; 3 (*bear*) supporter [1];
I can't stand her je ne la supporte pas; **I can't stand waiting** je ne supporte pas d'attendre.

● **to stand for something** (*be short for*) être [6] l'abréviation de; **'UN' stands for 'United Nations'** 'UN' est l'abréviation de 'United Nations'.

● **stand up** se lever [50]; **everybody stood up** tout le monde s'est levé.

standard *noun* niveau M; **her work is of a high standard** son travail est d'un bon niveau; **the standard of living** le niveau de vie.
adjective standard; **the standard price** le prix standard.

stands *plural noun* (*in a stadium*) tribune F *plural*.

staple *noun* agrafe F.
verb agrafer [1]; **to staple the pages together** agrafer les feuilles.

stapler *noun* agrafeuse F.

star *noun* 1 (*in the sky*) étoile F;
2 (*person*) vedette; **he's a film star** c'est une vedette de cinéma.

verb **to star in a film** être [6] la vedette d'un film.

stare *verb* regarder [1] fixement; **he was staring at me** il me regardait fixement; **what are you staring at?** qu'est-ce que tu regardes?

start *noun* **1** début M; **at the start** au début; **at the start of the book** au début du livre; **from the start** dès le début; **we knew from the start that it was dangerous** nous savions dès le début que c'était dangereux; **2 to make a start on something** commencer à faire quelque chose; **I've made a start on my homework** j'ai commencé à faire mes devoirs; **3** (*of a race*) départ M.
verb **1** commencer [61]; **the film starts at eight** le film commence à huit heures; **I've started the book** j'ai commencé le livre; **2 to start doing** commencer [61] à faire; **I've started learning Spanish** j'ai commencé à apprendre l'espagnol; **3 to start a business** créer [32] une entreprise; **4 to start a car** faire [10] démarrer une voiture; **she started the car** elle a fait démarrer la voiture; **the car wouldn't start** la voiture n'a pas voulu démarrer.

starter *noun* (*in a meal*) entrée F; **what would you like as a starter?** qu'est-ce que vous voulez comme entrée?

starve *verb* mourir [54] de faim; **I'm starving!** je meurs de faim!

state *noun* **1** état M; **the house is in a very bad state** la maison est en très mauvais état; **2** (*administrative*) état M; **the state** l'État; **3 the States** les États-Unis M *plural*; **they live in the States** ils habitent aux États-Unis.
verb **1** déclarer [1] (*intention, opinion*); **2** indiquer [1] (*address, income, occupation, reason, etc*).

stately home *noun* château M (*plural* châteaux).

statement *noun* déclaration F.

station *noun* gare F; **the railway station** la gare; **the bus station** la gare routière; **the police station** le commissariat; **a radio station** une station de radio.

stationer's *noun* papeterie F.

statistics *noun* **1** (*subject*) statistique F; **2 the statistics** (*figures*) les statistiques.

statue *noun* statue F.

stay *noun* séjour M; **our stay in Paris** notre séjour à Paris; **enjoy your stay!** bon séjour!
verb **1** rester [1]; **I'll stay here** je reste ici; **how long are you staying?** vous restez combien de temps?; **2** (*with time*) **we're going to stay in Berlin for three days** nous allons passer trois jours à Berlin; **3** (*at somebody's house*) **to stay with somebody** aller [7] chez quelqu'un; **I'm going to stay with my sister this weekend** je vais chez ma sœur ce weekend; **4** (*be temporarily lodged*) loger [52]; **where are you staying?** où est-ce que vous logez?
● **to stay in** rester [1] à la maison; **I'm staying in tonight** je reste à la maison ce soir.

steady *adjective* **1** stable; **a steady job** un emploi stable; **2** régulier (F régulière); **a steady increase** une augmentation régulière; **3** (*hand, voice*) ferme; **4 to hold something steady** bien tenir quelque chose.

steak *noun* steak M; **steak and chips** un steak frites.

steal *verb* voler [1].

steam *noun* vapeur F.

steam engine *noun* locomotive F à vapeur.

steam iron *noun* fer M à vapeur.

steel *noun* acier M.

steep *adjective* raide; **a steep slope** une pente raide.

steeple *noun* **1** (*spire*) flèche F; **2** (*bell tower*) clocher M.

steering wheel *noun* volant M.

step *noun* **1** pas M; **to take a step forwards** faire un pas en avant; **to take a step backwards** faire un pas en arrière; **2** (*stair*) marche F; **'mind the step'** 'attention à la marche'.
● **to step back** faire [10] un pas en arrière.
● **to step forward** faire [10] un pas en avant.
● **to step into** entrer [1] dans (*a lift*).

stepbrother *noun* demi-frère M (*plural* demi-frères).

stepdaughter *noun* belle-fille F (*plural* belles-filles).

stepfather *noun* beau-père M.

stepladder *noun* escabeau M (*plural* escabeaux).

stepmother *noun* belle-mère F.

stepsister *noun* demi-sœur F (*plural* demi-sœurs).

stepson *noun* beau-fils M (*plural* beaux-fils).

stereo *noun* chaîne F stéréo (*plural* chaînes stéréo).

sterling *noun* sterling M; **in sterling** en livres sterling.

stew *noun* ragoût M.

steward *noun* steward M.

stewardess *noun* hôtesse F.

stick *noun* **1** bâton M; **2 a walking stick** une canne; **3 a hockey stick** une crosse de hockey.
verb **1** (*with glue*) coller [1]; **2** (*put*) mettre [11]; **stick them on my desk** mets-les sur mon bureau.

sticker *noun* autocollant M.

sticky *adjective* **1** poisseux (F poisseuse); **my hands are sticky** j'ai les mains poisseuses; **2** adhésif (F adhésive); **sticky paper** le papier adhésif.

sticky tape *noun* Scotch™ M.

stiff *adjective* **1 to feel stiff** avoir des courbatures; **to have stiff legs** avoir des courbatures dans les jambes; **2 to be bored stiff** s'ennuyer à mourir; **to be scared stiff** être mort de peur.

still *adjective* **1 sit still!** tiens-toi tranquille!; **keep still!** ne bouge pas!; **2 still mineral water** l'eau minérale non-gazeuse.
adverb **1** toujours; **do you still live in London?** est-ce que tu habites toujours à Londres?; **I've still not finished** je n'ai toujours pas fini; **he's still working** il est toujours en train de travailler; **2** encore; **there's still a lot of beer left** il reste encore

beaucoup de bière; **3 better still** encore mieux.

sting *noun* piqûre F; **a wasp sting** une piqûre de guêpe.
verb piquer [1]; **I was stung by a bee** je me suis fait piquer par une abeille.

stink *noun* odeur F; **what a stink!** ça pue!
verb puer [1]; **it stinks of cigarette smoke in here** ça pue la cigarette ici.

stir *verb* remuer [1].

stitch *noun* **1** (*in sewing*) point M; **2** (*in knitting*) maille F; **3** (*surgical*) point M de suture (*plural* points de suture).

stock *noun* **1** (*in a shop*) stock M; **to have something in stock** avoir quelque chose en stock; **2** (*supply*) réserve F; **I always have a stock of pencils** j'ai toujours une réserve de crayons; **3** (*for cooking*) bouillon M; **chicken stock** le bouillon de poulet.
verb (*in a shop*) vendre [3]; **they don't stock dictionaries** ils ne vendent pas les dictionnaires.
● **to stock up on something** s'approvisionner [1] en quelque chose.

stock cube *noun* bouillon-cube M.

stocking *noun* bas M.

stomach *noun* estomac M.

stomachache *noun* **to have stomachache** avoir mal au ventre.

stone *noun* **1** pierre F; **a stone wall** un mur en pierre; **2** (*pebble*)

caillou M (*plural* cailloux); **3** (*in fruit*) noyau M (*plural* noyaux).

stool *noun* tabouret M.

stop *noun* arrêt M; **the bus stop** l'arrêt de bus.
verb **1** s'arrêter [1]; **he stopped in front of the shop** il s'est arrêté devant le magasin; **the music stopped** la musique s'est arrêtée; **does the train stop in Dijon?** est-ce que le train s'arrête à Dijon?; **2 to stop somebody/something** arrêter [1] quelqu'un/quelque chose; **she stopped me in the street** elle m'a arrêté dans la rue; **3 to stop doing** arrêter [1] de faire; **he's stopped smoking** il a arrêté de fumer; **she never stops asking questions** elle n'arrête pas de poser des questions; **4 to stop somebody doing** empêcher [1] quelqu'un de faire; **there's nothing to stop you going on your own** rien ne t'empêche d'y aller tout seul.

stopwatch *noun* chronomètre M.

store *noun* (*shop*) magasin M.
verb **1** garder [1]; **2** (*on a computer*) mémoriser [1].

storey *noun* étage M; **a three-storey house** une maison à trois étages.

storm *noun* **1** (*wind*) tempête F; **a snowstorm** une tempête de neige; **a rainstorm** une tempête de pluie; **2** (*thunderstorm*) orage M.

stormy *adjective* orageux (F orageuse).

story *noun* histoire F; **to tell a story** raconter une histoire.

stove *noun* (*cooker*) cuisinière F.

straight *adjective* **1** droit; **a straight line** une ligne droite; **2 to have straight hair** avoir les cheveux raides.
adverb **1** (*in direction*) droit; **go straight ahead** continuez tout droit; **2** (*in time*) directement; **he went straight to the doctor's** il est allé directement chez le médecin; **3 straight away** tout de suite.

straightforward *adjective* simple.

strain *noun* stress M; **the strain of the last few weeks** le stress de ces dernières semaines; **to be a strain** être stressant.
verb se faire [10] mal à (*part of the body*); **he's strained his back** il s'est fait mal au dos.

strange *adjective* bizarre; **a strange situation** une situation bizarre.

stranger *noun* inconnu M, inconnue F.

strangle *verb* étrangler [1].

strap *noun* **1** (*on case, bag, camera*) courroie F; **2** (*on a garment*) bretelle F; **3** (*of a watch*) bracelet M; **a watchstrap** un bracelet de montre; **4** (*on a shoe*) lanière F.

strapless *adjective* sans bretelles.

straw *noun* paille F (*both the material and for drinking with*); **a straw hat** un chapeau de paille.

strawberry *noun* fraise F; **strawberry jam** la confiture de fraises; **a strawberry yoghurt** un yaourt à la fraise.

stray *adjective* **a stray dog** un chien perdu.

stream *noun* (*small river*) ruisseau M (*plural* ruisseaux).

street *noun* rue F; **I met Simon in the street** j'ai croisé Simon dans la rue.

streetlamp *noun* réverbère M.

street map *noun* plan M de la ville.

streetwise *adjective* dégourdi.

strength *noun* force F.

stress *noun* stress M.
verb (*emphasize*) souligner [1]; **to stress the importance of something** souligner l'importance de quelque chose.

stretch *verb* **1** (*garment*) se déformer [1]; **this jumper has stretched** ce pull s'est déformé; **2** (*shoes*) s'élargir [2].

stretcher *noun* brancard M.

stretchy *adjective* élastique.

strict *adjective* strict.

strike *noun* grève F; **to go on strike** faire grève; **to be on strike** être en grève.
verb **1** (*hit*) frapper [1]; **2** (*clock*) sonner [1]; **the clock struck six** l'horloge a sonné six heures; **3** (*go on strike*) faire [10] grève.

striker *noun* **1** (*in football*) buteur M; **2** (*person on strike*) gréviste M & F.

striking *adjective* frappant; **a striking resemblance** une ressemblance frappante.

string *noun* **1** (*for tying*) ficelle F; **2** (*for a musical instrument*) corde F.

strip noun bande F.
verb (undress) se déshabiller [1].

strip cartoon noun bande
dessinée F.

stripe noun rayure F.

striped adjective rayé.

stroke noun 1 (style of swimming)
nage F; 2 (medical) attaque F; **to
have a stroke** avoir une attaque;
★ **a stroke of luck** un coup de
chance.
verb caresser [1].

stroll noun **to go for a stroll** faire
une petite promenade.
verb se promener [50].

strong adjective 1 (person, drink)
fort; 2 (feeling) puissant;
3 (material) solide.

strongly adverb 1 (believe)
fermement; 2 (support)
fortement; 3 (advise, oppose)
vivement.

struggle noun 1 lutte F; **the
struggle for independence** la lutte
pour l'indépendance; **a power
struggle** une lutte pour le pouvoir;
2 **it's been a struggle** ça a été très
dur.
verb 1 (to obtain something) se
battre [21]; **they have struggled to
survive** ils se sont battus pour
survivre; 2 (physically, in order to
escape or reach something) se
débattre [21]; 3 (have difficulty in
doing) avoir [5] du mal à faire; **I'm
struggling to finish my homework**
j'ai du mal à finir mes devoirs.

stub noun **a cigarette stub** un
mégot.
● **to stub out** écraser [1] (a cigarette).

stubborn adjective têtu.

stuck adjective 1 (jammed) coincé;
the drawer's stuck le tiroir est
coincé; 2 (person) **to get stuck**
rester coincé (in a lift, traffic jam, or
place).

stud noun 1 (on a belt or jacket) clou
M; 2 (on a boot) clou M;
3 (earring) boucle F d'oreille.

student noun étudiant M,
étudiante F.

studio noun 1 (film, TV) studio
M; 2 (artist's) atelier M.

studio flat noun studio M.

study verb 1 réviser [1]; **he's busy
studying for his exams** il est en
train de réviser pour ses examens;
2 faire [10] des études de (a subject);
she's studying medicine elle fait
des études de médecine.

stuff noun 1 (things) trucs M
plural (informal); **we can put all
that stuff in the attic** on peut mettre
tous ces trucs au grenier;
2 (personal belongings) affaires F
plural; **you can leave your stuff at
my house** tu peux laisser tes affaires
chez moi; 3 (substance) truc M
(informal); **some antiseptic stuff**
un truc antiséptique.
verb 1 (shove) fourrer [1]
(informal); **she stuffed some
things into a suitcase** elle a fourré
quelques affaires dans une valise;
2 farcir [2] (chicken, turkey,
vegetables); **stuffed aubergines** des
aubergines farcies.

stuffing noun (for cooking) farce F.

stuffy adjective (airless) étouffant.

stumble *verb* (*trip*) trébucher [1].

stunned *adjective* (*amazed*) stupéfait.

stunning *adjective* sensationnel (F sensationnelle).

stunt *noun* (*in a film*) cascade F.

stuntman *noun* cascadeur M.

stuntwoman *noun* cascadeuse F.

stupid *adjective* bête; **that was really stupid** c'était vraiment bête; **to do something stupid** faire une bêtise.

stutter *noun* **to have a stutter** bégayer [59].
verb bégayer [59].

style *noun* **1** style M; **a style of living** un style de vie; **he has his own style** il a son propre style; **2** (*fashion*) mode F; **it's the latest style** c'est la dernière mode.

subject *noun* **1** sujet M; **the subject of my talk** le sujet de mon exposé; **2** (*at school*) matière F; **my favourite subject is biology** ma matière préférée c'est la biologie.

submarine *noun* sous-marin M (*plural* sous-marins).

subscription *noun* abonnement M; **to take out a subscription to** s'abonner à.

subsidy *noun* subvention F.

substance *noun* substance F.

substitute *noun* (*person*) remplaçant M, remplaçante F.
verb substituer [1].

subtitled *adjective* (*film*) sous-titré.

subtitles *plural noun* sous-titres M *plural*.

subtle *adjective* subtil.

subtract *verb* soustraire [78].

suburb *noun* banlieue F; **a suburb of Edinburgh** une banlieue d'Édimbourg; **in the suburbs of London** dans la banlieue de Londres.

suburban *adjective* de banlieue.

subway *noun* (*underpass*) passage souterrain M.

succeed *verb* réussir [2]; **to succeed in doing** réussir à faire; **we've succeeded in contacting her** nous avons réussi à la contacter.

success *noun* succès M; **a great success** un grand succès.

successful *adjective* **1** réussi; **he's a successful writer** c'est un écrivain réussi; **2 to be successful in doing** réussir à faire.

successfully *adverb* avec succès.

such *adjective, adverb* **1** tellement; **they're such nice people!** ils sont tellement gentils!; **I've had such a busy day!** j'ai eu une journée tellement chargée!; **it's such a long way** c'est tellement loin; **it's such a pity** c'est tellement dommage; **2 such a lot of** tellement de; **I've got such a lot of things to tell you!** j'ai tellement de choses à te dire!; **3 such as** comme; **in big cities such as Glasgow** dans les grandes villes comme Glasgow; **4 there's no such thing** ça n'existe pas.

suck *verb* sucer [61].

sudden *adjective* soudain; ★ **all of a sudden** tout d'un coup.

suddenly *adverb* **1** tout d'un coup; **he suddenly started to laugh** tout d'un coup il s'est mis à rire; **suddenly the light went out** tout d'un coup la lumière s'est éteinte; **2 to die suddenly** mourir subitement.

suede *noun* daim M; **a suede jacket** une veste en daim.

suffer *verb* souffrir [73].

sufficiently *adverb* suffisamment.

sugar *noun* sucre M; **would you like sugar?** est-ce que tu veux du sucre?; **brown sugar** le sucre roux.

suggest *verb* suggérer [24]; **he suggested I should speak to you about it** il m'a suggéré de vous en parler.

suggestion *noun* suggestion F; **to make a suggestion** faire une suggestion.

suicide *noun* suicide M; **to commit suicide** se suicider.

suit *noun* **1** (*man's*) costume M; **2** (*woman's*) tailleur M.

suitable *adjective* **1** (*clothing*) approprié; **I don't have any suitable shoes** je n'ai pas de chaussures appropriées. **2** convenable; **a suitable hotel** un hôtel convenable; **3 to be suitable for** convenir à.

suitcase *noun* valise F.

sulk *verb* bouder [1].

sum *noun* **1** somme F; **a sum of money** une somme d'argent; **a large**

sum une grosse somme; **2** (*calculation*) calcul M.
● **to sum up** résumer [1].

summarize *verb* résumer [1].

summary *noun* résumé M.

summer *noun* été M; **in summer** en été; **summer clothes** les vêtements d'été; **the summer holidays** les grandes vacances.

summertime *noun* été M; **in summertime** en été.

summit *noun* sommet M.

sun *noun* soleil M; **in the sun** au soleil.

sunbathe *verb* se bronzer [1].

sunblock *noun* crème F écran total.

sunburn *noun* coup M de soleil.

sunburned *adjective* **1** (*tanned*) bronzé; **2 to get sunburned** (*burned*) attraper un coup de soleil.

Sunday *noun* dimanche M; **on Sunday** dimanche; **I'm going out on Sunday** je sors dimanche; **see you on Sunday!** à dimanche!; **on Sundays** le dimanche; **the museum is closed on Sundays** le musée est fermé le dimanche; **every Sunday** tous les dimanches; **last Sunday** dimanche dernier; **next Sunday** dimanche prochain.

sunflower *noun* tournesol M; **sunflower oil** l'huile F de tournesol.

sunglasses *plural noun* lunettes F *plural* de soleil.

sunlight *noun* soleil M.

sunny *adjective* **1 it's a sunny day** il fait du soleil; **it's going to be**

sunny il va faire du soleil; **2** (*place*) ensoleillé; **in a sunny corner of the garden** dans un coin ensoleillé du jardin.

sunrise *noun* lever M du soleil.

sunroof *noun* toit ouvrant M.

sunset *noun* coucher M du soleil.

sunshine *noun* soleil M.

sunstroke *noun* insolation F; **to get sunstroke** attraper une insolation.

suntan *noun* bronzage M; **to get a suntan** bronzer.

suntan lotion *noun* lotion solaire F.

suntan oil *noun* huile solaire F.

super *adjective* formidable; **we had a super time!** c'était formidable!

supermarket *noun* supermarché M.

supernatural *adjective* surnaturel (F surnaturelle).

superstitious *adjective* superstitieux (F superstitieuse).

supervise *verb* surveiller [1].

supper *noun* dîner M; **I had supper at Sandy's** j'ai dîné chez Sandy.

supplement *noun* supplément M.

supplies *plural noun* (*of food*) provisions F *plural*.

supply *noun* **1** (*stock*) réserves F *plural*; **2 to be in short supply** être difficile à trouver.
verb fournir [2]; **the school supplies the paper** c'est l'école qui fournit le papier; **to supply somebody with**

something fournir quelque chose à quelqu'un.

supply teacher *noun* suppléant M, suppléante F.

support *noun* soutien M; **he has a lot of support** il a beaucoup de soutien.
verb **1** (*back up*) soutenir [77]; **her teachers have really supported her** ses professeurs l'ont vraiment soutenue; **2** être [6] supporter de (*a team*); **Graeme supports Liverpool** Graeme est supporter de Liverpool; **3** (*financially*) **to support a family** subvenir [81] aux besoins d'une famille.

supporter *noun* supporter M; **a Manchester United supporter** un supporter de Manchester United.

suppose *verb* **I suppose she's forgotten** elle a sans doute oublié.

supposed *adjective* **to be supposed to do** être censé faire; **you're supposed to wear a helmet** on est censé porter un casque; **he was supposed to be here at six** il était censé être là à six heures.

sure *adjective* sûr; **are you sure?** tu es sûr?; **are you sure you've had enough to eat?** tu es sûr que tu as assez mangé?; **are you sure you saw her?** tu es sûr de l'avoir vue?; **'can you shut the door?' – 'sure!'** 'peux-tu fermer la porte?' – 'bien sûr!'

surely *adverb* quand même; **surely she couldn't have forgotten!** elle ne peut quand même pas avoir oublié!

surface *noun* surface F.

surfboard noun planche F de surf (plural planches de surf).

surfing noun surf M; **to go surfing** faire du surf.

surgeon noun chirurgien M; **she's a surgeon** elle est chirurgien.

surgery noun 1 **to have surgery** se faire opérer; 2 (doctor's) cabinet médical M; **the dentist's surgery** le cabinet dentaire.

surname noun nom M de famille (plural noms de famille).

surprise noun surprise F; **what a surprise!** quelle surprise!

surprised adjective surpris; **I was surprised to see her** j'ai été surpris de la voir.

surprising adjective surprenant.

surround verb 1 encercler [1]; 2 **to be surrounded by** être [6] entouré de; **she's surrounded by friends** elle est entourée d'amis.

survey noun enquête F.

survive verb survivre [82].

survivor noun survivant M, survivante F.

suspect noun suspect M, suspecte F.
adjective douteux (F douteuse).
verb soupçonner [1].

suspend verb 1 (hang) suspendre [3]; 2 **to be suspended** (from school) être [6] exclu.

suspense noun suspense M.

suspicious adjective 1 méfiant; **to be suspicious of** se méfier de; 2 **a suspicious parcel** un paquet suspect; 3 **a suspicious-looking individual** un individu louche.

swallow noun (bird) hirondelle F.
verb avaler [1].

swan noun cygne M.

swap verb 1 échanger [52]; **do you want to swap?** tu veux qu'on échange?; **he's swapped his bike for a computer** il a échangé son vélo contre un ordinateur; 2 **to swap seats with somebody** changer [52] de place avec quelqu'un.

swear verb (use bad language) utiliser [1] des gros mots; **he swears a lot** il utilise beaucoup de gros mots.

swearword noun gros mot M.

sweat noun transpiration F.
verb transpirer [1].

sweater noun pull M.

Swede noun Suédois M, Suédoise F.

swede noun (vegetable) rutabaga M.

Sweden noun Suède F; **in Sweden** en Suède; **to Sweden** en Suède.

Swedish noun (language) suédois M.
adjective suédois.

sweep verb balayer [59].

sweet noun 1 bonbon M; **I bought her some sweets** je lui ai acheté des bonbons; 2 (dessert) dessert M.
adjective 1 (food) sucré; **I try not to eat sweet things** j'essaie d'éviter les choses sucrées; 2 (kind) gentil (F gentille); **she's a really sweet person** elle est vraiment gentille; **it**

was really sweet of him c'était vraiment gentil de sa part; **3** (*cute*) mignon (F mignonne); **he looks really sweet in that hat!** il est mignon avec ce chapeau!

sweetcorn *noun* maïs M.

swell *verb* (*part of the body*) enfler [1].

swim *noun* **to go for a swim** aller [7] se baigner;
verb nager [52]; **can he swim?** est-ce qu'il sait nager?; **to swim across something** traverser [1] quelque chose à la nage.

swimmer *noun* nageur M, nageuse F; **she's a strong swimmer** c'est une bonne nageuse.

swimming *noun* natation F; **to go swimming** faire de la natation.

swimming cap *noun* bonnet M de bain.

swimming costume *noun* maillot M de bain.

swimming pool *noun* piscine F.

swimming trunks *noun* maillot M de bain.

swimsuit *noun* maillot M de bain.

swing *noun* balançoire F.

Swiss *noun* (*person*) Suisse M & F; **the Swiss** les Suisses M *plural*
adjective suisse.

switch *noun* **1** (*button type*) bouton M; **2** (*up-down type*) interrupteur M.
verb (*change*) changer [52] de; **to switch places** changer de place.
● **to switch something off** éteindre [60] quelque chose.

● **to switch something on** allumer [1] quelque chose.

Switzerland *noun* Suisse F; **in Switzerland** en Suisse; **to Switzerland** en Suisse.

swollen *adjective* enflé.

swop *verb* SEE **swap**.

sword *noun* épée F.

sycamore *noun* sycomore M.

syllabus *noun* programme M; **to be on the syllabus** être au programme.

symbol *noun* symbole M.

symbolic *adjective* symbolique.

sympathetic *adjective* compréhensif (F compréhensive).

sympathize *verb* **to sympathize with somebody** comprendre [64] quelqu'un; **I sympathize with her** je la comprends.

sympathy *noun* compassion F.

symphony *noun* symphonie F.

symphony orchestra *noun* orchestre symphonique M.

symptom *noun* symptôme M.

synthesizer *noun* synthétiseur M.

synthetic *adjective* synthétique.

syringe *noun* seringue F.

system *noun* système M.

T t

table *noun* table F; **on the table** sur

la table; **to lay the table** mettre la table; **to clear the table** débarrasser la table.

tablecloth *noun* nappe F.

tablespoon *noun* grande cuillère F; (*in recipes*) **a tablespoon of flour** une cuillère à soupe de farine.

tablet *noun* comprimé M.

table tennis *noun* ping-pong™ M; **to play table tennis** jouer au ping-pong.

tabloid *noun* quotidien populaire M.

tackle *verb* **1** (*in football or hockey*) tacler [1]; **2** s'attaquer [1] à (*a job or problem*).

tact *noun* tact M.

tactful *adjective* plein de tact; **that wasn't very tactful** ça a manqué un peu de tact.

tadpole *noun* têtard M.

tail *noun* **1** queue F; **2 'heads or tails?' – 'tails'** 'pile ou face?' – 'pile'.

take *verb* **1** prendre [64]; **he took a chocolate** il a pris un chocolat; **take my hand** prends ma main; **I took the bus** j'ai pris le bus; **to take a holiday** prendre des vacances; **do you take sugar?** est-ce que vous prenez du sucre?; **who's taken my keys?** qui a pris mes clefs?; **it takes two hours** ça prend deux heures; **he took the news badly** il a mal pris la nouvelle; **2** (*to accompany*) emmener [50] (*a person*); **I'm taking Jake to the doctor's** j'emmène Jake chez le médecin; **I must take the car to the garage** je dois emmener la

voiture au garage; **3** (*carry away*) emporter [1]; **she's taken some work to do at home** elle a emporté du travail pour faire chez elle; **4 to take something up(stairs)** monter [1] quelque chose; **could you take these towels up?** est-ce que tu peux monter ces serviettes?; **5 to take something down(stairs)** descendre [3] quelque chose; **Cheryl's taken the cups down** Cheryl a descendu les tasses; **6** accepter [1] (*a credit card or a cheque*); **do you take cheques?** est-ce que vous acceptez les chèques?; **7** passer [1] (*an exam*); **she's taking her driving test tomorrow** elle passe son permis demain; **8 it takes a lot of courage** il faut beaucoup de courage; **9 what size do you take?** quelle taille faites-vous?

● **to take something apart** démonter [1] quelque chose.

● **to take something back** rapporter [1] quelque chose.

● **to take off 1** (*a plane*) décoller [1]; **2** enlever [50] (*clothes or shoes*); **he took off his shirt** il a enlevé sa chemise; **3** déduire [26] (*money*); **he took five pounds off the price** il a déduit cinq livres du prix.

● **to take out 1** (*from a bag or pocket*) sortir [72]; **Eric took out his wallet** Eric a sorti son porte-feuille; **2 he's taking me out to lunch** il m'emmène déjeuner; **she took me out to the theatre** elle m'a emmenée au théâtre.

takeaway *noun* **1** (*a meal*) repas M à emporter; **an Indian takeaway** un repas indien à emporter; **2** (*where you buy it*) restaurant M qui fait des plats à emporter.

take-off *noun* décollage M (*of a plane*).

talent *noun* talent M; **to have a talent for something** être doué pour quelque chose.

talented *adjective* doué; **he's really talented** il est vraiment doué.

talk *noun* 1 (*a chat*) conversation F; **I had a talk with Roy about it** j'ai eu une conversation avec Roy à ce sujet; 2 exposé M; **she's giving a talk on Hungary** elle fait un exposé sur la Hongrie.
verb 1 parler [1]; **I was talking to Jeevan about football** je parlais du foot avec Jeevan; **what's he talking about?** il parle de quoi?; **we'll talk about it later** on en parlera plus tard; 2 (*to gossip*) bavarder [1]; **they're always talking** ils n'arrêtent pas de bavarder.

talkative *adjective* bavard; **he's not exactly talkative!** on ne pourrait pas dire qu'il est bavard!

tall *adjective* 1 grand; **she's very tall** elle est très grande; **I'm 1.7 metres tall** je mesure un virgule sept mètres; 2 haut (*a building or tree*).

tame *adjective* apprivoisé (*an animal*).

tampon *noun* tampon M.

tan *noun* bronzage M; **to get a tan** bronzer.
verb bronzer [1]; **I tan easily** je bronze facilement.

tank *noun* 1 (*for petrol or water*) réservoir M; 2 **a fish tank** un aquarium; 3 (*military*) char M.

tanned *adjective* bronzé.

tap *noun* 1 robinet M; **to turn on the tap** ouvrir le robinet; **to turn off the tap** fermer le robinet; **the hot tap** le robinet d'eau chaude; 2 (*a pat*) petite tape F.
verb taper [1].

tap-dancing *noun* claquettes F *plural*; **to do tap-dancing** faire des claquettes.

tape *noun* 1 cassette F; **my tape of the Stones** ma cassette des Stones; **I've got it on tape** je l'ai en cassette; 2 **sticky tape** Scotch™ M.
verb enregistrer [1]; **I want to tape the film** je veux enregistrer le film.

tape measure *noun* mètre M à ruban.

tape recorder *noun* magnétophone M.

tapestry *noun* tapisserie F.

target *noun* cible F.

tart *noun* tarte F; **a raspberry tart** une tarte aux framboises.

tartan *adjective* écossais; **a tartan skirt** une jupe écossaise.

task *noun* tâche F.

taste *noun* goût M; **the taste of onions** le goût des oignons; **in bad taste** de mauvais goût.
verb 1 goûter [1]; **do you want to taste?** tu veux goûter?; **the soup tastes horrible** la soupe a un goût infect; 2 **to taste of** avoir [5] un goût de; **it tastes of strawberries** ça a un goût de fraises.

tasty *adjective* savoureux (F savoureuse).

tattoo *noun* tatouage M; **he's got a**

tattoo on his arm il a un tatouage sur le bras.

Taurus *noun* Taureau M; **Josephine's Taurus** Josephine est Taureau.

tax *noun* 1 impôts M *plural*; 2 (*on goods*) taxe F.

taxi *noun* taxi M; **by taxi** en taxi; **to take a taxi** prendre un taxi.

taxi driver *noun* chauffeur M de taxi.

taxi rank *noun* station F de taxis.

TB *noun* tuberculose F.

tea *noun* 1 thé M; **a cup of tea** une tasse de thé; **to have tea** prendre le thé; 2 (*evening meal*) dîner M.

teabag *noun* sachet M de thé.

teach *verb* 1 apprendre [64]; **she's teaching me Italian** elle m'apprend l'italien; **that'll teach you!** ça t'apprendra!; 2 enseigner [1]; **her mum teaches maths** sa mère enseigne les maths; 3 **to teach yourself something** apprendre [64] quelque chose tout seul; **Anne taught herself Italian** Anne a appris l'italien toute seule.

teacher *noun* 1 (*in a secondary school*) professeur M; **my mother's a teacher** ma mère est professeur; **our biology teacher** notre professeur de biologie; 2 (*in primary school*) instituteur M, institutrice F; **she's a primary school teacher** elle est institutrice.

teaching *noun* enseignement M.

team *noun* équipe F; **a football**

team une équipe de foot; **our team won** notre équipe a gagné.

teapot *noun* théière F.

tear[1] *noun* (*a rip*) accroc M; **I've got a tear in my jeans** j'ai un accroc dans mon jean.
verb 1 déchirer [1]; **you've torn your shirt** tu as déchiré ta chemise; **she tore up my letter** elle a déchiré ma lettre; 2 se déchirer [1]; **be careful, it tears easily** attention, ça se déchire facilement.
● **to tear off, to tear open** 1 (*carefully*) détacher [1]; 2 (*violently*) arracher [1].

tear[2] *noun* (*when you cry*) larme F; **to be in tears** être en larmes; **to burst into tears** fondre en larmes.

tease *verb* 1 taquiner [1] (*a person*); 2 tourmenter [1] (*an animal*).

teaspoon *noun* petite cuillère F; (*in recipes*) **a teaspoonful of...** une cuillère à café de...

teatime *noun* l'heure F du dîner (*evening meal*).

tea towel *noun* torchon M.

technical *adjective* technique.

technical college *noun* lycée technique M.

technician *noun* technicien M, technicienne F.

technique *noun* technique F.

techno *noun* techno F (*music*).

technological *adjective* technologique.

technology *noun* technologie F;

information technology
l'informatique F.

teddy bear *noun* nounours M.

teenage *adjective* **1** adolescent (F adolescente); **they have a teenage son** ils ont un fils adolescent; **2** (*films, magazines, etc*) pour les jeunes; **a teenage magazine** un magazine pour les jeunes.

teenager *noun* **1** jeune M & F; **a group of teenagers** une bande de jeunes; **2** (*more precisely*) adolescent M, adolescente F; **when I was a teenager** quand j'étais adolescent.

teens *plural noun* adolescence F; **he's in his teens** c'est un adolescent.

tee-shirt *noun* tee-shirt M.

telephone *noun* téléphone M; **on the telephone** au téléphone. *verb* appeler [18]; **I'll telephone the bank** je vais appeler la banque.

telephone box *noun* cabine F téléphonique.

telephone call *noun* coup M de téléphone.

telephone directory *noun* annuaire M.

telephone number *noun* numéro M de téléphone.

telescope *noun* téléscope M.

televise *verb* téléviser [1]; **they're televising the match** on va téléviser le match.

television *noun* télévision F; **she was watching television** elle regardait la télévision; **I saw it on television** je l'ai vu à la télévision.

television programme *noun* émission F de télévision.

tell *verb* **1** **to tell somebody something** dire [9] quelque chose à quelqu'un; **that's what she told me** c'est ce qu'elle m'a dit; **I told him it was silly** je lui ai dit que c'était idiot; **have you told Sara?** est-ce que tu l'as dit à Sara?; **2** **to tell somebody to do** dire [9] à quelqu'un de faire; **he told me to do it myself** il m'a dit de le faire moi-même; **she told me not to wait** elle m'a dit de ne pas attendre; **3** (*explain*) **can you tell me how to do it?** est-ce que vous pouvez m'expliquer comment on le fait? **4** raconter [1] (*a story*); **tell me about your holiday** raconte-moi tes vacances; **5** (*to see*) voir [13]; **you can tell it's old** on voit bien que c'est ancien; **you can tell she's cross** on voit bien qu'elle est fâchée; **I can't tell them apart** je n'arrive pas à les distinguer.

telly *noun* télé F; **to watch telly** regarder la télé; **I saw her on telly** je l'ai vue à la télé.

temp *noun* intérimaire M & F.

temper *noun* **to be in a temper** être en colère; **to lose your temper** se mettre en colère.

temperature *noun* **1** température F; **the oven temperature** la température du four; **2** **to have a temperature** avoir de la fièvre.

temple *noun* temple M.

temporary *adjective* temporaire.

temptation *noun* tentation F.

tempted *adjective* tenté; **I'm really tempted to go** je suis vraiment tenté d'y aller.

tempting *adjective* tentant.

ten *number* dix M; **Harry's ten** Harry a dix ans.

tend *verb* **to tend to do** avoir [5] tendance à faire; **he tends to talk a lot** il a tendance à beaucoup parler.

tender *adjective* tendre.

tennis *noun* tennis M; **to play tennis** jouer au tennis.

tennis ball *noun* balle F de tennis.

tennis court *noun* tennis M.

tennis player *noun* joueur de tennis M, joueuse de tennis F.

tennis racket *noun* raquette F de tennis.

tenor *noun* ténor M.

tenpin bowling *noun* bowling M; **to go tenpin bowling** jouer au bowling.

tense *noun* **the present tense** le présent; **in the future tense** au futur.
adjective tendu.

tent *noun* tente F.

tenth *number* dixième M; **on the tenth floor** au dixième étage; **the tenth of April** le dix avril.

term *noun* 1 (*in school*) trimestre M; 2 **to be on good terms with somebody** être en bons termes avec quelqu'un.

terminal *noun* 1 (*at an airport*) aérogare F; **terminal two** l'aérogare numéro deux; 2 **a ferry**

terminal une gare maritime; 3 (*a computer terminal*) terminal M (*plural* terminaux).

terrace *noun* 1 (*of a house or hotel*) terrasse F; 2 **the terraces** (*at a stadium*) les gradins M *plural*.

terrible *adjective* épouvantable; **the weather was terrible** il a fait un temps épouvantable.

terribly *adverb* 1 (*very*) très; **not terribly clean** pas très propre; 2 (*badly*) affreusement mal; **I played terribly** j'ai joué affreusement mal.

terrific *adjective* 1 **at a terrific speed** à une vitesse folle; **a terrific amount** une quantité énorme; 2 **terrific!** formidable!

terrified *adjective* terrifié.

terrorism *noun* terrorisme M.

terrorist *noun* terroriste M & F.

test *noun* 1 (*in school*) contrôle M; **we've got a maths test tomorrow** nous avons un contrôle de maths demain; 2 (*of your skills or patience*) test M; 3 (*medical*) analyse F; **a blood test** une analyse de sang; 4 **a driving test** un examen de permis de conduire; **she's doing her driving test on Friday** elle passe son permis vendredi; **he passed his driving test** il a eu son permis.
verb 1 (*in school*) contrôler [1]; 2 **to test something out** essayer quelque chose.

test tube *noun* éprouvette F.

text *noun* texte M.

textbook *noun* manuel M.

Thames *noun* **the Thames** la Tamise.

than *preposition, conjunction* **1** que; **their new album's better than the last one** leur nouveau CD est meilleur que le dernier; **they have more money than we do** ils ont plus d'argent que nous; **2** (*for quantities*) de; **more than forty** plus de quarante; **more than thirty years** plus de trente ans.

thank *verb* remercier [1].

thanks *plural noun* **1** merci; **no thanks** non merci; **thanks a lot** merci beaucoup; **thanks for your letter** merci pour ta lettre; **2 with thanks for** avec mes remerciements pour; **3 thanks to** grâce à; **it was thanks to Micky** c'était grâce à Micky.

thank you *adverb* merci; **thank you very much for the cheque** merci beaucoup pour le chèque; **no thank you** non merci; **a thank-you letter** une lettre de remerciements.

that *adjective* **1** ce (F cette) (*but 'ce' becomes 'cet' before a masculine noun beginning with a vowel or a silent 'h'*); **that dog** ce chien; **that man** cet homme; **that blue car** cette voiture bleue; **2 that one** celui-là M, celle-là F; **'which cake would you like?' – 'that one, please'** 'tu veux quel gâteau?' – 'celui-là, s'il te plaît'; **I like all the dresses but I'm going to buy that one** j'aime toutes les robes mais je vais acheter celle-là.
adverb **1 it's not that silly** ce n'est pas si idiot que ça; **their house isn't that big** leur maison n'est pas si grande que ça; **2 it was that high** c'était haut comme ça.
pronoun **1** ce, c' (*before a vowel or a silent 'h'*); **that's not true** ce n'est pas vrai; **that's not what you told me** ce n'est pas ce que tu m'as dit; **what's that?** qu'est-ce que c'est?; **who's that?** c'est qui?; **where's that?** c'est où?; **is that Mandy?** c'est Mandy?; **2** ça; **did you see that?** est-ce que tu as vu ça?; **that's my bedroom** ça c'est ma chambre; **3** qui; **the book that's on the table** le livre qui est sur la table; **4** que, qu' (*before a vowel or a silent 'h'*); **the book that I lent you** le livre que je t'ai prêté.
conjunction que, qu' (*before a vowel or a silent 'h'*); **I knew that he was wrong** je savais qu'il avait tort.

the *definite article* **1** (*before a noun which is masculine in French*) le, l' (*before a vowel or silent 'h'*); **the cat** le chat; **the tree** l'arbre; **2** (*before a noun which is feminine in French*) la, l' (*before a vowel or silent 'h'*); **the table** la table; **the orange** l'orange; **3** les (*before all plural nouns*); **the windows** les fenêtres.

theatre *noun* théâtre M; **to go to the theatre** aller au théâtre.

theft *noun* vol M.

their *adjective* leur (*plural* leurs); **their flat** leur appartement; **their mother** leur mère; **their presents** leurs cadeaux.

theirs *pronoun* **1** le leur (*when standing for a masculine noun*); **our garden's smaller than theirs** notre jardin est plus petit que le leur; **2** la leur (*when standing for a feminine* *noun*); **your house is bigger than theirs** votre maison est plus grande que la leur; **3** les leurs (*when standing for a plural noun*); **our children are older than theirs** nos enfants sont plus âgés que les leurs; **4** à eux; **the yellow car's theirs** la voiture jaune est à eux; **it's theirs** c'est à eux.

them *pronoun* **1** les; **I know them** je les connais; **I don't know them** je ne les connais pas; **listen to them!** écoute-les!; **I saw them last week** je les ai vus la semaine dernière; **2** (*to them*) leur; **I gave them my address** je leur ai donné mon adresse; **3** (*after a preposition*) eux (F elles); **I'll go with them** j'irai avec eux; (*if they are all female*) j'irai avec elles; **without them** sans eux; sans elles; (*in comparisons*) **she's older than them** elle est plus âgée qu'eux; (*if all female*) elle est plus âgée qu'elles.

theme *noun* thème F.

theme park *noun* parc M de loisirs.

themselves *pronoun* **1** se; **they've helped themselves** ils se sont servis; **2** (*for emphasis*) eux-mêmes M, elles-mêmes F; **the boys can do it themselves** les garçons peuvent le faire eux-mêmes; **the girls will tell you themselves** les filles vous le diront elles-mêmes.

then *adverb* **1** (*next*) ensuite; **I wash up and then I make the bed** je fais la vaisselle et ensuite je fais le lit; **I went to the post office and then the bank** je suis allé à la poste et ensuite à la banque; **2** (*at that time*) à l'époque; **we were living in York**

then nous habitions à York à l'époque; **3** (*in that case*) alors; **then why worry?** alors pourquoi s'inquiéter?; **that's all right then** ça va alors; **4** by then déjà; **by then it was too late** il était déjà trop tard.

theory *noun* théorie F; **in theory** en théorie.

there *adverb* **1** là; **put it there** mets-le là; **stand there** mettez-vous là; **they're in there** ils sont là; **look up there!** regarde là-haut!; **2** over there là-bas; **she's over there talking to Mark** elle est là-bas en train de discuter avec Mark; **down there** là-bas; **3** up there là-haut; **4** y (*when the place 'there' stands for has already been mentioned*); **I've seen photos of Oxford but I've never been there** j'ai vu des photos d'Oxford mais je n'y suis jamais allé; **yes, I'm going there on Tuesday** oui, j'y vais mardi; **5** there is il y a; **there's a cat in the garden** il y a un chat dans le jardin; **there was no bread** il n'y avait pas de pain; **yes, there's enough** oui, il y en a assez; **6** there are il y a; **there are plenty of seats** il y a beaucoup de places; **7** there they are! les voilà!; **there she is!** la voilà!; **there's the bus coming!** voilà le bus qui arrive!

therefore *adverb* donc.

thermometer *noun* thermomètre M.

these *adjective* ces.

they *pronoun* **1** ils (*when standing for a masculine noun*); 'where are the knives?' – 'they're in the drawer' 'où sont les couteaux?' – 'ils sont dans le tiroir'; **2** elles (*when* *standing for a feminine noun*); **I bought some apples but they're not very nice** j'ai acheté des pommes mais elles ne sont pas très bonnes.

thick *adjective* épais (F épaisse); **a thick layer of butter** une couche épaisse de beurre.

thief *noun* voleur M, voleuse F.

thigh *noun* cuisse F.

thin *adjective* 1 mince (*a slice or a person*); 2 (*too thin, skinny*) maigre; **she's got terribly thin** elle a beaucoup maigri.

thing *noun* 1 (*an object*) chose F; **shops full of pretty things** des magasins remplis de jolies choses; **she told me some surprising things** elle m'a raconté des choses étonnantes; 2 (*a whatsit*) truc M (*informal*); **you can use that thing to open it** tu peux utiliser ce truc-là pour l'ouvrir; **that thing next to the hammer** ce truc à côté du marteau; 3 **things** (*belongings*) affaires F *plural*; **you can put your things in my room** tu peux mettre tes affaires dans ma chambre; 4 **the best thing to do is …** ce qu'il faut faire, c'est …; **the thing is, I've lost her address** ce qu'il y a, c'est que j'ai perdu son adresse; **how are things with you?** comment ça va?

think *verb* 1 (*believe*) croire [33]; **do you think they'll come?** tu crois qu'ils vont venir?; **no, I don't think so** non, je ne crois pas; **I think he's already left** je crois qu'il est déjà parti; 2 penser [1]; **I'm thinking about you** je pense à toi; **Tony thinks it's silly** Tony pense que c'est bête; **what do you think of my new jacket?** qu'est-ce que tu penses de ma nouvelle veste?; **what do you think of that?** qu'en penses-tu?; 3 (*to think carefully*) réfléchir [2]; **he thought for a moment** il a réfléchi un instant; **I've thought it over carefully** j'y ai bien réfléchi; 4 (*imagine*) imaginer [1]; **just think! we'll soon be in Spain!** imagine! on va bientôt être en Espagne!; **I never thought it would be like this!** je n'ai jamais imaginé que ce serait comme ça!

third *noun* tiers M; **a third of the population** un tiers de la population.
adjective troisième; **on the third floor** au troisième étage; **the third of March** le trois mars.

thirdly *adverb* troisièmement.

Third World *noun* tiers-monde M.

thirst *noun* soif M.

thirsty *adjective* **to be thirsty** avoir soif; **I'm thirsty** j'ai soif; **we were all thirsty** nous avions tous soif.

thirteen *number* treize M; **Ahmed's thirteen** Ahmed a treize ans.

thirty *number* trente M.

this *adjective* 1 ce (*before a masculine noun*), cet (*before a masculine noun beginning with a vowel or a silent 'h'*), cette (*before a feminine noun*); **this paintbrush** ce pinceau; **this tree** cet arbre; **this cup** cette tasse; **this morning** ce matin; **this evening** ce soir; **this afternoon** cet après-midi; 2 **this one** celui-ci M, celle-ci F; **if you need a pen you can use this one** si

tu as besoin d'un stylo tu peux utiliser celui-ci; **if you want a lamp you can borrow this one** si tu veux une lampe tu peux emprunter celle-ci.
pronoun **1** ça; **can you hold this for a moment?** est-ce que tu peux prendre ça un instant?; **2 what's this?** qu'est-ce que c'est?; **this is Tracy speaking** (*on the phone*) c'est Tracy à l'appareil; **3** (*in introductions*) **this is my sister Carla** je te présente ma sœur Carla.

thistle *noun* chardon M.

thorn *noun* épine F.

those *adjective* ces; **those books** ces livres.
pronoun ceux-là M, celles-là F; **if you want some knives you can take those** si tu veux des couteaux tu peux prendre ceux-là; **if you want some plates you can take those** si tu veux des assiettes tu peux prendre celles-là.

though *conjunction* **1** bien que (*followed by a verb in the subjunctive*); **though it's cold** bien qu'il fasse froid; **though he's older than she is** bien qu'il soit plus âgé qu'elle; **2 it was a good idea, though** et pourtant, c'était une bonne idée.

thought *noun* pensée F.

thoughtful *adjective* **1** (*considerate*) gentil (F gentille); **it was really thoughtful of you** c'était vraiment gentil de ta part; **2** (*deep in thought*) pensif (F pensive).

thoughtless *adjective* irréfléchi.

thousand *number* **1** mille M; **a**

thousand mille; **three thousand** trois mille; **2 thousands of** des milliers de; **there were thousands of tourists in Venice** il y avait des milliers de touristes à Venise.

thread *noun* fil M.
verb enfiler [1] (*a needle*).

threat *noun* menace F.

threaten *verb* menacer [61]; **to threaten to do** menacer de faire.

three *number* trois M; **Oskar's three** Oskar a trois ans.

three-quarters *noun* trois-quarts M *plural*; **three-quarters full** plein aux trois-quarts.

thrilled *adjective* ravi; **I was thrilled to hear from you** j'ai été ravi d'avoir de tes nouvelles.

thriller *noun* thriller M.

thrilling *adjective* palpitant.

throat *noun* gorge F; **to have a sore throat** avoir mal à la gorge.

through *preposition* **1** (*across*) à travers; **through the forest** à travers la forêt; **the water went right through** l'eau est passée à travers; **the police let us through** la police nous a laissés passer; **2** (*via*) par; **the train went through Leeds** le train est passé par Leeds; **through the window** par la fenêtre; **I know them through my cousins** je les connais par mes cousins; **3 to go through something** traverser quelque chose; **we went through the park** nous avons traversé le parc; **4 right through the day** toute la journée.
adjective direct (*a train or flight*).

throw verb 1 jeter [48]; **I threw the letter into the bin** j'ai jeté la lettre dans la poubelle; **he threw the book on the floor** il a jeté le livre par terre; 2 (*taking aim*) lancer [61]; **throw me the ball!** lance-moi le ballon!; **we were throwing snowballs** on lançait des boules de neige.

● **to throw something away** jeter [48] quelque chose; **I've thrown away the old newspapers** j'ai jeté les vieux journaux.

● **to throw somebody out** expulser [1] quelqu'un.

● **to throw something out** jeter [48] quelque chose (*rubbish*).

● **to throw up** vomir [2].

thumb noun pouce M.

thump verb taper [1].

thunder noun tonnerre M; **a peal of thunder** un roulement de tonnerre.

thunderstorm noun orage M.

thundery adjective orageux (F orageuse).

Thursday noun jeudi M; **on Thursday** jeudi; **I'm going out on Thursday** je sors jeudi; **see you on Thursday!** à jeudi!; **on Thursdays** le jeudi; **the museum is closed on Thursdays** le musée est fermé le jeudi; **every Thursday** tous les jeudis; **last Thursday** jeudi dernier; **next Thursday** jeudi prochain.

thyme noun thym M.

tick verb 1 (*tick-tock*) faire [10] tic-tac; 2 (*on paper*) cocher [1]; **tick the box** cochez la case.

ticket noun 1 billet M; (*for a plane,*

a train, an exhibition, a theatre or cinema) **two tickets for the concert** deux billets pour le concert; 2 (*for the underground, the bus, or left luggage*) ticket M; **a bus ticket** un ticket de bus; 3 **a parking ticket** un PV (*informal*).

ticket inspector noun contrôleur M.

ticket office noun (*at a station*) guichet M.

tickle verb chatouiller [1].

tide noun marée F; **at high tide** à marée haute; **the tide is out** c'est la marée basse.

tidy adjective 1 bien rangé (*a room*); 2 soigné (*homework*); 3 ordonné (*a person*). verb ranger [52]; **I'll tidy (up) the kitchen** je rangerai la cuisine.

tie noun 1 cravate F; **a red tie** une cravate rouge; 2 (*in a match*) match M nul. verb 1 nouer [1]; **to tie your shoelaces** nouer ses lacets; 2 **to tie a knot in something** faire [10] un nœud à quelque chose; 3 (*in a match*) **we tied two all** nous avons fait match nul, deux partout.

tiger noun tigre M.

tight adjective 1 juste; **the skirt's a bit tight** la jupe est un peu juste; **these shoes are too tight** ces chaussures me serrent; 2 (*close-fitting*) moulant; **she was wearing a tight dress** elle portait une robe moulante.

tighten verb serrer [1].

tightly adverb fermement.

tights *plural noun* collant M
singular; **a pair of purple tights** un
collant violet.

tile *noun* **1** (*on a floor or wall*)
carreau M (*plural* carreaux);
2 (*on a roof*) tuile F.

till[1] *preposition, conjunction*
1 jusqu'à; **they're here till Sunday**
ils sont là jusqu'à dimanche; **till
then** jusque-là; **till now** jusqu'à
présent; **2 not till** pas avant; **she
won't be back till ten** elle ne sera
pas rentrée avant dix heures; **we
won't know till Monday** nous ne le
saurons pas avant lundi.

till[2] *noun* caisse F; **pay at the till**
payez à la caisse.

time *noun* **1** (*on the clock*) heure F;
what time is it? quelle heure est-il?;
it's time for lunch c'est l'heure du
déjeuner; **on time** à l'heure; **ten
o'clock French time** dix heures
heure française; **2** (*an amount of
time*) temps M; **we've got lots of
time** nous avons beaucoup de
temps; **there's not much time left** il
ne reste plus beaucoup de temps; **for
a long time** longtemps; **from time to
time** de temps en temps;
3 (*moment*) moment M; **is this a
good time to phone?** est-ce que
c'est le bon moment pour vous
appeler?; **at times** par moments; **for
the time being** pour le moment; **any
time now** d'un moment à l'autre;
4 (*in a series*) fois F; **six times** six
fois; **the first time** la première fois;
the first time I saw you la première
fois que je t'ai vu; **three times a year**
trois fois par an; **three times two is
six** trois fois deux égale six; **5 to
have a good time** bien s'amuser [1];
we had a really good time nous

sommes très bien amusés; **have
a good time!** amusez-vous bien!

time off *noun* **1** (*free time*) temps
M libre; **2** (*leave*) congé M.

timetable *noun* **1** (*in school*)
emploi M du temps; **2** (*for trains or
buses*) horaire M; **the bus
timetable** l'horaire des bus.

tin *noun* boîte F; **a tin of tomatoes**
une boîte de tomates.

tinned *adjective* en conserve; **tinned
peas** des petits pois en conserve.

tin opener *noun* ouvre-boîte M.

tinted *adjective* teinté.

tiny *adjective* minuscule.

tip *noun* **1** (*the end*) bout M; **the tip
of my finger** le bout de mon doigt;
2 (*money*) pourboire M; **3** (*a
useful hint*) tuyau M
(*plural* tuyaux) (*informal*).
verb **1** (*to give money to*) donner [1]
un pourboire à; **we tipped the
waiter** nous avons donné un
pourboire au garçon; **2** verser [1]
(*liquid*).

tiptoe *noun* **on tiptoe** sur la pointe
des pieds.

tired *adjective* **1** fatigué; **I'm tired** je
suis fatigué; **you look tired** tu as l'air
fatigué; **2 to be tired of** en avoir
assez de; **I'm tired of London** j'en ai
assez de Londres; **I'm tired of
watching TV** j'en ai assez de
regarder la télé.

tiring *adjective* fatigant.

tissue *noun* (*a paper hanky*)
kleenex™ M; **do you have a
tissue?** est-ce que tu as un kleenex?

tissue paper *noun* papier M de soie.

title *noun* titre M.

to *preposition* 1 (*to a place or person*) à (*note that 'à + le' becomes 'au' and 'à + les' becomes 'aux'*); **to go to London** aller à Londres; **give the book to Leila** donne le livre à Leila; **I'm going to school** je vais à l'école; **she's gone to the office** elle est partie au bureau; **a letter to parents** une lettre aux parents; **from Monday to Friday** du lundi au vendredi; 2 (*with names of countries*) **they're going to Spain** ils vont en Espagne; (*BUT*) **they're going to Japan** ils vont au Japon (*'en' with feminine countries, 'au' with most masculine countries*); 3 à; **I have nothing to do** je n'ai rien à faire; **I had a lot of homework to do** j'avais beaucoup de devoirs à faire; **we're ready to go** nous sommes prêts à partir; **it's easy to do** c'est facile à faire; 4 (*to somebody's house, shop, surgery*) chez; **I went round to Paul's house** je suis allé chez Paul; **we're going to the Browns' for supper** on va dîner chez les Brown; **I'm going to the dentist's tomorrow** je vais chez le dentiste demain; **she's gone to the hairdresser's** elle est allée chez le coiffeur; 5 (*talking about the time*) **it's ten to nine** il est neuf heures moins dix; **it's twenty to** il est moins vingt; 6 (*in order to*) pour; **he gave me some money to buy a sandwich** il m'a donné de l'argent pour acheter un sandwich.

toad *noun* crapaud M.

toadstool *noun* champignon M; **a**

poisonous toadstool un champignon vénéneux.

toast *noun* 1 pain grillé M; **two slices of toast** deux tranches de pain grillé; 2 (*to your health*) toast M; **to drink a toast to the future** lever un verre à l'avenir.

toaster *noun* grille-pain M.

tobacco *noun* tabac M.

tobacconist's *noun* bureau M de tabac.

today *noun* aujourd'hui M; **today's her birthday** c'est son anniversaire aujourd'hui.

toe *noun* doigt M de pied; **my big toe** mon gros orteil.

toffee *noun* caramel M.

together *adverb* 1 ensemble; **Kate and Lenny arrived together** Kate et Lenny sont arrivés ensemble; 2 (*at the same time*) en même temps; **they all left together** ils sont tous partis en même temps.

toilet *noun* toilettes F *plural*; **where's the toilet?** où sont les toilettes?; **she's gone to the toilet** elle est allé aux toilettes.

toilet paper *noun* papier M hygiénique.

toilet roll *noun* rouleau M de papier hygiénique.

token *noun* 1 (*for a machine or game*) jeton M; 2 **a record token** un chèque-cadeaux pour disque.

tolerant *adjective* tolérant.

toll *noun* péage M.

tomato *noun* tomate F; **a tomato**

salad une salade de tomates; **tomato sauce** la sauce tomate.

tomorrow *adverb* demain; **I'll do it tomorrow** je le ferai demain; **tomorrow afternoon** demain après-midi; **tomorrow morning** demain matin; **tomorrow night** demain soir; **the day after tomorrow** après-demain.

tone *noun* **1** (*on an answerphone*) tonalité F; **speak after the tone** parlez après la tonalité; **2** (*of a voice or a letter*) ton M.

tongue *noun* langue F; **to stick your tongue out** tirer la langue; ★ **it's on the tip of my tongue** je l'ai sur le bout de la langue.

tonic *noun* Schweppes™ M; **a gin and tonic** un gin tonic.

tonight *adverb* **1** (*this evening*) ce soir; **I'm going out with my mates tonight** je sors avec les copains ce soir; **2** (*after bedtime*) cette nuit.

tonsillitis *noun* angine F.

too *adverb* **1** trop; **it's too expensive** c'est trop cher; **too often** trop souvent; **2 too much, too many** trop; **it takes too much time** ça prend trop de temps; **there are too many accidents** il y a trop d'accidents; **he eats too much** il mange trop; **3** (*as well*) aussi; **Karen's coming too** Karen vient aussi; **me too!** moi aussi!

tool *noun* outil M.

tool box *noun* boîte F à outils.

tool kit *noun* trousse F à outils.

tooth *noun* dent F; **to brush your teeth** se brosser les dents.

toothache *noun* mal M de dents; **to have toothache** avoir mal aux dents.

toothbrush *noun* brosse F à dents.

toothpaste *noun* dentifrice M.

top *noun* **1** haut M (*of a page, a ladder, or stairs*); **at the top of the stairs** en haut de l'escalier; **2** (*of a container or box*) dessus M; **it's on top of the chest-of-drawers** c'est sur la commode; **3** (*of a mountain*) sommet M; **4** (*a lid*) (*of a pen*) capuchon M; (*of a bottle*) capsule F; **5 to be at the top of the list** être en tête de la liste. *adjective* **1** (*a step or floor*) dernier (F dernière); **it's on the top floor** c'est au dernier étage; **2** de haut (*a bunk*); **3** du haut (*a shelf*); **4 in the top left-hand corner** en haut à gauche; ★ **and on top of all that** et par-dessus le marché; ★ **it was a bit over the top** c'était un peu exagéré.

topic *noun* sujet M.

torch *noun* lampe F de poche.

torn *adjective* déchiré.

tortoise *noun* tortue F.

torture *noun* torture F. *verb* torturer [1].

Tory *noun* conservateur M, conservatrice F.

total *noun* total M. *adjective* total (M *plural* totaux).

totally *adverb* complètement.

touch *noun* **1** (*contact*) **to get in touch with somebody** prendre contact avec quelqu'un; **to stay in touch with somebody** rester en contact avec quelqu'un; **2 we've**

lost touch on s'est perdu de vue; **I've lost touch with her recently** je l'ai perdue de vue récemment; **3** (*a little bit*) petit peu M; **a touch of vanilla** un petit peu de vanille; **it was a touch embarrassing** c'était un petit peu gênant. *verb* toucher [1].

touched *adjective* touché.

touching *adjective* touchant.

tough *adjective* **1** dur; **the meat's a bit tough** la viande est un peu dure; **it's a tough area** c'est un quartier dur; **things are a bit tough at the moment** la vie est un peu dure en ce moment; **a tough guy** un dur; **2** robuste; **you need to be tough to survive** il faut être robuste pour survivre!; **a tough fabric** un tissu robuste; **3** (*tough luck*) tant pis; **tough, you're too late** tant pis pour toi, tu arrives trop tard.

tour *noun* **1** visite F; **we did the tour of the castle** nous avons fait la visite du château; **a tour of the city** une visite de la ville; **2 a package tour** un voyage organisé; **3** (*by a band or theatre group*) tournée F; **to go on tour** partir en tournée. *verb* (*performer*) être [6] en tournée; **they're touring the States** ils sont en tournée aux États-Unis.

tourism *noun* tourisme M.

tourist *noun* touriste M & F.

tourist information office *noun* syndicat M d'initiative.

tournament *noun* tournoi M; **a tennis tournament** un tournoi de tennis.

tow *verb* **to be towed away** (*by the police*) être [6] emmené à la fourrière; (*by a breakdown truck*) être [6] remorqué.

towards *adverb* en direction de; **she went off towards the lake** elle est parti en direction du lac.

towel *noun* serviette F.

tower *noun* tour F; **the Eiffel Tower** la tour Eiffel.

tower block *noun* tour F.

town *noun* ville F; **to go into town** aller en ville.

town centre *noun* centre-ville M.

town hall *noun* mairie F.

toy *noun* jouet M; **a toy car** une petite voiture.

toyshop *noun* magasin M de jouets.

trace *noun* trace F; **there was no trace of it** il n'en restait aucune trace. *verb* retrouver [1].

tracing paper *noun* papier calque M.

track *noun* **1** (*for sport*) piste F; **a track event** une épreuve de vitesse; **a racing track** (*for cars*) un circuit; **2** (*a path*) chemin M; **3** (*song*) chanson; **this is my favourite track** c'est ma chanson préférée.

track suit *noun* survêtement M.

tractor *noun* tracteur M.

trade *noun* (*a profession*) métier M.

trade union *noun* syndicat M.

tradition *noun* tradition F.

traditional *adjective* traditionnel (F traditionnelle).

traffic *noun* circulation F.

traffic island *noun* refuge M.

traffic jam *noun* embouteillage M.

traffic lights *plural noun* feux M *plural*.

traffic warden *noun* contractuel M, contractuelle F.

tragedy *noun* tragédie F.

tragic *adjective* tragique.

trail *noun* (*a path*) sentier M; **a nature trail** un sentier écologique.

trailer *noun* remorque F.

train *noun* train M; **he's coming by train** il prend le train; **I met her on the train** je l'ai rencontrée dans le train; **the train for York** le train pour York.
verb **1** former [1] (*a student*); **2 to train to be something** suivre [75] une formation de quelque chose; **he's training to be a nurse** il suit une formation d'infirmier; **3** (*in sport*) s'entraîner [1]; **the team trains on Saturdays** l'équipe s'entraîne le samedi.

train ticket *noun* billet M de train.

train timetable *noun* horaire M des trains.

trainee *noun* stagiaire M & F.

trainer *noun* **1** (*of an athlete or a horse*) entraîneur M, entraîneuse F; **2** (*shoe*) basket M; **my new trainers** mes nouveaux baskets.

training *noun* **1** (*for a career*) formation F; **2** (*for sport*) entraînement M.

tram *noun* tramway M.

tramp *noun* clochard M, clocharde F.

transfer *noun* (*sticker*) décalcomanie F.

transform *verb* transformer [1].

transistor *noun* transistor M.

translate *verb* traduire [26]; **to translate something into French** traduire quelque chose en français.

translation *noun* traduction F.

translator *noun* traducteur M, traductrice F; **I'd like to be a translator** j'aimerais être traducteur.

transparent *adjective* transparent.

transport *noun* transport M; **air transport** le transport aérien; **public transport** les transports en commun.

trap *noun* piège M.

travel *noun* voyages M *plural*; **foreign travel** les voyages à l'étranger; **a travel brochure** une brochure de voyages.
verb voyager [52].

travel agency *noun* agence F de voyages.

travel agent *noun* agent M de voyages.

traveller *noun* **1** voyageur M, voyageuse F. **2** (*gypsy*) nomade M & F.

traveller's cheque *noun* chèque-voyage M (*plural* chèques-voyage).

travelling *noun* voyages M *plural*;

I like travelling j'aime partir en voyage.

travel-sick *noun* **to be** or **get travel-sick** souffrir [73] du mal de voyage.

tray *noun* plateau M (*plural* plateaux)

tread *verb* **to tread on something** marcher [1] sur quelque chose.

treasure *noun* trésor M.

treat *noun* **1 I took them to the circus as a treat** je les ai emmenés au cirque pour leur faire plaisir; **2** (*food*) gâterie F; **it's a little treat** c'est une petite gâterie. *verb* **1** traiter [1]; **he treats his dog well** il traite bien son chien; **the doctor who treated you** le médecin qui vous a traité; **2 to treat somebody to something** offrir [56] quelque chose à quelqu'un; **I'll treat you to a drink** je vous offre à boire; **I treated myself to a new dress** je me suis offert une nouvelle robe.

treatment *noun* traitement M.

tree *noun* arbre M.

tree trunk *noun* tronc M d'arbre.

tremble *verb* trembler [1].

trend *noun* **1** (*a fashion*) mode F; **2** (*a tendency*) tendance F.

trendy *adjective* branché.

trial *noun* procès M (*legal*).

triangle *noun* triangle M.

trick *noun* **1** (*by a conjuror, or as a joke*) tour M; **to play a trick on somebody** jouer un tour à quelqu'un; **2** (*a knack*) astuce F; **it**

doesn't work, there must be a trick to it ça ne marche pas, il doit y avoir une astuce. *verb* rouler [1]; **he tricked me!** il m'a roulé!

tricky *adjective* délicat; **it's a tricky situation** c'est une situation délicate.

tricycle *noun* tricycle M.

trim *verb* couper [1] (*hair or fabric*).

trip *noun* voyage M; **a trip to Florida** un voyage en Floride; **he's on a business trip** il est en voyage d'affaires; **a day trip to France** une excursion d'une journée en France. *verb* (*to stumble*) trébucher [1]; **Nicky tripped over a stone** Nicky a trébuché sur un gros caillou.

triumph *noun* triomphe M.

trolley *noun* chariot M.

trombone *noun* trombone M; **to play the trombone** jouer du trombone.

troops *plural noun* troupes M *plural*.

trophy *noun* trophée M.

tropical *adjective* tropical (M *plural* tropicaux).

trot *verb* trotter [1].

trouble *noun* **1** problèmes M *plural*; **we've had trouble with the car** nous avons eu des problèmes avec la voiture; **the trouble is, I've forgotten the number** le problème, c'est que j'ai oublié le numéro; **2** (*personal problems*) ennuis M *plural*; **Steph's in trouble** Steph a des ennuis; **what's the trouble?** qu'est-ce qui ne va pas?;

3 (*difficulty*) **to have trouble doing** avoir du mal à faire; **I had trouble finding a seat** j'ai eu du mal à trouver une place; **it's not worth the trouble** cela ne vaut pas la peine; **it's no trouble!** ça ne me dérange pas!

trousers *plural noun* pantalon M singular; **my old trousers** mon vieux pantalon; **a new pair of trousers** un pantalon neuf.

trout *noun* truite F.

truck *noun* camion M.

true *adjective* vrai; **a true story** une histoire vraie; **is that true?** c'est vrai?; **it's true she's absent-minded** c'est vrai qu'elle est distraite.

trump *noun* atout M; **spades are trumps** atout pique.

trumpet *noun* trompette F; **to play the trumpet** jouer de la trompette.

trunk *noun* **1** (*of a tree*) tronc M; **2** (*of an elephant*) trompe F; **3** (*a suitcase*) malle F.

trunks *plural noun* **swimming trunks** maillot M singular de bain.

trust *noun* confiance F.
verb **I trust her** je lui fais confiance.

truth *noun* vérité F; **to tell the truth, I'd completely forgotten** à vrai dire, j'avais complètement oublié.

try *noun* essai M; **it's my first try** c'est mon premier essai; **to have a try** essayer [59]; **you should give it a try** tu devrais l'essayer.
verb essayer [59]; **to try to do** essayer de faire; **I'm trying to open the door** j'essaie d'ouvrir la porte; **to try hard to do** faire [10] de gros efforts pour faire.

● **to try something on** essayer [59] quelque chose (*a garment*).

T-shirt *noun* tee-shirt M.

tube *noun* tube M.

tuberculosis *noun* tuberculose F.

Tuesday *noun* mardi M; **on Tuesday** mardi; **I'm going out on Tuesday** je sors mardi; **see you on Tuesday!** à mardi!; **on Tuesdays** le mardi; **the museum is closed on Tuesdays** le musée est fermé le mardi; **every Tuesday** tous les mardis; **last Tuesday** mardi dernier; **next Tuesday** mardi prochain.

tug *verb* tirer [1].

tuition *noun* cours M *plural*; **piano tuition** les cours de piano; **private tuition** des cours particuliers.

tulip *noun* tulipe F.

tumble-drier *noun* sèche-linge M.

tumbler *noun* verre M droit.

tuna *noun* thon M.

tune *noun* air M.

Tunisia *noun* Tunisie F; **in Tunisia** en Tunisie.

tunnel *noun* tunnel M; **the Channel Tunnel** le tunnel sous la Manche.

turf *noun* gazon M.

turkey *noun* dinde F.

Turkey *noun* Turquie F; **in Turkey** en Turquie; **to Turkey** en Turquie.

Turkish *noun* turc M (*language*).
adjective turc (F turque).

turn *noun* **1** (*in a game*) tour M; **it's your turn** c'est ton tour; **whose turn**

is it? c'est à qui le tour?; **it's Jane's turn to play** c'est à Jane de jouer; **to take turns driving** conduire à tour de rôle; **2** (*in a road*) virage M.
verb **1** tourner [1]; **turn your chair round** tourne ta chaise; **turn left at the next set of lights** tournez à gauche aux prochains feux;
2 (*become*) devenir [81]; **she turned red** elle est devenue rouge.

• **to turn back** faire [10] demi-tour; **we turned back** nous avons fait demi-tour.

• **to turn off 1** (*from a road*) tourner [1]; **2** (*switch off*) éteindre [60] (*a light, an oven, a TV or radio*); fermer [1] (*a tap*); couper [1] (*gas or electricity*).

• **to turn on** allumer [1] (*the oven, TV, radio, or a light*); ouvrir [30] (*a tap*).

• **to turn out 1 to turn out well** bien se terminer [1]; **the holiday turned out badly** les vacances se sont mal terminées; **it all turned out alright in the end** finalement tout s'est arrangé; **2 it turned out that I was wrong** il s'est avéré que j'avais tort.

• **to turn over 1** (*roll over*) se retourner [1]; **2** tourner [1] (*a page*).

• **to turn up 1** (*to arrive*) arriver [1]; **they turned up an hour later** ils sont arrivés une heure plus tard;
2 augmenter [1] (*the gas or the heating*); **3** (*make louder*) **can you turn up the volume?** est-ce que tu peux monter le son?

turnip *noun* navet M.

turquoise *adjective* turquoise.

turtle *noun* tortue F.

TV *noun* télé F; **I saw her on TV** je l'ai vue à la télé.

tweezers *plural noun* pince à épiler F singular.

twelfth *number* douzième; **on the twelfth floor** au douzième étage; **the twelfth of May** le douze mai.

twelve *number* **1** douze M; **Tara's twelve** Tara a douze ans; **2 at twelve o'clock** (*midday*) à midi; (*midnight*) à minuit.

twenty *number* vingt M; **Marie's twenty** Marie a vingt ans; **twenty-one** vingt-et-un; **twenty-five** vingt-cinq.

twice *adverb* deux fois; **I've asked him twice** je lui ai demandé deux fois; **twice as much** deux fois plus.

twig *noun* brindille F.

twin *noun* jumeau M (*plural* jumeaux), jumelle F; **Helen and Tim are twins** Helen et Tim sont jumeaux; **her twin sister** sa sœur jumelle.
verb **Oxford is twinned with Grenoble** Oxford est jumelée avec Grenoble.

twist *verb* tordre [3].

two *number* deux M; **Ben's two** Ben a deux ans; **two by two** deux par deux.

type *noun* type M; **what type of computer is it?** c'est quel type d'ordinateur?
verb (*on a typewriter*) taper [1]; **I'm learning to type** j'apprends à taper à la machine; **I was busy typing**

some letters j'étais en train de taper des lettres.

typewriter *noun* machine F à écrire.

typical *adjective* typique.

tyre *noun* pneu M.

U u

ugly *adjective* laid.

UK *noun* (*short for United Kingdom*) Royaume-Uni M.

Ulster *noun* Irlande du Nord F.

umbrella *noun* parapluie M.

umpire *noun* arbitre M.

UN *noun* ONU F (*short for Organisation des Nations Unies*).

unable *adjective* **to be unable to do** ne pas pouvoir faire; **he's unable to come** il ne peut pas venir.

unanimous *adjective* unanime.

unattractive *adjective* peu attrayant (*person, place*).

unavoidable *adjective* inévitable.

unbearable *adjective* insupportable.

unbelievable *adjective* incroyable.

uncertain *adjective* **1** (*not sure*) incertain; **2** (*unpredictable*) variable (*weather, for example*).

unchanged *adjective* inchangé.

uncivilized *adjective* barbare.

uncle *noun* oncle M; **my Uncle Julian** mon oncle Julian.

uncomfortable *adjective* **1** inconfortable (*shoes or a chair*); **2** pénible (*a journey or a situation*).

uncommon *adjective* rare.

unconscious *adjective* (*out cold*) sans connaissance; **Tessa's still unconscious** Tessa est toujours sans connaissance.

under *preposition* **1** (*underneath*) sous; **under the bed** sous le lit; **perhaps it's under there** c'est peut-être là-dessous; **2** (*less than*) moins de; **under £20** moins de vingt livres; **children under five** les enfants de moins de cinq ans.

under-age *noun* **to be under-age** être mineur (F mineure).

underclothes *plural noun* sous-vêtements M *plural*.

undercooked *adjective* pas assez cuit.

underestimate *verb* sous-estimer [1].

underground *noun* (*a railway*) métro M; **I saw her on the underground** je l'ai vue dans le métro; **shall we go by underground?** on prend le métro? *adjective* souterrain; **an underground carpark** un parking souterrain.

underline *verb* souligner [1].

underneath *preposition* sous; **it's underneath these papers** c'est sous ces papiers. *adverb* dessous; **look underneath** cherche dessous.

underpants *plural noun* slip M singular; **my underpants** mon slip.

underpass *noun* **1** (*pedestrian*) passage souterrain M; **2** (*for traffic*) passage inférieur M.

understand *verb* comprendre [64]; **I don't understand** je ne comprends pas; **I didn't understand what he was saying** je n'ai pas compris ce qu'il disait.

understandable *adjective* **that's understandable** ça se comprend.

understanding *noun* compréhension F. *adjective* compréhensif (F compréhensive); **he was very understanding** il a été très compréhensif.

underwear *noun* sous-vêtements M *plural*.

undo *verb* **1** défaire [10] (*a button or a lock*); **2** ouvrir [30] (*a parcel*).

undone *adjective* **to come undone** se défaire [10].

undress *verb* **to get undressed** se déshabiller [1]; **I got undressed** je me suis déshabillé.

unemployed *noun* **work for the unemployed** du travail pour les chômeurs. *adjective* au chômage; **she's unemployed** elle est au chômage; **the unemployed** les chômeurs.

unemployment *noun* chômage M.

uneven *adjective* irrégulier (F irrégulière).

unexpected *adjective* imprévu.

unexpectedly *adverb* (*to happen, arrive*) à l'improviste.

unfair *adjective* injuste; **it's unfair to young people** c'est injuste pour les jeunes.

unfashionable *adjective* démodé.

unfasten *verb* défaire [10].

unfit *adjective* **I'm terribly unfit** je ne suis pas du tout en forme.

unfold *verb* déplier [1].

unfortunate *adjective* regrettable.

unfortunately *adverb* malheureusement.

unfriendly *adjective* pas très sympathique.

unfurnished *adjective* non meublé.

ungrateful *adjective* ingrat.

unhappy *adjective* malheureux (F malheureuse).

unhealthy *adjective* **1** maladif (F maladive) (*a person*); **2** malsain (*food*).

uniform *noun* uniforme M; **in school uniform** en uniforme scolaire.

union *noun* (*a trade union*) syndicat M.

Union Jack *noun* **the Union Jack** le drapeau du Royaume-Uni.

unique *adjective* unique.

unit *noun* **1** (*for measuring, for example*) unité F; **2** (*in a kitchen*) élément M; **3** (*a hospital department*) service M.

United Kingdom *noun* Royaume-Uni M.

United Nations *noun* O.N.U. (*Organisation des Nations Unies*).

United States (of America) *plural noun* États-Unis M *plural*; **in the United States** aux États-Unis; **to the United States** aux États-Unis.

universe *noun* univers M.

university *noun* universitè F; **to go to university** aller à l'université.

unkind *adjective* pas gentil (F pas gentille).

unknown *adjective* inconnu.

unleaded petrol *noun* essence F sans plomb.

unless *conjunction* **unless he does it** à moins qu'il ne le fasse; **unless you tell her** à moins que tu ne le lui dises (*note that 'à moins que' is followed by a subjunctive*).

unlike *adjective* **1 unlike me, she hates dogs** contrairement à moi, elle déteste les chiens; **2 it's unlike her to be late** ce n'est pas son genre d'être en retard.

unlikely *adjective* peu probable; **it's unlikely** c'est peu probable.

unlimited *adjective* illimité.

unload *verb* décharger [52].

unlock *verb* ouvrir [30]; **the car's unlocked** la voiture est ouverte.

unlucky *adjective* **1 to be unlucky** (*a person*) ne pas avoir de chance; **I was unlucky, it was shut** je n'ai pas eu de chance, c'était fermé;

2 thirteen is an unlucky number le treize porte malheur.

unmarried *adjective* célibataire.

unnatural *adjective* anormal (M *plural* anormaux).

unnecessary *adjective* inutile; **it's unnecessary to book** il est inutile de réserver.

unpack *verb* défaire [10]; **I unpacked my rucksack** j'ai défait mon sac à dos; **I'll just unpack and then come down** je vais juste défaire ma valise et puis je descendrai.

unpaid *adjective* **1** impayé (*a bill*); **2** non rémunéré (*work*).

unpleasant *adjective* désagréable.

unplug *verb* débrancher [1].

unpopular *adjective* impopulaire.

unreasonable *adjective* pas raisonnable; **he's being really unreasonable** il n'est vraiment pas raisonnable.

unrecognizable *adjective* méconnaissable.

unreliable *adjective* peu fiable (*information or equipment*); **he's unreliable** on ne peut pas compter sur lui.

unroll *verb* dérouler [1].

unsafe *adjective* dangereux (F dangereuse) (*wiring, for instance*).

unsatisfactory *adjective* insatisfaisant.

unscrew *verb* dévisser [1].

unshaven *adjective* pas rasé.

unsuccessful *adjective* **to be**

unsuccessful ne pas réussir; **I tried, but I was unsuccessful** j'ai essayé mais je n'ai pas réussi; **an unsuccessful attempt** un essai vain.

unsuitable *adjective* inapproprié.

untidy *adjective* en désordre; **the house is always untidy** la maison est toujours en désordre.

until *preposition* 1 jusqu'à; **until Monday** jusqu'à lundi; **until the tenth** jusqu'au dix; **until now** jusqu'à présent; **until then** jusque-là; 2 **not until** pas avant; **not until September** pas avant septembre; **it won't be finished until Friday** ce ne sera pas fini avant vendredi.

unusual *adjective* peu commun; **an unusual beetle** un scarabée peu commun; **storms are unusual in June** c'est rare d'avoir des orages au mois de juin.

unwilling *adjective* **to be unwilling to do** ne pas vouloir faire; **he's unwilling to wait** il ne veut pas attendre.

unwrap *verb* déballer [1].

up *preposition, adverb* 1 (*out of bed*) **to be up** être levé; **Liz isn't up yet** Liz n'est pas encore levée; **to get up** se lever [50]; **we got up at six** nous nous sommes levés à six heures; **I was up late last night** je me suis couché tard hier soir; 2 (*higher up*) en haut; **hands up!** haut les mains!; **up on the roof** en haut sur le toit; **up here** ici; **up there** là-haut; **we went up the road** nous avons remonté la rue; **it's just up the road** c'est tout près; **up in Glasgow** à Glasgow;

3 (*wrong*) **what's up?** qu'est-ce qui se passe?; **what's up with him?** qu'est-ce qu'il a?; 4 **up to** jusqu'à; **up to here** jusqu'ici; **up to fifty people** jusqu'à cinquante personnes; **she came up to me** elle s'est approchée de moi; 5 **what's she up to?** qu'est-ce qu'elle fait?; **it's up to you (to decide)** c'est à toi de décider; ★ **time's up!** c'est l'heure!

update *noun* mise F à jour; **here's an update on the delays** voici une mise à jour des retards.
verb 1 (*revise*) mettre [11] à jour (*timetables or information*); 2 moderniser [1] (*styles or furnishings*).

upheaval *noun* bouleversement M.

upright *adjective* droit; **put it upright** mets-le droit; **to stand upright** se tenir droit.

upset *noun* **a stomach upset** une indigestion.
adjective contrarié; **he's upset** il est contrarié.
verb **to upset somebody** contrarier [1] quelqu'un.

upside down *adjective* à l'envers.

upstairs *adverb* en haut; **Mum's upstairs** maman est en haut; **to go upstairs** monter [1].

up-to-date *adjective* 1 (*in fashion*) moderne; 2 (*information*) à jour.

upwards *adjective* vers le haut.

urgent *adjective* urgent.

US *noun* U.S.A. M *plural*.

us *pronoun* nous; **she knows us** elle

nous connaît; **they saw us** ils nous ont vus; **he gave us a cheque** il nous a donné un chèque; **with us** avec nous.

USA *noun* U.S.A. M *plural*.

use *noun* **1** emploi M; **the instructions for use** le mode d'emploi; **2 it's no use** ça ne sert à rien; **it's no use phoning** ça ne sert à rien de téléphoner.
verb utiliser [1]; **we used the dictionary** nous avons utilisé le dictionnaire; **to use something to do** se servir [71] de quelque chose pour faire; **I used a knife to open the parcel** je me suis servi d'un couteau pour ouvrir le paquet.
●**to use up 1** consommer [1] (*food or petrol*); **2** dépenser [1] (*money*).

used *adjective* **1 to be used to something** avoir l'habitude de quelque chose; **I'm not used to cats** je n'ai pas l'habitude des chats; **I'm not used to it** je n'ai pas l'habitude; **I'm not used to eating in restaurants** je n'ai pas l'habitude de manger au restaurant; **2 to get used to** s'habituer à; **I've got used to living here** je me suis habitué à habiter ici; **you'll get used to it!** tu t'y habitueras!
verb **they used to live in the country** ils habitaient à la campagne avant; **she used to smoke** elle fumait avant.

useful *adjective* utile.

useless *adjective* nul (F nulle); **this knife's useless** ce couteau est nul; **you're completely useless!** tu es complètement nul!

user-friendly *adjective* convivial (M *plural* conviviaux).

usual *adjective* habituel (F habituelle); **it's the usual problem** c'est le problème habituel; **as usual** comme d'habitude; **it's colder than usual** il fait plus froid que d'habitude.

usually *adjective* d'habitude; **I usually leave at eight** d'habitude je pars à huit heures.

V v

vacancy *noun* **1** (*in a hotel*) 'vacancies' 'chambres libres'; 'no vacancies' 'complet'; **2 a job vacancy** un poste vacant.

vacant *adjective* libre.

vaccinate *verb* vacciner [1].

vaccination *noun* vaccination F.

vacuum *verb* passer [1] l'aspirateur; **I'm going to vacuum my room** je vais passer l'aspirateur dans ma chambre.

vacuum cleaner *noun* aspirateur M.

vagina *noun* vagin M.

vague *adjective* vague.

vaguely *adverb* vaguement.

vain *adjective* vaniteux (F vaniteuse); **in vain** en vain.

Valentine's Day *noun* la Saint-Valentin.

valid *adjective* valable.

valley noun vallée F.

valuable adjective **1** de valeur; **to be valuable** avoir de la valeur; **that watch is very valuable** cette montre a une grande valeur; **2** (appreciated) précieux (F précieuse); **he gave us some valuable information** il nous a donné des renseignements précieux.

value noun valeur F.
verb apprécier [1] (somebody's help, opinion, or friendship).

van noun (small) fourgon M; (large) camionnette F.

vandal noun vandale M & F.

vandalism noun vandalisme M.

vandalize verb vandaliser [1].

vanilla noun vanille F; **a vanilla ice-cream** une glace à la vanille.

vanish verb disparaître [27].

variety noun variété F.

various adjective plusieurs; **there are various ways of doing it** il y a plusieurs façons de le faire.

vary verb varier [1]; **it varies a lot** ça varie beaucoup.

vase noun vase M.

VAT noun TVA F.

VCR noun magnétoscope M.

VDU noun console F.

veal noun veau M.

vegan noun végétalien M, végétalienne F.

vegetable noun légume M.

vegetarian noun, adjective végétarien M, végétarienne F; **he's vegetarian** il est végétarien.

vehicle noun véhicule M.

vein noun veine F.

velvet noun velours M.

vending machine noun distributeur M automatique.

verb noun verbe M.

verdict noun verdict M.

verge noun **1** (the roadside) accotement M; **2 to be on the verge of doing** être [6] sur le point de faire; **I was on the verge of leaving** j'étais sur le point de partir.

version noun version F.

versus preposition contre; **Bath versus Chelsea** Bath contre Chelsea.

vertical adjective vertical (M plural verticaux).

vertigo noun vertige M.

very adverb **it's very difficult** c'est très difficile; **very well** très bien; **very much** beaucoup.
adjective **the very person I need!** exactement la personne qu'il me faut!; **the very thing he was looking for** exactement ce qu'il cherchait; **2 in the very middle** en plein milieu; **at the very end** tout à la fin; **at the very front** tout devant.

vest noun maillot M de corps.

vet noun vétérinaire M & F; **she's a vet** elle est vétérinaire.

via preposition **to go via** passer par;

we're going via Dover nous allons passer par Douvres; **we'll go via the bank** on va passer par la banque.

vicar *noun* pasteur M.

vicious *adjective* **1** méchant (*a dog*); **2** brutal (M *plural* brutaux) (*an attack*).

victim *noun* victime F.

victory *noun* victoire F.

video *noun* **1** (*film*) vidéo F; **to watch a video** regarder une vidéo; **I've got it on video** je l'ai en vidéo; **2** (*cassette*) cassette vidéo F; **I bought a video** j'ai acheté une cassette vidéo; **3** (*video recorder*) magnétoscope M.
verb enregistrer [1]; **I'll video it for you** je te l'enregistrerai.

video cassette *noun* cassette F vidéo.

video game *noun* jeu M vidéo (*plural* jeux vidéo).

video recorder *noun* magnétoscope M.

video shop *noun* vidéoclub M.

view *noun* **1** vue F; **a room with a view of the lake** une chambre avec vue sur le lac; **2** (*opinion*) avis M; **in my view** à mon avis; **a point of view** un point de vue.

viewer *noun* (*on TV*) téléspectateur M, téléspectatrice F.

viewpoint *noun* point M de vue.

vigorous *adjective* vigoureux (F vigoureuse).

vile *adjective* abominable.

villa *noun* villa F.

village *noun* village M.

vine *noun* vigne F.

vinegar *noun* vinaigre M.

vineyard *noun* vignoble M.

violence *noun* violence F.

violent *adjective* violent.

violin *noun* violon M; **to play the violin** jouer du violon.

violinist *noun* violoniste M & F.

virgin *noun* vierge F.

Virgo *noun* Vierge F; **Robert's Virgo** Robert est Vierge.

virtual reality *noun* réalité F virtuelle.

virus *noun* virus M.

visa *noun* visa M.

visible *adjective* visible.

visit *noun* **1** (*stay*) séjour M; **my last visit to France** mon dernier séjour en France; **2** visite F (*to a house, museum*).
verb **1** visiter [1] (*museum, castle, town*); **2** aller [7] voir (*a person*); **we visited Auntie Pat at Christmas** nous sommes allés voir tante Pat à Noël.

visitor *noun* **1** invité M, invitée F; **we've got visitors tonight** on a des invités ce soir; **2** (*a tourist*) visiteur M, visiteuse F.

visual *adjective* visuel (F visuelle).

vital *adjective* indispensable; **it's vital to book** il est indispensable de réserver.

vitamin *noun* vitamine F.

vivid *adjective* **1** (*colour*) vif (F vive); **2 to have a vivid imagination** exagérer.

vocabulary *noun* vocabulaire M.

vocational *adjective* professionnel (F professionnelle).

vodka *noun* vodka M.

voice *noun* voix F.

volcano *noun* volcan M.

volleyball *noun* volley-ball M; **to play volleyball** jouer au volley-ball.

volume *noun* volume M; **could you turn down the volume?** est-ce que tu peux baisser le volume?

voluntary *adjective* **1** (*not compulsory*) volontaire; **2 to do voluntary work** travailler bénévolement.

volunteer *noun* **1** (*for a job*) volontaire M & F; **2** (*in charity work*) bénévole M & F.

vomit *verb* vomir [2].

vote *verb* voter [1].

voucher *noun* bon M.

vowel *noun* voyelle F.

vulgar *adjective* vulgaire.

W w

waffle *noun* (*to eat*) gaufre F.

wage(s) (*plural*) *noun* salaire M.

waist *noun* taille F.

waistcoat *noun* gilet M.

waist measurement *noun* tour M de taille.

wait *noun* attente F; **an hour's wait** une heure d'attente.
verb **1** attendre [3]; **they're waiting in the car** ils attendent dans la voiture; **she kept me waiting** elle m'a fait attendre; **2 to wait for** attendre [3]; **wait for me!** attends-moi!; **wait for the signal** attendez le signal; **3 I can't wait to open it!** j'ai hâte de l'ouvrir!

waiter *noun* serveur M.

waiting list *noun* liste F d'attente.

waiting room *noun* salle F d'attente.

waitress *noun* serveuse F.

wake *verb* **1** réveiller [1] (*somebody else*); **Jess woke me at six** Jess m'a réveillé à six heures; **2** se réveiller [1]; **I woke (up) at six** je me suis réveillé à six heures; **wake up!** réveille-toi!

Wales *noun* pays M de Galles; **in Wales** au pays de Galles; **to Wales** au pays de Galles.

walk *noun* promenade F; (*a little stroll*) tour M; **to go for a walk** faire une promenade; **we went for a walk in the woods** nous avons fait une promenade dans la forêt; **we'll go for a little walk round the village** on va faire un petit tour au village; **to take the dog for a walk** promener [50] le chien; **it's about five minutes' walk from here** c'est à environ cinq minutes à pied d'ici.
verb **1** marcher [1]; **I like walking on sand** j'aime marcher sur le sable; **2** (*walk around*) se promener [50];

we walked around the old town
nous nous sommes promenés dans
la vieille ville; **3** (*go*) aller [7]; **I'll
walk to the bus stop with you** j'irai
avec toi jusqu'à l'arrêt de bus; **4** (*on
foot rather than by car or bus*) aller
[7] à pied; **it's not far, we can walk**
ce n'est pas loin, on peut y aller à
pied.

walkie-talkie *noun* talkie-walkie
M (*plural* talkies-walkies).

walking *noun* (*hiking*) randonnée
F; **we're going walking in
Scotland** nous allons faire de la
randonnée en Écosse.

walking distance *noun* **it's within
walking distance of the sea** c'est à
quelques minutes à pied de la mer.

walking stick *noun* canne F.

walkman™ *noun* walkman™ M.

wall *noun* mur M.

wallet *noun* portefeuille M.

wallpaper *noun* papier M peint.

walnut *noun* noix F (*plural* noix).

wander *verb* **to wander around
town** se balader [1] en ville; **to
wander off** s'éloigner [1].

want *noun* **all our wants** tous nos
besoins.
verb vouloir [14]; **do you want some
coffee?** est-ce que tu veux du café?;
what do you want to do? qu'est-ce
que tu veux faire?; **I don't want to
bother him** je ne veux pas le
déranger.

war *noun* guerre F.

ward *noun* salle F (*in a hospital*).

wardrobe *noun* **1** (*cupboard*)
armoire F; **2** (*clothes*) garde-robe
F.

warm *adjective* **1** chaud; **a warm
drink** une boisson chaude; **it's
warm today** il fait chaud
aujourd'hui; **I am warm** j'ai chaud;
are you warm enough? as-tu assez
chaud?; **I'll keep your dinner warm**
je tiendrai ton dîner au chaud;
2 (*friendly*) chaleureux (F
chaleureuse); **a warm welcome** un
accueil chaleureux.
verb chauffer [1]; **warm the plates**
chauffez les assiettes.
● **to warm up 1** (*the weather*)
s'adoucir [2]; **2** (*an athlete*)
s'échauffer [1]; **3** (*to heat up*)
réchauffer [1] (*food*); **I'll warm up
some soup for you** je vous
réchaufferai de la soupe.

warmth *noun* chaleur F.

warn *verb* prévenir [81]; **I warn you,
it's expensive** je vous préviens que
c'est cher; **to warn somebody to do**
conseiller [1] à quelqu'un de faire; **he
warned me to lock the car** il m'a
conseillé de fermer la voiture.

warning *noun* avertissement M.

wart *noun* verrue F.

wash *noun* **to give something a
wash** laver [1] quelque chose; **to
have a wash** se laver.
verb laver [1]; **I've washed your
jeans** j'ai lavé ton jean; **to wash
your hands** se laver les mains;
I washed my hands je me suis lavé
les mains; **to wash your hair** se laver
les cheveux; **to get washed** se laver;
to wash the dishes faire [10] la
vaisselle.

● **to wash up** faire [10] la vaisselle.

washbasin *noun* lavabo M.

washing *noun* 1 (*dirty*) linge M sale; 2 (*clean*) linge M.

washing machine *noun* machine F à laver.

washing powder *noun* lessive F.

washing-up *noun* vaisselle F; **to do the washing-up** faire la vaisselle.

washing-up liquid *noun* liquide M à vaisselle.

wasp *noun* guêpe F.

waste *noun* 1 (*of food, money, paper*) gaspillage M; 2 (*of time*) perte F; **it's a waste of time** c'est une perte de temps.
verb 1 gaspiller [1] (*food, money, paper*); 2 perdre [3] (*time*); **you're wasting your time** tu perds ton temps.

waste-bin *noun* poubelle F.

wastepaper-basket *noun* corbeille F à papier.

watch *noun* montre F; **my watch is fast** ma montre avance; **my watch is slow** ma montre retarde.
verb 1 (*to look at*) regarder [1]; **I was watching TV** je regardais la télé; 2 (*keep a check on*) surveiller [1]; **watch the time** surveille l'heure; 3 (*to be careful*) faire [10] attention; **watch you don't spill it** fais attention de ne pas le renverser; **watch out for black ice** faites attention au verglas; **watch out!** attention!

water *noun* eau F.

verb arroser [1]; **to water the plants** arroser les plantes.

waterfall *noun* cascade F.

watering can *noun* arrosoir M.

water melon *noun* pastèque F.

waterproof *adjective* imperméable.

water-skiing *noun* ski M nautique; **to go water-skiing** faire du ski nautique.

water sports *plural noun* sports M *plural* nautiques.

wave *noun* 1 (*in the sea*) vague F; 2 (*with your hand*) signe M; **she gave him a wave from the bus** elle lui a fait signe du bus.
verb 1 (*with your hand*) saluer [1] de la main; 2 (*flap*) agiter [1] (*your ticket or the newspaper, for example*).

wax *noun* cire F.

way *noun* 1 (*a route or road*) chemin M; **the way to town** le chemin pour aller en ville; **we asked the way to the station** nous avons demandé le chemin pour aller à la gare; **on the way back** sur le chemin de retour; **on the way** en route; **'way in'** 'entrée'; **'way out'** 'sortie'; 2 (*direction*) direction F; **which way did he go?** en quelle direction est-il parti?; **come this way** venez par ici; **to be in the way** gêner le passage; 3 (*side*) sens M; **the right way up** dans le bons sens; **the wrong way round** dans le mauvais sens; 4 (*distance*) **it's a long way** c'est loin; **Terry went all the way to York** Terry est allé jusqu'à York; 5 (*manner*) façon F; **a way of talking** une façon de parler; **he does**

it his way il le fait à sa façon; **either way, she's wrong** de toute façon elle a tort; **do it this way** fais-le comme ceci; **6 no way!** pas question!; **7 by the way** à propos.

we *pronoun* nous; (*informally*) on; **we live in Carlisle** nous habitons Carlisle; **we're going to the cinema tonight** on va au cinéma ce soir.

weak *adjective* **1** (*feeble*) faible; **her voice was weak** sa voix était faible; **2** léger (F légère) (*coffee or tea*).

wealthy *adjective* riche.

weapon *noun* arme F.

wear *noun* **children's wear** vêtements M *plural* pour enfants; **sports wear** vêtements de sport. *verb* porter [1]; **Tamsin's wearing her trainers** Tamsin porte ses baskets; **she often wears red** elle est souvent en rouge; **to wear make-up** se maquiller [1].

weather *noun* temps M; **what's the weather like?** quel temps fait-il?; **in fine weather** quand il fait beau; **the weather was cold** il faisait froid; **the weather here is terrible** il fait un temps affreux ici.

weather forecast *noun* météo F; **the weather forecast says it will rain** selon la météo il va pleuvoir.

wedding *noun* mariage M.

Wednesday *noun* mercredi M; **on Wednesday** mercredi; **I'm going out on Wednesday** je sors mercredi; **see you on Wednesday!** à mercredi!; **on Wednesdays** le mercredi; **the museum is closed on Wednesdays** le musée est fermé le mercredi; **every Wednesday** tous les mercredis; **last Wednesday** mercredi dernier; **next Wednesday** mercredi prochain.

weed *noun* mauvaise herbe F.

week *noun* semaine F; **last week** la semaine dernière; **next week** la semaine prochaine; **this week** cette semaine; **for weeks** pendant des semaines; **a week today** aujourd'hui en huit.

weekday *noun* **on weekdays** en semaine.

weekend *noun* week-end M; **last weekend** le week-end dernier; **next weekend** le week-end prochain; **they're coming for the weekend** ils vont passer le week-end chez nous; **I'll do it at the weekend** je le ferai pendant le week-end; **have a nice weekend!** bon week-end!

weigh *verb* peser [50]; **to weigh something** peser quelque chose; **how much do you weigh?** combien pèses-tu?; **I weigh 50 kilos** je pèse cinquante kilos; **to weigh yourself** se peser.

weight *noun* poids M; **to put on weight** prendre du poids; **to lose weight** perdre du poids.

weird *adjective* bizarre.

welcome *noun* accueil M; **they gave us a warm welcome** ils nous ont fait un accueil chaleureux; **welcome to Oxford!** bienvenue à Oxford! *adjective* bienvenu; **you're welcome any time** vous êtes toujours les bienvenus; **'thank you!' – 'you're welcome!'**

'merci!' – 'de rien!'
verb accueillir [35].

well[1] *noun* puits M.

well[2] *adverb* **1 to feel well** se sentir bien; **I'm very well, thank you** ça va très bien, merci; **2** bien; **Terry played well** Terry a bien joué; **the operation went well** l'opération s'est bien passée; **well done!** bravo!; **3 as well** aussi; **Kevin's coming as well** Kevin vient aussi; **4** alors; **well then, what's the problem?** alors, quel est le problème?; **5 very well then, you can go** très bien, tu peux y aller.

well-behaved *adjective* sage.

well-done *adjective* bien cuit (*a steak*).

wellington (boot) *noun* botte F en caoutchouc.

well-known *adjective* célèbre.

well-off *adjective* aisé.

Welsh *noun* **1 the Welsh** (*people*) les Gallois M *plural*; **2** (*language*) gallois M.
adjective gallois.

Welshman *noun* Gallois M.

Welshwoman *noun* Galloise F.

west *noun* ouest M; **in the west** à l'ouest.
adjective, adverb ouest (*never agrees*); **the west side** le côté ouest; **a west wind** un vent d'ouest; **west of Paris** à l'ouest de Paris.

western *noun* (*a film*) western M.

West Indian *noun* Antillais M, Antillaise F.
adjective antillais.

West Indies *plural noun* Antilles F *plural*; **in the West Indies** aux Antilles.

wet *adjective* **1** (*damp*) mouillé; **the grass is wet** l'herbe est mouillée; **we got wet** nous nous sommes fait mouiller; **2 a wet day** un jour de pluie.

whale *noun* baleine F.

what *pronoun, adjective* **1** qu'est-ce que (*in questions*); **what did you say?** qu'est-ce que tu as dit?; **what's she doing?** qu'est-ce qu'elle fait?; **what did you buy?** qu'est-ce que tu as acheté?; **what is it?** qu'est-ce que c'est?; **what's the matter?** qu'est-ce qu'il y a?; **2** qu'est-ce qui (*in questions as the subject of the verb*); **what's happening?** qu'est-ce qui se passe?; **3** ce que (*relative pronoun*); **tell me what you bought** dis-moi ce que tu as acheté; **4** ce qui (*relative pronoun as subject of a verb*); **she told me what had happened** elle m'a dit ce qui s'était passé; **5** quel (F quelle); **what's your address?** quelle est ton adresse?; **what country is it in?** c'est dans quel pays?; **what colour is it?** c'est de quelle couleur?; **what make is it?** c'est quelle marque?; **6 what's her name?** elle s'appelle comment?; **what?** comment?

wheat *noun* blé M.

wheel *noun* roue F; **the spare wheel** la roue de rechange; **the steering wheel** le volant.

wheelbarrow *noun* brouette F.

wheelchair *noun* fauteuil roulant M.

when *adverb, conjunction* quand; **when is she arriving?** quand est-ce qu'elle arrive?; **when's your birthday?** c'est quand, ton anniversaire?; **it was raining when I went out** il pleuvait quand je suis sorti.

where *adverb, conjunction* où; **where are the plates?** où sont les assiettes?; **where do you live?** tu habites où?; **where are you going?** où vas-tu?; **I don't know where they live** je ne sais pas où ils habitent.

whether *conjunction* si; **I don't know whether he's back or not** je ne sais pas s'il est rentré ou non.

which *adjective* quel (F quelle); **which CD did you buy?** quel CD as-tu acheté? *pronoun* **1** (*which one*) lequel, laquelle (*depending on whether it is standing for a masculine or a feminine noun*); **'I saw your brother' – 'which one?'** 'j'ai vu ton frère' – 'lequel?'; **'I saw your sister' – 'which one?'** 'j'ai vu ta sœur' – 'laquelle?'; **which of these jackets is yours?** laquelle de ces vestes est à toi?; **2** (*relative pronoun*) qui (*as subject of the verb*); **the lamp which is on the table** la lampe qui est sur la table; **3** (*relative pronoun*) que (*as object of the verb*); **the book which you borrowed from me** le livre que tu m'as emprunté.

while *noun* **for a while** pendant quelque temps; **she worked here for a while** elle a travaillé ici pendant quelque temps; **after a while** au bout d'un moment. *conjunction* pendant que; **you can make some tea while I'm finishing my homework** tu peux faire du thé pendant que je finirai mes devoirs.

whip *noun* (*for a horse*) cravache F. *verb* fouetter [1]; **whipped cream** la crème fouettée.

whiskers *plural noun* moustaches F *plural*.

whisky *noun* whisky M.

whisper *noun* chuchotement M; **to speak in a whisper** chuchoter [1]. *verb* chuchoter [1].

whistle *noun* sifflet M. *verb* siffler [1].

white *noun* blanc M; **an egg white** un blanc d'œuf. *adjective* blanc (F blanche); **a white shirt** une chemise blanche.

white coffee *noun* café M au lait.

Whitsun *noun* Pentecôte F.

who *pronoun* **1** (*in questions*) qui; **who wants some chocolate?** qui veut du chocolat?; **2** (*relative pronoun*) qui (*as subject of the verb*); **my friend who lives in Paris** mon ami qui habite à Paris; **3** (*relative pronoun*) que (*as object of the verb*); **the friends who we invited** les amis que nous avons invités.

whole *noun* **the whole of the class** la classe tout entière; **on the whole** dans l'ensemble. *adjective* tout; **the whole family** toute la famille; **the whole morning**

toute la matinée; **the whole time** tout le temps; **the whole world** le monde entier.

wholemeal *adjective* complet (F complète); **wholemeal bread** le pain complet.

whom *pronoun* **1** que; **the person whom I saw** la personne que j'ai vue; **2** (*after a preposition*) qui; **the person to whom I wrote** la personne à qui j'ai écrit.

whose *pronoun, adjective* **1** à qui; **whose is this jacket?** à qui est cette veste?; **whose shoes are these?** à qui sont ces chaussures?; **whose is it?** à qui c'est?; **I know whose it is** je sais à qui c'est; **2** dont; **the man whose car has been stolen** le monsieur dont la voiture a été volée.

why *adverb* pourquoi; **why did she phone?** pourquoi est-ce qu'elle a appelé?; **nobody knows why he did it** personne ne sait pourquoi il l'a fait.

wicked *adjective* **1** (*bad*) méchant; **2** (*brilliant*) génial (M *plural* géniaux).

wide *adjective* **1** large; **the Thames is very wide here** la Tamise est très large ici; **a piece of paper 20 cm wide** une feuille de papier de vingt centimètres de large; **2 a wide range** une vaste gamme.
adverb **the door was wide open** la porte était grande ouverte.

wide awake *adjective* complètement éveillé.

widow *noun* veuve F.

widower *noun* veuf M.

width *noun* largeur F.

wife *noun* femme F.

wig *noun* perruque F.

wild *adjective* **1** sauvage (*an animal or plant*); **wild birds** les oiseaux sauvages; **2** (*crazy*) fou (F folle) (*idea, party, person*); **3 to be wild about something** être un fana de quelque chose.

wild life *noun* **a programme on wild life in Africa** un programme sur la nature en Afrique.

wild life park *noun* réserve F naturelle.

will *verb* **1** (*if you are unsure of the future tense of a French verb, you can check in the verb tables in the centre of the dictionary*); **I'll see you soon** je te reverrai bientôt; **he'll be pleased to see you** il sera content de te voir; **it won't rain** il ne pleuvra pas; **there won't be a problem** il n'y aura pas de problème; **2** aller [7](*can be used for the immmediate future*); **I'll phone them at once** je vais les appeler tout de suite; **3** (*in questions and requests*) **will you have a drink?** est-ce que vous prenez quelque chose à boire?; **will you help me?** est-ce que tu peux m'aider?; **'will you write to me?'** – **'of course I will!'** 'est-ce que tu m'écriras?' – 'bien sûr que oui!'; **4** he won't open the door il ne veut pas ouvrir la porte; **the car won't start** la voiture ne veut pas démarrer; **the drawer won't open** je n'arrive pas à ouvrir le tiroir.

willing *adjective* **to be willing to do**

être prêt à faire; **I'm willing to pay half** je suis prêt à payer la moitié.

willingly *adverb* volontiers.

willow *noun* saule M; **a weeping willow** un saule pleureur.

win *noun* victoire F; **our win over Everton** notre victoire sur Everton. *verb* gagner [1]; **we won!** nous avons gagné!; **Rovers won by two goals** Rovers ont gagné de deux buts.

wind[1] *noun* vent M; **the North wind** le vent du nord.

wind[2] *verb* 1 enrouler [1] (*a wire or a rope, for example*); 2 remonter [1] (*a clock*).

wind instrument *noun* instrument M à vent.

window *noun* 1 (*in a building*) fenêtre F; **to look out of the window** regarder par la fenêtre; 2 (*in a car, bus, train*) vitre F.

windscreen *noun* pare-brise M (*plural* pare-brise).

windscreen wipers *plural noun* essuie-glace M.

windy *adjective* 1 venteux (F venteuse) (*a place*); 2 **it's windy today** il fait du vent aujourd'hui.

wine *noun* vin M; **a glass of white wine** un verre de vin blanc.

wing *noun* 1 aile F; 2 (*in sport*) ailier M.

wink *verb* **to wink at somebody** faire [10] un clin d'œil à quelqu'un.

winner *noun* gagnant M, gagnante F.

winning *adjective* gagnant.

winnings *plural noun* gains M *plural*.

winter *noun* hiver M; **in winter** en hiver.

wipe *verb* essuyer [41]; **I'll just wipe the table** je vais juste essuyer la table; **to wipe your nose** se moucher [1].

●**to wipe up** (*dishes*) essuyer [41] la vaisselle.

wire *noun* fil M; **an electric wire** un fil électrique.

wire netting *noun* grillage M.

wise *adjective* sage.

wish *noun* 1 vœu M (*plural* vœux); **make a wish!** fais un vœu!; 2 (*a desire*) désir M; 3 **best wishes on your birthday** meilleurs vœux pour ton anniversaire. *verb* 1 **I wish he were here** si seulement il était ici; 2 **I wished him happy birthday** je lui ai souhaité un bon anniversaire.

wit *noun* esprit M.

with *preposition* 1 avec; **with James** avec James; **with me** avec moi; **with pleasure** avec plaisir; **beat the eggs with a fork** battez les œufs avec une fourchette; **he took his umbrella with him** il a pris son parapluie; 2 (*at the house of*) chez; **we're staying the night with Frank** on va passer la nuit chez Frank; 3 (*in descriptions*) **a girl with red hair** une fille aux cheveux roux; **the boy with the broken arm** le garçon au bras cassé; 4 de; **filled with water** rempli d'eau; **covered with mud**

couvert de boue; **red with rage** rouge de colère.

without *preposition* sans; **without you** sans toi; **without sugar** sans sucre; **without a sweater** sans pull; **without looking** sans regarder.

witness *noun* témoin M.

witty *adjective* spirituel (F spirituelle).

wolf *noun* loup M.

woman *noun* femme F; **a woman friend** une amie; **a woman doctor** une femme médecin.

wonder *noun* 1 merveille F; **2 it's no wonder you're tired** ce n'est pas étonnant si tu es fatigué.
verb se demander [1]; **I wonder why** je me demande pourquoi; **I wonder where Jake is** je me demande où est Jake.

wonderful *adjective* merveilleux (F merveilleuse).

wood *noun* bois M; **the lamp is made of wood** la lampe est en bois.

wooden *adjective* en bois.

woodwork *noun* menuiserie F.

wool *noun* laine F.

word *noun* 1 mot M; **a long word** un mot long; **what's the French word for 'window'?** comment dit-on 'window' en français?; **in other words** autrement dit; **to have a word with somebody** parler avec quelqu'un; **2** (*promise*) **to give somebody your word** donner sa parole à quelqu'un; **he broke his word** il n'a pas tenu parole; **3 the**

words of a song les paroles d'une chanson.

word processing *noun* traitement M de texte.

word processor *noun* machine F à traitement de texte.

work *noun* travail M (*plural* travaux); **Mum's at work** maman est au travail; **I've got some work to do** j'ai du travail à faire; **he's out of work** il est sans emploi; **Ben's off work** (*sick*) Ben est en arrêt de travail; (*on holiday*) Ben est en congé.
verb 1 travailler [1]; **she works in an office** elle travaille dans un bureau; **Dad works at home** papa travaille à domicile; **Ruth works in advertising** Ruth travaille dans la publicité; **he works nights** il travaille de nuit; **2** (*to operate*) se servir [71] de; **can you work the video?** sais-tu te servir du magnétoscope?; **3** (*function*) marcher [1]; **the dishwasher's not working** le lave-vaisselle est en panne; **that worked really well!** ça a bien marché!
● **to work out** 1 (*understand*) comprendre [64]; **I can't work out why** je ne comprends pas pourquoi; **2** (*exercise*) s'entraîner [1]; **3** (*to go well*) (*a plan*) marcher [1]; **4** (*calculate*) calculer [1]; **I'll work out how much it would cost** je vais calculer combien ça coûterait.

worked up *adjective* **to get worked up** s'énerver [1].

worker *noun* ouvrier M, ouvrière F.

work experience *noun* stage M; **to do work experience** faire un stage; **to be on work experience** être en stage.

worker noun (*in a factory*) ouvrier M, ouvrière F.

working-class adjective ouvrier (F ouvrière); **a working-class background** un milieu ouvrier.

work of art noun œuvre F d'art.

workshop noun atelier M.

workstation noun (*computer*) poste M de travail (*plural* postes de travail).

world noun monde M; **the best in the world** le meilleur du monde; **the Western world** les pays occidentaux.

World Cup noun **the World Cup** la Coupe du Monde.

world war noun guerre F mondiale; **the Second World War** la Seconde Guerre mondiale.

worm noun ver M.

worn out adjective **1** (*a person*) épuisé; **2** (*clothes or shoes*) complètement usé.

worried adjective inquiet (F inquiète); **they're worried** ils s'inquiètent; **to be worried about** s'inquiéter pour; **we're worried about Susan** nous nous inquiétons pour Susan.

worry noun soucis M *plural*. verb s'inquiéter [24]; **don't worry!** ne t'inquiète pas!; **there's nothing to worry about** il n'y a pas de quoi s'inquiéter.

worrying adjective inquiétant.

worse adjective pire; **it was even worse than the last time** c'était encore pire que la dernière fois; **to get worse** empirer [1]; **the weather's getting worse** le temps empire; **things are getting worse and worse** ça va de pire en pire.

worst adjective **the worst** le plus mauvais; **it was the worst day of my life** ça a été la journée la plus mauvaise de ma vie; **if the worst comes to the worst** au pire.

worth adjective **to be worth** valoir [80]; **how much is it worth?** ça vaut combien?; **to be worth doing** valoir la peine de faire; **it's worth trying** ça vaut la peine d'essayer; **it's not worth it** ça ne vaut pas la peine.

would verb **1 would you like something to eat?** voulez-vous quelque chose à manger?; **2 he wouldn't answer** il n'a pas voulu répondre; **the car wouldn't start** la voiture n'a pas voulu démarrer; **3 I would like an omelette** je voudrais une omelette; **I'd like to go to the cinema** j'aimerais aller au cinéma; **that would be a good idea** ce serait une bonne idée; **if we asked her she would help us** elle nous aiderait, si nous le lui demandions.

wound noun blessure F. verb blesser [1].

wrap verb emballer [1]; **I'm going to wrap (up) my presents** je vais emballer mes cadeaux; **could you wrap it for me please?** voulez-vous me faire un paquet cadeau, s'il vous plaît?

wrapping paper noun papier cadeau M.

wreck noun **1** (of a crashed car or plane) épave F; **2 I feel a wreck!** je suis une loque!
verb **1** détruire [26]; **2** gâcher [1] (plans, occasion); **it completely wrecked my evening!** ça m'a complètement gâché la soirée!

wrestler noun catcheur M, catcheuse F.

wrestling noun catch M.

wrinkled adjective ridé.

wrist noun poignet M.

write verb écrire [38] (a letter or a story); **I'll write her a letter** je lui écrirai une lettre; **to write to somebody** écrire à quelqu'un; **I wrote to Jean yesterday** j'ai écrit à Jean hier.
● **to write down** noter [1]; **I wrote down her name** j'ai noté son nom.

writer noun écrivain M.

writing noun écriture F.

wrong adjective **1** (not correct) mauvais; **the wrong answer** la mauvaise réponse; **it's the wrong address** ce n'est pas la bonne adresse; **I've brought the wrong file** je n'ai pas apporté le bon classeur; **you've got the wrong number** vous vous êtes trompé de numéro; **2 to be wrong** (mistaken) se tromper; **I was wrong** je me suis trompé; **I was wrong when I said it was finished** je me suis trompé en disant que c'était fini; **3 what's wrong?** qu'est-ce qu'il y a?; **4** (false) faux (F fausse); **the information was wrong** les renseignements étaient faux.

X x

xerox™ noun photocopie F.
verb photocopier [1].

X-ray noun radio F; **I saw the X-rays** j'ai vu les radios.
verb faire [10] une radio de; **they X-rayed her ankle** ils ont fait une radio de sa cheville.

Y y

yacht noun **1** (sailing boat) voilier M; **2** (large luxury boat) yacht M.

yawn verb bâiller [1].

year noun **1** an M; (the whole period) année F; **six years ago** il y a six ans; **the whole year** toute l'année; **they lived in Moscow for years** ils ont habité Moscou pendant des années; **2** (for someone's age) an M; **he's seventeen years old** il a dix-sept ans; **a two-year-old child** un enfant de deux ans; **3** (in secondary schools in France the years go from 'sixième', the equivalent of Year 7, to 'terminale', the equivalent of Year 13); **I'm in Year 10** je suis en troisième; **I'm in Year 11** je suis en seconde.

yell verb hurler [1].

yellow adjective jaune.

yes adverb **1** oui; **yes, I know** oui, je

sais; **'is Tom in his room?'** – **'yes, he is'** 'est-ce que Tom est dans sa chambre?' – 'oui'; **2** (*answering a negative*) si; **'you don't want to go, do you?'** – **'yes I do!'** 'tu ne veux pas y aller, n'est-ce pas?' – 'mais si!'; **'you haven't finished, have you?'** – **'yes, I have'** 'tu n'as pas fini?' – 'si si'.

yesterday *adverb* hier; **I saw her yesterday** je l'ai vue hier; **yesterday afternoon** hier après-midi; **yesterday morning** hier matin; **the day before yesterday** avant-hier.

yet *adverb* **not yet** pas encore; **it's not ready yet** ce n'est pas encore prêt.

yoghurt *noun* yaourt M; **a banana yoghurt** un yaourt à la banane.

yolk *noun* jaune d'œuf M (*plural* jaunes d'œuf).

you *pronoun* **1** tu (*'tu' is the familiar way of talking to family members, close friends, and people of your own age; 'vous' is more polite*); **do you want to go to the cinema tonight?** est-ce que tu veux aller au cinéma ce soir?; **2** te (*the object form of 'tu'*); **I'll lend you my bike** je te prêterai mon vélo; **I'll invite you** je t'inviterai; **I'll write to you** je t'écrirai; **3** toi (*after prepositions and in comparisons*); **I'll go with you** j'irai avec toi; **he's older than you** il est plus âgé que toi; **4** (*more polite or to several people*) vous; **can you tell me where the station is, please?** est-ce que vous pouvez m'indiquer la gare, s'il vous plaît?; **I'll invite you all!** je vous inviterai tous!

young *adjective* jeune; **he's younger than me** il est plus jeune que moi; **Tessa's two years younger than me** Tessa a deux ans de moins que moi; **young people** les jeunes.

your *adjective* **1** ton (F ta) (*plural* tes) (*this is the familiar way of talking to family members, close friends, and people of your own age; 'vous' is more polite*); **I met your Dad** j'ai rencontré ton père; **I like your skirt!** j'aime bien ta jupe!; **you've forgotten your CDs!** tu as oublié tes CD; **2** (*more polite or to several people*) votre (*plural* vos); **thank you for your hospitality** merci pour votre hospitalité; **you can all bring your friends** vous pouvez tous amener vos amis.

yours *pronoun* **1** le tien (*plural* les tiens), la tienne (*plural* les tiennes) (*this is the familiar way of talking to somebody of your own age or belonging to your family; otherwise you should use 'vôtre'*); **my brother's younger than yours** mon frère est plus jeune que le tien; **2** (*formally or to several people*) le vôtre (F la vôtre) (*plural* les vôtres); **my children are younger than yours** mes enfants sont plus jeunes que les vôtres; **3** à toi; à vous (*polite form*); **is this pen yours?** est-ce que ce stylo est à toi?

yourself *pronoun* **1** te; (*formally*) vous; **you'll hurt yourself** tu vas te faire mal; **2** (*for emphasis*) toi-même; (*formally*) vous-même; **did you do it yourself?** est-ce que tu l'as fait toi-même?; **3** **all by yourself** tout seul (F toute seule).

yourselves *pronoun* **1** vous; **help yourselves** servez-vous; **2** (*for* *emphasis*) vous-mêmes; **did you do it yourselves?** est-ce que vous l'avez fait vous-mêmes?

youth hostel *noun* auberge F de jeunesse (*plural* auberges de jeunesse).

Yugoslavia *noun* Yougoslavie F.

Z z

zany *adjective* loufoque.

zebra *noun* zèbre M.

zebra crossing *noun* passage M pour piétons.

zero *noun* zéro M.

zigzag *verb* zigzaguer [1].

zip *noun* fermeture F éclair™.

zodiac *noun* zodiaque M; **the signs of the zodiac** les signes du zodiaque.

zone *noun* zone F.

zoo *noun* zoo M.

zoom lens *noun* zoom M.

la France

Régions

①	Alsace	⑧	Champagne	⑮	Nord
②	Aquitaine	⑨	Franche-Comté	⑯	Pays de la Loire
③	Auvergne	⑩	Haute Normandie	⑰	Picardie
④	Basse Normandie	⑪	Languedoc-Roussillon	⑱	Poitou-Charentes
⑤	Bourgogne	⑫	Limousin	⑲	Provence-Côte d'Azur
⑥	Bretagne	⑬	Lorraine	⑳	Rhône-Alpes
⑦	Centre	⑭	Midi-Pyrénées	㉑	Ile de France